S0-CPU-296

STUDIES IN THE NATIONAL BALANCE SHEET OF THE UNITED STATES

Volume II

Basic Data on Balance Sheets and Fund Flows

NATIONAL BUREAU OF ECONOMIC RESEARCH

STUDIES IN CAPITAL FORMATION AND FINANCING

1. *Capital Formation in Residential Real Estate: Trends and Prospects*
   Leo Grebler, David M. Blank, and Louis Winnick
2. *Capital in Agriculture: Its Formation and Financing since 1870*
   Alvin S. Tostlebe
3. *Financial Intermediaries in the American Economy Since 1900*
   Raymond W. Goldsmith
4. *Capital in Transportation, Communications, and Public Utilities: Its Formation and Financing*
   Melville J. Ulmer
5. *Postwar Market for State and Local Government Securities*
   Roland I. Robinson
6. *Capital in Manufacturing and Mining: Its Formation and Financing*
   Daniel Creamer, Sergei P. Dobrovolsky, and Israel Borenstein
7. *Trends in Government Financing*
   Morris A. Copeland
8. *The Postwar Residential Mortgage Market*
   Saul B. Klaman
9. *Capital in the American Economy: Its Formation and Financing*
   Simon Kuznets
10. *The National Wealth of the United States in the Postwar Period*
    Raymond W. Goldsmith
11. *Studies in the National Balance Sheet of the United States*
    Volume I, Raymond W. Goldsmith and Robert E. Lipsey
    Volume II, Raymond W. Goldsmith, Robert E. Lipsey, and Morris Mendelson

Studies in the National Balance Sheet of the United States

VOLUME II

Basic Data on Balance Sheets and Fund Flows

BY

RAYMOND W. GOLDSMITH,

ROBERT E. LIPSEY,

AND

MORRIS MENDELSON

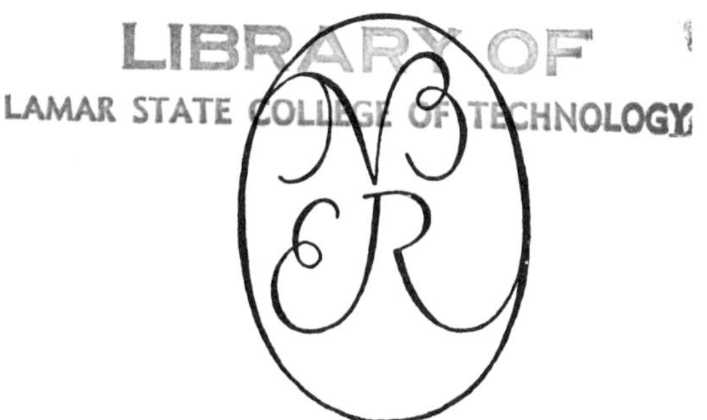

A STUDY BY THE

NATIONAL BUREAU OF ECONOMIC RESEARCH

PUBLISHED BY

PRINCETON UNIVERSITY PRESS

1963

L.C. Card No. 63-7520

Printed in the United States of America

RELATION OF THE DIRECTORS TO THE WORK AND PUBLICATIONS OF THE NATIONAL BUREAU OF ECONOMIC RESEARCH

1. The object of the National Bureau of Economic Research is to ascertain and to present to the public important economic facts and their interpretation in a scientific and impartial manner. The Board of Directors is charged with the responsibility of ensuring that the work of the National Bureau is carried on in strict conformity with this object.

2. To this end the Board of Directors shall appoint one or more Directors of Research.

3. The Director or Directors of Research shall submit to the members of the Board, or to its Executive Committee, for their formal adoption, all specific proposals concerning researches to be instituted.

4. No report shall be published until the Director or Directors of Research shall have submitted to the Board a summary drawing attention to the character of the data and their utilization in the report, the nature and treatment of the problems involved, the main conclusions, and such other information as in their opinion would serve to determine the suitability of the report for publication in accordance with the principles of the National Bureau.

5. A copy of any manuscript proposed for publication shall also be submitted to each member of the Board. For each manuscript to be so submitted a special committee shall be appointed by the President, or at his designation by the Executive Director, consisting of three Directors selected as nearly as may be one from each general division of the Board. The names of the special manuscript committee shall be stated to each Director when the summary and report described in paragraph (4) are sent to him. It shall be the duty of each member of the committee to read the manuscript. If each member of the special committee signifies his approval within thirty days, the manuscript may be published. If each member of the special committee has not signified his approval within thirty days of the transmittal of the report and manuscript, the Director of Research shall then notify each member of the Board, requesting approval or disapproval of publication, and thirty additional days shall be granted for this purpose. The manuscript shall then not be published unless at least a majority of the entire Board and a two-thirds majority of those members of the Board who shall have voted on the proposal within the time fixed for the receipt of votes on the publication proposed shall have approved.

6. No manuscript may be published, though approved by each member of the special committee, until forty-five days have elapsed from the transmittal of the summary and report. The interval is allowed for the receipt of any memorandum of dissent or reservation, together with a brief statement of his reasons, that any member may wish to express; and such memorandum of dissent or reservation shall be published with the manuscript if he so desires. Publication does not, however, imply that each member of the Board has read the manuscript, or that either members of the Board in general, or of the special committee, have passed upon its validity in every detail.

7. A copy of this resolution shall, unless otherwise determined by the Board, be printed in each copy of every National Bureau book.

(Resolution adopted October 25, 1926,
as revised February 6, 1933, and February 24, 1941)

This report is one of a series emerging from an investigation of postwar capital market developments in the United States. The costs of the study were financed in large part by a grant to the National Bureau from the Life Insurance Association of America supplemented by funds from the Research and Educational Trust Fund of the Mortgage Bankers Association of America. Neither of these organizations, however, is responsible for any of the statements made or views expressed in the report.

CONTENTS

TABLES

Reconciliation of NBER and FRB Estimates

TABLES

STUDIES IN THE NATIONAL BALANCE SHEET OF THE UNITED STATES

Volume II

Basic Data on Balance Sheets and Fund Flows

INTRODUCTION

This volume contains the basic data underlying the three parts of Volume I as well as the forthcoming book by Raymond W. Goldsmith, *The Flow of Capital Funds in the Postwar Economy.* Also included are national and sectoral balance sheets for prewar years from Volume III of Goldsmith's *A Study of Saving in the United States* (1956), rearranged with some corrections and revisions to make them more comparable with the postwar data. The tables and notes presented here, together with Appendixes A and B of Goldsmith's *The National Wealth of the United States in the Postwar Period* (1962), will enable a reader to reproduce or extend the balance sheets, asset and liability tables, and fund flow data.

This introduction describes the main features of the National Bureau accounts, some of which were outlined in Volume I, Part One, Chapter 2. It includes the definitions of types of assets and liabilities and of sectors, and identifies the main differences between these accounts and those published by the Federal Reserve Board. The FRB accounts appear in *Flow of Funds/Saving Accounts, 1946-1960,* Supplement 5 (1961),[1] and the most recent explanation can be found in "A Quarterly Presentation of Flow of Funds, Saving, and Investment" (*Federal Reserve Bulletin,* August 1959). Where possible, reconciliations between the NBER and FRB accounts were prepared. These are shown below for 1954-58, which appeared to be long enough to include almost all the main differences between the two sets of accounts. Some of these reconciliations are incomplete, particularly where completeness would have required an examination of the unpublished worksheets underlying the FRB data. However, where the sources of discrepancy could be identified from published information or inferred from the general principles followed by the Federal Reserve Board and the NBER, a reconciliation was made, and these accounted for most of the major discrepancies.

The basic tables are divided into eight sections, as follows:

Assets and Liabilities

- I. National Balance Sheets, 1945-58
- Ia. National Balance Sheets, 1900-45, Selected Years
- II. Finance Sector Balance Sheets, 1945-58
- III. Sector Balance Sheets, 1945-58 and Selected Earlier Years
- IV. Asset and Liability Tables, 1945-58 and Selected Earlier Years

Flow of Funds

- V. Flow of Funds Through Sectors, 1946-58
- VI. Flow of Funds Through Finance Subsectors, 1946-58
- VII. Sector Flow of Funds, 1946-58
- VIII. Transaction Flow of Funds, 1946-58

Section I consists of fourteen balance sheets, one for each year 1945 through 1958, showing, for each major asset and liability, the amount held by each of seven major sectors and by the nation as a whole. These are patterned after the national balance sheets for eight benchmark years between 1900 and 1949 presented in Volume III of *A Study of Saving* (Tables W-9 to W-16). These balance sheets for earlier years, revised to include new data and to improve comparability with later years, are presented in Section Ia. The revision is not complete, however, as can be seen from a comparison of the 1945 balance sheets in Sections I and Ia.

The Section II balance sheets are an expansion of the finance columns in Section I, giving the same information (except on tangible assets) for thirteen subsectors of finance.

[1]Hereinafter referred to as *Supplement 5.*

Sections I and II are both derived from the data for individual sectors and items in Sections III and IV. For each major sector in Section I, for each finance sector in Section II, and for many subdivisions of these, Section III contains a table showing assets, liabilities, and equity for every year from 1945 through 1958. These are similar to the sector balance sheets in *A Study of Saving* (Tables W-22 to W-43 of Volume III for major sectors and various tables in Volume I for subsectors). However, the definitions of some major sectors in the postwar tables are different from those in *A Study of Saving* and there have been some changes in the treatment or estimation of several asset and liability items. We have therefore included, as supplementary tables, revised balance sheets for the major sectors for 1900-45.

The Federal Reserve Board has published partial sector balance sheets for 1945-60, excluding tangible assets and many miscellaneous assets and liabilities, in *Supplement 5* (pp. 34-71, particularly Table 8).

Section IV gives, for each asset and liability listed in Sections I, II, and III, the amount held or owed by each of the major sectors and thirteen finance subsectors. These tables correspond to the FRB tables on "amounts outstanding, year-end" in *Supplement 5* (pp. 74-119).

Tables numbered IV-a (for tangible assets) or IV-b (for intangible assets) show the amount of the asset held by each of the main sectors of the economy and the total held by all domestic sectors combined. For those categories which are liabilities as well (all except tangibles and equities), tables numbered IV-c show the amount outstanding against each sector and the total outstanding against all domestic sectors. An attempt is made in each table numbered IV-b to reconcile the total outstanding with the total held, in terms of foreign (rest-of-world) holdings and outstandings, various types of float, valuation differences between holders' and obligors' records, and other sources of discrepancy.

Sections V through VIII are flow tables corresponding to the four sets of stock tables in Sections I through IV. Sections V and VI are annual flow-of-funds tables for the nation, major sectors, and thirteen finance subsectors. The tables in Section V show inventory change in two versions: one at book value, and one (in the notes to the tables) in which only changes in inventories that reflect quantity changes are entered. These real inventory changes are estimated by subtracting the inventory valuation adjustment (IVA) of the Department of Commerce National Income Division.

Data on flows (sources and uses of funds) for the sectors and many of the subsectors listed in Section III are shown in Section VII. Here again, for several of the major sectors, data on inventories are shown both at book value and with IVA.

The Federal Reserve Board's analogous set of tables are the "sector statements of sources and uses of funds," which include estimates of saving from the income account as well as from the balance sheet. These appear in *Supplement 5*, Table 4, pages 11-31, and for subsectors on pages 41-73. They cover 1946-60 in annual data and 1952-60 in quarterly data.

Section VIII provides data on sources and uses of funds, showing, for each type, the sectoral distribution in every year. For structures and durable goods, the flow tables (VIII-a) show expenditures at original and constant cost and net investment at current replacement and constant cost. Inventory flows are shown in constant and in current dollars, and the latter both at book value and with inventory valuation adjustment. No flow of funds into land is estimated; all changes in land value are treated as capital gains, ignoring intersectoral land sales. Financial flows (Tables VIII-b, VIII-c, and VIII-d) are mostly estimated by taking the net change in assets and liabilities between the beginning and end of the year, assuming that valuation changes are small enough to be ignored. However, the flow of funds into equity securities and net worth must be estimated directly because this assumption cannot be made. Net purchases are therefore used as the flow of funds into common stock, and net issues of stock and saving as the net worth flow.

Part b of Section VIII shows uses of funds while parts c and d deal with sources. Part c gives data on the issuance of financial liabilities and part d presents estimates of the flow of funds through common and preferred stock and of gross and net saving, by sector. The analogous FRB tables are shown on pages 74-119 of *Supplement 5* as "annual flows, 1946-1960" and "quarterly flows, 1952-1960."

Assets and Liabilities

Some of the asset and liability tables have self-explanatory titles, but others are somewhat ambiguous or have a different coverage from that of the closest corresponding groups in the

FRB accounts. In this section the NBER categories are defined and reconciled with the corresponding FRB transactions categories.[2]

Most of the large differences between the asset and liability totals listed here and those shown by the Federal Reserve Board arise from the fact that the FRB consolidates its sectors, netting out intrasector holdings, while the NBER does not. By this process the FRB eliminates, for example, interbank deposits, corporate stocks and bonds owned by other corporations, and holdings of federal government debt by federal agencies and trust funds.

Holdings of tangible assets are not included in the FRB accounts. Data given here on the market or current value of tangible assets, mainly derived by the perpetual inventory method, are from *The National Wealth of the United States*, and definitions of the asset categories can be found there. The only substantial change from that source is that monetary metals, included there under tangible assets, have been shifted to intangible or financial assets, under currency and demand deposits.

Currency and Demand Deposits (Tables IV-b-1 and IV-c-1) encompass two FRB classifications: gold and Treasury currency, and demand deposits and currency. The former category is made up mainly of monetary gold and silver held by the Treasury monetary funds plus official gold holdings of the rest of the world, which were omitted in the NBER accounts. The only liability item under this heading is Treasury currency liability, consisting of seigniorage on coins and revalued silver plus minor coin outstanding and the sum of Federal Reserve bank notes, national bank notes, and U.S. notes outstanding, minus gold reserves against U.S. notes. All the rest of the difference between assets and liabilities appears as discrepancy, since monetary metals are not considered to be a liability of any sector.

TABLE 1

Currency and Demand Deposits: Reconciliation of NBER and FRB Estimates

(billion dollars)

	1954	1955	1956	1957	1958
1. FRB currency and demand deposits, assets	134.7	135.5	137.2	137.9	144.8
2. Less NBER rest-of-world assets	4.3	4.3	4.5	4.7	4.8
3. Plus NBER Federal Reserve banks and Treasury monetary funds, assets	48.6	48.7	49.2	50.9	46.8
4. Plus NBER commercial banks, assets	34.0	34.3	35.6	35.5	35.1
5. Total of lines 1-4	213.0	214.2	217.5	219.6	221.9
6. NBER currency and demand deposits, assets	213.1	214.2	217.5	219.5	221.9
7. FRB currency and demand deposits, liabilities	141.9	144.2	145.9	145.2	151.0
8. Plus NBER gold certificates	21.0	21.0	21.3	22.1	20.0
9. Plus NBER FR bank holdings of FR notes	0.2	0.3	0.4	0.4	0.5
10. Plus NBER Exch. Stab. Fund deposits with FR banks	0.2	0.2	0.1	--	0.2
11. Plus NBER FR bank holdings of Treasury currency	0.4	0.3	0.3	0.3	0.3
12. Plus NBER commercial bank demand deposits	12.8	12.9	13.7	13.2	13.5
13. Plus NBER cash items in process of collection	10.0	13.3	13.9	13.7	14.6
14. Plus FRB Federal Reserve float	0.8	1.6	1.7	1.4	1.3
15. Plus FRB member-bank reserves	18.9	19.0	19.1	19.0	18.5
16. Plus FRB other domestic bank deposits	0.1	0.1	0.1	0.1	0.1
17. Plus FRB other vault cash	2.5	2.7	3.3	3.3	3.2
18. Plus FRB federal currency liabilities	2.5	2.5	2.5	2.6	2.6
19. Total of lines 7-18	211.3	218.1	222.3	221.3	225.8
20. NBER currency and demand deposits, liabilities	211.5	218.2	222.2	221.5	225.8

[2]For an earlier discussion of the differences between NBER and FRB accounts, see Morris Mendelson, *The Flow-of-Funds Through the Financial Markets, 1953-1955*, New York, NBER, 1959, pp. 3-20.

Source to Table 1

Line

1: *Supplement* 5, Table 19L, line K.
2: Table IV-b-1, line 9.
3-4: Table IV-b-1, lines 5a and 5b.
5: Sum of lines 1, 3, and 4, minus line 2.
6: Table IV-b-1, line 8.
7: *Supplement* 5, Table 19L, line A.
8: See notes to Table III-5a-2, line III-1.
9: From various issues of *Annual Report of the Board of Governors of the Federal Reserve System*, table on condition of Federal Reserve Banks.

Line

10: See notes to Table III-5a-2, line II-1.
11: Same source as line 9.
12: Table IV-b-1c, column 5.
13: Table IV-b-1, line 12.
14: *Supplement* 5, Table 16L, line i.
15-17: *Supplement* 5, Table 17L, lines W, Z, and a.
18: *Supplement* 5, Table 8, federal government sector, "Treasury currency liability."
19: Sum of lines 7-18.
20: Table IV-b-1, line 15.

TABLE 2

Gold and Treasury Currency: Reconciliation of NBER and FRB Estimates

(billion dollars)

	1954	1955	1956	1957	1958
1. FRB gold and Treasury currency	41.7	42.5	43.1	43.9	44.7
2. Plus NBER cash assets of Exch. Stab. Fund	0.3	0.3	0.2	0.1	0.2
3. Less FRB rest-of-world gold	15.1	15.9	16.1	16.0	19.3
4. Less FRB nonmonetary silver bullion held at cost in acct. of U.S. Treasury	--	--	0.1	0.1	0.1
5. Total of lines 1-4	26.9	26.9	27.1	27.9	25.5
6. NBER Treasury monetary funds, currency and demand deposits	27.0	27.0	27.2	28.0	26.0

Line

1: *Supplement* 5, Table 18L, sum of lines A and G.
2: See notes to Table III-5a-2, line II-1.

Line

3-4: *Supplement* 5, Table 18L, lines E and K.
5: Sum of lines 1-4.
6: Table III-5a-2, line II-1.

The NBER total for other currency and demand deposits is much larger than that of the FRB because the FRB nets out all the currency and demand deposits held by commercial banks and the Treasury monetary funds, although it does take in foreign currency and deposit holdings. The main items disappearing in the FRB consolidation are bank reserves with the Federal Reserve Banks, gold certificates, interbank deposits, cash items in process of collection, Federal Reserve float, and vault cash.

There is a very large discrepancy between assets and liabilities in this item of the NBER accounts because monetary metals appear in assets but not in liabilities. Furthermore, several large items of float also enter into the discrepancy. Nonfarm households' assets are estimated as a residual by subtracting known holdings by other groups from total currency and demand deposits of individuals, partnerships, and corporations, after adjusting that total to a holder record basis.

Other Bank Deposits and Shares (Tables IV-b-2 and IV-c-2) consist of time deposits at commercial and mutual savings banks and postal savings deposits plus shares in savings and loan associations and credit unions. The Federal Reserve Board includes these items, along with consumer-held U.S. government savings bonds, in a category called "fixed-value redeemable claims" (*Supplement* 5, Table 20L, p. 78), which differs from the NBER asset totals by including rest-of-world time deposits as well as savings bonds.

It is assumed, for this category, that there is no discrepancy between total assets and total liabilities (as there is for currency and demand deposits) except for rest-of-world holdings. Total assets are estimated from total liabilities and the household sector is calculated as a residual.

TABLE 3

Other Bank Deposits and Shares: Reconciliation of NBER and FRB Estimates

(billion dollars)

	1954	1955	1956	1957	1958
1. FRB fixed-value redeemable claims, assets	156.9	165.3	174.3	184.4	200.6
2. Less FRB U.S. savings bonds (consumer-held)	50.0	50.2	50.1	48.2	47.7
3. Less NBER rest-of-world time deposits	1.8	1.7	1.6	1.6	2.6
4. Total of lines 1-3	105.1	113.4	122.6	134.6	150.3
5. NBER other bank deposits and shares, assets	104.9	113.3	122.5	134.6	150.2
6. FRB fixed-value redeemable claims, liabilities	156.9	165.3	174.3	184.4	200.6
7. Less FRB U.S. savings bonds (consumer-held)	50.0	50.2	50.1	48.2	47.7
8. Total of lines 6-7	106.9	115.1	124.2	136.2	152.9
9. NBER other bank deposits and shares, liabilities	106.7	114.9	124.1	136.1	152.8

Line
1: *Supplement 5*, Table 20L, line M.
2: *Ibid.*, line S.
3: Table IV-b-2, line 9.
4: Line 1 minus lines 2 and 3.
5: Table IV-b-2, line 8.

Line
6: *Supplement 5*, Table 20L, line A.
7: *Ibid.*, line I.
8: Line 6 minus line 7.
9: Table IV-c-2, line 8.

Private Life Insurance Reserves (Tables IV-b-3 and IV-c-3) include all liabilities of life insurance companies, fraternal orders, savings bank life insurance (SBLI), and group health insurance plans except for small amounts of specifically identified "other liabilities." The method of estimation treats all insurance organizations as if they were organized as mutuals,

TABLE 4

Private Life Insurance Reserves: Reconciliation of NBER and FRB Estimates

(billion dollars)

	1954	1955	1956	1957	1958
1. FRB saving through life ins., assets and liab.	70.2	73.4	77.2	80.0	83.4
2. Plus FRB savings through life ins. co. pension funds	10.0	11.2	12.4	14.0	15.5
3. Plus FRB assets minus liab., life ins. co.	7.4	8.3	8.6	9.2	10.3
4. Plus FRB assets minus liab., fraternal orders	0.8	0.9	0.9	0.8	0.8
5. Plus NBER life ins. co., tangible assets	3.3	3.8	4.1	4.5	4.5
6. Plus NBER life ins. co., other intang. assets	2.3	2.5	2.8	3.0	3.2
7. Plus NBER group health and SBLI reserves	.8	.9	1.0	1.0	1.1
8. Plus NBER fraternal order tangibles and other intangibles	0.1	0.1	0.1	0.2	0.2
9. Less FRB saving through fed. govt. life ins.	6.0	5.9	6.0	6.2	6.2
10. Less NBER other liabilities and equities, life ins. cos.	2.8	3.2	3.6	3.7	3.9
11. Less NBER other liab., fraternal orders	0.2	0.2	0.2	0.2	0.3
12. Total of lines 1-11	85.9	91.8	97.3	102.6	108.6
13. NBER private life ins. reserves, liabilities	85.7	91.6	97.1	102.2	108.5
14. Less NBER rest-of-world holdings of ins. reserves	1.6	1.8	1.9	2.0	2.1
15. Total of lines 13-14	84.3	90.0	95.4	100.6	106.5
16. NBER private life ins. reserves, assets	84.0	89.9	95.2	100.2	106.4

Source to Table 4

Line
1: *Supplement 5*, Table 21L, line F.
2: *Ibid.*, Table 22L, line G.
3: *Ibid.*, Table 12L, line C minus line M.
4: FRB worksheets.
5-6: Table III-5h, lines I-7 and II-20.
7: Tables III-5k-2 and III-5k-3, line III-14.
8: Table III-5k-1, lines I-7 and II-20.
9: *Supplement 5*, Table 21L, line B.

Line
10: Table III-5h, lines III-13 and IV.
11: Table III-5k-1, line III-13.
12: Lines 1-8 minus lines 9-11.
13: Table IV-c-3, line 8.
14: Table IV-b-3, line 9.
15: Line 12 minus line 14.
16: Table IV-b-3, line 8.

with all assets, except those specifically earmarked, belonging to the policyholders. This procedure understates the equity of stockholders in stock life insurance companies. However, it was not possible to subdivide the sector into stock and mutual companies. Fortunately, for this purpose, more than half the outstanding life insurance is with mutual companies. This category is not confined strictly to life insurance reserves, including as it does the reserves of life insurance companies against other types of policies (pensions, annuities, accident and health insurance) and the reserves of nonprofit medical plans.

The closest FRB transactions category is saving through life insurance, which includes government life insurance reserves but excludes pension reserves of life insurance companies. Even when these two adjustments are made, however, the NBER item is much larger, mainly because it includes all liabilities not allocable to categories other than policyholders. This procedure adds to the FRB estimates the difference between financial assets and liabilities, as estimated by the FRB for life insurance companies and fraternal orders, plus total assets (tangible and "other intangible") not included by the FRB, minus "other liabilities" and equities (life insurance company stock outstanding). The NBER data also make a rough adjustment for rest-of-world insurance assets, not calculated by the FRB.

Private Pension and Retirement Funds (Tables IV-b-4 and IV-c-4) consist of the reserves (assumed equal to total assets) of noninsured private pension plans, that is, plans not managed by insurance companies. Corporate pension funds, covered in SEC surveys, own the great bulk of the assets, but union-administered and multiemployer funds and those of nonprofit organizations are also included.

This category is approximately equivalent to that part of the FRB transactions item "saving through pension funds" which is the liability of noninsured pension plans. However, the

TABLE 5

Private Pension and Retirement Funds: Reconciliation of NBER and FRB Estimates

(billion dollars)

	1954	1955	1956	1957	1958
1. FRB saving through pension funds, private noninsured pension plans	12.6	14.9	17.2	20.0	23.0
2. Less SEC common stock of corporate pension funds, book value	2.3	3.0	3.8	4.8	6.0
3. Plus SEC common stock, corporate pension funds, market value	3.2	4.8	5.6	6.0	9.5
4. Plus NBER misc. assets of noninsured pension plans	0.5	0.6	0.8	0.9	1.0
5. Total of lines 1-4	14.0	17.3	19.8	22.1	27.5
6. NBER private pension and retirement funds	14.3	17.4	20.0	22.3	27.8

Line
1: *Supplement* 5, Table 22L, line H.
2: SEC, *Corporate Pension Funds*, 1959 (Statistical Series, Release No. 1680, 1960), Table 1.
3: *Ibid.*, Table 3, and Table III-5j-1, line II-17.

Line
4: Table III-5j, line II-20.
5: Sum of lines 1, 3, and 4, minus line 2.
6: Table IV-b-4, line 8.

FRB excludes miscellaneous intangible assets and apparently includes stock at book rather than market value, presumably on the assumption that it is only the book value which enters into the obligation to pension holders. The NBER method, as for life insurance and government pension reserves, treats all assets as belonging to policyholders.

The coverage of the FRB category is slightly narrower in 1945-49. Union-administered, multiemployer, and nonprofit plans are excluded, as are mortgage holdings of corporate plans.

Government Pension and Insurance Funds (Tables IV-b-5 and IV-c-5) consist of retirement funds for federal, state, and local government employees, the Old Age and Survivors' Insurance and railroad retirement trust funds, federal government life insurance funds, the unemployment insurance trust fund, and state-administered workmen's compensation funds. All the assets of these funds are credited to the policyholders or beneficiaries.

TABLE 6

Government Pension and Insurance Funds: Reconciliation of NBER and FRB Estimates

(billion dollars)

	1954	1955	1956	1957	1958
1. FRB saving through pension funds, fed. govt.	9.4	10.0	10.9	11.3	12.3
2. FRB saving through pension funds, state and local govt.	9.3	10.6	12.1	13.7	15.6
3. FRB saving through life insur., federal govt.	6.0	5.9	6.0	6.2	6.2
4. Plus FRB OASI fund assets	20.6	21.7	22.5	22.4	21.9
5. Plus NBER unemployment trust fund assets	8.7	8.8	9.1	9.1	7.1
6. Plus NBER state-adm. workmen's compensation fund assets	0.9	1.0	1.1	1.2	1.3
7. Total of lines 1-6	54.9	58.0	61.7	63.9	64.4
8. NBER govt. pension and insurance funds	55.2	58.4	62.0	64.9	66.1

Line
1-2: *Supplement 5*, Table 22L, lines B and E.
3: *Ibid.*, Table 21L, line B.
4: *Ibid.*, Table 8, p. 36.
5: See note to Table III-5b-1, line II-1.

Line
6: See note to Table III-5b-2, line II-21.
7: Sum of lines 1-6.
8: Table IV-b-5, line 8.

The corresponding Federal Reserve Board categories are the government parts of saving through life insurance and saving through pension funds, but these exclude the unemployment, workmen's compensation and OASI funds. They also measure the liabilities of the government life insurance funds by policy reserves rather than by total assets as in the NBER estimates.

Consumer Credit (Tables IV-b-6 and IV-c-6) includes short- and intermediate-term credit extended to consumers, but excludes mortgage and security credit. The item has the same

TABLE 7

Consumer Credit: Reconciliation of NBER and FRB Estimates

(billion dollars)

	1954	1955	1956	1957	1958
1. FRB consumer credit	32.5	38.9	42.5	45.3	45.5
2. Plus FRB commercial bank loans offset by hypothecated deposits	0.5	0.5	0.6	0.6	0.6
3. Total of lines 1-2	33.0	39.4	43.1	45.9	46.1
4. NBER consumer credit	32.9	39.4	43.1	45.9	46.1

Line
1: *Supplement 5*, Table 29L, line F.
2: *Ibid.*, Table 32L, line z.

Line
3: Sum of lines 1 and 2.
4: Table IV-b-6, line 8.

coverage as the FRB series. The only difference is that in the NBER figures hypothecated deposits are not netted out of the data for consumer credit extended by commercial banks and classified under other loans as is done by the FRB. Supplementary Table IV-b-6a consists of a rearrangement of prewar data to fit more closely into the postwar sectoral classification.

Trade Credit (Tables IV-b-7 and IV-c-7) consists in theory of book credit extended by one business to another in connection with the sale of goods and services. It should thus exclude all consumer credit and most debts to financial institutions, as well as all debts represented by financial instruments, such as bonds or commercial paper. In practice, the estimates are made by subtracting identifiable items other than trade credit from business payables and receivables; they are thus residuals which contain other types of debt. The FRB figures are lower than those presented here mainly because financial institutions have been more thoroughly eliminated from the corporate sector in their accounts. The effect of this difference can be seen in the attempt at reconciliation in Table 8. The receivables of "credit agencies other than banks," deducted from corporate receivables by the FRB, are considerably larger than the consumer and trade credit and other loans of finance companies and other finance deducted in arriving at the NBER estimates. The FRB method probably removes more items inappropriate under the definition of trade credit but runs a greater risk of excluding debts from the nonfinancial sector which fail to be picked up in the finance sector. An even lower recent estimate made at the NBER by Martin Seiden ("The Quality of Trade Credit," ms.) eliminates more doubtful items, but it uses a narrower definition of nonfinancial corporations without any necessity of insuring that every item excluded from trade credit was included somewhere else.

TABLE 8

Trade Credit: Reconciliation of NBER and FRB Estimates

(billion dollars)

	1954	1955	1956	1957	1958
1. FRB trade credit	57.1	67.2	73.5	75.4	81.4
2. Plus FRB nonfarm unincorp. bus. trade credit assets	9.1	9.7	10.6	10.9	11.6
3. Plus NBER finance co. trade credit	0.9	1.1	1.3	1.5	1.7
4. Plus NBER other finance trade credit	0.2	0.2	0.3	0.4	0.4
5. Plus difference bet. NBER fin. co. rcvbles. and FRB rcvbles. of credit agen. other than banks	1.6	1.9	3.0	3.9	5.1
6. Total of lines 1-5	68.9	80.1	88.7	92.1	100.2
7. NBER trade credit	68.8	80.4	88.8	92.1	100.4
8. FRB trade debt	45.6	54.7	59.7	60.6	63.6
9. Plus FRB noncorp. nonfinan. bus. trade credit assets	9.1	9.7	10.6	10.9	11.6
10. Total of lines 8-9	54.7	64.4	70.3	71.5	75.2
11. NBER trade debt	58.6	69.7	76.9	80.0	87.0

Line
1: *Supplement 5*, Table 33L, line A.
2: *Ibid.*, line J.
3-4: Tables III-5l and III-5m, line II-7.
5: NBER from Table III-5l, lines II-6, II-7, and II-10; FRB from unpublished worksheets on trade credit.

Line
6: Sum of lines 1-5.
7: Table IV-b-7, line 8.
8: *Supplement 5*, Table 33L, line E.
9: *Ibid.*, line J.
10: Sum of lines 8-9.
11: Table IV-c-7, line 8.

Another contribution to the lower level of the FRB estimates is the fact that they include, for nonfarm unincorporated business, only net trade credit (trade credit minus trade debt), counted as a negative liability. The NBER data show gross trade credit and trade debt.

The trade debt figures from the two sources differ considerably, even though their derivations both start from the same SEC working capital series for corporate payables. It is not possible to find any simple explanation for the discrepancy because of differences in method: the NBER deducts specific types of debt, such as bank loans, while the FRB deducts all payables of certain institutions such as brokers and dealers and credit agencies other than banks and then deducts bank loans for the remaining group. It seems likely that the FRB method eliminates from the total more liabilities that are not strictly trade debt. Supplementary Table IV-b-7a consists of a rearrangement of prewar data to fit more closely into the postwar sectoral classification.

Loans on Securities (Tables IV-b-8 and IV-c-8) consist of loans for purchasing and carrying securities. Mainly these are loans by commercial banks but they also include credit granted by security brokers and dealers (customer debit balances). No estimates are made of security credit extended by others, except for agencies of foreign banks. The NBER estimates differ from those of the FRB mainly by excluding customer credit balances, treated as security credit by the FRB but as other loans (Table IV-b-10) here.

TABLE 9

Loans on Securities: Reconciliation of NBER and FRB Estimates

(billion dollars)

	1954	1955	1956	1957	1958
1. FRB security credit, assets	8.6	9.6	9.0	8.7	10.4
2. Less FRB consumer and nonprofit customers' credit balances with brokers and dealers	1.0	.9	.9	.9	1.2
3. Less FRB rest-of-world sec. cred. assets	0.1	0.1	0.1	0.1	0.1
4. Total of lines 1-3	7.5	8.6	8.0	7.7	9.1
5. NBER loans on securities, assets	7.6	8.7	8.0	7.6	9.2
6. FRB security credit, liabilities	8.6	9.6	9.0	8.7	10.4
7. Less FRB consumer and nonprofit customers' cred. balances with brokers and dealers	1.0	0.9	0.9	0.9	1.2
8. Less FRB rest-of-world sec. cred. liab.	0.1	0.1	0.1	0.1	0.1
9. Total of lines 6-8	7.5	8.6	8.0	7.7	9.1
10. NBER loans on securities, liabilities	7.9	9.0	8.3	8.0	9.6

Line
1-3: *Supplement 5*, Table 30L, lines J, K, and N.
4: Sum of lines 1-3.
5: Table IV-b-8, line 8.

Line
6-8: *Supplement 5*, Table 30L, lines A, K, and I.
9: Sum of lines 6-8.
10: Table IV-c-8, line 8.

The NBER liability estimates are higher than the FRB figures because a larger ratio (derived from earlier FRB estimating procedures) was used here to raise customer debit balances at New York Stock Exchange member firms to a level covering all brokers and dealers.

There is no residual line in either Table IV-b-8 or Table IV-c-8. The two total lines have not been forced into agreement and the difference between them (line 10 of IV-b-8) is therefore simply an unexplained discrepancy.

Bank Loans, n.e.c. (Tables IV-b-9 and IV-c-9) are all commercial bank loans (and a small amount by Federal Reserve banks) not included in the other specified loan categories. The specified classes of loans are mainly mortgages, consumer credit, security credit, and bonds and notes.

TABLE 10

Bank Loans, N.E.C.: Reconciliation of NBER and FRB Estimates

(billion dollars)

	1954	1955	1956	1957	1958
1. FRB bank loans, n.e.c., assets	34.2	42.1	47.9	50.2	51.5
2. Plus FRB loans to domestic banks by Federal Reserve banks	--	0.1	--	--	--
3. Plus FRB CCC-guar. loans and certificates of interest	2.3	1.2	0.9	0.5	0.8
4. Plus FRB open-market paper	1.0	0.8	0.9	1.1	1.2
5. Total of lines 1-4	37.5	44.2	49.7	51.8	53.5
6. NBER bank loans, n.e.c., assets	37.6	44.4	50.0	52.1	53.8
7. FRB bank loans, n.e.c., liabilities	34.2	42.1	47.9	50.2	51.5
8. Plus lines 3, 4, and 5	3.3	2.1	1.8	1.6	2.0
9. Less FRB rest-of-world liabilities	1.0	1.4	1.8	2.1	2.6
10. Total of lines 7-9	36.5	42.8	47.9	49.7	50.9
11. NBER bank loans, n.e.c., liabilities	36.6	43.0	48.3	50.0	51.2

Line
1: *Supplement 5*, Table 31L, line H. (The published figure for 1958 seems to be an error.)
2: *Ibid.*, Table 8 (G.1), line v.
3-4: *Ibid.*, Table 8(G), lines X and Y.
5: Sum of lines 1-4.
6: Table IV-b-9, line 8.

Line
7: *Supplement 5*, Table 31L, line I.
8: Lines 3, 4, and 5.
9: *Supplement 5*, line R.
10: Sum of lines 7-8, minus line 9.
11: Table IV-c-9, line 8.

The NBER estimates for this category are generally larger than those in *Supplement 5* (the composition of which is described in *Federal Reserve Bulletin*, August 1959, pp. 855-856), because they include several additional items. The main ones are loans to commercial banks by the Federal Reserve banks, netted out in the FRB accounts, and CCC-guaranteed loans and certificates of interest and open-market paper, both included by the FRB in "other loans."

A rough division of bank loans into short- and long-term is made in Tables IV-c-9a and IV-c-9b, using SEC series on long-term bank debt which are derived from the FRB loan surveys in 1946, 1955, and 1957.

Other Loans (Tables IV-b-10 and IV-c-10) consist essentially of all loans not made by banks and not included in the categories specified separately, namely, consumer credit, trade credit, security credit, mortgages, and bonds and notes. The major components are federal government loans to business and to other countries, insurance policy loans, loans to business by finance companies, and household credit balances with brokers and dealers.

The corresponding FRB category differs considerably from this one. Among the additional assets included by the FRB are open-market paper (mostly placed under bonds and notes, Table IV-b-12 in the NBER accounts), federal government loans to states (under state and local obligations, Table IV-b-14), CCC-guaranteed loans and certificates of interest (under bank loans, n.e.c., Table IV-b-9), consumer loans offset by hypothecated deposits (under consumer credit, Table IV-b-6), and other loans of business finance companies (under trade credit, Table IV-b-7). In addition, loans from the rest of the world are also included by the FRB in total assets, but excluded here. The FRB data appear to exclude loans to farmers by agricultural credit cooperatives (Table III-5m-4) which are included in the NBER totals.

The differences on the liability side are much the same, except that rest-of-world liabilities to the federal government must also be deducted from the FRB figures.

Total liabilities for this item were derived from total assets after adjusting for rest-of-world liabilities. Other loan liabilities of nonfarm unincorporated business were the residual in this calculation.

TABLE 11

Other Loans: Reconciliation of NBER and FRB Estimates

(billion dollars)

	1954	1955	1956	1957	1958
1. FRB other loans, assets	28.7	29.7	30.6	33.3	35.3
2. Less FRB open-market paper	2.8	2.6	3.1	4.0	4.0
3. Less FRB fed. govt. loans to states	0.5	0.5	0.6	0.8	1.0
4. Less FRB CCC-guar. loans and certificates of interest	2.3	1.2	0.9	0.5	0.8
5. Less FRB consumer bank loans offset by hypothecated deposits	0.5	0.5	0.6	0.6	0.6
6. Less NBER finance co. trade credit	0.9	1.1	1.3	1.4	1.7
7. Plus NBER nonfarm household other loan assets	2.4	2.3	2.3	2.3	3.1
8. Plus NBER other loans of agric. credit org.	0.7	0.7	0.8	0.9	1.2
9. Plus NBER fed. loans to farm coops., ex. tobacco	0.1	0.3	0.1	0.1	0.1
10. Total of lines 1-9	24.9	27.1	27.3	29.3	31.6
11. NBER other loans, assets	25.0	27.2	27.3	29.3	31.6
12. FRB other loans, liabilities	28.4	29.4	30.3	32.8	34.7
13. Less lines 2-6	7.0	5.9	6.5	7.3	8.1
14. Less FRB rest-of-world loans from federal government	10.7	10.6	10.7	11.0	11.6
15. Plus lines 7-9	3.2	3.3	3.2	3.3	4.4
16. Total of lines 12-15	13.9	16.2	16.3	17.8	19.4
17. NBER other loans, liabilities	14.0	16.1	16.2	17.8	19.4

Line
1-5: *Supplement 5*, Table 32L, lines A, S, n, r, and z.
6: Table III-51, line II-7.
7: Table III-1, line II-10.
8: Table III-5m-4, line II-10.
9: Table III-7d, column 6.
10: Sum of lines 1 and 7-9 minus the sum of lines 2-6.
11: Table IV-b-10, line 8.

Line
12: *Supplement 5*, Table 32L, line H.
13: Sum of lines 2-6.
14: *Supplement 5*, Table 32L, line q.
15: Sum of lines 7-9.
16: Sum of lines 12 and 15 minus lines 13 and 14.
17: Table IV-c-10, line 8.

Mortgages, which are debt secured by real property, are set out in considerable detail, by type, in Tables IV-b-11, IV-c-11, IV-b-12, and subsidiary tables. The coverage of this category is the same as that of the series published regularly by the Federal Reserve Board and of the data in Saul B. Klaman, *The Volume of Mortgage Debt in the Postwar Decade* (1958). The latter source gives an account of the construction of mortgage estimates and an appraisal of their quality.

The data on mortgage holdings are divided here into nonfarm (Table IV-b-11) and farm mortgages (Table IV-b-12), and the former are further broken down into residential (IV-b-11a) and nonresidential (IV-b-11b). Residential mortgage holdings are then subdivided again by type of property (one- to four-family versus multifamily) and by type of mortgage (FHA-insured, VA-guaranteed, and conventional).

Mortgage assets and liabilities are shown at the same total value, with nonfarm households the residual holders and debtors. No rest-of-world debts or holdings are shown, although it is known (see Table IV-c-11) that U.S. life insurance companies, for example, own over $700 million of foreign—mainly Canadian—mortgages. The presumption is that the U.S. holdings of foreign mortgages are approximately offset by foreign holdings of U.S. mortgages and that the estimate of household mortgage holdings, which is a residual, is therefore not seriously distorted.

The FRB tabulations in *Supplement 5* distinguish one- to four-family, multifamily, nonfarm nonresidential, and farm mortgages. No reconciliations are shown for any of these categories because the estimates used here, derived mainly from Klaman, *The Volume of Mortgage Debt* and from data of the Federal Reserve Board and the Home Loan Bank Board, are virtually identical with those in *Supplement 5*.

Several supplementary tables (IV-b-11c, IV-b-11c-1 through IV-b-11c-4, and IV-b-12a are included here for benchmark years from 1900 through 1945. These put data from *A Stud of Saving* into a form more comparable with the later information, changing the coverage o sectors and, in some cases, taking advantage of later studies and estimates of mortgage debt particularly by Klaman and the Home Loan Bank Board. The most extensive of these revi sions were in the data on multifamily and nonresidential mortgages, where the totals and th amounts held by households were scaled down sharply.

U.S. Government Securities (Tables IV-b-13, IV-b-13a, IV-b-13b, and IV-b-13c) cover di rect federal debt and guaranteed securities issued by federal agencies, including deman notes issued to the IMF. Nonguaranteed federal agency bonds and notes are excluded an placed under other bonds and notes (Table IV-b-15). Also excluded is privately held stoc issued by federal agencies, the largest element of which is Federal Home Loan Bank stoc owned by insured savings and loan associations.

In supplementary tables this category is divided into several parts, the estimates for whic are less reliable than those for the totals. The subcategories are short-term securitie (Table IV-b-13a), savings bonds (Table IV-b-13b), and other long-term securities (Table IV-b-13c). The estimates of short-term holdings are taken mainly from FRB worksheets, an those for savings bonds from the Treasury ownership survey. The estimates for long-term securities other than savings bonds are thus a residual.

Both the FRB and the NBER balance sheets consolidate government corporations with the federal government to the extent that investments by the government in these corporations are netted out. Therefore there is no entry for agency securities held by the federal govern-ment or for federal advances to these agencies.

TABLE 12

U.S. Government Securities: Reconciliation of NBER and FRB Estimates

(billion dollars)

	1954	1955	1956	1957	1958
1. FRB federal obligations, assets	179.4	180.2	174.6	175.7	184.8
2. Plus FRB consumer-held savings bonds	50.0	50.2	50.1	48.2	47.7
3. Plus NBER U.S. govt. secur. held by fed. govt.	5.2	5.2	5.5	5.9	5.8
4. Plus NBER U.S. govt. secur. held by federal insur. and pension funds	44.4	46.5	48.4	49.4	48.4
5. Less FRB nonguar. federal obligations	2.1	3.6	4.2	6.3	5.8
6. Less FRB rest-of-world holdings of federal obligations	4.8	5.8	6.6	6.8	6.8
7. Plus difference between FRB and NBER est. of valuation discrepancy	--	--	0.2	0.4	0.1
8. Total of lines 1-7	272.1	272.7	268.0	266.5	274.2
9. NBER U.S. government securities, assets	272.1	272.7	268.1	266.4	274.3
10. FRB federal obligations, liabilities	179.3	180.4	175.3	176.7	185.7
11. Plus lines 2-4	99.6	101.9	104.0	103.5	101.9
12. Plus FRB demand notes issued to IMF	1.5	1.6	1.1	0.7	0.8
13. Less FRB nonguar. fed. obligations	2.1	3.6	4.2	6.3	5.8
14. Total of lines 10-13	278.3	280.3	276.2	274.6	282.6
15. NBER U.S. government securities, liabilities	278.4	280.4	276.3	274.6	282.7

Line
1-2: *Supplement* 5, Table 23L, lines E and I.
3: Table III-7, line II-13.
4: Table III-5b-1, line II-13.
5-6: *Supplement* 5, Table 23L, lines D and p.
7: *Ibid.*, line 5 (with sign reversed) minus Table IV-b-13, line 10.
8: Sum of lines 1-4 and line 7, minus lines 5 and 6.

Line
9: Table IV-b-13, line 8.
10: *Supplement* 5, Table 23L, line A.
11: Sum of lines 2-4.
12: *Supplement* 5, Table 34L, line 5.
13: *Ibid.*, Table 23L, line D.
14: Sum of lines 10-12, minus line 13.
15: Table IV-c-12, line 7a.

The FRB's federal obligation item differs from this one by including nonguaranteed securities but excluding consumer-held savings bonds, demand notes issued to the IMF, and all federal securities held by the federal government and federal agencies and trust funds, particularly the large social insurance funds.

On the liability side, these items account for all of the divergence between FRB and NBER figures, but, on the asset side, there is a difference in the estimate of the discrepancy between total assets and total liabilities. The discrepancy arises because liabilities are listed at par value and assets at book value. For most assets this type of discrepancy disappears in the process of estimating one sector (usually households) as a residual. For government bonds, however, the Treasury ownership survey, giving data by holder on a par value basis, permits direct estimation of the discrepancy for several holder groups. The NBER data estimate this only for banks, but the FRB makes a more comprehensive estimate, covering all sectors except households.

A supplementary table (IV-b-13d) revises the sectoral allocation of U.S. government securities given in *A Study of Saving* for benchmark years back to 1900. Aside from the redefinition of the sectors, the main change to match later years is elimination of the estimate for nonfarm unincorporated business holdings of these securities. The amounts have been added into the household sector.

State and Local Government Securities are all debts of state and local governments except for their trade debt and the obligations of their retirement and other insurance funds. The amounts shown here are larger than in *Supplement 5* because we have included state and local debts to the federal government (included in "other loans" by the FRB) and an estimate of non-interest-bearing debt.

TABLE 13

State and Local Government Securities: Reconciliation of NBER and FRB Estimates

(billion dollars)

	1954	1955	1956	1957	1958
1. FRB state and local oblig., assets and liab.	42.5	46.0	49.2	53.8	59.5
2. Plus FRB fed. govt. loans to state and local governments	0.5	0.5	0.6	0.8	1.0
3. Plus NBER non-interest-bearing state and local govt. debt	0.6	0.6	0.6	0.7	0.7
4. Total of lines 1-3	43.6	47.1	50.4	55.3	61.2
5. NBER state and local govt. sec., liabilities	43.6	47.0	50.4	55.2	61.2
6. Less NBER rest-of-world holdings of state and local securities	0.1	0.1	0.1	0.1	0.1
7. Total of lines 5-6	43.5	47.0	50.3	55.2	61.1
8. NBER state and local govt. sec., assets	43.5	47.0	50.3	55.1	61.1

Line
1: *Supplement 5*, Table 24L, line A.
2: *Ibid.*, Table 32L, line n.
3: See note to Table III-6, line III-12.
4: Sum of lines 1-3.

Line
5: Table IV-c-12, line 6.
6: Table IV-b-14, line 9.
7: Line 4 minus line 6.
8: Table IV-b-14, line 8.

In the NBER accounts, total assets are estimated from total liabilities, with only a small estimate of foreign holdings as a discrepancy item, and nonfarm households as the residual sector. The state and local government sector is one case in which the FRB accounts do not completely consolidate a sector; total assets are shown including state and local securities held by the state and local governments themselves.

A supplementary table (IV-b-14a) gives data from *A Study of Saving* for benchmark years back to 1900 according to the postwar classification of sectors.

Other Bonds and Notes (Table IV-b-15) are made up mainly of corporate bonds, but also include foreign bonds, nonguaranteed bonds issued by U.S. government agencies, and commercial paper held outside banks. Total assets are derived from the liabilities of domestic nonfinancial corporations and finance companies (Table IV-c-12) by adding foreign bonds held in the United States and subtracting U.S. corporate bonds held abroad. Nonfarm household assets are calculated as a residual.

The closest FRB category, corporate and foreign bonds (*Supplement 5*, Table 25L, p. 89), excludes commercial paper and nonguaranteed bonds, listing the former under "other loans" and the latter under "U.S. government securities." A further divergence between the two sources arises from the use of different estimates of corporate bond liability. The NBER and FRB series start with the same 1945 value but the former (derived in David Meiselman's and Eli Shapiro's manuscript "Corporate Sources and Uses of Funds" from SEC data on "net change in outstanding corporate securities") rise faster, by about $1 billion between 1945 and 1958.

A supplementary table (IV-b-15a) gives data for corporate bonds from *A Study of Saving* at benchmark dates back to 1900. These have been allocated according to the postwar definitions of the sectors.

TABLE 14

Other Bonds and Notes: Reconciliation of NBER and FRB Estimates

(billion dollars)

	1954	1955	1956	1957	1958
1. FRB corporate and foreign bonds, assets	57.6	61.4	66.5	73.8	80.2
2. Plus FRB federal nonguaranteed sec.	2.1	3.6	4.2	6.3	5.8
3. Plus NBER com. paper held outside banks	1.4	1.6	1.7	2.0	2.1
4. Less FRB rest-of-world holdings of U.S. corporate bonds	0.2	0.3	0.3	0.4	0.5
5. Total of lines 1-4	60.9	66.3	72.1	81.7	87.6
6. NBER other bonds and notes, assets	61.4	67.1	72.9	82.8	88.7

Line
1: *Supplement 5*, Table 25L, line E.
2: *Ibid.*, Table 23L, line D.
3: Table III-51-a, sum of columns 4, 8, and 11.
4: *Supplement 5*, Table 25L, line O.
5: Sum of lines 1 through 3, minus line 4.
6: Table IV-b-15, line 8.

Preferred Stock (Table IV-b-16) is calculated by cumulating new issues, less retirements and conversions, starting from a 1949 benchmark estimate (in Goldsmith's *Supplementary Appendixes to Financial Intermediaries in the American Economy since 1900*, 1958, Appendix F). No adjustment for price changes is made, and it is assumed in effect that holdings are reported at the original cost. The Federal Reserve Board combines preferred with common stock and it is therefore impossible to make any comparisons with their data.

Common Stock (Tables IV-b-17 and IV-b-17a) presents more serious problems. It is a much more important category and is subject to large changes in price whose influence far outweighs that of new issues. Furthermore, most common stock is held by households and there is thus relatively little direct information from the asset side. This situation contrasts with that for most other instruments, which are held mainly by financial institutions.

Even the definition of the total amount of stock outstanding presents difficulties, particularly for intercorporate holdings. The 1949 benchmark from Goldsmith's *Supplementary Appendixes to Financial Intermediaries*, which is the starting point for both the NBER and FRB series, includes some intercorporate stockholdings but not stock of wholly owned subsidiaries (Table F-5, pp. F-32 to F-34), even though the line is entitled "all stock outstanding." The estimated intercorporate holdings thus refer essentially to holdings of those stocks which are also held by others.

TABLE 15

Corporate Stock: Reconciliation of NBER and FRB Estimates

(billion dollars)

	1954	1955	1956	1957	1958
1. FRB corporate stock, assets	258.0	317.0	338.0	299.0	418.0
2. Plus NBER stock held by nonfin. corp.	52.7	63.6	66.1	59.7	79.0
3. Plus NBER stock held by closed-end investment companies	4.7	5.7	5.2	4.9	6.1
4. Less FRB rest-of-world corp. stockholdings	5.3	6.6	7.0	6.1	8.3
5. Total of lines 1-4	310.1	379.7	402.3	357.5	494.8
6. NBER common and preferred stock, assets	298.6	364.3	381.6	347.5	465.4

Line
1: *Supplement 5*, Table 26L, line G.
2: Table III-4, sum of lines II-16 and II-17.
3: Table III-5f-2, sum of lines II-16 and II-17.
4: *Supplement 5*, Table 26L, line Q.
5: Sum of lines 1-3, minus line 4.
6: Sum of Table IV-b-16, line 8, and Table IV-b-17, line 8.

The 1945 and 1949 figures from *Financial Intermediaries* are interpolated and extrapolated to 1958 by new stock issues and capital gains and losses. New stock issues are SEC estimates, with some additions, especially for new incorporations not covered by the SEC (Table IV-b-17a). The change in value of outstanding issues is calculated from Standard and Poor's 500-stock price index. New stock issues accounted for only a little over 10 per cent of the total change in the market value of stock outstanding between 1945 and 1958. All the rest was the effect of price changes on outstanding stock (including new stock after issuance). Corporate stockholdings were estimated, starting from the 1949 benchmark, by assuming that corporations purchased 5 per cent of new stock issues and that price changes on their existing stockholdings were identical with those for stocks in general. Since their share in new stock issues was assumed to be less than a third of their share in stock outstanding in 1945, a very high proportion—over 95 per cent—of the change from 1945 to 1958 was attributed to gains in the value of stock held.

The Federal Reserve Board used an entirely different method of estimating outstanding stock. Starting from a similar benchmark, they extrapolated by means of SEC data on the value of stock traded on exchanges (which accounted for almost two-thirds of the benchmark total). The underlying assumption is that stock traded on exchanges is a constant proportion of total (except intercorporate) stock outstanding.

The resulting FRB estimates rise more rapidly than the NBER series over the postwar period as a whole, and particularly after the 1949 benchmark. The FRB series also fluctuates more violently; after 1950 both its rises and its falls are greater than those in the NBER series, and some of the differences are substantial.

One reason for the sharper movements in the FRB series is that the dates involved are the last trading days of each year. The index underlying the NBER series uses an average of December and January to represent end-of-year levels, a process which involves some smoothing. The effect of this difference in dating can be estimated by measuring the price changes implied by the NBER and FRB series (calculated roughly by subtracting new issues from changes in value outstanding) and comparing them with changes in the stock price index measured from December 31 to December 31 and from December-January to December-January.

For example, in 1953 the index implied by the FRB series declined 5.9 per cent and the one implied by the NBER series only 2.4 per cent. The difference can be explained largely by the fact that the year-end price index fell by 6.6 per cent as against 2.2 per cent for the index actually used in the calculation. Similarly, in 1954, the FRB implied price index rose 46.4 per cent and the NBER one only 38.8 per cent. Again the dating was mainly responsible. The stock price index used rose by 38.1 per cent while the end-of-year index rose 45 per cent. Much the same story was repeated during the 1957 decline and the 1958 increase in stock prices.

The greater volatility of the FRB series thus seems to be mainly attributable to its use of single-date valuations rather than the two-month averages used by the NBER. On the other hand, the relatively rising trend of the FRB series might be explained in several ways. One possibility is that the stock price index used in the NBER calculation is biased: that prices have been rising more quickly outside of the realm of the 500 stocks, either on exchanges other than the New York Stock Exchange or on stocks not traded on any exchanges. Another possibility, more favorable to the NBER estimates, is that the value of stocks traded on the exchanges is a biased extrapolator because the proportion of stocks so traded has been increasing. A third possible source of error is the estimate of stock held by corporations. An overestimate of the rise in this series would produce a downward bias in the NBER series for other stockholdings. The only events that could have brought about a substantial overestimate in the NBER figures would have been a slower rise in prices for corporation-owned stocks than for others or substantial net sales of stock investments by corporations.

There is no liability table corresponding to the asset categories for corporate stock. The matching item on the liability side of the nonfinancial corporation balance sheet is line IV, "equity," which is the difference between the market value of assets and the value of liabilities. The corporate stock asset category includes financial corporations too, and it is therefore necessary to include on the liability side the equity line for commercial banks, investment companies, life insurance, fire and casualty insurance, and finance companies. The matching is still not perfect, however. Stock life insurance companies' equity includes no estimate of retained earnings, all of which are attributed here to policyholders. And equity of brokers and dealers is all included here under unincorporated business although some of them are incorporated.

A supplementary table (IV-b-17c) shows the sectoral distribution of corporate stock at benchmark dates back to 1900. Data from *A Study of Saving* were arranged according to the sector definitions used for the postwar years.

Equity in Mutual Financial Organizations (Table IV-b-18) consists of the equity, all assumed to be owned by nonfarm households, of mutual savings banks, savings and loan associations, and credit unions. Equity in other mutual financial organizations has been dispersed over several categories. That of mutual insurance companies appears in the reserves of private pension and insurance organizations (Tables IV-c-3 and IV-c-4) and the equity of farm cooperatives appears to be scattered among insurance organizations and nonfarm unincorporated business. On the asset side, farm cooperative equity is listed under "other assets" of agriculture.

Equity in Other Business (Table IV-b-19) consists mainly of equity of unincorporated business (including brokers and dealers) but includes also the equity of the federal government in the Exchange Stabilization Fund. All unincorporated business equity is allocated to the nonfarm household sector, but part of it duplicates equity in farm cooperatives already covered in agriculture sector assets. Another part represents the equity of incorporated brokers and dealers which is already presumably covered by household sector holdings of corporate stock.

Other Intangible Assets and Liabilities (Tables IV-b-20 and IV-c-13) are a miscellany best described in connection with the individual sector estimates below. They include many unidentifiable items estimated in the course of making up complete balance sheets for sectors, and many types of current assets not specified elsewhere, such as accruals and prepayments. Among the major assets included are direct investments abroad by U.S. corporations, the U.S. subscription to the IMF and IBRD, and corporation income taxes owed to the U.S. government. Data were not considered adequate for estimation of personal income tax liability to the federal government or other tax liabilities to state and local governments. Among the important items in other liabilities are the previously mentioned tax accruals and policyholders' equity in fire and casualty companies.

The FRB category "miscellaneous financial transactions" contains the same direct investment assets and liabilities and other foreign assets as the NBER group but does not attempt to cover the accrual, current, and unidentified items which make up the rest of the class. This is partly because the FRB did not attempt complete balance sheets for all the sectors included; many of the NBER figures for other assets and liabilities were estimated by subtracting identified from total assets and liabilities.

Equities or Net Worth, although not shown in a separate table in Section IV, is an important part of the sectoral and national balance sheets. It is defined as the difference between the market value of a sector's assets and the value of its liabilities. Two equity classifications—equity in mutual financial organizations and equity in other (mainly nonfarm unincorporated) business—are listed at the same value on both sides of the balance sheets. The net worth of corporate business, as mentioned earlier, is valued independently on the asset side, and the two valuations are often far apart.

Classification of Sectors

The accounts presented here are divided into eight major sectors, one of which is finance. The finance sector is subdivided into thirteen subsectors in Section II and many of these are further subdivided in Section III. Most of these detailed finance subsectors need little description or explanation but the boundaries of the major sectors are much more hazy. Although those delineated here are similar to the corresponding sectors in *A Study of Saving* and in the Federal Reserve Board flow-of-funds accounts, there are considerable divergencies in detail. This section lists the NBER sectors, defines them, and describes the most important respects in which they differ from those in other sources.

A number of reconciliation tables are included which identify the most important items of discrepancy between the NBER and FRB accounts for specific assets and liabilities within sectors.

Nonfarm Household estimates (Table III-1) are derived almost entirely as residuals. The sector's holdings of almost every asset and its debt on almost every liability are calculated by first estimating the total value of that asset outstanding and then deducting the estimated holdings of every other sector. The balance sheet of this sector therefore includes all items mistakenly omitted from other sectors and the consequences of all errors made in estimating total outstandings for any instrument.

In principle, the nonfarm household sector includes all individuals except farmers and all nonprofit organizations. Personal trust funds are consolidated with households, but separate balance sheets have been drawn up for total personal trust funds (Table III-1a), personal trust funds other than common trust funds (Table III-1b), and common trust funds (Table III-1c). These funds can therefore be separated from the household sector. If this were done, an entry would have to be added to household assets for equity in personal trust funds.

It should be noted that owners of farms are treated differently from owners of nonfarm unincorporated businesses. The latter's personal assets are segregated from their businesses and retained in the household sector, while farmers are consolidated into a combined farm business and farm household sector. The Federal Reserve Board does attempt to make the separation for farmers, placing certain of their assets and liabilities in the household sector.

The combination of households with nonprofit organizations is clearly undesirable and can only be justified on the grounds of lack of data. Some pieces of information are available, however. Tangible assets of nonprofit organizations are estimated annually for 1945 to 1958 in Goldsmith's *National Wealth* (Table A-51, p. 206). The FRB has made estimates of nonprofit organizations' liability on bank loans, n.e.c. (*Supplement 5*, p. 102), federal government loans (*ibid.*, p. 105), trade debt (*ibid.*, p. 111), and commercial mortgages (*ibid.*, p. 95). Rough estimates of complete balance sheets for a number of years can be found in *A Study of Saving* (Vol. III, Table W-25, p. 72) and in Mendelson's *The Flow-of-Funds* (Tables 24-1 and 24-2, p. I-220).

One of the major differences between the FRB and NBER balance sheets for households arises from the arbitrary nature of the division between personal and unincorporated business assets. The FRB accounts show mortgage debt on rented one- to four-family houses as a liability of unincorporated nonfinancial business. The NBER accounts place these houses, and therefore the mortgage debt on them, in the household sector, thus treating them as investments rather than as businesses.

The differences between the FRB and NBER accounts in the treatment of farm households are reflected in several lines of the balance sheet, as can be seen in the reconciliation Tables 16 and 17. Among assets, time deposits, private and government insurance policies, and savings bonds are placed in the agriculture sector by the NBER and in the consumer sector by the FRB, and among liabilities the same is true of consumer debt and insurance policy loans of farmers.

Other discrepancies between the two sets of accounts arise from differences in estimating total outstandings (as in the case of state and local government securities, corporate stock, and insurance reserves) or holdings by other sectors (as in federal obligations and corporate stock). Some discrepancies arise from the use of different estimating methods, such as in

TABLE 16

Nonfarm Household Assets: Reconciliation of NBER and FRB Estimates

(billion dollars)

	1954	1955	1956	1957	1958
Line II-1					
1. FRB demand deposits and currency	59.0	58.2	59.1	58.2	60.9
2. NBER currency and demand deposits	59.3	58.6	59.5	58.5	61.4
Line II-2					
3. FRB fixed-value redeemable claims	150.6	159.3	168.3	178.1	191.7
4. Less FRB U.S. savings bonds	50.0	50.2	50.1	48.2	47.7
5. Less NBER agric. sector, other bank deposits and shares	2.5	2.6	2.6	2.9	3.1
6. Total of lines 3-5	98.1	106.5	115.6	127.0	140.9
7. NBER other bank deposits and shares	97.8	106.2	115.4	126.8	140.6
Line II-3					
8. FRB savings in life insurance, private	64.2	67.6	71.1	73.8	77.2
9. Plus FRB savings in life ins. co. pension funds	10.0	11.2	12.4	14.0	15.5
10. Plus NBER additional assets incl. in insur. reserves	14.7	16.5	17.5	18.7	20.1
11. Less NBER other liab. and equities, fraternal orders and life insur.	3.0	3.4	3.8	3.9	4.2
12. Less NBER rest-of-world holdings of insur. reserves	1.6	1.8	1.9	2.0	2.1
13. Less NBER agric. sector insur. reserves	5.6	5.9	6.2	6.4	6.7
14. Total of lines 8-13	78.7	84.2	89.1	94.2	99.8
15. NBER life insurance reserves, private	78.4	84.0	89.0	93.8	99.7
Line II-4					
16. FRB savings in pension funds, private	22.6	26.1	29.7	34.0	38.5
17. Plus NBER adjustment to total private pens. funds	1.4	2.4	2.6	2.1	4.5
18. Less FRB saving in life ins. co. pens. funds	10.0	11.2	12.4	14.0	15.5
19. Total of lines 16-18	14.0	17.3	19.9	22.1	27.5
20. NBER pension and retirement funds, private	14.3	17.4	20.0	22.3	27.8
Line II-5					
21. FRB savings in life insurance, govt.	6.0	5.9	6.0	6.2	6.2
22. FRB savings in pension funds, govt.	18.7	20.7	23.0	25.1	27.9
23. Plus NBER adjustment to total govt. pens. and ins. funds	30.2	31.5	32.7	32.7	30.3
24. Less NBER agric. sector, govt. life ins. funds	.4	.4	.4	.4	.4
25. Total of lines 21-24	54.5	57.7	61.3	63.6	64.0
26. NBER pension and ins. funds, govt.	54.8	58.0	61.6	64.4	65.7
Lines II-6, II-7, and II-9 — No household assets					
Line II-8 — No assets; see line II-10					
Line II-10					
27. FRB security credit	1.0	0.9	0.9	0.9	1.2
28. Plus NBER sav. and loan assoc. loans in process	0.8	0.9	0.9	0.9	1.1
29. Total of lines 27-28	1.8	1.8	1.8	1.8	2.3
30. NBER other loans	2.4	2.3	2.3	2.3	3.1

(continued)

TABLE 16 (continued)

	1954	1955	1956	1957	1958
Line II-11a (1- to 4-family)					
31. FRB 1- to 4-family mortgages	8.9	9.2	9.7	10.6	11.2
32. Less NBER face amt. invest. co. holdings	0.3	0.3	0.3	0.3	0.2
33. Total of lines 31-32	8.6	8.9	9.4	10.3	11.0
34. NBER 1- to 4-family mortgages	8.6	8.9	9.6	10.3	11.0
Line II-11a (multifamily)					
35. FRB multifamily and com. mortgages	8.3	8.9	9.6	10.4	11.6
36. Less NBER nonfarm nonresident. mortg.	6.9	7.6	8.3	8.9	9.9
37. Total of lines 35-36	1.4	1.3	1.3	1.5	1.7
38. NBER multifamily mortages	1.4	1.5	1.6	1.7	1.8
Line II-11b					
39. FRB multifamily and com. mortgages	8.3	8.9	9.6	10.4	11.6
40. Less NBER multifamily mortgages	1.4	1.5	1.6	1.7	1.8
41. Total of lines 39-40	6.9	7.4	8.0	8.7	9.8
42. NBER nonfarm nonresidential mortgages	6.9	7.6	8.3	8.9	9.9
Line II-12					
43. FRB farm mortgages	3.5	3.7	4.0	4.3	4.6
44. NBER farm mortgages	3.4	3.6	4.0	4.2	4.5
Line II-13b					
45. FRB U.S. savings bonds	50.0	50.2	50.1	48.2	47.7
46. Plus FRB nonprofit org. savings bonds	1.2	1.2	1.0	0.7	0.6
47. Less NBER agric. sector savings bonds	5.0	5.2	5.1	5.1	5.2
48. Total of lines 45-47	46.2	46.2	46.0	43.8	43.1
49. NBER savings bonds	46.4	46.5	46.2	43.9	43.0
Lines II-13a and II-13c					
50. FRB federal obligations	13.9	16.1	17.1	18.0	15.6
51. Less FRB nonguar. federal obligations	0.3	0.9	1.2	1.9	1.6
52. Less FRB nonprofit org. savings bonds	1.2	1.2	1.0	0.7	0.6
53. Less NBER nonfinancial corp. holdings of govt. bonds	18.8	22.8	18.2	17.4	17.6
54. Plus FRB nonfinancial corp. holdings of federal obligations	19.0	23.2	18.8	18.4	19.2
55. Total of lines 50-54	12.6	14.4	15.5	16.4	15.0
56. NBER U.S. govt. sec. excl. savings bonds	12.4	14.2	15.6	16.7	15.6
Line II-14					
57. FRB state and local obligations	17.7	19.4	21.0	23.1	24.3
58. Plus NBER non-interest-bearing debt of state and local govts.	0.6	0.6	0.6	0.7	0.7
59. Total of lines 57-58	18.3	20.0	21.6	23.8	25.0
60. NBER state and local govt. securities	17.9	19.6	21.2	23.4	24.8
Line II-15					
61. FRB corporate and foreign bonds	4.2	5.4	6.6	7.7	8.3
62. Plus FRB nonguar. federal securities	0.3	0.9	1.2	1.9	1.6
63. Plus FRB nonguar. federal secur. held by savings and loan assoc.	0.1	0.1	0.3	0.5	0.5
64. Total of lines 61-63	4.6	6.4	8.1	10.1	10.4
65. NBER other bonds and notes	5.3	7.2	8.9	10.7	11.0

(continued)

TABLE 16 (concluded)

	1954	1955	1956	1957	1958
Lines II-16 and II-17					
66. FRB corporate stock	233.6	287.5	306.3	268.2	376.9
67. Less differences bet. FRB and NBER estimates of total stock outstanding	11.5	15.4	20.7	10.0	29.4
68. Less NBER corporate stock held by noninsured pension plans	4.0	5.6	6.6	7.0	10.8
69. Plus FRB corporate stock held by noninsured pension plans	2.9	3.7	4.6	5.7	7.1
70. Total of lines 66-69	221.0	270.2	283.6	256.9	343.8
71. NBER corporate stock	220.8	269.9	283.1	256.1	343.0
Lines II-18, II-19, and II-20	Not estimated by FRB				

Line
1: *Supplement* 5, Table 8(A), line V.
2: Table III-1, line II-1.
3-4: *Supplement* 5, Table 8(A), lines W and Z.
5: Table III-3, line II-2.
6: Line 3 minus lines 4 and 5.
7: Table III-1, line II-2.
8: *Supplement* 5, Table 8(A).
9: *Ibid.*, Table 22L, line G.
10: Table 4, sum of lines 3-8.
11: Table 4, sum of lines 10-11.
12: Table 4, line 14.
13: Table III-3, line II-3.
14: Sum of lines 8-10, minus lines 11-13.
15: Table III-1, line II-3.
16: *Supplement* 5, Table 8(A).
17: Table 5, sum of lines 3-4, minus line 2.
18: Line 9, above.
19: Sum of lines 16-17, minus line 18.
20: Table III-1, line II-4.
21-22: *Supplement* 5, Table 8(A).
23: Table 6, sum of lines 4-6.
24: Table III-3, line II-5.
25: Sum of lines 21-24.
26: Table III-1, line II-5.
27: *Supplement* 5, Table 30L, line K.
28: See Table III-5e, note to line III-10.
29: Sum of lines 27-28.
30: Table III-1, line II-10. Almost all the discrepancy between lines 29 and 30 is due to differences between NBER and FRB estimates of customer credit balances at brokers and dealers. The NBER estimates are higher by the following amounts (billion dollars): 1954 0.7, 1955 0.6, 1956 0.6, 1957 0.7, 1958 0.9.

Line
31: *Supplement* 5, Table 27L, line B.
32: Table IV-b-11a-2, line f.
33: Line 31 minus line 32.
34: Table IV-b-11a-2, line 1.
35,39: *Supplement* 5, Table 28L, line O.
36,42: Table IV-b-11b, line 1.
37: Line 35 minus line 36.
38,40: Table IV-b-11a-1, line 1.
41: Line 39 minus line 40.
43: *Supplement* 5, Table 28L, line P.
44: Table III-1, line II-12.
45: *Supplement* 5, Table 8(A), line Z.
46: FRB worksheets.
47: Table III-3, line II-13b.
48: Sum of lines 45-46, minus line 47.
49: Table III-1, line II-13b.
50-51: *Supplement* 5, Table 23L, lines F and H.
52: FRB worksheets.
53: Table III-4, line II-13.
54: *Supplement* 5, Table 23L, line J.
55: Sum of lines 50-54, minus lines 51-53.
56: Table III-1, sum of lines II-13a and II-13c.
57: *Supplement* 5, Table 8(A), line e.
58: See note to Table III-6, line III-12.
59: Sum of lines 57-58.
60: Table III-1, line II-14.
61: *Supplement* 5, Table 8(A), line f.
62-63: *Ibid.*, Table 23L, lines H and d.
64: Sum of lines 61-63.
65: Table III-1, line II-15.
66: *Supplement* 5, Table 8(A), line g.
67: Table 15, line 5 minus line 6.
68: Table III-5j, sum of lines II-16 and II-17.
69: *Supplement* 5, Table 12L, line U.
70: Sum of lines 66-69, minus lines 67-68.
71: Table III-1, sum of lines II-16 and II-17.

the case of security credit where the NBER data used a larger ratio in estimating total customers' credit balances from those for New York Stock Exchange member firms.

A supplementary table (III-1d) shows nonfarm household balance sheets for benchmark years from 1900 through 1945. These are from Volume III of *A Study of Saving*, but they have been revised to improve comparability with the postwar data. Among the major changes were the substitution of revised mortgage estimates (see Table IV-b-11c), the inclusion of government bond holdings allocated to unincorporated business by Goldsmith (with a corresponding reduction in equity in unincorporated business), and the elimination of tax accruals, which were not estimated for the postwar years. Also, payables to financial intermediaries were subdivided by type of debt; monetary metals were transferred to intangible assets; and time deposits were separated from demand deposits.

TABLE 17

Nonfarm Household Liabilities: Reconciliation of NBER and FRB Estimates

(billion dollars)

	1954	1955	1956	1957	1958
Lines III-1 through III-5	No household liabilities				
Line III-6					
1. FRB consumer credit liabilities	32.5	38.9	42.5	45.3	45.5
2. Plus FRB consumer bank loans offset by hypothecated deposits	0.5	0.5	0.6	0.6	0.6
3. Less NBER agric. sector consumer debt	1.0	1.2	1.2	1.2	1.3
4. Total of lines 1-3	32.0	38.2	41.9	44.7	44.8
5. NBER consumer debt	31.9	38.2	41.9	44.8	44.8
Line III-7	No discrepancy				
Line III-8					
6. FRB security credit liabilities	4.1	4.8	4.8	4.4	5.5
7. NBER loans on securities	4.6	5.4	5.3	4.9	6.2
Line III-9	No discrepancy				
Line III-10					
8. FRB other loans	3.9	4.2	4.5	5.0	5.5
9. Less FRB consumer bank loans offset by hypothecated deposits	0.5	0.5	0.6	0.6	0.6
10. Less FRB federal govt. loans to nonprofit organizations	--	--	--	0.1	0.2
11. Less NBER agric. sector policy loans	0.2	0.2	0.2	0.3	0.3
12. Total of lines 8-11	3.2	3.5	3.7	4.0	4.4
13. NBER other loans	3.2	3.4	3.7	4.0	4.4
Line III-11					
14. FRB consumer debt: 1- to 4-family mortg.	69.2	81.5	92.6	101.3	110.9
15. FRB nonprofit orgs.: other mortg.	0.6	0.7	0.7	0.8	0.9
16. Plus FRB noncorporate nonfinancial bus.: 1- to 4-family mortg. liability	5.0	5.2	5.0	5.0	5.2
17. Total of lines 14-16	74.8	87.4	98.3	107.1	117.0
18. NBER mortgage debt	74.8	87.4	98.4	107.1	117.0
Lines III-12 and III-13	No liabilities				

Line
1: *Supplement 5*, Table 8(A), line m.
2: *Ibid.*, Table 32L, line z.
3: Table III-3, line III-6.
4: Sum of lines 1-2, minus line 3.
5: Table III-1, line III-6.
6: *Supplement 5*, Table 8(A), line n.
7: Table III-1, line III-8.
8: *Supplement 5*, Table 8 (A), line o.
9-10: *Ibid.*, Table 32L, lines z and qq.
11: See Table III-3, note to line III-10.
12: Line 8 minus sum of lines 9-11.
13: Table III-1, line III-10.
14-15: *Supplement 5*, Table 8(A), lines 1 and "other mortgages."
16: *Ibid.*, Table 8(C).
17: Sum of lines 14-16.
18: Table III-1, line III-11.

The Nonfarm Unincorporated Business balance sheet (Table III-2) is probably the least reliable of all except households. Estimates are made only for certain assets and liabilities which seem clearly to be business rather than personal (multifamily and commercial structures and land, producer durables, consumer and trade credit, trade debt, and multifamily and commercial mortgage debt). For only a few items (such as currency and demand deposits) is an attempt made to split assets between households and unincorporated business.

Aside from the treatment of one- to four-family homes, described earlier, the FRB and NBER sectors are very similar, because the latter is constructed mainly from FRB data. Both estimates treat farm cooperatives ambiguously. Their tangible assets (roughly $5 billion in 1958, according to Table III-3a) are probably scattered among unincorporated busi-

TABLE 18

Nonfarm Unincorporated Business: Reconciliation of NBER and FRB Estimates

(billion dollars)

	1954	1955	1956	1957	1958
Line II-1 — No discrepancy					
Lines II-2 through II-5 — No nonfarm unincorporated business assets					
Lines II-6 and II-7 — No discrepancy					
Lines II-8 through II-20 — No nonfarm unincorporated business assets					
Lines III-1 through III-6 — No nonfarm unincorporated business liabilities					
Line III-7 — No discrepancy					
Line III-8 — No nonfarm unincorporated business liabilities					
Line III-9					
1. FRB bank loans, n.e.c.	8.2	9.2	9.8	9.6	10.1
2. Plus FRB bank-held open-market paper	1.0	0.8	0.9	1.1	1.2
3. Plus difference between NBER and FRB corporate bank debt	-0.4	0.1	--	--	1.4
4. Total of lines 1-3	8.8	10.1	10.7	10.7	12.7
5. NBER bank loans, n.e.c.	8.6	10.0	10.7	10.6	12.4
Line III-10					
6. FRB other loans	4.5	5.3	5.7	6.2	6.4
7. Less FRB noncorp. nonfin. bus. liab. on acceptances	0.3	0.2	0.2	0.3	0.3
8. Total of lines 6-7	4.2	5.1	5.5	5.9	6.1
9. NBER other loans	3.9	4.9	5.0	5.3	5.4
Line III-11 — No discrepancy between NBER mortgage debt and FRB multifamily and commercial mortgage debt					
Lines III-12 and III-13 — No nonfarm unincorporated business liabilities					

Line
1: *Supplement 5*, Table 8(C), line Q.
2: *Ibid.*, Table 32L, sum of lines V, a, and d.
3: Table 20.
4: Sum of lines 1-3.
5: Table III-2, line III-9.

Line
6: *Supplement 5*, Table 8(C), line R.
7: *Ibid.*, Table 32L, line g.
8: Line 6 minus line 7.
9: Table III-2, line III-10.

ness, corporate business, and agriculture, as are many of their other assets and liabilities, but most of them are probably in this sector. It is clear that the unincorporated business indebtedness to the federal government (included in line III-10) consists largely of loans to farm cooperatives.

The two items for which a reconciliation is attempted in Table 18, bank loans, n.e.c., and other loans, are both estimated as residuals in the NBER accounts. It is therefore difficult to know exactly what is contained in the figures for the nonfarm unincorporated business sector and to explain the discrepancies with the FRB accounts.

Supplementary Table III-2a gives earlier balance sheets for this sector with some adjustments for comparability with later years. The main change was elimination of the estimate for holdings of government bonds, which were transferred to the household sector, a shift of some cash assets to nonfarm households, and subdivision of the category "payables to financial intermediaries."

Agriculture (Table III-3) includes all households engaged primarily in farming, and its balance sheet contains all their assets and liabilities including those not used in agriculture. It also contains agricultural assets owned by nonfarm households and corporations even though no specific entry is made for agricultural assets in the nonfarm household balance sheet. Stock in agricultural corporations presumably is included there but not ownership of farms themselves.

TABLE 19

Agriculture: Reconciliation of NBER and FRB Estimates

(billion dollars)

		1954	1955	1956	1957	1958
Line II-1	No discrepancy					
Lines II-2, II-3, II-5, and II-13	Not estimated by FRB; included in nonfarm household (consumer) sector					
Lines II-4, II-6 through II-12, II-14 through II-19	No agriculture sector assets					
Line II-20	Mostly not estimated by FRB; only a very small item for equity in federal land banks is shown in farm business sector balance sheet					
Lines III-1 through III-5, III-8, III-12, and III-13	No agriculture sector liabilities					
Line III-6	Not estimated by FRB; included in nonfarm household (consumer) sector					
Lines III-7 and III-9	No discrepancy					
Line III-10						
1. FRB other loans		1.1	1.1	1.2	1.4	1.6
2. Plus NBER agric. sec. life insur. policy loans		0.2	0.2	0.2	0.3	0.3
3. Total of lines 1-2		1.3	1.3	1.4	1.7	1.9
4. NBER other loans		1.3	1.3	1.4	1.6	1.9
Line III-11	No discrepancy					

Line
1: *Supplement 5*, Table 8(B), line P.
2: See Table III-3, note to line III-10.
3: Sum of lines 1-2.
4: Table III-3, line III-10.

The Federal Reserve Board, as mentioned above, includes only farm business assets, leaving such items as equity in insurance and consumer debt in the household or "consumer" sector.

In *A Study of Saving* farm cooperatives were consolidated into the agriculture sector; their total assets, rather than just farmers' equity as in Table III-3, were therefore included. In this volume most of their assets are in the nonfarm unincorporated business sector, as was mentioned earlier. However, a separate balance sheet for agricultural cooperatives was calculated (Table III-3a) along with supporting balance sheets for specific types of cooperatives. These include cooperatives for purchase, supply, and related services (Table III-3a-1), rural electric cooperatives and farmers' mutual telephone companies (Table III-3a-2), and farmers' mutual irrigation companies (Table III-3a-3). The farm cooperative balance sheets draw together assets and liabilities which are scattered through the other sectors.

Almost all the differences between these figures and those of the Federal Reserve Board (Table 19) involve the inclusion of nonbusiness assets and liabilities of farm households, such as time deposits, insurance and pension funds, savings bonds, consumer debt, and life insurance policy loans.

Supplementary Table III-3b revises the prewar balance sheets to match the new ones, by moving monetary metals to intangible assets, separating time from demand deposits, breaking payables into components, and substituting equity in farm cooperatives for the total assets of these organizations.

Nonfinancial Corporations (Table III-4) include all except corporate farms and those corporations specifically listed as part of the finance sector. Banks, insurance companies, investment companies, and finance companies (sales, personal, and business finance, and mortgage companies) are all excluded, but real estate corporations, including lessors, are included.

Data for all corporations are based on *Statistics of Income* tabulations in which industry and balance sheet categories are broadly defined and are, furthermore, obscured by consolidation of parent and subsidiary accounts. Data for financial corporations, on the other hand, are from sources in which the industries and the individual assets and liabilities are more precisely defined. It is often not clear, therefore, whether the financial sectors and items eliminated from the corporation total correspond with those entered in the finance sector. There is a considerable chance that some items are included under both nonfinancial corporations and finance, and that others are omitted from both. For example, incorporated brokers and dealers in securities are in the finance sector, combined with the unincorporated ones, which are more important. However, corporate brokers and dealers have not been removed from nonfinancial corporations, and there is therefore some overlapping between the two groups.

The main differences between the NBER and FRB corporate sector balance sheets follow from the fact that the latter consolidate this sector, netting out most intercorporate assets. This process eliminates several lines which appear in the NBER balance sheet and virtually removes holding companies and closed-end investment companies from the corporate sector. An exception to the netting of intercorporate assets by the Federal Reserve Board is trade credit, for which the amounts extended to other corporations are included in the balance sheet.

The reconciliation with FRB estimates (Table 20) is incomplete for several items. The main differences in the trade credit estimates have been discussed earlier in connection with the calculation of total trade credit outstanding, and those for corporate bonds in connection with the totals for that item. The FRB data include closed-end investment companies (except intercorporate investments), which are in the NBER finance sector, and at least in some assets appear to include corporate farms, even though conceptually they should have been removed.

It is impossible to make a real reconciliation for "other assets" and "other liabilities," since the Federal Reserve Board shows only foreign investments in these categories while the NBER figures include large amounts, only vaguely identified, which arise in the estimation of a complete corporate balance sheet. Part of the assets and most of the liabilities are current items excluded in all the FRB data.

Supplementary Table III-4b, which provides a nonfinancial corporation balance sheet for earlier years, is substantially different from that in *A Study of Saving*. The major changes resulted from the adjustment of the finance sector to the postwar definition and can best be described in connection with that sector.

TABLE 20

Nonfinancial Corporations: Reconciliation of NBER and FRB Estimates

(billion dollars)

	1954	1955	1956	1957	1958
Line II-1					
1. FRB demand deposits and currency	30.9	32.0	32.1	32.1	33.8
2. Less NBER closed-end investment cos.	0.1	0.1	0.1	0.1	0.1
3. Less NBER corporate farms	0.2	0.2	0.2	0.2	0.3
4. Total of lines 1-3	30.6	31.7	31.8	31.8	33.4
5. NBER currency and demand deposits	30.5	31.5	31.6	31.6	33.3
Line II-2	No discrepancy				
Lines II-3, II-4, and II-5	No nonfinancial corporation assets				
Line II-6	No discrepancy				
Line II-7					
6. FRB trade credit	53.7	63.8	69.8	71.6	78.1
7. Plus FRB receivables deducted, brokers and dealers	0.3	0.4	0.5	0.4	0.6
8. Plus FRB receivables deducted, credit agencies other than banks	13.2	17.6	19.9	22.4	22.8
9. Less NBER rcvbl. deducted, finance cos.	11.6	15.7	16.9	18.5	17.7
10. Less NBER rcvbl. deducted, corp. farms	.4	.3	.4	.4	.5
11. Total of lines 6-10	55.2	65.8	72.9	75.5	83.3
12. NBER trade credit	55.1	65.9	73.0	75.7	83.4
Lines II-8 through II-12	No nonfinancial corporation assets				
Line II-13					
13. FRB federal obligations	19.1	23.5	19.2	19.2	19.8
14. Less FRB nonguar. federal obligations	0.1	0.3	0.4	0.8	0.6
15. Less NBER closed-end invest. cos.	0.1	0.1	0.1	0.1	0.1
16. Less NBER corporate farms	0.1	0.1	0.1	0.1	0.1
17. Total of lines 13-16	18.8	23.0	18.6	18.2	19.0
18. NBER U.S. government securities	18.8	22.8	18.2	17.4	17.6
Line II-14	No discrepancy				
Lines II-15, II-16, and II-17	Not estimated by FRB; considered to be intercorporate holdings eliminated in consolidation				
Lines II-18 and II-19	No nonfinancial corporation assets				
Line II-20					
19. FRB miscellaneous financial assets	17.9	19.5	22.4	25.4	27.5
20. Plus nonfin. corp., other cur. assets	2.2	3.0	4.5	5.2	5.4
21. Plus nonfin. corp., other assets	10.8	11.2	10.9	12.0	11.8
22. Total of lines 19-21	30.9	33.7	37.8	42.6	44.7
23. NBER other intangible assets	29.7	34.5	40.5	47.1	48.1
Lines III-1 through III-6	No nonfinancial corporation liabilities				

(continued)

TABLE 20 (concluded)

	1954	1955	1956	1957	1958
Line III-7					
24. FRB trade debt	40.8	49.7	54.0	53.9	57.0
25. NBER trade debt	44.6	54.9	60.5	62.5	68.8
Line III-8 — No discrepancy					
Line III-9					
26. FRB bank loans, n.e.c.	16.7	19.5	24.8	26.8	27.3
27. NBER bank loans, n.e.c.	17.1	19.4	24.8	26.8	25.9
Line III-10					
28. FRB other loans	2.8	3.0	3.2	3.7	3.8
29. Less NBER finance company trade credit	0.9	1.1	1.3	1.4	1.7
30. Total of lines 28-29	1.9	1.9	1.9	2.3	2.1
31. NBER other loans	1.6	2.1	2.0	2.3	2.2
Line III-11 — No discrepancy					
Line III-12					
32. FRB corporate bonds	50.1	52.8	56.4	62.6	68.4
33. Plus NBER com. paper other than finance co., held outside banks	0.2	0.2	0.2	0.2	0.3
34. Total of lines 32-33	50.3	53.0	56.6	62.8	68.7
35. NBER bonds and notes	51.0	53.7	57.4	63.8	69.7
Line III-13					
36. FRB miscellaneous liabilities	4.0	4.3	4.5	4.8	4.9
37. Plus NBER tax liability	15.5	19.3	17.6	15.4	12.9
38. Plus NBER other current liabilities	22.5	25.7	29.0	31.1	33.3
39. Total of lines 36-38	42.0	49.3	51.1	51.3	51.1
40. NBER other liabilities	48.1	54.7	58.1	60.6	60.8

Line

1: *Supplement 5*, Table 8(D), line o.
2: Table III-5f-2, line II-1.
3: Meiselman and Shapiro, "Corporate Sources and Uses of Funds," Table C-9, column 2.
4: Line 1 minus lines 2 and 3.
5: Table III-4, line II-1.
6: *Supplement 5*, Table 8(D), line T.
7-8: FRB worksheets.
9: Table III-51, sum of lines II-6 and II-7.
10: "Corporate Sources and Uses of Funds," Table C-11, column 2.
11: Sum of lines 6-8, minus lines 9 and 10.
12: Table III-4, line II-7.
13: *Supplement 5*, Table 8(D), line Q.
14: *Ibid.*, Table 23L, line K.
15: Table III-5f-2, line II-13.
16: "Corporate Sources and Uses of Funds," Table C-10, column 3.
17: Line 13 minus the sum of lines 14-16.
18: Table III-4, line II-13.
19: *Supplement 5*, Table 8(D).

Line

20-21: "Corporate Sources and Uses of Funds," Table C-1a, lines 9 and 10.
22: Sum of lines 19-22.
23: Table III-4, line II-20.
24: *Supplement 5*, Table 8(D), line c.
25: Table III-4, line III-7.
26: *Supplement 5*, Table 8(D), line a.
27: Table III-4, line III-9.
28: *Supplement 5*, Table 8(D), line b.
29: Table III-51, line II-7.
30: Line 28 minus line 29.
31: Table III-4, line III-10.
32: *Supplement 5*, Table 8(D), line X.
33: Table III-51-a, column 11.
34: Sum of lines 32-33.
35: Table III-4, line III-12.
36: *Supplement 5*, Table 8(D).
37-38: "Corporate Sources and Uses of Funds," Table C-1b, lines 7 and 8.
39: Sum of lines 36-38.
40: Table III-4, line III-13.

Finance (Table III-5) is a mixture of government and private agencies: corporations, cooperatives, and unincorporated businesses, all of which perform some sort of financial services. Among government or quasigovernmental agencies are the Federal Reserve banks, Treasury monetary funds, and federal, state, and local government pension, retirement, and other insurance funds. Corporations include banks, stock insurance, investment, and finance companies. Also included are several types of mutual or cooperative organizations such as mutual insurance companies, savings banks, savings and loan associations, credit unions, and cooperative agricultural credit agencies.

The FRB accounts do not show any total finance sector, and the reconciliations for finance are therefore performed for each type of institution separately.

The finance sector balance sheet for 1900-45 (Table III-5o) is much narrower in coverage than the sector defined in *A Study of Saving*. It consists mainly of the banking system, financial intermediaries other than the banking system and government corporations, and unincorporated brokers and dealers. To these were added finance companies (using data from *Financial Intermediaries*), mortgage companies, and Treasury monetary funds, while investment holding companies and the postal savings system were subtracted. Excluded from the finance sector were financial corporations other than financial intermediaries (except for finance companies), consisting mainly of real estate and holding companies. These were placed, along with investment holding companies, in the nonfinancial corporation sector. Also excluded from finance were government lending agencies which, together with the postal savings system, were moved into the federal government sector.

Financial intermediaries, as covered by the broadest definition used in Goldsmith's *Financial Intermediaries* (Table A-28), are also a wider group than the present one. They include government corporations and credit agencies, federal land banks, the postal savings system, and investment holding companies, all excluded here, and personal trust funds, which are placed in the household sector in these balance sheets. However, they do not cover the Treasury monetary funds.

Most of the individual finance subsectors are self-explanatory as far as sector coverage is concerned, but there are many differences in the treatment of individual items, as well as a few points of sectoring, that should be mentioned.

Federal Reserve Banks (Table III-5a-1) and *Treasury Monetary Funds* (Table III-5a-2) are combined into a monetary authorities subsector in the FRB accounts and into Table III-5a here. The Treasury monetary funds are not, strictly speaking, an institution. They consist of the Exchange Stabilization Fund and the Treasury's stock of monetary metals and liability on gold certificates. The monetary funds are excluded from *Financial Intermediaries* and placed in the federal government sector in *A Study of Saving*.

TABLE 21

Federal Reserve Banks and Treasury Monetary Funds: Reconciliation of NBER and FRB Estimates

(billion dollars)

	1954	1955	1956	1957	1958
Line II-1					
1. FRB monetary authorities, gold and Treasury currency	26.6	26.7	27.0	27.9	25.7
2. Plus NBER cash assets of FR banks	21.6	21.7	21.9	22.9	20.8
3. Plus NBER cash assets of Exch. Stab. Fund	0.3	0.3	0.2	0.1	0.2
4. Total of lines 1-3	48.5	48.7	49.1	50.9	46.7
5. NBER currency and demand deposits	48.6	48.7	49.2	50.9	46.8
Lines II-2 through II-8	No Federal Reserve bank and Treasury monetary fund assets				

(continued)

TABLE 21 (concluded)

	1954	1955	1956	1957	1958
Line II-9					
6. FRB Fed. Res. bank loans to domestic banks	--	0.1	--	--	--
7. NBER bank loans, n.e.c.	0.1	0.1	0.1	0.1	0.1
Lines II-10 through II-12	No Federal Reserve bank and Treasury monetary fund assets				
Line II-13	No discrepancy				
Lines II-14 through II-19	No FR bank and Treasury monetary fund assets				
Line II-20					
8. FRB miscellaneous assets	--	--	--	0.2	--
9. Plus NBER FR banks uncol. cash items, etc.	4.1	5.7	5.9	5.7	5.8
10. Total of lines 8-9	4.1	5.7	5.9	5.9	5.8
11. NBER other intangible assets	4.1	5.7	5.9	5.9	5.8
Line III-1					
12. FRB demand deposits and currency	29.8	30.0	30.0	30.0	30.1
13. Plus FRB member bank reserves	18.9	19.0	19.1	19.0	18.5
14. Plus FRB other domestic bank deposits	0.1	0.1	0.1	0.1	0.1
15. Plus FRB other vault cash	2.5	2.7	3.3	3.3	3.2
16. Plus NBER gold certificates	21.0	21.0	21.3	22.1	20.0
17. Plus NBER FR bank holdings of FR notes	0.2	0.3	0.4	0.4	0.5
18. Plus NBER Exch. Stab. Fund deposits with FR banks	0.2	0.2	0.1	--	0.2
19. Plus NBER FR bank holdings of Treasury cur.	0.4	0.3	0.3	0.3	0.3
20. Total of lines 12-19	73.1	73.6	74.6	75.2	72.9
21. NBER currency and demand deposits	73.2	73.7	74.5	75.4	73.0
Lines III-2 through III-12	No FR bank and Treasury monetary fund liabilities				
Line III-13					
22. FRB miscellaneous liabilities	0.2	0.2	0.2	0.2	0.2
23. Plus NBER FR banks, other liabilities	3.6	4.5	4.5	4.6	4.9
24. Total of lines 22-23	3.8	4.7	4.7	4.8	5.1
25. NBER other liabilities	3.8	4.7	4.7	4.8	5.1

Line
1: *Supplement 5*, Table 17L, sum of lines C and D.
2: Table III-5a-1, line II-1.
3: See Table III-5a-2, note to line II-1.
4: Sum of lines 1-3.
5: Table III-5a, line II-1.
6: *Supplement 5*, Table 17L, line N.
7: Table III-5a, line II-9.
8: *Supplement 5*, Table 17L, line K.
9: Table III-5a-1, line II-20.
10: Sum of lines 8-9.
11: Table III-5a, line II-20.
12-15: *Supplement 5*, Table 17L, lines Q, W, Z, and a.
16: See Table III-5a-2, note to line III-1.
17-19: See Table III-5a-1, note to line II-1.
20: Sum of lines 12-19.
21: Table III-5a, line III-1.
22: *Supplement 5*, Table 17L, line U.
23: Table III-5a-1, line III-13.
24: Sum of lines 22-23.
25: Table III-5a, line III-13.

The differences between the NBER and FRB accounts listed in Table 21 are accounted for by the usual factors: the netting out of intrabanking system assets and liabilities by the FRB and the inclusion of miscellaneous current and other assets and liabilities by the NBER.

Government Pension and Insurance Funds (Table III-5b) are the sum of two components: federal government pension and insurance funds (Table III-5b-1), which include the retirement system for federal employees, the two federal government life insurance funds, and social insurance funds such as the Old Age and Survivors Insurance, railroad retirement, and unemployment insurance trust funds; and state and local government pension and insurance funds (Table III-5b-2), which cover retirement systems for state and local government employees as well as state-administered workmen's compensation funds.

All the assets and liabilities of these funds are included with other government assets in the FRB accounts, and there is therefore no reconciliation table for them here. They do, however, play a part in the reconciliations for the government sectors.

These funds make up almost all of the category government trust funds in *Financial Intermediaries* and they are included in financial intermediaries both there and in *A Study of Saving*.

Commercial Banks (Table III-5c) have the same coverage as the FRB flow-of-funds category and as the regularly published FRB series on commercial bank assets and liabilities. Banks in possessions are excluded from this category and placed under other finance below.

Most of the differences between the NBER and FRB estimates (Table 22) involve asset and liability items which disappear in the process of consolidating the banking sector.

TABLE 22

Commercial Banks: Reconciliation of NBER and FRB Estimates

(billion dollars)

	1954	1955	1956	1957	1958
Line II-1					
1. FRB FR bank deposits and vault cash	21.3	21.5	22.1	22.4	21.7
2. Plus NBER interbank deposits, com. banks	12.8	12.9	13.7	13.2	13.5
3. Total of lines 1-2	34.1	34.4	35.8	35.6	35.2
4. NBER currency and demand deposits	34.0	34.3	35.6	35.5	35.1
Line II-2	Not estimated by FRB; netted out in consolidation of banking sector				
Lines II-3 through II-5	No commercial bank assets				
Line II-6					
5. FRB consumer credit	10.9	13.2	14.6	15.8	15.9
6. Plus FRB consumer bank loans offset by hypothecated deposits	0.5	0.5	0.6	0.6	0.6
7. Total of lines 5-6	11.4	13.7	15.2	16.4	16.5
8. NBER consumer credit	11.4	13.7	15.2	16.4	16.6
Line II-7	No commercial bank assets				
Line II-8	No discrepancy				
Line II-9					
9. FRB bank loans, n.e.c.	34.0	42.1	47.9	50.2	51.5
10. Plus FRB CCC-guar. loans and certif. of inter.	2.3	1.2	0.9	0.5	0.8
11. Plus FRB open-market paper	1.0	0.8	0.8	1.0	1.1
12. Total of lines 9-11	37.3	44.1	49.6	51.7	53.4
13. NBER bank loans, n.e.c.	37.5	44.3	49.9	52.0	53.7
Line II-10	No commercial bank assets				
Lines II-11 and II-12	No discrepancy				

(continued)

TABLE 22 (concluded)

	1954	1955	1956	1957	1958
<u>Line II-13</u>					
14. FRB federal obligations	70.4	63.4	60.2	60.3	68.6
15. Less FRB nonguar. federal obligations	1.4	1.8	1.6	2.1	2.2
16. Total of lines 14-15	69.0	61.6	58.6	58.2	66.4
17. NBER U.S. government securities	69.0	61.6	58.6	58.2	66.2
<u>Line II-14</u>	No discrepancy				
<u>Line II-15</u>					
18. FRB corporate bonds	1.9	1.7	1.3	1.4	1.3
19. Plus FRB nonguar. federal obligations	1.4	1.8	1.6	2.1	2.2
20. Total of lines 18-19	3.3	3.5	2.9	3.5	3.5
21. NBER other bonds and notes	3.3	3.5	2.9	3.5	3.5
<u>Lines II-16, II-18, and II-19</u>	No commercial bank assets				
<u>Line II-17</u>	Not estimated by FRB				
<u>Line II-20</u>					
22. FRB misc. assets and FR bank stock	0.5	0.5	0.4	0.5	0.6
23. NBER other intangible assets	11.0	14.0	14.9	15.1	16.1
<u>Line III-1</u>					
24. FRB demand deposits, net	112.1	114.2	115.9	115.2	120.8
25. Plus FRB Federal Reserve float	0.8	1.6	1.7	1.4	1.3
26. Plus NBER cash items in process of col.	10.0	13.3	13.9	13.7	14.6
27. Plus NBER interbank dep. of com. banks	12.8	12.9	13.7	13.2	13.5
28. Total of lines 24-27	135.7	142.0	145.2	143.5	150.2
29. NBER currency and demand deposits	135.8	142.0	145.2	143.5	150.2
<u>Line III-2</u>	No discrepancy				
<u>Lines III-3 through III-8</u>	No commercial bank liabilities				
<u>Line III-9</u>	Not estimated by FRB; netted out in consolidation of banking sector				
<u>Line III-10</u>	No discrepancy; see *Supplement 5*, Table 32L, line o				
<u>Lines III-11 and III-12</u>	No commercial bank liabilities				
<u>Line III-13</u>					
30. FRB other liabilities	0.5	0.6	0.6	0.4	0.3
31. NBER other liabilities	3.0	3.0	3.6	3.9	3.9

Line
1: *Supplement 5*, Table 16L, line T.
2: Table IV-b-1c, column 5.
3: Sum of lines 1-2.
4: Table III-5c, line II-1.
5: *Supplement 5*, Table 16L, line L.
6: *Ibid.*, Table 32L, line z.
7: Sum of lines 5-6.
8: Table III-5c, line II-6.
9-11: *Supplement 5*, Table 16L, lines N, P, and Q.
12: Sum of lines 9-11.
13: Table III-5c, line II-9.
14-15: *Supplement* 5, Table 16L, lines D and G.
16: Line 14 minus line 15.
17: Table III-5c, line II-13.
18-19: *Supplement 5*, Table 16L, lines I and G.
20: Sum of lines 18-19.
21: Table III-5c, line II-15.
22: *Supplement 5*, Table 16L, lines R and U.
23: Table III-5c, line II-20.
24-25: *Supplement 5*, Table 16L, lines X and i.
26: Table IV-b-1h, column 6.
27: Table IV-b-1c, column 5.
28: Sum of lines 24-27.
29: Table III-5c, line III-1.
30: *Supplement 5*, Table 16L, line g.
31: Table III-5c, line III-13.

Mutual Savings Banks (Table III-5d) cover the same group as the corresponding category in *Supplement 5*, and all the estimates agree closely. The only differences (Table 23) are that a few more lines are estimated in the NBER accounts and the calculation of other bonds and notes is slightly different.

TABLE 23

Mutual Savings Banks: Reconciliation of NBER and FRB Estimates

(billion dollars)

		1954	1955	1956	1957	1958
Lines II-1 and II-2	No discrepancy					
Lines II-3, II-4, II-5, II-7, and II-9	No mutual savings bank assets					
Lines II-6 and II-10	No discrepancy; FRB includes in *Supplement 5*, Table 10L, line P					
Line II-8	Not estimated by FRB					
Lines II-11 and II-12	No discrepancy					
Line II-13	No discrepancy with federal obligations, direct and fully guaranteed, *Supplement 5*, Table 10L, line H					
Line II-14	No discrepancy					
Line II-15						
1. FRB savings inst. (mutual sav. banks), corporate and foreign bonds		2.9	2.6	2.6	3.2	3.8
2. NBER other bonds and notes		3.0	2.7	2.8	3.6	4.1
Line II-16	No mutual savings bank assets					
Line II-17	No discrepancy with *Supplement 5*, Table 26L, line I					
Lines II-18 and II-19	No mutual savings bank assets					
Line II-20	Not estimated by FRB					
Lines III-1, III-3 through III-8, and III-10 through III-12	No mutual savings bank liabilities					
Line III-2	No discrepancy					
Lines III-9 and III-13	Not estimated by FRB					

Line
1: *Supplement 5*, Table 25L, line I.
2: Table III-5d, line II-15.

Savings and Loan Associations (Table III-5e) have the same coverage as the FRB class. The discrepancies in two lines result from the treatment of loans in process as a loan liability of the associations and from the incorrect location of nonguaranteed federal government securities in other assets in the NBER accounts. These nonguaranteed government se-

TABLE 24

Savings and Loan Associations: Reconciliation of NBER and FRB Estimates

(billion dollars)

	1954	1955	1956	1957	1958
Lines II-1, II-6, and II-11	No discrepancy				
Lines II-2 through II-5, II-7 through II-10, and II-12	No savings and loan association assets				
Line II-13	No discrepancy with *Supplement 5*, Table 10L, line V (direct and fully guaranteed)				
Lines II-14 through II-19	No savings and loan association assets				
Line II-20					
1. FRB misc. financial transactions	1.2	1.2	1.3	1.3	1.6
2. Plus FRB nonguar. fed. obligations	0.1	0.1	0.3	0.5	0.5
3. Total of lines 1-2	1.3	1.3	1.6	1.8	2.1
4. NBER other intangible assets	1.5	1.6	1.8	2.1	2.4
Lines III-1, III-3 through III-8, III-11 and III-12	No savings and loan association liabilities				
Lines III-2 and III-9	No discrepancy				
Line III-10					
5. FRB other loans	0.9	1.4	1.2	1.3	1.3
6. Plus NBER loans in process	0.8	0.9	0.9	0.9	1.1
7. Total of lines 5-6	1.7	2.3	2.1	2.2	2.4
8. NBER other loans	1.7	2.3	2.1	2.1	2.4
Line III-13	Not estimated by FRB				

Line
1-2: *Supplement 5*, Table 10L, lines c and W.
3: Sum of lines 1-2.
4: Table III-5e, line II-20.
5: *Supplement 5*, Table 10L, line h.
6: See note to Table III-5e, line III-10.
7: Sum of lines 5-6.
8: Table III-5e, line III-10.

curities are mainly notes of the Federal Home Loan Banks and the Federal National Mortgage Association and should have been included under other bonds and notes (line II-15). However, data on these holdings were not shown separately in the Federal Home Loan Bank Board reports used for this sector and appeared in the Treasury Ownership Survey only starting with June 1960 (*Treasury Bulletin*, September 1960) when the survey was expanded to include savings and loan associations.

For FRB estimates of these holdings, see Table III-5e, note to line II-20.

Investment Companies (Table III-5f) include open-end (Table III-5f-1), closed-end (Table III-5f-2), and face-amount investment companies (Table III-5f-3), as does the corresponding sector in *Financial Intermediaries*. The latter source adds an estimate (very small for recent years) for fixed and semifixed investment trust companies.

The Federal Reserve Board includes only the open-end companies among financial institutions, leaving the closed-end in the nonfinancial corporation sector where their main asset, common stock, is netted out in consolidation. No reconciliation with the FRB data is shown here because there is almost perfect agreement between the two estimates.

Credit Unions (Table III-5g), covering both federal- and state-chartered organizations, coincide with the FRB sector, although details of assets and liabilities are not given in Table

10L of *Supplement 5*. However, most of the FRB estimates can be inferred from the asset and liability tables, usually by subtracting savings and loan associations from a total including them and credit unions. The resulting figures agree closely with the NBER calculations.

Life Insurance Companies (Table III-5h) include all the activities of these companies, including pension plans administered by them and accident, health, and other insurance. The NBER and FRB asset figures, both derived mainly from Institute of Life Insurance data published in the *Life Insurance Fact Book*, agree closely, with the exception of small offsetting discrepancies for lines II-10 and II-15. In addition, the FRB makes an estimate for life insurance company trade credit (receivables from agents) which never gets above $.1 billion.

The more substantial differences on the liability side of the life insurance account have been explained earlier in connection with the asset category, private life insurance reserves (Table 4).

Fire and Casualty Insurance Companies (Table III-5i) consist of the groups called "fire and marine insurance" and "casualty and miscellaneous insurance" in *Financial Intermediaries*, with some adjustments to eliminate overlapping with the life insurance category. The data were derived mainly from various issues of Best's *Fire and Casualty Aggregates and Averages*.

The FRB did not publish a separate balance sheet for fire and casualty companies in *Supplement 5*, but merged them into other insurance companies, of which they are, however, the major part. A comparison of the NBER estimates with unpublished FRB worksheets reveals no major discrepancies. There were some small differences such as the assumption by the FRB that all mortgage holdings were of commercial mortgages, whereas the NBER split them between commercial and multifamily.

Noninsured Pension Plans (Table III-5j) cover all plans not administered by insurance companies. Mainly these are corporate pension funds (Table III-5j-1) but estimates are also included for union-administered and multiemployer plans (Table III-5j-2) and for pension funds of nonprofit organizations, such as churches (Table III-5j-3). Estimates for corporate plans were derived from Securities and Exchange Commission surveys, and those for the other funds made use of unpublished data from the National Bureau's pension study and estimates by the U.S. Social Security Administration. These were supplemented by examination of a sample of plans of nonprofit organizations.

The FRB estimates cover the same universe, conceptually, but only corporate funds were calculated before 1950. The rough estimates in *Financial Intermediaries* and *A Study of Saving*, made before the SEC data became available, were intended to cover only the corporate pension funds, although the total assets shown are larger than the aggregate for all funds in Table III-5j.

The only major discrepancies between the FRB and NBER balance sheets, the valuation of common stockholdings and the treatment of miscellaneous assets, have been discussed earlier in connection with the asset category private pension and retirement funds (Table 5).

Other Private Insurance (Table III-5k) is the sum of three groups, fraternal orders (Table III-5k-1), group health insurance (Table III-5k-2), and savings bank life insurance (Table III-5k-3). Most of the information on fraternal orders was from the *Annual Report* of the New York State Insurance Department, combined with aggregate data from the *Life Insurance Fact Book* and data published by *The Fraternal Monitor*. The balance sheets for group health insurance (nonprofit medical plans) were calculated from totals given in *Best's Insurance Reports* and asset distributions supplied by the Blue Cross Commission of the American Hospital Association. Savings bank life insurance aggregates from the *Life Insurance Fact Book* were distributed among the various asset categories by using data on New York and Massachusetts savings banks.

Group health insurance was not included in the tabulations in *Financial Intermediaries* or *A Study of Saving*, but is a part of the FRB category other insurance companies. Savings bank life insurance is omitted by the FRB. The total of Tables III-5i and III-5k, however, matches the FRB other insurance category almost exactly in each item.

Finance Companies (Table III-5l) consist of sales finance, consumer (or personal) finance, industrial loan, commercial finance (factors), and mortgage companies. The last were shown separately from other finance companies in *Financial Intermediaries* and included only in the broad definition of financial intermediaries. In *A Study of Saving*, all finance companies, including mortgage companies, were removed from the financial intermediaries group and combined with financial corporations other than financial intermediaries.

The data for finance companies were all taken from FRB calculations, based in recent

TABLE 25

Finance Companies: Reconciliation of NBER and FRB Estimates
(billion dollars)

		1954	1955	1956	1957	1958
Lines II-1 and II-6	No discrepancy					
Lines II-2 through II-5	No finance company assets					
Line II-7	Not estimated by FRB; included in other loans					
Lines II-8 and II-9	No finance company assets					
Line II-10						
1. FRB other loans		2.6	3.8	3.9	4.6	4.5
2. Less FRB other loans of com. fin. cos.		0.9	1.1	1.3	1.5	1.7
3. Total of lines 1-2		1.7	2.7	2.6	3.1	2.8
4. NBER other loans		1.7	2.6	2.5	3.2	2.8
Line II-11	No discrepancy					
Lines II-12 through II-20, III-1 through III-8, III-10, III-11, and III-13	No finance company assets or liabilities					
Line III-9						
5. FRB bank loans, n.e.c.		4.6	7.2	6.6	6.2	5.0
6. Plus NBER bank-held fin. co. com. paper		0.4	0.3	0.4	0.4	0.4
7. Total of lines 5-6		5.0	7.5	7.0	6.6	5.4
8. NBER bank loans, n.e.c.		4.9	7.5	6.9	6.6	5.5
Line III-12						
9. FRB corporate bonds		4.0	5.3	6.4	7.1	7.3
10. FRB other loans (open-market paper)		1.5	1.7	1.9	2.3	2.2
11. Less NBER bank-held fin. co. com. paper		0.4	0.3	0.4	0.4	0.4
12. Total of lines 9-11		5.1	6.7	7.9	9.0	9.1
13. NBER bonds and notes		5.1	6.8	8.0	9.1	9.1

Line
1: *Supplement 5*, Table 14L, line H.
2: Table III-51, line II-7.
3: Sum of lines 1-2.
4: Table III-51, line II-10.
5: *Supplement 5*, Table 14L, line K.
6: Table III-51-a, sum of columns 3 and 7.

Line
7: Sum of lines 5-6.
8: Table III-51, line III-9.
9-10: *Supplement 5*, Table 14L, lines J and L.
11: Table III-51-a, sum of columns 3 and 7.
12: Sum of lines 9-11.
13. Table III-51, line III-12.

years on their surveys of finance companies. There are, therefore, no real discrepancies between the two sets of balance sheets. However, several items have been treated differently in the NBER accounts, as can be seen in Table 25. Other loans of commercial finance companies have been listed here as trade credit, and commercial paper liabilities have been included with bonds and notes, rather than other loans, except for bank-held paper, which has been carried as bank loans. Estimates of the distribution of commercial paper are made in Table III-51-a.

Other Finance (Table III-5m) is a heterogeneous group united by nothing but the fact that they are institutions performing financial functions and have not been included in any of the previous groups. The components are brokers and dealers (Table III-5m-1), banks in possessions (Table III-5m-2), agencies of foreign banks (Table III-5m-3), and agricultural credit organizations (Table III-5m-4).

TABLE 26

Brokers and Dealers: Reconciliation of NBER and FRB Estimates

(billion dollars)

	1954	1955	1956	1957	1958
Line II-1 — No discrepancy					
Lines II-2 through II-7 — No brokers and dealers assets					
Line II-8					
1. FRB security credit	2.7	3.1	3.1	2.8	3.8
2. NBER loans on securities	2.9	3.4	3.4	3.1	4.1
Lines II-9 through II-12 — No brokers and dealers assets					
Line II-13					
3. FRB federal obligations	0.8	0.4	0.4	0.7	0.7
4. NBER U.S. government securities	0.8	0.3	0.3	0.5	0.7
Lines II-14 through II-17, combined					
5. FRB other securities	2.2	2.2	1.5	1.6	1.5
6. NBER state and local secur., other bonds and notes, corporate stock	1.4	1.4	0.8	1.3	0.9
Lines II-18 and II-19 — No brokers and dealers assets					
Lines III-1 through III-7 — No brokers and dealers liabilities					
Line III-8					
7. FRB security loans from agencies of foreign banks	0.4	0.5	0.6	0.7	0.7
8. Plus FRB security loans from banks	2.9	3.3	2.6	2.6	2.8
9. Total of lines 7-8	3.3	3.8	3.2	3.3	3.5
10. NBER loans on securities	3.3	3.6	3.0	3.1	3.4
Lines III-9, III-11, and III-12 — No brokers and dealers liabilities					
Line III-10					
11. FRB customer credit balances	1.1	1.0	1.0	1.0	1.3
12. NBER other loans	1.6	1.4	1.4	1.5	2.0

Line
1: *Supplement 5*, Table 14L, line R.
2: Table III-5m-1, line II-8.
3: *Supplement 5*, Table 14L, line P.
4: Table III-5m-1, line II-13.
5: *Supplement 5*, Table 14L, line Q.
6: Table III-5m-1, sum of lines II-14 through II-17.
7-8: *Supplement 5*, Table 14L, lines U and V.
9: Sum of lines 7-8.
10: Table III-5m-1, line III-8.
11: *Supplement 5*, Table 14L, line T.
12: Table III-5m-1, line III-10.

Brokers and dealers, combining both unincorporated and incorporated businesses, are the most important of these four groups and the only one for which a separate balance sheet is published in *Supplement 5*. For several categories the NBER estimates differ from those of the FRB despite the fact that they are both based, to a considerable extent, on the same data for New York Stock Exchange member firms (Table III-5m-1a). The ratios used by the NBER to estimate national from N.Y. Stock Exchange totals for customer debit and credit balances appear to be larger than those of the FRB. Some of the NBER ratios come from earlier versions of the FRB accounts.

Banks in possessions are separated from the rest of commercial banking to match the official monetary statistics, which exclude them. The sector has recently become negligible with the shift of Hawaii and Alaska to statehood. Liabilities on demand and time deposits are calculated in Table III-5m-2, but they do not enter the totals in Tables IV-c-1 and IV-c-2 or the national balance sheets in this form. Instead they are entered there as other liabilities.

Data for banks in possessions are derived from the *Annual Report of Comptroller of the Currency*. Although *Supplement 5* does not show a separate account for these institutions, there is very little possibility that the FRB estimates are different from those shown here.

Agencies of foreign banks are a different case. Very little is known about the distribution of their assets and it is clear that the NBER and FRB estimates are far apart on some items. The NBER and FRB calculations started from the same asset totals but the NBER asset distribution was derived from that of the American Express Company (see Mendelson, *The Flow-of-Funds*, p. I-267, for a discussion of the method).

Agricultural credit organizations consist of livestock loan companies, production credit associations, and national farm loan associations. These are apparently consolidated with the farm business sector in the FRB accounts, which means that their main assets, loans to farmers, are netted out. It is because of this consolidation that agricultural credit organization loans appear as an element in the discrepancy between FRB and NBER other loan assets and liabilities (see Table 11).

State and Local Government (Table III-6) contains all the general government and enterprise activity of political subdivisions of the United States, including the District of Columbia, states, cities, counties, special districts and authorities, and other local government units. It excludes their pension and retirement funds, the unemployment insurance trust funds, and workmen's compensation trust funds, all of which are in Table III-5-b. Other trust and sinking funds, such as those for debt retirement, are included in the government sector.

TABLE 27

State and Local Governments, Including State and Local Pension and Retirement Funds: Reconciliation of NBER and FRB Estimates

(billion dollars)

	1954	1955	1956	1957	1958
<u>Lines II-1 and II-2</u> — No discrepancy					
<u>Lines II-3 through II-10, II-12</u> — No state and local government assets					
<u>Lines II-11, II-13, and II-14</u> — No discrepancy (II-13 with direct and guar. only)					
<u>Line II-15</u>					
1. FRB corporate bonds	2.7	3.2	3.8	4.6	5.6
2. Plus FRB nonguar. federal securities	0.1	0.2	0.3	0.4	0.3
3. Total of lines 1-2	2.8	3.4	4.1	5.0	5.9
4. NBER other bonds and notes	2.8	3.4	4.1	5.0	6.0
<u>Lines II-16 and II-17</u> — Not estimated by FRB					
<u>Lines II-18 through II-20</u> — No state and local government assets					
<u>Lines III-1 through III-4, III-6</u> — No state and local government liabilities					
<u>Line III-5</u>					
5. FRB consumer savings in retirement funds	9.3	10.6	12.1	13.7	15.6
6. Plus NBER workmen's compensation funds	0.9	1.0	1.1	1.2	1.3
7. Total of lines 5-6	10.2	11.6	13.2	14.9	16.9
8. NBER pension and insurance funds	9.7	11.0	12.5	14.2	16.2

(continued)

TABLE 27 (concluded)

	1954	1955	1956	1957	1958
Line III-6	No state and local government liabilities				
Line III-7	No discrepancy				
Lines III-8 through III-11, III-13	No state and local government liabilities				
Line III-12					
9. FRB state and local obligations	42.5	46.0	49.2	53.8	59.5
10. Plus FRB other loans (federal govt.)	0.5	0.5	0.6	0.8	1.0
11. Plus NBER non-interest-bearing state and local govt. debt	0.6	0.6	0.6	0.7	0.7
12. Total of lines 9-11	43.6	47.1	50.4	55.3	61.2
13. NBER bonds and notes	43.6	47.0	50.4	55.2	61.2

Line
1-2: *Supplement 5*, Table 8(F).
3: Sum of lines 1-2.
4: Table III-6, line II-15, plus Table III-5b-2, line II-15.
5: *Supplement 5*, Table 8(F), line W.
6: See note to Table III-5b-2, line II-21.
7: Sum of lines 5-6.

Line
8: Table III-5b-2, line III-5.
9: *Supplement 5*, Table 8(F), line T.
10: *Ibid.*, Table 8(F), line "other loans (federal government)."
11: See note to Table III-6, line III-12.
12: Sum of lines 9-11.
13: Table III-6, line III-12.

The combination of this sector with state and local pension and retirement funds (Table III-5b-2) is equivalent to the FRB state and local government sector. The coverage of this sector in *A Study of Saving* is the same as in the present volume.

The only differences between NBER and FRB data, aside from the location of nonguaranteed U.S. government securities, are in pension and insurance fund liabilities and in bonds and notes outstanding. The former discrepancy appears to be due to a difference in estimating procedure. The FRB figures are apparently based on the Census Bureau reports on *Governmental Finances*; those shown here are calculated by cumulating receipts and expenditures of the pension funds. The two sources also differ in the treatment of state-administered workmen's compensation funds, which are excluded by the FRB.

The discrepancy for bond liabilities arises from the inclusion here of loans from the federal government (other loans in the FRB accounts) and non-interest-bearing debt.

A large part of the NBER estimates for this sector were taken over directly from the Federal Reserve Board. The original sources, and the sources of information for the split between general government and pension fund assets, were the various Census Bureau publications on government finances, including the *1957 Census of Governments*.

Supplementary Table III-6a gives data for state and local governments back to 1900. Only a few changes have been made in the balance sheet from *A Study of Saving*, the most important one being the addition to structures of federal-aid highways, which were incorrectly omitted in the source.

Federal Government (Table III-7) covers all the departments, agencies, and trust funds of the federal government, with the exceptions noted below. Both general government functions and corporations and credit agencies are included, as well as federal land banks and federal home loan banks, even though they have passed into private ownership. Military assets are excluded, however, and are shown only in supplementary Table III-7a. Also excluded from this sector are the Federal Reserve banks (Table III-5a-1), Treasury monetary funds (Table III-5a-2), and federal government pension and insurance funds (Table III-5b-1).

The federal government sector in *Supplement 5* matches this one closely except that the FRB does not separate federal pension funds. The FRB accounts also do not include Old Age and Survivors' Insurance and unemployment trust fund assets as a federal government liability to the household sector, as was explained earlier.

Several supplementary tables give data for parts of the federal government, for use in computing the total balance sheet or to aid in comparisons with other sources. Table III-7b

TABLE 28

Federal Government, Including Federal Pension and Insurance Funds: Reconciliation of NBER and FRB Estimates

(billion dollars)

	1954	1955	1956	1957	1958
Lines II-1 and II-2 — No discrepancy					
Lines II-3 through II-6 — No federal government assets					
Line II-7 — No discrepancy					
Lines II-8 and II-9 — No federal government assets					
Line II-10					
1. FRB other loans	17.0	17.8	18.1	19.0	20.4
2. Plus NBER CCC loans to coops, except tobacco	0.1	0.3	0.1	0.1	0.1
3. Less FRB fed. govt. loans to states	0.5	0.5	0.6	0.8	1.0
4. Less FRB fed. govt. loans to nonprofit org.	--	--	--	0.1	0.2
5. Total of lines 1-4	16.6	17.6	17.6	18.2	19.3
6. NBER other loans	16.6	17.6	17.6	18.3	19.4
Lines II-11 and II-12					
7. FRB 1- to 4-family and other mortgages	4.6	5.2	6.0	7.5	7.8
8. NBER mortgages, nonfarm and farm	4.5	5.0	5.7	7.2	7.6
Line II-13 — Not estimated by FRB; netted out in consolidation of sector					
Line II-14 — No discrepancy; included under "other loans" by FRB					
Lines II-15 through II-18 — No federal government assets					
Line II-19					
9. FRB misc. assets, capital stock of Exch. Stab. Fund	0.2	0.2	0.2	0.2	0.2
10. Plus NBER other assets, postal sav. system	0.1	0.1	0.1	0.1	0.1
11. Plus NBER other equity in Exch. Stab. Fund	0.1	0.1	0.1	0.1	0.1
12. Total of lines 9-11	0.4	0.4	0.4	0.4	0.4
13. NBER equity in other business	0.4	0.4	0.4	0.4	0.4
Line II-20					
14. FRB miscellaneous assets	3.9	4.1	4.6	5.3	5.6
15. Plus FRB corp. profits tax liab. to federal government	15.5	19.3	17.6	15.4	12.9
16. Less FRB capital stock of Exch. Stab. Fund	0.2	0.2	0.2	0.2	0.2
17. Total of lines 14-16	19.2	23.2	22.0	20.5	18.3
18. NBER other intangible assets	19.2	23.2	22.0	20.5	18.3
Lines III-1 and III-2 — No discrepancy					
Lines III-3 and III-4 — No federal government liabilities					
Line III-5					
19. FRB cons. sav., life ins. and retirement funds	15.4	15.9	16.9	17.5	18.5
20. Plus FRB OASI fund assets	20.6	21.7	22.5	22.4	21.9
21. Plus NBER unemployment trust fund assets	8.7	8.8	9.1	9.1	7.1
22. Total of lines 19-21	44.7	46.4	48.5	49.0	47.5
23. NBER pension and insurance funds, govt.	45.5	47.4	49.5	50.6	49.9

(continued)

TABLE 28 (concluded)

	1954	1955	1956	1957	1958
Lines III-6 and III-8	No federal government liabilities				
Line III-7	No discrepancy				
Line III-9	No discrepancy; listed under "other loans" by FRB				
Lines III-10 and III-11	No federal government liabilities				
Line III-12					
24. FRB federal obligations	179.3	180.4	175.3	176.7	185.7
25. Plus FRB consumer-held savings bonds	50.0	50.2	50.1	48.2	47.7
26. Plus NBER U.S. govt. secur. held by fed. pension and insurance funds	44.4	46.5	48.4	49.4	48.4
27. Plus NBER U.S. govt. secur. held by fed. govt.	5.2	5.2	5.5	5.9	5.8
28. Plus FRB demand notes issued to IMF	1.5	1.6	1.1	0.7	0.8
29. Total of lines 24-28	280.4	283.9	280.4	280.9	288.4
30. NBER bonds and notes	280.5	284.0	280.5	280.9	288.5
Line III-13					
31. FRB misc. liabilities, other	0.8	0.9	1.0	1.4	1.3
32. Plus FRB misc. assets, deposits of savings and loan assoc. at FHLB	0.8	0.7	0.7	0.7	0.8
33. Less FRB unallocated foreign deposit liability of federal govt.	0.2	0.2	0.3	0.3	0.3
34. Less NBER Exch. Stab. Fund deposits with Treasurer of U.S.	--	--	--	0.2	--
35. Total of lines 31-34	1.4	1.4	1.4	1.6	1.8
36. NBER other liabilities	1.4	1.4	1.5	1.5	1.8

Line
1: *Supplement* 5, Table 8(E), line v.
2: Table III-7d, column 6.
3-4: *Supplement* 5, Table 32L, lines n and qq.
5: Sum of lines 1 and 2, minus lines 3 and 4.
6: Table III-7, line II-10, plus Table III-5b-1, line II-10.
7: *Supplement* 5, Table 8(E).
8: Table III-7, sum of lines II-11 and II-12.
9: *Supplement* 5, Table 34L, line o.
10: Table III-7b, line II-20.
11: See Table III-7, note to line II-19.
12: Sum of lines 9-11.
13: Table III-7, line II-19.
14: *Supplement* 5, Table 8(E).
15: FRB worksheets.
16: *Supplement* 5, Table 34L, line o.
17: Sum of lines 14 and 15, minus line 16.
18: Table III-7, line II-20.
19-20: *Supplement* 5, Table 8(E).
21: See note to Table III-5b-1, line II-1.
22: Sum of lines 19-21.
23: Table III-5b-1, line III-5.
24-25: *Supplement* 5, Table 8(E), lines c and a.
26: Table III-5b-1, line II-13.
27: Table III-7, line II-13.
28: *Supplement* 5, Table 8(E).
29: Sum of lines 24-28.
30: Table III-7, line III-12.
31-32: *Supplement* 5, Table 8(E).
33: *Ibid.*, Table 34L, line R.
34: See note to Table III-5a-2, line II-20.
35: Table III-7, line II-20.

is a balance sheet for the postal savings system, Table III-7c for government lending and credit agencies, and Table III-7e for the federal land banks. Table III-7d gives details on the distribution of federal government loans.

Another supplementary table (III-7f) is a reconstruction of the earlier balance sheets in *A Study of Saving*. Balance sheets for the federal government, government corporations and credit agencies, and the postal savings system were added together, and assets and liabilities of Treasury monetary funds were subtracted. Items for personal income and estate and gift tax accruals, equity in government corporations, and miscellaneous liabilities of the federal government were removed from the balance sheet and revisions were made in mortgage holdings.

The classification of sectors for Sections V, VI, and VII is identical with that described here for Section III and therefore requires no separate discussion. Most of the flow-of-funds categories are similarly described by the definitions of assets and liabilities. The ones which involve separate conceptual or estimative problems—tangible and equity flows—are discussed further in the notes to Section VIII.

Robert E. Lipsey

SECTION I

National Balance Sheets, 1945–58

TABLE I

National Balance Sheet—1945 (billion dollars)

	Nonfarm Households	Nonfarm Unincorporated Business
I. Tangible assets		
1. Residential structures	123.72	9.18
2. Nonresidential structures	6.97	8.21
3. Land	28.33	8.17
4. Producer durables	.13	5.31
5. Consumer durables	40.98	
6. Inventories		7.97
7. Total	200.13	38.84
II. Intangible assets		
1. Currency and demand deposits	49.89	8.93
a. Monetary metals	.84	.13
b. Other	49.05	8.80
2. Other bank deposits and shares	52.80	
3. Life insurance reserves, private	41.07	
4. Pension and retirement funds, private	2.68	
5. Pension and insurance funds, govt.	25.35	
6. Consumer credit		1.53
7. Trade credit		4.03
8. Loans on securities		
9. Bank loans, n.e.c.		
10. Other loans	1.00	
11. Mortgages, nonfarm	9.64	
a. Residential	6.23	
b. Nonresidential	3.42	
12. Mortgages, farm	1.92	
13. Securities, U.S. government	59.69	
a. Short-term	.51	
b. Savings bonds	40.42	
c. Other long-term	18.76	
14. Securities, state and local	11.92	
15. Securities, other bonds and notes	9.29	
16. Securities, preferred stock	8.15	
17. Securities, common stock	103.47	
18. Equity in mutual financial organizations	2.28	
19. Equity in other business	42.13	
20. Other intangible assets	1.33	
21. Total	422.61	14.49
III. Liabilities		
1. Currency and demand deposits		
2. Other bank deposits and shares		
3. Life insurance reserves, private		
4. Pension and retirement funds, private		
5. Pension and insurance funds, govt.		
6. Consumer debt	5.36	
7. Trade debt	.52	3.42
8. Loans on securities	3.34	
9. Bank loans, n.e.c.	.88	3.15
10. Other loans	1.97	.88
11. Mortgages	18.45	4.45
12. Bonds and notes		
13. Other liabilities		
14. Total	30.52	11.90
IV. Equities	592.22	41.43
V. Total assets or liabilities and equities	622.74	53.33

Agriculture	Nonfinancial Corporations	Finance	State and Local Govts.	Federal Govt.	Total	
						I.
9.22	8.09	.14	.87	1.21	152.43	1.
7.10	54.44	1.17	41.55	13.76	133.20	2.
43.47	20.03	.99	14.20	6.30	121.49	3.
5.79	33.94	.18	.62	2.64	48.61	4.
5.26					46.24	5.
15.68	26.31	.01	.07	2.58	52.62	6.
86.52	142.81	2.49	57.31	26.49	554.59	7.
						II.
6.60	19.68	77.30	5.21	26.81	194.42	1.
.16	.09	22.68			23.90	
6.44	19.59	54.62	5.21	26.81	170.52	
1.98	.90	.15	.53	.12	56.48	2.
3.40					44.47	3.
					2.68	4.
.48					25.83	5.
	1.66	2.52			5.71	6.
	22.73	.44		.90	28.10	7.
		8.25			8.25	8.
		13.29			13.29	9.
		2.86		4.06	7.92	10.
		20.16	.06	.92	30.78	11.
		16.08	.06	.90	23.27	
		4.07		.02	7.51	
		1.34		1.50	4.76	12.
4.15	20.72	181.65	4.99	4.52	275.72	13.
	17.00	57.61	2.40		77.52	
4.15	1.60	2.05			48.22	
	2.12	121.99	2.59	4.52	149.98	
	.32	6.98	1.45	.50	21.17	14.
	.18	17.70	.29		27.46	15.
	3.47	1.83			13.45	16.
	24.20	5.53			133.20	17.
					2.28	18.
				2.34	44.47	19.
1.38	14.36	9.66		11.12	37.85	20.
17.99	108.22	349.66	12.53	52.79	978.29	21.
						III.
		185.24		2.31	187.55	1.
		53.48		3.02	56.50	2.
		45.34			45.34	3.
		2.68			2.68	4.
		25.83			25.83	5.
.35					5.71	6.
.70	19.72	.03	.55	2.70	27.64	7.
	1.40	3.74			8.48	8.
1.04	6.42	1.17		.31	12.97	9.
.80	.81	1.71			6.17	10.
4.76	7.87				35.53	11.
	23.60	.19	21.27	278.98	324.04	12.
	28.42	11.21		.19	39.82	13.
7.65	88.24	330.62	21.82	287.51	778.26	14.
96.86	162.79	21.53	48.02	−208.23	754.62	IV.
104.51	251.03	352.15	69.84	79.28	1532.88	V.

TABLE I

National Balance Sheet—1946 (billion dollars)

	Nonfarm Households	Nonfarm Unincorporated Business
I. Tangible assets		
1. Residential structures	145.28	10.26
2. Nonresidential structures	9.26	11.02
3. Land	32.38	11.01
4. Producer durables	.18	6.88
5. Consumer durables	52.81	
6. Inventories		10.06
7. Total	239.91	49.23
II. Intangible assets		
1. Currency and demand deposits	54.04	8.94
a. Monetary metals	.89	.14
b. Other	53.15	8.80
2. Other bank deposits and shares	59.18	
3. Life insurance reserves, private	44.58	
4. Pension and retirement funds, private	3.25	
5. Pension and insurance funds, govt.	28.82	
6. Consumer credit		1.86
7. Trade credit		4.99
8. Loans on securities		
9. Bank loans, n.e.c.		
10. Other loans	1.16	
11. Mortgages, nonfarm	11.00	
a. Residential	7.11	
b. Nonresidential	3.89	
12. Mortgages, farm	2.04	
13. Securities, U.S. government	59.20	
a. Short-term	.67	
b. Savings bonds	41.62	
c. Other long-term	16.91	
14. Securities, state and local	11.76	
15. Securities, other bonds and notes	7.92	
16. Securities, preferred stock	8.15	
17. Securities, common stock	92.27	
18. Equity in mutual financial organizations	2.66	
19. Equity in other business	51.45	
20. Other intangible assets	1.32	
21. Total	438.80	15.79
III. Liabilities		
1. Currency and demand deposits		
2. Other bank deposits and shares		
3. Life insurance reserves, private		
4. Pension and retirement funds, private		
5. Pension and insurance funds, govt.		
6. Consumer debt	8.01	
7. Trade debt	.59	3.33
8. Loans on securities	1.86	
9. Bank loans, n.e.c.	.59	4.60
10. Other loans	1.90	1.22
11. Mortgages	22.71	4.97
12. Bonds and notes		
13. Other liabilities		
14. Total	35.66	14.12
IV. Equities	643.05	50.90
V. Total assets or liabilities and equities	678.71	65.02

Agriculture	Nonfinancial Corporations	Finance	State and Local Govts.	Federal Govt.	Total	
						I.
11.00	9.34	.15	1.35	1.15	178.53	1.
8.33	68.99	1.39	50.64	17.22	166.85	2.
46.53	24.99	1.14	18.90	7.00	141.95	3.
6.55	41.55	.20	.79	2.37	58.52	4.
6.82					59.63	5.
19.10	37.52	.03	.09	1.39	68.19	6.
98.33	182.40	2.91	71.77	29.13	673.68	7.
						II.
7.10	20.82	77.80	6.08	4.08	178.86	1.
.17	.10	23.09			24.39	
6.93	20.72	54.71	6.08	4.08	154.47	
2.18	.90	.29	.71	.13	63.39	2.
3.59					48.17	3.
					3.25	4.
.68					29.50	5.
	2.23	4.38			8.47	6.
	25.92	.77		.10	31.78	7.
		3.85			3.85	8.
		18.26			18.26	9.
		3.23		7.23	11.62	10.
		25.12	.07	.68	36.87	11.
		20.25	.07	.67	28.10	
		4.87		.01	8.77	
		1.54		1.32	4.90	12.
4.21	15.02	169.56	4.37	5.06	257.42	13.
	11.90	44.09	2.30		58.96	
4.21	1.60	2.43			49.86	
	1.52	123.04	2.07	5.06	148.60	
	.32	7.16	1.32	.48	21.04	14.
	.22	20.25	.30		28.69	15.
	3.48	2.01			13.64	16.
	21.67	5.41			119.35	17.
					2.66	18.
				2.34	53.79	19.
1.54	13.90	10.90		12.02	39.68	20.
19.30	104.48	350.53	12.85	33.44	975.19	21.
						III.
		170.36		2.44	172.80	1.
		60.03		3.38	63.41	2.
		49.11			49.11	3.
		3.25			3.25	4.
		29.50			29.50	5.
.46					8.47	6.
.90	23.45	.02	.70	.70	29.69	7.
	.49	1.70			4.05	8.
1.29	9.40	1.76		.10	17.74	9.
.82	.82	1.93			6.69	10.
4.90	9.19				41.77	11.
	24.48	.45	21.14	259.99	306.06	12.
	28.84	12.59		.23	41.66	13.
8.37	96.67	330.70	21.84	266.84	774.20	14.
109.26	190.21	22.74	62.78	−204.27	874.67	IV.
117.63	286.88	353.44	84.62	62.57	1648.87	V.

TABLE I

National Balance Sheet—1947 (billion dollars)

	Nonfarm Households	Nonfarm Unincorporated Business
I. Tangible assets		
1. Residential structures	177.58	11.89
2. Nonresidential structures	11.54	13.25
3. Land	39.41	12.81
4. Producer durables	.25	9.21
5. Consumer durables	65.00	
6. Inventories		11.59
7. Total	293.78	58.75
II. Intangible assets		
1. Currency and demand deposits	53.73	9.30
a. Monetary metals	.92	.15
b. Other	52.81	9.15
2. Other bank deposits and shares	62.81	
3. Life insurance reserves, private	47.87	
4. Pension and retirement funds, private	3.90	
5. Pension and insurance funds, govt.	32.61	
6. Consumer credit		2.19
7. Trade credit		5.36
8. Loans on securities		
9. Bank loans, n.e.c.		
10. Other loans	1.20	
11. Mortgages, nonfarm	12.21	
a. Residential	7.78	
b. Nonresidential	4.43	
12. Mortgages, farm	2.11	
13. Securities, U.S. government	61.02	
a. Short-term	.25	
b. Savings bonds	43.43	
c. Other long-term	17.34	
14. Securities, state and local	12.17	
15. Securities, other bonds and notes	7.23	
16. Securities, preferred stock	8.46	
17. Securities, common stock	90.20	
18. Equity in mutual financial organizations	2.87	
19. Equity in other business	59.20	
20. Other intangible assets	1.33	
21. Total	458.92	16.85
III. Liabilities		
1. Currency and demand deposits		
2. Other bank deposits and shares		
3. Life insurance reserves, private		
4. Pension and retirement funds, private		
5. Pension and insurance funds, govt.		
6. Consumer debt	11.20	
7. Trade debt	.68	2.80
8. Loans on securities	1.80	
9. Bank loans, n.e.c.	.34	6.82
10. Other loans	1.95	1.68
11. Mortgages	27.64	5.56
12. Bonds and notes		
13. Other liabilities		
14. Total	43.61	16.86
IV. Equities	709.09	58.74
V. Total assets or liabilities and equities	752.70	75.60

Agriculture	Nonfinancial Corporations	Finance	State and Local Govts.	Federal Govt.	Total	
						I.
13.08	11.13	.23	1.69	1.13	216.73	1.
9.86	80.74	1.45	60.49	20.61	197.94	2.
49.78	31.16	1.30	21.40	8.30	164.16	3.
8.39	52.58	.23	1.05	1.96	73.67	4.
8.38					73.38	5.
22.50	44.67	.02	.10	1.10	79.98	6.
111.99	220.28	3.23	84.73	33.10	805.86	7.
						II.
7.00	23.02	85.69	6.80	3.54	189.08	1.
.18	.10	25.31			26.66	
6.82	22.92	60.38	6.80	3.54	162.42	
2.10	.90	.33	.87	.12	67.13	2.
3.80					51.67	3.
					3.90	4.
.77					33.38	5.
	2.87	6.70			11.76	6.
	31.78	.90			38.04	7.
		2.79			2.79	8.
		22.85			22.85	9.
		3.56		11.36	16.12	10.
		30.94	.06	.64	43.85	11.
		25.28	.06	.63	33.75	
		5.66		.01	10.10	
		1.76		1.20	5.07	12.
4.38	13.82	165.19	5.03	5.10	254.54	13.
	11.00	41.26	2.60		55.11	
4.38	1.60	2.77			52.18	
	1.22	121.16	2.43	5.10	147.25	
	.36	8.15	1.27	.50	22.45	14.
	.34	24.10	.34		32.01	15.
	3.49	2.12			14.07	16.
	21.26	5.55			117.01	17.
					2.87	18.
				.55	59.75	19.
1.71	15.77	12.58		14.21	45.60	20.
19.76	113.61	373.21	14.37	37.22	1033.94	21.
						III.
		179.97		2.41	182.38	1.
		63.62		3.52	67.14	2.
		52.68			52.68	3.
		3.90			3.90	4.
		33.38			33.38	5.
.56					11.76	6.
1.10	28.09	.03	.85		33.55	7.
	.16	.99			2.95	8.
1.59	11.06	2.38		.07	22.26	9.
.85	.96	2.12			7.56	10.
5.06	10.66				48.92	11.
	27.32	.73	22.55	257.69	308.29	12.
	31.58	12.72		.27	44.57	13.
9.16	109.83	352.52	23.40	263.96	819.34	14.
122.59	224.06	23.92	75.70	−193.64	1020.46	IV.
131.75	333.89	376.44	99.10	70.32	1839.80	V.

TABLE I

National Balance Sheet—1948 (billion dollars)

	Nonfarm Households	Nonfarm Unincorporated Business
I. Tangible assets		
1. Residential structures	192.31	12.95
2. Nonresidential structures	12.49	14.11
3. Land	43.87	14.09
4. Producer durables	.35	11.35
5. Consumer durables	75.41	
6. Inventories		12.92
7. Total	324.43	65.42
II. Intangible assets		
1. Currency and demand deposits	51.67	9.15
a. Monetary metals	.95	.15
b. Other	50.72	9.00
2. Other bank deposits and shares	64.99	
3. Life insurance reserves, private	51.39	
4. Pension and retirement funds, private	4.55	
5. Pension and insurance funds, govt.	36.10	
6. Consumer credit		2.56
7. Trade credit		5.76
8. Loans on securities		
9. Bank loans, n.e.c.		
10. Other loans	1.07	
11. Mortgages, nonfarm	13.21	
a. Residential	8.38	
b. Nonresidential	4.84	
12. Mortgages, farm	2.23	
13. Securities, U.S. government	60.79	
a. Short-term	2.36	
b. Savings bonds	45.05	
c. Other long-term	13.38	
14. Securities, state and local	13.16	
15. Securities, other bonds and notes	6.95	
16. Securities, preferred stock	8.74	
17. Securities, common stock	90.41	
18. Equity in mutual financial organizations	3.33	
19. Equity in other business	65.24	
20. Other intangible assets	1.32	
21. Total	475.15	17.47
III. Liabilities		
1. Currency and demand deposits		
2. Other bank deposits and shares		
3. Life insurance reserves, private		
4. Pension and retirement funds, private		
5. Pension and insurance funds, govt.		
6. Consumer debt	14.00	
7. Trade debt	.76	3.56
8. Loans on securities	1.68	
9. Bank loans, n.e.c.	.44	6.12
10. Other loans	2.08	2.33
11. Mortgages	32.78	6.16
12. Bonds and notes		
13. Other liabilities		
14. Total	51.74	18.17
IV. Equities	747.84	64.72
V. Total assets or liabilities and equities	799.58	82.89

Agriculture	Nonfinancial Corporations	Finance	State and Local Govts.	Federal Govt.	Total	
						I.
13.63	12.33	.27	1.76	.99	234.24	1.
10.52	89.30	1.52	65.12	22.20	215.26	2.
51.93	37.06	1.51	21.50	8.90	178.86	3.
10.69	61.95	.26	1.35	1.56	87.51	4.
9.90					85.31	5.
22.20	48.88	.01	.11	1.92	86.04	6.
118.87	249.52	3.57	89.84	35.57	887.22	7.
						II.
6.70	23.22	90.43	7.29	4.62	193.08	1.
.18	.12	26.81			28.21	
6.52	23.10	63.62	7.29	4.62	164.87	
2.10	.90	.35	1.14	.12	69.60	2.
4.03					55.42	3.
					4.55	4.
.76					36.86	5.
	3.41	8.68			14.65	6.
	34.12	1.07			40.95	7.
		3.04			3.04	8.
		25.02			25.02	9.
		4.17		13.03	18.27	10.
		36.90	.07	.72	50.90	11.
		30.45	.07	.72	39.62	
		6.45		.01	11.30	
		1.92		1.14	5.29	12.
4.60	14.62	159.43	5.35	5.20	249.99	13.
	11.90	34.78	3.10		52.14	
4.60	1.80	3.75			55.20	
	.92	120.90	2.25	5.20	142.65	
	.41	9.25	1.27	.57	24.66	14.
	.48	29.27	.51		37.21	15.
	3.50	2.19			14.43	16.
	21.39	5.74			117.54	17.
					3.33	18.
				.54	65.78	19.
1.88	16.70	12.52		14.98	47.40	20.
20.07	118.75	389.98	15.63	40.92	1077.97	21.
						III.
		182.05		2.40	184.45	1.
		66.19		3.45	69.64	2.
		56.51			56.51	3.
		4.55			4.55	4.
		36.86			36.86	5.
.65					14.65	6.
1.40	28.53	.04	1.00		35.29	7.
		1.50			3.18	8.
1.95	12.12	2.84		.92	24.39	9.
.93	1.13	2.12			8.59	10.
5.29	11.97				56.20	11.
	31.55	1.31	24.76	253.88	311.50	12.
	33.35	13.66		.33	47.34	13.
10.22	118.65	367.63	25.76	260.98	853.15	14.
128.72	249.62	25.92	79.71	−184.49	1112.04	IV.
138.94	368.27	393.55	105.47	76.49	1965.19	V.

TABLE I

National Balance Sheet—1949 (billion dollars)

	Nonfarm Households	Nonfarm Unincorporated Business
I. Tangible assets		
1. Residential structures	189.39	12.79
2. Nonresidential structures	12.44	13.73
3. Land	43.28	13.89
4. Producer durables	.48	12.83
5. Consumer durables	80.69	
6. Inventories		11.97
7. Total	326.28	65.21
II. Intangible assets		
1. Currency and demand deposits	49.36	9.52
a. Monetary metals	.95	.16
b. Other	48.41	9.36
2. Other bank deposits and shares	67.47	
3. Life insurance reserves, private	55.21	
4. Pension and retirement funds, private	5.26	
5. Pension and insurance funds, govt.	38.59	
6. Consumer credit		2.81
7. Trade credit		5.82
8. Loans on securities		
9. Bank loans, n.e.c.		
10. Other loans	1.23	
11. Mortgages, nonfarm	13.80	
a. Residential	8.60	
b. Nonresidential	5.20	
12. Mortgages, farm	2.31	
13. Securities, U.S. government	61.76	
a. Short-term	3.33	
b. Savings bonds	46.35	
c. Other long-term	12.08	
14. Securities, state and local	13.77	
15. Securities, other bonds and notes	6.32	
16. Securities, preferred stock	8.75	
17. Securities, common stock	101.09	
18. Equity in mutual financial organizations	3.71	
19. Equity in other business	65.17	
20. Other intangible assets	1.31	
21. Total	495.11	18.15
III. Liabilities		
1. Currency and demand deposits		
2. Other bank deposits and shares		
3. Life insurance reserves, private		
4. Pension and retirement funds, private		
5. Pension and insurance funds, govt.		
6. Consumer debt	16.95	
7. Trade debt	.80	3.78
8. Loans on securities	2.00	
9. Bank loans, n.e.c.	.44	5.83
10. Other loans	2.27	2.42
11. Mortgages	37.04	6.69
12. Bonds and notes		
13. Other liabilities		
14. Total	59.50	18.72
IV. Equities	761.89	64.64
V. Total assets or liabilities and equities	821.39	83.36

Agriculture	Nonfinancial Corporations	Finance	State and Local Govts.	Federal Govt.	Total	
						I.
13.75	12.48	.32	1.93	.89	231.55	1.
10.82	89.02	2.43	63.77	22.34	214.55	2.
50.90	36.40	1.91	20.50	9.10	175.98	3.
12.47	67.94	.28	1.63	1.24	96.87	4.
10.51					91.20	5.
18.93	45.30	.01	.10	3.28	79.59	6.
117.38	251.14	4.95	87.93	36.85	889.74	7.
						II.
6.30	24.29	87.64	7.52	5.00	189.63	1.
.19	.12	27.03			28.45	
6.11	24.17	60.61	7.52	5.00	161.18	
2.10	.90	.36	1.29	.18	72.30	2.
4.27					59.48	3.
					5.26	4.
.81					39.40	5.
	3.85	10.93			17.59	6.
	33.18	1.17			40.17	7.
		3.79			3.79	8.
		23.40			23.40	9.
		4.29		13.70	19.22	10.
		41.93	.16	1.21	57.10	11.
		34.91	.16	1.20	44.87	
		7.01			12.21	
		2.11		1.16	5.58	12.
4.72	16.54	160.57	5.37	5.28	254.24	13.
	14.20	41.63	3.20		62.36	
4.72	1.80	4.04			56.91	
	.54	114.90	2.17	5.28	134.97	
	.46	10.74	1.55	.49	27.01	14.
	.62	32.98	.50		40.42	15.
	3.50	2.50			14.75	16.
	24.20	7.24			132.53	17.
					3.71	18.
				.52	65.69	19.
2.06	17.56	13.25		12.89	47.07	20.
20.26	125.10	402.90	16.39	40.43	1118.34	21.
						III.
		179.36		2.38	181.74	1.
		69.17		3.31	72.48	2.
		60.65			60.65	3.
		5.26			5.26	4.
		39.40			39.40	5.
.64					17.59	6.
1.60	27.19	.06	1.10		34.53	7.
		1.95			3.95	8.
2.05	10.19	3.23		1.00	22.74	9.
.96	1.21	2.20			9.06	10.
5.58	13.37				62.68	11.
	34.45	1.83	27.11	258.07	321.46	12.
	32.69	14.96		.49	48.14	13.
10.83	119.10	378.07	28.21	265.25	879.68	14.
126.81	257.14	29.78	76.11	−187.97	1128.40	IV.
137.64	376.24	407.85	104.32	77.28	2008.08	V.

TABLE I

National Balance Sheet—1950 (billion dollars)

	Nonfarm Households	Nonfarm Unincorporated Business
I. Tangible assets		
1. Residential structures	220.58	14.07
2. Nonresidential structures	13.94	14.84
3. Land	48.91	15.67
4. Producer durables	.65	14.81
5. Consumer durables	98.91	
6. Inventories		14.24
7. Total	382.99	73.63
II. Intangible assets		
1. Currency and demand deposits	51.26	9.74
a. Monetary metals	1.01	.17
b. Other	50.25	9.57
2. Other bank deposits and shares	69.56	
3. Life insurance reserves, private	59.23	
4. Pension and retirement funds, private	6.23	
5. Pension and insurance funds, govt.	40.15	
6. Consumer credit		3.30
7. Trade credit		7.04
8. Loans on securities		
9. Bank loans, n.e.c.		
10. Other loans	1.78	
11. Mortgages, nonfarm	14.16	
a. Residential	8.69	
b. Nonresidential	5.47	
12. Mortgages, farm	2.53	
13. Securities, U.S. government	61.43	
a. Short-term	2.15	
b. Savings bonds	46.80	
c. Other long-term	12.48	
14. Securities, state and local	14.15	
15. Securities, other bonds and notes	6.35	
16. Securities, preferred stock	8.69	
17. Securities, common stock	125.38	
18. Equity in mutual financial organizations	4.03	
19. Equity in other business	71.76	
20. Other intangible assets	1.08	
21. Total	537.77	20.08
III. Liabilities		
1. Currency and demand deposits		
2. Other bank deposits and shares		
3. Life insurance reserves, private		
4. Pension and retirement funds, private		
5. Pension and insurance funds, govt.		
6. Consumer debt	20.94	
7. Trade debt	.90	4.52
8. Loans on securities	2.78	
9. Bank loans, n.e.c.	.71	7.96
10. Other loans	2.45	2.78
11. Mortgages	44.31	7.26
12. Bonds and notes		
13. Other liabilities		
14. Total	72.09	22.52
IV. Equities	848.67	71.19
V. Total assets or liabilities and equities	920.76	93.71

Agriculture	Nonfinancial Corporations	Finance	State and Local Govts.	Federal Govt.	Total	
						I.
14.91	14.26	.40	2.33	.84	267.39	1.
11.93	101.29	2.41	70.75	24.72	239.88	2.
58.40	41.24	2.01	24.00	11.50	201.73	3.
14.09	77.08	.35	1.94	1.06	109.98	4.
12.41					111.32	5.
24.37	55.08	.02	.13	2.67	96.51	6.
136.11	288.96	5.19	99.15	40.79	1026.82	7.
						II.
6.30	25.60	87.72	7.98	4.32	192.92	1.
.18	.13	25.30			26.79	
6.12	25.47	62.42	7.98	4.32	166.13	
2.10	.90	.31	1.39	.19	74.45	2.
4.51					63.74	3.
					6.23	4.
.56					40.71	5.
	4.63	13.84			21.77	6.
	44.62	1.47		.38	53.51	7.
		4.59			4.59	8.
		28.92			28.92	9.
		4.91		14.40	21.09	10.
		50.87	.21	1.50	66.74	11.
		43.21	.21	1.49	53.60	
		7.66			13.13	
		2.37		1.21	6.11	12.
4.69	19.41	156.05	5.73	5.04	252.35	13.
	17.20	41.31	3.50		64.16	
4.69	1.80	4.96			58.25	
	.41	109.78	2.23	5.04	129.94	
	.53	13.03	1.85	.56	30.22	14.
	.65	35.93	.56		43.39	15.
	3.51	2.81			15.01	16.
	29.67	8.80			163.85	17.
					4.03	18.
				.49	72.25	19.
2.28	18.12	17.44		20.36	59.28	20.
20.44	147.64	429.06	17.72	48.45	1221.16	21.
						III.
		188.71		2.36	191.07	1.
		71.81		3.04	74.85	2.
		64.99			64.99	3.
		6.23			6.23	4.
		40.71			40.71	5.
.83					21.77	6.
1.80	35.20	.07	1.20	1.10	44.79	7.
		2.02			4.80	8.
2.52	12.34	4.29		.38	28.20	9.
1.02	1.34	3.19			10.78	10.
6.12	15.18				72.87	11.
	36.06	2.25	30.22	258.12	326.65	12.
	40.06	16.86		.49	57.41	13.
12.29	140.18	401.13	31.42	265.49	945.12	14.
144.26	296.42	33.12	85.45	−176.25	1302.86	IV.
156.55	436.60	434.25	116.87	89.24	2247.98	V.

TABLE I

National Balance Sheet—1951 (billion dollars)

	Nonfarm Households	Nonfarm Unincorporated Business
I. Tangible assets		
1. Residential structures	236.14	14.46
2. Nonresidential structures	15.15	15.83
3. Land	52.42	16.95
4. Producer durables	.83	16.63
5. Consumer durables	108.85	
6. Inventories		15.07
7. Total	413.39	78.94
II. Intangible assets		
1. Currency and demand deposits	54.33	10.78
a. Monetary metals	1.06	.19
b. Other	53.27	10.59
2. Other bank deposits and shares	73.76	
3. Life insurance reserves, private	63.22	
4. Pension and retirement funds, private	7.80	
5. Pension and insurance funds, govt.	44.26	
6. Consumer credit		3.60
7. Trade credit		7.26
8. Loans on securities		
9. Bank loans, n.e.c.		
10. Other loans	1.74	
11. Mortgages, nonfarm	14.66	
a. Residential	8.91	
b. Nonresidential	5.74	
12. Mortgages, farm	2.78	
13. Securities, U.S. government	59.98	
a. Short-term	.54	
b. Savings bonds	46.25	
c. Other long-term	13.19	
14. Securities, state and local	14.46	
15. Securities, other bonds and notes	6.42	
16. Securities, preferred stock	9.14	
17. Securities, common stock	142.96	
18. Equity in mutual financial organizations	4.28	
19. Equity in other business	78.94	
20. Other intangible assets	.85	
21. Total	579.58	21.64
III. Liabilities		
1. Currency and demand deposits		
2. Other bank deposits and shares		
3. Life insurance reserves, private		
4. Pension and retirement funds, private		
5. Pension and insurance funds, govt.		
6. Consumer debt	22.29	
7. Trade debt	.90	3.83
8. Loans on securities	2.63	
9. Bank loans, n.e.c.	.70	7.16
10. Other loans	2.65	3.28
11. Mortgages	51.08	7.91
12. Bonds and notes		
13. Other liabilities		
14. Total	80.25	22.18
IV. Equities	912.72	78.40
V. Total assets or liabilities and equities	992.97	100.58

Agriculture	Nonfinancial Corporations	Finance	State and Local Govts.	Federal Govt.	Total	
						I.
16.07	15.17	.43	2.95	.79	286.01	1.
13.18	109.79	2.26	77.27	25.89	259.37	2.
66.31	46.26	2.09	24.20	13.40	221.63	3.
15.68	86.80	.39	2.27	1.00	123.60	4.
13.60					122.45	5.
28.14	64.83	.02	.13	2.24	110.43	6.
152.98	322.85	5.19	106.82	43.32	1123.49	7.
						II.
6.50	27.42	92.39	8.41	4.38	204.21	1.
.20	.14	25.25			26.84	
6.30	27.28	67.14	8.41	4.38	177.37	
2.17	.90	.39	1.54	.28	79.04	2.
4.75					67.97	3.
					7.80	4.
.52					44.78	5.
	5.14	14.37			23.11	6.
	48.03	1.66		1.30	58.25	7.
		4.25			4.25	8.
		33.60			33.60	9.
		5.56		15.03	22.33	10.
		58.56	.29	2.11	75.62	11.
		50.08	.29	2.11	61.39	
		8.49			14.23	
		2.62		1.27	6.67	12.
4.71	20.34	158.78	6.10	4.95	254.86	13.
	17.50	32.10	3.30		53.44	
4.71	1.80	4.98			57.74	
	1.04	121.70	2.80	4.95	143.68	
	.58	14.69	1.98	.82	32.53	14.
	.95	39.96	.66		47.99	15.
	3.51	2.94			15.59	16.
	33.65	10.97			187.58	17.
					4.28	18.
				.48	79.42	19.
2.48	19.14	18.11		24.98	65.56	20.
21.13	159.66	458.85	18.98	55.60	1315.44	21.
						III.
		199.64		2.40	202.04	1.
		76.73		2.82	79.55	2.
		69.31			69.31	3.
		7.80			7.80	4.
		44.78			44.78	5.
.82					23.11	6.
2.20	37.48	.06	1.20	2.70	48.37	7.
		1.83			4.46	8.
3.12	17.30	4.25		.29	32.82	9.
1.13	1.49	3.24			11.79	10.
6.68	16.63				82.30	11.
	39.36	2.82	32.63	261.11	335.92	12.
	47.00	18.03		.64	65.67	13.
13.95	159.26	428.49	33.83	269.96	1007.92	14.
160.16	323.25	35.55	91.97	−171.04	1431.01	IV.
174.11	482.51	464.04	125.80	98.92	2438.93	V.

TABLE I

National Balance Sheet—1952 (billion dollars)

	Nonfarm Households	Nonfarm Unincorporated Business
I. Tangible assets		
1. Residential structures	249.61	14.71
2. Nonresidential structures	16.47	16.52
3. Land	56.78	17.10
4. Producer durables	.97	17.65
5. Consumer durables	113.97	
6. Inventories		14.79
7. Total	437.80	80.77
II. Intangible assets		
1. Currency and demand deposits	56.22	10.43
a. Monetary metals	1.14	.18
b. Other	55.08	10.25
2. Other bank deposits and shares	81.11	
3. Life insurance reserves, private	68.00	
4. Pension and retirement funds, private	9.52	
5. Pension and insurance funds, govt.	48.62	
6. Consumer credit		4.00
7. Trade credit		8.37
8. Loans on securities		
9. Bank loans, n.e.c.		
10. Other loans	1.63	
11. Mortgages, nonfarm	15.22	
a. Residential	9.20	
b. Nonresidential	6.02	
12. Mortgages, farm	3.03	
13. Securities, U.S. government	60.21	
a. Short-term	1.29	
b. Savings bonds	46.40	
c. Other long-term	12.52	
14. Securities, state and local	15.62	
15. Securities, other bonds and notes	6.27	
16. Securities, preferred stock	9.42	
17. Securities, common stock	154.00	
18. Equity in mutual financial organizations	4.59	
19. Equity in other business	80.29	
20. Other intangible assets	.62	
21. Total	614.37	22.80
III. Liabilities		
1. Currency and demand deposits		
2. Other bank deposits and shares		
3. Life insurance reserves, private		
4. Pension and retirement funds, private		
5. Pension and insurance funds, govt.		
6. Consumer debt	26.99	
7. Trade debt	1.14	4.14
8. Loans on securities	2.84	
9. Bank loans, n.e.c.	.64	7.64
10. Other loans	2.77	3.59
11. Mortgages	57.81	8.43
12. Bonds and notes		
13. Other liabilities		
14. Total	92.19	23.80
IV. Equities	959.98	79.77
V. Total assets or liabilities and equities	1052.17	103.57

Agriculture	Nonfinancial Corporations	Finance	State and Local Govts.	Federal Govt.	Total	
						I.
16.58	15.87	.53	3.62	.74	301.66	1.
13.76	116.34	2.53	83.84	27.60	277.06	2.
66.89	47.05	2.30	23.70	12.90	226.72	3.
16.41	92.95	.44	2.56	1.00	131.98	4.
13.65					127.62	5.
23.15	66.07	.03	.13	2.71	106.88	6.
150.45	338.28	5.83	113.85	44.95	1171.93	7.
						II.
6.40	28.22	93.53	8.88	6.33	210.01	1.
.20	.15	25.72			27.39	
6.20	28.07	67.81	8.88	6.33	182.62	
2.30	.90	.52	1.63	.35	86.81	2.
5.03					73.03	3.
					9.52	4.
.51					49.13	5.
	5.90	18.00			27.90	6.
	51.56	1.81		2.25	63.99	7.
		4.95			4.95	8.
		36.62			36.62	9.
		5.89		15.78	23.30	10.
		66.00	.36	2.58	84.16	11.
		56.74	.36	2.57	68.87	
		9.26			15.28	
		2.87		1.36	7.26	12.
4.63	19.54	165.16	7.18	5.05	261.77	13.
	16.40	37.51	4.00		59.20	
4.63	1.80	5.22			58.05	
	1.34	122.43	3.18	5.05	144.52	
	.64	16.23	2.08	1.14	35.71	14.
	1.36	45.01	.59		53.23	15.
	3.52	3.12			16.06	16.
	36.11	13.30			203.41	17.
					4.59	18.
				.48	80.77	19.
2.72	22.12	19.11		21.82	66.39	20.
21.59	169.87	492.12	20.72	57.14	1398.61	21.
						III.
		206.62		2.44	209.06	1.
		84.86		2.66	87.52	2.
		74.47			74.47	3.
		9.52			9.52	4.
		49.13			49.13	5.
.91					27.90	6.
2.30	41.07	.10	1.30	2.80	52.85	7.
		2.31			5.15	8.
3.19	18.49	5.16		.72	35.84	9.
1.21	1.58	3.21			12.36	10.
7.26	17.92				91.42	11.
	44.08	3.36	35.81	269.12	352.37	12.
	45.60	20.15		.90	66.65	13.
14.87	168.74	458.89	37.11	278.64	1074.24	14.
157.17	339.41	39.06	97.46	− 176.55	1496.30	IV.
172.04	508.15	497.95	134.57	102.09	2570.54	V.

TABLE I

National Balance Sheet—1953 (billion dollars)

	Nonfarm Households	Nonfarm Unincorporated Business
I. Tangible assets		
1. Residential structures	259.88	14.91
2. Nonresidential structures	17.55	17.32
3. Land	59.87	17.51
4. Producer durables	1.10	18.82
5. Consumer durables	120.57	
6. Inventories		15.21
7. Total	458.97	83.77
II. Intangible assets		
1. Currency and demand deposits	57.13	10.38
a. Monetary metals	1.20	.19
b. Other	55.93	10.19
2. Other bank deposits and shares	88.99	
3. Life insurance reserves, private	72.80	
4. Pension and retirement funds, private	11.42	
5. Pension and insurance funds, govt.	52.04	
6. Consumer credit		4.18
7. Trade credit		8.95
8. Loans on securities		
9. Bank loans, n.e.c.		
10. Other loans	1.68	
11. Mortgages, nonfarm	15.97	
a. Residential	9.60	
b. Nonresidential	6.37	
12. Mortgages, farm	3.22	
13. Securities, U.S. government	60.40	
a. Short-term	2.31	
b. Savings bonds	46.36	
c. Other long-term	11.73	
14. Securities, state and local	17.23	
15. Securities, other bonds and notes	6.39	
16. Securities, preferred stock	9.45	
17. Securities, common stock	151.93	
18. Equity in mutual financial organizations	4.99	
19. Equity in other business	82.52	
20. Other intangible assets	.61	
21. Total	636.77	23.51
III. Liabilities		
1. Currency and demand deposits		
2. Other bank deposits and shares		
3. Life insurance reserves, private		
4. Pension and retirement funds, private		
5. Pension and insurance funds, govt.		
6. Consumer debt	30.92	
7. Trade debt	1.20	5.24
8. Loans on securities	3.36	
9. Bank loans, n.e.c.	.56	7.45
10. Other loans	2.98	3.69
11. Mortgages	65.46	8.98
12. Bonds and notes		
13. Other liabilities		
14. Total	104.48	25.36
IV. Equities	991.26	81.92
V. Total assets or liabilities and equities	1095.74	107.28

Agriculture	Nonfinancial Corporations	Finance	State and Local Govts.	Federal Govt.	Total	
						I.
16.88	16.52	.54	4.14	.67	313.54	1.
14.07	124.27	2.79	87.42	28.75	292.17	2.
64.22	47.88	2.52	24.00	12.00	228.00	3.
16.64	99.87	.48	2.86	1.00	140.77	4.
14.20					134.77	5.
18.91	67.88	.03	.14	5.59	107.76	6.
144.92	356.42	6.36	118.56	48.01	1217.01	7.
						II.
6.30	28.14	92.36	9.48	4.86	208.65	1.
.19	.15	24.56			26.29	
6.11	27.99	67.80	9.48	4.86	182.36	
2.43	.90	.60	1.96	.34	95.22	2.
5.30					78.10	3.
					11.42	4.
.47					52.51	5.
	6.14	21.50			31.82	6.
	50.75	1.97		2.21	63.88	7.
		5.75			5.75	8.
		37.00			37.00	9.
		6.12		16.39	24.19	10.
		74.16	.50	2.93	93.56	11.
		64.08	.50	2.92	77.10	
		10.08			16.45	
		3.08		1.47	7.77	12.
4.73	21.12	169.01	8.49	5.07	268.82	13.
	18.20	49.28	5.20		74.99	
4.73	1.80	5.05			57.94	
	1.12	114.68	3.29	5.07	135.89	
	.73	18.35	2.17	.81	39.29	14.
	1.54	49.47	.64		58.04	15.
	3.52	3.47			16.44	16.
	35.46	14.11			201.50	17.
					4.99	18.
				.46	82.98	19.
2.87	24.75	19.67		22.35	70.25	20.
22.10	173.05	516.62	23.24	56.89	1452.18	21.
						III.
		206.27		2.47	208.74	1.
		94.01		2.47	96.48	2.
		79.64			79.64	3.
		11.42			11.42	4.
		52.51			52.51	5.
.90					31.82	6.
2.10	41.23	.12	1.40	2.60	53.89	7.
		2.61			5.97	8.
2.76	18.33	5.02		2.20	36.32	9.
1.19	1.92	3.25			13.03	10.
7.77	19.11				101.32	11.
	47.43	4.94	39.39	276.91	368.67	12.
	47.83	21.72		1.11	70.66	13.
14.72	175.85	481.51	40.79	287.76	1130.47	14.
152.30	353.62	41.47	101.01	− 182.86	1538.72	IV.
167.02	529.47	522.98	141.80	104.90	2669.19	V.

TABLE I

National Balance Sheet—1954 (billion dollars)

	Nonfarm Households	Nonfarm Unincorporated Business
I. Tangible assets		
1. Residential structures	270.18	14.83
2. Nonresidential structures	18.77	18.27
3. Land	64.24	18.30
4. Producer durables	1.27	19.79
5. Consumer durables	124.82	
6. Inventories		15.06
7. Total	479.28	86.25
II. Intangible assets		
1. Currency and demand deposits	59.33	10.91
a. Monetary metals	1.21	.20
b. Other	58.12	10.71
2. Other bank deposits and shares	97.82	
3. Life insurance reserves, private	78.41	
4. Pension and retirement funds, private	14.34	
5. Pension and insurance funds, govt.	54.75	
6. Consumer credit		4.27
7. Trade credit		9.15
8. Loans on securities		
9. Bank loans, n.e.c.		
10. Other loans	2.42	
11. Mortgages, nonfarm	16.96	
a. Residential	10.03	
b. Nonresidential	6.94	
12. Mortgages, farm	3.40	
13. Securities, U.S. government	58.87	
a. Short-term	1.66	
b. Savings bonds	46.45	
c. Other long-term	10.76	
14. Securities, state and local	17.89	
15. Securities, other bonds and notes	5.42	
16. Securities, preferred stock	9.44	
17. Securities, common stock	211.34	
18. Equity in mutual financial organizations	5.49	
19. Equity in other business	82.72	
20. Other intangible assets	.61	
21. Total	719.21	24.33
III. Liabilities		
1. Currency and demand deposits		
2. Other bank deposits and shares		
3. Life insurance reserves, private		
4. Pension and retirement funds, private		
5. Pension and insurance funds, govt.		
6. Consumer debt	31.93	
7. Trade debt	1.30	6.56
8. Loans on securities	4.64	
9. Bank loans, n.e.c.	.68	8.56
10. Other loans	3.22	3.87
11. Mortgages	74.83	9.73
12. Bonds and notes		
13. Other liabilities		
14. Total	116.60	28.72
IV. Equities	1081.89	81.86
V. Total assets or liabilities and equities	1198.49	110.58

Agriculture	Nonfinancial Corporations	Finance	State and Local Govts.	Federal Govt.	Total	
						I.
17.26	16.97	.56	4.41	.57	324.78	1.
14.43	129.36	3.17	92.85	29.68	306.53	2.
66.41	50.04	2.82	24.10	12.40	238.31	3.
16.86	106.85	.57	3.22	.93	149.49	4.
13.90					138.72	5.
18.75	66.28	.02	.15	6.83	107.09	6.
147.61	369.50	7.14	124.73	50.41	1264.92	7.
						II.
6.20	30.50	91.42	9.81	4.89	213.06	1.
.19	.15	24.29			26.04	
6.01	30.35	67.13	9.81	4.89	187.02	
2.53	1.10	.70	2.42	.36	104.93	2.
5.62					84.03	3.
					14.34	4.
.45					55.20	5.
	6.41	22.24			32.92	6.
	55.06	2.12		2.44	68.77	7.
		7.61			7.61	8.
		37.60			37.60	9.
		6.22		16.32	24.96	10.
		84.92	.61	2.94	105.43	11.
		73.62	.61	2.94	87.20	
		11.30			18.24	
		3.32		1.57	8.29	12.
4.97	18.83	174.26	9.93	5.20	272.06	13.
	15.60	40.61	5.20		63.07	
4.97	1.80	5.14			58.36	
	1.43	128.51	4.73	5.20	150.63	
	1.06	21.84	2.20	.48	43.47	14.
	1.47	53.77	.84		61.50	15.
	3.53	3.88			16.85	16.
	49.13	21.25			281.72	17.
					5.49	18.
				.45	83.17	19.
3.11	29.68	20.29		19.22	72.91	20.
22.88	196.77	551.44	25.81	53.87	1594.31	21.
						III.
		208.97		2.50	211.47	1.
		104.50		2.24	106.74	2.
		85.68			85.68	3.
		14.34			14.34	4.
		55.20			55.20	5.
.99					32.92	6.
2.10	46.70	.13	1.55	2.37	60.71	7.
		3.28			7.92	8.
2.93	17.11	5.02		2.27	36.57	9.
1.29	1.65	3.93			13.96	10.
8.29	20.87				113.72	11.
	50.97	5.13	43.57	280.46	380.13	12.
	48.15	23.16		1.39	72.70	13.
15.60	185.45	509.34	45.12	291.23	1192.06	14.
154.89	380.82	49.24	105.42	− 186.95	1667.17	IV.
170.49	566.27	558.58	150.54	104.28	2859.23	V.

TABLE I

National Balance Sheet—1955 (billion dollars)

	Nonfarm Households	Nonfarm Unincorporated Business
I. Tangible assets		
1. Residential structures	294.13	15.30
2. Nonresidential structures	20.40	20.06
3. Land	70.82	19.89
4. Producer durables	1.47	21.76
5. Consumer durables	136.92	
6. Inventories		15.81
7. Total	523.74	92.82
II. Intangible assets		
1. Currency and demand deposits	58.58	11.20
a. Monetary metals	1.27	.21
b. Other	57.31	10.99
2. Other bank deposits and shares	106.24	
3. Life insurance reserves, private	83.96	
4. Pension and retirement funds, private	17.35	
5. Pension and insurance funds, govt.	57.99	
6. Consumer credit		4.43
7. Trade credit		9.68
8. Loans on securities		
9. Bank loans, n.e.c.		
10. Other loans	2.30	
11. Mortgages, nonfarm	17.96	
a. Residential	10.41	
b. Nonresidential	7.56	
12. Mortgages, farm	3.62	
13. Securities, U.S. government	60.63	
a. Short-term	.65	
b. Savings bonds	46.48	
c. Other long-term	13.50	
14. Securities, state and local	19.57	
15. Securities, other bonds and notes	7.33	
16. Securities, preferred stock	9.30	
17. Securities, common stock	260.63	
18. Equity in mutual financial organizations	6.10	
19. Equity in other business	86.15	
20. Other intangible assets	.61	
21. Total	798.32	25.31
III. Liabilities		
1. Currency and demand deposits		
2. Other bank deposits and shares		
3. Life insurance reserves, private		
4. Pension and retirement funds, private		
5. Pension and insurance funds, govt.		
6. Consumer debt	38.19	
7. Trade debt	1.42	7.16
8. Loans on securities	5.39	
9. Bank loans, n.e.c.	1.36	10.05
10. Other loans	3.40	4.88
11. Mortgages	87.36	10.63
12. Bonds and notes		
13. Other liabilities		
14. Total	137.12	32.72
IV. Equities	1184.94	85.41
V. Total assets or liabilities and equities	1322.06	118.13

Agriculture	Nonfinancial Corporations	Finance	State and Local Govts.	Federal Govt.	Total	
						I.
17.92	18.18	.59	4.77	.52	351.41	1.
15.09	139.91	3.68	102.29	30.79	332.22	2.
68.94	54.89	3.18	24.80	13.60	256.12	3.
17.23	110.96	.64	3.71	.85	156.62	4.
13.85					150.77	5.
17.38	72.95	.02	.16	6.98	113.30	6.
150.41	396.89	8.11	135.73	52.74	1360.44	7.
						II.
6.20	31.48	92.04	10.20	4.48	214.18	1.
.20	.16	24.24			26.08	
6.00	31.32	67.80	10.20	4.48	188.10	
2.58	1.00	.72	2.36	.36	113.26	2.
5.92					89.88	3.
					17.35	4.
.45					58.44	5.
	7.07	27.87			39.37	6.
	65.92	2.51		2.27	80.38	7.
		8.69			8.69	8.
		44.44			44.44	9.
		7.50		17.35	27.15	10.
		98.92	.72	3.27	120.87	11.
		86.22	.72	3.27	100.62	
		12.69			20.25	
		3.68		1.76	9.06	12.
5.17	22.82	168.55	10.34	5.22	272.73	13.
	18.60	32.46	3.60		55.31	
5.17	1.80	5.10			58.55	
	2.42	130.99	6.74	5.22	158.87	
	1.24	23.41	2.25	.48	46.95	14.
	1.88	57.15	.88		67.24	15.
	3.54	4.08			16.92	16.
	60.09	26.69			347.41	17.
					6.10	18.
				.43	86.58	19.
3.25	34.51	25.26		23.24	86.87	20.
23.57	229.55	591.51	26.75	58.86	1753.87	21.
						III.
		215.69		2.51	218.20	1.
		112.95		1.99	114.94	2.
		91.65			91.65	3.
		17.35			17.35	4.
		58.44			58.44	5.
1.18					39.37	6.
2.10	54.87	.15	1.70	2.28	69.68	7.
		3.60			8.99	8.
3.31	19.38	7.77		1.17	43.04	9.
1.34	2.11	4.41			16.14	10.
9.07	22.88				129.94	11.
	53.74	6.76	47.05	284.04	391.59	12.
	54.70	25.27		1.36	81.33	13.
17.00	207.68	544.04	48.75	293.35	1280.66	14.
156.98	418.76	55.58	113.73	−181.75	1833.65	IV.
173.98	626.44	599.62	162.48	111.60	3114.31	V.

TABLE I

National Balance Sheet—1956 (billion dollars)

	Nonfarm Households	Nonfarm Unincorporated Business
I. Tangible assets		
1. Residential structures	315.54	15.80
2. Nonresidential structures	22.26	21.97
3. Land	77.89	20.99
4. Producer durables	1.69	24.26
5. Consumer durables	149.43	
6. Inventories		16.51
7. Total	566.81	99.53
II. Intangible assets		
1. Currency and demand deposits	59.54	11.55
a. Monetary metals	1.33	.22
b. Other	58.21	11.33
2. Other bank deposits and shares	115.38	
3. Life insurance reserves, private	89.05	
4. Pension and retirement funds, private	20.02	
5. Pension and insurance funds, govt.	61.57	
6. Consumer credit		4.69
7. Trade credit		10.57
8. Loans on securities		
9. Bank loans, n.e.c.		
10. Other loans	2.26	
11. Mortgages, nonfarm	19.46	
a. Residential	11.16	
b. Nonresidential	8.29	
12. Mortgages, farm	3.96	
13. Securities, U.S. government	61.74	
a. Short-term	2.15	
b. Savings bonds	46.19	
c. Other long-term	13.40	
14. Securities, state and local	21.25	
15. Securities, other bonds and notes	8.99	
16. Securities, preferred stock	9.90	
17. Securities, common stock	273.23	
18. Equity in mutual financial organizations	6.74	
19. Equity in other business	91.65	
20. Other intangible assets	.62	
21. Total	845.36	26.81
III. Liabilities		
1. Currency and demand deposits		
2. Other bank deposits and shares		
3. Life insurance reserves, private		
4. Pension and retirement funds, private		
5. Pension and insurance funds, govt.		
6. Consumer debt	41.89	
7. Trade debt	1.59	8.10
8. Loans on securities	5.34	
9. Bank loans, n.e.c.	1.49	10.72
10. Other loans	3.67	4.97
11. Mortgages	98.37	11.65
12. Bonds and notes		
13. Other liabilities		
14. Total	152.35	35.44
IV. Equities	1259.82	90.90
V. Total assets or liabilities and equities	1412.17	126.34

Agriculture	Nonfinancial Corporations	Finance	State and Local Govts.	Federal Govt.	Total	
						I.
18.53	19.43	.61	5.14	.48	375.53	1.
15.84	151.15	4.10	113.42	32.28	361.02	2.
73.96	57.99	3.52	26.30	13.40	274.05	3.
17.64	128.05	.73	4.27	.77	177.41	4.
13.95					163.38	5.
18.23	80.52	.02	.18	6.87	122.33	6.
158.15	437.14	8.98	149.31	53.80	1473.72	7.
						II.
6.00	31.62	94.24	10.35	4.18	217.48	1.
.21	.17	24.55			26.48	
5.79	31.45	69.69	10.35	4.18	191.00	
2.63	1.00	.77	2.40	.33	122.51	2.
6.18					95.23	3.
					20.02	4.
.45					62.02	5.
	7.48	30.89			43.06	6.
	72.98	2.93		2.35	88.83	7.
		8.01			8.01	8.
		50.02			50.02	9.
		7.76		17.32	27.34	10.
		110.75	.84	3.72	134.77	11.
		96.40	.84	3.72	112.12	
		14.36			22.65	
		3.94		2.01	9.91	12.
5.06	18.23	166.53	11.04	5.47	268.07	13.
	14.90	38.82	5.80		61.67	
5.06	1.60	4.17			57.02	
	1.73	123.54	5.24	5.47	149.38	
	1.35	24.79	2.32	.56	50.27	14.
	2.11	61.03	.89		73.02	15.
	3.54	3.95			17.39	16.
	62.54	28.39			364.16	17.
					6.74	18.
				.43	92.08	19.
3.42	40.50	27.25		22.03	93.82	20.
23.74	241.35	621.25	27.84	58.40	1844.75	21.
						III.
		219.67		2.53	222.20	1.
		122.36		1.74	124.10	2.
		97.10			97.10	3.
		20.02			20.02	4.
		62.02			62.02	5.
1.17					43.06	6.
2.10	60.48	.18	1.80	2.61	76.86	7.
		2.98			8.32	8.
3.28	24.76	7.14		.88	48.27	9.
1.42	1.96	4.22			16.24	10.
9.91	24.75				144.68	11.
	57.41	7.95	50.37	280.53	396.26	12.
	58.09	27.33		1.46	86.88	13.
17.88	227.45	570.97	52.17	289.75	1346.01	14.
164.01	451.04	59.26	124.98	− 177.55	1972.46	IV.
181.89	678.49	630.23	177.15	112.20	3318.47	V.

TABLE I

National Balance Sheet—1957 (billion dollars)

	Nonfarm Households	Nonfarm Unincorporated Business
I. Tangible assets		
1. Residential structures	330.28	15.99
2. Nonresidential structures	24.25	24.01
3. Land	85.56	22.25
4. Producer durables	1.90	26.44
5. Consumer durables	159.61	
6. Inventories		16.82
7. Total	601.60	105.51
II. Intangible assets		
1. Currency and demand deposits	58.52	12.36
a. Monetary metals	1.50	.25
b. Other	57.02	12.11
2. Other bank deposits and shares	126.80	
3. Life insurance reserves, private	93.80	
4. Pension and retirement funds, private	22.28	
5. Pension and insurance funds, govt.	64.43	
6. Consumer credit		4.79
7. Trade credit		10.85
8. Loans on securities		
9. Bank loans, n.e.c.		
10. Other loans	2.32	
11. Mortgages, nonfarm	20.88	
a. Residential	11.98	
b. Nonresidential	8.90	
12. Mortgages, farm	4.20	
13. Securities, U.S. government	60.60	
a. Short-term	4.53	
b. Savings bonds	43.92	
c. Other long-term	12.15	
14. Securities, state and local	23.37	
15. Securities, other bonds and notes	10.84	
16. Securities, preferred stock	10.33	
17. Securities, common stock	245.79	
18. Equity in mutual financial organizations	7.36	
19. Equity in other business	97.17	
20. Other intangible assets	.62	
21. Total	849.31	28.00
III. Liabilities		
1. Currency and demand deposits		
2. Other bank deposits and shares		
3. Life insurance reserves, private		
4. Pension and retirement funds, private		
5. Pension and insurance funds, govt.		
6. Consumer debt	44.75	
7. Trade debt	1.73	8.78
8. Loans on securities	4.88	
9. Bank loans, n.e.c.	1.70	10.63
10. Other loans	4.02	5.30
11. Mortgages	107.06	12.58
12. Bonds and notes		
13. Other liabilities		
14. Total	164.14	37.29
IV. Equities	1286.77	96.22
V. Total assets or liabilities and equities	1450.91	133.51

Agriculture	Nonfinancial Corporations	Finance	State and Local Govts.	Federal Govt.	Total	
						I.
18.79	20.30	.63	5.51	.64	392.14	1.
16.40	172.06	4.54	123.27	33.57	398.10	2.
79.94	62.98	3.92	27.40	13.60	295.65	3.
18.01	140.43	.82	4.85	.69	193.14	4.
14.00					173.61	5.
20.57	83.24	.03	.19	5.93	126.78	6.
167.71	479.01	9.94	161.22	54.43	1579.42	7.
						II.
5.90	31.62	96.31	10.56	4.19	219.46	1.
.24	.19	25.28			27.46	
5.66	31.43	71.03	10.56	4.19	192.00	
2.90	1.00	.77	2.78	.30	134.55	2.
6.42					100.22	3.
					22.28	4.
.44					64.87	5.
	7.69	33.42			45.90	6.
	75.70	3.27		2.30	92.12	7.
		7.65			7.65	8.
		52.08			52.08	9.
		9.07		17.95	29.34	10.
		119.05	1.20	4.99	146.12	11.
		103.12	1.20	4.99	121.29	
		15.93			24.83	
		4.07		2.24	10.51	12.
5.12	17.43	165.59	11.78	5.91	266.43	13.
	14.50	41.05	7.10		67.18	
5.12	1.40	2.77			53.21	
	1.53	121.77	4.68	5.91	146.04	
	1.50	27.12	2.39	.76	55.14	14.
	2.94	68.35	.79		82.92	15.
	3.55	3.92			17.80	16.
	56.12	27.78			329.69	17.
					7.36	18.
				.42	97.59	19.
3.59	47.14	28.38		20.54	100.27	20.
24.37	244.69	646.83	29.50	59.60	1882.30	21.
						III.
		218.93		2.56	221.49	1.
		134.69		1.42	136.11	2.
		102.20			102.20	3.
		22.28			22.28	4.
		64.87			64.87	5.
1.15					45.90	6.
2.20	62.50	.19	1.85	2.77	80.02	7.
		3.08			7.96	8.
3.60	26.82	6.77		.46	49.98	9.
1.64	2.33	4.53			17.82	10.
10.51	26.48				156.63	11.
	63.76	9.08	55.24	280.92	409.00	12.
	60.65	29.47		1.53	91.65	13.
19.10	242.54	596.09	57.09	289.66	1405.91	14.
172.98	481.16	60.68	133.63	– 175.63	2055.81	IV.
192.08	723.70	656.77	190.72	114.03	3461.72	V.

TABLE I

National Balance Sheet—1958 (billion dollars)

	Nonfarm Households	Nonfarm Unincorporated Business
I. Tangible assets		
1. Residential structures	346.81	16.26
2. Nonresidential structures	26.26	25.56
3. Land	92.16	22.74
4. Producer durables	2.07	26.94
5. Consumer durables	164.73	
6. Inventories		16.81
7. Total	632.03	108.31
II. Intangible assets		
1. Currency and demand deposits	61.36	13.46
a. Monetary metals	1.62	.27
b. Other	59.74	13.19
2. Other bank deposits and shares	140.56	
3. Life insurance reserves, private	99.70	
4. Pension and retirement funds, private	27.80	
5. Pension and insurance funds, govt.	65.67	
6. Consumer credit		4.70
7. Trade credit		11.64
8. Loans on securities		
9. Bank loans, n.e.c.		
10. Other loans	3.10	
11. Mortgages, nonfarm	22.72	
a. Residential	12.79	
b. Nonresidential	9.93	
12. Mortgages, farm	4.54	
13. Securities, U.S. government	58.57	
a. Short-term	3.16	
b. Savings bonds	43.02	
c. Other long-term	12.39	
14. Securities, state and local	24.79	
15. Securities, other bonds and notes	11.12	
16. Securities, preferred stock	10.37	
17. Securities, common stock	332.62	
18. Equity in mutual financial organizations	8.04	
19. Equity in other business	98.24	
20. Other intangible assets	.62	
21. Total	969.82	29.80
III. Liabilities		
1. Currency and demand deposits		
2. Other bank deposits and shares		
3. Life insurance reserves, private		
4. Pension and retirement funds, private		
5. Pension and insurance funds, govt.		
6. Consumer debt	44.77	
7. Trade debt	1.83	9.00
8. Loans on securities	6.20	
9. Bank loans, n.e.c.	2.12	12.45
10. Other loans	4.37	5.42
11. Mortgages	117.05	13.94
12. Bonds and notes		
13. Other liabilities		
14. Total	176.34	40.81
IV. Equities	1425.51	97.30
V. Total assets or liabilities and equities	1601.85	138.11

Agriculture	Nonfinancial Corporations	Finance	State and Local Govts.	Federal Govt.	Total	
						I.
19.28	21.31	.64	6.03	1.01	411.34	1.
16.75	180.83	4.78	133.20	35.00	422.38	2.
87.58	63.46	4.04	28.00	12.80	310.78	3.
18.59	145.53	.85	5.25	.61	199.84	4.
14.02					178.75	5.
26.15	78.81	.03	.20	7.89	129.89	6.
182.37	489.94	10.34	172.68	57.31	1652.98	7.
						II.
6.20	33.34	92.59	10.78	4.19	221.92	1.
.25	.21	23.06			25.41	
5.95	33.13	69.53	10.78	4.19	196.51	
3.07	1.60	1.08	3.58	.33	150.22	2.
6.71					106.41	3.
					27.80	4.
.43					66.10	5.
	8.21	33.19			46.10	6.
	83.37	3.64		1.70	100.35	7.
		9.23			9.23	8.
		53.80			53.80	9.
		9.42		19.05	31.57	10.
		131.22	1.61	5.10	160.65	11.
		113.52	1.61	5.10	133.02	
		17.70			27.63	
		4.26		2.46	11.26	12.
5.21	17.62	176.01	11.08	5.82	274.31	13.
	15.20	41.63	6.00		65.99	
5.21	1.22	2.43			51.88	
	1.20	131.95	5.08	5.82	156.44	
	1.63	31.23	2.44	.97	61.06	14.
	2.68	74.30	.67		88.77	15.
	3.55	4.36			18.28	16.
	75.45	39.10			447.17	17.
					8.04	18.
				.42	98.66	19.
3.81	48.14	29.78		18.28	100.63	20.
25.43	275.59	693.21	30.16	58.32	2082.33	21.
						III.
		223.18		2.60	225.78	1.
		151.62		1.22	152.84	2.
		108.51			108.51	3.
		27.80			27.80	4.
		66.10			66.10	5.
1.33					46.10	6.
2.30	68.78	.21	2.00	2.83	86.95	7.
		3.42			9.62	8.
4.16	25.94	5.69		.81	51.17	9.
1.87	2.18	5.55			19.39	10.
11.25	29.67				171.91	11.
	69.68	9.09	61.16	288.49	428.42	12.
	60.84	31.20		1.80	93.84	13.
20.91	257.09	632.37	63.16	297.75	1488.43	14.
186.89	508.44	71.18	139.68	182.12	2246.88	IV.
207.80	765.53	703.55	202.84	115.63	3735.31	V.

SECTION Ia

National Balance Sheets, 1900–45, Selected Years

TABLE Ia

National Balance Sheet—1900 (million dollars)

	Nonfarm Households	Nonfarm Unincorporated Business
I. Tangible assets		
1. Residential structures	15,205	260
2. Nonresidential structures	1,101	2,228
3. Land	7,491	1,194
4. Producer durables	90	911
5. Consumer durables	5,217	
6. Inventories		2,649
7. Total	29,104	7,242
II. Intangible assets		
1. Currency and demand deposits	1,529	1,280
a. Monetary metals		
b. Other		
2. Other bank deposits and shares	3,419	
3. Life insurance reserves, private	1,375	
4. Pension and retirement funds, private		
5. Pension and insurance funds, govt.	5	
6. Consumer credit		202
7. Trade credit		1,828
8. Loans on securities		
9. Bank loans, n.e.c.		
10. Other loans	100	
11. Mortgages, nonfarm	2,399	
a. Residential	1,604	
b. Nonresidential	795	
12. Mortgages, farm	1,441	299
13. Securities, U.S. government	576	
a. Short-term		
b. Savings bonds		
c. Other long-term		
14. Securities, state and local	521	
15. Securities, other bonds and notes	3,323	
16. Securities, preferred stock	}10,704	
17. Securities, common stock		
18. Equity in mutual financial organizations	240	
19. Equity in other business	6,666	
20. Other intangible assets	100	
21. Total	32,398	3,609
III. Liabilities		
1. Currency and demand deposits		
2. Other bank deposits and shares		
3. Life insurance reserves, private		
4. Pension and retirement funds, private		
5. Pension and insurance funds, govt.		
6. Consumer debt	532	
7. Trade debt		1,639
8. Loans on securities	908	
9. Bank loans, n.e.c.	200	1,609
10. Other loans	184	
11. Mortgages	2,606	1,081
12. Bonds and notes		6
13. Other liabilities	100	
14. Total	4,530	4,335
IV. Equities	56,972	6,516
V. Total assets or liabilities and equities	61,502	10,851

Agriculture	Nonfinancial Corporations	Finance	State and Local Govts.	Federal Govt.	Total	
						I.
1,692			1,574			1.
1,570	18,297	573		1,450	72,418	2.
14,546			3,000			3.
1,170			61	5		4.
831					6,048	5.
4,537	2,757		10		9,953	6.
24,346	21,054	573	4,645	1,455	88,419	7.
						II.
657	1,980	3,229	110	102	8,887	1.
160	64	1,197	6			
497	1,916	2,032	104			
115	120		35		3,689	2.
179					1,554	3.
						4.
					5	5.
	580	239			1,021	6.
	3,900				5,728	7.
		1,289			1,289	8.
		3,946			3,946	9.
		90			190	10.
		2,066			4,465	11.
		1,350			2,954	
		716			1,511	
140		432			2,312	12.
		663			1,239	13.
	50	889	554		2,014	14.
		1,828			5,151	15.
	2,818	380			13,902	16.
						17.
					240	18.
					6,666	19.
80	4,496	1,311	84		6,071	20.
1,171	13,944	16,361	783	102	68,368	21.
						III.
		7,428		58	7,486	1.
		3,706			3,706	2.
		1,554			1,554	3.
						4.
		5			5	5.
53					585	6.
425	3,066				5,130	7.
	81	300			1,289	8.
488	1,420	101			3,818	9.
10	52	103			349	10.
2,312	778				6,777	11.
	7,072		2,014	1,239	10,331	12.
100	2,569	762			3,531	13.
3,388	15,038	13,959	2,014	1,297	44,561	14.
22,129	19,960	2,974	3,414	260	112,225	IV.
25,517	34,998	16,933	5,428	1,557	156,786	V.

TABLE Ia

National Balance Sheet—1912 (million dollars)

	Nonfarm Households	Nonfarm Unincorporated Business
I. Tangible assets		
1. Residential structures	23,964	840
2. Nonresidential structures	2,035	3,843
3. Land	10,725	1,967
4. Producer durables	145	1,419
5. Consumer durables	11,724	
6. Inventories		3,115
7. Total	48,593	11,184
II. Intangible assets		
1. Currency and demand deposits	2,847	2,000
a. Monetary metals		
b. Other		
2. Other bank deposits and shares	8,153	
3. Life insurance reserves, private	3,672	
4. Pension and retirement funds, private		
5. Pension and insurance funds, govt.	17	
6. Consumer credit		491
7. Trade credit		1,889
8. Loans on securities		
9. Bank loans, n.e.c.		
10. Other loans	200	
11. Mortgages, nonfarm	2,826	
a. Residential	1,875	
b. Nonresidential	951	
12. Mortgages, farm	2,192	468
13. Securities, U.S. government	397	
a. Short-term		
b. Savings bonds		
c. Other long-term		
14. Securities, state and local	1,451	
15. Securities, other bonds and notes	9,481	
16. Securities, preferred stock	30,112 (16 and 17)	
17. Securities, common stock		
18. Equity in mutual financial organizations	406	
19. Equity in other business	9,772	
20. Other intangible assets	600	
21. Total	72,126	4,848
III. Liabilities		
1. Currency and demand deposits		
2. Other bank deposits and shares		
3. Life insurance reserves, private		
4. Pension and retirement funds, private		
5. Pension and insurance funds, govt.		
6. Consumer debt	1,463	
7. Trade debt		1,770
8. Loans on securities	1,704	
9. Bank loans, n.e.c.	400	2,821
10. Other loans	712	
11. Mortgages	4,059	1,928
12. Bonds and notes	47	41
13. Other liabilities	100	
14. Total	8,485	6,560
IV. Equities	112,234	9,472
V. Total assets or liabilities and equities	120,719	16,032

Agriculture	Nonfinancial Corporations	Finance	State and Local Govts.	Federal Govt.	Total	
						I.
2,919			4,825			1.
2,717	35,650	923		2,053	134,511	2.
31,574			6,500			3.
2,240			154	18		4.
1,863					13,587	5.
8,236	5,304		20	2	16,677	6.
49,549	40,954	923	11,499	2,073	164,775	7.
						II.
993	3,900	6,224	387	56	16,407	1.
152	91	2,132	7			
841	3,809	4,092	380			
573	350		126	26	9,228	2.
470					4,142	3.
						4.
					17	5.
	1,962	456			2,909	6.
	6,208				8,097	7.
		2,297			2,297	8.
		9,049			9,049	9.
		594			794	10.
		4,835			7,661	11.
		3,117			4,992	
		1,718			2,669	
219		1,469			4,348	12.
		794			1,191	13.
	100	1,729	1,150		4,430	14.
		5,043			14,524	15.
	7,134	740		2	37,988	16.
						17.
					406	18.
					9,772	19.
160	5,746	1,491	169	40	8,206	20.
2,415	25,400	34,721	1,832	124	141,466	21.
						III.
		14,421		135	14,556	1.
		9,310		28	9,338	2.
		4,142			4,142	3.
						4.
		17			17	5.
144					1,607	6.
1,312	4,355				7,437	7.
	93	500			2,297	8.
1,520	3,780	292			8,813	9.
64	60	214			1,050	10.
4,348	1,674				12,009	11.
	18,096		4,430	1,191	23,805	12.
100	5,188	717		2	6,107	13.
7,488	33,246	29,613	4,430	1,356	91,178	14.
44,476	33,108	6,033	8,901	841	215,065	IV.
51,964	66,354	35,646	13,331	2,197	306,243	V.

TABLE Ia

National Balance Sheet—1922 (million dollars)

	Nonfarm Households	Nonfarm Unincorporated Business
I. Tangible assets		
1. Residential structures	52,444	2,400
2. Nonresidential structures	4,056	8,215
3. Land	21,504	4,119
4. Producer durables	175	3,424
5. Consumer durables	27,235	
6. Inventories		6,679
7. Total	105,414	24,837
II. Intangible assets		
1. Currency and demand deposits	9,862	2,610
a. Monetary metals		
b. Other		
2. Other bank deposits and shares	18,328	
3. Life insurance reserves, private	7,769	
4. Pension and retirement funds, private	90	
5. Pension and insurance funds, govt.	240	
6. Consumer credit		694
7. Trade credit		2,878
8. Loans on securities		
9. Bank loans, n.e.c.		
10. Other loans	500	
11. Mortgages, nonfarm	6,707	
a. Residential	4,377	
b. Nonresidential	2,330	
12. Mortgages, farm	4,761	946
13. Securities, U.S. government	10,806	
a. Short-term		
b. Savings bonds		
c. Other long-term		
14. Securities, state and local	4,983	
15. Securities, other bonds and notes	15,923	
16. Securities, preferred stock	55,520 (16 and 17)	
17. Securities, common stock		
18. Equity in mutual financial organizations	803	
19. Equity in other business	21,647	
20. Other intangible assets	4,000	
21. Total	161,939	7,128
III. Liabilities		
1. Currency and demand deposits		
2. Other bank deposits and shares		
3. Life insurance reserves, private		
4. Pension and retirement funds, private		
5. Pension and insurance funds, govt.		
6. Consumer debt	2,979	
7. Trade debt		2,471
8. Loans on securities	4,534	
9. Bank loans, n.e.c.	600	4,657
10. Other loans	1,305	
11. Mortgages	8,310	3,948
12. Bonds and notes	256	242
13. Other liabilities	100	
14. Total	18,084	11,318
IV. Equities	249,269	20,647
V. Total assets or liabilities and equities	267,353	31,965

Agriculture	Nonfinancial Corporations	Finance	State and Local Govts.	Federal Govt.	Total	
						I.
6,569			}13,342			1.
5,822	}74,706	}1,584		}3,981	}258,404	2.
41,541			11,100			3.
3,266			121	35		4.
3,705					30,940	5.
8,454	17,347		40	30	32,550	6.
69,357	92,053	1,584	24,603	4,046	321,894	7.
						II.
1,962	5,587	13,799	1,097	544	35,461	1.
117	57	3,991	6			
1,845	5,530	9,808	1,091			
1,377	700		365	56	20,826	2.
931					8,700	3.
					90	4.
11					251	5.
	4,040	916			5,650	6.
	12,027				14,905	7.
	450	6,253			6,703	8.
		18,211			18,211	9.
		1,162		83	1,745	10.
		9,947			16,654	11.
		6,715			11,092	
		3,232			5,562	
910		3,518		651	10,786	12.
450	3,563	7,715	232	229	22,995	13.
	337	2,854	2,210		10,384	14.
		7,762		2	23,687	15.
	19,234	1,339			}76,093	16.
						17.
					803	18.
					21,647	19.
410	14,300	7,006	312	1,310	27,338	20.
6,051	60,238	80,482	4,216	2,875	322,929	21.
						III.
		33,841		467	34,308	1.
		20,942		135	21,077	2.
		8,700			8,700	3.
		90			90	4.
		251			251	5.
167					3,146	6.
2,797	12,450				17,718	7.
	219	1,950			6,703	8.
3,088	8,694	740			17,779	9.
173	67	574			2,119	10.
10,786	4,396				27,440	11.
	24,516	233	10,384	23,638	59,269	12.
	14,081	3,603		183	17,967	13.
17,011	64,423	70,924	10,384	24,423	216,567	14.
58,397	87,868	11,141	18,435	−17,502	428,255	IV.
75,408	152,291	82,065	28,819	6,921	644,822	V.

TABLE Ia

National Balance Sheet—1929 (million dollars)

	Nonfarm Households	Nonfarm Unincorporated Business
I. Tangible assets		
1. Residential structures	79,408	5,480
2. Nonresidential structures	5,568	11,241
3. Land	33,815	8,705
4. Producer durables	372	4,562
5. Consumer durables	38,423	
6. Inventories		6,426
7. Total	157,586	36,414
II. Intangible assets		
1. Currency and demand deposits	8,602	2,842
a. Monetary metals		
b. Other		
2. Other bank deposits and shares	30,542	
3. Life insurance reserves, private	15,851	
4. Pension and retirement funds, private	500	
5. Pension and insurance funds, govt.	1,356	
6. Consumer credit		1,280
7. Trade credit		2,946
8. Loans on securities		
9. Bank loans, n.e.c.		
10. Other loans	1,200	
11. Mortgages, nonfarm	13,570	
a. Residential	8,527	
b. Nonresidential	5,043	
12. Mortgages, farm	3,551	681
13. Securities, U.S. government	5,053	
a. Short-term		
b. Savings bonds		
c. Other long-term		
14. Securities, state and local	7,642	
15. Securities, other bonds and notes	24,078	
16. Securities, preferred stock	}138,296	
17. Securities, common stock		
18. Equity in mutual financial organizations	1,628	
19. Equity in other business	29,535	
20. Other intangible assets	9,100	
21. Total	290,504	7,749
III. Liabilities		
1. Currency and demand deposits		
2. Other bank deposits and shares		
3. Life insurance reserves, private		
4. Pension and retirement funds, private		
5. Pension and insurance funds, govt.		
6. Consumer debt	6,428	
7. Trade debt		2,701
8. Loans on securities	11,579	
9. Bank loans, n.e.c.	800	4,734
10. Other loans	3,049	
11. Mortgages	17,985	7,697
12. Bonds and notes	1,704	1,696
13. Other liabilities	300	
14. Total	41,845	16,828
IV. Equities	406,245	27,335
V. Total assets or liabilities and equities	448,090	44,163

Agriculture	Nonfinancial Corporations	Finance	State and Local Govts.	Federal Govt.	Total	
						I.
6,377			21,170			1.
5,855	99,293	2,990		4,935	342,340	2.
34,930			13,200			3.
3,871			505	63		4.
3,806					42,229	5.
9,487	22,001		60	3	37,977	6.
64,326	121,294	2,990	34,935	5,001	422,546	7.
						II.
1,782	7,449	17,079	1,767	234	39,755	1.
96	71	4,474	5			
1,686	7,378	12,605	1,762			
1,726	1,410		712	138	34,528	2.
1,651					17,502	3.
					500	4.
114					1,470	5.
	3,979	3,305			8,564	6.
	21,861	909			25,716	7.
	2,000	14,345			16,345	8.
		20,513			20,513	9.
		2,616		226	4,042	10.
		23,281			36,851	11.
		16,385			24,912	
		6,896			11,939	
318		3,881		1200	9,631	12.
	3,158	7,658	255	52	16,176	13.
	644	4,956	3,631		16,873	14.
	543	13,465		13	38,099	15.
	42,309	6,080			186,685	16.
						17.
					1,628	18.
					29,535	19.
600	23,421	11,473	520	1,375	46,489	20.
6,191	106,774	129,561	6,885	3,238	550,902	21.
						III.
		40,865		411	41,276	1.
		34,720		168	34,888	2.
		17,502			17,502	3.
		500			500	4.
		1,470			1,470	5.
462					6,890	6.
1,691	15,970				20,362	7.
	566	4,200			16,345	8.
2,491	9,446	2,214			19,685	9.
310	128	1,325			4,812	10.
9,631	11,169				46,482	11.
	36,258	1,577	16,873	17,539	75,647	12.
	22,755	6,777		35	29,867	13.
14,585	96,291	111,150	16,873	18,153	315,725	14.
55,932	131,777	21,402	24,947	−9,914	657,724	IV.
70,517	228,068	132,552	41,820	8,239	973,449	V.

TABLE Ia

National Balance Sheet—1933 (million dollars)

	Nonfarm Households	Nonfarm Unincorporated Business
I. Tangible assets		
1. Residential structures	61,737	4,360
2. Nonresidential structures	4,766	9,799
3. Land	24,647	4,572
4. Producer durables	283	3,204
5. Consumer durables	23,765	
6. Inventories		3,092
7. Total	115,198	25,027
II. Intangible assets		
1. Currency and demand deposits	11,181	1,914
a. Monetary metals		
b. Other		
2. Other bank deposits and shares	25,846	
3. Life insurance reserves, private	18,899	
4. Pension and retirement funds, private	700	
5. Pension and insurance funds, govt.	2,722	
6. Consumer credit		740
7. Trade credit		1,818
8. Loans on securities		
9. Bank loans, n.e.c.		
10. Other loans	300	
11. Mortgages, nonfarm	10,537	
a. Residential	7,152	
b. Nonresidential	3,385	
12. Mortgages, farm	2,741	508
13. Securities, U.S. government	6,845	
a. Short-term		
b. Savings bonds		
c. Other long-term		
14. Securities, state and local	9,478	
15. Securities, other bonds and notes	24,577	
16. Securities, preferred stock 17. Securities, common stock	} 57,113	
18. Equity in mutual financial organizations	1,746	
19. Equity in other business	18,632	
20. Other intangible assets	4,100	
21. Total	195,417	4,980
III. Liabilities		
1. Currency and demand deposits		
2. Other bank deposits and shares		
3. Life insurance reserves, private		
4. Pension and retirement funds, private		
5. Pension and insurance funds, govt.		
6. Consumer debt	3,235	
7. Trade debt		1,802
8. Loans on securities	4,015	
9. Bank loans, n.e.c.	500	2,230
10. Other loans	5,284	
11. Mortgages	14,584	6,169
12. Bonds and notes	1,536	1,774
13. Other liabilities	200	
14. Total	29,354	11,975
IV. Equities	281,261	18,032
V. Total assets or liabilities and equities	310,615	30,007

Agriculture	Nonfinancial Corporations	Finance	State and Local Govts.	Federal Govt.	Total	
						I.
4,634			}24,036			1.
4,047	}75,322	}4,824		}5,552	}270,899	2.
22,800			13,150			3.
2,572			483	111		4.
1,954					25,719	5.
4,946	13,796		60	3	21,897	6.
40,953	89,118	4,824	37,729	5,666	318,515	7.
						II.
1,199	5,599	15,952	1,736	1,219	38,800	1.
73	33	4,611	4			
1,126	5,566	11,341	1,732			
1,177	1,010		360	914	29,307	2.
1,963					20,862	3.
					700	4.
234					2,956	5.
	1,938	1,621			4,299	6.
	15,915	464			18,197	7.
		5,152			5,152	8.
		9,967			9,967	9.
		5,503		1,989	7,792	10.
		19,797		132	30,466	11.
		13,768		132	21,052	
		6,029			9,414	
237		2,954		1,245	7,685	12.
	2,837	13,659	219	309	23,869	13.
	607	5,908	3,041	50	19,084	14.
	83	13,043		45	37,748	15.
	40,473	3,869		249	}101,704	16.
						17.
					1,746	18.
					18,632	19.
600	11,929	5,814	492	1,415	24,350	20.
5,410	80,390	103,703	5,848	7,567	403,315	21.
						III.
		36,600		414	37,014	1.
		26,858		1,230	28,088	2.
		20,862			20,862	3.
		700			700	4.
		2,956			2,956	5.
198					3,433	6.
786	11,888				14,476	7.
	137	1,000			5,152	8.
913	5,210	913			9,766	9.
840	1,277	480			7,881	10.
7,685	9,713				38,151	11.
	35,629	1,016	19,084	25,494	84,533	12.
	15,660	2,857	417	56	19,190	13.
10,422	79,514	94,242	19,501	27,194	272,202	14.
35,941	89,994	14,285	24,076	−13,961	449,628	IV.
46,363	169,508	108,527	43,577	13,233	721,830	V.

TABLE Ia

National Balance Sheet—1939 (million dollars)

	Nonfarm Households	Nonfarm Unincorporated Business
I. Tangible assets		
1. Residential structures	76,839	5,250
2. Nonresidential structures	5,368	11,453
3. Land	26,117	5,474
4. Producer durables	153	3,840
5. Consumer durables	29,964	
6. Inventories		4,145
7. Total	138,441	30,162
II. Intangible assets		
1. Currency and demand deposits	15,541	3,248
a. Monetary metals		
b. Other		
2. Other bank deposits and shares	29,158	
3. Life insurance reserves, private	26,629	
4. Pension and retirement funds, private	1,050	
5. Pension and insurance funds, govt.	6,120	
6. Consumer credit		1,168
7. Trade credit		2,602
8. Loans on securities		
9. Bank loans, n.e.c.		
10. Other loans	400	
11. Mortgages, nonfarm	8,568	
a. Residential	5,879	
b. Nonresidential	2,689	
12. Mortgages, farm	1,632	311
13. Securities, U.S. government	9,140	
a. Short-term		
b. Savings bonds		
c. Other long-term		
14. Securities, state and local	8,274	
15. Securities, other bonds and notes	16,836	
16. Securities, preferred stock 17. Securities, common stock	} 73,231	
18. Equity in mutual financial organizations	1,678	
19. Equity in other business	28,307	
20. Other intangible assets	5,800	
21. Total	232,364	7,329
III. Liabilities		
1. Currency and demand deposits		
2. Other bank deposits and shares		
3. Life insurance reserves, private		
4. Pension and retirement funds, private		
5. Pension and insurance funds, govt.		
6. Consumer debt	7,197	
7. Trade debt		2,664
8. Loans on securities	1,869	
9. Bank loans, n.e.c.	567	1,716
10. Other loans	3,530	
11. Mortgages	15,525	4,544
12. Bonds and notes	702	660
13. Other liabilities	600	
14. Total	29,990	9,584
IV. Equities	340,815	27,907
V. Total assets or liabilities and equities	370,805	37,491

Agriculture	Nonfinancial Corporations	Finance	State and Local Govts.	Federal Govt.	Total	
						I.
4,906			28,713			1.
4,092	83,580	5,560		9,687	313,155	2.
23,237			14,600			3.
3,509			476	301		4.
2,550					32,514	5.
7,304	17,999		60	937	30,445	6.
45,598	101,579	5,560	43,849	10,925	376,114	7.
						II.
2,000	8,698	60,140	2,986	1,596	94,209	1.
91	74	20,177	6			
1,909	8,624	39,663	2,980			
1,200	700	2	553	303	31,916	2.
2,599					29,228	3.
					1,050	4.
110					6,230	5.
	2,966	3,688			7,822	6.
	11,067	1,010			14,679	7.
		2,696			2,696	8.
		9,834			9,834	9.
		3,499		1,947	5,846	10.
		18,153		2,182	28,903	11.
		12,781		2,182	20,842	
		5,372			8,061	
145		1,697		2,801	6,586	12.
249	1,776	33,506	250	2,080	47,001	13.
	379	8,054	2,762	296	19,765	14.
	112	14,692		862	32,502	15.
	21,969	4,359		572	100,131	16.
						17.
					1,678	18.
					28,307	19.
826	4,238	5,348	601	2,023	18,836	20.
7,129	51,905	166,678	7,152	14,662	487,219	21.
						III.
		78,068		1,128	79,196	1.
		30,348		1,315	31,663	2.
		29,228			29,228	3.
		1,050			1,050	4.
		6,230			6,230	5.
417					7,614	6.
763	12,807				16,234	7.
	127	700			2,696	8.
900	4,344	1,439		235	9,201	9.
924	571	625			5,650	10.
6,586	8,834				35,489	11.
	31,446	778	19,765	55,070	108,421	12.
	7,952	4,623	54	217	13,446	13.
9,590	66,081	153,089	19,819	57,965	346,118	14.
43,137	87,403	19,149	31,182	−32,378	517,214	IV.
52,727	153,484	172,238	51,001	25,587	863,333	V.

TABLE Ia

National Balance Sheet—1945 (million dollars)

	Nonfarm Households	Nonfarm Unincorporated Business
I. Tangible assets		
1. Residential structures	111,915	7,260
2. Nonresidential structures	6,400	15,018
3. Land	33,820	6,585
4. Producer durables	128	5,191
5. Consumer durables	46,714	
6. Inventories		7,829
7. Total	198,977	41,883
II. Intangible assets		
1. Currency and demand deposits	54,217	8,990
a. Monetary metals		
b. Other		
2. Other bank deposits and shares	51,649	
3. Life insurance reserves, private	40,772	
4. Pension and retirement funds, private	2,900	
5. Pension and insurance funds, govt.	24,948	
6. Consumer credit		1,046
7. Trade credit		4,030
8. Loans on securities		
9. Bank loans, n.e.c.		
10. Other loans	850	
11. Mortgages, nonfarm	9,564	
a. Residential	6,945	
b. Nonresidential	2,619	
12. Mortgages, farm	1,491	257
13. Securities, U.S. government	64,945	
a. Short-term		
b. Savings bonds		
c. Other long-term		
14. Securities, state and local	6,939	
15. Securities, other bonds and notes	9,751	
16. Securities, preferred stock	}115,790	
17. Securities, common stock		
18. Equity in mutual financial organizations	2,219	
19. Equity in other business	45,747	
20. Other intangible assets	6,500	
21. Total	438,282	14,323
III. Liabilities		
1. Currency and demand deposits		
2. Other bank deposits and shares		
3. Life insurance reserves, private		
4. Pension and retirement funds, private		
5. Pension and insurance funds, govt.		
6. Consumer debt	5,491	
7. Trade debt		3,420
8. Loans on securities	4,946	
9. Bank loans, n.e.c.	620	2,719
10. Other loans	2,177	
11. Mortgages	17,661	4,313
12. Bonds and notes	403	407
13. Other liabilities	500	
14. Total	31,798	10,859
IV. Equities	605,461	45,347
V. Total assets or liabilities and equities	637,259	56,206

Agriculture	Nonfinancial Corporations	Finance	State and Local Govts.	Federal Govt.	Total	
						I.
8,975			} 40,034			1.
6,755	} 110,255	} 2,227		} 20,977	} 447,202	2.
44,508			17,450			3.
6,272			405	3,027		4.
4,238					50,952	5.
15,374	26,317		150	2,584	52,254	6.
86,122	136,572	2,227	58,039	26,588	550,408	7.
						II.
6,600	20,353	74,331	5,311	25,783	195,585	1.
179	48	22,444	13			
6,421	20,305	51,887	5,298			
1,980	700	71	521	27	54,948	2.
3,490					44,262	3.
					2,900	4.
519					25,467	5.
	2,412	2,340			5,798	6.
	19,464	505		900	24,899	7.
		8,129			8,129	8.
		12,955			12,955	9.
		2,183		1,865	4,898	10.
		20,369		859	30,792	11.
		15,487		859	23,291	
		4,882			7,501	
120		1,363		1,451	4,682	12.
4,150	17,442	178,935	4,390	4,520	274,382	13.
	278	6,579	1,633	484	15,913	14.
		16,135			25,886	15.
	28,193	6,516		304	}150,803	16.
						17.
					2,219	18.
					45,747	19.
1,333	6,841	10,926	428	12,372	38,400	20.
18,192	95,683	341,337	12,283	48,565	968,665	21.
						III.
		180,112		2,536	182,648	1.
		53,033		3,014	56,047	2.
		44,262			44,262	3.
		2,900			2,900	4.
		25,467			25,467	5.
339					5,830	6.
625	16,961			2,700	23,706	7.
	1,933	1,250			8,129	8.
1,034	6,894	698		143	12,108	9.
873	281	1,215			4,546	10.
4,760	8,818				35,552	11.
	27,934	681	15,913	278,484	323,822	12.
	21,089	8,200	343	1,796	31,928	13.
7,631	83,910	317,818	16,256	288,673	756,945	14.
96,683	148,345	25,745	54,066	−213,520	762,127	IV.
104,314	232,255	343,563	70,322	75,153	1,519,072	V.

SECTION II

Finance Sector Balance Sheets, 1945–58

TABLE II

Finance Sector Balance Sheets—1945

(billion dollars)

	Federal Reserve Banks & Treasury Monetary Funds	Govt. Pension and Insurance Funds	Commercial Banks	Mutual Savings Banks
I. Tangible assets	.03		1.12	.14
II. Intangible assets				
1. Currency and demand deposits	42.91	.27	29.83	.60
a. Monetary metals	22.68			
b. Other	20.23	.27	29.83	.60
2. Other bank deposits and shares			.07	.01
3. Life insurance reserves, private				
4. Pension and retirement funds, private				
5. Pension and insurance funds, govt.				
6. Consumer credit			1.47	.02
7. Trade credit				
8. Loans on securities			6.82	
9. Bank loans, n.e.c.	.25		13.04	
10. Other loans		.12		.05
11. Mortgages, nonfarm		.02	4.23	4.18
a. Residential		.02	3.38	3.39
b. Nonresidential			.85	.80
12. Mortgages, farm			.52	.02
13. Securities, U.S. government	24.29	24.05	90.61	10.68
a. Short-term	23.20		32.30	.16
b. Savings bonds		.20	.94	.21
c. Other long-term	1.09	23.85	57.37	10.31
14. Securities, state and local		1.19	3.97	.09
15. Securities, other bonds and notes		.14	2.96	1.02
16. Securities, preferred stock		.02		
17. Securities, common stock		.02	.22	.14
18. Equity in mutual financial organizations				
19. Equity in other business				
20. Other intangible assets	2.27		5.54	.07
21. Total	69.72	25.83	159.28	16.88
III. Liabilities				
1. Currency and demand deposits	65.36		119.88	
2. Other bank deposits and shares			30.34	15.38
3. Life insurance reserves, private				
4. Pension and retirement funds, private				
5. Pension and insurance funds, govt.		25.83		
6. Consumer debt				
7. Trade debt				
8. Loans on securities				
9. Bank loans, n.e.c.			.22	
10. Other loans			.28	
11. Mortgages				
12. Bonds and notes				
13. Other liabilities	3.89		.63	.05
14. Total	69.25	25.83	151.35	15.43
IV. Equities	.50		9.05	1.59
V. Total assets or liabilities and equities	69.75	25.83	160.40	17.02

Savings and Loan Associations	Investment Companies	Credit Unions	Life Insurance Companies	Fire and Casualty Insurance Companies	Non-insured Pension Plans	Other Private Insurance	Finance Companies	Other Finance	Total	
.11			.93	.13		.04			2.49	I.
										II.
.40	.15	.06	.78	.67	.08	.07	.64	.84	77.30	1.
									22.68	
.40	.15	.06	.78	.67	.08	.07	.64	.84	54.62	
		.07		0					.15	2.
										3.
										4.
										5.
.02		.10					.91		2.52	6.
				.32			.08	.04	.44	7.
								1.43	8.25	8.
									13.29	9.
			1.96			.08	.32	.33	2.86	10.
5.38	.10	.03	5.86	.06	.02	.18	.07	.02	20.16	11.
5.27	.09	.03	3.70	.02	.02	.07	.07	.02	16.08	
.11	.01		2.15	.04		.10			4.07	
			.78			.02			1.34	12.
2.42	.23	.18	20.58	3.22	1.47	.52		3.40	181.65	13.
.20			.31	.34				1.10	57.61	
.20			.10	.19	.18	.03			2.05	
2.02	.23	.18	20.17	2.69	1.29	.49		2.30	121.99	
			.72	.24		.37		.40	6.98	14.
	.22		11.30	.46	.78	.50		.32	17.70	15.
	.25		.82	.59	.09	.04		.02	1.83	16.
	2.65		.18	1.81	.20	.01		.30	5.53	17.
										18.
										19.
.43	.03		.96	.14	.04	.02		.16	9.66	20.
8.65	3.63	.44	43.94	7.51	2.68	1.80	2.02	7.26	349.66	21.
										III.
									185.24	1.
7.39		.37							53.48	2.
			43.57			1.77			45.34	3.
					2.68				2.68	4.
									25.83	5.
										6.
		.03							.03	7.
			.37					3.37	3.74	8.
.14							.81		1.17	9.
.31								1.12	1.71	10.
										11.
							.19		.19	12.
.26			.64	3.85		.07		1.82	11.21	13.
8.10		.40	44.58	3.85	2.68	1.84	1.00	6.30	330.62	14.
.65	3.63	.04	.29	3.79			1.02	.95	21.53	IV.
8.76	3.63	.44	44.87	7.64	2.68	1.84	2.02	7.26	352.15	V.

TABLE II

Finance Sector Balance Sheets—1946

(billion dollars)

	Federal Reserve Banks & Treasury Monetary Funds	Govt. Pension and Insurance Funds	Commercial Banks	Mutual Savings Banks
I. Tangible assets	.04		1.36	.15
II. Intangible assets				
1. Currency and demand deposits	44.17	.28	28.53	.66
a. Monetary metals	23.09			
b. Other	21.08	.28	28.53	.66
2. Other bank deposits and shares			.06	.16
3. Life insurance reserves, private				
4. Pension and retirement funds, private				
5. Pension and insurance funds, govt.				
6. Consumer credit			2.66	.02
7. Trade credit				
8. Loans on securities			3.16	
9. Bank loans, n.e.c.	.16		18.10	
10. Other loans		.11		.07
11. Mortgages, nonfarm		.03	6.50	4.42
a. Residential		.03	5.12	3.59
b. Nonresidential			1.38	.83
12. Mortgages, farm			.70	.03
13. Securities, U.S. government	23.37	27.81	74.78	11.78
a. Short-term	22.30		18.80	.44
b. Savings bonds		.30	.96	.25
c. Other long-term	1.07	27.51	55.02	11.09
14. Securities, state and local		1.09	4.40	.06
15. Securities, other bonds and notes		.14	3.31	1.19
16. Securities, preferred stock		.02		
17. Securities, common stock		.02	.19	.15
18. Equity in mutual financial organizations				
19. Equity in other business				
20. Other intangible assets	2.65		6.32	.07
21. Total	70.35	29.50	148.71	18.61
III. Liabilities				
1. Currency and demand deposits	65.50		104.86	
2. Other bank deposits and shares			34.17	16.87
3. Life insurance reserves, private				
4. Pension and retirement funds, private				
5. Pension and insurance funds, govt.		29.50		
6. Consumer debt				
7. Trade debt				
8. Loans on securities				
9. Bank loans, n.e.c.			.05	
10. Other loans			.21	
11. Mortgages				
12. Bonds and notes				
13. Other liabilities	4.30		.84	.07
14. Total	69.80	29.50	140.13	16.94
IV. Equities	.59		9.94	1.82
V. Total assets or liabilities and equities	70.39	29.50	150.07	18.76

Savings and Loan Associations	Investment Companies	Credit Unions	Life Insurance Companies	Fire and Casualty Insurance Companies	Noninsured Pension Plans	Other Private Insurance	Finance Companies	Other Finance	Total	
.14			1.00	.16		.05			2.91	I.
										II.
.47	.15	.06	.77	.86	.10	.07	.63	1.05	77.80	1.
									23.09	
.47	.15	.06	.77	.86	.10	.07	.63	1.05	54.71	
		.07							.29	2.
										3.
										4.
										5.
.06		.15					1.49		4.38	6.
				.49			.25	.03	.77	7.
								.69	3.85	8.
									18.26	9.
			1.89			.08	.66	.42	3.23	10.
7.14	.14	.04	6.36	.06	.03	.18	.18	.03	25.12	11.
7.00	.13	.04	4.02	.02	.03	.07	.18	.03	20.25	
.14	.02		2.34	.04		.11		.01	4.87	
			.80			.02			1.54	12.
2.01	.18	.18	21.63	3.41	1.65	.53		2.23	169.56	13.
.20			.76	.39				1.20	44.09	
.20			.12	.22	.35	.03			2.43	
1.61	.18	.18	20.75	2.80	1.30	.50		1.03	123.04	
			.61	.24		.38		.38	7.16	14.
	.20		13.11	.46	1.04	.56		.24	20.25	15.
	.24		.97	.60	.12	.05		.01	2.01	16.
	2.56		.28	1.73	.24	.02		.22	5.41	17.
										18.
										19.
.43	.04		1.03	.12	.07	.03		.14	10.90	20.
10.11	3.53	.50	47.45	7.97	3.25	1.90	3.21	5.44	350.53	21.
										III.
									170.36	1.
8.56		.43							60.03	2.
			47.24			1.87			49.11	3.
					3.25				3.25	4.
									29.50	5.
										6.
		.02							.02	7.
								1.70	1.70	8.
.11							1.60		1.76	9.
.50								1.22	1.93	10.
										11.
							.45		.45	12.
.29			.70	4.60		.08		1.71	12.59	13.
9.46		.45	47.94	4.60	3.25	1.96	2.05	4.62	330.70	14.
.79	3.54	.05	.51	3.53			1.16	.82	22.74	IV.
10.25	3.54	.50	48.45	8.13	3.25	1.96	3.21	5.44	353.44	V.

TABLE II

Finance Sector Balance Sheets—1947

(billion dollars)

	Federal Reserve Banks & Treasury Monetary Funds	Govt. Pension and Insurance Funds	Commercial Banks	Mutual Savings Banks
I. Tangible assets	.04		1.48	.15
II. Intangible assets				
1. Currency and demand deposits	49.52	.30	30.74	.68
a. Monetary metals	25.31			
b. Other	24.21	.30	30.74	.68
2. Other bank deposits and shares			.06	.21
3. Life insurance reserves, private				
4. Pension and retirement funds, private				
5. Pension and insurance funds, govt.				
6. Consumer credit			3.97	.04
7. Trade credit				
8. Loans on securities			2.05	
9. Bank loans, n.e.c.	.09		22.76	
10. Other loans		.11		.05
11. Mortgages, nonfarm		.03	8.58	4.83
a. Residential		.03	6.90	3.94
b. Nonresidential			1.68	.89
12. Mortgages, farm			.82	.03
13. Securities, U.S. government	22.58	31.56	69.22	11.98
a. Short-term	19.90		19.20	.49
b. Savings bonds		.40	.93	.30
c. Other long-term	2.68	31.16	49.09	11.19
14. Securities, state and local		1.19	5.28	.06
15. Securities, other bonds and notes		.15	3.37	1.51
16. Securities, preferred stock		.02		
17. Securities, common stock		.02	.16	.15
18. Equity in mutual financial organizations				
19. Equity in other business				
20. Other intangible assets	3.11		7.44	.07
21. Total	75.30	33.38	154.45	19.61
III. Liabilities				
1. Currency and demand deposits	71.47		108.50	
2. Other bank deposits and shares			35.60	17.75
3. Life insurance reserves, private				
4. Pension and retirement funds, private				
5. Pension and insurance funds, govt.		33.38		
6. Consumer debt				
7. Trade debt				
8. Loans on securities				
9. Bank loans, n.e.c.			.07	
10. Other loans			.16	
11. Mortgages				
12. Bonds and notes				
13. Other liabilities	3.26		.99	.09
14. Total	74.73	33.38	145.32	17.84
IV. Equities	.61		10.61	1.92
V. Total assets or liabilities and equities	75.34	33.38	155.93	19.76

Savings and Loan Associations	Investment Companies	Credit Unions	Life Insurance Companies	Fire and Casualty Insurance Companies	Noninsured Pension Plans	Other Private Insurance	Finance Companies	Other Finance	Total	
.14			1.21	.17		.06			3.23	I.
										II.
.47	.14	.07	1.02	1.04	.13	.07	.57	.94	85.69	1.
									25.31	
.47	.14	.07	1.02	1.04	.13	.07	.57	.94	60.38	
		.06							.33	2.
										3.
										4.
										5.
.09		.24					2.36		6.70	6.
				.59			.26	.05	.90	7.
								.74	2.79	8.
									22.85	9.
			1.94			.08	.87	.51	3.56	10.
8.86	.22	.04	7.78	.07	.03	.20	.25	.05	30.94	11.
8.68	.20	.04	5.07	.03	.03	.08	.25	.04	25.28	
.18	.02		2.17	.05		.12		.01	5.66	
			.90			.02		.01	1.76	12.
1.74	.19	.18	20.02	4.00	1.81	.54		1.37	165.19	13.
.20			.23	.54				.70	41.26	
.20			.14	.26	.51	.03			2.77	
1.34	.19	.18	19.65	3.20	1.30	.51		.67	121.16	
			.61	.32		.39		.30	8.15	14.
	.18		16.13	.52	1.35	.62		.27	24.10	15.
	.25		1.03	.60	.16	.05		.01	2.12	16.
	2.52		.36	1.76	.32	.02		.24	5.55	17.
										18.
										19.
.43	.03		1.09	.14	.10	.03		.14	12.58	20.
11.59	3.54	.59	50.88	9.04	3.90	2.02	4.30	4.62	373.21	21.
										III.
									179.97	1.
9.76		.51							63.62	2.
			50.70			1.98			52.68	3.
					3.90				3.90	4.
									33.38	5.
										6.
		.03							.03	7.
								.99	.99	8.
.11							2.20		2.38	9.
.70								1.26	2.12	10.
										11.
							.73		.73	12.
.26			.78	5.59		.10		1.65	12.72	13.
10.83		.54	51.48	5.59	3.90	2.08	2.93	3.90	352.52	14.
.90	3.55	.05	.61	3.62			1.37	.72	23.92	IV.
11.73	3.55	.59	52.09	9.21	3.90	2.08	4.30	4.62	376.44	V.

TABLE II

Finance Sector Balance Sheets—1948

(billion dollars)

	Federal Reserve Banks & Treasury Monetary Funds	Govt. Pension and Insurance Funds	Commercial Banks	Mutual Savings Banks
I. Tangible assets	.04		1.53	.15
II. Intangible assets				
1. Currency and demand deposits	52.55	.38	32.26	.65
a. Monetary metals	26.81			
b. Other	25.74	.38	32.26	.65
2. Other bank deposits and shares			.05	.23
3. Life insurance reserves, private				
4. Pension and retirement funds, private				
5. Pension and insurance funds, govt.				
6. Consumer credit			4.98	.04
7. Trade credit				
8. Loans on securities			2.31	
9. Bank loans, n.e.c.	.22		24.80	
10. Other loans		.13		.07
11. Mortgages, nonfarm		.04	9.94	5.77
a. Residential		.04	8.00	4.76
b. Nonresidential			1.93	1.02
12. Mortgages, farm			.87	.03
13. Securities, U.S. government	23.35	34.70	62.62	11.48
a. Short-term	12.40		19.40	.54
b. Savings bonds		.50	1.23	.48
c. Other long-term	10.95	34.20	41.99	10.46
14. Securities, state and local		1.34	5.66	.07
15. Securities, other bonds and notes		.21	3.17	2.01
16. Securities, preferred stock		.03		
17. Securities, common stock		.03	.16	.16
18. Equity in mutual financial organizations				
19. Equity in other business				
20. Other intangible assets	3.02		7.18	.08
21. Total	79.14	36.86	154.00	20.59
III. Liabilities				
1. Currency and demand deposits	75.40		106.65	
2. Other bank deposits and shares			36.23	18.39
3. Life insurance reserves, private				
4. Pension and retirement funds, private				
5. Pension and insurance funds, govt.		36.86		
6. Consumer debt				
7. Trade debt				
8. Loans on securities				
9. Bank loans, n.e.c.			.06	
10. Other loans			.13	
11. Mortgages				
12. Bonds and notes				
13. Other liabilities	3.11		1.15	.09
14. Total	78.51	36.86	144.22	18.48
IV. Equities	.67		11.31	2.26
V. Total assets or liabilities and equities	79.18	36.86	155.53	20.74

Savings and Loan Associations	Investment Companies	Credit Unions	Life Insurance Companies	Fire and Casualty Insurance Companies	Non-insured Pension Plans	Other Private Insurance	Finance Companies	Other Finance	Total	
.15			1.45	.21		.06			3.57	I.
										II.
.53	.14	.08	.91	1.08	.16	.07	.74	.88	90.43	1.
									26.81	
.53	.14	.08	.91	1.08	.16	.07	.74	.88	63.62	
		.07						.01	.35	2.
										3.
										4.
										5.
.12		.33					3.21		8.68	6.
				.67			.28	.12	1.07	7.
								.73	3.04	8.
									25.02	9.
			2.06			.08	1.22	.61	4.17	10.
10.30	.28	.06	9.84	.08	.04	.23	.24	.09	36.90	11.
10.10	.24	.06	6.79	.03	.04	.09	.24	.06	30.45	
.21	.04		3.05	.05		.14		.02	6.45	
			.99			.02		.01	1.92	12.
1.46	.14	.16	16.75	4.49	1.94	.54		1.80	159.43	13.
.10			.25	.89				1.20	34.78	
.30			.24	.41	.56	.03			3.75	
1.06	.14	.16	16.26	3.19	1.38	.51		.60	120.90	
			.87	.53		.39		.39	9.25	14.
	.19		20.36	.69	1.70	.68		.26	29.27	15.
	.27		1.06	.59	.18	.05		.01	2.19	16.
	2.56		.37	1.82	.40	.02		.22	5.74	17.
										18.
										19.
.51	.05		1.24	.15	.13	.03		.13	12.52	20.
12.92	3.63	.70	54.45	10.10	4.55	2.12	5.68	5.25	389.98	21.
										III.
									182.05	1.
10.97		.60							66.19	2.
			54.44			2.07			56.51	3.
					4.55				4.55	4.
									36.86	5.
										6.
		.04							.04	7.
								1.50	1.50	8.
.07							2.71		2.84	9.
.74								1.25	2.12	10.
										11.
							1.31		1.31	12.
.28			.82	6.43		.10		1.68	13.66	13.
12.06		.64	55.26	6.43	4.55	2.17	4.01	4.44	367.63	14.
1.01	3.63	.06	.64	3.88			1.67	.81	25.92	IV.
13.07	3.63	.70	55.90	10.31	4.55	2.17	5.68	5.25	393.55	V.

TABLE II

Finance Sector Balance Sheets—1949

(billion dollars)

	Federal Reserve Banks & Treasury Monetary Funds	Govt. Pension and Insurance Funds	Commercial Banks	Mutual Savings Banks
I. Tangible assets	.05		1.99	.19
II. Intangible assets				
1. Currency and demand deposits	52.90	.36	28.90	.65
a. Monetary metals	27.03			
b. Other	25.87	.36	28.90	.65
2. Other bank deposits and shares			.04	.22
3. Life insurance reserves, private				
4. Pension and retirement funds, private				
5. Pension and insurance funds, govt.				
6. Consumer credit			6.01	.04
7. Trade credit				
8. Loans on securities			2.64	
9. Bank loans, n.e.c.	.08		23.32	
10. Other loans		.14		.07
11. Mortgages, nonfarm		.04	10.64	6.67
a. Residential		.04	8.60	5.57
b. Nonresidential			2.04	1.10
12. Mortgages, farm			.91	.04
13. Securities, U.S. government	18.90	36.89	67.00	11.43
a. Short-term	12.00		26.50	.44
b. Savings bonds		.60	1.18	.50
c. Other long-term	6.90	36.29	39.32	10.49
14. Securities, state and local		1.55	6.55	.09
15. Securities, other bonds and notes		.36	3.32	2.15
16. Securities, preferred stock		.03		
17. Securities, common stock		.03	.15	.16
18. Equity in mutual financial organizations				
19. Equity in other business				
20. Other intangible assets	3.06		7.58	.10
21. Total	74.94	39.40	157.06	21.62
III. Liabilities				
1. Currency and demand deposits	70.84		108.52	
2. Other bank deposits and shares			36.73	19.27
3. Life insurance reserves, private				
4. Pension and retirement funds, private				
5. Pension and insurance funds, govt.		39.40		
6. Consumer debt				
7. Trade debt				
8. Loans on securities				
9. Bank loans, n.e.c.			.02	
10. Other loans			.11	
11. Mortgages				
12. Bonds and notes				
13. Other liabilities	3.41		1.32	.11
14. Total	74.25	39.40	146.70	19.38
IV. Equities	.74		12.35	2.43
V. Total assets or liabilities and equities	74.99	39.40	159.05	21.81

Savings and Loan Associations	Investment Companies	Credit Unions	Life Insurance Companies	Fire and Casualty Insurance Companies	Noninsured Pension Plans	Other Private Insurance	Finance Companies	Other Finance	Total	
.24			2.12	.29		.07			4.95	I.
										II.
.61	.14	.08	.91	1.14	.20	.09	.85	.81	87.64	1.
									27.03	
.61	.14	.08	.91	1.14	.20	.09	.85	.81	60.61	
		.10							.36	2.
										3.
										4.
										5.
.14		.44					4.30		10.93	6.
				.74			.32	.11	1.17	7.
								1.15	3.79	8.
									23.40	9.
			2.24			.09	1.13	.62	4.29	10.
11.62	.30	.07	11.77	.09	.04	.26	.33	.10	41.93	11.
11.38	.26	.07	8.39	.04	.04	.11	.33	.08	34.91	
.23	.04		3.38	.06		.15		.02	7.01	
			1.14			.03			2.11	12.
1.46	.18	.14	15.29	5.00	2.09	.54		1.65	160.57	13.
.10			.30	1.19				1.10	41.63	
.40			.26	.46	.61	.03			4.04	
.96	.18	.14	14.73	3.35	1.47	.51		.55	114.90	
			1.05	.75		.38		.37	10.74	14.
	.21		22.93	.78	2.04	.74		.45	32.98	15.
	.27		1.26	.65	.21	.06		.02	2.50	16.
	3.24		.46	2.30	.51	.02		.37	7.24	17.
										18.
										19.
.65	.03		1.33	.17	.16	.03		.14	13.25	20.
14.48	4.39	.83	58.38	11.62	5.26	2.26	6.94	5.80	402.90	21.
										III.
									179.36	1.
12.47		.70							69.17	2.
			58.45			2.20			60.65	3.
					5.26				5.26	4.
									39.40	5.
										6.
		.06							.06	7.
								1.95	1.95	8.
.07							3.14		3.23	9.
.70								1.39	2.20	10.
										11.
							1.83		1.83	12.
.28			.90	7.20		.12		1.62	14.96	13.
13.52		.76	59.35	7.20	5.26	2.32	4.97	4.96	378.07	14.
1.21	4.38	.07	1.15	4.71			1.97	.84	29.78	IV.
14.72	4.38	.83	60.50	11.91	5.26	2.32	6.94	5.80	407.85	V.

TABLE II

Finance Sector Balance Sheets—1950

(billion dollars)

	Federal Reserve Banks & Treasury Monetary Funds	Govt. Pension and Insurance Funds	Commercial Banks	Mutual Savings Banks
I. Tangible assets	.06		1.99	.19
II. Intangible assets				
1. Currency and demand deposits	49.52	.82	31.18	.63
a. Monetary metals	25.30			
b. Other	24.22	.82	31.18	.63
2. Other bank deposits and shares			.04	.17
3. Life insurance reserves, private				
4. Pension and retirement funds, private				
5. Pension and insurance funds, govt.				
6. Consumer credit			7.67	.06
7. Trade credit				
8. Loans on securities			2.86	
9. Bank loans, n.e.c.	.07		28.85	
10. Other loans		.16		.07
11. Mortgages, nonfarm		.10	12.58	8.22
a. Residential		.10	10.33	7.05
b. Nonresidential			2.24	1.16
12. Mortgages, farm			.96	.04
13. Securities, U.S. government	20.80	37.30	62.03	10.87
a. Short-term	16.00		22.20	.11
b. Savings bonds		.70	1.47	.58
c. Other long-term	4.80	36.60	38.36	10.18
14. Securities, state and local		1.74	8.12	.09
15. Securities, other bonds and notes		.51	3.90	2.07
16. Securities, preferred stock		.04		
17. Securities, common stock		.04	.15	.18
18. Equity in mutual financial organizations				
19. Equity in other business				
20. Other intangible assets	4.40		10.02	.12
21. Total	74.79	40.71	168.36	22.52
III. Liabilities				
1. Currency and demand deposits	70.41		118.30	
2. Other bank deposits and shares			36.96	20.01
3. Life insurance reserves, private				
4. Pension and retirement funds, private				
5. Pension and insurance funds, govt.		40.71		
6. Consumer debt				
7. Trade debt				
8. Loans on securities				
9. Bank loans, n.e.c.			.09	
10. Other loans			.09	
11. Mortgages				
12. Bonds and notes				
13. Other liabilities	3.66		1.90	.14
14. Total	74.07	40.71	157.34	20.15
IV. Equities	.78		13.01	2.56
V. Total assets or liabilities and equities	74.85	40.71	170.35	22.71

Savings and Loan Associations	Investment Companies	Credit Unions	Life Insurance Companies	Fire and Casualty Insurance Companies	Noninsured Pension Plans	Other Private Insurance	Finance Companies	Other Finance	Total	
.29			2.30	.30		.06			5.19	I.
										II.
.70	.18	.10	1.00	1.20	.27	.10	1.02	1.00	87.72	1.
									25.30	
.70	.18	.10	1.00	1.20	.27	.10	1.02	1.00	62.42	
		.10							.31	2.
										3.
										4.
										5.
.20		.59					5.32		13.84	6.
				.76			.61	.10	1.47	7.
								1.73	4.59	8.
									28.92	9.
		.01	2.41			.10	1.44	.72	4.91	10.
13.66	.34	.08	14.78	.11	.05	.31	.54	.12	50.87	11.
13.38	.30	.08	11.09	.04	.05	.14	.54	.10	43.21	
.27	.04		3.68	.06		.17		.02	7.66	
			1.33			.03			2.37	12.
1.49	.20	.12	13.46	5.35	2.30	.55		1.58	156.05	13.
.10			.56	1.24				1.10	41.31	
.50			.31	.57	.80	.03			4.96	
.89	.20	.12	12.59	3.54	1.50	.52		.48	109.78	
			1.15	1.06		.37		.50	13.03	14.
	.25		24.76	.83	2.48	.79		.34	35.93	15.
	.30		1.45	.68	.27	.06		.01	2.81	16.
	4.04		.65	2.76	.67	.03		.28	8.80	17.
										18.
										19.
.67	.04		1.59	.19	.19	.04		.18	17.44	20.
16.72	5.34	1.00	62.58	12.94	6.23	2.38	8.91	6.56	429.06	21.
										III.
									188.71	1.
13.99		.85							71.81	2.
			62.67			2.32			64.99	3.
					6.23				6.23	4.
									40.71	5.
										6.
		.07							.07	7.
								2.02	2.02	8.
.08							4.12		4.29	9.
1.22								1.88	3.19	10.
										11.
							2.25		2.25	12.
.33			1.01	7.92		.13		1.77	16.86	13.
15.62		.92	63.68	7.92	6.23	2.45	6.38	5.67	401.13	14.
1.39	5.35	.08	1.20	5.32			2.54	.90	33.12	IV.
17.01	5.35	1.00	64.88	13.24	6.23	2.45	8.91	6.57	434.25	V.

TABLE II

Finance Sector Balance Sheets—1951

(billion dollars)

	Federal Reserve Banks & Treasury Monetary Funds	Govt. Pension and Insurance Funds	Commercial Banks	Mutual Savings Banks
I. Tangible assets	.06		1.94	.17
II. Intangible assets				
1. Currency and demand deposits	49.68	.88	35.10	.70
a. Monetary metals	25.25			
b. Other	24.43	.88	35.10	.70
2. Other bank deposits and shares			.04	.19
3. Life insurance reserves, private				
4. Pension and retirement funds, private				
5. Pension and insurance funds, govt.				
6. Consumer credit			7.84	.06
7. Trade credit				
8. Loans on securities			2.56	
9. Bank loans, n.e.c.	.02		33.58	
10. Other loans		.18		.07
11. Mortgages, nonfarm		.16	13.58	9.87
a. Residential		.16	11.14	8.60
b. Nonresidential			2.44	1.27
12. Mortgages, farm			1.00	.05
13. Securities, U.S. government	23.82	40.90	61.52	9.82
a. Short-term	13.40		15.80	.18
b. Savings bonds		.70	1.49	.58
c. Other long-term	10.40	40.20	44.23	9.06
14. Securities, state and local		1.81	9.20	.15
15. Securities, other bonds and notes		.75	3.77	2.20
16. Securities, preferred stock		.05		
17. Securities, common stock		.05	.14	.23
18. Equity in mutual financial organizations				
19. Equity in other business				
20. Other intangible assets	4.05		10.60	.17
21. Total	77.57	44.78	178.93	23.51
III. Liabilities				
1. Currency and demand deposits	73.49		126.15	
2. Other bank deposits and shares			38.69	20.89
3. Life insurance reserves, private				
4. Pension and retirement funds, private				
5. Pension and insurance funds, govt.		44.78		
6. Consumer debt				
7. Trade debt				
8. Loans on securities				
9. Bank loans, n.e.c.			.03	
10. Other loans			.08	
11. Mortgages				
12. Bonds and notes				
13. Other liabilities	3.34		2.30	.15
14. Total	76.83	44.78	167.25	21.04
IV. Equities	.80		13.62	2.64
V. Total assets or liabilities and equities	77.63	44.78	180.87	23.68

Savings and Loan Associations	Investment Companies	Credit Unions	Life Insurance Companies	Fire and Casualty Insurance Companies	Noninsured Pension Plans	Other Private Insurance	Finance Companies	Other Finance	Total	
.30			2.35	.32		.06		.01	5.19	I.
										II.
.80	.21	.15	1.10	1.24	.31	.11	1.14	.97	92.39	1.
									25.25	
.80	.21	.15	1.10	1.24	.31	.11	1.14	.97	67.14	
		.15		.01					.39	2.
										3.
										4.
										5.
.23		.64					5.60		14.37	6.
				.88			.65	.13	1.66	7.
								1.69	4.25	8.
									33.60	9.
		.02	2.59			.11	1.71	.88	5.56	10.
15.56	.33	.10	17.79	.12	.10	.36	.45	.15	58.56	11.
15.25	.29	.10	13.64	.05	.10	.17	.45	.12	50.08	
.31	.04		4.15	.07		.19		.02	8.49	
			1.53			.04			2.62	12.
1.60	.20	.14	11.01	5.48	2.42	.57		1.30	158.78	13.
.20			.65	.87				1.00	32.10	
.50			.31	.59	.77	.04			4.98	
.90	.20	.14	10.05	4.02	1.65	.53		.30	121.70	
			1.17	1.45		.36		.55	14.69	14.
	.30		27.47	.88	3.36	.85		.38	39.96	15.
	.34		1.40	.72	.36	.05		.02	2.94	16.
	5.17		.82	3.15	1.03	.04		.34	10.97	17.
										18.
										19.
.82	.04		1.77	.24	.22	.04		.16	18.11	20.
19.01	6.60	1.20	66.65	14.17	7.80	2.53	9.55	6.56	458.85	21.
										III.
									199.64	1.
16.11		1.04							76.73	2.
			66.85			2.46			69.31	3.
					7.80				7.80	4.
									44.78	5.
										6.
		.06							.06	7.
								1.83	1.83	8.
.09							4.13		4.25	9.
1.22								1.94	3.24	10.
										11.
							2.82		2.82	12.
.35			1.08	8.77		.14		1.90	18.03	13.
17.77		1.10	67.93	8.77	7.80	2.59	6.95	5.66	428.49	14.
1.54	6.61	.10	1.07	5.72			2.60	.90	35.55	IV.
19.31	6.61	1.20	69.00	14.49	7.80	2.59	9.55	6.56	464.04	V.

TABLE II

Finance Sector Balance Sheets—1952

(billion dollars)

	Federal Reserve Banks & Treasury Monetary Funds	Govt. Pension and Insurance Funds	Commercial Banks	Mutual Savings Banks
I. Tangible assets	.07		2.04	.20
II. Intangible assets				
1. Currency and demand deposits	50.83	.77	35.04	.70
a. Monetary metals	25.72			
b. Other	25.11	.77	35.04	.70
2. Other bank deposits and shares			.04	.22
3. Life insurance reserves, private				
4. Pension and retirement funds, private				
5. Pension and insurance funds, govt.				
6. Consumer credit			9.73	.07
7. Trade credit				
8. Loans on securities			3.16	
9. Bank loans, n.e.c.	.16		36.46	
10. Other loans		.19		.07
11. Mortgages, nonfarm		.20	14.66	11.33
a. Residential		.20	12.06	9.88
b. Nonresidential			2.59	1.44
12. Mortgages, farm			1.05	.05
13. Securities, U.S. government	24.72	44.82	63.32	9.42
a. Short-term	14.80		19.20	.26
b. Savings bonds		.80	1.51	.59
c. Other long-term	9.92	44.02	42.61	8.57
14. Securities, state and local		1.94	10.19	.32
15. Securities, other bonds and notes		1.09	3.55	2.57
16. Securities, preferred stock		.06		
17. Securities, common stock		.06	.15	.34
18. Equity in mutual financial organizations				
19. Equity in other business				
20. Other intangible assets	4.41		10.72	.17
21. Total	80.12	49.13	188.07	25.26
III. Liabilities				
1. Currency and demand deposits	75.44		131.18	
2. Other bank deposits and shares			41.76	22.59
3. Life insurance reserves, private				
4. Pension and retirement funds, private				
5. Pension and insurance funds, govt.		49.13		
6. Consumer debt				
7. Trade debt				
8. Loans on securities				
9. Bank loans, n.e.c.			.19	
10. Other loans			.05	
11. Mortgages				
12. Bonds and notes				
13. Other liabilities	3.88		2.54	.16
14. Total	79.32	49.13	175.72	22.75
IV. Equities	.87		14.39	2.71
V. Total assets or liabilities and equities	80.19	49.13	190.11	25.46

Savings and Loan Associations	Investment Companies	Credit Unions	Life Insurance Companies	Fire and Casualty Insurance Companies	Noninsured Pension Plans	Other Private Insurance	Finance Companies	Other Finance	Total	
.39			2.72	.34		.07		.01	5.83	I.
										II.
.87	.20	.15	1.15	1.32	.28	.12	1.17	.93	93.53	1.
									25.72	
.87	.20	.15	1.15	1.32	.28	.12	1.17	.93	67.81	
		.24		.02					.52	2.
										3.
										4.
										5.
.30		.84					7.06		18.00	6.
				.95			.72	.14	1.81	7.
								1.79	4.95	8.
									36.62	9.
		.03	2.71			.11	1.84	.94	5.89	10.
18.40	.34	.12	19.55	.12	.13	.40	.60	.15	66.00	11.
18.03	.30	.12	15.04	.05	.13	.19	.60	.12	56.74	
.37	.04		4.50	.07		.21		.03	9.26	
			1.70			.06			2.87	12.
1.79	.19	.14	10.25	5.82	2.42	.60		1.67	165.16	13.
.20			.54	1.01				1.50	37.51	
.50			.32	.60	.78	.12			5.22	
1.09	.19	.14	9.39	4.21	1.64	.48		.17	122.43	
			1.15	1.87		.36		.40	16.23	14.
	.40		30.57	1.04	4.42	.92		.45	45.01	15.
	.29		1.49	.80	.41	.05		.02	3.12	16.
	6.29		.96	3.52	1.55	.04		.39	13.30	17.
										18.
										19.
1.03	.04		1.95	.28	.30	.04		.17	19.11	20.
22.39	7.76	1.52	71.48	15.74	9.52	2.70	11.39	7.05	492.12	21.
										III.
									206.62	1.
19.20		1.31							84.86	2.
			71.85			2.62			74.47	3.
					9.52				9.52	4.
									49.13	5.
										6.
		.10							.10	7.
								2.31	2.31	8.
.08							4.89		5.16	9.
1.37								1.79	3.21	10.
										11.
							3.36		3.36	12.
.36			1.16	9.85		.16		2.04	20.15	13.
21.01		1.41	73.01	9.85	9.52	2.78	8.25	6.15	458.89	14.
1.77	7.76	.11	1.19	6.23			3.15	.91	39.06	IV.
22.78	7.76	1.52	74.20	16.08	9.52	2.78	11.39	7.06	497.95	V.

TABLE II

Finance Sector Balance Sheets—1953

(billion dollars)

	Federal Reserve Banks & Treasury Monetary Funds	Govt. Pension and Insurance Funds	Commercial Banks	Mutual Savings Banks
I. Tangible assets	.07		2.22	.22
II. Intangible assets				
1. Currency and demand deposits	49.15	.73	35.28	.74
a. Monetary metals	24.56			
b. Other	24.59	.73	35.28	.74
2. Other bank deposits and shares			.04	.24
3. Life insurance reserves, private				
4. Pension and retirement funds, private				
5. Pension and insurance funds, govt.				
6. Consumer credit			11.33	.08
7. Trade credit				
8. Loans on securities			3.56	
9. Bank loans, n.e.c.	.03		36.97	
10. Other loans		.21		.08
11. Mortgages, nonfarm		.23	15.62	12.89
a. Residential		.23	12.80	11.33
b. Nonresidential			2.81	1.56
12. Mortgages, farm			1.08	.05
13. Securities, U.S. government	25.94	47.51	63.43	9.18
a. Short-term	17.00		28.20	.48
b. Savings bonds		.80	1.49	.56
c. Other long-term	8.94	46.71	33.74	8.14
14. Securities, state and local		2.18	10.82	.41
15. Securities, other bonds and notes		1.49	3.43	2.86
16. Securities, preferred stock		.08		
17. Securities, common stock		.08	.15	.43
18. Equity in mutual financial organizations				
19. Equity in other business				
20. Other intangible assets	4.38		10.73	.20
21. Total	79.50	52.51	192.44	27.16
III. Liabilities				
1. Currency and demand deposits	74.73		131.54	
2. Other bank deposits and shares			45.16	24.36
3. Life insurance reserves, private				
4. Pension and retirement funds, private				
5. Pension and insurance funds, govt.		52.51		
6. Consumer debt				
7. Trade debt				
8. Loans on securities				
9. Bank loans, n.e.c.			.06	
10. Other loans			.04	
11. Mortgages				
12. Bonds and notes				
13. Other liabilities	3.94		2.65	.21
14. Total	78.67	52.51	179.45	24.57
IV. Equities	.90		15.21	2.81
V. Total assets or liabilities and equities	79.57	52.51	194.66	27.38

Savings and Loan Associations	Investment Companies	Credit Unions	Life Insurance Companies	Fire and Casualty Insurance Companies	Non-insured Pension Plans	Other Private Insurance	Finance Companies	Other Finance	Total	
.46			2.91	.37		.08		.01	6.36	I.
										II.
.92	.24	.17	1.22	1.37	.33	.16	1.19	.86	92.36	1.
									24.56	
.92	.24	.17	1.22	1.37	.33	.16	1.19	.86	67.80	
		.30		.02					.60	2.
										3.
										4.
										5.
.35		1.12					8.62		21.50	6.
				1.00			.78	.19	1.97	7.
								2.19	5.75	8.
									37.00	9.
		.03	2.91			.12	1.92	.85	6.12	10.
21.96	.36	.15	21.44	.14	.17	.44	.62	.15	74.16	11.
21.52	.31	.15	16.56	.06	.17	.21	.62	.12	64.08	
.44	.05		4.88	.08		.23		.03	10.08	
			1.89			.06			3.08	12.
1.92	.19	.13	9.83	6.03	2.58	.61		1.66	169.01	13.
.20			.47	1.43				1.50	49.28	
.50			.30	.58	.76	.07			5.05	
1.22	.19	.13	9.06	4.02	1.83	.54		.16	114.68	
			1.30	2.62		.37		.65	18.35	14.
	.41		33.28	1.16	5.49	.99		.36	49.47	15.
	.46		1.53	.85	.48	.05		.02	3.47	16.
	6.47		1.04	3.61	1.96	.04		.33	14.11	17.
										18.
										19.
1.26	.04		2.07	.34	.41	.05		.19	19.67	20.
26.41	8.16	1.90	76.51	17.14	11.42	2.89	13.14	7.46	516.62	21.
										III.
									206.27	1.
22.85		1.64							94.01	2.
			76.84			2.80			79.64	3.
					11.42				11.42	4.
									52.51	5.
										6.
		.12							.12	7.
								2.61	2.61	8.
.08							4.88		5.02	9.
1.51								1.70	3.25	10.
										11.
							4.94		4.94	12.
.39			1.26	10.95		.17		2.15	21.72	13.
24.83		1.76	78.10	10.95	11.42	2.97	9.82	6.46	481.51	14.
2.04	8.18	.14	1.32	6.56			3.32	1.01	41.47	IV.
26.87	8.18	1.90	79.42	17.51	11.42	2.97	13.14	7.48	522.98	V.

TABLE II

Finance Sector Balance Sheets—1954

(billion dollars)

	Federal Reserve Banks & Treasury Monetary Funds	Govt. Pension and Insurance Funds	Commercial Banks	Mutual Savings Banks
I. Tangible assets	.07		2.40	.25
II. Intangible assets				
1. Currency and demand deposits	48.63	1.05	34.05	.76
a. Monetary metals	24.29			
b. Other	24.34	1.05	34.05	.76
2. Other bank deposits and shares			.04	.27
3. Life insurance reserves, private				
4. Pension and retirement funds, private				
5. Pension and insurance funds, govt.				
6. Consumer credit			11.36	.08
7. Trade credit				
8. Loans on securities			4.45	.01
9. Bank loans, n.e.c.	.14		37.46	
10. Other loans		.23		.09
11. Mortgages, nonfarm		.30	17.26	14.95
a. Residential		.30	14.03	13.21
b. Nonresidential			3.23	1.74
12. Mortgages, farm			1.16	.06
13. Securities, U.S. government	24.95	48.95	68.98	8.75
a. Short-term	19.40		17.60	.16
b. Savings bonds		.80	1.50	.55
c. Other long-term	5.55	48.15	49.88	8.04
14. Securities, state and local		2.49	12.59	.60
15. Securities, other bonds and notes		1.98	3.29	2.95
16. Securities, preferred stock		.10		
17. Securities, common stock		.10	.15	.57
18. Equity in mutual financial organizations				
19. Equity in other business				
20. Other intangible assets	4.10		10.99	.21
21. Total	77.82	55.20	201.78	29.30
III. Liabilities				
1. Currency and demand deposits	73.18		135.79	
2. Other bank deposits and shares			48.97	26.30
3. Life insurance reserves, private				
4. Pension and retirement funds, private				
5. Pension and insurance funds, govt.		55.20		
6. Consumer debt				
7. Trade debt				
8. Loans on securities				
9. Bank loans, n.e.c.			.03	
10. Other loans			.02	
11. Mortgages				
12. Bonds and notes				
13. Other liabilities	3.80		2.99	.28
14. Total	76.98	55.20	187.80	26.58
IV. Equities	.91		16.38	2.97
V. Total assets or liabilities and equities	77.89	55.20	204.18	29.55

Savings and Loan Associations	Investment Companies	Credit Unions	Life Insurance Companies	Fire and Casualty Insurance Companies	Noninsured Pension Plans	Other Private Insurance	Finance Companies	Other Finance	Total	
.56			3.34	.42		.09		.01	7.14	I.
										II.
1.18	.24	.22	1.24	1.32	.33	.17	1.24	.99	91.42	1.
									24.29	
1.18	.24	.22	1.24	1.32	.33	.17	1.24	.99	67.13	
		.37		.02					.70	2.
										3.
										4.
										5.
.40		1.34					9.06		22.24	6.
				1.06			.88	.18	2.12	7.
								3.15	7.61	8.
									37.60	9.
		.03	3.13			.13	1.67	.94	6.22	10.
26.11	.35	.18	23.93	.14	.20	.49	.84	.15	84.92	11.
25.59	.31	.18	18.56	.06	.20	.23	.84	.12	73.62	
.52	.04		5.37	.09		.27		.03	11.30	
			2.05			.06			3.32	12.
2.02	.19	.13	9.07	6.14	2.59	.65		1.84	174.26	13.
.20			.55	.90				1.80	40.61	
.50			.29	.57	.83	.10			5.14	
1.32	.19	.13	8.23	4.67	1.76	.55		.04	128.51	
			1.85	3.40		.39		.52	21.84	14.
	.55		35.38	1.19	6.70	1.05		.68	53.77	15.
	.54		1.73	.90	.53	.05		.03	3.88	16.
	9.74		1.54	5.04	3.46	.06		.59	21.25	17.
										18.
										19.
1.53	.04		2.27	.39	.52	.05		.19	20.29	20.
31.24	11.66	2.27	82.19	19.60	14.34	3.10	13.71	9.28	551.44	21.
										III.
									208.97	1.
27.25		1.98							104.50	2.
			82.68			3.00			85.68	3.
					14.34				14.34	4.
									55.20	5.
										6.
		.13							.13	7.
								3.28	3.28	8.
.08							4.91		5.02	9.
1.66								2.25	3.93	10.
										11.
							5.13		5.13	12.
.45			1.34	11.64		.19		2.47	23.16	13.
29.44		2.11	84.02	11.64	14.34	3.20	10.04	8.00	509.34	14.
2.36	11.66	.16	1.51	8.38			3.67	1.29	49.24	IV.
31.80	11.66	2.27	85.53	20.02	14.34	3.20	13.71	9.29	558.58	V.

TABLE II

Finance Sector Balance Sheets—1955

(billion dollars)

	Federal Reserve Banks & Treasury Monetary Funds	Govt. Pension and Insurance Funds	Commercial Banks	Mutual Savings Banks
I. Tangible assets	.09		2.73	.26
II. Intangible assets				
1. Currency and demand deposits	48.68	.83	34.28	.74
a. Monetary metals	24.24			
b. Other	24.44	.83	34.28	.74
2. Other bank deposits and shares			.04	.22
3. Life insurance reserves, private				
4. Pension and retirement funds, private				
5. Pension and insurance funds, govt.				
6. Consumer credit			13.72	.10
7. Trade credit				
8. Loans on securities			5.04	.02
9. Bank loans, n.e.c.	.14		44.30	
10. Other loans		.26		.09
11. Mortgages, nonfarm		.34	19.52	17.40
a. Residential		.34	15.74	15.57
b. Nonresidential			3.78	1.83
12. Mortgages, farm			1.29	.06
13. Securities, U.S. government	24.80	51.35	61.59	8.46
a. Short-term	20.70		9.00	.26
b. Savings bonds		.80	1.48	.52
c. Other long-term	4.10	50.55	51.11	7.68
14. Securities, state and local		2.83	12.70	.64
15. Securities, other bonds and notes		2.57	3.53	2.69
16. Securities, preferred stock		.13		
17. Securities, common stock		.13	.16	.66
18. Equity in mutual financial organizations				
19. Equity in other business				
20. Other intangible assets	5.67		13.96	.23
21. Total	79.29	58.44	210.13	31.31
III. Liabilities				
1. Currency and demand deposits	73.74		141.95	
2. Other bank deposits and shares			50.30	28.13
3. Life insurance reserves, private				
4. Pension and retirement funds, private				
5. Pension and insurance funds, govt.		58.44		
6. Consumer debt				
7. Trade debt				
8. Loans on securities				
9. Bank loans, n.e.c.			.16	
10. Other loans			.01	
11. Mortgages				
12. Bonds and notes				
13. Other liabilities	4.67		3.01	.33
14. Total	78.41	58.44	195.43	28.46
IV. Equities	.97		17.43	3.11
V. Total assets or liabilities and equities	79.38	58.44	212.86	31.57

Savings and Loan Associations	Investment Companies	Credit Unions	Life Insurance Companies	Fire and Casualty Insurance Companies	Noninsured Pension Plans	Other Private Insurance	Finance Companies	Other Finance	Total	
.70			3.77	.48		.10		.02	8.11	I.
										II.
1.37	.24	.23	1.26	1.35	.39	.17	1.50	1.00	92.04	1.
									24.24	
1.37	.24	.23	1.26	1.35	.39	.17	1.50	1.00	67.80	
		.44		.02					.72	2.
										3.
										4.
										5.
.48		1.68					11.89		27.87	6.
				1.15			1.13	.23	2.51	7.
								3.63	8.69	8.
									44.44	9.
		.05	3.29			.14	2.64	1.03	7.50	10.
31.41	.34	.21	27.17	.15	.24	.57	1.37	.19	98.92	11.
30.78	.30	.21	21.21	.06	.24	.26	1.37	.15	86.23	
.63	.04		5.96	.10		.32		.04	12.70	
			2.27			.06		.01	3.69	12.
2.34	.33	.13	8.58	6.00	2.89	.72		1.36	168.55	13.
.30			.41	.49				1.30	32.46	
.53			.27	.56	.85	.09			5.10	
1.51	.33	.13	7.90	4.95	2.04	.63		.06	130.99	
			2.04	4.19		.44		.57	23.41	14.
	.73		37.13	1.18	7.61	1.07		.64	57.15	15.
	.65		1.74	.90	.58	.05		.03	4.08	16.
	12.10		1.89	6.02	5.07	.06		.60	26.69	17.
										18.
										19.
1.57	.07		2.48	.43	.58	.06		.21	25.26	20.
37.17	14.46	2.74	87.85	21.39	17.35	3.34	18.52	9.51	591.51	21.
										III.
									215.69	1.
32.14		2.38							112.95	2.
			88.42			3.23			91.65	3.
					17.35				17.35	4.
									58.44	5.
										6.
		.15							.15	7.
								3.60	3.60	8.
.13							7.48		7.77	9.
2.34								2.06	4.41	10.
										11.
							6.76		6.76	12.
.48			1.48	12.42		.21		2.67	25.27	13.
35.09		2.53	89.90	12.42	17.35	3.44	14.24	8.33	544.04	14.
2.78	14.46	.21	1.72	9.45			4.28	1.20	55.58	IV.
37.87	14.46	2.74	91.62	21.87	17.35	3.44	18.52	9.53	599.62	V.

TABLE II

Finance Sector Balance Sheets—1956

(billion dollars)

	Federal Reserve Banks & Treasury Monetary Funds	Govt. Pension and Insurance Funds	Commercial Banks	Mutual Savings Banks
I. Tangible assets	.10		3.02	.29
II. Intangible assets				
1. Currency and demand deposits	49.16	.97	35.64	.76
a. Monetary metals	24.55			
b. Other	24.61	.97	35.64	.76
2. Other bank deposits and shares			.04	.16
3. Life insurance reserves, private				
4. Pension and retirement funds, private				
5. Pension and insurance funds, govt.				
6. Consumer credit			15.17	.13
7. Trade credit				
8. Loans on securities			4.28	.02
9. Bank loans, n.e.c.	.12		49.90	
10. Other loans		.29		.10
11. Mortgages, nonfarm		.43	21.18	19.69
a. Residential		.43	16.85	17.70
b. Nonresidential			4.33	1.98
12. Mortgages, farm			1.33	.06
13. Securities, U.S. government	25.02	53.60	58.55	7.97
a. Short-term	22.10		13.80	.24
b. Savings bonds		.70	1.09	.45
c. Other long-term	2.92	52.90	43.66	7.28
14. Securities, state and local		3.23	12.90	.67
15. Securities, other bonds and notes		3.20	2.89	2.82
16. Securities, preferred stock		.15		
17. Securities, common stock		.15	.16	.70
18. Equity in mutual financial organizations				
19. Equity in other business				
20. Other intangible assets	5.88		14.90	.25
21. Total	80.18	62.02	216.94	33.33
III. Liabilities				
1. Currency and demand deposits	74.52		145.15	
2. Other bank deposits and shares			52.37	30.00
3. Life insurance reserves, private				
4. Pension and retirement funds, private				
5. Pension and insurance funds, govt.		62.02		
6. Consumer debt				
7. Trade debt				
8. Loans on securities				
9. Bank loans, n.e.c.			.08	
10. Other loans				
11. Mortgages				
12. Bonds and notes				
13. Other liabilities	4.72		3.56	.36
14. Total	79.24	62.02	201.16	30.36
IV. Equities	1.04		18.80	3.26
V. Total assets or liabilities and equities	80.28	62.02	219.96	33.62

Savings and Loan Associations	Investment Companies	Credit Unions	Life Insurance Companies	Fire and Casualty Insurance Companies	Non-insured Pension Plans	Other Private Insurance	Finance Companies	Other Finance	Total	
.86			4.09	.53		.10		.02	8.98	I.
										II.
1.44	.27	.26	1.28	1.28	.38	.16	1.52	1.12	94.24	1.
									24.55	
1.44	.27	.26	1.28	1.28	.38	.16	1.52	1.12	69.69	
		.55		.02				.01	.77	2.
										3.
										4.
										5.
.56		2.01					13.02		30.89	6.
				1.29			1.31	.33	2.93	7.
								3.71	8.01	8.
									50.02	9.
		.04	3.52			.16	2.55	1.10	7.76	10.
35.73	.33	.27	30.51	.16	.34	.64	1.27	.20	110.75	11.
35.01	.29	.27	23.74	.06	.34	.27	1.27	.16	96.40	
.72	.04		6.76	.10		.37		.05	14.36	
			2.48			.06		.01	3.94	12.
2.78	.35	.14	7.56	5.67	2.69	.75		1.45	166.53	13.
.20			.28	.75				1.45	38.82	
.40			.23	.49	.70	.11			4.17	
2.18	.35	.14	7.05	4.43	1.99	.64		0	123.54	
			2.27	4.82		.44		.46	24.79	14.
	.84		39.28	1.21	9.20	1.13		.46	61.03	15.
	.73		1.55	.82	.64	.04		.02	3.95	16.
	12.63		1.95	6.40	5.95	.06		.39	28.39	17.
										18.
										19.
1.77	.05		2.79	.47	.82	.07		.25	27.25	20.
42.28	15.20	3.27	93.19	22.14	20.02	3.51	19.67	9.49	621.25	21.
										III.
									219.67	1.
37.15		2.84							122.36	2.
			93.71			3.39			97.10	3.
					20.02				20.02	4.
									62.02	5.
										6.
		.18							.18	7.
								2.98	2.98	8.
.12							6.94		7.14	9.
2.13								2.09	4.22	10.
										11.
							7.95		7.95	12.
.51			1.67	13.08		.22		3.21	27.33	13.
39.91		3.02	95.38	13.08	20.02	3.61	14.89	8.28	570.97	14.
3.23	15.22	.25	1.90	9.59			4.78	1.23	59.26	IV.
43.14	15.22	3.27	97.28	22.67	20.02	3.61	19.67	9.52	630.23	V.

TABLE II

Finance Sector Balance Sheets—1957

(billion dollars)

	Federal Reserve Banks & Treasury Monetary Funds	Govt. Pension and Insurance Funds	Commercial Banks	Mutual Savings Banks
I. Tangible assets	.11		3.33	.31
II. Intangible assets				
1. Currency and demand deposits	50.89	1.21	35.49	.76
a. Monetary metals	25.28			
b. Other	25.61	1.21	35.49	.76
2. Other bank deposits and shares			.04	.12
3. Life insurance reserves, private				
4. Pension and retirement funds, private				
5. Pension and insurance funds, govt.				
6. Consumer credit			16.38	.13
7. Trade credit				
8. Loans on securities			4.22	.01
9. Bank loans, n.e.c.	.12		51.96	
10. Other loans		.32		.13
11. Mortgages, nonfarm		.45	21.75	21.11
a. Residential		.45	17.00	19.01
b. Nonresidential			4.76	2.10
12. Mortgages, farm			1.36	.06
13. Securities, U.S. government	24.26	54.67	58.24	7.55
a. Short-term	21.40		15.70	.45
b. Savings bonds		.60	.62	.30
c. Other long-term	2.86	54.07	41.92	6.80
14. Securities, state and local		3.68	13.92	.68
15. Securities, other bonds and notes		4.16	3.49	3.56
16. Securities, preferred stock		.19		
17. Securities, common stock		.19	.18	.77
18. Equity in mutual financial organizations				
19. Equity in other business				
20. Other intangible assets	5.92		15.11	.28
21. Total	81.19	64.87	222.14	35.16
III. Liabilities				
1. Currency and demand deposits	75.43		143.50	
2. Other bank deposits and shares			57.82	31.66
3. Life insurance reserves, private				
4. Pension and retirement funds, private				
5. Pension and insurance funds, govt.		64.87		
6. Consumer debt				
7. Trade debt				
8. Loans on securities				
9. Bank loans, n.e.c.			.08	
10. Other loans			.01	
11. Mortgages				
12. Bonds and notes				
13. Other liabilities	4.79		3.93	.44
14. Total	80.22	64.87	205.34	32.10
IV. Equities	1.08		20.13	3.37
V. Total assets or liabilities and equities	81.30	64.87	225.47	35.47

Savings and Loan Associations	Investment Companies	Credit Unions	Life Insurance Companies	Fire and Casualty Insurance Companies	Non-insured Pension Plans	Other Private Insurance	Finance Companies	Other Finance	Total	
1.03			4.46	.57		.11		.02	9.94	I.
										II.
1.49	.30	.29	1.29	1.27	.44	.15	1.59	1.14	96.31	1.
									25.28	
1.49	.30	.29	1.29	1.27	.44	.15	1.59	1.14	71.03	
		.63		.02					.81	2.
										3.
										4.
										5.
.64		2.43					13.84		33.42	6.
				1.44			1.46	.37	3.27	7.
								3.42	7.65	8.
									52.08	9.
		.06	3.87			.16	3.16	1.37	9.07	10.
40.01	.31	.27	32.65	.16	.52	.66	.94	.22	119.05	11.
39.21	.27	.27	24.99	.05	.52	.26	.94	.16	103.12	
.80	.04		7.66	.11		.40		.06	15.93	
			2.58			.06		.01	4.07	12.
3.17	.35	.13	7.03	5.46	2.42	.74		1.57	165.59	13.
.50			.25	1.18				1.57	41.05	
.32			.13	.32	.36	.12			2.77	
2.35	.35	.13	6.65	3.96	2.05	.62		0	121.77	
			2.38	5.44		.42		.60	27.12	14.
	.98		41.95	1.39	10.93	1.16		.73	68.35	15.
	.62		1.52	.84	.68	.04		.03	3.92	16.
	11.89		1.87	5.83	6.36	.06		.63	27.78	17.
										18.
										19.
2.11	.06		3.05	.55	.93	.08		.29	28.38	20.
47.42	14.51	3.81	98.19	22.40	22.28	3.53	20.99	10.39	646.87	21.
										III.
									218.93	1.
41.91		3.30							134.69	2.
			98.79			3.41			102.20	3.
					22.28				22.28	4.
									64.87	5.
										6.
		.19							.19	7.
								3.08	3.08	8.
.11							6.58		6.77	9.
2.13								2.39	4.53	10.
										11.
							9.08		9.08	12.
.63			1.84	14.13		.24		3.47	29.47	13.
44.78		3.49	100.63	14.13	22.28	3.64	15.66	8.94	596.09	14.
3.67	14.51	.32	2.02	8.84			5.33	1.47	60.72	IV.
48.45	14.51	3.81	102.65	22.97	22.28	3.64	20.99	10.41	656.81	V.

TABLE II

Finance Sector Balance Sheets—1958

(billion dollars)

	Federal Reserve Banks & Treasury Monetary Funds	Govt. Pension and Insurance Funds	Commercial Banks	Mutual Savings Banks
I. Tangible assets	.12		3.47	.32
II. Intangible assets				
1. Currency and demand deposits	46.76	1.34	35.13	.76
a. Monetary metals	23.06			
b. Other	23.70	1.34	35.13	.76
2. Other bank deposits and shares			.08	.16
3. Life insurance reserves, private				
4. Pension and retirement funds, private				
5. Pension and insurance funds, govt.				
6. Consumer credit			16.56	.14
7. Trade credit				
8. Loans on securities			4.66	.01
9. Bank loans, n.e.c.	.11		53.69	
10. Other loans		.36		.17
11. Mortgages, nonfarm		.40	23.79	23.21
a. Residential		.40	18.41	20.94
b. Nonresidential			5.38	2.27
12. Mortgages, farm			1.46	.05
13. Securities, U.S. government	26.44	54.05	66.18	7.26
a. Short-term	21.00		16.60	.30
b. Savings bonds		.50	.59	.22
c. Other long-term	5.44	53.55	48.99	6.74
14. Securities, state and local		4.14	16.50	.73
15. Securities, other bonds and notes		5.31	3.52	4.11
16. Securities, preferred stock		.25		
17. Securities, common stock		.25	.19	.86
18. Equity in mutual financial organizations				
19. Equity in other business				
20. Other intangible assets	5.78		16.07	.30
21. Total	79.09	66.10	237.83	37.76
III. Liabilities				
1. Currency and demand deposits	73.03		150.15	
2. Other bank deposits and shares			65.86	34.01
3. Life insurance reserves, private				
4. Pension and retirement funds, private				
5. Pension and insurance funds, govt.		66.10		
6. Consumer debt				
7. Trade debt				
8. Loans on securities				
9. Bank loans, n.e.c.			.07	.01
10. Other loans				
11. Mortgages				
12. Bonds and notes				
13. Other liabilities	5.06		3.88	.53
14. Total	78.09	66.10	219.96	34.55
IV. Equities	1.12		21.34	3.53
V. Total assets or liabilities and equities	79.21	66.10	241.30	38.08

Savings and Loan Associ-ations	Invest-ment Com-panies	Credit Unions	Life Insur-ance Com-panies	Fire and Casualty Insur-ance Com-panies	Non-insured Pension Plans	Other Private Insur-ance	Finance Com-panies	Other Finance	Total	
1.15			4.54	.62		.12		.03	10.34	I.
										II.
1.76	.30	.33	1.37	1.33	.47	.17	1.70	1.17	92.59	1.
									23.06	
1.76	.30	.33	1.37	1.33	.47	.17	1.70	1.17	69.53	
		.82		.02				.01	1.08	2.
										3.
										4.
										5.
.70		2.66					13.13		33.19	6.
				1.58			1.70	.36	3.64	7.
								4.56	9.23	8.
									53.80	9.
		.06	4.19			.17	2.83	1.64	9.42	10.
45.63	.28	.35	34.40	.16	.65	.70	1.40	.26	131.22	11.
44.72	.24	.35	25.92	.05	.65	.27	1.40	.18	113.52	
.91	.04		8.47	.11		.43		.08	17.70	
			2.67			.07		.01	4.26	12.
3.82	.49	.13	7.18	5.40	2.45	.80		1.81	176.01	13.
.30			.52	1.10				1.81	41.63	
.32			.10	.25	.35	.10			2.43	
3.20	.49	.13	6.56	4.05	2.10	.70		0	131.95	
			2.68	6.15		.43		.60	31.23	14.
	1.22		44.37	1.48	12.44	1.24		.61	74.30	15.
	.93		1.56	.83	.73	.04		.02	4.36	16.
	17.15		2.55	7.51	10.07	.08		.44	39.10	17.
										18.
										19.
2.38	.07		3.25	.55	.98	.08		.32	29.78	20.
54.29	20.45	4.35	104.22	25.01	27.80	3.78	20.75	11.82	693.21	21.
										III.
									223.18	1.
47.98		3.77							151.62	2.
			104.87			3.64			108.51	3.
					27.80				27.80	4.
									66.10	5.
										6.
		.21							.21	7.
								3.42	3.42	8.
.15							5.46		5.69	9.
2.44								3.11	5.55	10.
										11.
							9.09		9.09	12.
.73			1.97	14.97		.26		3.80	31.20	13.
51.30		3.98	106.84	14.97	27.80	3.90	14.56	10.33	632.37	14.
4.14	20.45	.37	1.92	10.66			6.20	1.52	71.18	IV.
55.44	20.45	4.35	108.76	25.63	27.80	3.90	20.75	11.84	703.55	V.

SECTION III

Sector Balance Sheets, 1945–58 and Selected Earlier Years

(Some tables have been extended through 1959.)

TABLE III-1

Nonfarm Households, 1945-58
(billion dollars)

	1945	1946	1947	1948
I. Tangible assets				
1. Residential structures	123.72	145.28	177.58	192.31
2. Nonresidential structures	6.97	9.26	11.54	12.49
3. Land	28.33	32.38	39.41	43.87
4. Producer durables	.13	.18	.25	.35
5. Consumer durables	40.98	52.81	65.00	75.41
7. Total	200.13	239.91	293.78	324.43
II. Intangible assets				
1. Currency and demand deposits	49.89	54.04	53.73	51.67
a. Monetary metals	.84	.89	.92	.95
b. Other	49.05	53.15	52.81	50.72
2. Other bank deposits and shares	52.80	59.18	62.81	64.99
3. Life insurance reserves, private	41.07	44.58	47.87	51.39
4. Pension and retirement funds, private	2.68	3.25	3.90	4.55
5. Pension and insurance funds, govt.	25.35	28.82	32.61	36.10
10. Other loans	1.00	1.16	1.20	1.07
11. Mortgages, nonfarm	9.64	11.00	12.21	13.21
a. Residential	6.23	7.11	7.78	8.38
b. Nonresidential	3.42	3.89	4.43	4.84
12. Mortgages, farm	1.92	2.04	2.11	2.23
13. Securities, U.S. government	59.69	59.20	61.02	60.79
a. Short-term	.51	.67	.25	2.36
b. Savings bonds	40.42	41.62	43.43	45.05
c. Other long-term	18.76	16.91	17.34	13.38
14. Securities, state and local	11.92	11.76	12.17	13.16
15. Securities, other bonds and notes	9.29	7.92	7.23	6.95
16. Securities, preferred stock	8.15	8.15	8.46	8.74
17. Securities, common stock	103.47	92.27	90.20	90.41
18. Equity in mutual financial organizations	2.28	2.66	2.87	3.33
19. Equity in other business	42.13	51.45	59.20	65.24
20. Other intangible assets	1.33	1.32	1.33	1.32
21. Total	422.61	438.80	458.92	475.15
III. Liabilities				
6. Consumer debt	5.36	8.01	11.20	14.00
7. Trade debt	.52	.59	.68	.76
8. Loans on securities	3.34	1.86	1.80	1.68
9. Bank loans, n.e.c.	.88	.59	.34	.44
10. Other loans	1.97	1.90	1.95	2.08
11. Mortgages	18.45	22.71	27.64	32.78
14. Total	30.52	35.66	43.61	51.74
IV. Equities	592.22	643.05	709.09	747.84
V. Total assets or liabilities and equities	622.74	678.71	752.70	799.58

Line

I-1 through I-7	From line 1 of Tables IV-a-1 through IV-a-7 respectively.
II-1 through II-17	Line 1 of Tables IV-b-1 through IV-b-17.
18	Sum of line IV of Tables III-5d, III-5e, and III-5g.
19	Sum of line IV of Tables III-2 and III-5m-1.
20	Table III-1a, line II-20.

1949	1950	1951	1952	1953	1954	1955	1956	1957	1958	
										I.
189.39	220.58	236.14	249.61	259.88	270.18	294.13	315.54	330.28	346.81	1.
12.44	13.94	15.15	16.47	17.55	18.77	20.40	22.26	24.25	26.26	2.
43.28	48.91	52.42	56.78	59.87	64.24	70.82	77.89	85.58	92.16	3.
.48	.65	.83	.97	1.10	1.27	1.47	1.69	1.90	2.07	4.
80.69	98.91	108.85	113.97	120.57	124.82	136.92	149.43	159.61	164.73	5.
326.28	382.99	413.39	437.80	458.97	479.28	523.74	566.81	601.60	632.03	7.
										II.
49.36	51.26	54.33	56.22	57.13	59.33	58.58	59.54	58.52	61.36	1.
.95	1.01	1.06	1.14	1.20	1.21	1.27	1.33	1.50	1.62	
48.41	50.25	53.27	55.08	55.93	58.12	57.31	58.21	57.02	59.74	
67.47	69.56	73.76	81.11	88.99	97.82	106.24	115.38	126.80	140.56	2.
55.21	59.23	63.22	68.00	72.80	78.41	83.96	89.05	93.80	99.70	3.
5.26	6.23	7.80	9.52	11.42	14.34	17.35	20.02	22.28	27.80	4.
38.59	40.15	44.26	48.62	52.04	54.75	57.99	61.57	64.43	65.67	5.
1.23	1.78	1.74	1.63	1.68	2.42	2.30	2.26	2.32	3.10	10.
13.80	14.16	14.66	15.22	15.97	16.96	17.96	19.46	20.88	22.72	11.
8.60	8.69	8.91	9.20	9.60	10.03	10.41	11.16	11.98	12.79	
5.20	5.47	5.74	6.02	6.37	6.94	7.56	8.29	8.90	9.93	
2.31	2.53	2.78	3.03	3.22	3.40	3.62	3.96	4.20	4.54	12.
61.76	61.43	59.98	60.21	60.40	58.87	60.63	61.74	60.60	58.57	13.
3.33	2.15	.54	1.29	2.31	1.66	.65	2.15	4.53	3.16	
46.35	46.80	46.25	46.40	46.36	46.45	46.48	46.19	43.92	43.02	
12.08	12.48	13.19	12.52	11.73	10.76	13.50	13.40	12.15	12.39	
13.77	14.15	14.46	15.62	17.23	17.89	19.57	21.25	23.37	24.79	14.
6.32	6.35	6.42	6.27	6.39	5.42	7.33	8.99	10.84	11.12	15.
8.75	8.69	9.14	9.42	9.45	9.44	9.30	9.90	10.33	10.37	16.
101.09	125.38	142.96	154.00	151.93	211.34	260.63	273.23	245.79	332.62	17.
3.71	4.03	4.28	4.59	4.99	5.49	6.10	6.74	7.36	8.04	18.
65.17	71.76	78.94	80.29	82.52	82.72	86.15	91.65	97.17	98.24	19.
1.31	1.08	.85	.62	.61	.61	.61	.62	.62	.62	20.
495.11	537.77	579.58	614.37	636.77	719.21	798.32	845.36	849.31	969.82	21.
										III.
16.95	20.94	22.29	26.99	30.92	31.93	38.19	41.89	44.75	44.77	6.
.80	.90	.90	1.14	1.20	1.30	1.42	1.59	1.73	1.83	7.
2.00	2.78	2.63	2.84	3.36	4.64	5.39	5.34	4.88	6.20	8.
.44	.71	.70	.64	.56	.68	1.36	1.49	1.70	2.12	9.
2.27	2.45	2.65	2.77	2.98	3.22	3.40	3.67	4.02	4.37	10.
37.04	44.31	51.08	57.81	65.46	74.83	87.36	98.37	107.06	117.05	11.
59.50	72.09	80.25	92.19	104.48	116.60	137.12	152.35	164.14	176.34	14.
761.89	848.67	912.72	959.98	991.26	1081.89	1184.94	1259.82	1286.77	1425.51	IV.
821.39	920.76	992.97	1052.17	1095.74	1198.49	1322.06	1412.17	1450.91	1601.85	V.

Line

Line	
II-21	Sum of lines II-1 through II-20.
III-6 through III-11	Line 1 of Tables IV-c-6 through IV-c-11.
14	Sum of lines III-6 through III-11.
IV	Line V minus line III-14.
V	Sum of lines I-7 and II-21.

TABLE III-1a

Personal Trust Funds, Including Common Trust Funds, 1945-59 (billion dollars)

	1945	1946	1947	1948	1949
I. Tangible assets					
7. Total	.88	.82	.76	.71	.66
II. Intangible assets					
1. Currency and demand deposits	.50	.51	.53	.54	.55
11. Mortgages, nonfarm	.89	.83	.77	.71	.66
13. Securities, U.S. government	8.15	8.61	9.07	9.52	9.98
14. Securities, state and local	2.95	3.03	3.11	3.19	3.27
15. Securities, other bonds and notes	2.39	2.47	2.54	2.61	2.68
16. Securities, preferred stock	1.68	1.68	1.67	1.67	1.66
17. Securities, common stock	10.18	9.47	9.63	10.02	11.67
20. Other intangible assets	1.33	1.32	1.33	1.32	1.31
21. Total	28.07	27.92	28.65	29.58	31.78
III. Liabilities					
IV. Equities	28.95	28.74	29.41	30.29	32.44
V. Total assets or liabilities and equities	28.95	28.74	29.41	30.29	32.44

Sum of Tables III-1b and III-1c.

TABLE III-1b

Personal Trust Funds Other Than Common Trust Funds, 1945-59 (billion dollars)

	1945	1946	1947	1948	1949
I. Tangible assets					
7. Total	.88	.82	.76	.71	.66
II. Intangible assets					
1. Currency and demand deposits	.50	.51	.52	.54	.55
11. Mortgages, nonfarm	.88	.83	.77	.71	.66
13. Securities, U.S. government	8.10	8.53	8.96	9.39	9.82
14. Securities, state and local	2.95	3.03	3.11	3.19	3.27
15. Securities, other bonds and notes	2.36	2.42	2.49	2.55	2.62
16. Securities, preferred stock	1.65	1.63	1.61	1.59	1.57
17. Securities, common stock	10.14	9.40	9.54	9.90	11.52
20. Other intangible assets	1.33	1.32	1.33	1.32	1.31
21. Total	27.91	27.67	28.33	29.19	31.32
III. Liabilities					
IV. Equities	28.79	28.49	29.09	29.90	31.98
V. Total assets or liabilities and equities	28.79	28.49	29.09	29.90	31.98

1957-59: The estimates for mid-1959 and mid-1958 contained in the *Report of National Survey of Trust Accounts* (American Bankers Association, mimeo., 1958 and 1959) were used as a benchmark. Assets as of December 31, 1957 and December 31, 1959 were estimated by assuming that all types, other than common stock and participation in common trust funds, were at the same level as on June 30, 1958 and June 30, 1959 and that holdings of common stock varied only with stock prices, represented by Standard and Poor's combined index (500 stocks). Assets as of end-of-year 1958 were derived by straight-line interpolation of figures in the mid-1958 and mid-1959 ABA reports, except common stock which was interpolated via Standard and Poor's combined index. Participation in common trust funds was subtracted out and estimated separately as indicated below. Real estate was separated from all other assets using the 1955 ratio in Raymond W. Goldsmith and Eli Shapiro, "An Estimate of Bank-Administered Personal Trust Funds," *The Journal of Finance*, March 1959.

1956: Assets for 1956 were estimated by interpolating between 1955 and 1957. Common stock was interpolated via the common stock price index; all other assets were interpolated on a straight line.

1950	1951	1952	1953	1954	1955	1956	1957	1958	1959	
										I.
.87	1.09	1.30	1.29	1.28	1.26	1.27	1.28	1.29	1.30	7.
										II.
.60	.65	.70	.59	.42	.98	.70	.39	.45	.49	1.
.67	.70	.72	.82	.94	1.00	.86	.70	.73	.78	11.
8.64	7.29	5.93	5.10	5.00	5.18	3.97	2.72	2.70	2.76	13.
3.95	4.61	5.27	5.41	6.13	6.65	7.25	7.83	7.84	7.83	14.
2.28	1.87	1.52	2.37	2.94	2.94	2.88	2.86	3.11	3.30	15.
1.64	1.61	1.60	1.55	1.87	1.82	1.66	1.49	1.50	1.48	16.
14.52	16.73	18.26	17.83	24.49	29.42	31.63	28.15	37.11	39.68	17.
1.08	.85	.62	.61	.61	.61	.62	.62	.62	.63	20.
33.38	34.32	34.62	34.29	42.41	48.61	49.57	44.76	54.06	56.95	21.
										III.
34.25	35.41	35.92	35.58	43.69	49.87	50.84	46.04	55.35	58.25	IV.
34.25	35.41	35.92	35.58	43.69	49.87	50.84	46.04	55.35	58.25	V.

1950	1951	1952	1953	1954	1955	1956	1957	1958	1959	
										I.
.87	1.09	1.30	1.29	1.28	1.26	1.27	1.28	1.29	1.30	7.
										II.
.60	.64	.69	.58	.41	.97	.68	.38	.43	.47	1.
.67	.69	.71	.81	.93	.98	.83	.67	.70	.74	11.
8.41	7.00	5.59	4.77	4.68	4.86	3.69	2.51	2.53	2.55	13.
3.94	4.60	5.26	5.40	6.10	6.62	7.21	7.79	7.79	7.79	14.
2.21	1.80	1.39	2.15	2.65	2.58	2.46	2.33	2.46	2.59	15.
1.54	1.50	1.47	1.39	1.68	1.61	1.45	1.29	1.28	1.27	16.
14.30	16.42	17.85	17.29	23.74	28.51	30.65	27.21	35.82	38.24	17.
1.08	.85	.62	.61	.61	.61	.62	.62	.62	.63	20.
32.75	33.50	33.58	33.00	40.80	46.74	47.59	42.80	51.63	54.28	21.
										III.
33.62	34.59	34.88	34.29	42.08	48.00	48.86	44.08	52.92	55.58	IV.
33.62	34.59	34.88	34.29	42.08	48.00	48.86	44.08	52.92	55.58	V.

1952-55: A December 31, 1955 total, comparable to those for 1957 and 1958, was derived by adjusting common stock holdings by the stock price index and bond holdings by Standard and Poor's Treasury, domestic municipal, and industrial bond price indexes, assuming other assets the same as 1958, and then rounding the resulting figure of $48.2 billion down to $48.0 billion to allow for some net increase in these funds.

Assets for 1952 through 1955 were estimated on the basis of the figures in Goldsmith and Shapiro, in *The Journal of Finance*. These Goldsmith and Shapiro estimates were first corrected for the apparent overstatement of cash holdings in the Federal Reserve Board figures which they had used. (The corrected cash holdings, estimated in the same manner as other assets, were $1.05 billion in 1952, $.88 billion in 1953, $.62 billion in 1954, and $1.48 billion in 1955.) Then all assets were scaled down by the ratio of the 1955 total derived from the ABA survey to the corrected Goldsmith-Shapiro total.

(Notes continued on page 123)

TABLE III-1c

Common Trust Funds, 1945-59

(billion dollars)

	1945	1946	1947	1948	1949
I. Tangible assets					
II. Intangible assets					
1. Currency and demand deposits	a	a	a	a	a
11. Mortgages, nonfarm	a	a	a	a	a
13. Securities, U.S. government	.05	.08	.11	.13	.16
14. Securities, state and local	a	a	a	a	a
15. Securities, other bonds and notes	.03	.05	.05	.06	.06
16. Securities, preferred stock	.03	.05	.06	.08	.09
17. Securities, common stock	.04	.07	.09	.12	.15
20. Other intangible assets	0	0	0	0	a
21. Total	.16	.26	.33	.39	.47
III. Liabilities					
IV. Equities	.16	.26	.33	.39	.47
V. Total assets or liabilities and equities	.16	.26	.33	.39	.47

1955-59: Data taken from Federal Reserve Board surveys of common trust funds, *Federal Reserve Bulletin*, June 1957, May 1958, May 1959, and May 1960.

1954: Asset estimates reported in the *Federal Reserve Bulletin*, August 1956, were raised by the 1955 ratio to adjust for the omission of funds operating less than twelve months and those in U.S. possessions. The FRB figure for "other investments" was split between savings accounts and mortgages in the same proportion as in 1955.

1945-53: Figures for 1954 were extrapolated back to 1945 using published and unpublished data from *Trusts and Estates* (see Morris Mendelson, *The Flow-of-Funds Through the Financial Markets, 1953-1955*, NBER Working Memorandum, 1959, pp. I-238 to I-239 for a description of the NBER estimates). The 1954 figure for corporate bonds was extrapolated back by NBER corporate bond estimates. The 1954 figures for other bonds and notes and state and local securities were extrapolated back by NBER estimates for "other bonds," and those for mortgages and savings accounts by NBER estimates for "mortgages and miscellaneous."

[a]Less than $5 million.

1950	1951	1952	1953	1954	1955	1956	1957	1958	1959	
										I.
										II.
a	.01	.01	.01	.01	.01	.02	.01	.02	.02	1.
a	.01	.01	.01	.01	.02	.03	.03	.03	.04	11.
.23	.29	.34	.33	.32	.32	.28	.21	.17	.21	13.
.01	a	.01	.01	.03	.03	.04	.04	.05	.04	14.
.07	.09	.13	.22	.29	.36	.42	.53	.65	.71	15.
.10	.11	.13	.16	.19	.21	.21	.20	.22	.21	16.
.22	.31	.41	.54	.75	.91	.98	.94	1.29	1.44	17.
a	a	a	a	a	a	a	a	a	a	20.
.63	.82	1.04	1.29	1.61	1.87	1.97	1.96	2.43	2.67	21.
										III.
.63	.82	1.04	1.29	1.61	1.87	1.97	1.96	2.43	2.67	IV.
.63	.82	1.04	1.29	1.61	1.87	1.97	1.96	2.43	2.67	V.

Notes to Table III-1b (*concluded*)

1945-51: For 1945 and 1949, Raymond W. Goldsmith's estimates from *Financial Intermediaries in the American Economy Since 1900* (Princeton University Press for National Bureau of Economic Research, 1958) and *A Study of Saving in the United States*, Princeton, N.J., 1956, Vol. III, were used after reducing the figures for cash assets in the same proportion as for 1955. Assets for 1946-48 and 1950-51 were then estimated by straight-line interpolation, except for common stock which was interpolated via Standard and Poor's combined index.

TABLE III-1d

Nonfarm Households, 1900-45, Selected Years

(million dollars)

	1900	1912	1922	1929	1933	1939	1945[a]
I. Tangible assets							
1. Residential structures	15,205	23,964	52,444	79,408	61,737	76,839	111,915
2. Nonresidential structures	1,101	2,035	4,056	5,568	4,766	5,368	6,400
3. Land	7,491	10,725	21,504	33,815	24,647	26,117	33,820
4. Producer durables	90	145	175	372	283	153	128
5. Consumer durables	5,217	11,724	27,235	38,423	23,765	29,964	46,714
7. Total	29,104	48,593	105,414	157,586	115,198	138,441	198,977
II. Intangible assets							
1. Currency and demand deposits	1,529	2,847	9,862	8,602	11,181	15,541	54,217
2. Other bank deposits and shares	3,419	8,153	18,328	30,542	25,846	29,158	51,649
3. Life insurance reserves, private	1,375	3,672	7,769	15,851	18,899	26,629	40,772
4. Pension and retirement funds, private			90	500	700	1,050	2,900
5. Pension and insurance funds, govt.	5	17	240	1,356	2,722	6,120	24,948
10. Other loans	100	200	500	1,200	300	400	850
11. Mortgages, nonfarm	2,399	2,826	6,707	13,570	10,537	8,568	9,564
a. Residential	1,604	1,875	4,377	8,527	7,152	5,879	6,945
b. Nonresidential	795	951	2,330	5,043	3,385	2,689	2,619
12. Mortgages, farm	1,441	2,192	4,761	3,551	2,741	1,632	1,491
13. Securities, U.S. government	576	397	10,806	5,053	6,845	9,140	64,945
14. Securities, state and local	521	1,451	4,983	7,642	9,478	8,274	6,939
15. Securities, other bonds and notes	3,323	9,481	15,923	24,078	24,577	16,836	9,751
16. Securities, preferred stock 17. Securities, common stock	10,704	30,112	55,520	138,296	57,113	73,231	115,790
18. Equity in mutual financial organizations	240	406	803	1,628	1,746	1,678	2,219
19. Equity in other business	6,666	9,772	21,647	29,535	18,632	28,307	45,747
20. Other intangible assets	100	600	4,000	9,100	4,100	5,800	6,500
21. Total	32,398	72,126	161,939	290,504	195,417	232,364	438,282

III. Liabilities							
6. Consumer debt	532	1,463	2,979	6,428	3,235	7,197	5,491
8. Loans on securities	908	1,704	4,534	11,579	4,015	1,869	4,946
9. Bank loans, n.e.c.	200	400	600	800	500	567	620
10. Other loans	184	712	1,305	3,049	5,284	3,530	2,177
11. Mortgages	2,606	4,059	8,310	17,985	14,584	15,525	17,661
12. Bonds and notes		47	256	1,704	1,536	702	403
13. Other liabilities	100	100	100	300	200	600	500
14. Total	4,530	8,485	18,084	41,845	29,354	29,990	31,798
IV. Equities	56,972	112,234	249,269	406,245	281,261	340,815	605,464
V. Total assets or liabilities and equities	61,502	120,719	267,353	448,090	310,615	370,805	637,259

Source: All data not specified below are from Goldsmith, *A Study of Saving*, Vol. III, lines of Table W-22 corresponding to those given here. All other "W" tables listed below are also from this source.

Line	
I-1	W-22, line I-1, minus our Table III-2a, line I-1.
3	W-22, line I-3, minus nonfarm unincorporated business residential land (see note to Table III-2a, line I-3).
7	W-22, line I-10, minus the sum of W-22, line I-9 and nonfarm unincorporated business residential property (see notes to lines I-1 and I-3 of this table).
II-1	W-18, sum of lines I-9, II-1, II-2, and II-3, minus our tables: III-2a, line II-1; III-3b, lines II-1 and II-2; III-4b, lines II-1 and II-2; III-5o, lines II-1 and II-2; III-6a, lines II-1 and II-2; III-7f, lines II-1 and II-2; III-1d, line II-2.
2	Sum of W-22, line II-3; Goldsmith, *Financial Intermediaries*, Table A-3.c, lines 6 and 12; and Goldsmith, *A Study of Saving*, Vol. I, Table L-9, column 10.
3	W-22, line II-4.
4	W-22, line II-5.
5	W-22, line II-6.
10	W-22, line II-7.
11	Our Table IV-b-11c, line 1.
11a	IV-b-11c-1, line 1.
11b	IV-b-11c-4, line 1.
12	W-22, line II-11.
13	IV-b-13d, line 1.
II-14	IV-b-14a, line 1.
15	IV-b-15a, line 1.
16, 17	IV-b-17b, line 1.
18	W-22, line II-18.
19	Sum of our Table III-2a, line IV, and W-37, line IV.
20	W-22, line II-21. Most of this line is foreign stocks and bonds, included in lines II-15, II-16, and II-17 in later years.
21	Sum of lines II-1 through II-20 of this table.
III-6	Sum of W-24, lines 1a and 1h, and W-22, line III-8; minus W-28, line 1, and our Tables III-3b, line III-6, and III-1d, line III-9.
8	W-22, line III-10.
9	Goldsmith, *Financial Intermediaries*, Table A-3.a, line 18.
10	W-22, lines III-7 and III-8, minus lines III-6 and III-9 of this table.
11	IV-c-11e, line 1.
12	W-22, line III-12.
13	W-22, line III-14.
14	Sum of lines III-6 through III-13 of this table.
IV	Line V minus line III-14 of this table.
V	Sum of lines I-7 and II-21 of this table.

[a] The 1945 figures in this table have been superseded by those in Table III-1; they are included here for comparability with earlier years.

TABLE III-2

Nonfarm Unincorporated Business, 1945-58

(billion dollars)

	1945	1946	1947	1948
I. Tangible assets				
1. Residential structures	9.18	10.26	11.89	12.95
2. Nonresidential structures	8.21	11.02	13.25	14.11
3. Land	8.17	11.01	12.81	14.09
4. Producer durables	5.31	6.88	9.21	11.35
6. Inventories	7.97	10.06	11.59	12.92
7. Total	38.84	49.23	58.75	65.42
II. Intangible assets				
1. Currency and demand deposits	8.93	8.94	9.30	9.15
a. Monetary metals	.13	.14	.15	.15
b. Other	8.80	8.80	9.15	9.00
6. Consumer credit	1.53	1.86	2.19	2.56
7. Trade credit	4.03	4.99	5.36	5.76
21. Total	14.49	15.79	16.85	17.47
III. Liabilities				
7. Trade debt	3.42	3.33	2.80	3.56
9. Bank loans, n.e.c.	3.15	4.60	6.82	6.12
10. Other loans	.88	1.22	1.68	2.33
11. Mortgages	4.45	4.97	5.56	6.16
14. Total	11.90	14.12	16.86	18.17
IV. Equities	41.43	50.90	58.74	64.72
V. Total assets or liabilities and equities	53.33	65.02	75.60	82.89

Line	
I-1 through I-7	From line 2 of Tables IV-a-1 through IV-a-7 respectively.
II-1	From Federal Reserve Board worksheets.
1a	Table IV-b-1a, line 2.
1b	Table IV-b-1b, line 2.
6	Table IV-b-6, line 2.
7	Table IV-b-7, line 2.
21	Sum of lines II-1 through II-7.

1949	1950	1951	1952	1953	1954	1955	1956	1957	1958	
										I.
12.79	14.07	14.46	14.71	14.91	14.83	15.30	15.80	15.99	16.26	1.
13.73	14.84	15.83	16.52	17.32	18.27	20.06	21.97	24.01	25.56	2.
13.89	15.67	16.95	17.10	17.51	18.30	19.89	20.99	22.25	22.74	3.
12.83	14.81	16.63	17.65	18.82	19.79	21.76	24.26	26.44	26.94	4.
11.97	14.24	15.07	14.79	15.21	15.06	15.81	16.51	16.82	16.81	6.
65.21	13.63	78.94	80.77	83.77	86.25	92.82	99.53	105.51	108.31	7.
										II.
9.52	9.74	10.78	10.43	10.38	10.91	11.20	11.55	12.36	13.46	1.
.16	.17	.19	.18	.19	.20	.21	.22	.25	.27	
9.36	9.57	10.59	10.25	10.19	10.71	10.99	11.33	12.11	13.19	
2.81	3.30	3.60	4.00	4.18	4.27	4.43	4.69	4.79	4.70	6.
5.82	7.04	7.26	8.37	8.95	9.15	9.68	10.57	10.85	11.64	7.
18.15	20.08	21.64	22.80	23.51	24.33	25.31	26.81	28.00	29.80	21.
										III.
3.78	4.52	3.83	4.14	5.24	6.56	7.16	8.10	8.78	9.00	7.
5.83	7.96	7.16	7.64	7.45	8.56	10.05	10.72	10.63	12.45	9.
2.42	2.78	3.28	3.59	3.69	3.87	4.88	4.97	5.30	5.42	10.
6.69	7.26	7.91	8.43	8.98	9.73	10.63	11.65	12.58	13.94	11.
18.72	22.52	22.18	23.80	25.36	28.72	32.72	35.44	37.29	40.81	14.
64.64	71.19	78.40	79.77	81.92	81.86	85.41	90.90	96.22	97.30	IV.
83.36	93.71	100.58	103.57	107.28	110.58	118.13	126.34	133.51	138.11	V.

Line

III-7 Table IV-c-7, line 2.
9 Table IV-c-9, line 2.
10 Table IV-c-10, line 2.
11 Table IV-c-11, line 2.
14 Sum of lines III-7 through III-11.

IV Line V minus line III-14.

V Line I-7 plus line II-21.

TABLE III-2a

Nonfarm Unincorporated Business, 1900-45, Selected Years

(million dollars)

	1900	1912	1922	1929	1933	1939	1945[a]
I. Tangible assets							
1. Residential structures	260	840	2,400	5,480	4,360	5,250	7,260
2. Nonresidential structures	2,228	3,843	8,215	11,241	9,799	11,453	15,018
3. Land	1,194	1,967	4,119	8,705	4,572	5,474	6,585
4. Producer durables	911	1,419	3,424	4,562	3,204	3,840	5,191
6. Inventories	2,649	3,115	6,679	6,426	3,092	4,145	7,829
7. Total	7,242	11,184	24,837	36,414	25,027	30,162	41,883
II. Intangible assets							
1. Currency and demand deposits	1,280	2,000	2,610	2,842	1,914	3,248	8,990
6. Consumer credit	202	491	694	1,280	740	1,168	1,046
7. Trade credit	1,828	1,889	2,878	2,946	1,818	2,602	4,030
12. Mortgages, farm	299	468	946	681	508	311	257
21. Total	3,609	4,848	7,128	7,749	4,980	7,329	14,323
III. Liabilities							
7. Trade debt	1,639	1,770	2,471	2,701	1,802	2,664	3,420
9. Bank loans, n.e.c.	1,609	2,821	4,657	4,734	2,230	1,716	2,719
11. Mortgages	1,081	1,928	3,948	7,697	6,169	4,544	4,313
12. Bonds and notes	6	41	242	1,696	1,774	660	407
14. Total	4,335	6,560	11,318	16,828	11,975	9,584	10,859
IV. Equities	6,516	9,472	20,647	27,335	18,032	27,907	45,347
V. Total assets or liabilities and equities	10,851	16,032	31,965	44,163	30,007	37,491	56,206

Notes to Table III-2a

Source: Goldsmith, *A Study of Saving*, Vol. III, Table W-29, plus additional sources listed below.

Line	
I-1	Raymond W. Goldsmith, *The National Wealth of the U.S. in the Postwar Period*, Princeton University Press for NBER, 1962, Table A-52, column 2.
3	Table W-29, line I-4, plus Goldsmith, *National Wealth*, Table A-52, column 4.
7	Table W-29, line I-10, plus Goldsmith, *National Wealth*, Table A-52, columns 2 and 4.
II-1	1900-12: Table W-29, line II-2. 1922-45: 58 per cent of Table W-29, line II-2. The original figures were based on old Federal Reserve Board estimates which have since been revised downward, as indicated.
7	48.8 per cent of Table W-29, line II-7. See note to line II-1.
21	Sum of lines II-1 through II-12 of this table.
III-7	44.4 per cent of Table W-29, line III-8. See note to line II-1.
11	Table IV-c-11e, line 2.
14	Sum of lines III-7 through III-12 of this table.
IV	Line V minus line III-14 of this table.
V	Sum of lines I-7 and II-21 of this table.

[a]The 1945 figures in this table have been superseded by those in Table III-2; they are included here for comparability with earlier years.

TABLE III-3

Agriculture, 1945-58

(billion dollars)

	1945	1946	1947	1948
I. Tangible assets				
1. Residential structures	9.22	11.00	13.08	13.63
2. Nonresidential structures	7.10	8.33	9.86	10.52
3. Land	43.47	46.53	49.78	51.93
4. Producer durables	5.79	6.55	8.39	10.69
5. Consumer durables	5.26	6.82	8.38	9.90
6. Inventories	15.68	19.10	22.50	22.20
7. Total	86.52	98.33	111.99	118.87
II. Intangible assets				
1. Currency and demand deposits	6.60	7.10	7.00	6.70
a. Monetary metals	.16	.17	.18	.18
b. Other	6.44	6.93	6.82	6.52
2. Other bank deposits and shares	1.98	2.18	2.10	2.10
3. Life insurance reserves, private	3.40	3.59	3.80	4.03
5. Pension and insurance funds, govt.	.48	.68	.77	.76
13. Securities, U.S. government	4.15	4.21	4.38	4.60
b. Savings bonds	4.15	4.21	4.38	4.60
20. Other intangible assets	1.38	1.54	1.71	1.88
21. Total	17.99	19.30	19.76	20.07
III. Liabilities				
6. Consumer debt	.35	.46	.56	.65
7. Trade debt	.70	.90	1.10	1.40
9. Bank loans, n.e.c.	1.04	1.29	1.59	1.95
10. Other loans	.80	.82	.85	.93
11. Mortgages	4.76	4.90	5.06	5.29
14. Total	7.65	8.37	9.16	10.22
IV. Equities	96.86	109.26	122.59	128.72
V. Total assets or liabilities and equities	104.51	117.63	131.75	138.94

Line

I-1 through I-7 From line 3 of Tables IV-a-1 through IV-a-7 respectively.

II-1 Board of Governors of the Federal Reserve System, *Flow of Funds/Saving Accounts, 1946-60, Supplement 5* (December 1961), p. 35.

1a Table IV-b-1a, line 3.

1b Table IV-b-1b, line 3.

2 Time deposits owned by farmers. Estimates in billions are published in U.S. Department of Agriculture, *The Balance Sheet of Agriculture*, various issues. Estimates in millions obtained directly from USDA.

3 Life insurance reserves (Table III-5h, line III-3) multiplied by the estimated ratio of farmers' equity to total policyholders' equity in life insurance companies. The ratio for 1945-49 is from R. W. Goldsmith, *A Study of Saving*, Vol. I, Table A-53, col. 4, divided by Table I-2, col. 8. From 1950-58 the ratio is assumed to decline one-tenth of one percentage point yearly from the 1949 level of .073.

5 Total equity in veterans' funds multiplied by estimated ratio of farmers' equity to total equity in veterans' funds. The 1943 ratio, 10% (See Goldsmith, *A Study of Saving*, Vol. I, p. 1036), was extrapolated by the ratio of farm population to total population. Population data from Bureau of the Census, *Statistical Abstract of the U.S.*, 1960, Table 822, p. 615. Total equity in veterans' funds from the following sources:
1945-49: Goldsmith, *A Study of Saving*, Vol. I, Table F-25, col. 11, p. 1033.

1949	1950	1951	1952	1953	1954	1955	1956	1957	1958	
										I.
13.75	14.91	16.07	16.58	16.88	17.26	17.92	18.53	18.79	19.28	1.
10.82	11.93	13.18	13.76	14.07	14.43	15.09	15.84	16.40	16.75	2.
50.90	58.40	66.31	66.89	64.22	66.41	68.94	73.96	79.94	87.58	3.
12.47	14.09	15.68	16.41	16.64	16.86	17.23	17.64	18.01	18.59	4.
10.51	12.41	13.60	13.65	14.20	13.90	13.85	13.95	14.00	14.02	5.
18.93	24.37	28.14	23.15	18.91	18.75	17.38	18.23	20.57	26.15	6.
117.38	136.11	152.98	150.45	144.92	147.61	150.41	158.15	167.71	182.37	7.
										II.
6.30	6.30	6.50	6.40	6.30	6.20	6.20	6.00	5.90	6.20	1.
.19	.18	.20	.20	.19	.19	.20	.21	.24	.25	
6.11	6.12	6.30	6.20	6.11	6.01	6.00	5.79	5.66	5.95	
2.10	2.10	2.17	2.30	2.43	2.53	2.58	2.63	2.90	3.07	2.
4.27	4.51	4.75	5.03	5.30	5.62	5.92	6.18	6.42	6.71	3.
.81	.56	.52	.51	.47	.45	.45	.45	.44	.43	5.
4.72	4.69	4.71	4.63	4.73	4.97	5.17	5.06	5.12	5.21	13.
4.72	4.69	4.71	4.63	4.73	4.97	5.17	5.06	5.12	5.21	
2.06	2.28	2.48	2.72	2.87	3.11	3.25	3.42	3.59	3.81	20.
20.26	20.44	21.13	21.59	22.10	22.88	23.57	23.74	24.37	25.43	21.
										III.
.64	.83	.82	.91	.90	.99	1.18	1.17	1.15	1.33	6.
1.60	1.80	2.20	2.30	2.10	2.10	2.10	2.10	2.20	2.30	7.
2.05	2.52	3.12	3.19	2.76	2.93	3.31	3.28	3.60	4.16	9.
.96	1.02	1.13	1.21	1.19	1.29	1.34	1.42	1.64	1.87	10.
5.58	6.12	6.68	7.26	7.77	8.29	9.07	9.91	10.51	11.25	11.
10.83	12.29	13.95	14.87	14.72	15.60	17.00	17.88	19.10	20.91	14.
126.81	144.26	160.16	157.17	152.30	154.89	156.98	164.01	172.98	186.89	IV.
137.64	156.55	174.11	172.04	167.02	170.49	173.98	181.89	192.08	207.80	V.

Line

II-5 1950-58: Sum of special issues of federal obligations held by the Government Life Insurance Fund, the National Service Life Insurance Fund, the Adjusted Service Certificate Fund, and the cash balance of the National Service Life Insurance Fund. For all, except the last, the sources are: 1950-52—*Treasury Bulletin*, e.g., December 1953, p. 11; and 1953-58—*Daily Treasury Statement*, e.g., December 31, 1958, p. 5. The cash balance of the National Service Life Insurance Fund is from *Treasury Bulletin*, e.g., August 1951, p. 11 (item on unexpended balance).

13 Estimates in billions are published in *Balance Sheet of Agriculture*, 1960, Table 22, p. 28. Estimates in millions obtained directly from USDA.

13b Same as line 13.

20 Same as line 13 (equity in farm cooperatives).

21 Sum of lines II-1 through II-20.

III-6 Table IV-c-6, line 3.

7 Farm business trade debt from FRB, *Flow of Funds/Saving Accounts, 1946-60, Supplement 5*, December 1961, p. 35.

9 1945-46: Bank loans to farms, excluding loans guaranteed by the Commodity Credit Corporation, from *Annual Report of the Comptroller of the Currency*, e.g., 1945, p. 117.

1947-58: Total loans by commercial banks to farms, from *Federal Reserve Bulletin*, e.g., June 1955, p. 668, plus loans to farms by mutual savings banks, from *Annual Report of the Comptroller of the Currency*, e.g., 1949, p. 154, minus CCC guaranteed loans to farms by commercial banks, from *ibid.*, e.g., 1955, p. 173.

(Notes continued on following page)

TABLE III-3a

Agricultural Cooperatives, 1945-59

(million dollars)

	1945	1946	1947	1948	1949
I. Tangible assets					
7. Total	1306	1546	1986	2452	2709
II. Intangible assets					
1. Currency and demand deposits	206	242	318	386	381
2. Other bank deposits and shares	9	12	16	21	28
7. Trade credit	209	244	321	386	373
13. Securities, U.S. government	64	78	105	132	146
20. Other intangible assets	200	226	284	329	318
21. Total	688	802	1044	1254	1246
III. Liabilities					
7. Trade debt	246	274	340	385	347
9. Bank loans, n.e.c.	10	11	9	6	2
10. Other loans	602	781	1223	1688	1850
13. Other liabilities	138	156	201	237	229
14. Total	996	1222	1773	2316	2428
IV. Equities	998	1126	1257	1390	1527
V. Total assets or liabilities and equities	1994	2348	3030	3706	3955

Sum of Tables III-3a-1 through III-3a-3.

Notes to Table III-3 (*concluded*)

Line

III-10 Sum of loans to farmers by:
Life insurance companies (Table III-5h, line II-10, multiplied by the estimated ratio of farmers' equity to total policyholders' equity in life insurance companies. See note to line II-3 above for source of ratio);
Federal Land Banks (from Farm Credit Administration, *Combined Statements of the Federal Land Banks*—various issues. Item includes loans in the process of closing and loans called for foreclosure, judgment, etc.);
The Farmers Home Administration (from *Agricultural Finance Review*, e.g., Vol. 22, September 1960, Table 16, p. 140. Item includes operating and emergency loans and emergency crop and feed loans);
Production credit associations and livestock loan companies (Table III-5m-4, line II-10).

11 Table IV-b-12, line 8.

14 Sum of lines III-6 through III-11.

IV Line V minus line III-14.

V Sum of lines I-7 and II-21.

1950	1951	1952	1953	1954	1955	1956	1957	1958	1959	
										I.
2997	3375	3704	4106	4328	4579	4730	4830	5101	5301	7.
										II.
399	451	493	560	586	626	636	633	675	685	1.
33	37	41	47	53	61	69	77	85	94	2.
386	437	478	542	563	597	598	585	622	622	7.
162	184	201	230	248	274	296	315	343	364	13.
320	343	352	372	395	426	446	460	498	513	20.
1300	1452	1565	1751	1845	1984	2045	2070	2223	2278	21.
										III.
332	345	340	342	311	289	245	239	254	254	7.
4	12	26	555	615	90	105	106	103	113	9.
2033	2378	2649	2582	2684	3504	3638	3634	3880	3930	10.
226	230	219	222	203	200	173	179	191	196	13.
2595	2965	3234	3701	3813	4083	4161	4158	4428	4493	14.
1702	1862	2035	2156	2360	2480	2614	2742	2896	3086	IV.
4297	4827	5269	5857	6173	6563	6775	6900	7324	7579	V.

TABLE III-3a-1

Cooperatives for Purchase, Supply, and Related Services, 1945-59

(million dollars)

	1945	1946	1947	1948	1949
I. Tangible assets					
2. Nonresidential structures	318	385	522	649	646
6. Inventories	296	344	450	540	519
7. Total	614	729	972	1189	1165
II. Intangible assets					
1. Currency and demand deposits	196	229	301	362	350
7. Trade credit	209	244	321	386	373
13. Securities, U.S. government	41	48	63	76	73
20. Other intangible assets	179	199	246	277	252
21. Total	625	720	931	1101	1048
III. Liabilities					
7. Trade debt	246	274	340	385	347
9. Bank loans, n.e.c.					
10. Other loans	158	213	452	657	526
13. Other liabilities	136	151	188	213	192
14. Total	540	638	980	1255	1065
IV. Equities	699	811	923	1035	1148
V. Total assets or liabilities and equities	1239	1449	1903	2290	2213

Line

I-2 Estimated from line V using proportions calculated as follows:
1945: Fred Koller, *Financing of Farmers' Cooperatives* (unpublished manuscript, Financial Research Program, NBER, 1950), ratio of net fixed assets to total assets.
1953: U.S. Treasury Department, Internal Revenue Service, *Farmers' Cooperative Income Tax Returns for 1953*, p. 8, ratio of net capital assets plus land to total assets.
Straight-line interpolation of proportions was used between the benchmark years, and the 1953 proportion was carried forward to 1958.

6 See line I-2 above.

7 Sum of lines I-2 and I-6.

II-1 Same proportion of total assets as in Koller, *Financing of Farmers' Cooperatives.*

7 See line II-1 above.

13 See line II-1 above.

20 Line II-21 minus lines II-1, II-7 and II-13.

21 Line V minus line I-7.

III-7 Same proportion of line V minus lines III-9, III-10, and IV as in 1945. Trade debt for 1945 derived by multiplying Koller's "accounts payable, general" and "accounts payable, patrons" by ratio of 1945 equity to Koller's equity figure.

9 Loans guaranteed, but not held by Commodity Credit Corporation. Data obtained directly from the Agricultural Stabilization and Conservation Service, Fiscal Division.

10 Sum of loans from Banks for Cooperatives and loans held by CCC, from *Agricultural Finance Review*, Vol. 22, September 1960, p. 149. (The FRB considers all CCC held and guaranteed loans to be liabilities of the federal government, except CCC loans to tobacco cooperatives, which are considered liabilities of the nonfarm, noncorporate business sector.)

13 Line III-14 minus lines III-7, III-9, and III-10.

14 Line V minus line IV.

1950	1951	1952	1953	1954	1955	1956	1957	1958	1959	
										I.
689	803	903	1053	1094	1159	1162	1136	1208	1208	2.
534	602	656	740	769	815	816	798	848	849	6.
1223	1405	1559	1793	1863	1974	1978	1934	2056	2057	7.
										II.
362	410	448	508	528	559	561	548	582	583	1.
386	437	478	542	563	597	598	585	622	622	7.
76	86	94	107	111	117	118	115	122	122	13.
241	254	254	263	274	290	292	286	304	304	20.
1065	1187	1274	1420	1476	1563	1569	1534	1630	1631	21.
										III.
332	345	340	342	311	289	245	239	254	254	7.
			512	543						9.
474	627	735	515	505	1229	1262	1138	1267	1180	10.
184	190	188	189	172	159	135	132	141	141	13.
990	1162	1263	1558	1531	1677	1642	1509	1662	1575	14.
1298	1430	1570	1655	1808	1860	1905	1959	2024	2113	IV.
2288	2592	2833	3213	3339	3537	3547	3468	3686	3688	V.

Line

IV Sum of farmers' financial interest in marketing and purchasing cooperatives. Estimates in billions published in various issues of *The Balance Sheet of Agriculture*. Estimates in millions obtained directly from U.S. Department of Agriculture.

V Estimated from sum of lines III-9, III-10, and IV, using proportions computed as follows:
1945: Total assets derived by multiplying Koller's figure for total assets by the ratio of 1945 equity to Koller's equity figure.
1954: Total assets, consolidated, from the Farmer Cooperative Service, *Methods of Financing Farmer Cooperatives*, General Report #32, pp. 3 and 8. (Total assets, combined, minus combined equity, plus consolidated equity, equals consolidated assets.)
1956: Total assets, consolidated, from Farmer Cooperative Service, *News for Farmer Cooperatives*, April 1959, pp. 6 and 18.
Straight-line interpolation of ratios was used between the benchmark years, and the 1956 ratio was carried forward to 1958.

TABLE III-3a-2

Rural Electric Cooperatives and Farmers' Mutual Telephone Companies, 1945-59
(million dollars)

	1945	1946	1947	1948	1949
I. Tangible assets					
7. Total	402	515	701	939	1209
II. Intangible assets					
1. Currency and demand deposits	10	13	17	24	31
2. Other bank deposits and shares	9	12	16	21	28
13. Securities, U.S. government	23	30	42	56	73
20. Other intangible assets	21	27	38	52	66
21. Total	63	82	113	153	198
III. Liabilities					
9. Bank loans, n.e.c.	10	11	9	6	2
10. Other loans	391	510	709	964	1253
13. Other liabilities	2	5	13	24	37
14. Total	403	526	731	994	1292
IV. Equities	62	71	83	98	115
V. Total assets or liabilities and equities	465	597	814	1092	1407

Line

I-7 Sum of tangible assets for farmers' mutual telephone companies and rural electric cooperatives.
Telephone: Same as total assets for telephone cooperatives.
Electric: 1945-51: Same proportion of total assets of electric cooperatives as in 1952.
1952-59: *Annual Statistical Report*, Rural Electrification Administration (REA), U.S. Department of Agriculture, e.g., 1956, p. XVI.

II-1 1945-51: Same proportion of total assets of electric cooperatives as in 1952.
1952-59: Estimated by assuming, for cooperative borrowers, the same ratio of cash to investments and special funds plus current and accrued assets less reserves (REA, *Annual Statistical Reports*) as for all borrowers in 1958. Cash and demand deposit holdings, for all borrowers, 1958, in U.S. Congress, House of Representatives, *Hearing Before the Subcommittee of the House Committee of Appropriations*, March 7, 1960, p. 398.

2 Same method as for line II-1 above. Item includes savings and loan associations, savings accounts certificates of deposit, and time deposits.

13 See line II-1 above.

20 Line II-21 minus lines II-1, II-2, and II-13.

21 Line V minus line I-7.

TABLE III-3a-3

Farmers' Mutual Irrigation Companies, 1945-59 (million dollars)

	1945	1946	1947	1948	1949
I. Tangible assets					
7. Total	290	302	313	324	335
II. Intangible assets					
III. Liabilities					
10. Other loans	53	58	62	67	71
14. Total	53	58	62	67	71
IV. Equities	237	244	251	257	264
V. Total assets or liabilities and equities	290	302	313	324	335

Line

I-7 Same as line V.

III-10 Same as line III-14.

14 1939 and 1949: Sum of total indebtedness of unincorporated and incorporated mutual enterprises (1950 *Census of Agriculture*, Vol. III, p. 95).
1945-48: Obtained by straight-line interpolation.
1950-59: Same rate of increase as for 1939-49.

1950	1951	1952	1953	1954	1955	1956	1957	1958	1959	
										I.
1428	1613	1777	1933	2074	2193	2320	2450	2579	2759	7.
										II.
37	41	45	52	58	67	75	85	93	102	1.
33	37	41	47	53	61	69	77	85	94	2.
86	98	107	123	137	157	178	200	221	242	13.
79	89	98	109	121	136	154	174	194	209	20.
235	265	291	331	369	421	476	536	593	647	21.
										III.
4	12	26	43	72	90	105	106	103	113	9.
1484	1671	1830	1978	2086	2178	2274	2390	2502	2635	10.
42	40	31	33	31	41	38	47	50	55	13.
1530	1723	1887	2054	2189	2309	2417	2543	2655	2803	14.
133	155	181	210	254	305	379	443	517	603	IV.
1663	1878	2068	2264	2443	2614	2796	2986	3172	3406	V.

Line

III-9 Long-term debt, electric cooperatives (see line I-7 above), minus other loans, electric cooperatives.

10 Sum of REA electrification and telephone loans, *Agricultural Finance Review*, Vol. 22, September 1960, p. 149.

13 Line III-14 minus lines III-9 and III-10.

14 Line V minus line IV.

IV Farmers' financial interest in rural electric cooperatives and farmers' mutual telephone companies. Estimates in billions published in various issues of *The Balance Sheet of Agriculture*. Estimates in millions obtained directly from U.S. Department of Agriculture.

V Sum of total assets for farmers' mutual telephone companies and rural electric cooperatives.
Telephone: Sum of equities and REA loans to telephone cooperatives.
Electric: 1945-51: Same ratio to sum of equities and REA loans to electric cooperatives, as in 1952.
1952-59: REA, *Annual Statistical Reports*.

1950	1951	1952	1953	1954	1955	1956	1957	1958	1959	
										I.
346	357	368	380	391	412	432	446	466	485	7.
										II.
										III.
75	80	84	89	93	97	102	106	111	115	10.
75	80	84	89	93	97	102	106	111	115	14.
271	277	284	291	298	315	330	340	355	370	IV.
346	357	368	380	391	412	432	446	466	485	V.

Line

IV Farmers' financial interest in mutual irrigation companies. Data in billions published in various issues of *The Balance Sheet of Agriculture*. Estimates in millions obtained directly from U.S. Department of Agriculture.

V Sum of lines III-14 and IV.

TABLE III-3b

Agriculture, 1900-45, Selected Years

(million dollars)

	1900	1912	1922	1929	1933	1939	1945[a]
I. Tangible assets							
1. Residential structures	1,692	2,919	6,569	6,377	4,634	4,906	8,975
2. Nonresidential structures	1,570	2,717	5,822	5,855	4,047	4,092	6,755
3. Land	14,546	31,574	41,541	34,930	22,800	23,237	44,508
4. Producer durables	1,170	2,240	3,266	3,871	2,572	3,509	6,272
5. Consumer durables	831	1,863	3,705	3,806	1,954	2,550	4,238
6. Inventories	4,537	8,236	8,454	9,487	4,946	7,304	15,374
7. Total	24,346	49,549	69,357	64,326	40,953	45,598	86,122
II. Intangible assets							
1. Currency and demand deposits	657	993	1,962	1,782	1,199	2,000	6,600
a. Monetary metals	160	152	117	96	73	91	179
b. Other	497	841	1,845	1,686	1,126	1,909	6,421
2. Other bank deposits and shares	115	573	1,377	1,726	1,177	1,200	1,980
3. Life insurance reserves, private	179	470	931	1,651	1,963	2,599	3,490
5. Pension and insurance funds, govt.			11	114	234	110	519
12. Mortgages, farm	140	219	910	318	237	145	120
13. Securities, U.S. government			450			249	4,150
20. Other intangible assets	80	160	410	600	600	826	1,333
21. Total	1,171	2,415	6,051	6,191	5,410	7,129	18,192
III. Liabilities							
6. Consumer debt	53	144	167	462	198	417	339
7. Trade debt	425	1,312	2,797	1,691	786	763	625
9. Bank loans, n.e.c.	488	1,520	3,088	2,491	913	900	1,034
10. Other loans	10	64	173	310	840	924	873
11. Mortgages	2,312	4,348	10,786	9,631	7,685	6,586	4,760
13. Other liabilities	100	100					
14. Total	3,388	7,488	17,011	14,585	10,422	9,590	7,631
IV. Equities	22,129	44,476	58,397	55,932	35,941	43,137	96,683
V. Total assets or liabilities and equities	25,517	51,964	75,408	70,517	46,363	52,727	104,314

Notes to Table III-3b

Source: Goldsmith, *A Study of Saving*, Volume III, Table W-27, plus other sources specified below.

Line	
I-7	Table W-27, line I-10 minus line I-9.
II-1	Table W-27, sum of lines I-9, II-1, and II-2 minus line II-2 of this table. For 1939 and 1945, revised *Balance Sheet of Agriculture* and unpublished U.S. Department of Agriculture data have been substituted.
2	Goldsmith, *A Study of Saving*, Vol. I, sum of Tables L-6, column 7 and L-9, column 9. For 1939 and 1945, revised *Balance Sheet of Agriculture* and unpublished USDA data have been substituted.
13	For 1945, revised figure from Table III-3 is used.
20	Table W-27, sum of lines II-18 and II-19.
21	1900-33: Table W-27, sum of lines I-9 and II-22, minus line II-21. 1939, 1945: Sum of lines II-1 through II-20 of this table.
III-6	Goldsmith, *A Study of Saving*, Vol. III, Table W-28, line 2.
7	*Ibid.*, line 6.
9	*Ibid.*, line 1.
10	*Ibid.*, sum of lines 3, 4, and 5.
11	Table W-27, line III-11, corrected, for 1945, from *Agricultural Finance Review*, Vol. 23, April 1962, p. 59.
13	Goldsmith, *A Study of Saving*, Vol. III, Table W-17, column 6. Other liabilities of farm cooperatives have been removed here for comparability with later years.
14	Sum of lines III-6 through III-13. All liabilities of cooperatives and tax accruals have been removed for comparability with later years.
IV	Line V minus line III-14.
V	1900-33: Table W-27, line V minus line II-21. 1939, 1945: Sum of lines II-7 and II-21 of this table.

[a]The 1945 figures in this table have been superseded by those in Table III-3; they are included here for comparability with earlier years.

TABLE III-4

Nonfinancial Corporations, 1945 – 58

(billion dollars)

	1945	1946	1947	1948
I. Tangible assets				
1. Residential structures	8.09	9.34	11.13	12.33
2. Nonresidential structures	54.44	68.99	80.74	89.30
3. Land	20.03	24.99	31.16	37.06
4. Producer durables	33.94	41.55	52.58	61.95
6. Inventories	26.31	37.52	44.67	48.88
7. Total	142.81	182.40	220.28	249.52
II. Intangible assets				
1. Currency and demand deposits	19.68	20.82	23.02	23.22
a. Monetary metals	.09	.10	.10	.12
b. Other	19.59	20.72	22.92	23.10
2. Other bank deposits and shares	.90	.90	.90	.90
6. Consumer credit	1.66	2.23	2.87	3.41
7. Trade credit	22.73	25.92	31.78	34.12
13. Securities, U.S. government	20.72	15.02	13.82	14.62
a. Short-term	17.00	11.90	11.00	11.90
b. Savings bonds	1.60	1.60	1.60	1.80
c. Other long-term	2.12	1.52	1.22	.92
14. Securities, state and local	.32	.32	.36	.41
15. Securities, other bonds and notes	.18	.22	.34	.48
16. Securities, preferred stock	3.47	3.48	3.49	3.50
17. Securities, common stock	24.20	21.67	21.26	21.39
20. Other intangible assets	14.36	13.90	15.77	16.70
21. Total	108.22	104.48	113.61	118.75
III. Liabilities				
7. Trade debt	19.72	23.45	28.09	28.53
8. Loans on securities	1.40	.49	.16	
9. Bank loans, n.e.c.	6.42	9.40	11.06	12.12
10. Other loans	.81	.82	.96	1.13
11. Mortgages	7.87	9.19	10.66	11.97
12. Bonds and notes	23.60	24.48	27.32	31.55
13. Other liabilities	28.42	28.84	31.58	33.35
14. Total	88.24	96.67	109.83	118.65
IV. Equities	162.79	190.21	224.06	249.62
V. Total assets or liabilities and equities	251.03	286.88	333.89	368.27

Notes to Table III-4 are on page 144.

Table 3

1949	1950	1951	1952	1953	1954	1955	1956	1957	1958	
										I.
12.48	14.26	15.17	15.87	16.52	16.97	18.18	19.43	20.30	21.31	1.
89.02	101.29	109.79	116.34	124.27	129.36	139.91	151.15	172.06	180.83	2.
36.40	41.24	46.26	47.05	47.88	50.04	54.89	57.99	62.98	63.46	3.
67.94	77.08	86.80	92.95	99.87	106.85	110.96	128.05	140.43	145.53	4.
45.30	55.08	64.83	66.07	67.88	66.28	72.95	80.52	83.24	78.81	6.
251.14	288.96	322.85	338.28	356.42	369.50	396.89	437.14	479.01	489.94	7.
										II.
24.29	25.60	27.42	28.22	28.14	30.50	31.48	31.62	31.62	33.34	1.
.12	.13	.14	.15	.15	.15	.16	.17	.19	.21	
24.17	25.47	27.28	28.07	27.99	30.35	31.32	31.45	31.43	33.13	
.90	.90	.90	.90	.90	1.10	1.00	1.00	1.00	1.60	2.
3.85	4.63	5.14	5.90	6.14	6.41	7.07	7.48	7.69	8.21	6.
33.18	44.62	48.03	51.56	50.75	55.06	65.92	72.98	75.70	83.37	7.
16.54	19.41	20.34	19.54	21.12	18.83	22.82	18.23	17.43	17.62	13.
14.20	17.20	17.50	16.40	18.20	15.60	18.60	14.90	14.50	15.20	
1.80	1.80	1.80	1.80	1.80	1.80	1.80	1.60	1.40	1.22	
.54	.41	1.04	1.34	1.12	1.43	2.42	1.73	1.53	1.20	
.46	.53	.58	.64	.73	1.06	1.24	1.35	1.50	1.63	14.
.62	.65	.95	1.36	1.54	1.47	1.88	2.11	2.94	2.68	15.
3.50	3.51	3.51	3.52	3.52	3.53	3.54	3.54	3.55	3.55	16.
24.20	29.67	33.65	36.11	35.46	49.13	60.09	62.54	56.12	75.45	17.
17.56	18.12	19.14	22.12	24.75	29.68	34.51	40.50	47.14	48.14	20.
125.10	147.64	159.66	169.87	173.05	196.77	229.55	241.35	244.69	275.59	21.
										III.
27.19	35.20	37.48	41.07	41.23	44.63	54.87	60.48	62.50	68.78	7.
										8.
10.19	12.34	17.30	18.49	18.33	17.11	19.38	24.76	26.82	25.94	9.
1.21	1.34	1.49	1.58	1.92	1.65	2.11	1.96	2.33	2.18	10.
13.37	15.18	16.63	17.92	19.11	20.87	22.88	24.75	26.48	29.67	11.
34.45	36.06	39.36	44.08	47.43	50.97	53.74	57.41	63.76	69.68	12.
32.69	40.06	47.00	45.60	47.83	48.14	54.70	58.09	60.65	60.84	13.
119.10	140.18	159.26	168.74	175.85	183.37	207.68	227.45	242.54	257.09	14.
257.14	296.42	323.25	339.41	353.62	372.90	418.76	451.04	481.16	508.44	IV.
376.24	436.60	482.51	508.15	529.47	566.27	626.44	678.49	723.70	765.53	V.

Source: Raymond W. Goldsmith, Robert E. Lipsey, and Morris Mendelson, _Studies in the National Balance Sheet of the United States_, National Bureau of Economic Research Studies in Capital Formation and Financing, Vol. II (Princeton: Princeton University Press, 1963), p. 140.

TABLE III-4a

Real Estate Corporations, 1945-58

(million dollars)

	1945	1946	1947	1948
I. Tangible assets				
1. Residential structures 2. Nonresidential structures 3. Land 4. Producer durables 5. Consumer durables	13,363	16,561	17,364	19,213
6. Inventories	36	44	32	
7. Total	13,399	16,605	17,396	19,213
II. Intangible assets				
1. Currency and demand deposits	750	884	904	933
a. Monetary metals				
b. Other	750	884	904	933
6. Consumer credit	445	529	598	682
7. Trade credit	444	529	597	682
11. Mortgages, nonfarm				
13. Securities, U.S. government	350	333	300	317
14. Securities, state and local	95	91	81	86
17. Securities, common stock	1,692	1,963	2,024	2,395
20. Other intangible assets	423	494	512	542
21. Total	4,199	4,823	5,016	5,637
III. Liabilities				
7. Trade debt	798	894	990	1,096
9. Bank loans, n.e.c.	291	384	560	606
11. Mortgages	6,719	7,419	7,411	8,319
12. Bonds and notes	2,348	2,293	2,208	2,222
13. Other liabilities	1,072	1,227	1,288	1,241
14. Total	11,228	12,217	12,457	13,484
IV. Equities	6,370	9,211	9,955	11,366
V. Total assets or liabilities and equities	17,598	21,428	22,412	24,850

Notes to Table III-4a are on page 145.

1949	1950	1951	1952	1953	1954	1955	1956	1957	1958	
										I.
19,666	22,700	24,499	26,246	24,395	26,109	26,531	29,199	32,279	33,550	{ 1. 2. 3. 4. 5.
		1	2	2	30	27	35	80	62	6.
19,666	22,700	24,500	26,248	24,397	26,139	26,558	29,234	32,359	33,612	7.
										II.
1,017	1,164	1,216	1,286	1,333	1,582	1,790	1,930	1,859	2,125	1.
1,017	1,164	1,216	1,286	1,333	1,582	1,790	1,930	1,859	2,125	
758	910	914	1,018	1,070	1,271	1,563	1,765	1,922	2,123	6.
757	910	914	1,017	1,070	1,271	1,562	1,765	1,922	2,123	7.
								550	801	11.
342	344	365	360	344	296	363	318	352	367	13.
93	93	99	98	93	81	112	156	98	161	14.
2,666	3,073	2,966	4,635	5,064	5,809	7,430	7,682	7,054	7,498	17.
573	703	647	715	919	1,015	1,098	1,399	1,429	1,409	20.
6,206	7,197	7,121	9,129	9,893	11,325	13,918	15,015	15,186	16,607	21.
										III.
1,128	1,377	1,351	1,267	1,287	1,551	1,957	2,338	2,543	2,885	7.
559	636	683	650	677	1,188	1,662	1,970	2,037	2,385	9.
9,518	10,768	11,627	12,537	13,545	14,027	14,949	16,186	18,021	19,413	11.
2,108	2,167	2,154	2,042	1,966	2,761	3,133	3,407	3,173	3,593	12.
1,252	1,364	1,501	1,568	1,720	2,031	2,454	2,736	2,769	3,118	13.
14,565	16,312	17,316	18,064	19,195	21,558	24,155	26,637	28,543	31,394	14.
11,307	13,585	14,305	17,313	15,095	15,906	16,321	17,612	19,002	18,825	IV.
25,872	29,897	31,621	35,377	34,290	37,464	40,476	44,249	47,545	50,219	V.

Notes to Table III-4

Line	
I-1 through I-7	From line 4 of Tables IV-a-1 through IV-a-7 respectively.
II-1	David Meiselman and Eli Shapiro, "Corporate Sources and Uses of Funds" (in preparation), Table C-1a, line 1, minus: "Rest of the world" deposit liability to corporate business (FRB worksheets); line II-2 of this table; and line II-1 of Table III-51.
1a	Table IV-b-1a, line 4.
1b	Line II-1 minus line II-1a.
2	FRB, *Flow of Funds/Saving Accounts, 1946-1960, Supplement 5,* December 1961, p. 35.
6	Table IV-b-6, line 4.
7	Meiselman and Shapiro, "Corporate Sources," Table C-1a, line 3, minus line II-6 of this table and lines II-6, II-7, and II-10 of Table III-51.
13	*Ibid.*, Table C-1a, line 2, minus nonguaranteed government bonds held by corporations (from F[illegible] worksheets).
13a	Table IV-b-13a, line 4.
13b	Table IV-b-13b, line 4.
13c	Table IV-b-13c, line 4.
14	Meiselman and Shapiro, "Corporate Sources," Table C-1a, line 10.
15	Nonguaranteed U.S. Government bonds held by corporations (from FRB worksheets), plus commercial paper held outside banks (Table III-51-a, col. 4, col. 8 and col. 11).
16	$3,500 million in 1949 (R. W. Goldsmith, *Financial Intermediaries*, Appendix F Supplement, Table F-5, line 3 minus line 31) cumulated by assuming that 1 per cent of net new issues (see notes to Table IV-b-16), were purchased by nonfinancial corporations.
17	1945 and 1949: Goldsmith, *Financial Intermediaries*, Appendix F (Supplement), Table F-4, line 2 minus line 17. 1946-48: Interpolated by estimates derived from 1945, using method described for 1950-58. 1950-58: 1949 figure extrapolated to 1958 by cumulating net purchases of stock and capital gains. Net purchases are assumed to be 5 per cent of net new issues of domestic common stock (Table IV-b-17a, line 10). Capital gains for each year consist of two parts; gains on stock held at the beginning of the year and gains on stock purchased during the year. The former are estimated by taking the previous end-of-year holdings and multiplying by the change in stock prices during the year (Table IV-b-17a, line 13). The latter are estimated by multiplying purchases by the ratio of end-of-year prices to average prices during the year (Table IV-b-17a, line 15).
20	Line II-21 minus sum of lines II-1 through II-17.
21	Meiselman and Shapiro, "Corporate Sources," Table C-1a, lines 11 through 13, and line 19, minus line 8 and minus line II-21 of Table III-51. Capital gains included in line II-17 of this table were added to this total because the Meiselman and Shapiro balance sheet includes stock only at book value. Capital gains were estimated as the difference between line II-17 and the cumulation from 1945 of purchases at original cost (see note to line II-17).
III-7	Table IV-c-7, line 4.
8	FRB worksheets.
9	Meiselman and Shapiro, "Corporate Sources," Table C-1b, sum of lines 2 and 11, minus line III-9 of Table III-51 and minus loans to corporations by mutual savings banks (estimated as 20% of total commercial and industrial loans, from *Annual Report of the Comptroller of the Currency*, e.g., 1955, Table 42, p. 202).
10	Federal government loans to corporate business (FRB worksheets) plus one half of line II-10 of Table III-51, and plus loans to corporations by mutual savings banks (see note to line III-9 above).
11	Table IV-c-11, line 4.
12	Table IV-c-12, line 4.
13	Line III-14 minus the sum of lines III-7 through III-12.
14	Liabilities of nonfinancial corporations (Meiselman and Shapiro, "Corporate Sources," Table C-1b, sum of lines 9, 10 and 15) less finance company liabilities (Table III-51, line III-14).
IV	Line V minus line III-14.
V	Line I-7 plus line II-21.

Notes to Table III-4a

Source: Except as noted below, data are from various issues of *Statistics of Income*: part 2, U.S. Treasury Department, Internal Revenue Service. Balance sheet data were raised by the ratio of compiled receipts for all corporate returns to compiled receipts for all corporate returns with balance sheets.

Line	
I-1	Estimated from total corporate tangibles (other than inventories) in Goldsmith, *National Wealth*, Table A-54, by using proportion for book values of tangibles from *Statistics of Income*.
II-6, 7	Each estimated to be one half of "notes and accounts receivable."
13, 14	1954-58: Holdings of "government obligations not stated" allocated between U.S. obligations and "states, territories, and U.S. possessions" by the proportion for those stated. 1945-53: The 1954 ratio of U.S. obligations to total government obligations was extrapolated back by the ratio for all corporations. (Table III-4).
17	*Statistics of Income* category, "other investments."
III-9	Long-term plus short-term bank debt. Long-term bank debt was estimated by interpolating and extrapolating the 1955 and 1957 estimates from the Federal Reserve Board Commercial Loan Survey (*Federal Reserve Bulletin*, April 1959, pp. 354, 356, 365) by long-term bank debt of trade-service corporations (Meiselman and Shapiro, "Corporate Sources," Table C-6b, line 11). Short-term bank debt was estimated by interpolating and extrapolating 1955 and 1957 estimates from the Federal Reserve Board Commercial Loan Survey (*Federal Reserve Bulletin*, April 1959) by *Statistics of Income* category "bonds and notes payable, maturity less than one year."
11	*Statistics of Income*, item: "bonds and notes payable, maturity one year or more," minus long-term bank debt (see note to line III-9) and minus estimate of real estate bonds (Leo Grebler, David M. Blank, and Louis Winnick, *Capital Formation in Residential Real Estate*, Princeton University Press for NBER, 1956, page 446). The figures were continued to 1958 by the same method.
12	*Statistics of Income*, item: "bonds and notes payable, maturity less than one year" minus short-term bank debt (see note to line III-9) plus real estate bonds (see note to line III-11).
IV	Line V minus line III-14.
V	Line I-7 plus line II-21.

TABLE III-4b

Nonfinancial Corporations, 1900-45, Selected Years (million dollars)

	1900	1912	1922	1929	1933	1939	1945[a]
I. Tangible assets							
1. Residential structures; 2. Nonresidential structures; 3. Land; 4. Producer durables	18,297	35,650	74,706	99,293	75,322	83,580	110,255
6. Inventories	2,757	5,304	17,347	22,001	13,796	17,999	26,317
7. Total	21,054	40,954	92,053	121,294	89,118	101,579	136,572
II. Intangible assets							
1. Currency and demand deposits	1,980	3,900	5,587	7,449	5,599	8,698	20,353
a. Monetary metals	64	91	57	71	33	74	48
b. Other	1,916	3,809	5,530	7,378	5,566	8,624	20,305
2. Other bank deposits and shares	120	350	700	1,410	1,010	700	700
6. Consumer credit	580	1,962	4,040	3,979	1,938	2,966	2,412
7. Trade credit	3,900	6,208	12,027	21,861	15,915	11,067	19,464
8. Loans on securities			450	2,000			
13. Securities, U.S. government			3,563	3,158	2,837	1,776	17,442
14. Securities, state and local	50	100	337	644	607	379	278
15. Securities, other bonds and notes				543	83	112	
16. Securities, preferred stock; 17. Securities, common stock	2,818	7,134	19,234	42,309	40,473	21,969	28,193
20. Other intangible assets	4,496	5,746	14,300	23,421	11,929	4,238	6,841
21. Total	13,944	25,400	60,238	106,774	80,391	51,905	95,683
III. Liabilities							
7. Trade debt	3,066	4,355	12,450	15,970	11,888	12,807	16,961
8. Loans on securities	81	93	219	566	137	127	1,933
9. Bank loans, n.e.c.	1,420	3,780	8,694	9,446	5,210	4,344	6,894
10. Other loans	52	60	67	128	1,277	571	281
11. Mortgages	778	1,674	4,396	11,169	9,713	8,834	8,818
12. Bonds and notes	7,072	18,096	24,516	36,258	35,629	31,446	27,934
13. Other liabilities	2,569	5,188	14,081	22,755	15,660	7,952	21,089
14. Total	15,038	33,246	64,423	96,292	79,514	66,081	83,910
IV. Equities	19,960	33,108	87,868	131,777	89,994	87,403	148,345
V. Total assets or liabilities and equities	34,998	66,354	152,291	228,068	169,508	153,484	232,255

Notes to Table III-4b

Source: Goldsmith, *A Study of Saving,* Vol. III, for the W tables; and Goldsmith, *Financial Intermediaries*, for the A tables.

Line	
I-1 through I-4	Sum of W-31, lines I-1 through I-5, and W-36, lines I-1 through I-4; minus A-25, line 2, and A-26, line 2.
6	Sum of W-31, line I-7, and W-36, line I-7.
7	Sum of W-31, line I-10, and W-36, line I-10; minus A-25, line 2, A-26, line 2, and W-31, line I-9.
II-1	Sum of W-31, lines I-9, II-1, II-2, and W-36, line II-1, 2; minus A-3.c, line 15, A-25, line 3, A-26, line 3, and A-27, line 2 (one-half of line 2 in 1945).
1a	W-31, line I-9.
1b	Line II-1, this table, minus line II-1a.
2	A-3.c, line 15.
6	1900-22: Sum of W-31, line II-8 and W-24, line 2c. 1929-45: Sum of W-31, line II-8 and W-36, line II-8; minus A-25, line 6, and A-26, line 5.
7	Sum of W-31, line II-7, and W-36, line II-7; minus A-25, line 7, and A-27, lines 3 and 4.
8	W-31, line II-9.
13	Sum of W-31, line II-12, and W-36, lines II-12 and 13; minus W-35, line II-13, A-25, line 8, A-26, line 6 (1945 only), and A-27, 1/2 of line 2 (for 1945 only).
14	Sum of W-31, line II-13, and W-35, line II-13.
15	III-4b-1, line 4.
16, 17	Sum of W-31, lines II-15 and 16, W-36, lines II-15 and 16, and III-4b-1, line 8; minus A-26, line 6 (1929 and 1933 only).
20	Sum of W-31, line II-21, W-36, line II-21, and III-4b-1, line 11; minus A-25, line 9, A-26, line 7, and A-27, line 5.
21	Sum of W-31, lines I-9 and II-22, W-36, line II-22, and A-28, line 4; minus A-25 (line 1 minus line 2), A-26 (line 1 minus line 2), A-27, line 1, A-28, line 2, and W-24, lines 2a and 2b (1900-22).
III-7	Sum of W-31, line III-8, and W-36, line III-8; minus A-25, line 12, A-26, line 10, and A-27, line 8.
8	W-36, line III-10.
9	Sum of A-2, line 9, A-3.a, line 4, and A-4, lines 20 and 21; minus A-25, line 11 (1900-39) and line 13 (1945), A-26, line 9 (1900-39) and line 11 (1945), A-27, line 9, and A-28, one-third of line 2.
10	Sum of W-31, line III-7, and W-36, line III-7; minus A-2, line 9, A-3.a, line 4, and A-4, lines 20 and 21.
11	Table IV-c-11e, line 4.
12	Sum of W-31, lines III-11 and 12, and W-36, lines III-11 and 12; minus A-25, line 15, A-26, line 13, and line III-11 of this table.
13	Sum of W-31, lines III-13 and III-14, and W-36, lines III-13 and III-14; minus A-25, lines 14 and 16, A-26, lines 12 and 14, A-27, line 11, and A-28, one-third of line 2.
14	Sum of W-31, line III-15, and W-36, line III-15; minus A-25 (line 10 minus line 17), A-26 (line 8 minus line 15), A-27 (line 6 minus line 12), and A-28 (two-thirds of line 2).
IV	Line V minus line III-14.
V	Sum of lines I-7 and II-21.

[a]The 1945 figures in this table have been superseded by those in Table III-4; they are included here for comparability with earlier years.

TABLE III-4b-1

Investment Holding Companies, 1929-45, Selected Years

(million dollars)

	1929	1933	1939	1945
Corporate bonds				
1. Financial intermediaries, except banking system and government corporations	7,006	6,846	9,963	12,302
2. Insurance organizations	6,331	6,667	9,724	12,074
3. Investment companies	132	96	127	228
4. Estimate: investment holding companies	543	83	112	[illegible]
Corporate stock				
5. Financial intermediaries, except banking system and government corporations	7,287	3,953	4,740	7,872
6. Insurance organizations	1,963	1,628	2,248	3,809
7. Investment companies	2,191	1,006	1,216	2,017
8. Estimate: investment holding companies	3,133	1,319	1,276	2,046
Other assets				
9. Investment holding companies, total assets	4,354	1,724	1,553	2,272
10. Corporate stock and bonds	3,676	1,402	1,388	2,046
11. Estimate: investment holding companies, other assets	678	322	165	226

Notes to Table III-4b-1

Line	
1	1929-39: Goldsmith, *A Study of Saving*, Vol. III, Table W-41, line II-14. 1945: Sum of lines 2 and 3 of this table.
2	Goldsmith, *Financial Intermediaries*, Table A-7, line 19.
3	*Ibid.*, Table A-21, line 10.
4	Line 1 minus lines 2 and 3.
5	Goldsmith, *A Study of Saving*, Vol. III, Table W-41, sum of lines II-15 and II-16.
6	Goldsmith, *Financial Intermediaries*, Table A-7, line 20.
7	*Ibid.*, Table A-21, line 14
8	Line 5 minus lines 6 and 7. It is assumed that the corporate stock figures in line 5 do not include Federal Home Loan Bank stock owned by savings and loan associations (*Ibid.*, Table A-19, line 10), or savings and loan shares owned by credit unions (*Ibid.*, Table A-20, line 9), both of which are included as stock in *Ibid.*, Table A-18, line 20.
9	*Ibid.*, Table A-28, line 4.
10	Sum of lines 4 and 8 of this table.
11	Line 9 minus line 10.

TABLE III-5

Total Finance, 1945-58

(billion dollars)

	1945	1946	1947	1948
I. Tangible assets				
1. Residential structures	.14	.15	.23	.27
2. Nonresidential structures	1.17	1.39	1.45	1.52
3. Land	.99	1.14	1.30	1.51
4. Producer durables	.18	.20	.23	.26
6. Inventories	.01	.03	.02	.01
7. Total	2.49	2.91	3.23	3.57
II. Intangible assets				
1. Currency and demand deposits	77.30	77.80	85.69	90.43
a. Monetary metals	22.68	23.09	25.31	26.81
b. Other	54.62	54.71	60.38	63.62
2. Other bank deposits and shares	.15	.29	.33	.35
6. Consumer credit	2.52	4.38	6.70	8.68
7. Trade credit	.44	.77	.90	1.07
8. Loans on securities	8.25	3.85	2.79	3.04
9. Bank loans, n.e.c.	13.29	18.26	22.85	25.02
10. Other loans	2.86	3.23	3.56	4.17
11. Mortgages, nonfarm	20.16	25.12	30.94	36.90
a. Residential	16.08	20.25	25.28	30.45
b. Nonresidential	4.07	4.87	5.66	6.45
12. Mortgages, farm	1.34	1.54	1.76	1.92
13. Securities, U.S. government	181.65	169.56	165.19	159.43
a. Short-term	57.61	44.09	41.26	34.78
b. Savings bonds	2.05	2.43	2.77	3.75
c. Other long-term	121.99	123.04	121.16	120.90
14. Securities, state and local	6.98	7.16	8.15	9.25
15. Securities, other bonds and notes	17.70	20.25	24.10	29.27
16. Securities, preferred stock	1.83	2.01	2.12	2.19
17. Securities, common stock	5.53	5.41	5.55	5.74
20. Other intangible assets	9.66	10.90	12.58	12.52
21. Total	349.66	350.53	373.21	389.98
III. Liabilities				
1. Currency and demand deposits	185.24	170.36	179.97	182.05
2. Other bank deposits and shares	53.48	60.03	63.62	66.19
3. Life insurance reserves, private	45.34	49.11	52.68	56.51
4. Pension and retirement funds, private	2.68	3.25	3.90	4.55
5. Pension and insurance funds, govt.	25.83	29.50	33.38	36.86
7. Trade debt	.03	.02	.03	.04
8. Loans on securities	3.74	1.70	.99	1.50
9. Bank loans, n.e.c.	1.17	1.76	2.38	2.84
10. Other loans	1.71	1.93	2.12	2.12
12. Bonds and notes	.19	.45	.73	1.31
13. Other liabilities	11.21	12.59	12.72	13.66
14. Total	330.62	330.70	352.52	367.63
IV. Equities	21.53	22.74	23.92	25.92
V. Total assets or liabilities and equities	352.15	353.44	376.44	393.55

Line

I-1 through I-7 — Tables IV-a-1 through IV-a-7.

Other lines: Sum of Tables III-5a through III-5m.

1949	1950	1951	1952	1953	1954	1955	1956	1957	1958	
										I.
.32	.40	.43	.53	.54	.56	.59	.61	.63	.64	1.
2.43	2.41	2.26	2.53	2.79	3.17	3.68	4.10	4.54	4.78	2.
1.91	2.01	2.09	2.30	2.52	2.82	3.18	3.52	3.92	4.04	3.
.28	.35	.39	.44	.48	.57	.64	.73	.82	.85	4.
.01	.02	.02	.03	.03	.02	.02	.02	.03	.03	6.
4.95	5.19	5.19	5.83	6.36	7.14	8.11	8.98	9.94	10.34	7.
										II.
87.64	87.72	92.39	93.53	92.36	91.42	92.04	94.24	96.31	92.59	1.
27.03	25.30	25.25	25.72	24.56	24.29	24.24	24.55	25.28	23.06	
60.61	62.42	67.14	67.81	67.80	67.13	67.80	69.69	71.03	69.53	
.36	.31	.39	.52	.60	.70	.72	.77	.77	1.08	2.
10.93	13.84	14.37	18.00	21.50	22.24	27.87	30.89	33.42	33.19	6.
1.17	1.47	1.66	1.81	1.97	2.12	2.51	2.93	3.27	3.64	7.
3.79	4.59	4.25	4.95	5.75	7.61	8.69	8.01	7.65	9.23	8.
23.40	28.92	33.60	36.62	37.00	37.60	44.44	50.02	52.08	53.80	9.
4.29	4.91	5.56	5.89	6.12	6.22	7.50	7.76	9.07	9.42	10.
41.93	50.87	58.56	66.00	74.16	84.92	98.92	110.75	119.05	131.22	11.
34.91	43.21	50.08	56.74	64.08	73.62	86.22	96.40	103.12	113.52	
7.01	7.66	8.49	9.26	10.08	11.30	12.69	14.36	15.93	17.70	
2.11	2.37	2.62	2.87	3.08	3.32	3.68	3.94	4.07	4.26	12.
160.57	156.05	158.78	165.16	169.01	174.26	168.55	166.53	165.59	176.01	13.
41.63	41.31	32.10	37.51	49.28	40.61	32.46	38.82	41.05	41.63	
4.04	4.96	4.98	5.22	5.05	5.14	5.10	4.17	2.77	2.43	
114.90	109.78	121.70	122.43	114.68	128.51	130.99	123.54	121.77	131.95	
10.74	13.03	14.69	16.23	18.35	21.84	23.41	24.79	27.12	31.23	14.
32.98	35.93	39.96	45.01	49.47	53.77	57.15	61.03	68.35	74.30	15.
2.50	2.81	2.94	3.12	3.47	3.88	4.08	3.95	3.92	4.36	16.
7.24	8.80	10.97	13.30	14.11	21.25	26.69	28.39	27.78	39.10	17.
13.25	17.44	18.11	19.11	19.67	20.29	25.26	27.25	28.38	29.78	20.
402.90	429.06	458.85	492.12	516.62	551.44	591.51	621.25	646.83	693.21	21.
										III.
179.36	188.71	199.64	206.62	206.27	208.97	215.69	219.67	218.93	223.18	1.
69.17	71.81	76.73	84.86	94.01	104.50	112.95	122.36	134.69	151.62	2.
60.65	64.99	69.31	74.47	79.64	85.68	91.65	97.10	102.20	108.51	3.
5.26	6.23	7.80	9.52	11.42	14.34	17.35	20.02	22.28	27.80	4.
39.40	40.71	44.78	49.13	52.51	55.20	58.44	62.02	64.87	66.10	5.
.06	.07	.06	.10	.12	.13	.15	.18	.19	.21	7.
1.95	2.02	1.83	2.31	2.61	3.28	3.60	2.98	3.08	3.42	8.
3.23	4.29	4.25	5.16	5.02	5.02	7.77	7.14	6.77	5.69	9.
2.20	3.19	3.24	3.21	3.25	3.93	4.41	4.22	4.53	5.55	10.
1.83	2.25	2.82	3.36	4.94	5.13	6.76	7.95	9.08	9.09	12.
14.96	16.86	18.03	20.15	21.72	23.16	25.27	27.33	29.47	31.20	13.
378.07	401.13	428.49	458.89	481.51	509.34	544.04	570.97	596.09	632.37	14.
29.78	33.12	35.55	39.06	41.47	49.24	55.58	59.26	60.68	71.18	IV.
407.85	434.25	464.04	497.95	522.98	558.58	599.62	630.23	656.77	703.55	V.

TABLE III-5a

Federal Reserve Banks and Treasury Monetary Funds, 1945-58 (billion dollars)

	1945	1946	1947	1948
I. Tangible assets				
7. Total	.03	.04	.04	.04
II. Intangible assets				
1. Currency and demand deposits	42.91	44.17	49.52	52.55
a. Monetary metals	22.68	23.09	25.31	26.81
b. Other	20.23	21.08	24.21	25.74
9. Bank loans, n.e.c.	.25	.16	.09	.22
13. Securities, U.S. government	24.29	23.37	22.58	23.35
a. Short-term	23.20	22.30	19.90	12.40
c. Other long-term	1.09	1.07	2.68	10.95
20. Other intangible assets	2.27	2.65	3.11	3.02
21. Total	69.72	70.35	75.30	79.14
III. Liabilities				
1. Currency and demand deposits	65.36	65.50	71.47	75.40
13. Other liabilities	3.89	4.30	3.26	3.11
14. Total	69.25	69.80	74.73	78.51
IV. Equities	.50	.59	.61	.67
V. Total assets or liabilities and equities	69.75	70.39	75.34	79.18

Sum of Tables III-5a-1 and III-5a-2.

TABLE III-5a-1

Federal Reserve Banks, 1945-58 (billion dollars)

	1945	1946	1947	1948
I. Tangible assets				
7. Total	.03	.04	.04	.04
II. Intangible assets				
1. Currency and demand deposits	18.25	18.81	21.93	23.44
a. Monetary metals	.02	.03	.03	.04
b. Other	18.23	18.78	21.90	23.40
9. Bank loans, n.e.c.	.25	.16	.09	.22
13. Securities, U.S. government	24.26	23.35	22.56	23.33
20. Other intangible assets	2.26	2.65	3.10	3.01
21. Total	45.02	44.97	47.68	50.00
III. Liabilities				
1. Currency and demand deposits	42.76	42.21	44.15	46.57
13. Other liabilities	1.89	2.30	3.06	2.91
14. Total	44.65	44.51	47.21	49.48
IV. Equities	.40	.50	.51	.56
V. Total assets or liabilities and equities	45.05	45.01	47.72	50.04

Line

I-7 Table III-5n, column 2 multiplied by column 11.

II-1 Cash assets of the Federal Reserve Banks (*Annual Report of the Board of Governors of the Federal Reserve System*, Table 1 for all years).

1a Goldsmith, *National Wealth*, Table B-183, column 3.

1b Line II-1 minus line II-1a.

9 Sum of Federal Reserve Banks' loans to member banks, foreign banks, and independent firms, and acceptances (same source as II-1 above).

13 Federal obligations held by Federal Reserve Banks (same source as II-1 above).

20 Sum of Federal Reserve Banks uncollected cash items and other assets (same source as II-1 above).

1949	1950	1951	1952	1953	1954	1955	1956	1957	1958	
										I.
.05	.06	.06	.07	.07	.07	.09	.10	.11	.12	7.
										II.
52.90	49.52	49.68	50.83	49.15	48.63	48.68	49.16	50.89	46.76	1.
27.03	25.30	25.25	25.72	24.56	24.29	24.24	24.55	25.28	23.06	
25.87	24.22	24.43	25.11	24.59	24.34	24.44	24.61	25.61	23.70	
.08	.07	.02	.16	.03	.14	.14	.12	.12	.11	9.
18.90	20.80	23.82	24.72	25.94	24.95	24.80	25.02	24.26	26.44	13.
12.00	16.00	13.40	14.80	17.00	19.40	20.70	22.10	21.40	21.00	
6.90	4.80	10.42	9.92	8.94	5.55	4.10	2.92	2.86	5.44	
3.06	4.40	4.05	4.41	4.38	4.10	5.67	5.88	5.92	5.78	20.
74.94	74.79	77.57	80.12	79.50	77.82	79.29	80.18	81.19	79.09	21.
										III.
70.84	70.41	73.49	75.44	74.73	73.18	73.74	74.52	75.43	73.03	1.
3.41	3.66	3.34	3.88	3.94	3.80	4.67	4.72	4.79	5.06	13.
74.25	74.07	76.83	79.32	78.67	76.98	78.41	79.24	80.22	78.09	14.
.74	.78	.80	.87	.90	.91	.97	1.04	1.08	1.12	IV.
74.99	74.85	77.63	80.19	79.57	77.89	79.38	80.28	81.30	79.21	V.

1949	1950	1951	1952	1953	1954	1955	1956	1957	1958	
										I.
.05	.06	.06	.07	.07	.07	.09	.10	.11	.12	7.
										II.
23.60	21.90	21.99	22.55	21.94	21.65	21.70	21.93	22.87	20.76	1.
.04	.03	.02	.02	.04	.07	.05	.04	.06	.06	
23.56	21.87	21.97	22.53	21.90	21.58	21.65	21.89	22.81	20.70	
.08	.07	.02	.16	.03	.14	.14	.12	.12	.11	9.
18.88	20.78	23.80	24.70	25.92	24.93	24.78	24.92	24.24	26.35	13.
3.05	4.39	4.04	4.40	4.38	4.10	5.66	5.88	5.72	5.78	20.
45.61	47.14	49.85	51.81	52.27	50.82	52.28	52.85	52.95	53.00	21.
										III.
41.82	43.07	46.09	47.44	47.81	46.48	47.04	47.50	47.50	47.26	1.
3.21	3.46	3.14	3.68	3.74	3.60	4.47	4.52	4.59	4.86	13.
45.03	46.53	49.23	51.12	51.55	50.08	51.51	52.02	52.09	52.12	14.
.63	.67	.68	.76	.79	.81	.86	.93	.97	1.00	IV.
45.66	47.20	49.91	51.88	52.34	50.89	52.37	52.95	53.06	53.12	V.

Line	
II-21	Sum of lines II-1 through II-20.
III-1	Deposits with the Federal Reserve Banks by member and nonmember banks, U.S. Treasury, and foreign banks (same source as II-1 above), and deposits of the Exchange Stabilization Fund (*Treasury Bulletin* table, "Balance Sheet-Exchange Stabilization Fund," May issue each year).
13	Miscellaneous liabilities of the Federal Reserve Banks, the sum of officers' and certified checks and Federal Reserve exchange drafts, deposits of international organizations, deferred liabilities, paid-in capital, and other deposits and misc. liabilities (see II-1 above).
14	Line III-1 plus line III-13.
IV	Line V minus line III-14.
V	Sum of lines I-7 and II-21.

TABLE III-5a-2

Treasury Monetary Funds, 1945-58 (billion dollars)

	1945	1946	1947	1948
I. Tangible assets				
II. Intangible assets				
1. Currency and demand deposits	24.66	25.36	27.59	29.11
a. Monetary metals	22.66	23.06	25.28	26.77
b. Other	2.00	2.30	2.31	2.34
13. Securities, U.S. government	.03	.02	.02	.02
20. Other intangible assets	a	a	.01	.01
21. Total	24.69	25.38	27.62	29.14
III. Liabilities				
1. Currency and demand deposits	22.60	23.29	27.32	28.83
13. Other liabilities	2.00	2.00	.20	.20
14. Total	24.60	25.29	27.52	29.03
IV. Equities	.09	.09	.10	.11
V. Total assets or liabilities and equities	24.69	25.38	27.62	29.14

Line

II-1 Cash assets of the Treasury monetary funds. This is the sum of gold; standard silver dollars; silver bullion; subsidiary silver coin; minor coin; U.S. notes; Federal Reserve Bank notes; National Bank notes (*Federal Reserve Bulletin*, e.g., February 1946, p. 155); and special account no. 1 gold, total due from foreign banks and countries, and cash—except Treasurer of the U.S. (*Treasury Bulletin* table, "Balance Sheet-Exchange Stabilization Fund," May issue for all years).

1a Goldsmith, *National Wealth*, Table A-44, column 7.

1b Line II-1 minus line II-1a.

13 Federal obligations held by Exchange Stabilization Fund, (*Treasury Bulletin*, line on "Federal Reserve Bank of N.Y. Special Account," May issue for all years).

20 Securities of U.S. government, Treasurer of U.S. checking account (same source as for II-13).

21 Sum of lines II-1 through II-20.

TABLE III-5b

Government Pension and Insurance Funds, 1945-58 (billion dollars)

	1945	1946	1947	1948
I. Tangible assets				
II. Intangible assets				
1. Currency and demand deposits	.27	.28	.30	.38
b. Other	.27	.28	.30	.38
10. Other loans	.12	.11	.11	.13
11. Mortgages, nonfarm	.02	.03	.03	.04
a. Residential	.02	.03	.03	.04
13. Securities, U.S. government	24.05	27.81	31.56	34.70
b. Savings bonds	.20	.30	.40	.50
c. Other long-term	23.85	27.51	31.16	34.20
14. Securities, state and local	1.19	1.09	1.19	1.34
15. Securities, other bonds and notes	.14	.14	.15	.21
16. Securities, preferred stock	.02	.02	.02	.03
17. Securities, common stock	.02	.02	.02	.03
21. Total	25.83	29.50	33.38	36.86
III. Liabilities				
5. Pension and insurance funds, govt.	25.83	29.50	33.38	36.86
14. Total	25.83	29.50	33.38	36.86
IV. Equities				
V. Total assets or liabilities and equities	25.83	29.50	33.38	36.86

Sum of corresponding lines in Tables III-5b-1 and III-5b-2, except line II-13b (for which see Table IV-b-13b, line 5b), and line II-13c (which is line II-13 minus line II-13b).

1949	1950	1951	1952	1953	1954	1955	1956	1957	1958	
										I.
										II.
29.30	27.62	27.69	28.28	27.21	26.98	26.98	27.23	28.02	26.00	1.
26.99	25.27	25.23	25.70	24.52	24.22	24.19	24.51	25.22	23.00	
2.31	2.35	2.46	2.58	2.69	2.76	2.79	2.72	2.80	3.00	
.02	.02	.02	.02	.02	.02	.02	.10	.02	.09	13.
.01	.01	.01	.01	.01	.01	[a]	[a]	.20	[a]	20.
29.33	27.65	27.72	28.31	27.24	27.01	27.00	27.33	28.24	26.09	21.
										III.
29.02	27.34	27.40	28.00	26.92	26.70	26.70	27.02	27.93	25.77	1.
.20	.20	.20	.20	.20	.20	.20	.20	.20	.20	13.
29.22	27.54	27.60	28.20	27.12	26.90	26.90	27.22	28.13	25.97	14.
.11	.11	.12	.11	.12	.11	.10	.11	.11	.12	IV.
29.33	27.65	27.72	28.31	27.24	27.01	27.00	27.33	28.24	26.09	V.

Line

III-1 Currency of the Treasury monetary funds. Sum of Treasury currency outstanding, gold certificates, money held in Treasury for Federal Reserve Banks and agents, and money held by Federal Reserve Banks and agents, currency in circulation, $156 million of U.S. Notes and Treasury notes of 1890 (*Federal Reserve Bulletin*, e.g., February 1946, p. 155), and gold in general fund, e.g., *Treasury Bulletin*, May 1946, p. 71, col. 5).

13 Capital account (*Treasury Bulletin* table, "Balance Sheet-Exchange Stabilization Fund," May issue all years).

14 Line III-1 plus line III-13.

IV Line V minus line III-14.

V Same as line II-21.

[a]Under $5 million.

1949	1950	1951	1952	1953	1954	1955	1956	1957	1958	
										I.
										II.
.36	.82	.88	.77	.73	1.05	.83	.97	1.21	1.34	1.
.36	.82	.88	.77	.73	1.05	.83	.97	1.21	1.34	
.14	.16	.18	.19	.21	.23	.26	.29	.32	.36	10.
.04	.10	.16	.20	.23	.30	.34	.43	.45	.40	11.
.04	.10	.16	.20	.23	.30	.34	.43	.45	.40	
36.89	37.30	40.90	44.82	47.51	48.95	51.35	53.60	54.67	54.05	13.
.60	.70	.70	.80	.80	.80	.80	.70	.60	.50	
36.29	36.60	40.20	44.02	46.71	48.15	50.55	52.90	54.07	53.55	
1.55	1.74	1.81	1.94	2.18	2.49	2.83	3.23	3.68	4.14	14.
.36	.51	.75	1.09	1.49	1.98	2.57	3.20	4.16	5.31	15.
.03	.04	.05	.06	.08	.10	.13	.15	.19	.25	16.
.03	.04	.05	.06	.08	.10	.13	.15	.19	.25	17.
39.40	40.71	44.78	49.13	52.51	55.20	58.44	62.02	64.87	66.10	21.
										III.
39.40	40.71	44.78	49.13	52.51	55.20	58.44	62.02	64.87	66.10	5.
39.40	40.71	44.78	49.13	52.51	55.20	58.44	62.02	64.87	66.10	14.
										IV.
39.40	40.71	44.78	49.13	52.51	55.20	58.44	62.02	64.87	66.10	V.

TABLE III-5b-1

Federal Government Pension and Insurance Funds, 1945-58

(billion dollars)

	1945	1946	1947	1948
I. Tangible assets				
II. Intangible assets				
1. Currency and demand deposits	.20	.20	.20	.27
a. Monetary metals				
b. Other	.20	.20	.20	.27
10. Other loans	.12	.11	.11	.13
13. Securities, U.S. government	22.47	25.81	29.31	32.17
21. Total	22.79	26.12	29.62	32.57
III. Liabilities				
5. Pension and insurance funds, govt.	22.79	26.12	29.62	32.57
14. Total	22.79	26.12	29.62	32.57
IV. Equities				
V. Total assets or liabilities and equities	22.79	26.12	29.62	32.57

Line

II-1 1945-49: Goldsmith, *A Study of Saving*, Vol. I, Table F-23, col. 7, p. 1027.
1950-58: Sum of the unexpended balances of the Old Age and Survivors Insurance Trust Fund, Unemployment Trust Fund, Railway Retirement Fund, and National Service Life Insurance Fund (*Treasury Bulletin*, e.g., February 1956, Table 6, p. 9) and the cash balance of the Civil Service Retirement and Disability Fund (*Annual Report of the Secretary of the Treasury*, e.g., 1956, Table 55, p. 509. December 31 figures obtained by linear interpolation of fiscal year figures).

1949	1950	1951	1952	1953	1954	1955	1956	1957	1958	
										I.
										II.
.24	.69	.76	.64	.56	.85	.65	.77	.97	1.09	1.
.24	.69	.76	.64	.56	.85	.65	.77	.97	1.09	
.14	.16	.18	.19	.21	.23	.26	.29	.32	.36	10.
34.13	34.20	37.36	40.85	43.25	44.42	46.52	48.45	49.35	48.45	13.
34.51	35.05	38.30	41.68	44.02	45.50	47.43	49.51	50.64	49.90	21.
										III.
34.51	35.05	38.30	41.68	44.02	45.50	47.43	49.51	50.64	49.90	5.
34.51	35.05	38.30	41.68	44.02	45.50	47.43	49.51	50.64	49.90	14.
										IV.
34.51	35.05	38.30	41.68	44.02	45.50	47.43	49.51	50.64	49.90	V.

Line

II-10 1945-47: Goldsmith, *A Study of Saving*, Vol. I, Table F-25, col. 10, p. 1033.

1948-58: Sum of national service life insurance and U.S. government life insurance policy loans (U.S. Bureau of the Budget, *The Budget of the United States Government*, e.g., fiscal 1956, pp. 1059-1060). Where June figures appeared in the Budget, straight-line interpolations were made to arrive at December figures. Figures for 1949 and 1954, not available in the Budget, were interpolated between adjoining years.

13 Sum of public issues and special issues of federal securities held by federal pension and retirement funds. See notes to Tables III-5b-1a and III-5b-1b.

21 Sum of lines II-1 through II-13.

III-5, 14 Same as line II-21.

V Same as line II-21.

TABLE III-5b-1a

Special Issues of Federal Securities Held by Federal Government Pension and Insurance Funds, 1945-58

(million dollars)

Year	*Special Issues Held by:* Farm Tenant Mortgage Insurance Corporation (1)	Federal Deposit Insurance Corporation (2)	Federal Home Loan Banks (3)	Federal Housing Administration (4)	Federal Savings and Loan Insurance Corporation (5)	Highway Trust Fund (6)	Postal Savings System (7)	Total (8)	Total Special Issues Held by U.S. Govt. Investment Accounts (9)	Special Issues of Federal Govt. Securities Held by Federal Pension and Insurance Funds (10)
1945			54				456	510	20,000	19,490
1946			263				938	1,201	24,585	23,384
1947			586				1,882	2,468	28,955	26,487
1948			768				1,867	2,635	31,714	29,079
1949			966				1,882	2,848	33,896	31,048
1950	1	839	50		81		1,630	2,601	33,707	31,106
1951	1	862	52		79		632	1,626	35,902	34,276
1952	1	854	44		56		520	1,475	39,150	37,675
1953	1	813	53		60		358	1,285	41,197	39,912
1954	1	860	263	80	91		164	1,459	42,566	41,107
1955	1	667	64	77	93		26	928	43,926	42,998
1956		674	50	102	95		6	927	45,639	44,712
1957		640	50	29	83	587	5	1,394	45,799	44,405
1958		631	165	62	104	386		1,348	44,840	43,492

Cols. 1 through 7: 1945-49: Goldsmith, *A Study of Saving*, Vol. I, Tables F-23, F-24.
1950-52: U.S. Treasury Department, *Treasury Bulletin*, e.g., December 1953, p. 11.
1953-58: U.S. Treasury Department, *Daily Treasury Statement*, e.g., December 31, 1958, p. 5.

Col. 8 : Sum of columns 1 through 7.
Col. 9 : *Treasury Bulletin*, e.g., June 1959, p. 44.
Col. 10 : Col. 9 minus col. 8.

TABLE III-5b-1b

Public Issues of Federal Securities Held by Federal Government Pension and Insurance Funds, 1945-58

(million dollars)

Year	Public Issues Held by U.S. Gov't. Investment Accounts (1)	*Federal Credit Agencies* Total (2)	*Federal Credit Agencies* Special Issues (3)	*Federal Credit Agencies* Public Issues (4)	Public Issues Held by the Postal Savings System (5)	Issues Held by the District of Columbia (6)	Issues Held by Exchange Stabilization Fund (7)	Public Issues Held by Federal Govt. Pension and Insurance Funds (8)
1945	7,041	1,683	54	1,629	2,381	23	30	2,978
1946	6,329	1,873	263	1,610	2,244	30	20	2,425
1947	5,397	1,685	586	1,099	1,426	31	20	2,821
1948	5,603	1,854	768	1,086	1,377	32	20	3,088
1949	5,450	2,047	966	1,081	1,236	30	20	3,083
1950	5,490	2,075	971	1,104	1,238	31	20	3,097
1951	6,379	2,226	994	1,232	2,012	36	20	3,079
1952	6,742	2,421	955	1,466	2,031	51	20	3,174
1953	7,116	2,602	927	1,675	2,031	54	20	3,336
1954	7,043	2,967	1,295	1,672	1,970	61	25	3,315
1955	7,798	3,236	902	2,334	1,848	71	25	3,520
1956	8,363	3,739	921	2,818	1,622	87	95	3,741
1957	9,379	3,804	802	3,002	1,310	100	25	4,942
1958	9,498	4,198	962	3,236	1,128	90	90	4,954

Col. 1: U.S. Treasury Department, *Treasury Bulletin*, e.g., June 1959, Table 1, p. 44.
Col. 2: *Federal Reserve Bulletin*, e.g., June 1959, p. 618 ("U.S. Government Securities-Total").
Col. 3: Sum of columns 1-5 of Table III-5b-1a.
Col. 4: Column 2 minus column 3.
Col. 5: Total issues held by the Postal Savings System (1945-54: *Federal Reserve Bulletin*, e.g., June 1955, p. 662; 1955-58: Federal Reserve Board worksheets) minus special issues held by Postal Savings System (see notes to Table III-5b-1a).
Col. 6: *Annual Report of the Secretary of the Treasury* (e.g., fiscal 1956 report, p. 504) for June 30 figures. End-of-year figures are linear interpolations of June 30 figures, except those for 1950-53, which are estimated from net investment in government securities by these D.C. funds (*Daily Treasury Statement*).
Col. 7: *Treasury Bulletin*, e.g., November 1955, p. 49.
Col. 8: Col. 1 minus the sum of cols. 4, 5, 6, and 7.

Columns 1, 2, and 4 include holdings of the Federal Land Banks for 1945 and 1946.

TABLE III-5b-2

State and Local Government Pension and Insurance Funds, 1945-59

(billion dollars)

	1945	1946	1947	1948
I. Tangible assets				
II. Intangible assets				
1. Currency and demand deposits	.07	.08	.10	.11
a. Monetary metals				
b. Other	.07	.08	.10	.11
11. Mortgages, nonfarm	.02	.03	.03	.04
13. Securities, U.S. government	1.58	2.00	2.25	2.53
14. Securities, state and local	1.19	1.09	1.19	1.34
15. Securities, other bonds and notes	.14	.14	.15	.21
16. Securities, preferred stock	.02	.02	.02	.03
17. Securities, common stock	.02	.02	.02	.03
21. Total	3.04	3.38	3.76	4.29
III. Liabilities				
5. Pension and insurance funds, govt.	3.04	3.38	3.76	4.29
14. Total	3.04	3.38	3.76	4.29
IV. Equities				
V. Total assets or liabilities and equities	3.04	3.38	3.76	4.29

Line

II-1, 13, 14 Line II-21 multiplied by the estimated share of cash and deposits, U.S. government securities, and state and local securities, in total assets. Fiscal-year data on distribution of assets of state and local government pension and retirement funds are from the following sources (calendar year estimates derived by linear interpolation):

Fiscal 1945-Fiscal 1953: Interpolated between 1954 benchmark, below, and 1941 benchmark from U.S. Bureau of the Census, *Retirement Systems for State and Local Government Employees*, State and Local Government Special Study No. 17. The interpolations used data from the Census Bureau's *Summary of Governmental Finances* (for the later years), *State Finances*, and *City Finances*, as well as information received directly from the Bureau of the Census.

Fiscal 1954-Fiscal 1958: Bureau of the Census, *Summary of Governmental Finances*, e.g., 1958, Table 10, p. 19.

11 1945-56: Total state and local government holdings of mortgages (FRB worksheets) were interpolated to obtain fiscal year figures. State debt outstanding to finance veterans' farm and home loans (Bureau of the Census, *State Finances*, various issues) was subtracted. Calendar-year remainders were estimated by interpolation of the fiscal-year ratios of veterans' farm and home loans to total state and local government holdings of mortgages. Calendar-year remainders were then multiplied by the 1957 ratio of employee pension and retirement fund mortgages (see 1957 and 1958, below) to the 1957 remainder.

1957-58: Fiscal 1957 figure for state and local employee retirement funds holdings of mortgages from Bureau of the Census, *1957 Census of Governments*, Vol. IV, No. 1. Calendar 1957 and 1958 figures assumed to remain the same.

1949	1950	1951	1952	1953	1954	1955	1956	1957	1958	
										I.
										II.
.12	.13	.12	.13	.17	.20	.18	.20	.24	.25	1.
.12	.13	.12	.13	.17	.20	.18	.20	.24	.25	
.04	.10	.16	.20	.23	.30	.34	.43	.45	.40	11.
2.76	3.10	3.54	3.97	4.26	4.53	4.83	5.15	5.32	5.60	13.
1.55	1.74	1.81	1.94	2.18	2.49	2.83	3.23	3.68	4.14	14.
.36	.51	.75	1.09	1.49	1.98	2.57	3.20	4.16	5.31	15.
.03	.04	.05	.06	.08	.10	.13	.15	.19	.25	16.
.03	.04	.05	.06	.08	.10	.13	.15	.19	.25	17.
4.89	5.66	6.48	7.45	8.49	9.70	11.01	12.51	14.23	16.20	21.
										III.
4.89	5.66	6.48	7.45	8.49	9.70	11.01	12.51	14.23	16.20	5.
4.89	5.66	6.48	7.45	8.49	9.70	11.01	12.51	14.23	16.20	14.
										IV.
4.89	5.66	6.48	7.45	8.49	9.70	11.01	12.51	14.23	16.20	V.

Line

II-15 The sum of lines II-11, II-15, II-16, and II-17 was estimated in the same manner as line II-1, above. Line II-15 was calculated as a residual item after deduction of lines II-11, II-16, and II-17, which were estimated independently.

16,
17 Total common and preferred stock held by state and local government pension and retirement funds was assumed to be 7.444 per cent of total corporate securities held by state and local governments (FRB worksheets). Common stock was calculated as one half of total stock. These percentages were derived from the National Council of Teacher Retirement, *Compilation of Investment Questionnaire Returns*, June 30, 1955.

21 Sum of total assets of state and local government employee retirement funds and workmen's compensation funds.

Total assets of employee retirement funds were cumulated from the 1944 figure (Goldsmith, *A Study of Saving*, Vol. I, Table G-19, col. 5, p. 1073) by the fund increase, which is the sum of assessments, government contributions, and investment income, minus benefits paid out (*Survey of Current Business*, National Income Number, e.g., July 1957, Table 10, p. 14, lines 14, 15, and 18 minus line 20).

Total assets of workmen's compensation funds derived by cumulating from the 1944 figure (Goldsmith, *A Study of Saving*, Vol. I, Table G-19, col. 11, p. 1073) by the fund increase which is revenues minus benefits paid out (1945-49: *Ibid.*, cols. 7 and 8 minus col. 9, p. 1073; 1950-57: Bureau of the Census, *Summary of State Government Finances*, e.g., 1955, Table 1, pp. 6-7. Calendar year figures obtained by linear interpolation of fiscal year figures).

III-5
14 Same as line II-21.

V Same as line II-21.

TABLE III-5c

Commercial Banks, 1945-58 (billion dollars)

	1945	1946	1947	1948
I. Tangible assets				
7. Total	1.12	1.36	1.48	1.53
II. Intangible assets				
1. Currency and demand deposits	29.83	28.53	30.74	32.26
a. Monetary metals				
b. Other	29.83	28.53	30.74	32.26
2. Other bank deposits and shares	.07	.06	.06	.05
6. Consumer credit	1.47	2.66	3.97	4.98
8. Loans on securities	6.82	3.16	2.05	2.31
9. Bank loans, n.e.c.	13.04	18.10	22.76	24.80
11. Mortgages, nonfarm	4.23	6.50	8.58	9.94
a. Residential	3.38	5.12	6.90	8.00
b. Nonresidential	.85	1.38	1.68	1.93
12. Mortgages, farm	.52	.70	.82	.87
13. Securities, U.S. government	90.61	74.78	69.22	62.62
a. Short-term	32.30	18.80	19.20	19.40
b. Savings bonds	.94	.96	.93	1.23
c. Other long-term	57.37	55.02	49.09	41.99
14. Securities, state and local	3.97	4.40	5.28	5.66
15. Securities, other bonds and notes	2.96	3.31	3.37	3.17
17. Securities, common stock	.22	.19	.16	.16
20. Other intangible assets	5.54	6.32	7.44	7.18
21. Total	159.28	148.71	154.45	154.00
III. Liabilities				
1. Currency and demand deposits	119.88	104.86	108.50	106.65
2. Other bank deposits and shares	30.34	34.17	35.60	36.23
9. Bank loans, n.e.c.	.22	.05	.07	.06
10. Other loans	.28	.21	.16	.13
13. Other liabilities	.63	.84	.99	1.15
14. Total	151.35	140.13	145.32	144.22
IV. Equities	9.05	9.94	10.61	11.31
V. Total assets or liabilities and equities	160.40	150.07	155.93	155.53

Line

I-7 Table III-5n, col. 3 multiplied by col. 11.

[a]Under $5 million.

II-1 Table IV-b-1, line 5c.

2 *Annual Report of the Federal Deposit Insurance Corporation*, e.g., 1956, Table 105, p. 106. Other balances with banks in U.S. minus Table III-5m-2, line II-2.

6 Total instalment and noninstalment credit held by commercial banks (*Federal Reserve Bulletin*, e.g., October 1957, p. 1171) plus hypothecated deposits accumulated by consumers for the repayment of loans (FRB worksheets).

8 Sum of commercial bank loans on securities to brokers and dealers and to others. 1945-46: *Annual Report of the Comptroller of the Currency*, e.g., 1946, Table 29, p. 119; 1947-58: *Federal Reserve Bulletin*, e.g., March 1958, p. 319.

9 1945-46: Total loans, net, for all commercial banks (*Federal Reserve Bulletin*) minus lines II-6, II-8, II-11, and II-12 of this table; 1947-58: *Federal Reserve Bulletin*, e.g., June 1955, p. 668. Sum of commercial loans, agricultural loans, other loans to individuals, loans to financial institutions and other loans, minus line II-6 of this table.

11 Table IV-b-11, line 5c.

11a Table IV-b-11a, line 5c.

11b Table IV-b-11b, line 5c.

12 Table IV-b-12, line 5c.

13 *Federal Reserve Bulletin*, e.g., December 1956, p. 1329.

13a Table IV-b-13a, line 5c.

13b Table IV-b-13b, line 5c.

13c Table IV-b-13c, line 5c.

14 1945-46: FRB worksheets; 1947-58: *Federal Reserve Bulletin*, e.g., December 1956, p. 1332.

1949	1950	1951	1952	1953	1954	1955	1956	1957	1958	
										I.
1.99	1.99	1.94	2.04	2.22	2.40	2.73	3.02	3.33	3.47	7.
										II.
28.90	31.18	35.10	35.04	35.28	34.05	34.28	35.64	35.49	35.13	1.
28.90	31.18	35.10	35.04	35.28	34.05	34.28	35.64	35.49	35.13	
.04	.04	.04	.04	.04	.04	.04	.04	.04	.08	2.
6.01	7.67	7.84	9.73	11.33	11.36	13.72	15.17	16.38	16.56	6.
2.64	2.86	2.56	3.16	3.56	4.45	5.04	4.28	4.22	4.66	8.
23.32	28.85	33.58	6.46	36.97	37.46	44.30	49.90	51.96	53.69	9.
10.64	12.58	13.58	14.66	15.62	17.26	19.52	21.18	21.75	23.79	11.
8.60	10.33	11.14	12.06	12.80	14.03	15.74	16.85	17.00	18.41	
2.04	2.24	2.44	2.59	2.81	3.23	3.78	4.33	4.76	5.38	
.91	.96	1.00	1.05	1.08	1.16	1.29	1.33	1.36	1.46	12.
67.00	62.03	61.52	63.32	63.43	68.98	61.59	58.55	58.24	66.18	13.
26.50	22.20	15.80	19.20	28.20	17.60	9.00	13.80	15.70	16.60	
1.18	1.47	1.49	1.51	1.49	1.50	1.48	1.09	.62	.59	
39.32	38.36	44.23	42.61	33.74	49.88	51.11	43.66	41.92	48.99	
6.55	8.12	9.20	10.19	10.82	12.59	12.70	12.90	13.92	16.50	14.
3.32	3.90	3.77	3.55	3.43	3.29	3.53	2.89	3.49	3.52	15.
.15	.15	.14	.15	.15	.15	.16	.16	.18	.19	17.
7.58	10.02	10.60	10.72	10.73	10.99	13.96	14.90	15.11	16.07	20.
157.06	168.36	178.93	188.07	192.44	201.78	210.13	216.94	222.14	237.83	21.
										III.
108.52	118.30	126.15	131.18	131.54	135.79	141.95	145.15	143.50	150.15	1.
36.73	36.96	38.69	41.76	45.16	48.97	50.30	52.37	57.82	65.86	2.
.02	.09	.03	.19	.06	.03	.16	.08	.08	.07	9.
.11	.09	.08	.05	.04	.02	.01	a	.01	a	10.
1.32	1.90	2.30	2.54	2.65	2.99	3.01	3.56	3.93	3.88	13.
146.70	157.34	167.25	175.72	179.45	187.80	195.43	201.16	205.34	219.96	14.
12.35	13.01	13.62	14.39	15.21	16.38	17.43	18.80	20.13	21.34	IV.
159.05	170.35	180.87	190.11	194.66	204.18	212.86	219.96	225.47	241.30	V.

Line

II-15 Total investment of commercial banks (1945-46: FRB worksheets; 1947-58: *Federal Reserve Bulletin*, e.g., December 1956, p. 1332) minus lines II-13, II-14, II-17 of this table, and Federal Reserve Bank stock (see line II-17 below for source).

17 Stock held by all banks (*Annual Report of the Comptroller of the Currency*, e.g., 1954, Table 38, p. 161) less FRB stock held by commercial banks (*Annual Report, FDIC*, e.g., 1948, Table 108, p. 94), and stock held by mutual savings banks (Table III-5d, line II-17).

20 Line II-21 minus lines II-1 through II-17.

21 Total assets (1946, 1948, and 1949: FRB worksheets; 1945, 1947, and 1950-58: *Federal Reserve Bulletin*, e.g., December 1956, p. 1329) plus the difference between gross loans (sum of lines II-6 through II-12) and net loans (*Federal Reserve Bulletin*, e.g., June 1955, p. 668) minus the book value of tangible assets (Table III-5n, col. 3).

III-1 Total deposit liabilities of commercial banks (*Federal Reserve Bulletin*, e.g., March 1958, p. 315) minus line III-2.

2 1945-46, 1948-49: Sum of: time deposit liabilities to banks in U.S. and banks in foreign countries (*Annual Report of the Comptroller of the Currency*, e.g., 1946, p. 121), and other time deposit liabilities (see line III-1 above for source).
1947, 1950-58: Total time deposit liabilities (*Federal Reserve Bulletin*, e.g., March 1958, p. 319).

9 Item on "bills payable, rediscounts, and other liabilities for borrowed money" of all banks in continental U.S. (*Annual Report of the Comptroller of the Currency*, e.g., 1946, p. 117) minus same item for mutual savings banks (Table III-5d, line III-9).

10 FRB worksheets.

(Notes continued at foot of page 165)

TABLE III-5d

Mutual Savings Banks, 1945-58 (billion dollars)

	1945	1946	1947	1948
I. Tangible assets				
7. Total	.14	.15	.15	.15
II. Intangible assets				
1. Currency and demand deposits	.60	.66	.68	.65
a. Monetary metals				
b. Other	.60	.66	.68	.65
2. Other bank deposits and shares	.01	.16	.21	.23
6. Consumer credit	.02	.02	.04	.04
8. Loans on securities	a	a	a	a
10. Other loans	.05	.07	.05	.07
11. Mortgages, nonfarm	4.18	4.42	4.83	5.77
a. Residential	3.39	3.59	3.94	4.76
b. Nonresidential	.80	.83	.89	1.02
12. Mortgages, farm	.02	.03	.03	.03
13. Securities, U.S. government	10.68	11.78	11.98	11.48
a. Short-term	.16	.44	.49	.54
b. Savings bonds	.21	.25	.30	.48
c. Other long-term	10.31	11.09	11.19	10.46
14. Securities, state and local	.09	.06	.06	.07
15. Securities, other bonds and notes	1.02	1.19	1.51	2.01
17. Securities, common stock	.14	.15	.15	.16
20. Other intangible assets	.07	.07	.07	.08
21. Total	16.88	18.61	19.61	20.59
III. Liabilities				
2. Other bank deposits and shares	15.38	16.87	17.75	18.39
9. Bank loans, n.e.c.	a	a	a	a
13. Other liabilities	.05	.07	.09	.09
14. Total	15.43	16.94	17.84	18.48
IV. Equities	1.59	1.82	1.92	2.26
V. Total assets or liabilities and equities	17.02	18.76	19.76	20.74

[a]Under $5 million.

Line	
I-7	Table III-5n, col. 4 multiplied by col. 11.
II-1	Total currency and deposits of mutual savings banks (1945, 1947-58: *Federal Reserve Bulletin*, e.g., December 1956, p. 1329; 1946: *Annual Report of the Federal Deposit Insurance Corporation*, 1946, p. 123) less time deposits (line II-2).
2	FRB worksheets.
6	FRB worksheets.
8	*Annual Report, Comptroller of the Currency*, e.g., 1955, p. 166.
10	1945-46: Gross loans (*Annual Report, FDIC*, e.g., 1946, p. 123) minus lines II-6, II-8, II-11, and II-12; 1947-58: Non-real estate loans (*Annual Report, FDIC*, e.g., 1955, Table 105, p. 124) minus lines II-6 and II-8.
11	Table IV-b-11, line 5d.
11a	Table IV-b-11a, line 5d.
11b	Table IV-b-11b, line 5d.
12	Table IV-b-12, line 5d.
13	1945-46: *Annual Report, FDIC*, e.g., 1945, p. 111, Table 105. 1947-58: *Federal Reserve Bulletin*, e.g., December 1956, p. 1329.
13a	Table IV-b-13a, line 5d.
13b	Table IV-b-13b, line 5d.
13c	Table IV-b-13c, line 5d.
14	1945-46: See line II-13 above; 1947-58: *Annual Report, FDIC*, e.g., 1955, Table 105, p. 124.
15	Total securities (see line II-13 above for sources) less lines II-13, II-14, and II-17.
17	*Annual Report, FDIC*, e.g., 1955, Table 105, p. 124.
20	Total assets minus net loans (see note to line II-1 for sources), lines II-1, II-2, II-13 through II-17, and tangible assets at book value (Table III-5n).
21	Sum of lines II-1 through II-20.

1949	1950	1951	1952	1953	1954	1955	1956	1957	1958	
										I.
.19	.19	.17	.20	.22	.25	.26	.29	.31	.32	7.
										II.
.65	.63	.70	.70	.74	.76	.74	.76	.76	.76	1.
.65	.63	.70	.70	.74	.76	.74	.76	.76	.76	
.22	.17	.19	.22	.24	.27	.22	.16	.12	.16	2.
.04	.06	.06	.07	.08	.08	.10	.13	.13	.14	6.
a	a	a	a	a	.01	.02	.02	.01	.01	8.
.07	.07	.07	.07	.08	.09	.09	.10	.13	.17	10.
6.67	8.22	9.87	11.33	12.89	14.95	17.40	19.69	21.11	23.21	11.
5.57	7.05	8.60	9.88	11.33	13.21	15.57	17.70	19.01	20.94	
1.10	1.16	1.27	1.44	1.56	1.74	1.83	1.98	2.10	2.27	
.04	.04	.05	.05	.05	.06	.06	.06	.06	.05	12.
11.43	10.87	9.82	9.42	9.18	8.75	8.46	7.97	7.55	7.26	13.
.44	.11	.18	.26	.48	.16	.26	.24	.45	.30	
.50	.58	.58	.59	.56	.55	.52	.45	.30	.22	
10.49	10.18	9.06	8.57	8.14	8.04	7.68	7.28	6.80	6.74	
.09	.09	.15	.32	.41	.60	.64	.67	.68	.73	14.
2.15	2.07	2.20	2.57	2.86	2.95	2.69	2.82	3.56	4.11	15.
.16	.18	.23	.34	.43	.57	.66	.70	.77	.86	17.
.10	.12	.17	.17	.20	.21	.23	.25	.28	.30	20.
21.62	22.52	23.51	25.26	27.16	29.30	31.31	33.33	35.16	37.76	21.
										III.
19.27	20.01	20.89	22.59	24.36	26.30	28.13	30.00	31.66	34.01	2.
a	a	a	a	a	a	a	a	a	.01	9.
.11	.14	.15	.16	.21	.28	.33	.36	.44	.53	13.
19.38	20.15	21.04	22.75	24.57	26.58	28.46	30.36	32.10	34.55	14.
2.43	2.56	2.64	2.71	2.81	2.97	3.11	3.26	3.37	3.53	IV.
21.81	22.71	23.68	25.46	27.38	29.55	31.57	33.62	35.47	38.08	V.

Line

III-2 *Federal Reserve Bulletin*, e.g., March 1958, p. 314.

9 Bills payable, rediscounts, and other liabilities for borrowed money, from *Annual Report, Comptroller of the Currency*, e.g., 1955, Table 42, p. 201.

13 Line III-14 minus lines III-2 and III-9.

14 Line V minus line IV.

IV Surplus, undivided profits, and reserves and retirement account for capital notes and debentures (*Annual Report, Comptroller of the Currency*, e.g., 1955, Table 42, p. 201), plus difference between gross loans and net loans (see notes to lines II-10 and II-20 for source) and the difference between current value and book value of tangible assets (see line I-7).

V Line I-7 plus line II-21.

Notes to Table III-5c (concluded)

III-13 Line III-14 minus lines III-1 through III-10.

14 Line V minus line IV.

IV Sum of: capital stock; surplus; undivided profits; reserves and retirement account for preferred stock and capital notes and debentures, of all active banks in the U.S. (*Annual Report, Comptroller of the Currency*, e.g., 1955, Table 38, p. 170); plus the difference between gross loans and net loans (see note to line II-21 above); and the difference between current value and book value of tangible assets (see note to line I-7 above), minus the sum of: surplus; undivided profits; reserves and retirement account for capital notes and debentures, of all active mutual savings banks (*Annual Report, Comptroller of the Currency*, e.g., 1955, Table 42, p. 201).

V Sum of lines I-7 and II-21.

TABLE III-5e

Savings and Loan Associations, 1945-59

(billion dollars)

	1945	1946	1947	1948	1949
I. Tangible assets					
7. Total	.11	.14	.14	.15	.24
II. Intangible assets					
1. Currency and demand deposits	.40	.47	.47	.53	.61
a. Monetary metals					
b. Other	.40	.47	.47	.53	.61
6. Consumer credit	.02	.06	.09	.12	.14
11. Mortgages, nonfarm	5.38	7.14	8.86	10.30	11.62
a. Residential	5.27	7.00	8.68	10.10	11.38
b. Nonresidential	.11	.14	.18	.21	.23
13. Securities, U.S. government	2.42	2.01	1.74	1.46	1.46
a. Short-term	.20	.20	.20	.10	.10
b. Savings bonds	.20	.20	.20	.30	.40
c. Other long-term	2.02	1.61	1.34	1.06	.96
20. Other intangible assets	.43	.43	.43	.51	.65
21. Total	8.65	10.11	11.59	12.92	14.48
III. Liabilities					
2. Other bank deposits and shares	7.39	8.56	9.76	10.97	12.47
9. Bank loans, n.e.c.	.14	.11	.11	.07	.07
10. Other loans	.31	.50	.70	.74	.70
13. Other liabilities	.26	.29	.26	.28	.28
14. Total	8.10	9.46	10.83	12.06	13.52
IV. Equities	.65	.79	.90	1.01	1.21
V. Total assets or liabilities and equities	8.76	10.25	11.73	13.07	14.72

Line

I-7 Table III-5n, col. 8 multiplied by col. 11.

II-1 Cash assets of savings and loan associations less member deposits with Federal Home Loan Banks (from Federal Home Loan Bank Board, *Savings and Home Financing Source Book, 1961*, pp. 6 and 8).

6 FRB worksheets.

11 Table IV-b-11, line 5e.

11a Table IV-b-11a, line 5e.

11b Table IV-b-11b, line 5e.

13 *Savings and Home Financing Source Book, 1961*, p. 8.

13a Table IV-b-13a, line 5e.

13b Table IV-b-13b, line 5e.

13c Table IV-b-13c, line 5e.

20 Line II-21 minus the sum of lines II-1 through II-13. This line apparently includes a considerable amount of nonguaranteed federal agency securities, mainly notes of Federal Home Loan Banks and the Federal National Mortgage Association, which belong in line II-15, "Securities, other bonds and notes." Data on these holdings became available starting with June 1960 (*Treasury Bulletin*, September 1960) when the Treasury Ownership Survey was expanded. The FRB estimates savings and loan association holdings of nonguaranteed federal agency securities as follows: 1952-55, $.1 billion; 1956, .3 billion; 1957-58, .5 billion; and 1959, .6 billion.

1950	1951	1952	1953	1954	1955	1956	1957	1958	1959	
										I.
.29	.30	.39	.46	.56	.70	.86	1.03	1.15	1.35	7.
										II.
.70	.80	.87	.92	1.18	1.37	1.44	1.49	1.76	1.59	1.
.70	.80	.87	.92	1.18	1.37	1.44	1.49	1.76	1.59	
.20	.23	.30	.35	.40	.48	.56	.64	.70	.70	6.
13.66	15.56	18.40	21.96	26.11	31.41	35.73	40.01	45.63	53.09	11.
13.38	15.25	18.03	21.52	25.59	30.78	35.01	39.21	44.72	52.03	
.27	.31	.37	.44	.52	.63	.72	.80	.91	1.06	
1.49	1.60	1.79	1.92	2.02	2.34	2.78	3.17	3.82	4.48	13.
.10	.20	.20	.20	.20	.30	.20	.50	.30		
.50	.50	.50	.50	.50	.53	.40	.32	.32		
.89	.90	1.09	1.22	1.32	1.51	2.18	2.35	3.20		
.67	.82	1.03	1.26	1.53	1.57	1.77	2.11	2.38	2.67	20.
16.72	19.01	22.39	26.41	31.24	37.17	42.28	47.42	54.29	62.53	21.
										III.
13.99	16.11	19.20	22.85	27.25	32.14	37.15	41.91	47.98	54.58	2.
.08	.09	.08	.08	.08	.13	.12	.11	.15	.25	9.
1.22	1.22	1.37	1.51	1.66	2.34	2.13	2.13	2.44	3.46	10.
.33	.35	.36	.39	.45	.48	.51	.63	.73	.85	13.
15.62	17.77	21.01	24.83	29.44	35.09	39.91	44.78	51.30	59.14	14.
1.39	1.54	1.77	2.04	2.36	2.78	3.23	3.67	4.14	4.74	IV.
17.01	19.31	22.78	26.87	31.80	37.87	43.14	48.45	55.44	63.88	V.

Line

II-21 Total assets (from *Savings and Home Financing Source Book, 1961*, p. 8), minus tangible assets at book value, which are the sum of real estate owned, office building (net), and furniture and fixtures (net), from Federal Home Loan Bank Board, *Trends in the Savings and Loan Field*, 1960 and 1957, Table 2.

III-2 Savings capital, from *Savings and Home Financing Source Book, 1961*, p. 8, plus line on "government savings capital," from *Trends in the Savings and Loan Field, 1957*.

9 Column on "FHLB advances and other borrowed money" less "advances outstanding" of Federal Home Loan Banks, from *Savings and Home Financing Source Book, 1961*, pp. 6 and 8.

10 Federal Home Loan Bank advances outstanding, from *Savings and Home Financing Source Book, 1961*, Table 1, plus line on "loans in process" from *Trends in the Savings and Loan Field*, 1960 and 1957, Table 2.

13 Line III-14 minus the sum of lines III-2 through III-10.

14 Line V minus line IV.

IV Column on "reserves and undivided profits" from *Savings and Home Financing Source Book, 1961*, p. 8, Table 3-a, minus book value tangible assets (see note to Line II-21) plus current value tangible assets (Line I-7).

V Line I-7 plus line II-21.

TABLE III-5f

Investment Companies, 1945-58

(billion dollars)

	1945	1946	1947	1948
I. Tangible assets				
II. Intangible assets				
1. Currency and demand deposits	.15	.15	.14	.14
a. Monetary metals				
b. Other	.15	.15	.14	.14
11. Mortgages, nonfarm	.10	.14	.22	.28
a. Residential	.09	.13	.20	.24
b. Nonresidential	.01	.02	.02	.04
13. Securities, U.S. government	.23	.18	.19	.14
c. Other long-term	.23	.18	.19	.14
15. Securities, other bonds and notes	.22	.20	.18	.19
16. Securities, preferred stock	.25	.24	.25	.27
17. Securities, common stock	2.65	2.56	2.52	2.56
20. Other intangible assets	.03	.04	.03	.05
21. Total	3.63	3.53	3.54	3.63
III. Liabilities				
IV. Equities	3.63	3.54	3.55	3.63
V. Total assets or liabilities and equities	3.63	3.54	3.55	3.63

Sum of corresponding lines from Tables III-5f-1, III-5f-2, and III-5f-3; except line II-11-a, for which see notes to Table IV-b-11a, line 5f.

TABLE III-5f-1

Open-End Investment Companies, 1945-58

(billion dollars)

	1945	1946	1947	1948
I. Tangible assets				
II. Intangible assets				
1. Currency and demand deposits	.07	.07	.07	.07
13. Securities, U.S. government	.04	.03	.04	.06
15. Securities, other bonds and notes	.11	.12	.12	.13
16. Securities, preferred stock	.11	.12	.13	.14
17. Securities, common stock	.94	.95	1.05	1.12
21. Total	1.27	1.30	1.41	1.52
III. Liabilities				
IV. Equities	1.27	1.30	1.41	1.52
V. Total assets or liabilities and equities	1.27	1.30	1.41	1.52

Line

II-1, 13, 15, 16, 17 — 1945-53: Securities and Exchange Commission, *Statistical Bulletin*, e.g., June 1951, p. 17.
1954-58: National Association of Investment Companies worksheets.

1946-55: The sum of lines II-15, II-16, and II-17 was obtained by subtracting lines II-1 and II-13 from line II-21. Common stock of The Coca-Cola Company held by Coca-Cola International (a nondiversified open-end investment company) was estimated from Coca-Cola International, *Annual Report*, and subtracted from sum of lines II-15, II-1 and II-17 before estimating the breakdown of investments. Then it was readded to lin II-17. The residual was distributed by the percentage breakdown indicated in "Distribution of Assets of 20 Open-End Investment Companies, 1946-1955," *Institutional Investors and the Stock Market, 1953-1955*, Committee on Banking and Currency, U.S. Senate, December 1956, Table 12, p. 17.

1949	1950	1951	1952	1953	1954	1955	1956	1957	1958	
										I.
										II.
.14	.18	.21	.20	.24	.24	.24	.27	.30	.30	1.
.14	.18	.21	.20	.24	.24	.24	.27	.30	.30	
.30	.34	.33	.34	.36	.35	.34	.33	.31	.28	11.
.26	.30	.29	.30	.31	.31	.30	.29	.27	.24	
.04	.04	.04	.04	.05	.04	.04	.04	.04	.04	
.18	.20	.20	.19	.19	.19	.33	.35	.35	.49	13.
.18	.20	.20	.19	.19	.19	.33	.35	.35	.49	
.21	.25	.30	.40	.41	.55	.73	.84	.98	1.22	15.
.27	.30	.34	.29	.46	.54	.65	.73	.62	.93	16.
3.24	4.04	5.17	6.29	6.47	9.74	12.10	12.63	11.89	17.15	17.
.03	.04	.04	.04	.04	.04	.07	.05	.06	.07	20.
4.39	5.34	6.60	7.76	8.16	11.66	14.46	15.22	14.51	20.45	21.
										III.
4.38	5.35	6.61	7.76	8.18	11.66	14.46	15.22	14.51	20.45	IV.
4.38	5.35	6.61	7.76	8.18	11.66	14.46	15.22	14.51	20.45	V.

1949	1950	1951	1952	1953	1954	1955	1956	1957	1958	
										I.
										II.
.08	.10	.14	.13	.16	.17	.18	.22	.25	.23	1.
.10	.13	.13	.13	.13	.14	.26	.28	.28	.40	13.
.15	.20	.24	.33	.34	.44	.67		.78	.94	15.
.14	.20	.24	.20	.35	.42	.51	.59	.48	.76	16.
1.46	1.82	2.28	3.20	3.32	5.09	6.46	7.42	7.05	11.07	17.
1.94	2.44	3.04	3.99	4.29	6.25	7.99	9.17	8.83	13.40	21.
										III.
1.94	2.44	3.04	3.99	4.29	6.25	7.99	9.17	8.83	13.40	IV.
1.94	2.44	3.04	3.99	4.29	6.25	7.99	9.17	8.83	13.40	V.

ine

-15, 16, 17 — 1945 and 1956: Same method as above except 1946 and 1955 proportions were used.
1957-58: Line II-15, FRB worksheets.
Line II-16, 6.5 per cent of FRB worksheet figure for total stock.
Line II-17, 93.5 per cent of FRB worksheet figure for total stock, plus estimates of Coca-Cola International holdings of common stock.

21 — 1945-53: Securities and Exchange Commission, *Statistical Bulletin*, e.g., June 1951, p. 17;
1954-58: National Association of Investment Companies, *Investment Companies, A Statistical Summary 1940-1959* (New York, 1960), and estimates for Coca-Cola International, from *Moody's Industrials*, various issues.

Same as line II-21.

Same as line II-21.

TABLE III-5f-2

Closed-End Investment Companies, 1945-58 (billion dollars)

	1945	1946	1947	1948
I. Tangible assets				
II. Intangible assets				
1. Currency and demand deposits	.07	.07	.06	.06
13. Securities, U.S. government	.15	.12	.13	.07
15. Securities, other bonds and notes	.05	.03	.03	.03
16. Securities, preferred stock	.10	.07	.08	.10
17. Securities, common stock	1.71	1.61	1.47	1.44
20. Other intangible assets	.02	.03	.02	.03
21. Total	2.10	1.93	1.79	1.73
III. Liabilities				
IV. Equities	2.10	1.93	1.79	1.73
V. Total assets or liabilities and equities	2.10	1.93	1.79	1.73

Line

II-1 through II-20 — Total assets (line II-21) were allocated by type, using data from the following sources:

1945-51: SEC *Statistical Bulletin*, e.g., June 1952, p. 16. The distribution of corporate security holdings by type of security was estimated as follows: 1. The distribution for Christiana securities was taken from various issues of that company's annual report, and that for Delaware Realty from SEC worksheets. 2. The distribution for other investment companies, 1945-49, was taken from Goldsmith, *A Study of Saving*, Vol. I, Table V-62, p. 563. For 1950-51, bonds were interpolated geometrically between 1949 and 1952; preferred stock was interpolated roughly between those two years; and common stock was derived as a residual. From the 1952 figures, derived as indicated below, the Christiana and Delaware data were removed.

1952-55: Morris Mendelson, *The Flow-of-Funds through the Financial Markets, 1953-1955,*

TABLE III-5f-3

Face-Amount Investment Companies, 1945-58 (million dollars)

	1945	1946	1947	1948
I. Tangible assets				
II. Intangible assets				
1. Currency and demand deposits	9	8	12	10
11. Mortgages, nonfarm	103	145	222	277
13. Securities, U.S. government	38	33	20	5
15. Securities, other bonds and notes	58	52	36	33
16. Securities, preferred stock	42	53	36	33
17. Securities, common stock	4	4	4	5
20. Other intangible assets	6	10	14	19
21. Total	260	305	344	382
III. Liabilities				
IV. Equities				
V. Total assets or liabilities and equities	260	305	344	382

The universe of face-amount investment companies consists of two companies: Investors Diversified Services and Investors Syndicate of America. The former (prior to 1949 called Investors Syndicate) is the parent company of the latter. Investors Diversified Services no longer issues certificates but still has certificates outstanding. The data were taken from the published annual reports of the two companies and *Moody's Banking and Finance Manual* (various issues). Figures for Investors Diversified Services, 1945-46, are from Goldsmith, *A Study of Saving*, Vol. I, Table V-72, p. 573.

"U.S. government securities" and "other bonds and notes" (which includes a small amount of municipals) are at cost.

1949	1950	1951	1952	1953	1954	1955	1956	1957	1958	
										I.
										II.
.05	.06	.06	.06	.07	.06	.05	.05	.05	.06	1.
.07	.07	.06	.05	.06	.05	.07	.07	.07	.09	13.
.03	.03	.04	.05	.05	.06	.07	.06	.06	.08	15.
.10	.07	.06	.04	.05	.06	.06	.06	.06	.08	16.
1.77	2.21	2.88	3.07	3.13	4.62	5.61	5.17	4.80	6.03	17.
.01	.01		.01		.01	.03	.01	.01	.02	20.
2.03	2.45	3.10	3.28	3.36	4.86	5.89	5.42	5.05	6.36	21.
										III.
2.03	2.45	3.10	3.28	3.36	4.86	5.89	5.42	5.05	6.36	IV.
2.03	2.45	3.10	3.28	3.36	4.86	5.89	5.42	5.05	6.36	V.

Line

NBER Working Memorandum, 1959, p. I-210.

1956-58: Sum of Christiana, Delaware, and other companies. Other companies estimated by assuming the same percentage distribution of assets as in 1955 for all companies except Christiana, Delaware, and Newmont Mining.

21 1945-51: SEC, *Statistical Bulletin*, e.g., June, 1952, p. 16.

1952-55: Mendelson, *Flow-of-Funds*, p. I-210.

1956-58: Christiana Securities (from annual report, various issues) and Delaware Realty (stock data from New York Stock Exchange, other data extrapolated) added to other companies (estimated by assuming the same rate of growth of total assets from 1955 as indicated for closed end companies in National Association of Investment Companies, *Investment Companies, A Statistical Summary, 1940-1958*, New York, 1959.

IV See line II-21 above.

V See line II-21 above.

1949	1950	1951	1952	1953	1954	1955	1956	1957	1958	
										I.
										II.
7	16	9	11	6	6	6	4	4	3	1.
300	339	331	345	357	353	343	331	312	279	11.
12	3	10	3	3	4	1	1	1	1	13.
34	19	23	25	26	57	78	106	143	204	15.
34	29	38	52	63	65	78	84	80	91	16.
6	11	14	21	23	30	33	40	46	54	17.
23	28	36	30	34	33	44	44	50	54	20.
416	445	461	487	512	548	583	610	636	686	21.
										III.
										IV.
416	445	461	487	512	548	583	610	636	686	V.

"Common" and "preferred stocks" are at market except in the following cases:

a. Common stock of Investors Diversified Services is at cost throughout because it represents, almost entirely, stock of its wholly owned subsidiaries.
b. Preferred and common stock values of Investors Syndicate of America for 1945-51 are at cost. (The difference between cost and market values at this time is slight.)
c. Preferred stock of Investors Diversified Services for 1945-46 is at cost.
d. Common stock of Investors Diversified Services was assumed to be the same in 1945-46 as in 1947.

TABLE III-5g

Credit Unions, 1945-59

(billion dollars)

	1945	1946	1947	1948	1949
I. Tangible assets					
II. Intangible assets					
1. Currency and demand deposits	.06	.06	.07	.08	.08
a. Monetary metals					
b. Other	.06	.06	.07	.08	.08
2. Other bank deposits and shares	.07	.07	.06	.07	.10
6. Consumer credit	.10	.15	.24	.33	.44
10. Other loans	a	a	a	a	a
11. Mortgages, nonfarm	.03	.04	.04	.06	.07
a. Residential	.03	.04	.04	.06	.07
13. Securities, U.S. government	.18	.18	.18	.16	.14
c. Other long-term	.18	.18	.18	.16	.14
21. Total	.44	.50	.59	.70	.83
III. Liabilities					
2. Other bank deposits and shares	.37	.43	.51	.60	.70
7. Trade debt	.03	.02	.03	.04	.06
14. Total	.40	.45	.54	.64	.76
IV. Equities	.04	.05	.05	.06	.07
V. Total assets or liabilities and equities	.44	.50	.59	.70	.83

Line

II-1 FRB worksheets.

2 Line II-21 minus sum of lines II-1 and II-6 through II-13.

6 *Federal Reserve Bulletin*, e.g., June 1959, p. 630.

10 Loans outstanding for all credit unions, from Credit Union National Association, *Credit Union Yearbook*, 1960, Table I, p. 40.

11 1945-56: Saul B. Klaman, *The Volume of Mortgage Debt in the Postwar Decade*, New York, NBER, 1958, Table 2, column 13, p. 42.
1957-59: FRB worksheets.

13, 13c FRB worksheets.

21 1945-58: *Credit Union Yearbook, 1960*, Table I, p. 40.
1959: *Social Security Bulletin*, January 1961.

III-2 1945-57: *Credit Union Yearbook, 1960*, Table I, p. 40.
1958-59: *Social Security Bulletin*, January 1961.

7 Line III-14 minus line III-2.

14 Line V minus line IV.

1950	1951	1952	1953	1954	1955	1956	1957	1958	1959	
										I.
										II.
.10	.15	.15	.17	.22	.23	.26	.29	.33	.30	1.
.10	.15	.15	.17	.22	.23	.26	.29	.33	.30	
.10	.15	.24	.30	.37	.44	.55	.63	.82	.90	2.
.59	.64	.84	1.12	1.34	1.68	2.01	2.43	2.66	3.23	6.
.01	.02	.03	.03	.03	.05	.04	.06	.06	.08	10.
.08	.10	.12	.15	.18	.21	.27	.27	.35	.39	11.
.08	.10	.12	.15	.18	.21	.27	.27	.35	.39	
.12	.14	.14	.13	.13	.13	.14	.13	.13	.13	13.
.12	.14	.14	.13	.13	.13	.14	.13	.13	.13	
1.00	1.20	1.52	1.90	2.27	2.74	3.27	3.81	4.35	5.03	21.
										III.
.85	1.04	1.31	1.64	1.98	2.38	2.84	3.30	3.77	4.33	2.
.07	.06	.10	.12	.13	.15	.18	.19	.21	.27	7.
.92	1.10	1.41	1.76	2.11	2.53	3.02	3.49	3.98	4.60	14.
.08	.10	.11	.14	.16	.21	.25	.32	.37	.43	IV.
1.00	1.20	1.52	1.90	2.27	2.74	3.27	3.81	4.35	5.03	V.

Line

IV Sum of reserves and undivided profits.

1945-51: *Reserves* for state-chartered credit unions, from *Monthly Labor Review* (e.g., November 1947, p. 556); reserves for federally-chartered unions, from Federal Security Agency, *Federal Credit Unions, Report of Operations* (e.g., 1948, p. 4).

Undivided Profits: Sum of undivided profits of federally-chartered credit unions (*Federal Credit Unions, Report of Operations*) and undivided profits of state-chartered credit unions. The latter was estimated from the 1952 figure for undistributed profits by subtracting the addition to undistributed profits in each year. The addition to undistributed profits was estimated as net earnings less the sum of dividends and net addition to reserves. Data are from *Monthly Labor Review.*

1952-55: Morris Mendelson, *Flow-of-Funds*, pp. I-215 to I-217.

1956-59: Same method as 1945-51. All figures in *Social Security Bulletin* (e.g., November 1957, p. 20, Table 4).

V Same as line II-21.

[a]Under $5 million.

TABLE III-5h

Life Insurance Companies, 1945-59

(billion dollars)

	1945	1946	1947	1948	1949
I. Tangible assets					
7. Total	.93	1.00	1.21	1.45	2.12
II. Intangible assets					
1. Currency and demand deposits	.78	.77	1.02	.91	.91
a. Monetary metals					
b. Other	.78	.77	1.02	.91	.91
10. Other loans	1.96	1.89	1.94	2.06	2.24
11. Mortgages, nonfarm	5.86	6.36	7.78	9.84	11.77
a. Residential	3.70	4.02	5.07	6.79	8.39
b. Nonresidential	2.15	2.34	2.71	3.05	3.38
12. Mortgages, farm	.78	.80	.90	.99	1.14
13. Securities, U.S. government	20.58	21.63	20.02	16.75	15.29
a. Short-term	.31	.76	.23	.25	.30
b. Savings bonds	.10	.12	.14	.24	.26
c. Other long-term	20.17	20.75	19.65	16.26	14.73
14. Securities, state and local	.72	.61	.61	.87	1.05
15. Securities, other bonds and notes	11.30	13.11	16.13	20.36	22.93
16. Securities, preferred stock	.82	.97	1.03	1.06	1.26
17. Securities, common stock	.18	.28	.36	.37	.46
20. Other intangible assets	.96	1.03	1.09	1.24	1.33
21. Total	43.94	47.45	50.88	54.45	58.38
III. Liabilities					
3. Life insurance reserves, private	43.57	47.24	50.70	54.44	58.45
8. Loans on securities	.37				
13. Other liabilities	.64	.70	.78	.82	.90
14. Total	44.58	47.94	51.48	55.26	59.35
IV. Equities	.29	.51	.61	.64	1.15
V. Total assets or liabilities and equities	44.87	48.45	52.09	55.90	60.50

Line

I-7 Table III-5n, col. 5 multiplied by col. 11.

II-1 Institute of Life Insurance, *Life Insurance Fact Book*, e.g., 1955, p. 88.

10 Total life insurance policy loans from *ibid.*, 1961, p. 91.

11, 12 *Ibid.*, 1961, p. 87. Some foreign mortgages, chiefly Canadian, are included here. See Table IV-c-11.

11a Table IV-b-11a, line 5h.

11b Table IV-b-11b, line 5h.

13 *Life Insurance Fact Book*, 1961, p. 71.

13a Table IV-b-13a, line 5h.

13b Table IV-b-13b, line 5h.

13c Table IV-b-13c, line 5h.

14 *Life Insurance Fact Book*, 1961, p. 73.

15 *Ibid.*, pp. 72-82: Sum of foreign government bonds (including provincial and local), railroad bonds, public utility bonds, and industrial and miscellaneous bonds.

16, 17 1945-46: Total stock from *ibid.*, p. 84; common stock from Goldsmith, *A Study of Saving*, Vol. I, p. 456, col. 7.
1947-59: *Life Insurance Fact Book*, 1961, p. 83.

20 Line II-21 less the sum of lines II-1 through II-17.

21 Line V minus line I-7.

1950	1951	1952	1953	1954	1955	1956	1957	1958	1959	
										I.
2.30	2.35	2.72	2.91	3.34	3.77	4.09	4.46	4.54	4.93	7.
										II.
1.00	1.10	1.15	1.22	1.24	1.26	1.28	1.29	1.37	1.31	1.
1.00	1.10	1.15	1.22	1.24	1.26	1.28	1.29	1.37	1.31	
2.41	2.59	2.71	2.91	3.13	3.29	3.52	3.87	4.19	4.62	10.
14.78	17.79	19.55	21.44	23.93	27.17	30.51	32.65	34.40	36.37	11.
11.09	13.64	15.04	16.56	18.56	21.21	23.74	24.99	25.92	27.24	
3.68	4.15	4.50	4.88	5.37	5.96	6.76	7.66	8.47	9.12	
1.33	1.53	1.70	1.89	2.05	2.27	2.48	2.58	2.67	2.84	12.
13.46	11.01	10.25	9.83	9.07	8.58	7.56	7.03	7.18	6.87	13.
.56	.65	.54	.47	.55	.41	.28	.25	.52		
.31	.31	.32	.30	.29	.27	.23	.13	.10		
12.59	10.05	9.39	9.06	8.23	7.90	7.05	6.65	6.56		
1.15	1.17	1.15	1.30	1.85	2.04	2.27	2.38	2.68	3.20	14.
24.76	27.47	30.57	33.28	35.38	37.13	39.28	41.95	44.37	46.62	15.
1.45	1.40	1.49	1.53	1.73	1.74	1.55	1.52	1.56	1.61	16.
.65	.82	.96	1.04	1.54	1.89	1.95	1.87	2.55	2.95	17.
1.59	1.77	1.95	2.07	2.27	2.48	2.79	3.05	3.25	3.61	20.
62.58	66.65	71.48	76.51	82.19	87.85	93.19	98.19	104.22	110.00	21.
										III.
62.67	66.85	71.85	76.84	82.68	88.42	93.71	98.79	104.87	110.65	3.
										8.
1.01	1.08	1.16	1.26	1.34	1.48	1.67	1.84	1.97	2.19	13.
63.68	67.93	73.01	78.10	84.02	89.90	95.38	100.63	106.84	112.84	14.
1.20	1.07	1.19	1.32	1.51	1.72	1.90	2.02	1.92	2.09	IV.
64.88	69.00	74.20	79.42	85.53	91.62	97.28	102.65	108.76	114.93	V.

Line

III-3 Line III-14 less the sum of lines III-8 and III-13.

8 Federal Reserve Board worksheets.

13 1945-48: Goldsmith, *A Study of Saving*, Vol. I, p. 450, Table I-2, col. 3.
1949-52: *Spectator Life Insurance Yearbook*, e.g., 1954, p. 224a.
1953-59: *Life Insurance Fact Book*, e.g., 1956, p. 81, "Miscellaneous Assets—Due and Deferred Premiums."

14 Line V minus line IV.

IV Capital stock from the following sources, plus the difference between current value and book value of tangible assets (see note to I-7 above):
1945-51: *Spectator Life Insurance Yearbook*, e.g., 1954, p. 224a. (1945-48 also in Goldsmith, *A Study of Saving*, Vol. I, p. 450, Table I-2, col. 2.)
1952-59: *Life Insurance Fact Book*, 1961, p. 63, "Capital, Stock Companies."

V Total assets from: *Ibid.*, p. 65, plus the difference between current value and book value for tangible assets (see note I-7 above).

TABLE III-5i

Fire and Casualty Insurance Companies, 1945-58

(billion dollars)

	1945	1946	1947	1948
I. Tangible assets				
7. Total	.13	.16	.17	.21
II. Intangible assets				
1. Currency and demand deposits	.67	.86	1.04	1.08
a. Monetary metals				
b. Other	.67	.86	1.04	1.08
2. Other bank deposits and shares	0	a	a	a
7. Trade credit	.32	.49	.59	.67
11. Mortgages, nonfarm	.06	.06	.07	.08
a. Residential	.02	.02	.03	.03
b. Nonresidential	.04	.04	.05	.05
13. Securities, U.S. government	3.22	3.41	4.00	4.49
a. Short-term	.34	.39	.54	.89
b. Savings bonds	.19	.22	.26	.41
c. Other long-term	2.69	2.80	3.20	3.19
14. Securities, state and local	.24	.24	.32	.53
15. Securities, other bonds and notes	.46	.46	.52	.69
16. Securities, preferred stock	.59	.60	.60	.59
17. Securities, common stock	1.81	1.73	1.76	1.82
20. Other intangible assets	.14	.12	.14	.15
21. Total	7.51	7.97	9.04	10.10
III. Liabilities				
13. Other liabilities	3.85	4.60	5.59	6.43
14. Total	3.85	4.60	5.59	6.43
IV. Equities	3.79	3.53	3.62	3.88
V. Total assets or liabilities and equities	7.64	8.13	9.21	10.31

Source: All figures unless otherwise noted were derived as follows: Balance sheets were combined fo stock, mutual, reciprocals, and Lloyds groups (see *Best's Fire and Casualty Aggregates and Averages*, e.g., 1955, pp. 44, 132, 186, 188). Because all mutuals are not covered in the balance sheet, figures were stepped up by the ratio of total mutual company assets (*Ibid.*, p. 1) to the total asset figure of covered mutuals (e.g., *Ibid.*, p. 132). From these totals, assets for the Travelers Insurance Company's Accident Department (*Moody's Bank and Finance Manual* "Summary of Total Admitted Assets," e.g., 1950, p. 1130) were subtracted for every year.

Line

I-7 Table III-5n, col. 7 multiplied by col. 11.

II-2 Represents savings and loan shares held by fire and casualty companies (from *Best's*).

7 Trade credit was assumed to consist of "premium balances" as given in *Best's* (agents' balances and uncollected premiums) minus "miscellaneous assets" given for Travelers Accident Department in *Moody's*.

13 See Source. U.S. government securities are assumed to include direct and guaranteed government obligations only. Nonguaranteed issues are included in line II-15.

15 See Source and note to line II-13. Includes some Canadian government securities as well.

1949	1950	1951	1952	1953	1954	1955	1956	1957	1958	
										I.
.29	.30	.32	.34	.37	.42	.48	.53	.57	.62	7.
										II.
1.14	1.20	1.24	1.32	1.37	1.32	1.35	1.28	1.27	1.33	1.
1.14	1.20	1.24	1.32	1.37	1.32	1.35	1.28	1.27	1.33	
a	a	.01	.02	.02	.02	.02	.02	.02	.02	2.
.74	.76	.88	.95	1.00	1.06	1.15	1.29	1.44	1.58	7.
.09	.11	.12	.12	.14	.14	.15	.16	.16	.16	11.
.04	.04	.05	.05	.06	.06	.06	.06	.05	.05	
.06	.06	.07	.07	.08	.09	.10	.10	.11	.11	
5.00	5.35	5.48	5.82	6.03	6.14	6.00	5.67	5.46	5.40	13.
1.19	1.24	.87	1.01	1.43	.90	.49	.75	1.18	1.10	
.46	.57	.59	.60	.58	.57	.56	.49	.32	.25	
3.35	3.54	4.02	4.21	4.02	4.67	4.95	4.43	3.96	4.05	
.75	1.06	1.45	1.87	2.62	3.40	4.19	4.82	5.44	6.15	14.
.78	.83	.88	1.04	1.16	1.19	1.18	1.21	1.39	1.48	15.
.65	.68	.72	.80	.85	.90	.90	.82	.84	.83	16.
2.30	2.76	3.15	3.52	3.61	5.04	6.02	6.40	5.83	7.51	17.
.17	.19	.24	.28	.34	.39	.43	.47	.55	.55	20.
11.62	12.94	14.17	15.74	17.14	19.60	21.39	22.14	22.40	25.01	21.
										III.
7.20	7.92	8.77	9.85	10.95	11.64	12.42	13.08	14.13	14.97	13.
7.20	7.92	8.77	9.85	10.95	11.64	12.42	13.08	14.13	14.97	14.
4.71	5.32	5.72	6.23	6.56	8.38	9.45	9.59	8.84	10.66	IV.
11.91	13.24	14.49	16.08	17.51	20.02	21.87	22.67	22.97	25.63	V.

Line	
II-16, 17	See Source. Travelers total stock holdings were assumed to be all in common stock.
20	Line II-21 minus sum of lines II-1 to II-17.
III-13, 14	Line V minus line IV.
IV	Total policyholders' surplus (*Best's*, p. 1) adjusted by subtracting $14 million, the part of Travelers paid-up capital imputed to the accident and health department (see Mendelson, *Flow-of-Funds*, p. I-160).
V	Sum of lines I-7 and II-21.

[a] Under $5 million.

TABLE III-5j

Noninsured Pension Plans, 1945-59

(million dollars)

	1945	1946	1947	1948	1949
I. Tangible assets					
II. Intangible assets					
1. Currency and demand deposits	78	99	131	162	205
a. Monetary metals					
b. Other	78	99	131	162	205
11. Mortgages, nonfarm	24	30	34	38	44
a. Residential	24	30	34	38	44
13. Securities, U.S. government	1471	1647	1810	1943	2086
b. Savings bonds	180	350	510	560	612
c. Other long-term	1291	1297	1300	1383	1474
14. Securities, state and local					
15. Securities, other bonds and notes	781	1039	1347	1702	2042
16. Securities, preferred stock	94	123	155	179	212
17. Securities, common stock	195	244	322	398	508
20. Other intangible assets	40	69	96	127	160
21. Total	2683	3251	3896	4550	5255
III. Liabilities					
4. Pension and retirement funds, private	2683	3251	3896	4550	5255
14. Total	2683	3251	3896	4550	5255
IV. Equities					
V. Total assets or liabilities and equities	2683	3251	3896	4550	5255

Sum of Tables III-5j-1 through III-5j-3.

1950	1951	1952	1953	1954	1955	1956	1957	1958	1959	
										I.
										II.
267	308	282	331	329	386	381	444	474	513	1.
267	308	282	331	329	386	381	444	474	513	
51	96	129	166	199	235	344	515	652	877	11.
51	96	129	166	199	235	344	515	652	877	
2302	2425	2422	2584	2592	2894	2691	2417	2450	2720	13.
800	773	782	755	834	853	700	364	351		
1502	1652	1640	1829	1758	2041	1991	2053	2099		
				1			4	4	4	14.
2484	3359	4422	5486	6705	7611	9199	10933	12441	13662	15.
266	355	414	476	533	582	642	682	732	734	16.
671	1034	1550	1962	3460	5067	5951	6359	10068	12941	17.
191	224	301	414	522	576	817	930	984	1097	20.
6231	7802	9522	11419	14341	17351	20025	22282	27805	32549	21.
										III.
6231	7802	9522	11419	14341	17351	20025	22282	27805	32549	4.
6231	7802	9522	11419	14341	17351	20025	22282	27805	32549	14.
										IV.
6231	7802	9522	11419	14341	17351	20025	22282	27805	32549	V.

TABLE III-5j-1

Noninsured Pension Plans, Corporate, 1945-59

(million dollars)

	1945	1946	1947	1948	1949
I. Tangible assets					
II. Intangible assets					
1. Currency and demand deposits	70	90	120	150	193
11. Mortgages, nonfarm	0	4	8	12	16
13. Securities, U.S. government	1,353	1,490	1,630	1,760	1,890
15. Securities, other bonds and notes	663	928	1,223	1,544	1,863
16. Securities, preferred stock	53	68	92	116	147
17. Securities, common stock	159	204	275	346	439
20. Other intangible assets	29	59	88	118	147
21. Total	2,327	2,843	3,436	4,046	4,695
III. Liabilities					
4. Pension and retirement funds, private	2,327	2,843	3,436	4,046	4,695
14. Total	2,327	2,843	3,436	4,046	4,695
IV. Equities					
V. Total assets or liabilities and equities	2,327	2,843	3,436	4,046	4,695

Line

II-1 1945-50: FRB worksheets.
1951-59: SEC, *Corporate Pension Funds*, Release #1680 (May 31, 1960), Table 1, and Release #1533 (June 8, 1958), Table 1.

11 1945-49: Straight-line interpolation between 1945 (assumed to be zero) and 1950.
1950-54: FRB worksheets.
1955-59: SEC, Release #1680, Table 1.

13 See line II-1 above.

15 See line II-1 above.

16 1945-50: Same proportion of total corporate stock at book value (FRB workseets) as in 1951 (SEC, Release #1533, Table 1).
1951-59: See line II-1 above.

1950	1951	1952	1953	1954	1955	1956	1957	1958	1959	
										I.
										II.
253	291	265	313	296	343	332	368	383	407	1.
20	56	77	103	126	146	230	313	405	576	11.
2,080	2,170	2,162	2,297	2,284	2,536	2,293	2,032	1,985	2,148	13.
2,292	3,125	4,142	5,181	6,359	7,225	8,704	10,392	11,731	12,797	15.
194	272	331	397	454	510	570	611	655	657	16.
580	922	1,423	1,816	3,249	4,795	5,648	6,024	9,548	12,251	17.
176	206	277	384	473	511	736	833	892	1,008	20.
5,595	7,042	8,677	10,491	13,241	16,066	18,513	20,573	25,599	29,844	21.
										III.
5,595	7,042	8,677	10,491	13,241	16,066	18,513	20,573	25,599	29,844	4.
5,595	7,042	8,677	10,491	13,241	16,066	18,513	20,573	25,599	29,844	14.
										IV.
5,595	7,042	8,677	10,491	13,241	16,066	18,513	20,573	25,599	29,844	V.

Line

II-17 1945-50: Common stock at book value (see note to line II-16).

1951-54: Common stock at market value. Computed by working back from 1955 (see below) using net purchases of common stock (SEC Release #1680, p. 2), and adjusting by Standard and Poor's combined stock index. For example, the end-1954 market value is estimated from the 1955 market value as follows:

1. Subtract, from 1955 market value, purchases during 1955 (at end-1955 prices). Net purchases at book value (SEC) are adjusted to end-1955 market values by multiplying by the ratio of end-1955 to average 1955 stock prices.
2. Adjust the remaining stock to 1954 prices by multiplying by the ratio of end-1954 to end-1955 stock prices.

Before 1957, the Standard and Poor's index covered 90 stocks. It was used, instead of the index of Table IV-b-17a, because it gave a more logical relationship between book and market values before 1955.

1955-59: Common stock at market value. SEC, Release #1680, Table 3.

20 1945-50: Straight-line interpolation between 1944 (assumed to be zero) and 1951.

1951-59: See line II-1 above.

21 Sum of lines II-1 through II-20.

III-4 Same as line II-21.

14 Same as line II-21.

V Same as line II-21.

TABLE III-5j-2

Noninsured Pension Plans, Union Administered and Multiemployer, 1945-59

(million dollars)

	1945	1946	1947	1948	1949
I. Tangible assets					
II. Intangible assets					
1. Currency and demand deposits	0	1	3	4	5
11. Mortgages, nonfarm	0	1	1	2	3
13. Securities, U.S. government	0	16	31	46	59
15. Securities, other bonds and notes	0	2	3	7	10
16. Securities, preferred stock	0	0	1	2	2
17. Securities, common stock	0	0	1	2	3
20. Other intangible assets	0	1	1	2	4
21. Total	0	21	42	64	85
III. Liabilities					
4. Pension and retirement funds, private	0	21	42	64	85
14. Total	0	21	42	64	85
IV. Equities					
V. Total assets or liabilities and equities	0	21	42	64	85

Note: Ratios of market to book value for common stock are assumed equal to one before 1950; for 1950-59 they are assumed equal to those of corporate pension funds. See Table III-5j-3.

Totals: First computed at book value.

1945-49: Straight-line interpolation between 1945 (assumed to be zero) and 1950.

1950-56: Extrapolated from 1957 by totals obtained directly from U.S. Social Security Administration.

1957: Unpublished data from NBER pension study (in preparation); common stock at market value adjusted to book value via the estimated ratio of market to book value, 1957 (see headnote).

1958: Interpolated by U.S. Social Security Administration totals.

1959: Unpublished data from NBER pension study. Book value totals raised to market value by subtracting common stock at book value and adding common stock at market value (see notes below).

1950	1951	1952	1953	1954	1955	1956	1957	1958	1959	
										I.
										II.
6	9	10	12	23	31	38	62	74	87	1.
4	7	11	17	22	29	44	91	126	166	11.
73	104	126	158	183	223	273	284	363	452	13.
12	19	31	42	56	69	111	147	254	374	15.
3	4	6	7	8	8	11	13	17	22	16.
4	7	11	15	26	36	51	69	183	294	17.
5	7	11	16	28	39	54	70	60	49	20.
106	157	207	266	345	435	583	736	1,077	1,444	21.
										III.
106	157	207	266	345	435	583	736	1,077	1,444	4.
106	157	207	266	345	435	583	736	1,077	1,444	14.
										IV.
106	157	207	266	345	435	583	736	1,077	1,444	V.

Individual items: First computed at book value.

1945-56: 1957 values extrapolated by corresponding items in Table III-5j-3, except for line II-17, which was first adjusted to book values by means of the estimated ratio of market to book value (see headnote). Extrapolated distribution was then adjusted to match totals at book value.

1957: NBER pension study data, with common stock adjusted to book value by dividing by the estimating ratio (see headnote).

1958: Interpolated by U.S. Social Security Administration totals.

1959: NBER pension study data, with common stock at book value adjusted to market value by multiplying by estimating ratios (see headnote).

TABLE III-5j-3

Noninsured Pension Plans, Nonprofit Organizations, 1945-59

(million dollars)

	1945	1946	1947	1948	1949
I. Tangible assets					
II. Intangible assets					
1. Currency and demand deposits	8	8	8	8	7
11. Mortgages, nonfarm	24	25	25	24	25
13. Securities, U.S. government	118	141	149	137	137
14. Securities, state and local					
15. Securities, other bonds and notes	118	109	121	151	169
16. Securities, preferred stock	41	55	62	61	63
17. Securities, common stock	36	40	46	51	66
20. Other intangible assets	11	9	7	7	9
21. Total	356	387	418	440	475
III. Liabilities					
4. Pension and retirement funds, private	356	387	418	440	475
14. Total	356	387	418	440	475
IV. Equities					
V. Total assets or liabilities and equities	356	387	418	440	475

Totals:

1950-59: Totals at book value, directly from U.S. Social Security Administration, adjusted to market value by multiplying by the ratio of market to book value of total assets of sampled funds (see below). Total assets of sampled funds at book value derived by adjusting common stock at market value to book value, using the ratio of book to market value of common stock of corporate pension funds. For common stock of corporate pension reserves at market value, see Table III-5j-1, line II-17; at book value, 1950—see note to Table III-5j-1, line II-17; 1951-54—SEC Release #1533, Table 1; 1955-59—SEC Release #1680, Table 1.

1945-49: Extrapolated from 1950 by total funds (adjusted) reported at Annual Church Pensions Conferences (Huggins & Co. reports) plus total assets of the Red Cross pension fund. Red Cross fiscal year figures are averaged to estimate year-end figures, and Church Pensions Conference report data are ascribed to December of the preceding year. Church Pensions Conference totals include reserves of the YMCA and YWCA and are adjusted by us to omit Canadian funds and Evangelical Lutheran funds, which are insured.

Individual items:

1945-56: Allocated according to the combined asset distribution of seven pension funds in our sample: American Baptist; American Red Cross; Congregational Christian; Church Pension Fund; Presbyterian; United Lutheran; YMCA.
Year-end figures taken where available; otherwise, interpolations were made to derive year-end figures. Each item was calculated at book value, except for common stocks. The latter were taken at market value where available; otherwise, they were adjusted to market value by the ratio of common stocks at market to book values of corporate pension reserves. (See note to *Totals* above. Before 1951, book and market values are assumed equal.) Sources: Annual reports and balance sheets of individual pension funds.

1950	1951	1952	1953	1954	1955	1956	1957	1958	1959	
										I.
										II.
8	8	7	6	10	12	11	14	17	19	1.
27	33	41	46	51	60	70	111	121	135	11.
149	151	134	129	125	135	125	101	102	120	13.
				1			4	4	4	14.
180	215	249	263	290	317	384	394	456	491	15.
69	79	77	72	71	64	61	58	60	55	16.
87	105	116	131	185	236	252	266	337	396	17.
10	11	13	14	21	26	27	27	32	40	20.
530	603	638	662	755	850	929	973	1129	1261	21.
										III.
530	603	638	662	755	850	929	973	1129	1261	4.
530	603	638	662	755	850	929	973	1129	1261	14.
										IV.
530	603	638	662	755	850	929	973	1129	1261	V.

Individual items:

1957-59: Allocated according to unpublished data of the NBER pension study, the coverage of which is considerably higher than that of the sample used for earlier years. This method involved some discontinuity between 1956 and 1957.

The extent of this discontinuity may be judged by comparing the following asset distributions for 1957, the first of which was computed according to the sample breakdown, and the second according to the breakdown of the NBER pension study:

	Percentage Distribution	
	According to Sample	According to NBER Pension Study Coverage
Currency and demand deposits	1	1
Securities, U.S. government	10	11
Securities, state and local	0	0
Other bonds and notes	46	40
Preferred stock	6	6
Common stock—market value	26	27
Mortgages, nonfarm	8	11
Other intangible asset	2	3
Total Assets	100	100

TABLE III-5k

Other Private Insurance, 1945-58

(million dollars)

	1945	1946	1947	1948
I. Tangible assets				
7. Total	42	53	55	58
II. Intangible assets				
1. Currency and demand deposits	66	69	70	73
a. Monetary metals				
b. Other	66	69	70	73
10. Other loans	83	80	82	85
11. Mortgages, nonfarm	177	183	202	228
a. Residential	73	73	79	93
b. Nonresidential	104	110	123	135
12. Mortgages, farm	15	16	17	19
13. Securities, U.S. government	522	530	539	539
b. Savings bonds	30	30	30	30
c. Other long-term	492	500	509	509
14. Securities, state and local	366	375	388	388
15. Securities, other bonds and notes	500	558	625	679
16. Securities, preferred stock	37	49	51	51
17. Securities, common stock	10	16	21	20
20. Other intangible assets	22	27	29	33
21. Total	1797	1904	2023	2116
III. Liabilities				
3. Life insurance reserves, private	1772	1874	1981	2070
13. Other liabilities	67	83	97	104
14. Total	1839	1957	2078	2174
IV. Equities				
V. Total assets or liabilities and equities	1839	1957	2078	2174

Sum of corresponding items in Tables III-5k-1 through III-5k-3.

1949	1950	1951	1952	1953	1954	1955	1956	1957	1958	
										I.
66	64	65	74	82	93	99	100	113	119	7.
										II.
93	99	109	125	156	172	168	158	150	174	1.
93	99	109	125	156	172	168	158	150	174	
92	98	107	114	121	128	145	157	160	173	10.
262	308	359	400	439	494	573	636	661	697	11.
114	142	171	192	208	228	256	269	265	268	
148	166	188	208	231	266	317	367	396	429	
26	34	45	56	58	59	55	61	63	66	12.
544	552	570	598	613	652	723	749	738	799	13.
30	30	40	120	70	100	90	110	120	100	
514	522	530	478	543	552	633	639	618	699	
382	373	365	360	368	393	440	437	422	426	14.
741	792	847	915	989	1,048	1,066	1,130	1,158	1,241	15.
56	61	53	53	51	51	46	43	40	43	16.
24	31	35	39	41	55	61	65	60	80	17.
34	36	38	44	51	54	64	74	79	84	20.
2,255	2,384	2,529	2,703	2,887	3,105	3,341	3,511	3,532	3,783	21.
										III.
2,201	2,322	2,457	2,619	2,801	3,005	3,227	3,391	3,410	3,641	3.
120	126	137	158	168	193	213	220	235	261	13.
2,321	2,448	2,594	2,777	2,969	3,198	3,440	3,611	3,645	3,902	14.
										IV.
2,321	2,448	2,594	2,777	2,969	3,198	3,440	3,611	3,645	3,902	V.

TABLE III-5k-1

Fraternal Orders, 1945-59

(million dollars)

	1945	1946	1947	1948	1949
I. Tangible assets					
7. Total	42	53	55	58	66
II. Intangible assets					
1. Currency and demand deposits	44	42	38	34	45
10. Other loans	73	69	69	69	72
11. Mortgages, nonfarm	169	175	191	214	244
12. Mortgages, farm	15	16	17	19	26
13. Securities, U.S. government	427	417	407	384	370
14. Securities, state and local	366	375	388	388	382
15. Securities, other bonds and notes	489	544	607	657	708
16. Securities, preferred stock	36	48	50	50	55
17. Securities, common stock	8	14	18	18	20
20. Other intangible assets	18	23	23	26	26
21. Total	1,645	1,723	1,808	1,859	1,948
III. Liabilities					
3. Life insurance reserves, private	1,620	1,693	1,766	1,813	1,894
13. Other liabilities	67	83	97	104	120
14. Total	1,687	1,776	1,863	1,917	2,014
IV. Equities					
V. Total assets or liabilities and equities	1,687	1,776	1,863	1,917	2,014

All asset categories, except as specified below, are estimated by applying to total assets the percentage breakdown of assets for orders operating in New York State (New York State Insurance Department, *Annual Report of the Superintendent of Insurance*, 1945-59. Figures exclude Canadian orders operating in the United States.)

Line

I-7 Table III-5n, col. 6 multiplied by col. 11.

II-1 See headnote.

10 Certificate loans and liens, see headnote.

11, 12 Farm mortgages taken as 8.2% of total mortgages from 1945 to 1948 (1948 figure arrived at by correspondence with sixteen large orders. The same percentage was assumed for 1945-47). The 1952-54 percentage breakdown of mortgages was obtained by correspondence with ten fraternal orders. The distribution for 1949-51 was estimated by interpolation between the 1948 and 1952 percentages. Farm mortgages from 1955-59 were assumed to be 10 per cent of total mortgages.

13, 14, 15 Total bonds (see headnote) divided among U.S. government securities, state and local government securities, and other bonds and notes by applying percentage distribution for N.Y. State orders for the years 1945, 1948, 1952, 1953, 1954, 1955, and 1958 (percentages for intervening years obtained by interpolation), tabulated from detailed statements in N.Y. State Insurance Department, *Annual Report*. The 1959 distribution was assumed to be the same as that for 1958.

1950	1951	1952	1953	1954	1955	1956	1957	1958	1959	
										I.
64	65	74	82	93	99	100	113	119	129	7.
										II.
40	36	35	39	43	35	29	29	33	30	1.
74	78	79	81	86	92	95	95	103	110	10.
275	317	348	378	420	499	549	567	595	612	11.
34	45	56	58	59	55	61	63	66	68	12.
353	336	321	309	285	284	268	245	230	242	13.
372	363	357	364	388	433	430	414	416	438	14.
756	805	866	905	946	943	994	1,018	1,080	1,137	15.
59	51	51	48	47	42	38	35	37	38	16.
27	30	33	32	42	46	49	44	61	70	17.
27	30	31	31	32	37	44	48	46	49	20.
2,017	2,091	2,177	2,245	2,348	2,466	2,557	2,558	2,667	2,794	21.
										III.
1,955	2,019	2,093	2,159	2,248	2,352	2,437	2,436	2,525	2,633	3.
126	137	158	168	193	213	220	235	261	290	13.
2,081	2,156	2,251	2,327	2,441	2,565	2,657	2,671	2,786	2,923	14.
										IV.
2,081	2,156	2,251	2,327	2,441	2,565	2,657	2,671	2,786	2,923	V.

Line

II-16,
17 Total stock (see headnote) divided between preferred and common stock by the percentage breakdown for life insurance companies (see Table III-5h, lines II-16 and II-17).

20 Line II-21 minus lines II-1 through II-17.

21 Total assets of all domestic orders minus book value of real estate. Total assets for all orders from *Life Insurance Fact Book* (e.g., 1959 issue, p. 100). *Fact Book* figures adjusted to remove Independent Order of Foresters (a large Canadian order), for which data appear in the New York State Insurance Department *Annual Report*. The 1955 total assets were adjusted to remove all other Canadian orders (shown in The Fraternal Monitor, *The Consolidated Chart, 1956*, p. 3ff.); the ratio of total assets excluding all Canadian orders to total assets excluding the Foresters was used to adjust total assets down in every year.

III-3 Figures from N.Y. State Insurance Department, *Annual Report*, include all "reserve" items and "unassigned" funds; same procedure as for assets (see headnote).

13 Line III-14 minus line III-3.

14 Line I-7 plus line II-21.

V Same as line III-14.

TABLE III-5k-2

Group Health Insurance, 1945-59

(million dollars)

	1945	1946	1947	1948	1949
I. Tangible assets					
II. Intangible assets					
1. Currency and demand deposits	20	25	30	38	46
10. Other loans	6	8	9	11	14
13. Securities, U.S. government	53	65	80	99	123
14. Securities, state and local	a	a	a	a	a
15. Securities, other bonds and notes	7	9	11	14	17
16. Securities, preferred stock	1	1	1	1	1
17. Securities, common stock	1	1	2	2	3
20. Other intangible assets	2	2	4	4	5
21. Total	90	111	137	169	209
III. Liabilities					
3. Life insurance reserves, private	90	111	137	169	209
14. Total	90	111	137	169	209
IV. Equities					
V. Total assets or liabilities and equities	90	111	137	169	209

Note: Cash (line II-1), accounts and notes receivable (line II-10), and investments (sum of lines II-13 through II-17 and part of line II-20) estimated from line II-21 as follows:

1945-51: Distribution assumed the same as in 1952.

1952-59: Allocated according to distribution of assets of Blue Cross and Blue Shield plans in the continental United States from tabulation submitted by the Blue Cross Commission of the American Hospital Association.

Line

II-1 See headnote.

10 See headnote.

13,
16,
17 Estimated investments for 1945-51 (see headnote) allocated by type according to the distribution of investments of Blue Cross plans in the continental United States as of September 30, 1955; 1952-59 investments distributed according to investments of Blue Cross plans as of September 30, 1958, as submitted by the Blue Cross Commission.

1950	1951	1952	1953	1954	1955	1956	1957	1958	1959	
										I.
										II.
57	70	87	114	125	130	126	117	137	153	1.
17	22	27	31	32	42	50	52	56	63	10.
151	186	230	257	322	386	429	436	508	567	13.
1	1	1	2	2	3	3	3	4	4	14.
21	26	32	65	82	98	109	111	129	144	15.
2	2	2	3	4	4	5	5	6	6	16.
3	4	5	8	11	13	14	14	17	19	17.
6	7	9	16	18	23	26	27	33	38	20.
258	318	393	496	596	699	762	765	890	994	21.
										III.
258	318	393	496	596	699	762	765	890	994	3.
258	318	393	496	596	699	762	765	890	994	14.
										IV.
258	318	393	496	596	699	762	765	890	994	V.

Line

II-14,
15 See note to line II-13 above. The 1958 Blue Cross tabulation shows only a combined total for state and local securities and other bonds and notes. This total was divided by the 1955 percentage distribution.

20 Line II-21 minus lines II-1 through II-17.

21 1945-49: It was assumed that the annual rate of growth was the same as from 1950 to 1951.
1950-51: FRB worksheet figures reduced by the ratio of the 1952 total (see below) to FRB worksheet total for 1952.
1952-59: Tabulated from Best's *Insurance Reports*, excluding foreign associations and double counting.

III-13,
14 Same as line II-21.

V Same as line II-21.

[a] Under $500,000.

TABLE III-5k-3

Savings Bank Life Insurance, 1945-58

(million dollars)

	1945	1946	1947	1948
I. Tangible assets				
II. Intangible assets				
1. Currency and demand deposits	2	2	2	1
10. Other loans	4	3	4	5
11. Mortgages, nonfarm	8	8	11	14
13. Securities, U.S. government	42	48	52	56
14. Securities, state and local	a	a	a	a
15. Securities, other bonds and notes	4	5	7	8
17. Securities, common stock	1	1	1	a
20. Other intangible assets	2	2	2	3
21. Total	62	70	78	88
III. Liabilities				
3. Life insurance reserves, private	62	70	78	88
14. Total	62	70	78	88
IV. Equities				
V. Total assets or liabilities and equities	62	70	78	88

Line

II-1 through 20 — Total assets from line II-21, below, allocated by using percentage distributions of assets derived as follows:

1945-49: Massachusetts savings bank life insurance departments from Raymond W. Goldsmith, *A Study of Saving,* Vol. I, Table V-54, p. 551.

1950-54: For Massachusetts, from the Commonwealth of Massachusetts, *Statement of Savings —Insurance Banks; Assets and Liabilities,* and for New York, from the New York State Insurance Department, *Annual Report.*

1955-56: The Commonwealth of Massachusetts, *Statement of Savings.*

1957-58: Total assets from line II-21 below allocated by type, using 1956 percentage distribution of assets.

1949	1950	1951	1952	1953	1954	1955	1956	1957	1958	
										I.
										II.
2	2	3	3	3	4	3	3	4	4	1.
6	7	7	8	9	10	11	12	13	14	10.
18	33	42	52	61	74	74	87	94	102	11.
51	48	48	47	47	45	53	52	57	61	13.
a	a	1	2	2	3	4	4	5	6	14.
16	15	16	17	19	20	25	27	29	32	15.
1	1	1	1	1	2	2	2	2	2	17.
3	3	3	4	4	4	4	4	4	5	20.
98	109	120	133	146	161	176	192	209	226	21.
										III.
98	109	120	133	146	161	176	192	209	226	3.
98	109	120	133	146	161	176	192	209	226	14.
										IV.
98	109	120	133	146	161	176	192	209	226	V.

Line

II-21 *Life Insurance Fact Book*, e.g., 1959, p. 101. Figures for Massachusetts, which are given as of October 31, were converted to Dec. 31 by adding one-sixth of the next fiscal year's change in assets. For 1959 the change in the year ending October 31, 1959 was used.

III-3
14 *Life Insurance Fact Book*, e.g., 1957, p. 89.

V Line II-21.

[a]Under $500,000.

TABLE III-51

Finance Companies, 1945-59

(million dollars)

	1945	1946	1947	1948	1949
I. Tangible assets					
II. Intangible assets					
1. Currency and demand deposits	638	629	567	742	853
a. Monetary metals					
b. Other	638	629	567	742	853
6. Consumer credit	910	1,494	2,359	3,206	4,305
7. Trade credit	77	252	258	276	322
10. Other loans	322	656	867	1,222	1,134
11. Mortgages, nonfarm	71	181	249	237	326
a. Residential	71	181	249	237	326
21. Total	2,018	3,212	4,300	5,683	6,940
III. Liabilities					
9. Bank loans, n.e.c.	808	1,601	2,199	2,706	3,139
12. Bonds and notes	193	452	727	1,308	1,830
14. Total	1,001	2,053	2,926	4,014	4,969
IV. Equities	1,017	1,159	1,374	1,669	1,971
V. Total assets or liabilities and equities	2,018	3,212	4,300	5,683	6,940

Source: Includes sales finance, personal finance, industrial loan, commercial finance, and mortgage companies. All data from Federal Reserve Board worksheets except as indicated below.

Line

II-7 Trade credit represents "other loans" of commercial finance companies only.

10 Represents "other loans" for sales finance, consumer finance, and industrial loan companies.

III-9 FRB estimates of short-term bank debt plus NBER estimate of bank-held finance company commercial paper (Table III-51-a, cols. 3 and 7).

12 FRB estimates of corporate bonds plus commercial paper outstanding, less NBER estimate of bank-held finance company commercial paper (Table III-51-a, cols. 4 and 5).

1950	1951	1952	1953	1954	1955	1956	1957	1958	1959	
										I.
										II.
1,021	1,139	1,172	1,193	1,243	1,497	1,524	1,591	1,696	1,918	1.
1,021	1,139	1,172	1,193	1,243	1,497	1,524	1,591	1,696	1,918	
5,315	5,600	7,057	8,624	9,063	11,889	13,020	13,835	13,129	15,087	6.
606	653	723	776	884	1,127	1,312	1,463	1,697	2,277	7.
1,436	1,708	1,844	1,918	1,673	2,639	2,549	3,159	2,830	3,254	10.
536	454	598	624	845	1,372	1,268	943	1,400	1,644	11.
536	454	598	624	845	1,372	1,268	943	1,400	1,644	
8,914	9,554	11,394	13,135	13,708	18,524	19,673	20,991	20,752	24,180	21.
										III.
4,123	4,131	4,891	4,882	4,906	7,482	6,940	6,580	5,463	6,775	9.
2,253	2,820	3,356	4,937	5,131	6,760	7,954	9,078	9,093	10,564	12.
6,376	6,951	8,247	9,819	10,037	14,242	14,894	15,658	14,556	17,339	14.
2,538	2,603	3,147	3,316	3,671	4,282	4,779	5,333	6,196	6,841	IV.
8,914	9,554	11,394	13,135	13,708	18,524	19,673	20,991	20,752	24,180	V.

TABLE III-51-a

Commercial Paper, 1945-59

(million dollars)

	Total Commercial Paper (1)	*Directly Placed*			DEALER PLACED						
						Finance Company			*Other Than Finance Company*		
		Total (Finance Co.) (2)	Bank-Held (3)	Other (4)	Total (5)	Total (6)	Bank-Held (7)	Other (8)	Total (9)	Bank-Held (10)	Other (11)
1945	272	0	0	0	272	0	0	0	272	93	179
1946	344	116	18	98	228	0	0	0	228	106	122
1947	501	214	33	181	287	0	0	0	287	133	154
1948	674	397	62	335	277	0	0	0	277	129	148
1949	837	567	88	479	270	0	0	0	270	125	145
1950	920	575	89	486	345	100	68	32	245	114	131
1951	1,331	882	137	745	449	180	123	57	269	125	144
1952	1,745	1,193	185	1,008	552	221	150	71	331	154	177
1953	1,966	1,402	217	1,185	564	226	154	72	338	157	181
1954	1,924	1,191	153	1,038	733	293	199	94	440	204	236
1955	2,020	1,510	159	1,351	510	192	131	61	318	148	170
1956	2,166	1,660	174	1,486	506	202	138	64	304	141	163
1957	2,666	2,115	222	1,893	551	220	150	70	331	154	177
1958	2,744[a]	1,904[a]	200	1,704	840	336	229	107	504	234	270
1959	3,118	2,491	262	2,229	627	251	171	80	376	174	202

Notes to Table III-5l-a

Cols. 1, 2, and 5: *Federal Reserve Bulletin*, e.g., May 1955, p. 524. The Federal Reserve Board apparently attributes all directly placed commercial paper to finance companies.

Col. 3: 1945-51: 15.5 per cent of col. 2. See note for 1952-55.
1952-55: Proportions of total directly placed paper given in Morris Mendelson, *The Flow-of-Funds*, Table A5-1, p. II-26.
1956-59: 10.5 per cent of col. 2. See note for 1952-55.

Col. 4: Col. 2 minus col. 3.

Col. 6: Ratios from FRB worksheets
1945-49: Estimated to be zero.
1950: 30 per cent of col. 5.
1951-59: 40 per cent of col. 5.

Col. 7: 68.085 per cent of finance company dealer-placed commercial paper (see Morris Mendelson, *The Flow-of-Funds*, Table A5-1, note to line 2, p. II-26).

Col. 8: Col. 6 minus col. 7.

Col. 9: Col. 5 minus col. 6.

Col. 10: 46.5 per cent of col. 9.

Col. 11: Col. 9 minus col. 10.

[a]Beginning with 1958, includes all paper with maturity of 270 days and over. Figures on old basis were 2,731 and 1,891 (*Federal Reserve Bulletin*, October 1961, p. 1208).

TABLE III-5m

Other Finance, 1945-58

(billion dollars)

	1945	1946	1947	1948
I. Tangible assets				
7. Total				
II. Intangible assets				
1. Currency and demand deposits	.84	1.05	.94	.88
a. Monetary metals				
b. Other	.84	1.05	.94	.88
2. Other bank deposits and shares	a	a	a	.01
7. Trade credit	.04	.03	.05	.12
8. Loans on securities	1.43	.69	.74	.73
10. Other loans	.33	.42	.51	.61
11. Mortgages, nonfarm	.02	.03	.05	.09
a. Residential	.02	.03	.04	.06
b. Nonresidential		.01	.01	.02
12. Mortgages, farm			.01	.01
13. Securities, U.S. government	3.40	2.23	1.37	1.80
a. Short-term	1.10	1.20	.70	1.20
b. Savings bonds				
c. Other long-term	2.30	1.03	.67	.60
14. Securities, state and local	.40	.38	.30	.39
15. Securities, other bonds and notes	.32	.24	.27	.26
16. Securities, preferred stock	.02	.01	.01	.01
17. Securities, common stock	.30	.22	.24	.22
20. Other intangible assets	.16	.14	.14	.13
21. Total	7.26	5.44	4.62	5.25
III. Liabilities				
1. Currency and demand deposits[b]	.54	.48	.47	.42
2. Other bank deposits and shares[b]	.38	.42	.39	.37
8. Loans on securities	3.37	1.70	.99	1.50
10. Other loans	1.12	1.22	1.26	1.25
13. Other liabilities	.90	.81	.79	.89
14. Total	6.30	4.62	3.90	4.44
IV. Equities	.95	.82	.72	.81
V. Total assets or liabilities and equities	7.26	5.44	4.62	5.25

Sum of corresponding lines in Tables III-5m-1 through III-5m-4.

[a]Under $5 million.

[b]These deposit liabilities of banks in possessions are excluded from Tables IV-c-1 and IV-c-2 and are included under other liabilities in Tables I, II, III-5, and IV-c-13.

1949	1950	1951	1952	1953	1954	1955	1956	1957	1958	
										I.
a	a	.01	.01	.01	.01	.02	.02	.02	.03	7.
										II.
.81	1.00	.97	.93	.86	.99	1.00	1.12	1.14	1.17	1.
.81	1.00	.97	.93	.86	.99	1.00	1.12	1.14	1.17	
a	a	a	a	a	a	a	.01	a	.01	2.
.11	.10	.13	.14	.19	.18	.23	.33	.37	.36	7.
1.15	1.73	1.69	1.79	2.19	3.15	3.63	3.71	3.42	4.56	8.
.62	.72	.88	.94	.85	.94	1.03	1.10	1.37	1.64	10.
.10	.12	.15	.15	.15	.15	.19	.20	.22	.26	11.
.08	.10	.12	.12	.12	.12	.15	.16	.16	.18	
.02	.02	.02	.03	.03	.03	.04	.05	.06	.08	
						.01	.01	.01	.01	12.
1.65	1.58	1.30	1.67	1.66	1.84	1.36	1.45	1.57	1.81	13.
1.10	1.10	1.00	1.50	1.50	1.80	1.30	1.45	1.57	1.81	
.55	.48	.30	.17	.16	.04	.06	0	0	0	
.37	.50	.55	.40	.65	.52	.57	.46	.60	.60	14.
.45	.34	.38	.45	.36	.68	.64	.46	.73	.61	15.
.02	.01	.02	.02	.02	.03	.03	.02	.03	.02	16.
.37	.28	.34	.39	.33	.59	.60	.39	.63	.44	17.
.14	.18	.16	.17	.19	.19	.21	.25	.29	.32	20.
5.80	6.56	6.56	7.05	7.46	9.28	9.51	9.49	10.39	11.82	21.
										III.
.43	.47	.50	.51	.51	.53	.56	.62	.69	.73	1.
.34	.35	.35	.36	.37	.39	.40	.42	.49	.57	2.
1.95	2.02	1.83	2.31	2.61	3.28	3.60	2.98	3.08	3.42	8.
1.39	1.88	1.94	1.79	1.70	2.25	2.06	2.09	2.39	3.11	10.
.85	.95	1.05	1.17	1.27	1.55	1.71	2.17	2.29	2.50	13.
4.96	5.67	5.66	6.15	6.46	8.00	8.33	8.28	8.94	10.33	14.
.84	.90	.90	.91	1.01	1.29	1.20	1.23	1.47	1.52	IV.
5.80	6.57	6.56	7.06	7.48	9.29	9.53	9.52	10.41	11.84	V.

TABLE III-5m-1

Brokers and Dealers, 1945-58

(million dollars)

	1945	1946	1947	1948
I. Tangible assets				
II. Intangible assets				
1. Currency and demand deposits	516	752	648	576
8. Loans on securities	1,366	648	694	660
13. Securities, U.S. government	2,145	1,042	321	935
14. Securities, state and local	340	340	243	267
15. Securities, other bonds and notes	294	208	238	211
16. Securities, preferred stock	15	10	12	11
17. Securities, common stock	279	198	226	200
21. Total	4,955	3,198	2,382	2,860
III. Liabilities				
8. Loans on securities	3,370	1,696	990	1,504
10. Other loans	890	950	930	840
14. Total	4,260	2,646	1,920	2,344
IV. Equities	695	552	462	516
V. Total assets or liabilities and equities	4,955	3,198	2,382	2,860

Line

II-1, 8 FRB worksheets.

13 Bank loans on federal obligations to brokers and dealers (FRB worksheets), raised by 10 per cent.

14 FRB worksheets (1946-53 from Roland I. Robinson, *Postwar Market for State and Local Government Securities*, Princeton University Press for NBER, 1960, Table A-3, col. 6).

15 One-half of "corporate securities" (col. 11 of Table III-5m-1a minus lines II-8 and II-14 of this table).

16, 17 Sum of two lines assumed the same as line II-15. Preferred stock is assumed to be 5 per cent of total stock.

21 Sum of lines II-1 through II-17.

1949	1950	1951	1952	1953	1954	1955	1956	1957	1958	
										I.
										II.
505	655	624	566	490	574	546	554	540	540	1.
1,057	1,627	1,550	1,634	2,033	2,915	3,390	3,427	3,060	4,117	8.
880	759	484	780	770	825	341	319	549	719	13.
252	370	384	228	430	300	300	100	200	215	14.
371	276	322	378	308	575	574	344	572	360	15.
19	14	16	19	15	29	29	17	29	18	16.
352	262	306	359	293	546	545	327	543	342	17.
3,436	3,963	3,686	3,964	4,339	5,764	5,725	5,088	5,493	6,311	21.
										III.
1,947	2,017	1,827	2,311	2,614	3,285	3,605	2,981	3,082	3,417	8.
960	1,380	1,320	1,130	1,120	1,620	1,380	1,360	1,460	1,950	10.
2,907	3,397	3,147	3,441	3,734	4,905	4,985	4,341	4,542	5,367	14.
529	566	539	523	605	859	740	747	951	944	IV.
3,436	3,963	3,686	3,964	4,339	5,764	5,725	5,088	5,493	6,311	V.

Line

III-8 Line III-14 minus line III-10.

10 Table III-5m-1a, column 6, minus 125 per cent of foreign customers' credit balances with brokers and dealers (*Treasury Bulletin*, e.g., March 1959, p. 78).

14 Table III-5m-1a, sum of columns 6, 7, and 9.

IV Line V minus line III-14.

V Same as line II-21.

TABLE III-5m-1a

Assets of Brokers and Dealers, 1945-58

(million dollars)

	New York Stock Exchange Member Firms					*All Brokers and Dealers*					
	Customers' Debit Balances (1)	Debit Balances in Firm Trading Accounts (2)	Customers' Credit Balances (3)	Borrow-ings (4)	Ratio: Debit to Credit Balances (5)	Customers' Credit Balances (6)	Bank Loans on Securities (7)	Bank Loans on Federal Obligations (8)	Agencies of Foreign Banks, Loans on Securities (9)	Debt on Securities Except on Federal Obligations (10)	Assets Other Than Currency, Demand Deposits, and Federal Obligations (11)
1945	1,138	413	766	795	.99359	1,019	3,178	1,950	63	2,310	2,295
1946	540	312	814	218	.82558	1,083	1,524	947	39	1,699	1,403
1947	578	315	788	240	.86868	1,048	830	292	42	1,628	1,414
1948	550	312	698	257	.90262	928	1,344	850	72	1,494	1,349
1949	881	400	792	524	.97340	1,053	1,763	800	91	2,107	2,051
1950	1,356	399	1,120	744	.94152	1,490	1,802	690	105	2,707	2,549
1951	1,292	392	1,075	694	.95195	1,430	1,581	440	136	2,707	2,577
1952	1,362	406	924	920	.95879	1,229	2,060	709	152	2,732	2,619
1953	1,694	404	917	1,170	1.01527	1,220	2,361	700	153	3,034	3,080
1954	2,429	626	1,310	1,598	1.05055	1,742	2,929	750	234	4,155	4,365
1955	2,825	707	1,116	2,297	1.03487	1,484	3,263	310	238	4,675	4,838
1956	2,856	563	1,107	2,178	1.04079	1,472	2,589	290	280	4,051	4,216
1957	2,550	736[a]	1,185[c]	1,831	1.08952	1,576	2,601	499	365	4,043	4,405
1958	3,431	722[b]	1,570[c]	2,305	1.07174	2,088	2,832	654	447	4,713	5,051

Notes to Table III-5m-1a

Cols. 1 through 4:	*Federal Reserve Bulletin,* Table on "Stock Market Credit," covering member firms of the New York Stock Exchange carrying margin accounts, March 1957, p. 336, March 1959, p. 286, and March 1960, p. 295.
Col. 5:	Ratio of the sum of cols. 1 and 2 to the sum of cols. 3 and 4.
Col. 6:	FRB worksheets.
Col. 7:	*Annual Report of the Comptroller of the Currency,* e.g., 1946, Table 29, p. 110.
Col. 8:	FRB worksheets.
Col. 9:	Table III-5m-3, line II-8.
Col. 10:	Cols. 6, 7, and 9 minus col. 8.
Col. 11:	Col. 10 multiplied by col. 5.

[a]Interpolated between December 1956 and June 1958.

[b]Interpolated between June 1958 and June 1959.

[c]Customers' net free credit balances multiplied by ratio of total customers' credit balances to customers' net free credit balances (see notes to columns 1 through 4). Net free credit balances from *Federal Reserve Bulletin,* September 1959, p. 1167. The June 1958 ratio was used for 1958 and the ratio for 1957 was derived by interpolating between December 1956 and June 1958 ratios.

TABLE III-5m-2

Banks in Possessions, 1945-58

(million dollars)

	1945	1946	1947	1948
I. Tangible assets				
II. Intangible assets				
1. Currency and demand deposits	171	150	148	136
2. Other bank deposits and shares	3	3	3	7
10. Other loans	96	142	176	186
11. Mortgages, nonfarm	22	33	47	86
a. Residential	18	26	37	63
b. Nonresidential	4	7	10	23
12. Mortgages, farm	1	3	6	7
13. Securities, U.S. government	599	534	438	365
14. Securities, state and local	21	19	21	23
15. Securities, other bonds and notes	11	26	15	26
17. Securities, common stock	1	1	1	1
20. Other intangible assets	79	68	79	63
21. Total	1,004	979	934	900
III. Liabilities				
1. Currency and demand deposits	539	480	471	421
2. Other bank deposits and shares	377	420	392	372
13. Other liabilities	26	10	21	32
14. Total	942	910	884	825
IV. Equities	62	69	50	75
V. Total assets or liabilities and equities	1,004	979	934	900

Source: All figures come from columns in: *Annual Report of the Comptroller of the Currency* (e.g., 1958, Table 42, p. 167 ff.), except where otherwise indicated.

Line

II-1 Sum of: "currency and coin," from *Annual Report, Comptroller of the Currency*, and "demand deposits," from Federal Reserve Board worksheets. (FRB worksheets exclude "cash items in process of collection," included by Comptroller of the Currency in the category "balances with other banks, including reserve balances and cash items in process of collection.")

2 Federal Reserve Board worksheets.

10 Column on "loans and discounts including overdrafts," from *Annual Report, Comptroller of the Currency*, less the sum of lines II-11 and II-12 of this table.

11 Sum of II-11a and II-11b.

11a Column on "real estate loans secured by nonfarm residential property."

11b Column on "real estate loans secured by other nonfarm properties."

12 "Real estate loans secured by farm land."

13 "U.S. government obligations, direct and guaranteed."

14 "Obligations of states and political subdivisions."

15 "Other bonds, notes and debentures."

1949	1950	1951	1952	1953	1954	1955	1956	1957	1958	
										I.
										II.
133	124	156	144	143	135	131	143	156	169	1.
5	3	4	3	4	4	5	6	4	8	2.
183	202	242	262	247	288	324	344	422	453	10.
100	119	147	150	153	152	190	204	220	261	11.
78	100	125	123	123	123	147	157	157	185	
22	19	22	26	30	29	42	47	63	76	
2	4	4	5	3	4	6	8	10	11	12.
321	294	252	271	263	277	259	274	284	303	13.
23	43	48	50	54	59	61	66	73	81	14.
38	32	25	24	28	21	22	26	34	34	15.
a	1	1	1	1	1	1	3	3	3	17.
68	102	80	84	97	94	103	127	138	150	20.
873	924	959	994	993	1,035	1,102	1,201	1,344	1,473	21.
										III.
431	473	500	514	509	532	557	621	687	727	1.
345	351	348	365	370	387	399	417	491	569	2.
20	21	28	28	23	22	48	61	56	59	13.
796	845	876	907	902	941	1,004	1,099	1,234	1,355	14.
77	79	83	87	91	95	98	102	110	118	IV.
873	924	959	994	993	1,035	1,102	1,201	1,344	1,473	V.

Line

II-17 "Corporate stocks, including stocks of Federal Reserve Banks."
20 Line II-21 minus sum of lines II-1 through II-17.
21 "Total assets."

III-1 "Liabilities-demand deposits." (See note b, Table III-5m.)
2 "Liabilities-time deposits."
13 Line III-14 minus sum of lines III-1 and III-2.
14 Sum of: "total deposits," "bills payable, rediscounts and other liabilities for borrowed money," "acceptances executed by or for account of reporting banks and outstanding," and "other liabilities."

IV Sum of: "capital stock," "surplus," "undivided profits," and "reserves and retirement account."

V Line II-21 of this table.

[a]Under $500,000.

TABLE III-5m-3

Agencies of Foreign Banks, 1945-58

(million dollars)

	1945	1946	1947	1948
I. Tangible assets				
II. Intangible assets				
1. Currency and demand deposits	135	125	122	144
7. Trade credit	38	31	46	114
8. Loans on securities	63	39	42	72
13. Securities, U.S. government	541	538	487	372
14. Securities, state and local	34	23	34	102
15. Securities, other bonds and notes	17	8	15	25
17. Securities, common stock	17	16	15	17
21. Total	845	780	761	846
III. Liabilities				
13. Other liabilities	845	780	761	846
14. Total	845	780	761	846
IV. Equities				
V. Total assets or liabilities and equities	845	780	761	846

Very little is known about the distribution of the assets of agencies of foreign banks and this balance sheet is therefore only a very rough estimate. Totals from FRB worksheets were distributed using the asset distribution of the American Express Company and the method in Morris Mendelson, *The Flow-of-Funds*, page I-267, with some modifications and corrections. American Express Company figures were taken from *Moody's Bank and Finance Manual*, 1945-54, and annual reports thereafter.

1949	1950	1951	1952	1953	1954	1955	1956	1957	1958	
										I.
										II.
155	202	161	192	209	256	295	396	419	434	1.
106	101	131	136	184	180	229	323	364	362	7.
91	105	136	152	153	234	238	280	365	447	8.
311	376	402	452	454	556	574	667	551	603	13.
98	87	116	119	166	158	205	292	331	302	14.
41	27	30	45	25	75	49	63	88	168	15.
16	18	30	34	37	45	49	63	88	97	17.
818	916	1,006	1,130	1,228	1,504	1,639	2,084	2,206	2,413	21.
										III.
818	916	1,006	1,130	1,228	1,504	1,639	2,084	2,206	2,413	13.
818	916	1,006	1,130	1,228	1,504	1,639	2,084	2,206	2,413	14.
										IV.
818	916	1,006	1,130	1,228	1,504	1,639	2,084	2,206	2,413	V.

Line

II-8 Line II-21 minus the sum of lines II-1, II-7, II-13, and II-14 through II-17.
21 Federal Reserve Board worksheets.

III-13,
14 Same as II-21.

V Same as II-21.

TABLE III-5m-4

Agricultural Credit Organizations, 1945-58

(million dollars)

	1945	1946	1947	1948
I. Tangible assets				
7. Total	a	a	1	1
II. Intangible assets				
1. Currency and demand deposits	16	19	21	21
7. Trade credit	2	2	2	1
10. Other loans	231	274	334	428
13. Securities, U.S. government	116	115	121	130
15. Securities, other bonds and notes				
20. Other intangible assets	86	73	65	67
21. Total	451	483	543	647
III. Liabilities				
7. Trade debt	3	3	2	2
10. Other loans	226	265	327	414
13. Other liabilities	29	17	10	10
14. Total	258	285	339	426
IV. Equities	193	198	205	222
V. Total assets or liabilities and equities	451	483	544	648

Source: These figures are the sum of balance sheet items for:

a. Livestock loan companies (lines II-10 and III-10), from *Agricultural Finance Review*, Vol. 22, September 1960, p. 140, Table 16, col. 6.

b. Production credit associations (Farm Credit Administration, Finance and Accounts Division, *Combined Statement of Condition*).

c. National farm loan associations (June 1945 and June 1946: obtained directly from the Farm Credit Administration. June 1947-June 1959: *Annual Report of the Farm Credit Administration*). June 30th figures were interpolated on a straight line to obtain year-end figures.

Line

I-7 Book value of tangible assets held by agricultural credit organizations (notes b and c above), multiplied by Table III-5n, col. 11. Book values in millions are as follows:

1949	2
1950	3
1951	4
1952	6
1953	8
1954	9
1955	11
1956	14
1957	16
1958	19

1949	1950	1951	1952	1953	1954	1955	1956	1957	1958	
										I.
3	5	6	9	11	13	16	21	23	26	7.
										II.
21	23	25	24	23	23	24	22	22	23	1.
1	1	2	3	3	4	3	3	3	3	7.
441	515	641	683	606	654	705	755	948	1,190	10.
139	150	159	169	171	180	186	189	189	186	13.
				9	12	19	26	34	45	15.
71	73	80	87	92	99	110	126	151	174	20.
673	762	907	966	904	972	1,047	1,121	1,347	1,621	21.
										III.
1	2	2	2	1	1	2	3	3	3	7.
426	501	620	658	581	631	680	730	927	1,156	10.
11	11	13	15	17	20	22	25	30	32	13.
438	514	635	675	599	652	704	758	960	1,191	14.
238	253	278	300	316	333	359	384	410	456	IV.
676	767	913	975	915	985	1,063	1,142	1,370	1,647	V.

Line

II-1,
7 See notes b and c above.
10 See notes a and b above. For production credit associations, sum of loans net of reserves, and investments under CCC programs.
13 See notes b and c above (direct and guaranteed U.S. securities).
15 See notes b and c above (nonguaranteed U.S. securities plus Federal Land Bank notes held by national farm loan associations).
20 Line II-21 minus lines II-1 through II-15.
21 See notes a, b, and c above (total assets minus fixed assets at book value).

III-7 See notes b and c above.
10 See notes a and b above: For production credit associations, sum of loans rediscounted with federal intermediate credit banks, and notes payable to FICB's.
13 Line III-14 minus lines III-7 and III-10.
14 Line V minus line IV.

IV Sum of capital stock, surplus and reserves (notes b and c above), and difference between fixed assets at current and at book value (see note to line I-7).

V Sum of lines I-7 and II-21.

[a]Under $500,000.

TABLE III-5n

Tangible Assets of Financial Organizations, 1945-59

(billion dollars)

	Book Value					
	Total (1)	Federal Reserve Banks and Treasury Monetary Funds (2)	Commercial Banks (3)	Mutual Savings Banks (4)	Life Insurance (5)	Fraternal Orders (6)
1945	2.30	.03	1.03	.13	.86	.04
1946	2.15	.03	1.01	.11	.74	.04
1947	2.30	.03	1.05	.11	.86	.03
1948	2.60	.03	1.11	.11	1.06	.04
1949	2.91	.03	1.17	.11	1.25	.04
1950	3.25	.04	1.24	.12	1.44	.04
1951	3.60	.04	1.34	.12	1.63	.04
1952	4.09	.05	1.43	.14	1.90	.05
1953	4.41	.05	1.54	.15	2.02	.06
1954	4.93	.05	1.66	.17	2.30	.06
1955	5.58	.06	1.87	.18	2.58	.07
1956	6.20	.07	2.08	.20	2.82	.07
1957	6.97	.08	2.33	.22	3.12	.08
1958	7.68	.09	2.58	.24	3.36	.08
1959					3.65	

Col. 1: Sum of cols. 2 through 9.

Col. 2: *Annual Report of the Board of Governors of the Federal Reserve System*, various issues, e.g., 1954, p. 62.

Col. 3: Sum of "bank premises owned, furniture and fixtures" and "other real estate-direct and indirect" of all operating commercial banks in the U.S. and possessions (*Annual Report of the Federal Deposit Insurance Corporation*, e.g., 1954, p. 124), minus sum of "bank premises owned, furniture and fixtures," "real estate owned other than bank premises," and "investments and other assets indirectly representing bank premises or other real estate" of all active banks in U.S. possessions (*Annual Report of the Comptroller of the Currency*, e.g., 1954, p. 161).

Col. 4: *Annual Report of the Federal Deposit Insurance Corporation* (see note to col. 3 above), e.g., 1954, p. 124.

Book Value				
Fire and Casualty Insurance (7)	Savings and Loan Associations (8)	Agricultural Credit Organizations (9)	Current Value (Total) (10)	Ratio: Current to Book Value (Total) (11)
.11	.10		2.49	1.08
.12	.10		2.90	1.35
.12	.10		3.24	1.41
.14	.11		3.56	1.37
.17	.14		4.95	1.70
.19	.18		5.19	1.60
.22	.21		5.20	1.44
.24	.27	.01	5.83	1.43
.26	.32	.01	6.35	1.44
.29	.39	.01	7.14	1.45
.33	.48	.01	8.12	1.46
.36	.59	.01	8.99	1.45
.40	.72	.02	9.93	1.42
.46	.85	.02	10.33	1.35
	1.00			1.35

Col. 5: *Life Insurance Fact Book*, 1959, p. 86, and 1961, p. 90.
Col. 6: Estimated in same manner as intangible assets, Table III-5i.
Col. 7: 1945-49: Goldsmith, *A Study of Saving*, Vol. I, sum of Tables V-55, col. 4, and V-56, col. 4 (pp. 553 and 554).
1950-57: FRB worksheets.
1958: Estimated by using 1957 ratio of real estate to total assets excluding real estate, of fire, marine, and casualty companies (FRB worksheets).
Col. 8: Federal Home Loan Bank Board, *Trends in the Savings and Loan Field*, 1957 and 1961, Table 2.
Col. 9: Sum of fixed assets of production credit associations and national farm loan associations, from *Annual Report of the Farm Credit Administration*, e.g., 1954-55, Table 28, pp. 86-87 and Table 19, p. 75 (June 30th figures were interpolated to arrive at year-end figures).
Col. 10: Table III-5, line I-7.
Col. 11: Col. 10 divided by col. 1; 1959 assumed the same as 1958.

TABLE III-5o

Total Finance, 1900-45, Selected Years

(million dollars)

	1900	1912	1922
I. Tangible assets			
7. Total	573	923	1,584
II. Intangible assets			
1. Currency and demand deposits	3,229	6,224	13,799
a. Monetary metals	1,197	2,132	3,991
b. Other	2,032	4,092	9,808
2. Other bank deposits and shares			
6. Consumer credit	239	456	916
7. Trade credit			
8. Loans on securities	1,289	2,297	6,253
9. Bank loans, n.e.c.	3,946	9,049	18,211
10. Other loans	90	594	1,162
11. Mortgages, nonfarm	2,066	4,835	9,947
a. Residential	1,350	3,117	6,715
b. Nonresidential	716	1,718	3,232
12. Mortgages, farm	432	1,469	3,518
13. Securities, U.S. government	663	794	7,715
14. Securities, state and local	889	1,729	2,854
15. Securities, other bonds and notes	1,828	5,043	7,762
16. Securities, preferred stock 17. Securities, common stock	380	740	1,339
20. Other intangible assets	1,311	1,491	7,006
21. Total	16,361	34,721	80,482
III. Liabilities			
1. Currency and demand deposits	7,428	14,421	33,841
2. Other bank deposits and shares	3,706	9,310	20,942
3. Life insurance reserves, private	1,554	4,142	8,700
4. Pension and retirement funds, private			90
5. Pension and insurance funds, govt.	5	17	251
8. Loans and securities	300	500	1,950
9. Bank loans, n.e.c.	101	292	740
10. Other loans	103	214	574
12. Bonds and notes			233
13. Other liabilities	762	717	3,603
14. Total	13,959	29,613	70,924
IV. Equities	2,974	6,033	11,141
V. Total assets or liabilities and equities	16,933	35,646	82,065

1929	1933	1939	1945[a]	
				I.
2,990	4,824	5,560	2,227	7.
				II.
17,079	15,952	60,140	74,331	1.
4,474	4,611	20,177	22,444	
12,605	11,341	39,663	51,887	
		2	71	2.
3,305	1,621	3,688	2,340	6.
909	464	1,010	505	7.
14,345	5,152	2,696	8,129	8.
20,513	9,967	9,834	12,955	9.
2,616	5,503	3,499	2,183	10.
23,281	19,797	18,153	20,369	11.
16,385	13,768	12,781	15,487	
6,896	6,029	5,372	4,882	
3,881	2,954	1,697	1,363	12.
7,658	13,659	33,506	178,935	13.
4,956	5,908	8,054	6,579	14.
13,465	13,043	14,692	16,135	15.
6,080	3,869	4,359	6,516	16. 17.
11,473	5,814	5,348	10,926	20.
129,561	103,703	166,678	341,337	21.
				III.
40,865	36,600	78,068	180,112	1.
34,720	26,858	30,348	53,033	2.
17,502	20,862	29,228	44,262	3.
500	700	1,050	2,900	4.
1,470	2,956	6,230	25,467	5.
4,200	1,000	700	1,250	8.
2,214	913	1,439	698	9.
1,325	480	625	1,215	10.
1,577	1,016	778	681	12.
6,777	2,857	4,623	8,200	13.
111,150	94,242	153,089	317,818	14.
21,402	14,285	19,149	25,745	IV.
132,552	108,527	172,238	343,563	V.

(Notes to Table III-5o are on following page)

Notes to Table III-5o

Source: tables F, I, L, M, from Goldsmith, *A Study of Saving*, Vol. I; W tables, from Goldsmith, *A Study of Saving*, Vol. III; and A tables, from Goldsmith, *Financial Intermediaries*. Other tables referred to are in this volume.

Line		
I-7	Sum of:	W-39, line I-1 through I-5; W-41, line I-10; A-25, line 2; and A-26, line 2.
II-1	Sum of:	W-37, line II-1 and 2; W-39, lines I-9, II-1, II-2, and II-3; W-41, line II-1 and 2; W-43, line I-9; A-25, line 3; A-26, line 3; and A-27, line 2 (except 1945, one-half of line 2);
	minus:	A-6, line 2; and A-3.c, line 18.
1a	Sum of:	W-39, line I-9; and W-43, line I-9.
1b	Line II-1 minus line II-1a.	
2	Sum of:	W-41, line II-3; and A-3.c, line 18.
6	Sum of:	W-39, line II-8; W-41, line II-8; A-25, line 6; and A-26, line 5;
	minus:	A-3.a, lines 6, 12, and 18; and A-7, lines 9 and 12.
7	Sum of:	A-25, line 7; and A-27, lines 3 and 4.
8	Sum of:	W-37, line II-9; W-39, line II-9; and W-41, line II-9.
9	Sum of:	W-39, line II-7; and A-3.a, lines 6, 12, and 18.
10	Sum of:	W-41, line II-7; and A-7, lines 9 and 12.
11	IV-b-11c, line 5.	
11a	IV-b-11c-1, line 5.	
11b	IV-b-11c-4, line 5.	
12	Sum of:	W-39, line 11; W-41, line 11; and M-20, column 7.
13	Sum of:	W-37, lines II-12 and 13; W-39, line II-12; W-41, line II-12; A-25, line 8; A-26, line 6 (1945 only); and A-27, one-half of line 2 (1945 only) and an upward revision in estimated bond holdings of mutual savings banks of $20 million in 1945 (see L-29, column 7 and A-5, line 26);
	minus:	A-6, line 3, and a downward revision in estimated bond holdings of fraternal orders, of $20 million in 1939 and $51 million in 1945 (see I-10, column 7 and A-9, line 21).
14	IV-b-14a, line 5.	
15	IV-b-15a, line 5.	
16, 17	Sum of:	W-37, lines II-15 and 16; W-39, line II-16; W-41, lines II-15 and II-16; and A-26, line 6 (1929 and 1933);
	minus:	III-4b-1, line 8.
20	Line II-21 minus the sum of lines II-1 through II-17.	
21	Sum of:	W-37, line II-22; W-39, lines I-9 and II-22; W-41, line II-22; W-43, line I-9; A-25, (line 1 minus line 2); A-26 (line 1 minus line 2); A-27, line 1; and A-28, line 2;
	minus:	A-6, line 1; and A-28, line 4.

Line	
III-1	Sum of: W-39, line III-1; F-5, columns 1, 2, 4, and 5 (1900-1922); F-18, columns 1, 2, 4, and 5 (1929-1945); L-4, columns 2, 4; A-2, line 16; A-3.c, line 2; and A-4, line 28.
2	Sum of: W-39, line III-3; W-41, line III-3; and A-3.c, line 3; minus: A-2, line 16; and A-6, line 6.
3	W-41, line III-4.
4	W-41, line III-5.
5	W-41, line III-6.
8	W-37, line III-10.
9	Sum of: W-39, line III-7; W-41, line III-7; A-25, line 11 (1929-1939); A-25, line 13 (1945); A-26, line 9 (1929-1939); A-26, line 11 (1945); A-27, line 9; and A-28 (one-third of line 2); minus: A-19, line 15.
10	Sum of: W-37, line III-9; A-19, line 15; A-25, line 14; and A-26, line 12.
12	Sum of: W-41, line III-12; A-25, lines 12 and 15; A-26, lines 10 and 13; and A-27, line 8.
13	Line III-14 minus the sum of lines III-1 through III-12 of this table.
14	Sum of: W-37, line III-15; W-39, line III-15; W-41, line III-15; A-25 (line 10 minus line 17); A-26 (line 8 minus line 15); A-27 (line 6 minus line 12); A-28 (two-thirds of line 2); F-5, columns 1, 2, 4, and 5 (1900-1922); and F-18, columns 1, 2, 4, and 5 (1929-1945); minus: A-6 (line 5 minus line 8).
IV	Line V minus line III-14 of this table.
V	Line I-7 plus line II-21 of this table.

[a]The 1945 figures in this table have been superseded by those in Table III-5; they are included here for comparability with earlier years.

TABLE III-6

State and Local Governments, 1945-58

(billion dollars)

	1945	1946	1947	1948
I. Tangible assets				
1. Residential structures	.87	1.35	1.69	1.76
2. Nonresidential structures	41.55	50.64	60.49	65.12
3. Land	14.20	18.90	21.40	21.50
4. Producer durables	.62	.79	1.05	1.35
6. Inventories	.07	.09	.10	.11
7. Total	57.31	71.77	84.73	89.84
II. Intangible assets				
1. Currency and demand deposits	5.21	6.08	6.80	7.29
a. Monetary metals				
b. Other	5.21	6.08	6.80	7.29
2. Other bank deposits and shares	.53	.71	.87	1.14
11. Mortgages, nonfarm	.06	.07	.06	.07
a. Residential	.06	.07	.06	.07
13. Securities, U.S. government	4.99	4.37	5.03	5.35
a. Short-term	2.40	2.30	2.60	3.10
c. Other long-term	2.59	2.07	2.43	2.25
14. Securities, state and local	1.45	1.32	1.27	1.27
15. Securities, other bonds and notes	.29	.30	.34	.51
21. Total	12.53	12.85	14.37	15.63
III. Liabilities				
7. Trade debt	.55	.70	.85	1.00
12. Bonds and notes	21.27	21.14	22.55	24.76
14. Total	21.82	21.84	23.40	25.76
IV. Equities	48.02	62.78	75.70	79.71
V. Total assets or liabilities and equities	69.84	84.62	99.10	105.47

Line	
I-1 through I-7	Line 6 of Tables IV-a-1 through IV-a-7 respectively.
II-1	Sum of currency (FRB worksheets) and demand deposits (*Annual Report of the Comptroller of the Currency*, e.g., 1945, p. 119) minus line II-1 of Table III-5b-2.
2	*Annual Report of the Comptroller of the Currency*, e.g., 1945, p. 119.
11	Table IV-b-11, line 6.
13	Total direct and guaranteed U.S. government securities held by state and local governments (FRB worksheets) minus line II-13 of Table III-5b-2.
14	Total state and local government securities held by state and local governments (FRB worksheets) minus line II-14 of Table III-5b-2.
15	Sum of total corporate bonds held by state and local governments plus nonguaranteed U.S. government securities (FRB worksheets), minus corporate bonds held by state and local governments' pension and retirement funds (line II-15 of Table III-5b-2).
21	Sum of lines II-1 through II-15.

1949	1950	1951	1952	1953	1954	1955	1956	1957	1958	
										I.
1.93	2.33	2.95	3.62	4.14	4.41	4.77	5.14	5.51	6.03	1.
63.77	70.75	77.27	83.84	87.42	92.85	102.29	113.42	123.27	133.20	2.
20.50	24.00	24.20	23.70	24.00	24.10	24.80	26.30	27.40	28.00	3.
1.63	1.94	2.27	2.56	2.86	3.22	3.71	4.27	4.85	5.25	4.
.10	.13	.13	.13	.14	.15	.16	.18	.19	.20	6.
87.93	99.15	106.82	113.85	118.56	124.73	135.73	149.31	161.22	172.68	7.
										II.
7.52	7.98	8.41	8.88	9.48	9.81	10.20	10.35	10.56	10.78	1.
7.52	7.98	8.41	8.88	9.48	9.81	10.20	10.35	10.56	10.78	
1.29	1.39	1.54	1.63	1.96	2.42	2.36	2.40	2.78	3.58	2.
.16	.21	.29	.36	.50	.61	.72	.84	1.20	1.61	11.
.16	.21	.29	.36	.50	.61	.72	.84	1.20	1.61	
5.37	5.73	6.10	7.18	8.49	9.93	10.34	11.04	11.78	11.08	13.
3.20	3.50	3.30	4.00	5.20	5.20	3.60	5.80	7.10	6.00	
2.17	2.23	2.80	3.18	3.29	4.73	6.74	5.24	4.68	5.08	
1.55	1.85	1.98	2.08	2.17	2.20	2.25	2.32	2.39	2.44	14.
.50	.56	.66	.59	.64	.84	.88	.89	.79	.67	15.
16.39	17.72	18.98	20.72	23.24	25.81	26.75	27.84	29.50	30.16	21.
										III.
1.10	1.20	1.20	1.30	1.40	1.55	1.70	1.80	1.85	2.00	7.
27.11	30.22	32.63	35.81	39.39	43.57	47.05	50.37	55.24	61.16	12.
28.21	31.42	33.83	37.11	40.79	45.12	48.75	52.17	57.09	63.16	14.
76.11	85.45	91.97	97.46	101.01	105.42	113.73	124.98	133.63	139.68	IV.
104.32	116.87	125.80	134.57	141.80	150.54	162.48	177.15	190.72	202.84	V.

Line	
III-7	FRB worksheets.
12, 14	Sum of state and local government obligations outstanding (FRB worksheets), loans by the federal government (FRB worksheets), and noninterest-bearing debt. June 30 estimates for the last are derived by taking gross debt of state and local governments (*Survey of Current Business*, e.g., May 1957, Table 4, p. 19) minus total interest-bearing debt (*Annual Report of the Secretary of the Treasury*, e.g., 1955, Table 49, p. 512). December data are then derived by straight-line interpolation.
IV	Line V minus line III-14.
V	Sum of lines I-7 and II-21.

TABLE III-6a

State and Local Governments, 1900-45, Selected Years

(million dollars)

	1900	1912	1922	1929	1933	1939	1945[a]
I. Tangible assets							
1. Residential structures; 2. Nonresidential structures	1,574	4,825	13,342	21,170	24,036	28,713	40,034
3. Land	3,000	6,500	11,100	13,200	13,150	14,600	17,450
4. Producer durables	61	154	121	505	483	476	405
6. Inventories	10	20	40	60	60	60	150
7. Total	4,645	11,499	24,603	34,935	37,729	43,849	58,039
II. Intangible assets							
1. Currency and demand deposits	110	387	1,097	1,767	1,736	2,986	5,311
a. Monetary metals	6	7	6	5	4	6	13
b. Other	104	380	1,091	1,762	1,732	2,980	5,298
2. Other bank deposits and shares	35	126	365	712	360	553	521
13. Securities, U.S. government			232	255	219	250	4,390
14. Securities, state and local	554	1,150	2,210	3,631	3,041	2,762	1,633
20. Other intangible assets	84	169	312	520	492	601	428
21. Total	783	1,832	4,216	6,885	5,848	7,152	12,283
III. Liabilities							
12. Bonds and notes	2,014	4,430	10,384	16,873	19,084	19,765	15,913
13. Other liabilities					417	54	343
14. Total	2,014	4,430	10,384	16,873	19,501	19,819	16,256
IV. Equities	3,414	8,901	18,435	24,947	24,076	31,182	54,066
V. Total assets or liabilities and equities	5,428	13,331	28,819	41,820	43,577	51,001	70,322

Notes to Table III-6a

Source: All data were taken directly from Goldsmith, *A Study of Saving*, Volume III, Table W-42 xcept as specified below.

ine

-1 and
-2 Table W-42, lines I-1 and I-2, plus federal-aid highways (omitted from the table) as follows (million dollars):

1922	300
1929	630
1933	1,160
1939	1,850
1945	3,790

7 Table W-42, line I-10, plus federal-aid highways (see above), and minus monetary metals (Table W-42, line I-9).

I-1 Table W-42, sum of lines I-9, II-1, and II-2, minus line II-2 of this table.
2 Goldsmith, *Financial Intermediaries*, Table A-3.c, line 24.
21 Table W-42, line II-22 plus monetary metals (line I-9), and minus accruals (line II-20). The accruals, mainly on local property taxes but also on state income, gift, inheritance, and property taxes, are omitted here because they were not calculated for later years.

V Table W-42, line IV, plus federal-aid highways (see above), and minus accruals (line II-20).

V Table W-42, line V, plus federal-aid highways, and minus accruals.

[a]The 1945 figures in this table have been superseded by those in Table III-6; they are included here r comparability with earlier years.

TABLE III-7

Federal Government (Civil Only), 1945-58

(billion dollars)

	1945	1946	1947	1948
I. Tangible assets				
1. Residential structures	1.21	1.15	1.13	.99
2. Nonresidential structures	13.76	17.22	20.61	22.20
3. Land	6.30	7.00	8.30	8.90
4. Producer durables	2.64	2.37	1.96	1.56
6. Inventories	2.58	1.39	1.10	1.92
7. Total	26.49	29.13	33.10	35.57
II. Intangible assets				
1. Currency and demand deposits	26.81	4.08	3.54	4.62
a. Monetary metals				
b. Other	26.81	4.08	3.54	4.62
2. Other bank deposits and shares	.12	.13	.12	.12
7. Trade credit	.90	.10	0	0
10. Other loans	4.06	7.23	11.36	13.03
11. Mortgages, nonfarm	.92	.68	.64	.72
a. Residential	.90	.67	.63	.72
b. Nonresidential	.02	.01	.01	.01
12. Mortgages, farm	1.50	1.32	1.20	1.14
13. Securities, U.S. government	4.52	5.06	5.10	5.20
c. Other long-term	4.52	5.06	5.10	5.20
14. Securities, state and local	.50	.48	.50	.57
19. Equity in other business	2.34	2.34	.55	.54
20. Other intangible assets	11.12	12.02	14.21	14.98
21. Total	52.79	33.44	37.22	40.92
III. Liabilities				
1. Currency and demand deposits	2.31	2.44	2.41	2.40
2. Other bank deposits and shares	3.02	3.38	3.52	3.45
7. Trade debt	2.70	.70	0	0
9. Bank loans, n.e.c.	.31	.10	.07	.92
12. Bonds and notes	278.98	259.99	257.69	253.88
13. Other liabilities	.19	.23	.27	.33
14. Total	287.51	266.84	263.96	260.98
IV. Equities	–208.23	–204.27	–193.64	–184.49
V. Total assets or liabilities and equities	79.28	62.57	70.32	76.49

1949	1950	1951	1952	1953	1954	1955	1956	1957	1958	
										I.
.89	.84	.79	.74	.67	.57	.52	.48	.64	1.01	1.
22.34	24.72	25.89	27.60	28.75	29.68	30.79	32.28	33.57	35.00	2.
9.10	11.50	13.40	12.90	12.00	12.40	13.60	13.40	13.60	12.80	3.
1.24	1.06	1.00	1.00	1.00	.93	.85	.77	.69	.61	4.
3.28	2.67	2.24	2.71	5.59	6.83	6.98	6.87	5.93	7.89	6.
36.85	40.79	43.32	44.95	48.01	50.41	52.74	53.80	54.43	57.31	7.
										II.
5.00	4.32	4.38	6.33	4.86	4.89	4.48	4.18	4.19	4.19	1.
5.00	4.32	4.38	6.33	4.86	4.89	4.48	4.18	4.19	4.19	
.18	.19	.28	.35	.34	.36	.36	.33	.30	.33	2.
0	.38	1.30	2.25	2.21	2.44	2.27	2.35	2.30	1.70	7.
13.70	14.40	15.03	15.78	16.39	16.32	17.35	17.32	17.95	19.05	10.
1.21	1.50	2.11	2.58	2.93	2.94	3.27	3.72	4.99	5.10	11.
1.20	1.49	2.11	2.57	2.92	2.94	3.27	3.72	4.99	5.10	
a	a	a	a	a	—	—	—	—	—	
1.16	1.21	1.27	1.36	1.47	1.57	1.76	2.01	2.24	2.46	12.
5.28	5.04	4.95	5.05	5.07	5.20	5.22	5.47	5.91	5.82	13.
5.28	5.04	4.95	5.05	5.07	5.20	5.22	5.47	5.91	5.82	
.49	.56	.82	1.14	.81	.48	.48	.56	.76	.97	14.
.52	.49	.48	.48	.46	.45	.43	.43	.42	.42	19.
12.89	20.36	24.98	21.82	22.35	19.22	23.24	22.03	20.54	18.28	20.
40.43	48.45	55.60	57.14	56.89	53.87	58.86	58.40	59.60	58.32	21.
										III.
2.38	2.36	2.40	2.44	2.47	2.50	2.51	2.53	2.56	2.60	1.
3.31	3.04	2.82	2.66	2.47	2.24	1.99	1.74	1.42	1.22	2.
0	1.10	2.70	2.80	2.60	2.37	2.28	2.61	2.77	2.83	7.
1.00	.38	.29	.72	2.20	2.27	1.17	.88	.46	.81	9.
258.07	258.12	261.11	269.12	276.91	280.46	284.04	280.53	280.92	288.49	12.
.49	.49	.64	.90	1.11	1.39	1.36	1.46	1.53	1.80	13.
265.25	265.49	269.96	278.64	287.76	291.23	293.35	289.75	289.66	297.75	14.
−187.97	−176.25	−171.04	−176.55	−182.86	−186.95	−181.75	−177.55	−175.63	−182.12	IV.
77.28	89.24	98.92	102.09	104.90	104.28	111.60	112.20	114.03	115.63	V.

(Notes to Table III-7 are on following page)

Notes to Table III-7

Line

I-1 through I-7 From line 7 of Tables IV-a-1 through IV-a-7 respectively.

II-1 Total general fund assets (*Daily Treasury Statement*, category "account of the Treasurer of the U.S.," e.g., December 30, 1955, p. 1) plus domestic balance held outside the Treasury (FRB worksheets), minus the following:

1. time deposits in the general fund (*Federal Reserve Bulletin*, reserves and liabilities of commercial banks, e.g., March, 1958, p. 319, less cash assets of the Postal Savings System, from FRB worksheets).
2. deposits in foreign depositories for the general fund (FRB worksheets).
3. currency & demand deposits of federal government pension and insurance funds (line II-1 of Table III-5b-1).
4. silver bullion in general fund (*Treasury Bulletin*, e.g., Table 4, July, 1951, p. 50).
5. 1945-48: silver bullion deposits with Philippine Treasury (FRB worksheets).

2 Sum of federal government time deposits (*Federal Reserve Bulletin*, e.g., March, 1958, p. 319) and government savings capital in savings and loan associations (see note to line III-2, Table III-5e for source).

7 FRB worksheets.

10 Table III-7d, column 9.

11 Table IV-b-11, line 7.

11a Table IV-b-11a, line 7.

11b Table IV-b-11b, line 7.

12 Table IV-b-12, line 7.

13 The sum of Table III-5b-1a, column 8; Table III-5b-1b, columns 4 and 5; and Table III-7e, line II-13.

14 FRB worksheets.

19 Sum of:

1. stock and other equities of the Exchange Stabilization Fund (*Treasury Bulletin* table, "Exchange Stabilization Fund-Balance Sheet," e.g., February, 1956, p. 55).
2. other assets of the Postal Savings System (Table III-7b, line II-20).
3. capital stock in production credit associations held by the federal government (Farm Credit Administration, Accounting and Budget Division, *Production Credit Associations, Summary of Operations*).
4. federal government share of surplus and reserves of the production credit associations, estimated from *ibid.* as follows:

$$\frac{\text{PCA capital stock, held by Federal Government}}{\text{PCA capital stock, total}} \times \text{PCA surplus and reserves.}$$

20 Sum of federal government subscription in the International Monetary Fund and the International Bank for Reconstruction and Development (*Federal Reserve Bulletin*, e.g., February 1955, p. 168); rest of the world deposit liabilities to U.S. government (FRB worksheets); and corporate tax liabilities to U.S. government (FRB worksheets).

21 Sum of lines II-1 through II-20.

III-1 The sum of Federal Reserve Bank notes, National Bank notes, and U.S. notes outstanding, minus gold reserve against U.S. notes (*Federal Reserve Bulletin*, e.g., February 1959, p. 163, col. 1), seigniorage on coins and revalued silver (*Treasury Bulletin*, Table 5, e.g., April 1956, p. 50) and $131 million for minor coin outstanding, December, 1934 (*Banking and Monetary Statistics*, p. 420).

2 Deposit liabilities of the Postal Savings System (Table III-7b).

7 1945-53: Corporations' receivables from U.S. government (SEC, *Working Capital of U.S. Corporations*, e.g., Release No. 1448, April 1957).
1954-58: SEC, working capital worksheets.

9 Loans guaranteed by the Commodity Credit Corporation (*Annual Report of the Comptroller of the Currency*, e.g., 1955, p. 173). CCC pooled certificates of interest are included.

12 Sum of U.S. government direct, guaranteed, and nonguaranteed obligations outstanding. Direct and guaranteed obligations are estimated as follows:

Total gross debt (*Treasury Bulletin*, e.g., December 1956, Table 1, p. 16), minus currency items in public debt (*Daily Treasury Statement*, table on "statement of public debt," items: gold liabilities, National and Federal Reserve Bank notes assumed by the U.S., and old demand notes and fractional currency).

Nonguaranteed obligations are estimated as follows:

Debt of U.S. government corporations and agencies not guaranteed by the U.S. (*Treasury Bulletin*, "Corporations and certain other business-type activities," e.g., April 1959, pp. 73-97. This includes the debt of Federal Home Loan Bank Board, the Farm Credit Admin-

III-12 istration's Banks for Cooperatives, Federal Intermediate Credit Banks and the Federal National Mortgage Association), plus the debt of Federal Land Banks not guaranteed by U.S. government (Farm Credit Administration, *Combined Statements of the Federal Land Banks*).

13 Sum of:

	Source
Privately held capital stock of:	
Banks for Cooperatives	
Federal Home Loan Banks	*Treasury Bulletin*, see
Federal National Mortgage Association—secondary market operations	note to III-12 above
Federal Land Banks	*Combined Statements of the Federal Land Banks*
Trust interest on fund principal of Federal National Mortgage Association—secondary operations	*Treasury Bulletin*, see above
Trust and deposit liabilities of Federal Home Loan Banks	*Treasury Bulletin*, see above
Other liabilities of:	
Postal Savings System	Table III-7b

If the private share of the Federal Home Loan Banks and Federal Land Banks were included, the following amounts would be added:

(million dollars)

1945:	55
1946:	89
1947:	207
1948:	214
1949:	222
1950:	240
1951:	258
1952:	282
1953:	292
1954:	301
1955:	309
1956:	318
1957:	328
1958:	339

14 Sum of lines III-1 through III-13.

IV Line V minus line III-14.

V Sum of lines I-7 and II-21.

TABLE III-7a

Total Federal Government, Including Military, 1945-58

(billion dollars)

	1945	1946	1947	1948
I. Tangible assets				
1. Residential structures	1.29	1.24	1.25	1.14
2. Nonresidential structures	22.23	27.65	32.56	34.35
3. Land	6.30	7.00	8.30	8.90
4. Producer durables	66.16	65.43	56.95	50.94
6. Inventories	3.22	2.32	2.21	3.49
7. Total	99.20	103.64	101.27	98.82
II. Intangible assets				
1. Currency and demand deposits	26.81	4.08	3.54	4.62
a. Monetary metals				
b. Other	26.81	4.08	3.54	4.62
2. Other bank deposits and shares	.12	.13	.12	.12
7. Trade credit	.90	.10	0	0
10. Other loans	4.06	7.23	11.36	13.03
11. Mortgages, nonfarm	.92	.68	.64	.72
a. Residential	.90	.67	.63	.72
b. Nonresidential	.02	.01	.01	.01
12. Mortgages, farm	1.50	1.32	1.20	1.14
13. Securities, U.S. government	4.52	5.06	5.10	5.20
c. Other long-term	4.52	5.06	5.10	5.20
14. Securities, state and local	.50	.48	.50	.57
19. Equity in other business	2.34	2.34	.55	.54
20. Other intangible assets	11.12	12.02	14.21	14.98
21. Total	52.79	33.44	37.22	40.92
III. Liabilities				
1. Currency and demand deposits	2.31	2.44	2.41	2.40
2. Other bank deposits and shares	3.02	3.38	3.52	3.45
7. Trade debt	2.70	.70	0	0
9. Bank loans, n.e.c.	.31	.10	.07	.92
12. Bonds and notes	278.98	259.99	257.69	253.88
13. Other liabilities	.19	.23	.27	.33
14. Total	287.51	266.84	263.96	260.98
IV. Equities	−135.52	−129.76	−125.47	−121.24
V. Total assets or liabilities and equities	151.99	137.08	138.49	139.74

Data are from Table III-7, with the following additions, from the specified tables in Goldsmith, *National Wealth*, and corresponding adjustments to lines I-7, IV, and V of this table.

1949	1950	1951	1952	1953	1954	1955	1956	1957	1958	
										I.
1.07	1.05	1.01	.98	.91	.81	.76	.73	.89	1.26	1.
33.51	36.65	38.87	40.95	43.58	45.32	47.79	50.71	53.21	55.47	2.
9.10	11.50	13.40	12.90	12.00	12.40	13.60	13.40	13.60	12.80	3.
42.03	39.31	38.37	43.79	49.91	50.74	51.38	53.40	53.58	52.86	4.
5.44	6.69	6.48	9.07	12.88	15.77	18.45	19.84	19.74	23.80	6.
91.15	95.20	98.13	107.69	119.28	125.04	131.98	138.08	141.02	146.19	7.
										II.
5.00	4.32	4.38	6.33	4.86	4.89	4.48	4.18	4.19	4.19	1.
5.00	4.32	4.38	6.33	4.86	4.89	4.48	4.18	4.19	4.19	
.18	.19	.28	.35	.34	.36	.36	.33	.30	.33	2.
0	.38	1.30	2.25	2.21	2.44	2.27	2.35	2.30	1.70	7.
13.70	14.40	15.03	15.78	16.39	16.32	17.35	17.32	17.95	19.05	10.
1.21	1.50	2.11	2.58	2.93	2.94	3.27	3.72	4.99	5.10	11.
1.20	1.49	2.11	2.57	2.92	2.94	3.27	3.72	4.99	5.10	
a	a	a	a	a	0	0	0	0	0	
1.16	1.21	1.27	1.36	1.47	1.57	1.76	2.01	2.24	2.46	12.
5.28	5.04	4.95	5.05	5.07	5.20	5.22	5.47	5.91	5.82	13.
5.28	5.04	4.95	5.05	5.07	5.20	5.22	5.47	5.91	5.82	
.49	.56	.82	1.14	.81	.48	.48	.56	.76	.97	14.
.52	.49	.48	.48	.46	.45	.43	.43	.42	.42	19.
12.89	20.36	24.98	21.82	22.35	19.22	23.24	22.03	20.54	18.28	20.
40.43	48.45	55.60	57.14	56.89	53.87	58.86	58.40	59.60	58.32	21.
										III.
2.38	2.36	2.40	2.44	2.47	2.50	2.51	2.53	2.56	2.60	1.
3.31	3.04	2.82	2.66	2.47	2.24	1.99	1.74	1.42	1.22	2.
0	1.10	2.70	2.80	2.60	2.37	2.28	2.61	2.77	2.83	7.
1.00	.38	.29	.72	2.20	2.27	1.17	.88	.46	.81	9.
258.07	258.12	261.11	269.12	276.91	280.46	284.04	280.53	280.92	288.49	12.
.49	.49	.64	.90	1.11	1.39	1.36	1.46	1.53	1.80	13.
265.25	265.49	269.96	278.64	287.76	291.23	293.35	289.75	289.66	297.75	14.
−133.67	−121.84	−116.23	−113.81	−111.59	−112.32	−102.51	−93.27	−89.04	−93.24	IV.
131.58	143.65	153.73	164.83	176.17	178.91	190.84	196.48	200.62	204.51	V.

Line

I-1 Table B-177, column 11.

2 Table B-175, sum of columns 2, 3, and 4, minus Table B-177, column 11.

4 Table B-175, sum of columns 1, 5, and 8.

5 Table B-175, sum of columns 6 and 7.

[a]Under $5 million.

TABLE III-7b

Postal Savings System, 1945-58

(billion dollars)

	1945	1946	1947	1948
I. Tangible assets				
II. Intangible assets				
1. Currency and demand deposits	.01	.01	.01	.01
13. Securities, U.S. government	2.84	3.18	3.31	3.24
20. Other intangible assets	.18	.20	.21	.20
21. Total	3.02	3.39	3.52	3.45
III. Liabilities				
2. Other bank deposits and shares	3.02	3.38	3.52	3.45
13. Other liabilities	[a]	[a]	0	[a]
14. Total	3.02	3.39	3.52	3.45
IV. Equities				
V. Total assets or liabilities and equities	3.02	3.39	3.52	3.45

1945-54: All data are from *Federal Reserve Bulletin* table entitled "Postal Savings System," June 1955, p. 662.

1955-58: Federal Reserve Board worksheets.

[a]Under $5 million.

1949	1950	1951	1952	1953	1954	1955	1956	1957	1958	
										I.
										II.
.01	.01	.03	.03	.03	.03	.03	.03	.02	.02	1.
3.12	2.87	2.64	2.55	2.39	2.13	1.87	1.63	1.32	1.13	13.
.19	.17	.16	.15	.14	.13	.11	.11	.10	.09	20.
3.31	3.04	2.84	2.74	2.56	2.29	2.01	1.77	1.44	1.24	21.
										III.
3.31	3.04	2.82	2.66	2.47	2.24	1.99	1.74	1.42	1.22	2.
a	a	.02	.08	.09	.05	.03	.03	.02	.02	13.
3.31	3.04	2.84	2.74	2.56	2.29	2.01	1.77	1.44	1.24	14.
										IV.
3.31	3.04	2.84	2.74	2.56	2.29	2.01	1.77	1.44	1.24	V.

TABLE III-7c

Government Lending and Credit Agencies, Except Federal Land Banks, 1945-58

(million dollars)

	1945	1946	1947	1948
I. Tangible assets				
1. Residential structures 2. Nonresidential structures 3. Land 4. Producer durables	8,741	4,633	1,635	1,455
6. Inventories	2,168	1,139	686	437
7. Total	10,909	5,772	2,321	1,892
II. Intangible assets				
1. Currency and demand deposits	375	830	696	588
10. Other loans	2,717	3,761	5,149	6,802
11. Mortgages, nonfarm	917	681	638	724
a. Residential	902	672	631	717
b. Nonresidential	15	9	7	7
12. Mortgages, farm	426	341	306	270
13. Securities, U.S. government	1,507	1,717	1,663	1,855
15. Securities, other bonds and notes	320	220	151	133
20. Other intangible assets	1,208	865	540	208
21. Total	7,470	8,415	9,143	10,580
III. Liabilities				
12. Bonds and notes	876	756	771	1,004
13. Other liabilities	3,061	2,488	1,259	1,620
14. Total	3,937	3,244	2,030	2,624
IV. Equities	14,442	10,943	9,434	9,848
V. Total assets or liabilities and equities	18,379	14,187	11,464	12,472

Sum of balance sheet items for the following agencies.

Housing: Federal Home Loan Banks
Federal Housing Administration
Federal National Mortgage Association
Home Owners Loan Corporation
Office of the Administrator, Housing and Home Finance Agency
Public Housing Administration
R.F.C. Mortgage Corporation

Agriculture: Banks for Cooperatives
Commodity Credit Corporation
Farmers Home Administration
Federal Crop Insurance Corporation
Federal Farm Mortgage Corporation
Federal Intermediate Credit Banks
Production Credit Corporation
Rural Electrification Administration

Business: Small Business Administration

Finance: Federal Deposit Insurance Corporation
Federal Savings and Loan Insurance Corporation
Reconstruction Finance Corporation

1949	1950	1951	1952	1953	1954	1955	1956	1957	1958	
										I.
1,411	1,409	1,392	1,305	1,158	881	600	407	246	175	1. 2. 3. 4.
1,376	1,638	1,174	1,016	2,086	3,302	3,747	3,651	3,025	3,036	6.
2,787	3,047	2,566	2,321	3,244	4,183	4,347	4,058	3,271	3,211	7.
										II.
310	403	427	454	501	445	447	717	758	941	1.
7,377	7,581	8,129	9,616	11,189	12,042	12,499	12,440	12,856	15,959	10.
1,205	1,478	1,977	2,378	2,626	2,559	2,787	3,259	4,222	4,168	11.
1,200	1,474	1,973	2,375	2,623	2,559	2,787	3,259	4,222	4,168	
5	4	4	3	3	0	0	0	0	0	
252	265	279	294	301	301	279	291	341	391	12.
2,047	2,075	2,226	2,419	2,601	2,967	3,236	3,700	3,721	4,042	13.
104	84	74	42	40	5	6	8	13	5	15.
390	414	581	669	738	826	1,417	1,193	1,267	1,142	20.
11,685	12,300	13,693	15,872	17,996	19,145	20,671	21,608	23,178	26,648	21.
										III.
800	1,214	1,413	1,383	1,258	1,101	2,421	2,777	4,709	4,087	12.
1,692	1,161	1,051	1,625	3,514	3,896	2,438	2,193	1,695	2,325	13.
2,492	2,375	2,464	3,008	4,772	4,997	4,859	4,970	6,404	6,412	14.
11,980	12,972	13,795	15,185	16,468	18,331	20,159	20,696	20,045	23,447	IV.
14,472	15,347	16,259	18,193	21,240	23,328	25,018	25,666	26,449	29,859	V.

International Finance: Coordinator Inter-American Affairs
Export-Import Bank
International Cooperation Administration

(Not all these agencies existed during the whole period.)

Source:

Figures for all agencies are from *Federal Reserve Bulletin*, e.g., May 1951, p. 548, except those of the Public Housing Administration for 1945-47. For these years they are a sum of the balance sheets of the Federal Public Housing Administration (U.S. Housing Program Act) and the Public War Housing Program. The balance sheets for the FPHA from 1945-47 are in the *Federal Reserve Bulletin* (May 1946, p. 552, May 1947, p. 578, May 1948, p. 550). The PWHP balance sheet for 1946 is in the *Fifth Annual Report of the National Housing Agency*, Table 13, p. 281, and for 1947 is in the *First Annual Report of the Housing and Home Finance Agency*, Table 16, pp. 46-47. The total assets figure for the PWHP excludes unexpended appropriations. The difference between appropriated funds (asset) and unexpended appropriations (liability) is added into "other assets."

The 1945 balance sheet for the Public War Housing Program was obtained directly from the Public Housing Administration.

Lines II-11 and II-12 are taken from Saul B. Klaman, *The Volume of Mortgage Debt in the Postwar Decade*, New York, NBER, Technical Paper 13, 1958, Table 20. Veterans Administration and Federal Land Bank holdings are excluded. Klaman's estimates have been corrected and extended to 1958, using the same methods and sources.

TABLE III-7d

Estimate of Federal Government Loans, 1945-58

(million dollars)

	Unincorporated Business (1)	Corporate Business (2)	Banks (3)	Rest of the World (4)	Farms (5)	CCC Loans to Cooperatives, Other Than Tobacco (6)	Federal Intermediate Credit Bank Loans (7)	Financial Institutions (8)	Total (billion dollars) (9)
1945	610	647	281	1,610	414	-	231	267	4.06
1946	790	493	212	4,749	402	-	273	314	7.23
1947	1,177	525	155	8,343	372	1	336	447	11.36
1948	1,413	511	128	9,455	346	225	426	525	13.03
1949	1,717	638	110	9,934	352	72	437	445	13.70
1950	1,970	616	94	10,053	333	-	510	824	14.40
1951	2,290	634	76	10,251	307	19	633	814	15.03
1952	2,509	655	47	10,624	341	67	673	864	15.78
1953	2,611	953	41	10,853	380	10	590	952	16.39
1954	2,805	806	23	10,652	421	108	638	870	16.32
1955	3,161	784	9	10,619	412	260	689	1,419	17.35
1956	3,414	682	8	10,685	434	131	734	1,233	17.32
1957	3,444	741	7	11,019	439	93	935	1,270	17.95
1958	3,628	752	-	11,651	409	144	1,169	1,298	19.05

Notes to Table III-7d

Columns 1 through 4: Federal Reserve Board worksheets.
Column 1 includes loans to tobacco cooperatives.
Column 4 does not include investment in the IMF and IBRD.

Column 5: Loans to farmers by Federal Land Banks, Farmers Home Administration, production credit associations, and livestock loan companies. CCC price-support loans are not included. See note to line III-10 of Table III-3 for sources.

Column 6: Total CCC loans to cooperatives from *Agricultural Finance Review*, Vol. 22, September 1960, p. 149. CCC loans to tobacco cooperatives by correspondence from USDA, Agricultural Stabilization and Conservation Service, Fiscal Division.

Columns 7 and 8: *Federal Reserve Bulletin*, e.g., November 1960, p. 1268.

Column 9: Sum of columns 1 through 8.

TABLE III-7e

Federal Land Banks, 1945-58

(million dollars)

	1945	1946	1947	1948
I. Tangible assets				
7. Total	2	0	0	0
II. Intangible assets				
1. Currency and demand deposits	48	37	25	22
a. Monetary metals				
b. Other	48	37	25	22
10. Other loans	1	2	2	4
12. Mortgages, farm	1,079	977	889	868
13. Securities, U.S. government	145	136	104	101
c. Other long-term	145	136	104	101
14. Securities, state and local	0	0	0	2
20. Other intangible assets	29	29	28	29
21. Total	1,302	1,181	1,048	1,026
III. Liabilities				
12. Bonds and notes	792	757	702	682
13. Other liabilities	114	107	94	87
14. Total	906	864	796	769
IV. Equities	398	317	252	257
V. Total assets or liabilities and equities	1,304	1,181	1,048	1,026

Source: All data in this table (except Line II-12) come from Farm Credit Administration, *Combined Statements of the Federal Land Banks*.

Line

I-7 Real estate owned (investment).

II-1 Item of the same name; see headnote.
10 Includes loans in the process of closing, and loans called for foreclosure, judgment, etc.
12 Klaman, *Volume of Mortgage Debt*, Table 20, column 17.
13 Item of the same name (at amortized cost); see source.
14 Item of the same name (at amortized cost); see source.
20 Line II-21 minus lines II-1 through II-14.
21 Item of the same name, plus reserves for losses; see source.

1949	1950	1951	1952	1953	1954	1955	1956	1957	1958	
										I.
0	0	0	0	0	0	0	a	a	a	7.
										II.
20	20	18	15	18	18	19	20	16	15	1.
20	20	18	15	18	18	19	20	16	15	
5	4	3	3	4	4	6	3	3	3	10.
906	947	994	1,071	1,169	1,267	1,480	1,722	1,897	2,065	12.
106	88	83	82	86	101	107	109	109	109	13.
106	88	83	82	86	101	107	109	109	109	
0	1	20	0	10	4	0	8	2	a	14.
30	32	35	38	42	46	51	59	69	74	20.
1,067	1,092	1,153	1,209	1,329	1,440	1,663	1,921	2,096	2,266	21.
										III.
717	735	787	833	945	1,045	1,252	1,483	1,639	1,788	12.
86	80	77	61	56	57	59	70	74	80	13.
803	815	864	894	1,001	1,102	1,311	1,553	1,713	1,868	14.
264	277	289	315	328	338	352	368	383	398	IV.
1,067	1,092	1,153	1,209	1,329	1,440	1,663	1,921	2,096	2,266	V.

Line

III-12 Does not include bonds owned, but does include bank notes payable.

13 Line III-14 minus line III-12.

14 Line V minus line IV.

IV Includes capital stock owned by both National Farm Loan Associations and direct borrowers and, in 1945 ($68 million) and 1946 ($62 million), by the federal government.

V Sum of lines I-7 and II-21.

[a] Under $500,000.

TABLE III-7f

Federal Government (Civil Only), 1900-45, Selected Years

(million dollars)

	1900	1912	1922	1929	1933	1939	1945[a]
I. Tangible assets							
1. Residential structures, 2. Nonresidential structures, 3. Land (combined)	1,450	2,053	3,981	4,935	5,552	9,687	20,977
4. Producer durables	5	18	35	63	111	301	3,027
6. Inventories		2	30	3	3	937	2,584
7. Total	1,455	2,073	4,046	5,001	5,666	10,925	26,588
II. Intangible assets							
1. Currency and demand deposits	102	56	544	234	1,219	1,596	25,783
2. Other bank deposits and shares		26	56	138	914	303	27
7. Trade credit							900
10. Other loans			83	226	1,989	1,947	1,865
11. Mortgages, nonfarm					132	2,182	859
a. Residential					132	2,182	859
12. Mortgages, farm			651	1,200	1,245	2,801	1,451
13. Securities, U.S. government			229	52	309	2,080	4,520
14. Securities, state and local					50	296	484
15. Securities, other bonds and notes			2	13	45	862	
16. Securities, preferred stock		2			249	572	304
20. Other intangible assets		40	1,310	1,375	1,415	2,023	12,372
21. Total	102	124	2,875	3,238	7,567	14,662	48,565
III. Liabilities							
1. Currency and demand deposits	58	135	467	411	414	1,128	2,536
2. Other bank deposits and shares		28	135	168	1,230	1,315	3,014
7. Trade debt							2,700
9. Bank loans, n.e.c.						235	143
12. Bonds and notes	1,239	1,191	23,638	17,539	25,494	55,070	278,484
13. Other liabilities		2	183	35	56	217	1,796
14. Total	1,297	1,356	24,423	18,153	27,194	57,965	288,673
IV. Equities	260	841	−17,502	−9,914	−13,961	−32,378	−213,520
V. Total assets or liabilities and equities	1,557	2,197	6,921	8,239	13,233	25,587	75,153

Notes to Table III-7f

Source: All data were obtained by adding corresponding lines in Tables W-40 and W-43 of Goldsmith, *A Study of Saving*, Vol. III, except as specified below. The L, F, and K tables referred to are in Goldsmith, *A Study of Saving*, Vol. I.

Line	
I-7	Table W-40, line I-10, plus Table W-43, line I-10, minus Table W-43, line I-9.
II-1	Sum of: Table W-40, lines II-1 and II-2; and Table W-43, lines II-2 and II-3.
2	Sum of: Table W-40, line II-3 (savings and loan shares); and Table L-43, column 2.
7	Table W-43, line II-7.
10	Table W-40, sum of lines II-7 and II-8.
11	Table IV-b-11c, line 7.
11a	Table IV-b-11c-1, line 7.
12	Table W-40, line II-11.
13	Sum of: Table W-40, line II-12; and Table L-43, column 3.
20	Sum of: Tables W-40, line II-21; W-43, lines II-20 and II-21; and Table L-43, column 6, minus Table F-26, columns 2 and 4.
21	Sum of lines II-1 through II-20 of this table.
III-1	1900-22: Sum of: Table F-5, columns 3 and 6; and Table F-3, column 5. 1929-45: Sum of: Table F-18, columns 3 and 6; and Table F-13, column 5.
2	Table L-44, columns 2 and 3.
7	Table W-43, line III-8.
9	Table W-40, line III-7.
12	Sum of: Table W-40, line III-12; W-43, line III-12; and, for 1929-39, Table K-6, lines 13 and 16, with 1933 assumed the same as 1929; for 1945, Table IV-b-13, line 9.
13	Sum of: Table W-40, line III-14; and Table L-44, column 4.
14	Sum of lines III-1 through III-13 of this table.
IV	Line V minus line III-14 of this table.
V	Sum of lines I-7 and II-21 of this table.

[a]The 1945 figures in this table have been superseded by those in Table III-7; they are included here for comparability with earlier years.

TABLE III-8

Rest of the World, 1945-58

(billion dollars)

	1945	1946	1947	1948
I. Tangible assets				
II. Intangible assets				
1. Currency and demand deposits	4.37	4.44	4.49	4.83
2. Other bank deposits and shares	.02	.02	.01	.04
3. Life insurance reserves, private	.87	.94	1.01	1.09
8. Loans on securities	.09	.10	.09	.06
13. Securities, U.S. government	2.57	2.10	2.70	2.78
a. Short-term	2.08	1.54	.79	1.26
b. Savings bonds				
c. Other long-term	.49	.56	1.91	1.52
14. Securities, state and local	.10	.10	.10	.10
15. Securities, other bonds and notes	.17	.13	.09	.04
16. Securities, preferred stock	.28	.28	.27	.25
17. Securities, common stock	2.73	2.41	2.21	2.05
20. Other intangible assets	5.87	5.36	5.13	5.30
21. Total	17.07	15.88	16.10	16.54
III. Liabilities				
9. Bank loans, n.e.c.	.32	.52	.59	.63
10. Other loans	1.75	4.93	8.56	9.68
12. Bonds and notes	2.73	2.64	2.66	2.74
13. Other liabilities	8.71	9.15	13.84	15.05
14. Total	13.51	17.24	25.65	28.10
IV. Stock	1.26	1.45	1.39	1.34
V. Total stock and liabilities	14.77	18.69	27.04	29.44

Line

II-1 Table IV-b-1d, column 9.
2 Table IV-b-2, line 9.
3 Table IV-b-3, line 9.
8 Table IV-b-8, line 9.
13 Table IV-b-13, line 9.
13a Table IV-b-13a, line 9.
13c Table IV-b-13c, line 9.
14 Table IV-b-14, line 9.
15 Table IV-b-15, line 9.
16 Table IV-b-16, line 9.
17 Table IV-b-17, line 9.
20 Line II-21, minus the sum of lines II-1 through II-17.
21 Goldsmith, *National Wealth*, Table B-186, line 25.

1949	1950	1951	1952	1953	1954	1955	1956	1957	1958	
										I.
										II.
4.82	4.72	4.29	4.49	4.24	4.33	4.28	4.50	4.67	4.75	1.
.18	.40	.51	.71	1.26	1.81	1.68	1.59	1.56	2.62	2.
1.17	1.25	1.34	1.44	1.54	1.65	1.77	1.87	1.98	2.10	3.
.06	.08	.07	.07	.06	.06	.04	.05	.06	.07	8.
2.88	4.33	4.28	5.31	5.88	6.31	7.48	7.73	7.56	7.61	13.
1.54	2.44	2.16	3.40	4.11	4.23	4.89	5.93	5.92	5.91	
1.34	1.89	2.12	1.91	1.77	2.08	2.59	1.80	1.64	1.70	
.10	.10	.10	.10	.10	.10	.10	.10	.10	.10	14.
.08	.08	.09	.13	.17	.20	.16	.21	.32	.36	15.
.25	.25	.27	.27	.28	.30	.31	.32	.32	.33	16.
2.24	2.68	3.18	3.43	3.37	4.96	6.27	6.64	5.77	7.97	17.
5.10	5.57	6.42	6.58	6.73	7.05	7.47	8.60	9.09	8.91	20.
16.88	19.46	20.55	22.53	23.63	26.77	29.56	31.61	31.43	34.82	21.
										III.
.66	.72	.78	.78	.68	1.03	1.40	1.75	2.10	2.63	9.
10.16	10.30	10.54	10.94	11.16	11.00	11.01	11.10	11.52	12.18	10.
2.73	3.34	3.74	3.76	3.71	3.49	3.27	3.68	4.10	4.53	12.
16.04	17.49	18.89	20.86	23.30	25.05	27.06	30.78	34.66	36.72	13.
29.59	31.85	33.95	36.34	38.85	40.57	42.74	47.31	52.38	56.06	14.
1.07	.99	1.01	.91	.72	1.64	2.21	2.17	1.85	3.10	IV.
30.66	32.84	34.96	37.25	39.57	42.21	44.95	49.48	54.23	59.16	V.

Line

III-9 Table IV-b-9, line 9.
10 Table IV-b-10, line 9.
12 Table IV-b-15, line 10.
13 Line III-14 minus lines III-9, 10, and 12.
14 Goldsmith, *National Wealth*, Table B-185, line 27, minus line IV of this table.

IV Table IV-b-17, line 10.

V Line III-14 plus line IV.

SECTION IV

Asset and Liability Tables, 1945–58 and Selected Earlier Years

(Some tables have been extended through 1959.)

TABLE IV-a-1

Residential Structures, Assets

(billion dollars)

	1945	1946	1947	1948
1. Nonfarm households	123.72	145.28	177.58	192.31
2. Nonfarm unincorporated business	9.18	10.26	11.89	12.95
3. Agriculture	9.22	11.00	13.08	13.63
4. Nonfinancial corporations	8.09	9.34	11.13	12.33
5. Finance	.14	.15	.23	.27
6. State and local governments	.87	1.35	1.69	1.76
7. Federal government	1.21	1.15	1.13	.99
8. Total	152.43	178.53	216.73	234.24

Lines	
1-3, 6-8, and the sum of 4 and 5	Raymond W. Goldsmith, *The National Wealth of the United States in the Postwar Period*, (Princeton University Press for NBER, 1962) Table A-35, columns 1 to 7.
4	Total corporate, minus line 5.
5	Table IV-a-8, line B-1.

TABLE IV-a-2

Nonresidential Structures, Assets

(billion dollars)

	1945	1946	1947	1948
1. Nonfarm households	6.97	9.26	11.54	12.49
2. Nonfarm unincorporated business	8.21	11.02	13.25	14.11
3. Agriculture	7.10	8.33	9.86	10.52
4. Nonfinancial corporations	54.44	68.99	80.74	89.30
5. Finance	1.17	1.39	1.45	1.52
6. State and local governments	41.55	50.64	60.49	65.12
7. Federal government	13.76	17.22	20.61	22.20
8. Total	133.20	166.85	197.94	215.26

Lines	
1-3, 6-8, and the sum of 4 and 5	Goldsmith, *National Wealth*, Table A-36, columns 1 to 7.
4	Total corporate, minus line 5.
5	Tables IV-a-8, line B-2 and IV-a-9, line B.

1949	1950	1951	1952	1953	1954	1955	1956	1957	1958
189.39	220.58	236.14	249.61	259.88	270.18	294.13	315.54	330.28	346.81
12.79	14.07	14.46	14.71	14.91	14.83	15.30	15.80	15.99	16.26
13.75	14.91	16.07	16.58	16.88	17.26	17.92	18.53	18.79	19.28
12.48	14.26	15.17	15.87	16.52	16.97	18.18	19.43	20.30	21.31
.32	.40	.43	.53	.54	.56	.59	.61	.63	.64
1.93	2.33	2.95	3.62	4.14	4.41	4.77	5.14	5.51	6.03
.89	.84	.79	.74	,67	.57	.52	.48	.64	1.01
231.55	267.39	286.01	301.66	313.54	324.78	351.41	375.53	392.14	411.34

1949	1950	1951	1952	1953	1954	1955	1956	1957	1958
12.44	13.94	15.15	16.47	17.55	18.77	20.40	22.26	24.25	26.26
13.73	14.84	15.83	16.52	17.32	18.27	20.06	21.97	24.01	25.56
10.82	11.93	13.18	13.76	14.07	14.43	15.09	15.84	16.40	16.75
89.02	101.29	109.79	116.34	124.27	129.36	139.91	151.15	172.06	180.83
2.43	2.41	2.26	2.53	2.79	3.17	3.68	4.10	4.54	4.78
63.77	70.75	77.27	83.84	87.42	92.85	102.29	113.42	123.27	133.20
22.34	24.72	25.89	27.60	28.75	29.68	30.79	32.28	33.57	35.00
214.55	239.88	259.37	277.06	292.17	306.53	332.22	361.02	398.10	422.38

TABLE IV-a-3

Land, Assets

(billion dollars)

	1945	1946	1947	1948
1. Nonfarm households	28.33	32.38	39.41	43.87
2. Nonfarm unincorporated business	8.17	11.01	12.81	14.09
3. Agriculture	43.47	46.53	49.78	51.93
4. Nonfinancial corporations	20.03	24.99	31.16	37.06
5. Finance	.99	1.14	1.30	1.51
6. State and local governments	14.20	18.90	21.40	21.50
7. Federal government	6.30	7.00	8.30	8.90
8. Total	121.49	141.95	164.15	178.86

Lines

1-8 Sum of respective lines, Table IV-a-3a and IV-a-3b.

TABLE IV-a-3a

Residential Land, Assets

(billion dollars)

	1945	1946	1947	1948
1. Nonfarm households	18.46	21.66	26.47	28.65
2. Nonfarm unincorporated business	2.30	2.56	2.96	3.19
3. Agriculture				
4. Nonfinancial corporations	1.78	2.05	2.43	2.70
5. Finance	.04	.04	.06	.07
6. State and local governments				
7. Federal government				
8. Total	22.58	26.31	31.92	34.61

Lines

1, 2, 8, and the sum of 4 and 5 — Goldsmith, *National Wealth*, Table A-40, columns 1 through 4.

4 — Total corporate, minus line 5.

5 — Table IV-a-8, line A-1.

1949	1950	1951	1952	1953	1954	1955	1956	1957	1958
43.28	48.91	52.42	56.78	59.87	64.24	70.82	77.89	85.56	92.16
13.89	15.67	16.95	17.10	17.51	18.30	19.89	20.99	22.25	22.74
50.90	58.40	66.31	66.89	64.22	66.41	68.94	73.96	79.94	87.58
36.40	41.24	46.26	47.05	47.88	50.04	54.89	57.99	62.98	63.46
1.91	2.01	2.09	2.30	2.52	2.82	3.18	3.52	3.92	4.04
20.50	24.00	24.20	23.70	24.00	24.10	24.80	26.30	27.40	28.00
9.10	11.50	13.40	12.90	12.00	12.40	13.60	13.40	13.60	12.80
175.98	201.73	221.63	226.72	228.00	238.31	256.12	274.05	295.65	310.78

1949	1950	1951	1952	1953	1954	1955	1956	1957	1958
28.23	32.89	35.22	37.24	38.80	40.35	43.95	47.17	49.41	51.91
3.13	3.43	3.52	3.58	3.63	3.61	3.74	3.86	3.92	3.99
2.75	3.13	3.32	3.47	3.61	3.70	3.95	4.22	4.41	4.61
.08	.10	.11	.13	.14	.14	.15	.15	.16	.16
34.19	39.55	42.17	44.42	46.18	47.80	51.79	55.40	57.90	60.67

TABLE IV-a-3b

Nonresidential Land, Assets

(billion dollars)

	1945	1946	1947	1948
1. Nonfarm households	9.87	10.72	12.94	15.22
2. Nonfarm unincorporated business	5.87	8.45	9.85	10.90
3. Agriculture	43.47	46.53	49.78	51.93
4. Nonfinancial corporations	18.25	22.94	28.74	34.36
5. Finance	.95	1.10	1.23	1.44
6. State and local governments	14.20	18.90	21.40	21.50
7. Federal government	6.30	7.00	8.30	8.90
8. Total	98.91	115.64	132.23	144.25

Lines

1	Goldsmith, *National Wealth*, Table A-41, sum of columns 2 and 3.
2	*Ibid.*, Table A-41, column 4, Table A-42, column 2, and Table A-43, column 2.
3	*Ibid.*, Table A-41, column 5.
Sum of 4 and 5	*Ibid.*, Table A-41, column 6, Table A-42, column 3, and Table A-43, column 3.
4	Total corporate, minus line 5.
5	Table IV-a-8, line A-2 and Table IV-a-9, lines A-1 and A-2.
6-7	Goldsmith, *National Wealth*, Table A-41, columns 7 and 8.
8	*Ibid.*, Table A-41, column 1, Table A-42, column 1, and Table A-43, column 1.

TABLE IV-a-4

Producer Durables, Assets

(billion dollars)

	1945	1946	1947	1948
1. Nonfarm households	.13	.18	.25	.35
2. Nonfarm unincorporated business	5.31	6.88	9.21	11.35
3. Agriculture	5.79	6.55	8.39	10.69
4. Nonfinancial corporations	33.94	41.55	52.58	61.95
5. Finance	.18	.20	.23	.26
6. State and local governments	.62	.79	1.05	1.35
7. Federal government	2.64	2.37	1.96	1.56
8. Total	48.61	58.52	73.67	87.51

Lines

1-3, 6-8, and the sum of 4 and 5	Goldsmith, *National Wealth*, Table A-37, columns 1 through 7.
4	Total corporate, minus line 5.
5	Table IV-a-8, line C.

1949	1950	1951	1952	1953	1954	1955	1956	1957	1958
15.05	16.02	17.20	19.54	21.07	23.89	26.87	30.72	36.15	40.25
10.76	12.24	13.43	13.52	13.88	14.69	16.15	17.13	18.33	18.75
50.90	58.40	66.31	66.89	64.22	66.41	68.94	73.96	79.94	87.58
33.66	38.11	42.95	43.59	44.26	46.34	50.93	53.78	58.57	58.85
1.82	1.91	1.97	2.16	2.39	2.68	3.04	3.36	3.76	3.88
20.50	24.00	24.20	23.70	24.00	24.10	24.80	26.30	27.40	28.00
9.10	11.50	13.40	12.90	12.00	12.40	13.60	13.40	13.60	12.80
141.79	162.18	179.46	182.30	181.82	190.51	204.33	218.65	237.75	250.11

1949	1950	1951	1952	1953	1954	1955	1956	1957	1958
.48	.65	.83	.97	1.10	1.27	1.47	1.69	1.90	2.07
12.83	14.81	16.63	17.65	18.82	19.79	21.76	24.26	26.44	26.94
12.47	14.09	15.68	16.41	16.64	16.86	17.23	17.64	18.01	18.59
67.94	77.08	86.80	92.95	99.87	106.85	110.96	128.05	140.43	145.53
.28	.35	.39	.44	.48	.57	.64	.73	.82	.85
1.63	1.94	2.27	2.56	2.86	3.22	3.71	4.27	4.85	5.25
1.24	1.06	1.00	1.00	1.00	.93	.85	.77	.69	.61
96.87	109.98	123.60	131.98	140.77	149.49	156.62	177.41	193.14	199.84

TABLE IV-a-5

Consumer Durables, Assets

(billion dollars)

	1945	1946	1947	1948
1. Nonfarm households	40.98	52.81	65.00	75.41
2. Nonfarm unincorporated business				
3. Agriculture	5.26	6.82	8.38	9.90
4. Nonfinancial corporations				
5. Finance				
6. State and local governments				
7. Federal government				
8. Total	46.24	59.63	73.38	85.31

Lines

1, 3, 8 Goldsmith, *National Wealth,* Table A-38, columns 1 through 3.

TABLE IV-a-6

Inventories, Assets

(billion dollars)

	1945	1946	1947	1948
1. Nonfarm households				
2. Nonfarm unincorporated business	7.97	10.06	11.59	12.92
3. Agriculture	15.68	19.10	22.50	22.20
4. Nonfinancial corporations	26.31	37.52	44.67	48.88
5. Finance	.01	.03	.02	.01
6. State and local governments	.07	.09	.10	.11
7. Federal government	2.58	1.39	1.10	1.92
8. Total	52.62	68.19	79.98	86.04

Lines

2-3, 6-8, and the sum of 4 and 5 Goldsmith, *National Wealth,* Table A-39, columns 1 through 6.

4 Total corporate, minus line 5.

5 Tables IV-a-8 and IV-a-9, line E.

1949	1950	1951	1952	1953	1954	1955	1956	1957	1958
80.69	98.91	108.85	113.97	120.57	124.82	136.92	149.43	159.61	164.73
10.51	12.41	13.60	13.66	14.20	13.90	13.85	13.95	14.00	14.02
91.20	111.32	122.45	127.63	134.77	138.72	150.77	163.38	173.61	178.75

1949	1950	1951	1952	1953	1954	1955	1956	1957	1958
11.97	14.24	15.07	14.79	15.21	15.06	15.81	16.51	16.82	16.81
18.93	24.37	28.14	23.15	18.91	18.75	17.38	18.23	20.57	26.15
45.30	55.08	64.83	66.07	67.88	66.28	72.95	80.52	83.24	78.81
.01	.02	.02	.03	.03	.02	.02	.02	.03	.03
.10	.13	.13	.13	.14	.15	.16	.18	.19	.20
3.28	2.67	2.24	2.71	5.59	6.83	6.98	6.87	5.93	7.89
79.59	96.51	110.43	106.88	107.76	107.09	113.30	122.33	126.78	129.89

TABLE IV-a-7

Total Tangible Assets
(billion dollars)

	1945	1946	1947	1948
1. Nonfarm households	200.13	239.91	293.78	324.43
2. Nonfarm unincorporated business	38.84	49.23	58.75	65.42
3. Agriculture	86.52	98.33	111.99	118.87
4. Nonfinancial corporations	142.81	182.40	220.28	249.52
5. Finance	2.49	2.91	3.23	3.57
a. Federal Reserve Banks and Treasury monetary funds	.03	.04	.04	.04
c. Commercial banks	1.12	1.36	1.48	1.53
d. Mutual savings banks	.14	.15	.15	.15
e. Savings and loan associations	.11	.14	.14	.15
h. Life insurance	.93	1.00	1.21	1.45
i. Fire and casualty insurance	.13	.16	.17	.21
k. Other private insurance	.04	.05	.06	.06
m. Other finance				
6. State and local governments	57.31	71.77	84.73	89.84
7. Federal government	26.49	29.13	33.10	35.57
8. Total	554.59	673.68	805.86	887.22

Lines

1-5 Sum of corresponding lines, Tables IV-a-1 through IV-a-6.
5a Table III-5a-1, line I-7.
5c Table III-5c, line I-7.
5d Table III-5d, line I-7.
5e Table III-5e, line I-7.
5h Table III-5h, line I-7.
5i Table III-5i, line I-7.
5k Table III-5k, line I-7.
5m Table III-5m, line I-7.
[Lines 5a through 5m may not add up to total because of rounding.]
6-8 Sum of corresponding lines, Tables IV-a-1 through IV-a-6.

1949	1950	1951	1952	1953	1954	1955	1956	1957	1958	
326.28	382.99	413.39	437.80	458.97	479.28	523.74	566.81	601.60	632.03	1.
65.21	73.63	78.94	80.77	83.77	86.25	92.82	99.53	105.51	108.31	2.
117.38	136.11	152.98	150.45	144.92	147.61	150.41	158.15	167.71	182.37	3.
251.14	288.96	322.85	338.28	356.42	369.50	396.89	437.14	479.01	489.94	4.
4.95	5.19	5.19	5.83	6.36	7.14	8.11	8.98	9.94	10.34	5.
										a.
.05	.06	.06	.07	.07	.07	.09	.10	.11	.12	
1.99	1.99	1.94	2.04	2.22	2.40	2.73	3.02	3.33	3.47	c.
.19	.19	.17	.20	.22	.25	.26	.29	.31	.32	d.
.24	.29	.30	.39	.46	.56	.70	.86	1.03	1.15	e.
2.12	2.30	2.35	2.72	2.91	3.34	3.77	4.09	4.46	4.54	h.
.29	.30	.32	.34	.37	.42	.48	.53	.57	.62	i.
.07	.06	.06	.07	.08	.09	.10	.10	.11	.12	k.
		.01	.01	.01	.01	.02	.02	.02	.03	m.
87.93	99.15	106.82	113.85	118.56	124.73	135.73	149.31	161.22	172.68	6.
36.85	40.79	43.32	44.95	48.01	50.41	52.74	53.80	54.43	57.31	7.
889.74	1026.82	1123.49	1171.93	1217.01	1264.92	1360.44	1473.72	1579.42	1652.98	8.

TABLE IV-a-8

Tangible Assets of Financial Intermediaries

(million dollars)

Asset Item	1945	1946	1947	1948	1949	1950	1951	1952	1953	1954	1955	1956	1957	1958
A. Land, total	683	741	866	1,017	1,105	1,340	1,516	1,720	1,877	2,175	2,461	2,786	3,094	3,224
1. Residential	36	39	56	69	81	100	107	133	135	140	148	152	158	161
2. Nonresidential, other than agricultural, forest, and subsoil	647	702	810	948	1,024	1,240	1,409	1,587	1,742	2,035	2,313	2,634	2,936	3,063
B. Structures, total	1,112	1,207	1,443	1,697	1,858	2,260	2,541	2,911	3,154	3,615	4,061	4,561	5,033	5,237
1. Residential	144	154	225	274	323	399	427	533	541	560	592	609	630	643
2. Nonresidential	968	1,053	1,218	1,423	1,535	1,861	2,114	2,378	2,613	3,055	3,469	3,952	4,403	4,594
C. Producers' equipment, except vehicles	180	195	225	263	284	345	392	441	484	566	642	732	815	851
D. Land, structures, and equipment	1,975	2,143	2,534	2,977	3,247	3,945	4,449	5,072	5,515	6,356	7,164	8,079	8,942	9,312
E. Inventories, other than livestock, and stockpiles	4	5	-	-	-	15	22	24	26	18	18	21	25	25
F. Monetary metals	21	27	29	37	40	31	17	22	42	70	47	39	57	62

Holdings of structures, land, and equipment (line D) were estimated from total corporate holdings (Goldsmith, *National Wealth*, Table A-54). The share of financial intermediaries was assumed to be the same as their share in net depreciable assets of corporations (book value), from U.S. Internal Revenue Service, *Statistics of Income*, various issues.

Residential holdings (sum of lines A-1 and B-1) were estimated roughly from Life Insurance Company holdings, given in the *Life Insurance Fact Book*. They were allocated 80 per cent to structures (line B-1) and 20 per cent to land (line A-1).

Nonresidential land, structures, and equipment were allocated as follows: 10 per cent to producer durables (line C), 36 per cent to nonresidential land (line A-2), and 54 per cent to nonresidential structures (line B-2).

Inventories (line E) were estimated from *Statistics of Income* data, and monetary metals (line F) represent Federal Reserve System holdings.

TABLE IV-a-9

Tangible Assets of Other Financial Corporations (Excluding Real Estate Corporations)

(million dollars)

Asset Item	1945	1946	1947	1948	1949	1950	1951	1952	1953	1954	1955	1956	1957	1958
A. Land, total	308	396	425	493	798	673	564	578	644	643	723	730	831	822
1. Nonresidential, other than agricultural, forest, and subsoil	87	144	94	40	376	232	60	58	73	48	93	60	61	82
2. Subsoil	221	252	331	453	422	441	504	520	571	595	630	670	770	740
B. Structures, other than residential	204	343	231	98	889	546	147	147	182	112	210	147	140	189
C. Equipment, total[a]														
D. Land, structures, and equipment	512	739	656	591	1,687	1,219	711	725	826	755	933	877	971	1,011
E. Inventories, other than livestock, and stockpiles	8	12	16	11	6	4	0	1	3	2	2	3	5	5
F. Monetary metals[a]														

Holdings of structures, land, and equipment (Line D) estimated as in Table IV-a-8. The large increase in 1949 was in the *Statistics of Income* category, "Holding and Other Investment Companies" and probably represented a change in classification or method of reporting rather than a real growth in tangible assets.

Land and structures other than subsoil assets were allocated by assuming land to be approximately 40 per cent of structure values.

Inventories were estimated from *Statistics of Income* data.

[a]Assumed to be negligible.

TABLE IV-b-1

Currency and Demand Deposits, Assets

(billion dollars)

	1945	1946	1947	1948
1. Nonfarm households	49.89	54.04	53.73	51.67
2. Nonfarm unincorporated business	8.93	8.94	9.30	9.15
3. Agriculture	6.60	7.10	7.00	6.70
4. Nonfinancial corporations	19.68	20.82	23.02	23.22
5. Finance	77.30	77.80	85.69	90.43
a. Federal Reserve Banks and Treasury monetary funds	42.91	44.17	49.52	52.55
b. Govt. insurance and pension funds	.27	.28	.30	.38
c. Commercial banks	29.83	28.53	30.74	32.26
d. Mutual savings banks	.60	.66	.68	.65
e. Savings and loan associations	.40	.47	.47	.53
f. Investment companies	.15	.15	.14	.14
g. Credit unions	.06	.06	.07	.08
h. Life insurance	.78	.77	1.02	.91
i. Fire and casualty insurance	.67	.86	1.04	1.08
j. Noninsured pension plans	.08	.10	.13	.16
k. Other private insurance	.07	.07	.07	.07
l. Finance companies	.64	.63	.57	.74
m. Other finance	.84	1.05	.94	.88
6. State and local governments	5.21	6.08	6.80	7.29
7. Federal government	26.81	4.08	3.54	4.62
8. Total	194.42	178.86	189.08	193.08
9. Rest of world, assets	4.37	4.44	4.49	4.83
10. Monetary metals	22.04	22.40	23.72	25.20
11. Mail float	6.17	7.07	6.12	5.81
12. Commercial banks, cash items in process of collection	5.55	6.13	7.24	6.79
13. Currency and demand deposit assets, adjusted	188.47	174.10	183.21	185.31
14. Discrepancy	–.92	–1.30	–.83	–.86
15. Currency and demand deposits, liabilities	187.55	172.80	182.38	184.45

Lines

1	Domestic currency and demand deposits of individuals, partnerships and corporations (from holder records, Table IV-b-1g, column 1) minus lines 2, 3, 4, 5e through 5k of this table, and minus line II-1 of Tables III-5m-1, III-5m-3, III-5m-4, and III-5l.
2-5b	Line II-1 of Tables III-2 through III-5b.
5c	Table IV-b-1c, column 7.
5d-7	Line II-1 of Tables III-5d through III-7.
8	Sum of lines 1 through 7.
9	Rest-of-the-world demand deposit and currency assets, Table IV-b-1d, column 9.

1949	1950	1951	1952	1953	1954	1955	1956	1957	1958	
49.36	51.26	54.33	56.22	57.13	59.33	58.58	59.54	58.52	61.36	1.
9.52	9.74	10.78	10.43	10.38	10.91	11.20	11.55	12.36	13.46	2.
6.30	6.30	6.50	6.40	6.30	6.20	6.20	6.00	5.90	6.20	3.
24.29	25.60	27.42	28.22	28.14	30.50	31.48	31.62	31.62	33.34	4.
87.64	87.72	92.39	93.53	92.36	91.42	92.04	94.24	96.31	92.59	5.
52.90	49.52	49.68	50.83	49.15	48.63	48.68	49.16	50.89	46.76	a.
.36	.82	.88	.77	.73	1.05	.83	.97	1.21	1.34	b.
28.90	31.18	35.10	35.04	35.28	34.05	34.28	35.64	35.49	35.13	c.
.65	.63	.70	.70	.74	.76	.74	.76	.76	.76	d.
.61	.70	.80	.87	.92	1.18	1.37	1.44	1.49	1.76	e.
.14	.18	.21	.20	.24	.24	.24	.27	.30	.30	f.
.08	.10	.15	.15	.17	.22	.23	.26	.29	.33	g.
.91	1.00	1.10	1.15	1.22	1.24	1.26	1.28	1.29	1.37	h.
1.14	1.20	1.24	1.32	1.37	1.32	1.35	1.28	1.27	1.33	i.
.20	.27	.31	.28	.33	.33	.39	.38	.44	.47	j.
.09	.10	.11	.12	.16	.17	.17	.16	.15	.17	k.
.85	1.02	1.14	1.17	1.19	1.24	1.50	1.52	1.59	1.70	l.
.81	1.00	.97	.93	.86	.99	1.00	1.12	1.14	1.17	m.
7.52	7.98	8.41	8.88	9.48	9.81	10.20	10.35	10.56	10.78	6.
5.00	4.32	4.38	6.33	4.86	4.89	4.48	4.18	4.19	4.19	7.
189.63	192.92	204.21	210.01	208.65	213.06	214.18	217.48	219.46	221.92	8.
4.82	4.72	4.29	4.49	4.24	4.33	4.28	4.50	4.67	4.75	9.
25.43	23.75	23.75	24.27	23.64	23.33	23.34	23.71	24.62	22.63	10.
6.27	7.15	7.19	8.72	8.92	7.17	8.67	8.74	7.45	6.20	11.
7.31	9.63	10.02	10.15	10.15	10.03	13.28	13.88	13.70	14.58	12.
182.60	190.67	201.96	209.10	208.32	211.26	217.07	220.89	220.66	224.82	13.
−.86	.40	.08	−.04	.42	.21	1.13	1.31	.83	.96	14.
181.74	191.07	202.04	209.06	208.74	211.47	218.20	222.20	221.49	225.78	15.

Line

10 Value of monetary metals not included in liabilities (Table IV-b-1a, line 8), minus monetary metal items counted in liabilities (seigniorage on coins and revalued silver, minor coin outstanding, gold reserves against U.S. notes, and gold in general fund, see notes to line III-1, Tables III-5a-2 and III-7).

11 Table IV-b-1f, column 7, minus Table IV-b-1g, column 3. This is the discrepancy between holder and obligor records, which consists mainly of mail float.

12 Table IV-b-1h, column 6.

13 Sum of lines 8, 9, 11, and 12, minus line 10.

14 Line 15 minus line 13.

15 Table IV-c-1, line 8.

TABLE IV-b-1a

Monetary Metals, Assets

(billion dollars)

	1945	1946	1947	1948
1. Nonfarm households	.84	.89	.92	.95
2. Nonfarm unincorporated business	.13	.14	.15	.15
3. Agriculture	.16	.17	.18	.18
4. Nonfinancial corporations	.09	.10	.10	.12
5. Finance	22.68	23.09	25.31	26.81
a. Federal Reserve Banks and Treasury monetary funds	22.68	23.09	25.31	26.81
6. State and local governments				
7. Federal government				
8. Total	23.91	24.39	26.66	28.20

Lines

1-3 Goldsmith, *National Wealth*, Table A-44, columns 2, 3, and 4.
4 *Ibid.*, Table B-183, column 4.
5-5a Table III-5a, line II-1a.
8 Goldsmith, *National Wealth*, Table A-44, column 1. (Lines 1-5 may not add up to line 8 because of rounding.)

TABLE IV-b-1b

Currency and Demand Deposits, Other Than Monetary Metals, Assets

(billion dollars)

	1945	1946	1947	1948
1. Nonfarm households	49.05	53.15	52.81	50.72
2. Nonfarm unincorporated business	8.80	8.80	9.15	9.00
3. Agriculture	6.44	6.93	6.82	6.52
4. Nonfinancial corporations	19.59	20.72	22.92	23.10
5. Finance	54.62	54.71	60.38	63.62
a. Federal Reserve Banks and Treasury monetary funds	20.23	21.08	24.21	25.74
b. Govt. insurance and pension funds	.27	.28	.30	.38
c. Commercial banks	29.83	28.53	30.74	32.26
d. Mutual savings banks	.60	.66	.68	.65
e. Savings and loan associations	.40	.47	.47	.53
f. Investment companies	.15	.15	.14	.14
g. Credit unions	.06	.06	.07	.08
h. Life insurance	.78	.77	1.02	.91
i. Fire and casualty insurance	.67	.86	1.04	1.08
j. Noninsured pension plans	.08	.10	.13	.16
k. Other private insurance	.07	.07	.07	.07
l. Finance companies	.64	.63	.57	.74
m. Other finance	.84	1.05	.94	.88
6. State and local governments	5.21	6.08	6.80	7.29
7. Federal government	26.81	4.08	3.54	4.62
8. Total	170.51	154.47	162.42	164.88

Table IV-b-1, minus corresponding lines of Table IV-b-1a.

1949	1950	1951	1952	1953	1954	1955	1956	1957	1958
.95	1.01	1.06	1.14	1.20	1.21	1.27	1.33	1.50	1.62
.16	.17	.19	.18	.19	.20	.21	.22	.25	.27
.19	.18	.20	.20	.19	.19	.20	.21	.24	.25
.12	.13	.14	.15	.15	.15	.16	.17	.19	.21
27.03	25.30	25.25	25.72	24.56	24.29	24.24	24.55	25.28	23.06
27.03	25.30	25.25	25.72	24.56	24.29	24.24	24.55	25.28	23.06
28.45	26.79	26.83	27.39	26.30	26.04	26.08	26.48	27.46	25.41

1949	1950	1951	1952	1953	1954	1955	1956	1957	1958	
48.41	50.25	53.27	55.08	55.93	58.12	57.31	58.21	57.02	59.74	1.
9.36	9.57	10.59	10.25	10.19	10.71	10.99	11.33	12.11	13.19	2.
6.11	6.12	6.30	6.20	6.11	6.01	6.00	5.79	5.66	5.95	3.
24.17	25.47	27.28	28.07	27.99	30.35	31.32	31.45	31.43	33.13	4.
60.61	62.42	67.14	67.81	67.80	67.13	67.80	69.69	71.03	69.53	5.
										a.
25.87	24.22	24.43	25.11	24.59	24.34	24.44	24.61	25.61	23.70	
.36	.82	.88	.77	.73	1.05	.83	.97	1.21	1.34	b.
28.90	31.18	35.10	35.04	35.28	34.05	34.28	35.64	35.49	35.13	c.
.65	.63	.70	.70	.74	.76	.74	.76	.76	.76	d.
.61	.70	.80	.87	.92	1.18	1.37	1.44	1.49	1.76	e.
.14	.18	.21	.20	.24	.24	.24	.27	.30	.30	f.
.08	.10	.15	.15	.17	.22	.23	.26	.29	.33	g.
.91	1.00	1.10	1.15	1.22	1.24	1.26	1.28	1.29	1.37	h.
1.14	1.20	1.24	1.32	1.37	1.32	1.35	1.28	1.27	1.33	i.
.20	.27	.31	.28	.33	.33	.39	.38	.44	.47	j.
.09	.10	.11	.12	.16	.17	.17	.16	.15	.17	k.
.85	1.02	1.14	1.17	1.19	1.24	1.50	1.52	1.59	1.70	l.
.81	1.00	.97	.93	.86	.99	1.00	1.12	1.14	1.17	m.
7.52	7.98	8.41	8.88	9.48	9.81	10.20	10.35	10.56	10.78	6.
5.00	4.32	4.38	6.33	4.86	4.89	4.48	4.18	4.19	4.19	7.
161.18	166.13	177.38	182.62	182.35	187.02	188.10	191.00	192.00	196.51	8.

TABLE IV-b-1c

Calculation of Currency and Demand Deposit Holdings of Commercial Banks

(million dollars)

			Demand Deposits of				
	Currency (1)	Domestic Interbank Demand Deposits (2)	Mutual Savings Banks (3)	Banks in U.S. Possessions (4)	Commercial Banks (5)	Deposits with Federal Reserve (6)	Total (7)
1945	1,944	12,686	495	113	12,078	15,810	29,832
1946	2,138	11,010	543	86	10,381	16,013	28,532
1947	2,216	11,362	558	79	10,725	17,796	30,737
1948	1,978	10,476	520	81	9,875	20,404	32,257
1949	2,015	11,045	515	72	10,458	16,428	28,901
1950	2,174	12,102	489	66	11,547	17,458	31,179
1951	2,697	13,123	542	86	12,495	19,911	35,103
1952	2,753	13,109	543	83	12,483	19,809	35,045
1953	2,512	13,444	575	91	12,778	19,995	35,285
1954	2,469	13,511	582	79	12,850	18,734	34,053
1955	2,682	13,512	562	74	12,876	18,721	34,279
1956	3,261	14,338	587	82	13,669	18,706	35,636
1957	3,335	13,867	585	97	13,185	18,972	35,492
1958	3,249	14,142	575	109	13,458	18,427	35,134

Col. 1: *Federal Reserve Bulletin*, e.g., February 1959, p. 163.

Col. 2 1945-46: *Annual Report, Comptroller of the Currency*, e.g., 1946, p. 121.
1947-58: *Federal Reserve Bulletin*, e.g., March 1958, p. 319.

Col. 3 1945-46: Estimated by multiplying line 5d (Table IV-b-1) by the 1947 ratio of demand deposits (see note to 1947 below) to currency and demand deposits (line 5d).
1947: Line 5d (Table IV-b-1) less cash in vault—\$105 million (*Annual Report, Comptroller of the Currency*, 1947, p. 148), and less an estimate of cash items in process of collection (obtained by multiplying cash items in process of collection of insured mutuals by ratio of total cash of all mutuals to total cash of insured mutuals, from *Annual Report, Federal Deposit Insurance Corporation*).
1948-58: *Annual Report, FDIC*, e.g., 1956, Table 105, p. 106.

Col. 4: Federal Reserve Board worksheets.

Col. 5: Column 2, minus columns 3 and 4.

Col. 6: *Annual Report, FDIC*, e.g., 1949, Table 105, p. 142.

Col. 7: Sum of columns 1, 5, and 6.

TABLE IV-b-1d

Rest-of-the-World Demand Deposit and Currency Assets

(million dollars)

	U.S. Deposit Liability Per Balance of Payments (1)	Adjustment (2)	Balances At Brokers and Dealers (3)	Deposits in Branches of Foreign Banks (4)	Due to Foreign Branches of Domestic Banks (5)	U.S. Currency Held Abroad (6)	Currency and Deposits (7)	Time Deposits (8)	Currency and Demand Deposits (9)
1945	4,986	17	130	845	211	572	4,389	18	4,371
1946	4,894	17	136	780	195	663	4,463	19	4,444
1947	4,903	17	115	761	250	704	4,498	11	4,487
1948	5,298	17	87	846	262	746	4,866	35	4,831
1949	5,391	-	-	818	391	812	4,994	177	4,817
1950	5,821	-	-	916	552	772	5,125	404	4,721
1951	5,700	-	-	1,006	715	817	4,796	508	4,288
1952	6,150	-	-	1,130	661	848	5,207	715	4,492
1953	6,455	-	-	1,228	570	839	5,496	1,261	4,235
1954	7,316	-	-	1,504	509	838	6,141	1,811	4,330
1955	7,311	-	-	1,639	553	839	5,958	1,678	4,280
1956	7,949	-	-	2,084	614	847	6,098	1,593	4,505
1957	7,958	-	-	2,206	371	847	6,228	1,554	4,674
1958	9,040	-	-	2,401	293	890	7,236	2,486	4,750

Cols. 1 and 2: FRB worksheets.
Col. 3: *Treasury Bulletin*, Section IV, Table 4, e.g., March, 1956, p. 68. (Beginning with 1949, col. 1 is already adjusted for cols. 2 and 3.)
Col. 4: FRB worksheets.
Col. 5: Federal Reserve Board, *Member Bank Call Reports*.
Col. 6: *Survey of Current Business*, e.g., August, 1955, p. 12.
Col. 7: Cols. 1, 2, and 6 minus cols. 3, 4, and 5.
Col. 8: FRB worksheets.
Col. 9: Col. 7 minus col. 8.

TABLE IV-b-1e

Estimate of Commercial Bank Demand Deposit Liabilities, Other Than Interbank (million dollars)

	Total Deposits (1)	*Time Deposits* Total (2)	Cash Items In Process of Collection (3)	Domestic Interbank Demand Deposits (4)	*Demand Deposits Assets* Mutual Savings Banks (5)	Banks in U.S. Possessions (6)	Net Demand Deposits (7)
1945	150,227	30,343	5,551	12,686	495	110	102,252
1946	139,033	34,169	6,130	11,010	543	83	88,350
1947	144,103	35,600	7,244	11,362	558	76	90,531
1948	142,843	36,193	6,790	10,476	520	75	89,979
1949	145,174	36,649	7,308	11,045	515	72	90,759
1950	155,265	36,965	9,635	12,102	489	66	97,118
1951	164,840	38,687	10,015	13,123	542	86	103,643
1952	172,931	41,756	10,153	13,109	543	83	108,539
1953	176,702	45,164	10,152	13,444	575	91	108,608
1954	184,757	48,968	10,027	13,511	582	79	112,912
1955	192,254	50,300	13,283	13,512	562	74	115,795
1956	197,515	52,368	13,877	14,338	587	82	117,601
1957	201,326	57,825	13,700	13,867	585	97	116,616
1958	216,017	65,865	14,585	14,142	575	109	122,109

Col. 1: *Federal Reserve Bulletin*, e.g., March, 1958, p. 315.
Col. 2: Sum of interbank deposits and other time deposits.
Interbank deposits are from:
1945-46: *Annual Report, Comptroller of the Currency*, e.g., 1946, p. 121; (these figures include a small amount of mutual savings bank deposit liabilities).
1947-58: *Federal Reserve Bulletin*, e.g., March, 1958, p. 319.
Other time deposits: same source as col. 1.
Col. 3: Table IV-b-1g, col. 6.
Col. 4: Same sources as column 2.
Col. 5 1945-46: Roughly estimated by applying ratio of 1947 entry to Table III-5d, line II-1.
1947: Table III-5d, line II-1, less cash in vault (*Annual Report, Comptroller of the Currency*, 1947, p. 148), and rough estimate of cash items in the process of collection, approximated by blowing up cash items of insured mutuals (*Annual Report, FDIC*, 1948) by ratio of total cash of all mutuals to total cash of insured mutuals.
1948-58: *Annual Report, FDIC*, e.g., 1956, Table 105, p. 106.
Col. 6: FRB worksheets.
Col. 7: Col. 1 plus cols. 5 and 6, minus cols. 2, 3, and 4.

TABLE IV-b-1f

Estimate of Total Currency and Demand Deposit Liabilities

(million dollars)

	Net Demand Deposits (1)	Currency in Circulation (2)	Treasury Cash (3)	Federal Reserve Bank Liabilities (4)	Currency Held by Commercial Banks (5)	Federal Reserve Float (6)	Total (Obligor Record) (7)
1945	102,252	28,515	2,131	1,848	1,944	578	132,224
1946	88,350	28,952	2,116	919	2,138	540	117,659
1947	90,531	28,868	1,180	1,601	2,216	535	119,429
1948	89,979	28,224	1,169	2,072	1,978	541	118,925
1949	90,759	27,641	1,156	1,919	2,015	534	118,926
1950	97,118	27,741	1,137	1,638	2,174	1,368	124,092
1951	103,643	29,206	1,114	821	2,687	1,184	130,913
1952	108,539	30,433	1,114	988	2,753	967	137,354
1953	108,608	30,781	605	829	2,512	935	137,376
1954	112,912	30,509	640	1,102	2,469	808	141,886
1955	115,795	31,158	611	874	2,682	1,585	144,172
1956	117,601	31,790	619	836	3,261	1,665	145,920
1957	116,616	31,834	605	906	3,335	1,424	145,202
1958	122,109	32,193	527	699	3,249	1,296	150,983

Col. 1: Table IV-b-1e, col. 7.
Col. 2: *Federal Reserve Bulletin*, e.g., February 1957, p. 165.
Col. 3: *Ibid.*, e.g., February 1957, p. 166, less $156 million.
Col. 4: Sum of the following items:

Foreign deposits; U.S. Treasury general funds; officials' certified checks; Federal Reserve exchange drafts; and international organization deposits, 1945 and 1948-58 (*Annual Report of the Board of Governors of the Federal Reserve System*, various dates, e.g., 1956, page 72). International organization deposits, 1946-47, from FRB worksheets.

Col. 5: *Federal Reserve Bulletin*, e.g., March 1958, p. 319.
Col. 6: *Ibid.*, e.g., February 1957, p. 158.
Col. 7: Sum of cols. 1 through 4, minus cols. 5 and 6.

TABLE IV-b-1g

Estimation of Currency and Demand Deposit Assets (Holder Record)
(billion dollars)

	Domestic IPC (1)	Other (2)	Total (Holder Record) (3)
1945	88.62	37.43	126.05
1946	94.90	15.69	110.59
1947	97.35	15.96	113.31
1948	95.20	17.91	113.11
1949	94.18	18.48	112.66
1950	98.35	18.59	116.94
1951	104.90	18.82	123.72
1952	107.32	21.31	128.63
1953	108.27	20.19	128.46
1954	113.74	20.98	134.72
1955	114.84	20.66	135.50
1956	116.28	20.90	137.18
1957	116.20	21.55	137.75
1958	122.79	21.99	144.78

Col. 1: FRB worksheets (individuals, partnerships, and corporations).
Col. 2: Table IV-b-1, lines 5b, 5d, 6, 7, and 9; and Table III-5m-2, line II-1.
Col. 3: Sum of columns 1 and 2.

TABLE IV-b-1h

Commercial Banks: Estimate of Cash Items in Process of Collection

(million dollars)

	Demand Deposits					
	State and Local Government (1)	Certified and Officers' Checks (2)	IPC Deposits (3)	Total Unadjusted (4)	Total Adjusted (5)	Cash Items in Process of Collection (6)
1945	5,134	2,601	73,617	81,402	75,851	5,551
1946	6,059	2,383	81,002	89,444	83,314	6,130
1947	6,799	2,581	84,987	94,367	87,123	7,244
1948	7,299	2,135	82,882	92,316	85,526	6,790
1949	7,543	2,354	83,168	93,065	85,757	7,308
1950	8,012	2,918	90,986	101,916	92,282	9,634
1951	8,426	3,166	96,666	108,258	98,243	10,015
1952	8,910	2,956	99,793	111,659	101,506	10,153
1953	9,546	2,996	100,062	112,604	102,452	10,152
1954	9,902	3,199	103,466	116,567	106,540	10,027
1955	10,273	3,904	109,011	123,188	109,905	13,283
1956	10,449	3,785	111,048	125,282	111,405	13,877
1957	10,693	3,620	109,653	123,966	110,266	13,700
1958	10,928	4,043	115,132	130,103	115,518	14,585

Cols. 1 and 2: 1945-46: *Annual Report, Comptroller of the Currency*, e.g., 1946, p. 121.
1947-58: *Federal Reserve Bulletin*, e.g., March 1958, p. 319 (figures for 1945 and 1946 include a small amount of mutual savings bank liabilities).

Col. 3: 1945-46: Same source as column 2, adjusted to exclude demand deposit liabilities of mutual savings banks (Federal Reserve Board worksheets).
1947-58: Same source as col. 2.

Col. 4: Sum of cols. 1, 2, and 3.

Col. 5: 1945-46: Same source as col. 2.
1947-58: Same source as col. 2.

Col. 6: Col. 4 minus col. 5.

TABLE IV-b-2

Other Bank Deposits and Shares, Assets

(billion dollars)

	1945	1946	1947	1948
1. Nonfarm households	52.80	59.18	62.81	64.99
2. Nonfarm unincorporated business				
3. Agriculture	1.98	2.18	2.10	2.10
4. Nonfinancial corporations	.90	.90	.90	.90
5. Finance	.15	.29	.33	.35
c. Commercial banks	.07	.06	.06	.05
d. Mutual savings banks	.01	.16	.21	.23
g. Credit unions	.07	.07	.06	.07
i. Fire and casualty insurance	0	a	a	a
6. State and local governments	.53	.71	.87	1.14
7. Federal government	.12	.13	.12	.12
8. Total	56.48	63.39	67.13	69.60
9. Rest of world, assets	.02	.02	.01	.04
10. Total liabilities	56.50	63.41	67.14	69.64

Line

1 Line 8 minus lines 3 through 7.
3 Table III-3, line II-2.
4 Table III-4, line II-2.
5 Sum of lines 5c, 5d, 5g, and 5i.
5c Table III-5c, line II-2.

Line

5d Table III-5d, line II-2.
5g Table III-5g, line II-2.
5i Table III-5i, line II-2.
6 Table III-6, line II-2.
7 Table III-7, line II-2.

TABLE IV-b-3

Private Life Insurance Reserves, Assets

(billion dollars)

	1945	1946	1947	1948
1. Nonfarm households	41.07	44.58	47.87	51.39
2. Nonfarm unincorporated business				
3. Agriculture	3.40	3.59	3.80	4.03
4. Nonfinancial corporations				
5. Finance				
6. State and local governments				
7. Federal government				
8. Total	44.47	48.17	51.67	55.42
9. Rest of world, assets	.87	.94	1.01	1.09
10. Total liabilities	45.34	49.11	52.68	56.51

Line

1 Line 8 minus line 3.
3 Table III-3, line II-3.
8 98 per cent of line 5h, Table IV-c-3, plus line 5k, Table IV-c-3.
9 2 per cent of line 5h, Table IV-c-3, assumed to be life insurance reserves of foreigners.
10 Line 8 plus line 9.

1949	1950	1951	1952	1953	1954	1955	1956	1957	1958	
67.47	69.56	73.76	81.11	88.99	97.82	106.24	115.38	126.80	140.56	1.
										2.
2.10	2.10	2.17	2.30	2.43	2.53	2.58	2.63	2.90	3.07	3.
.90	.90	.90	.90	.90	1.10	1.00	1.00	1.00	1.60	4.
.36	.31	.39	.52	.60	.70	.72	.77	.77	1.08	5.
.04	.04	.04	.04	.04	.04	.04	.04	.04	.08	c.
.22	.17	.19	.22	.24	.27	.22	.16	.12	.16	d.
.10	.10	.15	.24	.30	.37	.44	.55	.59	.82	g.
a	a	.01	.02	.02	.02	.02	.02	.02	.02	i.
1.29	1.39	1.54	1.63	1.96	2.42	2.36	2.40	2.78	3.58	6.
.18	.19	.28	.35	.34	.36	.36	.33	.30	.33	7.
72.30	74.45	79.04	86.81	95.22	104.93	113.26	122.51	134.55	150.22	8.
.18	.40	.51	.71	1.26	1.81	1.68	1.59	1.56	2.62	9.
72.48	74.85	79.55	87.52	96.48	106.74	114.94	124.10	136.11	152.84	10.

Line

8 Line 10 minus line 9.

9 The sum of time deposits held by foreign banks (*Annual Report, Comptroller of the Currency*, e.g., 1956, Table 40, p. 195) and other time deposits held by "Rest of World" (27 per cent of time deposits held by foreign banks).

10 Table IV-c-2, line 8.

[a]Under $5 million.

1949	1950	1951	1952	1953	1954	1955	1956	1957	1958	
55.21	59.23	63.22	68.00	72.80	78.41	83.96	89.05	93.80	99.70	1.
										2.
4.27	4.51	4.75	5.03	5.30	5.62	5.92	6.18	6.42	6.71	3.
										4.
										5.
										6.
										7.
59.48	63.74	67.97	73.03	78.10	84.03	89.88	95.23	100.22	106.41	8.
1.17	1.25	1.34	1.44	1.54	1.65	1.77	1.87	1.98	2.10	9.
60.65	64.99	69.31	74.47	79.64	85.68	91.65	97.10	102.20	108.51	10.

TABLE IV-b-4

Private Pension and Retirement Funds, Assets

(billion dollars)

	1945	1946	1947	1948
1. Nonfarm households	2.68	3.25	3.90	4.55
2. Nonfarm unincorporated business				
3. Agriculture				
4. Nonfinancial corporations				
5. Finance				
6. State and local governments				
7. Federal government				
8. Total	2.68	3.25	3.90	4.55

Table III-5j, line III-4.

TABLE IV-b-5

Government Pension and Insurance Funds, Assets

(billion dollars)

	1945	1946	1947	1948
1. Nonfarm households	25.35	28.82	32.61	36.10
2. Nonfarm unincorporated business				
3. Agriculture	.48	.68	.77	.76
4. Nonfinancial corporations				
5. Finance				
6. State and local governments				
7. Federal government				
8. Total	25.83	29.50	33.38	36.86

Line

1 Line 8 minus line 3.
2 Table III-3, line II-5.
8 Table III-5b, line III-5.

1949	1950	1951	1952	1953	1954	1955	1956	1957	1958
5.26	6.23	7.80	9.52	11.42	14.34	17.35	20.02	22.28	27.80
5.26	6.23	7.80	9.52	11.42	14.34	17.35	20.02	22.28	27.80

1949	1950	1951	1952	1953	1954	1955	1956	1957	1958
38.59	40.15	44.26	48.62	52.04	54.75	57.99	61.57	64.43	65.67
.81	.56	.52	.51	.47	.45	.45	.45	.44	.43
39.40	40.71	44.78	49.13	52.51	55.20	58.44	62.02	64.87	66.10

TABLE IV-b-6

Consumer Credit, Assets

(billion dollars)

	1945	1946	1947	1948
1. Nonfarm households				
2. Nonfarm unincorporated business	1.53	1.86	2.19	2.56
3. Agriculture				
4. Nonfinancial corporations	1.66	2.23	2.87	3.41
5. Finance	2.52	4.38	6.70	8.68
c. Commercial banks	1.47	2.66	3.97	4.98
d. Mutual savings banks	.02	.02	.04	.04
e. Savings and loan associations	.02	.06	.09	.12
g. Credit unions	.10	.15	.24	.33
l. Finance companies	.91	1.49	2.36	3.21
6. State and local governments				
7. Federal government				
8. Total	5.71	8.47	11.76	14.65

Line

2 FRB worksheets.

4 Total consumer credit held by nonfinancial firms (Sum of instalment credit held by retail outlets, charge accounts, and service credit from *Federal Reserve Bulletin*, e.g., July 1961, pp. 826-827; and consumer credit held by pawnbrokers, from FRB worksheets), minus line 2, with minor adjustments made to correspond with FRB figures.

5 Sum of lines 5c through 5l.

TABLE IV-b-6a

Consumer Credit, Assets, 1900-45, Selected Years

(million dollars)

	1900	1912	1922
1. Nonfarm households			
2. Nonfarm unincorporated business	202	491	694
3. Agriculture			
4. Nonfinancial corporations	580	1,962	4,040
5. Finance	239	456	916
6. State and local governments			
7. Federal government			
8. Total	1,021	2,909	5,650

Line

2 Table III-2a, line II-6.

4 Table III-4b, line II-6.

5 Table III-5o, line II-6.

8 Sum of lines 2, 4, and 5.

[a]The 1945 figures in this table have been superseded by those in Table IV-b-6, but they are included here for comparability with earlier years.

1949	1950	1951	1952	1953	1954	1955	1956	1957	1958	
										1.
2.81	3.30	3.60	4.00	4.18	4.27	4.43	4.69	4.79	4.70	2.
										3.
3.85	4.63	5.14	5.90	6.14	6.41	7.07	7.48	7.69	8.21	4.
10.93	13.84	14.37	18.00	21.50	22.24	27.87	30.89	33.42	33.19	5.
6.01	7.67	7.84	9.73	11.33	11.36	13.72	15.17	16.38	16.56	c.
.04	.06	.06	.07	.08	.08	.10	.13	.13	.14	d.
.14	.20	.23	.30	.35	.40	.48	.56	.64	.70	e.
.44	.59	.64	.84	1.12	1.34	1.68	2.01	2.43	2.66	g.
4.30	5.32	5.60	7.06	8.62	9.06	11.89	13.02	13.84	13.13	l.
										6.
										7.
17.59	21.77	23.11	27.90	31.82	32.92	39.37	43.06	45.90	46.10	8.

Line

5c Table III-5c, line II-6.
5d Table III-5d, line II-6.
5e Table III-5e, line II-6.
5g Table III-5g, line II-6.
5l Table III-5l, line II-6.
8 Sum of lines 2, 4, and 5 of this table.

1929	1933	1939	1945[a]
1,280	740	1,168	1,046
3,979	1,938	2,966	2,412
3,305	1,621	3,688	2,340
8,564	4,299	7,822	5,798

TABLE IV-b-7

Trade Credit, Assets

(billion dollars)

	1945	1946	1947	1948
1. Nonfarm households				
2. Nonfarm unincorporated business	4.03	4.99	5.36	5.76
3. Agriculture				
4. Nonfinancial corporations	22.73	25.92	31.78	34.12
5. Finance	.44	.77	.90	1.07
i. Fire and casualty insurance	.32	.49	.59	.67
l. Finance companies	.08	.25	.26	.28
m. Other finance	.04	.03	.05	.12
6. State and local governments				
7. Federal government	.90	.10	0	0
8. Total	28.10	31.78	38.04	40.95
9. Net trade credit	.46	2.09	4.49	5.66
10. Trade debt	27.64	29.69	33.55	35.29

Line

2 FRB worksheets.
4 Table III-4, line II-7.
5 Sum of lines 5i, 5l, and 5m.
5i Table III-5i, line II-7.
5l Table III-5l, line II-7.

TABLE IV-b-7a

Trade Credit, Assets, 1900-45, Selected Years

(million dollars)

	1900	1912
1. Nonfarm households		
2. Nonfarm unincorporated business	1,828	1,889
3. Agriculture		
4. Nonfinancial corporations	3,900	6,208
5. Finance		
6. State and local governments		
7. Federal government		
8. Total	5,728	8,097

Line

2 Table III-2a, line II-7.
4 Table III-4b, line II-7.
5 Table III-5o, line II-7.
7 Table III-7f, line II-7.
8 Sum of lines 2, 4, 5, and 7.

1949	1950	1951	1952	1953	1954	1955	1956	1957	1958	
										1.
5.82	7.04	7.26	8.37	8.95	9.15	9.68	10.57	10.85	11.64	2.
										3.
33.18	44.62	48.03	51.56	50.75	55.06	65.92	72.98	75.70	83.37	4.
1.17	1.47	1.66	1.81	1.97	2.12	2.51	2.93	3.27	3.64	5.
.74	.76	.88	.95	1.00	1.06	1.15	1.29	1.44	1.58	i.
.32	.61	.65	.72	.78	.88	1.13	1.31	1.46	1.70	l.
.11	.10	.13	.14	.19	.18	.23	.33	.37	.36	m.
										6.
0	.38	1.30	2.25	2.21	2.44	2.27	2.35	2.30	1.70	7.
40.17	53.51	58.25	63.99	63.88	68.77	80.38	88.83	92.12	100.35	8.
5.64	8.72	9.88	11.14	9.99	10.13	10.70	11.97	12.10	13.40	9.
34.53	44.79	48.37	52.85	53.89	58.64	69.68	76.86	80.02	86.95	10.

Line

5m Table III-5m, line II-7.
7 Table III-7, line II-7.
8 Sum of lines 2, 4, 5 and 7.
9 Line 8 minus line 10.
10 Table IV-c-7, line 8.

1922	1929	1933	1939	1945[a]	
					1.
2,878	2,946	1,818	2,602	4,030	2.
					3.
12,027	21,861	15,915	11,067	19,464	4.
	909	464	1,010	505	5.
					6.
				900	7.
14,905	25,716	18,197	14,679	24,899	8.

[a]The 1945 figures in this table have been superseded by those in Table IV-b-7, but they are included here for comparability with earlier years.

TABLE IV-b-8

Loans on Securities, Assets

(billion dollars)

	1945	1946	1947	1948
1. Nonfarm households				
2. Nonfarm unincorporated business				
3. Agriculture				
4. Nonfinancial corporations				
5. Finance	8.25	3.85	2.79	3.04
c. Commercial banks	6.82	3.16	2.05	2.31
d. Mutual savings banks	a	a	a	a
m. Other finance	1.43	.69	.74	.73
6. State and local governments				
7. Federal government				
8. Total	8.25	3.85	2.79	3.04
9. Rest of world, net assets	.09	.10	.09	.06
10. Discrepancy	.14	.10	.07	.08
11. Total liabilities	8.48	4.05	2.95	3.18

Line

5 Sum of lines 5c, 5d, and 5m.
5c Table III-5c, line II-8.
5d Table III-5d, line II-8.
5m Table III-5m, line II-8.
8 Same as line 5.

TABLE IV-b-9

Bank Loans, N.E.C., Assets

(billion dollars)

	1945	1946	1947	1948
1. Nonfarm households				
2. Nonfarm unincorporated business				
3. Agriculture				
4. Nonfinancial corporations				
5. Finance	13.29	18.26	22.85	25.02
a. Federal Reserve Banks and Treasury monetary funds	.25	.16	.09	.22
c. Commercial banks	13.04	18.10	22.76	24.80
6. State and local governments				
7. Federal government				
8. Total	13.29	18.26	22.85	25.02
9. Rest of world, liabilities	.32	.52	.59	.63
10. Total liabilities	12.97	17.74	22.26	24.39

Line

5 Sum of lines 5a and 5c.
5a Table III-5a, line II-9.
5c Table III-5c, line II-9.
8 Same as line 5.
9 Rest-of-world liabilities (bank loans, n.e.c.) from FRB worksheets.
10 Line 8 minus line 9.

1949	1950	1951	1952	1953	1954	1955	1956	1957	1958	
										1.
										2.
										3.
										4.
3.79	4.59	4.25	4.95	5.75	7.61	8.69	8.01	7.65	9.23	5.
2.64	2.86	2.56	3.16	3.56	4.45	5.04	4.28	4.22	4.66	c.
a	a	a	a	a	.01	.02	.02	.01	.01	d.
1.15	1.73	1.69	1.79	2.19	3.15	3.63	3.71	3.42	4.56	m.
										6.
										7.
3.79	4.59	4.25	4.95	5.75	7.61	8.69	8.01	7.65	9.23	8.
.06	.08	.07	.07	.06	.06	.04	.05	.06	.07	9.
.10	.13	.14	.13	.16	.25	.26	.26	.25	.32	10.
3.95	4.80	4.46	5.15	5.97	7.92	8.99	8.32	7.96	9.62	11.

Line

9 Foreign customers net credit balances with brokers and dealers (125 per cent of credit balances minus debit balances, see note to line 1 of Table IV-c-8).

10 Line 11 minus lines 8 and 9.

11 Table IV-c-8, line 8.

[a]Under $5 million.

1949	1950	1951	1952	1953	1954	1955	1956	1957	1958	
										1.
										2.
										3.
										4.
23.40	28.92	33.60	36.62	37.00	37.60	44.44	50.02	52.08	53.80	5.
.08	.07	.02	.16	.03	.14	.14	.12	.12	.11	a.
23.32	28.85	33.58	36.46	36.97	37.46	44.30	49.90	51.96	53.69	c.
										6.
										7.
23.40	28.92	33.60	36.62	37.00	37.60	44.44	50.02	52.08	53.80	8.
.66	.72	.78	.78	.68	1.03	1.40	1.75	2.10	2.63	9.
22.74	28.20	32.82	35.84	36.32	36.57	43.04	48.27	49.98	51.17	10.

TABLE IV-b-10

Other Loans, Assets

(billion dollars)

	1945	1946	1947	1948
1. Nonfarm households	1.00	1.16	1.20	1.07
2. Nonfarm unincorporated business				
3. Agriculture				
4. Nonfinancial corporations				
5. Finance	2.86	3.23	3.56	4.17
b. Govt. insurance and pension funds	.12	.11	.11	.13
d. Mutual savings banks	.05	.07	.05	.07
g. Credit unions	a	a	a	a
h. Life insurance	1.96	1.89	1.94	2.06
k. Other private insurance	.08	.08	.08	.08
l. Finance companies	.32	.66	.87	1.22
m. Other finance	.33	.42	.51	.61
6. State and local governments				
7. Federal government	4.06	7.23	11.36	13.03
8. Total	7.92	11.62	16.12	18.27
9. Rest of world, liabilities	1.75	4.93	8.56	9.68
10. Total liabilities	6.17	6.69	7.56	8.59

Line

1 Loans in process of savings and loan associations (see note to line III-10 of Table III-5e) and line III-10, Table III-5m-1.
5 Sum of lines 5b through 5m.
5b Table III-5b, line II-10.
5d Table III-5d, line II-10.
5g Table III-5g, line II-10.
5h Table III-5h, line II-10.
5k Table III-5k, line II-10.
5l Table III-5l, line II-10.
5m Table III-5m, line II-10.

1949	1950	1951	1952	1953	1954	1955	1956	1957	1958	
1.23	1.78	1.74	1.63	1.68	2.42	2.30	2.26	2.32	3.10	1.
										2.
										3.
										4.
4.29	4.91	5.56	5.89	6.12	6.22	7.50	7.76	9.07	9.42	5.
.14	.16	.18	.19	.21	.23	.26	.29	.32	.36	b.
.07	.07	.07	.07	.08	.09	.09	.10	.13	.17	d.
a	.01	.02	.03	.03	.03	.05	.04	.06	.06	g.
2.24	2.41	2.59	2.71	2.91	3.13	3.29	3.52	3.87	4.19	h.
.09	.10	.11	.11	.12	.13	.14	.16	.16	.17	k.
1.13	1.44	1.71	1.84	1.92	1.67	2.64	2.55	3.16	2.83	l.
.62	.72	.88	.94	.85	.94	1.03	1.10	1.37	1.64	m.
										6.
13.70	14.40	15.03	15.78	16.39	16.32	17.35	17.32	17.95	19.05	7.
19.22	21.09	22.33	23.30	24.19	24.96	27.15	27.34	29.34	31.57	8.
10.16	10.30	10.54	10.94	11.16	11.00	11.01	11.10	11.52	12.18	9.
9.06	10.78	11.79	12.36	13.03	13.96	16.14	16.24	17.82	19.39	10.

Line

7 Table III-7, line II-10.

8 Sum of lines 1, 5, and 7.

9 Sum of federal government loans to "Rest of World" (see notes to Table III-7, line II-10), other loans of banks in possessions (Table III-5m-2, line II-10), and life insurance company policy loans to foreigners—2 per cent of line 5h.

10 Line 8 minus line 9.

[a] Under $5 million.

TABLE IV-b-11

Nonfarm Mortgages, Assets

(million dollars)

	1945	1946	1947	1948
1. Nonfarm households	9,643	11,000	12,211	13,211
2. Nonfarm unincorporated business				
3. Agriculture				
4. Nonfinancial corporations				
5. Finance	20,155	25,115	30,941	36,905
a. Federal Reserve Banks and Treasury monetary funds				
b. Govt. insurance and pension funds	21	26	31	36
c. Commercial banks	4,229	6,500	8,576	9,937
d. Mutual savings banks	4,184	4,415	4,828	5,773
e. Savings and loan associations	5,376	7,141	8,856	10,305
f. Investment companies	103	145	222	277
g. Credit unions	26	36	44	61
h. Life insurance	5,860	6,360	7,780	9,843
i. Fire and casualty insurance	62	65	72	84
j. Noninsured pension plans	24	30	34	38
k. Other private insurance	177	183	202	228
l. Finance companies	71	181	249	237
m. Other finance	22	33	47	86
6. State and local governments	61	66	63	69
7. Federal government	917	681	638	725
8. Total	30,776	36,862	43,853	50,910

Line

1 Line 8 minus the sum of lines 5, 6, and 7.

5 Sum of lines 5b to 5m.

5b Table III-5b, line II-11.

Nonfarm mortgage loans held by commercial banks (Saul B. Klaman, *The Volume of Mortgage Debt in the Postwar Decade*, New York, NBER, 1958, Table 18, column 2, extended by using the sources cited by Klaman), less nonfarm mortgages held by banks in possessions, from Table III-5m-2, line II-11.

5d Klaman, *Mortgage Debt*, Table 19, column 2, extended by using *Federal Reserve Bulletin*, August 1961, page 961.

5e Klaman, *Mortgage Debt*, Table 16, column 1, extended by using *Federal Reserve Bulletin*, August 1961, page 962.

1949	1950	1951	1952	1953	1954	1955	1956	1957	1958	
13,798	14,165	14,659	15,219	15,966	16,964	17,964	19,457	20,880	22,720	1.
										2.
										3.
										4.
41,927	50,868	58,565	65,995	74,159	84,915	98,915	110,752	119,052	131,220	5.
										a.
41	103	164	199	229	302	343	434	451	401	b.
10,636	12,576	13,581	14,659	15,615	17,263	19,517	21,179	21,750	23,791	c.
6,668	8,218	9,869	11,327	12,890	14,951	17,399	19,687	21,112	23,210	d.
11,616	13,657	15,564	18,396	21,962	26,108	31,408	35,729	40,007	45,627	e.
300	339	331	345	357	353	343	331	312	279	f.
72	80	95	122	150	176	210	271	271	350	g.
11,768	14,775	17,787	19,546	21,436	23,928	27,172	30,508	32,652	34,395	h.
94	106	118	124	138	144	153	161	158	157	i.
44	51	96	129	166	199	235	344	515	652	j.
262	308	359	400	439	494	573	636	661	697	k.
326	536	454	598	624	845	1,372	1,268	943	1,400	l.
100	119	147	150	153	152	190	204	220	261	m.
163	213	286	364	501	606	725	835	1,197	1,614	6.
1,209	1,495	2,112	2,576	2,927	2,942	3,267	3,724	4,993	5,105	7.
57,097	66,741	75,622	84,154	93,553	105,427	120,871	134,768	146,122	160,659	8.

Line

5f-5l Line II-11 of Tables III-5f-3 through III-5l.

5m Table III-5m-2, line II-11. (Banks in possessions are the only holders in this group.)

6 Total state and local government holdings (Federal Reserve Board worksheets) minus line 5b.

7 Klaman, *Mortgage Debt*, Table 21, column 2, corrected and extended by using data from sources cited by Klaman, *Federal Reserve Bulletin* tables on "Federal Business-Type Activities" and "Real Estate Credit," and correspondence with the Federal Housing Administration.

8 Klaman, *Mortgage Debt*, Table 3, column 1, corrected and extended by using sources cited by Klaman.

TABLE IV-b-11a

Nonfarm Residential Mortgages, Assets

(million dollars)

	1945	1946	1947	1948
1. Nonfarm households	6,226	7,114	7,782	8,375
2. Nonfarm unincorporated business				
3. Agriculture				
4. Nonfinancial corporations				
5. Finance	16,085	20,246	25,279	30,451
a. Federal Reserve Banks and Treasury monetary funds				
b. Govt. insurance and pension funds	21	26	31	36
c. Commerical banks	3,377	5,120	6,896	8,003
d. Mutual savings banks	3,387	3,588	3,937	4,758
e. Savings and loan associations	5,268	6,998	8,679	10,099
f. Investment companies	90	128	197	242
g. Credit unions	26	36	44	61
h. Life insurance	3,706	4,015	5,070	6,789
i. Fire and casualty insurance	24	25	26	32
j. Noninsured pension plans	24	30	34	38
k. Other private insurance	73	73	79	93
l. Finance companies	71	181	249	237
m. Other finance	18	26	37	63
6. State and local governments	61	66	63	69
7. Federal government	902	672	631	718
8. Total	23,274	28,098	33,755	39,613

Line	
1	Line 8 minus lines 5, 6, and 7.
5	Sum of lines 5b through 5m.
5b	Table III-5b, line II-11a.
5c	Holdings of all commercial banks (Klaman, *Mortgage Debt*, Table 18, column 3, extended by using *Federal Reserve Bulletin*, August 1961, page 961) minus holdings of banks in possessions, line II-11-a, Table III-5m-2.
5d	*Ibid.*, Table 19, column 3, extended by using *Federal Reserve Bulletin*, August 1961, page 961.
5e	*Ibid.*, Table 16, column 2, extended by using *Federal Reserve Bulletin*, August 1961, page 962.
5f	Line 5f, Table IV-b-11 multiplied by the ratio of column 3 to column 1 from Goldsmith, *A Study of Saving*, Vol. I, page 741, Table M-19 (ratio for 1950-58 assumed the same as for 1949). Face amount investment companies are the only investment companies listed as holding mortgages.
5g	Federal Reserve Board worksheets.
5h	Federal Home Loan Bank Board, *Nonfarm Mortgage Investments of Life Insurance Companies*, 1960, p. 5.

1949	1950	1951	1952	1953	1954	1955	1956	1957	1958	
8,603	8,694	8,914	9,197	9,600	10,028	10,406	11,165	11,975	12,787	1.
										2.
										3.
										4.
34,914	43,213	50,077	56,736	64,084	73,620	86,221	96,396	103,123	113,523	5.
										a.
41	103	164	199	229	302	343	434	451	401	b.
8,598	10,331	11,145	12,065	12,802	14,029	15,741	16,847	16,990	18,406	c.
5,569	7,054	8,595	9,883	11,334	13,211	15,568	17,703	19,010	20,936	d.
11,384	13,384	15,253	18,028	21,523	25,586	30,780	35,014	39,207	44,715	e.
261	295	288	300	311	308	299	288	272	243	f.
72	80	95	122	150	176	210	271	271	350	g.
8,389	11,093	13,641	15,045	16,558	18,557	21,213	23,745	24,992	25,921	h.
38	44	50	52	56	56	57	56	50	46	i.
44	51	96	129	166	199	235	344	515	652	j.
114	142	171	192	208	228	256	269	265	268	k.
326	536	454	598	624	845	1,372	1,268	943	1,400	l.
78	100	125	123	123	123	147	157	157	185	m.
163	213	286	364	501	606	725	835	1,197	1,614	6.
1,204	1,491	2,108	2,573	2,924	2,942	3,267	3,724	4,992	5,104	7.
44,884	53,611	61,385	68,870	77,109	87,196	100,619	112,120	121,287	133,028	8.

Line

5i Fire and casualty co. holdings, assumed to consist solely of multifamily and nonresidential mortgages, are divided between these two categories by the ratio for life insurance companies (see Tables IV-b-11a-l and IV-b-11b, line 5h).

5j Table III-5j, line II-11.

5k Composed of holdings of fraternal orders and savings bank life insurance departments. Fraternal orders' residential holdings are estimated in the same way as those for fire and casualty companies (see above). For savings bank life insurance departments, the percentage distribution for mutual savings banks was used.

5l Table III-5l, line II-11.

5m Table III-5m-2, line II-11a.

6 Total state and local government holdings (Federal Reserve Board worksheets) minus line 5b.

7 Klaman, *Mortgage Debt*, Table 21, column 3, corrected and extended by sources and methods cited by Klaman.

8 *Ibid.*, Table 4, column 1, corrected and extended by sources and methods cited by Klaman.

TABLE IV-b-11a-1

Multifamily Nonfarm Residential Mortgages, Assets

(million dollars)

	1945	1946	1947	1948
1. Nonfarm households	1,000	1,134	1,299	1,414
2. Nonfarm unincorporated business				
3. Agriculture				
4. Nonfinancial corporations				
5. Finance	3,645	3,891	4,219	4,878
a. Federal Reserve Banks and Treasury monetary funds				
b. Govt. insurance and pension funds	10	13	16	18
c. Commercial banks	517	567	627	665
d. Mutual savings banks	1,493	1,555	1,654	1,923
e. Savings and loan associations	112	158	204	258
f. Investment companies	7	9	13	17
g. Credit unions				
h. Life insurance	1,400	1,470	1,573	1,846
i. Fire and casualty insurance	24	25	26	32
j. Noninsured pension plans				
k. Other private insurance	70	70	74	86
l. Finance companies	9	21	29	28
m. Other finance	3	3	3	5
6. State and local governments	30	33	32	34
7. Federal government	8	6	6	8
8. Total	4,683	5,064	5,556	6,334

Table IV-b-11a minus Table IV-b-11a-2.

1949	1950	1951	1952	1953	1954	1955	1956	1957	1958	
1,445	1,408	1,384	1,378	1,373	1,407	1,476	1,568	1,659	1,812	1.
										2.
										3.
										4.
5,710	6,901	8,099	8,752	9,231	9,612	10,228	10,756	11,037	12,209	5.
										a.
20	52	82	100	114	151	172	217	226	200	b.
714	941	984	929	892	845	806	752	755	953	c.
2,205	2,742	3,264	3,689	3,961	4,209	4,468	4,713	4,900	5,296	d.
267	268	409	383	524	582	779	1,010	1,211	1,824	e.
20	23	22	23	24	24	23	22	21	19	f.
										g.
2,296	2,615	3,031	3,288	3,363	3,404	3,552	3,615	3,551	3,547	h.
38	44	50	52	56	56	57	56	50	46	i.
										j.
105	125	148	164	173	184	209	212	202	200	k.
39	82	98	115	116	150	155	152	114	114	l.
6	9	11	9	8	7	7	7	7	10	m.
82	106	143	182	250	303	362	418	598	807	6.
28	26	48	58	161	197	303	341	376	514	7.
7,265	8,441	9,674	10,370	11,015	11,519	12,369	13,083	13,670	15,342	8.

TABLE IV-b-11a-2

One- to Four-Family Nonfarm Residential Mortgages, Assets

(million dollars)

	1945	1946	1947	1948
1. Nonfarm households	5,226	5,980	6,483	6,961
2. Nonfarm unincorporated business				
3. Agriculture				
4. Nonfinancial corporations				
5. Finance	12,440	16,355	21,060	25,573
a. Federal Reserve Banks and Treasury monetary funds				
b. Govt. insurance and pension funds	11	13	15	18
c. Commercial banks	2,860	4,553	6,269	7,338
d. Mutual savings banks	1,894	2,033	2,283	2,835
e. Savings and loan associations	5,156	6,840	8,475	9,841
f. Investment companies	83	119	184	225
g. Credit unions	26	36	44	61
h. Life insurance	2,306	2,545	3,497	4,943
i. Fire and casualty insurance				
j. Noninsured pension plans	24	30	34	38
k. Other private insurance	3	3	5	7
l. Finance companies	62	160	220	209
m. Other finance	15	23	34	58
6. State and local governments	31	33	31	35
7. Federal government	894	666	625	710
8. Total	18,591	23,034	28,199	33,279

Line

1	Line 8 minus lines 5, 6, and 7.
5	Sum of lines 5b through 5m.
5b	Half of line 5b, Table IV-b-11a.
5c, 5d, 5e, 5h	Federal Home Loan Bank Board, *Estimated Home Mortgage Debt and Financing Activity*, 1961, p. 2. (Residential mortgage holdings of commercial banks, excluding banks in possession, divided between 1-4 and multifamily by same percentage distribution as that given in Klaman for all commercial banks, in *Mortgage Debt*, Table 18, columns 3 and 4).
5f	See note to line 5f, Table IV-b-11a.
5g	FRB worksheets.

1949	1950	1951	1952	1953	1954	1955	1956	1957	1958	
7,158	7,286	7,530	7,819	8,227	8,621	8,930	9,597	10,316	10,976	1.
										2.
										3.
										4.
29,204	36,312	41,978	47,984	54,853	64,008	75,993	85,640	92,086	101,314	5.
										a.
21	51	82	99	115	151	171	217	225	201	b.
7,884	9,390	10,161	11,136	11,910	13,184	14,935	16,095	16,235	17,453	c.
3,364	4,312	5,331	6,194	7,373	9,002	11,100	12,990	14,110	15,640	d.
11,117	13,116	14,844	17,645	20,999	25,004	30,001	34,004	37,996	42,890	e.
241	272	266	277	287	284	276	266	251	224	f.
72	80	95	122	150	176	210	271	271	350	g.
6,093	8,478	10,610	11,757	13,195	15,153	17,661	20,130	21,441	22,374	h.
										i.
44	51	96	129	166	199	235	344	515	652	j.
9	17	23	28	35	44	47	57	63	68	k.
288	454	356	483	508	695	1,217	1,116	829	1,288	l.
72	91	114	113	115	116	140	150	150	176	m.
81	107	143	182	251	303	363	417	599	807	6.
1,176	1,465	2,060	2,515	2,763	2,745	2,964	3,383	4,616	4,590	7.
37,619	45,170	51,711	58,500	66,094	75,677	88,250	99,037	107,617	117,686	8.

Line

5j Table III-5j, line II-11.

5k Savings bank life insurance total mortgage holdings are assumed to be distributed in the same proportions as mutual savings banks holdings.

5l FRB worksheets.

5m Klaman, *Mortgage Debt*, Table 5, column 5, minus line 5c of this table.

6 Half of line 6, Table IV-b-11a. The Federal Reserve Board distributes the total mortgage holdings of state and local government, including pension and retirement funds, in this way.

7 Klaman, *Mortgage Debt*, Table 21, column 8, extended by methods and sources cited by Klaman.

8 Federal Home Loan Bank Board, *Estimated Home Mortgage Debt*, p. 2.

TABLE IV-b-11a-3

Multifamily Nonfarm Residential Mortgages, Conventional, Assets
(million dollars)

	1945	1946	1947	1948	1949
1. Nonfarm households and others[a]	1,103	1,274	1,242	1,255	1,080
2. Nonfarm unincorporated business					
3. Agriculture					
4. Nonfinancial corporations					
5. Finance[b]	3,335	3,570	3,759	3,929	4,041
c. Commercial banks	487	541	514	412	287
d. Mutual savings banks	1,471	1,528	1,599	1,769	1,892
e. Savings and loan associations	106	151	190	240	235
h. Life insurance	1,271	1,350	1,456	1,508	1,627
6. State and local governments					
7. Federal government	8	6	6	6	8
8. Total	4,446	4,850	5,007	5,190	5,129
9. Banks in possessions[c]	3	3	3	3	3

Data are mainly from Klaman, *Mortgage Debt*, Table 15, corrected and extended by using the sources and methods cited by Klaman.

Data on banks in possessions are from Table IV-b-11a-1, divided between conventional and FHA mortgages by the ratios for commercial banks.

TABLE IV-b-11a-4

Multifamily Nonfarm Residential Mortgages, FHA-Insured, Assets
(million dollars)

	1945	1946	1947	1948	1949
1. Nonfarm households and others[a]	50	34	251	379	676
2. Nonfarm unincorporated business					
3. Agriculture					
4. Nonfinancial corporations					
5. Finance[b]	187	180	298	763	1,440
c. Commercial banks	30	26	112	253	426
d. Mutual savings banks	22	27	55	154	313
e. Savings and loan associations	6	7	14	18	32
h. Life insurance	129	120	117	338	669
6. State and local governments					
7. Federal government	c	c	c	2	20
8. Total	237	214	549	1,144	2,136
9. Banks in possessions[d]	c	c	1	2	4

Data are mainly from Klaman, *Mortgage Debt*, Table 11, corrected and extended by using the sources and methods cited by Klaman.

Data on banks in possessions are from Table IV-b-11a-1, divided between conventional and FHA by the ratio for commercial banks.

1950	1951	1952	1953	1954	1955	1956	1957	1958	1959	
764	1,044	1,312	1,397	1,491	1,789	1,951	1,935	2,074	2,338	1.
										2.
										3.
										4.
4,445	4,899	5,102	5,524	5,825	6,454	7,033	7,189	8,042	9,206	5.
352	382	452	512	531	534	467	306	259	439	c.
2,136	2,240	2,314	2,492	2,643	2,894	3,201	3,371	3,624	3,825	d.
232	383	364	496	561	765	996	1,171	1,776	2,378	e.
1,725	1,894	1,972	2,024	2,090	2,261	2,369	2,341	2,383	2,564	h.
										6.
13	25	36	66	92	132	161	180	194	229	7.
5,222	5,968	6,450	6,987	7,408	8,375	9,145	9,304	10,310	11,773	8.
3	4	5	5	5	5	4	3	3	1	9.

[a]Includes sectors 5b, 5f, 5i, 5k, 5l, 5m, and 6, not classified separately by Klaman.
[b]Not including sectors which are combined in "nonfarm households and others."
[c]Included in line 1.

1950	1951	1952	1953	1954	1955	1956	1957	1958	1959	
1,085	894	712	718	792	673	702	942	1,133	1,218	1.
										2.
										3.
										4.
2,121	2,789	3,186	3,215	3,214	3,150	3,057	3,228	3,579	3,619	5.
589	602	476	379	313	271	285	449	694	678	c.
606	1,024	1,375	1,469	1,566	1,574	1,512	1,529	1,672	1,774	d.
36	26	19	28	21	14	14	40	49	66	e.
890	1,137	1,316	1,339	1,314	1,291	1,246	1,210	1,164	1,101	h.
										6.
13	23	22	95	105	171	179	196	320	592	7.
3,219	3,706	3,920	4,028	4,111	3,994	3,938	4,366	5,032	5,429	8.
6	7	5	4	3	3	3	4	7	2	9.

[a]Includes sectors 5b, 5f, 5i, 5k, 5l, 5m, and 6 not classified separately by Klaman.
[b]Not including sectors which are combined in "nonfarm households and others."
[c]Under $500,000.
[d]Included in line 1.

TABLE IV-b-11a-5

One- to Four-Family Nonfarm Residential Mortgages, Conventional, Assets
(million dollars)

	1945	1946	1947	1948	1949
1. Nonfarm households and others[a]	4,878	5,793	6,455	6,684	7,181
2. Nonfarm unincorporated business					
3. Agriculture					
4. Nonfinancial corporations					
5. Finance[b]	8,572	10,494	11,958	13,740	15,184
c. Commercial banks	1,354	2,312	3,023	3,432	3,572
d. Mutual savings banks	1,567	1,551	1,531	1,613	1,682
e. Savings and loan associations	4,610	5,448	6,031	6,899	7,846
h. Life insurance	1,041	1,183	1,373	1,796	2,084
6. State and local governments					
7. Federal government	863	655	505	386	250
8. Total	14,313	16,942	18,918	20,810	22,615
9. Banks in possessions[c]	7	13	16	27	32

Data are mainly from Klaman, *Mortgage Debt*, Table 14, corrected and extended by using the sources and methods cited by Klaman.

Data on banks in possessions are from Table IV-b-11a-2, divided among conventional, FHA, and VA b the ratios for commercial banks.

TABLE IV-b-11a-6

One- to Four-Family Nonfarm Residential Mortgages, FHA- and VA-Insured, Assets
(million dollars)

	1945	1946	1947	1948	1949
1. Nonfarm households and others[a]	603	604	595	928	805
2. Nonfarm unincorporated business					
3. Agriculture					
4. Nonfinancial corporations					
5. Finance[b]	3,644	5,477	8,566	11,217	13,274
c. Commercial banks	1,506	2,241	3,246	3,906	4,312
d. Mutual savings banks	327	482	752	1,222	1,682
e. Savings and loan associations	546	1,392	2,444	2,942	3,271
h. Life insurance	1,265	1,362	2,124	3,147	4,009
6. State and local governments					
7. Federal government	31	11	120	324	926
8. Total	4,278	6,092	9,281	12,469	15,004
9. Banks in possessions[c]	8	10	18	31	40

Table IV-b-11a-2 (combining lines 1, 5b, 5f, 5g, 5j, 5k, 5l, 5m, and 6) minus Table IV-b-11a-5.

Data on banks in possessions are from Table IV-b-11a-2, divided among conventional, FHA, and VA by the ratios for commercial banks.

1950	1951	1952	1953	1954	1955	1956	1957	1958	1959	
8,023	7,898	8,343	9,035	9,719	9,818	10,572	10,489	11,359	12,710	1.
										2.
										3.
										4.
18,245	20,784	24,568	28,645	33,464	38,973	44,044	49,089	55,191	63,096	5.
4,299	4,492	4,993	5,383	6,106	7,012	7,756	8,348	9,423	10,561	c.
1,846	2,062	2,164	2,300	2,506	2,751	2,954	3,180	3,450	3,737	d.
9,331	10,871	13,366	16,000	19,144	22,727	25,889	29,382	33,656	39,477	e.
2,769	3,359	4,045	4,962	5,708	6,483	7,445	8,179	8,662	9,321	h.
										6.
44	159	227	332	415	521	516	838	1,010	1,249	7.
26,312	28,841	33,138	38,012	43,598	49,312	55,132	60,416	67,560	77,055	8.
42	50	51	52	54	66	72	78	95	36	9.

[a]Includes sectors 5b, 5f, 5g, 5k, 5m, and 6 not classified separately by Klaman.
[b]Not including sectors which are combined in "nonfarm households and others."
[c]Included in line 1.

1950	1951	1952	1953	1954	1955	1956	1957	1958	1959	
386	807	909	819	870	1,771	1,863	2,730	3,383	2,817	1.
										2.
										3.
										4.
17,051	20,162	22,164	24,832	28,879	34,724	39,175	40,693	43,166	46,099	5.
5,091	5,669	6,143	6,527	7,078	7,923	8,339	7,887	8,030	8,574	c.
2,466	3,269	4,030	5,073	6,496	8,349	10,036	10,930	12,190	13,150	d.
3,785	3,973	4,279	4,999	5,860	7,274	8,115	8,614	9,234	10,110	e.
5,709	7,251	7,712	8,233	9,445	11,178	12,685	13,262	13,712	14,265	h.
										6.
1,421	1,901	2,288	2,431	2,330	2,443	2,867	3,778	3,580	4,938	7.
18,858	22,870	25,362	28,082	32,079	38,938	43,905	47,201	50,127	53,854	8.
49	64	62	61	62	74	79	73	81	29	9.

[a]Includes sectors 5b, 5f, 5g, 5j, 5k, 5l, 5m, and 6 not classified separately by Klaman.
[b]Not including sectors which are combined in "nonfarm households and others."
[c]Included in line 1.

TABLE IV-b-11b

Nonfarm Nonresidential Mortgages, Assets
(million dollars)

	1945	1946	1947	1948
1. Nonfarm households	3,417	3,886	4,429	4,836
2. Nonfarm unincorporated business				
3. Agriculture				
4. Nonfinancial corporations				
5. Finance	4,070	4,869	5,662	6,454
c. Commercial banks	852	1,380	1,680	1,934
d. Mutual savings banks	797	827	891	1,015
e. Savings and loan associations	108	143	177	206
f. Investment companies	13	17	25	35
h. Life insurance	2,154	2,345	2,710	3,054
i. Fire and casualty insurance	38	40	46	52
k. Other private insurance	104	110	123	135
m. Other finance	4	7	10	23
6. State and local governments				
7. Federal government	15	9	7	7
8. Total	7,502	8,764	10,098	11,297

Table IV-b-11 minus Table IV-b-11a.

TABLE IV-b-11c

Nonfarm Mortgages, Assets, 1900-45, Selected Years
(million dollars)

	1900	1912
1. Nonfarm households	2,399	2,826
2. Nonfarm unincorporated business		
3. Agriculture		
4. Nonfinancial corporations		
5. Finance	2,066	4,835
c. Commercial banks	376	1,153
d. Mutual savings banks	839	1,679
e. Savings and loan associations	371	847
f. Investment companies		
h. Life insurance	357	913
i. Fire and casualty insurance	55	79
k. Other private insurance	2	15
l. Finance companies	66	149
6. State and local governments		
7. Federal government		
8. Total	4,465	7,661

Sum of corresponding lines of Tables IV-b-11c-1 and IV-b-11c-4.

[a] The 1945 figures in this table have been superseded by those in Table IV-b-11; they are included here for comparability with earlier years.

1949	1950	1951	1952	1953	1954	1955	1956	1957	1958	
5,195	5,471	5,745	6,022	6,366	6,936	7,558	8,292	8,905	9,933	1.
										2.
										3.
										4.
7,013	7,655	8,488	9,259	10,075	11,295	12,694	14,356	15,929	17,697	5.
2,038	2,245	2,436	2,594	2,813	3,234	3,776	4,332	4,760	5,385	c.
1,099	1,164	1,274	1,444	1,556	1,740	1,831	1,984	2,102	2,274	d.
232	273	311	368	439	522	628	715	800	912	e.
39	44	43	45	46	45	44	43	40	36	f.
3,379	3,682	4,146	4,501	4,878	5,371	5,959	6,763	7,660	8,474	h.
56	62	68	72	82	88	96	105	108	111	i.
148	166	188	208	231	266	317	367	396	429	k.
22	19	22	27	30	29	43	47	63	76	m.
										6.
5	4	4	3	3				1	1	7.
12,213	13,130	14,237	15,284	16,444	18,231	20,252	22,648	24,835	27,631	8.

1922	1929	1933	1939	1945[a]	
6,707	13,570	10,537	8,568	9,564	1.
					2.
					3.
					4.
9,947	23,281	19,797	18,153	20,369	5.
2,504	5,526	4,205	4,187	4,764	c.
2,878	5,367	5,457	4,775	4,177	d.
2,468	6,182	4,473	3,748	5,162	e.
	27	30	91	93	f.
1,534	5,219	5,022	4,782	5,796	h.
120	194	173	100	80	i.
50	139	161	143	167	k.
389	627	276	327	130	l.
					6.
		132	2,182	859	7.
16,654	36,851	30,466	28,903	30,792	8.

TABLE IV-b-11c-1

Nonfarm Residential Mortgages, Assets, 1900-45, Selected Years

(million dollars)

	1900	1912	1922	1929	1933	1939	1945[a]
1. Nonfarm households	1,604	1,875	4,377	8,527	7,152	5,879	6,945
2. Nonfarm unincorporated business							
3. Agriculture							
4. Nonfinancial corporations							
5. Finance	1,350	3,117	6,715	16,385	13,768	12,781	15,487
c. Commercial banks	194	596	1,295	3,316	2,668	2,814	3,504
d. Mutual savings banks	529	1,058	1,813	3,518	3,595	3,187	2,807
e. Savings and loan associations	371	847	2,468	6,182	4,473	3,748	5,162
f. Investment companies				14	15	79	81
h. Life insurance	183	469	788	2,704	2,626	2,562	3,680
i. Fire and casualty insurance	28	40	60	97	87	50	40
k. Other private insurance	1	7	25	72	84	77	106
l. Finance companies	44	100	264	482	220	264	107
6. State and local governments							
7. Federal government					132	2,182	859
8. Total	2,954	4,992	11,092	24,912	21,052	20,842	23,291

Sum of corresponding lines of Tables IV-b-11c-2 and IV-b-11c-3.

[a] The 1945 figures in this table have been superseded by those in Table IV-b-11a; they are included here for comparability with earlier years.

TABLE IV-b-11c-2

One- to Four-Family Nonfarm Residential Mortgages, Assets, 1900-45, Selected Years

(million dollars)

	1900	1912	1922	1929	1933	1939	1945[a]
1. Nonfarm households	1,469	1,676	3,509	6,156	4,631	4,319	5,249
2. Nonfarm unincorporated business							
3. Agriculture							
4. Nonfinancial corporations							
5. Finance	1,190	2,517	5,165	12,756	10,589	9,841	12,483
c. Commercial banks	156	409	737	2,213	1,901	2,128	2,875
d. Mutual savings banks	445	794	1,191	2,286	2,354	2,128	1,894
e. Savings and loan associations	371	847	2,468	6,182	4,473	3,748	5,162
f. Investment companies				7	8	73	75
h. Life insurance	153	348	507	1,626	1,599	1,495	2,306
i. Fire and casualty insurance	24	30	39	58	52	30	24
k. Other private insurance	1	5	16	43	51	45	66
l. Finance companies	40	84	206	341	151	194	81
6. State and local governments							
7. Federal government					132	2,182	859
8. Total	2,659	4,193	8,674	18,912	15,352	16,342	18,591

Line

1 Line 8 minus the sum of lines 5 and 7.
8 Column 3 of Tables IV-b-11c-5 and IV-b-11c-6.

Other lines

1900-22: Goldsmith, *A Study of Saving*, Vol. I, Table M-5; columns as indicated.

Line	Column
5	3
5c	4
5d	5
5e	6
5h	7
5i	8
5k	9
5l	10

1929-45: *A Study of Saving*, Vol. I, Table M-9; and Federal Home Loan Bank Board (FHLBB), *Estimated Home Mortgage Debt and Financing Activity, 1957*, page 2.

Line	Source
5	Sum of lines 5c through 5m of this table.
5c	FHLBB, column 4, plus Table M-9, column 5.
5d	FHLBB, column 3.
5e	FHLBB, column 1, plus Table M-9, column 12.
5f	Table M-9, column 13.
5h	FHLBB, column 2.
5i	Table M-9, column 9.
5k	Table M-9, column 8.
5l	Table M-9, column 10.
7	FHLBB, column 5 plus column 6.

[a] The 1945 figures in this table have been superseded by those in Table IV-b-11a-2; they are included here for comparability with earlier years.

TABLE IV-b-11c-3

Multifamily Nonfarm Residential Mortgages, Assets, 1900-45, Selected Years

(million dollars)

	1900	1912	1922	1929	1933	1939	1945[a]
1. Nonfarm households	135	199	868	2,371	2,521	1,560	1,696
2. Nonfarm unincorporated business							
3. Agriculture							
4. Nonfinancial corporations							
5. Finance	160	600	1,550	3,629	3,179	2,940	3,004
c. Commercial banks	38	187	558	1,103	767	686	629
d. Mutual savings banks	84	264	622	1,232	1,241	1,059	913
f. Investment companies				7	7	6	6
h. Life insurance	30	121	281	1,078	1,027	1,067	1,374
i. Fire and casualty insurance	4	10	21	39	35	20	16
k. Other private insurance		2	9	29	33	32	40
l. Finance companies	4	16	58	141	69	70	26
6. State and local governments							
7. Federal government							
8. Total	295	799	2,418	6,000	5,700	4,500	4,700

Line

1 Line 8 minus line 5.

8 Column 4 of Tables IV-b-11c-5 and IV-b-11c-6.

Other lines

1900-22: Goldsmith, *A Study of Saving*, Vol. I, Table M-6; columns as indicated.

Line	Column
5	3
5c	4
5d	5
5h	6
5i	8
5k	7
5l	9

1929-45: *A Study of Saving*, Vol. I, Table M-10; columns as indicated.

Line	Column
5	3
5c	Sum of columns 4 and 5
5d	6
5f	11
5h	7
5i	9
5k	8
5l	10

[a] The 1945 figures in this table have been superseded by those in Table IV-b-11a-1; they are included here for comparability with earlier years.

TABLE IV-b-11c-4

Nonfarm Nonresidential Mortgages, Assets, 1900-45, Selected Years

(million dollars)

	1900	1912	1922	1929	1933	1939	1945[a]
1. Nonfarm households	795	951	2,330	5,043	3,385	2,689	2,619
2. Nonfarm unincorporated business							
3. Agriculture							
4. Nonfinancial corporations							
5. Finance	716	1,718	3,232	6,896	6,029	5,372	4,882
c. Commercial banks	182	557	1,209	2,210	1,537	1,373	1,260
d. Mutual savings banks	310	621	1,065	1,849	1,862	1,588	1,370
f. Investment companies				13	15	12	12
h. Life insurance	174	444	746	2,515	2,396	2,220	2,116
i. Fire and casualty insurance	27	39	60	97	86	50	40
k. Other private insurance	1	8	25	67	77	66	61
l. Finance companies	22	49	125	145	56	63	23
6. State and local governments							
7. Federal government							
8. Total	1,511	2,669	5,362	11,939	9,414	8,061	7,501

Line

1 Line 8 minus line 5.

8 Column 5 of Tables IV-b-11c-5 and IV-b-11c-6.

Other lines

1900-22: Goldsmith, *A Study of Saving*, Vol. I, Table M-7; columns as indicated.

Line	Column
5	3
5c	4
5d	5
5h	6
5i	8
5k	7
5l	9

1929-45: Goldsmith, *A Study of Saving*, Vol. I, Table M-11; columns as indicated.

Line	Column
5	3
5c	Sum of columns 4 and 5.
5d	6
5f	11
5h	7
5i	9
5k	8
5l	10

[a]The 1945 figures in this table have been superseded by those in Table IV-b-11b; they are included here for comparability with earlier years.

TABLE IV-b-11c-5

Nonfarm Mortgages (Excluding Real Estate Bonds), Assets, 1890 and 1896-1929

(million dollars)

End of Year	Total Nonfarm Mortgage Debt (1)	Residential: Total (2)	Residential: One- to Four-Family (3)	Residential: Multifamily (4)	Non-residential (5)
1890	3,430	2,293	2,110	183	1,137
1896	4,272	2,840	2,579	261	1,432
1897	4,277	2,840	2,573	267	1,437
1898	4,313	2,860	2,585	275	1,453
1899	4,359	2,887	2,604	283	1,472
1900	4,465	2,954	2,659	295	1,511
1901	4,574	3,022	2,705	317	1,552
1902	4,734	3,124	2,780	344	1,610
1903	4,919	3,241	2,868	373	1,678
1904	5,137	3,381	2,975	406	1,756
1905	5,415	3,560	3,115	445	1,855
1906	5,727	3,760	3,271	489	1,967
1907	5,956	3,905	3,378	527	2,051
1908	6,184	4,050	3,483	567	2,134
1909	6,566	4,295	3,672	623	2,271
1910	6,959	4,546	3,864	682	2,413
1911	7,299	4,762	4,024	738	2,537
1912	7,661	4,992	4,193	799	2,669
1913	8,341	5,429	4,533	896	2,912
1914	8,936	5,810	4,822	988	3,126
1915	9,362	6,080	5,016	1,064	3,282
1916	9,921	6,436	5,278	1,158	3,485
1917	10,984	7,110	5,795	1,315	3,874
1918	11,339	7,409	6,001	1,408	3,930
1919	11,929	7,783	6,265	1,518	4,146
1920	13,819	9,042	7,234	1,808	4,777
1921	15,118	9,978	7,893	2,085	5,140
1922	16,654	11,092	8,674	2,418	5,562
1923	19,252	12,918	9,999	2,919	6,334
1924	21,969	14,873	11,378	3,495	7,096
1925	25,158	17,184	12,984	4,200	7,974
1926	28,347	19,409	14,809	4,600	8,938
1927	31,772	21,433	16,433	5,000	10,339
1928	34,961	23,304	17,904	5,400	11,657
1929	36,851	24,912	18,912	6,000	11,939

This is a revision of Table R-34 in Goldsmith, *A Study of Saving*, Vol. I.

Col. 1
- 1929: Table IV-b-11c-6.
- 1916-28: Extrapolated from 1929 using nonfarm mortgage debt, individual and noncorporate, from *Survey of Current Business*, July 1960, p. 35.
- 1913-15: Interpolated between 1912 and 1916 by column 1 of Table R-34, in Goldsmith, *A Study of Saving*, Vol. I.
- 1912: 46 per cent of 1922. See *ibid.*, note to column 1.
- 1896-1911: Interpolated between 1890 and 1912 by *ibid.*, Table R-34, column 1.
- 1890: *Ibid.*, Table R-34, column 1.

(Notes continued at foot of following page)

TABLE IV-b-11c-6

Nonfarm Mortgages (Excluding Real Estate Bonds), Assets, 1929-45

(million dollars)

End of Year	Total (1)	Residential: Total (2)	Residential: One- to Four-Family (3)	Residential: Multifamily (4)	Non-residential (5)
1929	36,851	24,912	18,912	6,000	11,939
1930	37,726	25,391	18,891	6,500	12,335
1931	36,511	24,304	18,104	6,200	12,207
1932	34,362	22,655	16,655	6,000	11,707
1933	30,466	21,052	15,352	5,700	9,414
1934	29,486	20,730	15,630	5,100	8,756
1935	28,415	20,237	15,437	4,800	8,178
1936	28,046	19,985	15,385	4,600	8,061
1937	27,995	20,018	15,518	4,500	7,977
1938	28,218	20,175	15,775	4,400	8,043
1939	28,903	20,842	16,342	4,500	8,061
1940	29,986	21,991	17,391	4,600	7,995
1941	31,250	23,151	18,351	4,800	8,099
1942	30,771	22,912	18,212	4,700	7,859
1943	29,906	22,411	17,811	4,600	7,495
1944	29,744	22,424	17,924	4,500	7,320
1945	30,792	23,291	18,591	4,700	7,501

This is a revision of Table R-35 in Goldsmith, *A Study of Saving*, Vol. I.

Col. 1: *Survey of Current Business*, September 1953, p. 18.
Col. 2: Column 3 plus column 4.
Col. 3: Federal Home Loan Bank Board, *Estimated Home Mortgage Debt and Financing Activity*, 1957, p. 2.
Col. 4: U.S. Housing and Home Finance Agency. *Housing Statistics*, Vol. 14, no. 3, March 1961, p. 57.
Col. 5: Column 1 minus column 2.

Notes to Table IV-11c-5 (concluded)

Col. 2
- 1925-29: Column 3 plus column 4.
- 1921-24: Column 1 multiplied by share of residential in total nonfarm mortgages (column 2 divided by column 1, interpolated between 1920 and 1925).
- 1890-1920: Goldsmith, *A Study of Saving*, Vol. I, Table R-34, column 2.

Col. 3
- 1925-29: Federal Home Loan Bank Board, *Estimated Home Mortgage Debt and Financing Activity*, 1957, p. 2.
- 1921-24: Column 2 minus column 4.
- 1890-1920: Goldsmith, *A Study of Saving*, Vol. I, Table R-34, column 3.

Col. 4
- 1925-29: U.S. Housing and Home Finance Agency, *Housing Statistics*, Vol. 14, No. 3, March 1961, p. 57.
- 1921-24: Column 2 multiplied by share of multifamily in total residential mortgages (column 4 divided by column 2, interpolated between 1920 and 1925).
- 1890-1920: Goldsmith, *A Study of Saving*, Vol. I, Table R-34, column 4.

Col. 5 : Column 1 minus column 2.

TABLE IV-b-12

Farm Mortgages, Assets

(million dollars)

	1945	1946	1947	1948	1949
1. Nonfarm households	1,919	2,040	2,106	2,232	2,311
2. Nonfarm unincorporated business					
3. Agriculture					
4. Nonfinancial corporations					
5. Finance	1,336	1,539	1,763	1,917	2,110
c. Commercial banks	520	699	817	867	907
d. Mutual savings banks	24	26	28	34	37
h. Life insurance	776	795	895	990	1,138
k. Other private insurance	15	16	17	19	26
m. Other finance	1	3	6	7	2
6. State and local governments					
7. Federal government	1,505	1,318	1,195	1,139	1,158
8. Total	4,760	4,897	5,064	5,288	5,579

Line

1 Line 8 minus the sum of lines 5 and 7.

5 Sum of lines 5c, 5d, 5h, 5k, and 5m.

5c Farm mortgage loans of commercial banks in the U.S. and possessions (Klaman, *Mortgage Debt*, Table 18, column 12, extended by using the *Federal Reserve Bulletin*, August 1961, page 961), minus farm mortgage loans of banks in U.S. possessions (Table III-5m-2 of this volume).

5d Klaman, *Mortgage Debt*, Table 19, column 12, extended by using the *Federal Reserve Bulletin*, August 1961, page 961.

TABLE IV-b-12a

Farm Mortgages, 1900-45, Selected Years

(million dollars)

	1900	1912
1. Nonfarm households	1,441	2,192
2. Nonfarm unincorporated business	299	468
3. Agriculture	140	219
4. Nonfinancial corporations		
5. Finance	432	1,469
6. State and local governments		
7. Federal government		
8. Total	2,312	4,348

Line

1 Table III-1d, line II-12.

2 Table III-2a, line II-12.

3 Table III-3b, line II-12.

5 Table III-5o, line II-12.

7 Table III-7f, line II-12.

8 Sum of lines 1 through 7.

1950	1951	1952	1953	1954	1955	1956	1957	1958	1959	
2,533	2,780	3,026	3,223	3,399	3,623	3,958	4,198	4,541	4,961	1.
										2.
										3.
										4.
2,373	2,623	2,872	3,079	3,322	3,683	3,937	4,071	4,257	4,555	5.
964	1,000	1,053	1,079	1,155	1,291	1,328	1,357	1,460	1,577	c.
44	47	53	53	56	58	59	57	53	55	d.
1,327	1,527	1,705	1,886	2,048	2,273	2,481	2,584	2,667	2,844	h.
34	45	56	58	59	55	61	63	66	68	k.
4	4	5	3	4	6	8	10	11	11	m.
										6.
1,212	1,273	1,365	1,470	1,568	1,760	2,013	2,238	2,456	2,775	7.
6,118	6,676	7,263	7,772	8,289	9,066	9,908	10,507	11,254	12,291	8.

Line

5h Table III-5h, line II-12.

5k Table III-5k, line II-12. Fraternal orders are the only holders of farm mortgages in this sector.

5m Table III-5m, line II-12. Represents only holdings by banks in possessions.

7 Klaman, *Mortgage Debt*, Table 21, column 12, extended by using the *Agricultural Finance Review*, September 1960, p. 121.

8 *Agricultural Finance Review*, September 1960, Table 2, p. 121.

1922	1929	1933	1939	1945[a]
4,761	3,551	2,741	1,632	1,491
946	681	508	311	257
910	318	237	145	120
3,518	3,881	2,954	1,697	1,363
651	1,200	1,245	2,801	1,451
10,786	9,631	7,685	6,586	4,682

[a]The 1945 figures in this table have been superseded by those in Table IV-b-12; they are included here for comparability with earlier years.

TABLE IV-b-13

U.S. Government Securities, Assets

(billion dollars)

	1945	1946	1947	1948
1. Nonfarm households	59.69	59.20	61.02	60.79
2. Nonfarm unincorporated business				
3. Agriculture	4.15	4.21	4.38	4.60
4. Nonfinancial corporations	20.72	15.02	13.82	14.62
5. Finance	181.65	169.56	165.19	159.43
a. Federal Reserve Banks and Treasury monetary funds	24.29	23.37	22.58	23.35
b. Govt. insurance and pension funds	24.05	27.81	31.56	34.70
c. Commercial banks	90.61	74.78	69.22	62.62
d. Mutual savings banks	10.68	11.78	11.98	11.48
e. Savings and loan associations	2.42	2.01	1.74	1.46
f. Investment companies	.23	.18	.19	.14
g. Credit unions	.18	.18	.18	.16
h. Life insurance	20.58	21.63	20.02	16.75
i. Fire and casualty insurance	3.22	3.41	4.00	4.49
j. Noninsured pension plans	1.47	1.65	1.81	1.94
k. Other private insurance	.52	.53	.54	.54
m. Other finance	3.40	2.23	1.37	1.80
6. State and local governments	4.99	4.37	5.03	5.35
7. Federal government	4.52	5.06	5.10	5.20
8. Total	275.72	257.42	254.54	249.99
9. Rest of world, assets	2.57	2.10	2.70	2.78
10. Difference between obligor and holder records, all banks	−.42	−.78	−.94	−.54
11. Total liabilities	277.87	258.74	256.30	252.23

Line

1 Line 8 minus lines 3, 4, 5, 6 and 7.

3-7 Line II-13 from Tables III-3 through III-7.

8 Line 11 minus lines 9 and 10.

9 Rest-of-the-world assets, plus International Monetary Fund demand notes (FRB worksheets).

10 Obligor record of U.S. government securities held by commercial banks and mutual savings banks (*Treasury Bulletin*, e.g., May 1959, p. 49, Table 3) minus U.S. government securities held by banks in possessions (Table III-5m-2, line II-13), and by mutual savings banks and commercial banks (lines 5c and 5d of this table).

11 Table IV-c-12, line 7a.

1949	1950	1951	1952	1953	1954	1955	1956	1957	1958	
61.76	61.43	59.98	60.21	60.40	58.87	60.63	61.74	60.60	58.57	1.
										2.
4.72	4.69	4.71	4.63	4.73	4.97	5.17	5.06	5.12	5.21	3.
16.54	19.41	20.34	19.54	21.12	18.83	22.82	18.23	17.43	17.62	4.
160.57	156.05	158.78	165.16	169.01	174.26	168.55	166.53	165.59	176.01	5.
18.90	20.80	23.82	24.72	25.94	24.95	24.80	25.02	24.26	26.44	a.
36.89	37.30	40.90	44.82	47.51	48.95	51.35	53.60	54.67	54.05	b.
67.00	62.03	61.52	63.32	63.43	68.98	61.59	58.55	58.24	66.18	c.
11.43	10.87	9.82	9.42	9.18	8.75	8.46	7.97	7.55	7.26	d.
1.46	1.49	1.60	1.79	1.92	2.02	2.34	2.78	3.17	3.82	e.
.18	.20	.20	.19	.19	.19	.33	.35	.35	.49	f.
.14	.12	.14	.14	.13	.13	.13	.14	.13	.13	g.
15.29	13.46	11.01	10.25	9.83	9.07	8.58	7.56	7.03	7.18	h.
5.00	5.35	5.48	5.82	6.03	6.14	6.00	5.67	5.46	5.40	i.
2.09	2.30	2.42	2.42	2.58	2.59	2.89	2.69	2.42	2.45	j.
.54	.55	.57	.60	.61	.65	.72	.75	.74	.80	k.
1.65	1.58	1.30	1.67	1.66	1.84	1.36	1.45	1.57	1.81	m.
5.37	5.73	6.10	7.18	8.49	9.93	10.34	11.04	11.78	11.08	6.
5.28	5.04	4.95	5.05	5.07	5.20	5.22	5.47	5.91	5.82	7.
254.24	252.35	254.86	261.77	268.82	272.06	272.73	268.07	266.43	274.31	8.
2.88	4.33	4.28	5.31	5.88	6.31	7.48	7.73	7.56	7.61	9.
–.54	–.48	–.19	–.12	.08	–.02	.20	.54	.63	.74	10.
256.58	256.20	258.95	266.96	274.78	278.35	280.41	276.34	274.62	282.66	11.

TABLE IV-b-13a

Short-Term U.S. Government Securities, Assets

(billion dollars)

	1945	1946	1947	1948
1. Nonfarm households	.51	.67	.25	2.36
2. Nonfarm unincorporated business				
3. Agriculture				
4. Nonfinancial corporations	17.00	11.90	11.00	11.90
5. Finance	57.61	44.09	41.26	34.78
a. Federal Reserve Banks and Treasury monetary funds	23.20	22.30	19.90	12.40
c. Commercial banks	32.30	18.80	19.20	19.40
d. Mutual savings banks	.16	.44	.49	.54
e. Savings and loan associations	.20	.20	.20	.10
h. Life insurance	.31	.76	.23	.25
i. Fire and casualty insurance	.34	.39	.54	.89
m. Other finance	1.10	1.20	.70	1.20
6. State and local governments	2.40	2.30	2.60	3.10
7. Federal government				
8. Total	77.52	58.96	55.11	52.14
9. Rest of world, assets	2.08	1.54	.79	1.26
10. Total liabilities	79.60	60.50	55.90	53.40

Line	
1	Line 8 minus the sum of lines 4 through 6.
5a, 5c, and 10	Federal Reserve Board, *Flow of Funds/Saving Accounts, 1946-1960, Supplement 5*, p. 84.
4, 5d, 5e, 5h, 5i, 5m, 6, and 9	FRB worksheets. Line 5i may include some holdings of noninsured pension plans or other private insurance.
5	Sum of lines 5a through 5m.
8	Line 10 minus line 9.

1949	1950	1951	1952	1953	1954	1955	1956	1957	1958	
3.33	2.15	.54	1.29	2.31	1.66	.65	2.15	4.53	3.16	1.
										2.
										3.
14.20	17.20	17.50	16.40	18.20	15.60	18.60	14.90	14.50	15.20	4.
41.63	41.31	32.10	37.51	49.28	40.61	32.46	38.82	41.05	41.63	5.
										a.
12.00	16.00	13.40	14.80	17.00	19.40	20.70	22.10	21.40	21.00	
26.50	22.20	15.80	19.20	28.20	17.60	9.00	13.80	15.70	16.60	c.
.44	.11	.18	.26	.48	.16	.26	.24	.45	.30	d.
.10	.10	.20	.20	.20	.20	.30	.20	.50	.30	e.
.30	.56	.65	.54	.47	.55	.41	.28	.25	.52	h.
1.19	1.24	.87	1.01	1.43	.90	.49	.75	1.18	1.10	i.
1.10	1.10	1.00	1.50	1.50	1.80	1.30	1.45	1.57	1.81	m.
3.20	3.50	3.30	4.00	5.20	5.20	3.60	5.80	7.10	6.00	6.
										7.
62.36	64.16	53.44	59.20	74.99	63.07	55.31	61.67	67.18	65.99	8.
1.54	2.44	2.16	3.40	4.11	4.23	4.89	5.93	5.92	5.91	9.
63.90	66.60	55.60	62.60	79.10	67.30	60.20	67.60	73.10	71.90	10.

TABLE IV-b-13b
U.S. Government Savings Bonds, Assets
(billion dollars)

	1945	1946	1947	1948
1. Nonfarm households	40.42	41.62	43.43	45.05
2. Nonfarm unincorporated business				
3. Agriculture	4.15	4.21	4.38	4.60
4. Nonfinancial corporations	1.60	1.60	1.60	1.80
5. Finance	2.05	2.43	2.77	3.75
b. Govt. insurance and pension funds	.20	.30	.40	.50
c. Commercial banks	.94	.96	.93	1.23
d. Mutual savings banks	.21	.25	.30	.48
e. Savings and loan associations	.20	.20	.20	.30
h. Life insurance	.10	.12	.14	.24
i. Fire and casualty insurance	.19	.22	.26	.41
j. Noninsured pension plans	.18	.35	.51	.56
k. Other private insurance	.03	.03	.03	.03
6. State and local governments				
7. Federal government				
8. Total	48.22	49.86	52.18	55.20

Notes to Table IV-b-13b are on page 302.

TABLE IV-b-13c
Long-Term U.S. Government Securities Other Than Savings Bonds, Assets
(billion dollars)

	1945	1946	1947	1948
1. Nonfarm households	18.76	16.91	17.34	13.38
2. Nonfarm unincorporated business				
3. Agriculture				
4. Nonfinancial corporations	2.12	1.52	1.22	.92
5. Finance	121.99	123.04	121.16	120.90
a. Federal Reserve Banks and Treasury monetary funds	1.09	1.07	2.68	10.95
b. Govt. insurance and pension funds	23.85	27.51	31.16	34.20
c. Commercial banks	57.37	55.02	49.09	41.99
d. Mutual savings banks	10.31	11.09	11.19	10.46
e. Savings and loan associations	2.02	1.61	1.34	1.06
f. Investment companies	.23	.18	.19	.14
g. Credit unions	.18	.18	.18	.16
h. Life insurance	20.17	20.75	19.65	16.26
i. Fire and casualty insurance	2.69	2.80	3.20	3.19
j. Noninsured pension plans	1.29	1.30	1.30	1.38
k. Other private insurance	.49	.50	.51	.51
m. Other finance	2.30	1.03	.67	.60
6. State and local governments	2.59	2.07	2.43	2.25
7. Federal government	4.52	5.06	5.10	5.20
8. Total	149.98	148.60	147.25	142.65
9. Rest of world, assets	.49	.56	1.91	1.52
10. Difference between obligor and holder records, all banks	–.42	–.78	–.94	–.54
11. Total liabilities	150.05	148.38	148.22	143.63

Table IV-b-13 minus IV-b-13a and IV-b-13b.

1949	1950	1951	1952	1953	1954	1955	1956	1957	1958	
46.35	46.80	46.25	46.40	46.36	46.45	46.48	46.19	43.92	43.02	1.
										2.
4.72	4.69	4.71	4.63	4.73	4.97	5.17	5.06	5.12	5.21	3.
1.80	1.80	1.80	1.80	1.80	1.80	1.80	1.60	1.40	1.22	4.
4.04	4.96	4.98	5.22	5.05	5.14	5.10	4.17	2.77	2.43	5.
.60	.70	.70	.80	.80	.80	.80	.70	.60	.50	b.
1.18	1.47	1.49	1.51	1.49	1.50	1.48	1.09	.62	.59	c.
.50	.58	.58	.59	.56	.55	.52	.45	.30	.22	d.
.40	.50	.50	.50	.50	.50	.53	.40	.32	.32	e.
.26	.31	.31	.32	.30	.29	.27	.23	.13	.10	h.
.46	.57	.59	.60	.58	.57	.56	.49	.32	.25	i.
.61	.80	.77	.78	.75	.83	.85	.70	.36	.35	j.
.03	.03	.04	.12	.07	.10	.09	.11	.12	.10	k.
										6.
										7.
56.91	58.25	57.74	58.05	57.94	58.36	58.55	57.02	53.21	51.88	8.

1949	1950	1951	1952	1953	1954	1955	1956	1957	1958	
12.08	12.48	13.19	12.52	11.73	10.76	13.50	13.40	12.15	12.39	1.
										2.
										3.
.54	.41	1.04	1.34	1.12	1.43	2.42	1.73	1.53	1.20	4.
114.90	109.78	121.70	122.43	114.68	128.51	130.99	123.54	121.77	131.95	5.
										a.
6.90	4.80	10.42	9.92	8.94	5.55	4.10	2.92	2.86	5.44	
36.29	36.60	40.20	44.02	46.71	48.15	50.55	52.90	54.07	53.55	b.
39.32	38.36	44.23	42.61	33.74	49.88	51.11	43.66	41.92	48.99	c.
10.49	10.18	9.06	8.57	8.14	8.04	7.68	7.28	6.80	6.74	d.
.96	.89	.90	1.09	1.22	1.32	1.51	2.18	2.35	3.20	e.
.18	.20	.20	.19	.19	.19	.33	.35	.35	.49	f.
.14	.12	.14	.14	.13	.13	.13	.14	.13	.13	g.
14.73	12.59	10.05	9.39	9.06	8.23	7.90	7.05	6.65	6.56	h.
3.35	3.54	4.02	4.21	4.02	4.67	4.95	4.43	3.96	4.05	i.
1.48	1.50	1.65	1.64	1.83	1.76	2.04	1.99	2.06	2.10	j.
.51	.52	.53	.48	.54	.55	.63	.64	.62	.70	k.
.55	.48	.30	.17	.16	.04	.06				m.
2.17	2.23	2.80	3.18	3.29	4.73	6.74	5.24	4.68	5.08	6.
5.28	5.04	4.95	5.05	5.07	5.20	5.22	5.47	5.91	5.82	7.
134.97	129.94	143.68	144.52	135.89	150.63	158.87	149.38	146.04	156.44	8.
1.34	1.89	2.12	1.91	1.77	2.08	2.59	1.80	1.64	1.70	9.
										10.
−.54	−.48	−.19	−.12	.08	−.02	.20	.54	.63	.74	
135.77	131.35	145.61	146.31	137.74	152.69	161.66	151.72	148.31	158.88	11.

Notes to Table IV-b-13b

Line

1 Individuals' holdings of federal securities (*Treasury Bulletin*, e.g., March 1958, p. 39) plus nonprofit organizations' holdings (FRB worksheets), minus line 3 of this table. The 1958 figure for nonprofit organizations was assumed to be the same as 1957.

3 Table III-3, line II-13b.

4 1945-57: FRB worksheets. For 1958, it was assumed that the decline of the previous few years continued.

5 Total of lines 5b through 5k.

5b 1945-57: FRB worksheets. The 1958 figure was estimated by assuming the same decline as in the previous two years.

5c *Ibid.* The 1958 figure was extrapolated from 1957 by the *Treasury Bulletin* (e.g., March 1958, p. 42) sample of commercial banks.

5d *Treasury Bulletin* (e.g., March 1958, p. 42), holdings of mutual savings banks.

5e Total holdings of savings institutions, from FRB worksheets, minus line 5d of this table. The 1958 figure is from *Savings and Loan Fact Book*, e.g., 1960, p. 85.

5h *Treasury Bulletin* (e.g., March 1958, p. 42), holdings of "Life Insurance."

Sum of lines 5i through 5k.

FRB worksheets. 1958 figure extrapolated from 1957 by the sum of *Treasury Bulletin* figures for "Fire, Casualty and Marine" and "Corporate Pension Trust Funds."

5i Treasury survey estimates (*Treasury Bulletin*, e.g., March 1958, p. 42, Table 4) raised to cover all fire and casualty companies by the ratio of Table IV-b-13, line 5i to Treasury survey estimates for holdings of marketable and nonmarketable bonds.

5j 1945-48: Total of lines 5i through 5k minus lines 5i and 5k.
1949-58: Same method as for line 5i.

5k 1945-48: Assumed the same as 1949.
1949-58: Total of lines 5i through 5k minus lines 5i and 5j.

8 *Treasury Bulletin* (e.g., March, 1958, p. 34, Table 2). Includes matured debt plus interest-bearing debt.

TABLE IV-b-13d
U.S. Government Securities, Assets, 1900-45, Selected Years
(million dollars)

	1900	1912	1922	1929	1933	1939	1945[a]
1. Nonfarm households	576	397	10,806	5,053	6,845	9,140	64,945
2. Nonfarm unincorporated business							
3. Agriculture			450			249	4,150
4. Nonfinancial corporations			3,563	3,158	2,837	1,776	17,442
5. Finance	663	794	7,715	7,658	13,659	33,506	178,935
a. Federal Reserve Banks and Treasury monetary funds			436	511	2,438	2,484	24,262
b. Govt. insurance and pension funds			105	769	500	4,580	24,095
c. Commercial banks	516	772	4,584	4,670	8,332	16,316	90,606
d. Mutual savings banks	102	12	1,088	533	839	3,102	10,682
e. Savings and loan associations			27	19	56	102	2,420
f. Investment companies			1	26	8	18	123
g. Credit unions					2	6	210
h. Life insurance	6	1	878	336	860	5,396	20,583
i. Fire and casualty insurance	38	7	492	464	432	1,168	3,274
j. Noninsured pension plans			9	50	70	158	1,305
k. Other private insurance	1	2	16	3	3	71	386
l. Finance companies				41	27	18	282
m. Other finance			79	236	92	87	707
6. State and local governments			232	255	219	250	4,390
7. Federal government			229	52	309	2,080	4,520
8. Total[b]	1,239	1,191	22,995	16,176	23,869	47,001	274,382

Line	
1	Line 8 minus the sum of lines 3-7.
3	Table III-3b, line II-13.
4	Table III-4b, line II-13.
5	Table III-5o, line II-13.
5a	Goldsmith, *Financial Intermediaries*, Table A-2, line 12.
5b	*Ibid.*, Table A-11, line 10.
5c	*Ibid.*, Table A-3, line 33, plus Table A-4, line 25.
5d	*Ibid.*, Table A-5, line 26.
5e	*Ibid.*, Table A-19, line 12.
5f	*Ibid.*, Table A-21, line 19.
5g	*Ibid.*, Table A-20, line 10.
5h	*Ibid.*, Table A-8, line 28.
5i	*Ibid.*, Table A-12, line 21, plus Table A-13, line 21.
5j	*Ibid.*, Table A-10, line 8.
5k	*Ibid.*, Table A-9, line 21, plus Table A-14, line 11.
5l	*Ibid.*, sum of Table A-25, line 8; Table A-26, line 6 (1945 only); and Table A-27, one-half of line 2 (1945 only).
5m	Line 5 minus lines 5a through 5m.
6	Table III-6a, line II-13.
7	Table III-7f, line II-13.
8	Goldsmith, *A Study of Saving*, Vol. III, Table W-18, line II-12.

[a]The 1945 figures in this table have been superseded by those in Table IV-b-13; they are included here for comparability with earlier years.

[b]See note b, Table IV-b-15a.

TABLE IV-b-14

State and Local Government Securities, Assets

(billion dollars)

	1945	1946	1947	1948
1. Nonfarm households	11.92	11.76	12.17	13.16
2. Nonfarm unincorporated business				
3. Agriculture				
4. Nonfinancial corporations	.32	.32	.36	.41
5. Finance	6.98	7.16	8.15	9.25
b. Govt. insurance and pension funds	1.19	1.09	1.19	1.34
c. Commercial banks	3.97	4.40	5.28	5.66
d. Mutual savings banks	.09	.06	.06	.07
h. Life insurance	.72	.61	.61	.87
i. Fire and casualty insurance	.24	.24	.32	.53
k. Other private insurance	.37	.38	.39	.39
m. Other finance	.40	.38	.30	.39
6. State and local governments	1.45	1.32	1.27	1.27
7. Federal government	.50	.48	.50	.57
8. Total	21.17	21.04	22.45	24.66
9. Rest of world, assets	.10	.10	.10	.10
10. Total liabilities	21.27	21.14	22.55	24.76

Line

1 Line 8 minus lines 4-7.
4-7 Line II-14 of Tables III-4 through III-7.
8 Line 10 minus line 9.
9 Goldsmith, *National Wealth*, Table B-186, line 10.
10 Table IV-c-12, line 6.

1949	1950	1951	1952	1953	1954	1955	1956	1957	1958	
13.77	14.15	14.46	15.62	17.23	17.89	19.57	21.25	23.37	24.79	1.
										2.
										3.
.46	.53	.58	.64	.73	1.06	1.24	1.35	1.50	1.63	4.
10.74	13.03	14.69	16.23	18.35	21.84	23.41	24.79	27.12	31.23	5.
1.55	1.74	1.81	1.94	2.18	2.49	2.83	3.23	3.68	4.14	b.
6.55	8.12	9.20	10.19	10.82	12.59	12.70	12.90	13.92	16.50	c.
.09	.09	.15	.32	.41	.60	.64	.67	.68	.73	d.
1.05	1.15	1.17	1.15	1.30	1.85	2.04	2.27	2.38	2.68	h.
.75	1.06	1.45	1.87	2.62	3.40	4.19	4.82	5.44	6.15	i.
.38	.37	.36	.36	.37	.39	.44	.44	.42	.43	k.
.37	.50	.55	.40	.65	.52	.57	.46	.60	.60	m.
1.55	1.85	1.98	2.08	2.17	2.20	2.25	2.32	2.39	2.44	6.
.49	.56	.82	1.14	.81	.48	.48	.56	.76	.97	7.
27.01	30.12	32.53	35.71	39.29	43.47	46.95	50.27	55.14	61.06	8.
.10	.10	.10	.10	.10	.10	.10	.10	.10	.10	9.
27.11	30.22	32.63	35.81	39.39	43.57	47.05	50.37	55.24	61.16	10.

TABLE IV-b-14a

State and Local Government Securities, Assets, 1900-45, Selected Years

(million dollars)

	1900	1912	1922	1929	1933	1939	1945[a]
1. Nonfarm households	521	1,451	4,983	7,642	9,478	8,274	6,939
2. Nonfarm unincorporated business							
3. Agriculture							
4. Nonfinancial corporations	50	100	337	644	607	379	278
5. Finance	889	1,729	2,854	4,956	5,908	8,054	6,579
a. Federal Reserve Banks and Treasury monetary funds				12	1		
b. Govt. insurance and pension funds	5	15	132	459	692	1,313	1,100
c. Commercial banks	181	526	1,132	2,057	2,635	3,497	3,981
d. Mutual savings banks	580	787	699	908	904	620	93
e. Savings and loan associations		3	9	31	32	12	36
f. Investment companies			1	2	3	6	1
h. Life insurance	71	183	363	574	864	1,758	722
i. Fire and casualty insurance	39	119	228	427	321	316	274
k. Other private insurance	13	96	290	486	456	532	372
6. State and local governments	554	1,150	2,210	3,631	3,041	2,762	1,633
7. Federal government					50	296	484
8. Total	2,014	4,430	10,384	16,873	19,084	19,765	15,913

Notes to Table IV-b-14a

Line	
1	Line 8 minus the sum of lines 4-7.
4	Table III-4b, line II-14.
5	Goldsmith, *Financial Intermediaries*, Table A-1, line 22, plus Table A-7, line 21, plus Table A-18, line 21, minus Table A-24, line 12. These incorporate the following revisions of, or additions to, estimates in Goldsmith, *A Study of Saving*: Federal Reserve Banks—an additional $12 million in 1929 and $1 million in 1933 (*Financial Intermediaries*, Table A-2, line 11, for which there is no comparable estimate in *A Study of Saving*); life insurance—an additional $103 million in 1945 (revision in *Financial Intermediaries*, Table A-8, line 27, of figures in *A Study of Saving*, Vol. I, Table I-6, col. 2); fraternal orders—an addition of $50 million in 1939 and subtraction of $65 million in 1945 (revision in *Financial Intermediaries*, Table A-9, line 20, of figures in *A Study of Saving*, Vol. I, Table I-10, col. 8). In addition there are some minor unidentifiable revisions in the *Financial Intermediaries* estimates which are included in the total here.
5a	Goldsmith, *Financial Intermediaries*, Table A-2, line 11.
5b	*Ibid.*, Table A-11, line 9.
5c	*Ibid.*, Table A-3, line 32, plus Table A-4, line 24.
5d	*Ibid.*, Table A-5, line 25.
5e	*Ibid.*, Table A-19, line 11.
5f	*Ibid.*, Table A-21, line 18.
5h	*Ibid.*, Table A-8, line 27.
5i	*Ibid.*, Table A-12, line 20, plus Table A-13, line 20.
5k	*Ibid.*, Table A-9, line 20, plus Table A-14, line 10.
6	Table III-6a, line II-14.
7	Table III-7f, line II-14.
8	Goldsmith, *A Study of Saving*, Vol. III, Table W-18, line II-13.

[a]The 1945 figures in this table have been superseded by those in Table IV-b-14, but they are included here for comparability with earlier years.

TABLE IV-b-15

Other Bonds and Notes, Assets
(billion dollars)

	1945	1946	1947	1948
1. Nonfarm households	9.29	7.92	7.23	6.95
2. Nonfarm unincorporated business				
3. Agriculture				
4. Nonfinancial corporations	.18	.22	.34	.48
5. Finance	17.70	20.25	24.10	29.27
b. Govt. insurance and pension funds	.14	.14	.15	.21
c. Commercial banks	2.96	3.31	3.37	3.17
d. Mutual savings banks	1.02	1.19	1.51	2.01
f. Investment companies	.22	.20	.18	.19
h. Life insurance	11.30	13.11	16.13	20.36
i. Fire and casualty insurance	.46	.46	.52	.69
j. Noninsured pension plans	.78	1.04	1.35	1.70
k. Other private insurance	.50	.56	.62	.68
m. Other finance	.32	.24	.27	.26
6. State and local governments	.29	.30	.34	.51
7. Federal government				
8. Total	27.46	28.69	32.01	37.21
9. Rest of world, assets	.17	.13	.09	.04
10. Rest of world, liabilities	2.73	2.64	2.66	2.74
11. Total liabilities	24.90	26.18	29.44	34.51

Line

1	Line 8 minus lines 4-6.
4-6	Line II-15 of Tables III-4 through III-6.
8	Sum of lines 10 and 11, minus line 9.
9	Goldsmith, *National Wealth*, Table B-186, line 9.
10	*Ibid.*, Table B-185, lines 7 and 8.
11	Sum of lines 4, 5, and 7b of Table IV-c-12.

1949	1950	1951	1952	1953	1954	1955	1956	1957	1958	
6.32	6.35	6.42	6.27	6.39	5.42	7.33	8.99	10.84	11.12	1.
										2.
										3.
.62	.65	.95	1.36	1.54	1.47	1.88	2.11	2.94	2.68	4.
32.98	35.93	39.96	45.01	49.47	53.77	57.15	61.03	68.35	74.30	5.
.36	.51	.75	1.09	1.49	1.98	2.57	3.20	4.16	5.31	b.
3.32	3.90	3.77	3.55	3.43	3.29	3.53	2.89	3.49	3.52	c.
2.15	2.07	2.20	2.57	2.86	2.95	2.69	2.82	3.56	4.11	d.
.21	.25	.30	.40	.41	.55	.73	.84	.98	1.22	f.
22.93	24.76	27.47	30.57	33.28	35.38	37.13	39.28	41.95	44.37	h.
.78	.83	.88	1.04	1.16	1.19	1.18	1.21	1.39	1.48	i.
2.04	2.48	3.36	4.42	5.49	6.70	7.61	9.20	10.93	12.44	j.
.74	.79	.85	.92	.99	1.05	1.07	1.13	1.16	1.24	k.
.45	.34	.38	.45	.36	.68	.64	.46	.73	.61	m.
.50	.56	.66	.59	.64	.84	.88	.89	.79	.67	6.
										7.
40.42	43.49	47.99	53.23	58.04	61.50	67.24	73.02	82.92	88.77	8.
.08	.08	.09	.13	.17	.20	.16	.21	.32	.36	9.
2.73	3.34	3.74	3.76	3.71	3.49	3.27	3.68	4.10	4.53	10.
37.77	40.23	44.34	49.60	54.50	58.21	64.13	69.55	79.14	84.60	11.

TABLE IV-b-15a

Corporate Bonds, Assets, 1900-45, Selected Years

(million dollars)

	1900	1912	1922	1929	1933	1939	1945[a]
1. Nonfarm households	3,323	9,481	15,923	24,078	24,577	16,836	9,751
2. Nonfarm unincorporated business							
3. Agriculture							
4. Nonfinancial corporations				543	83	112	
5. Finance	1,828	5,043	7,762	13,465	13,043	14,692	16,135
b. Govt. insurance and pension funds			4	18	28	58	131
c. Commercial banks	675	2,024	3,363	4,734	4,112	3,421	2,846
d. Mutual savings banks	444	966	1,240	2,018	2,118	1,370	934
f. Investment companies			14	132	96	127	228
h. Life insurance	547	1,591	2,219	4,666	5,117	8,277	10,060
i. Fire and casualty insurance	111	350	645	1,273	979	661	383
j. Noninsured pension plans			55	300	420	578	1,045
k. Other private insurance	1	12	18	74	122	149	455
m. Other finance	50	100	204	250	51	51	53
6. State and local governments							
7. Federal government			2	13	45	862	
8. Total[b]	5,151	14,524	23,687	38,099	37,748	32,502	25,886

Notes to Table IV-b-15a

Line	
1	Line 8 minus the sum of lines 4, 5, and 7.
4	Table III-4b-1, line 4.
5	1900-39: Sum of Goldsmith, *A Study of Saving*, Vol. III, Table W-37, line II-14, and Table W-41, line II-14; plus Goldsmith, *Financial Intermediaries*, Table A-1, line 20, minus Table III-4b-1, line 4, in this volume.
	1945: Same as 1900-39, except that $28 million is added to investment companies' holdings and $404 million to noninsured pension plan holdings to take account of Goldsmith's revisions in *Financial Intermediaries* of data originally given in his *A Study of Saving*. For investment companies, the relevant tables were: *Financial Intermediaries*, Table A-21, lines 10 and 20, and *A Study of Saving*, Vol. I, Tables V-60 (column 4), V-62 (column 4), and V-72 (column 8). For noninsured pension plans, the sources were: *Financial Intermediaries*, Table A-10, line 5, and *A Study of Saving*, Vol. I, Table I-16.
5b	Goldsmith, *Financial Intermediaries*, Table A-11, line 6.
5c	*Ibid.*, Table A-3, line 25, plus Table A-4, line 22.
5d	*Ibid.*, Table A-5, line 20.
5f	*Ibid.*, Table A-21, line 10.
5h	*Ibid.*, Table A-8, line 19.
5i	*Ibid.*, Table A-12, line 12, plus Table A-13, line 12.
5j	*Ibid.*, Table A-10, line 5.
5k	*Ibid.*, Table A-9, line 15, plus Table A-14, line 8.
5m	Line 5 minus the sum of lines 5b through 5k.
7	Table III-7f, line II-15.
8	Goldsmith, *A Study of Saving*, Table W-18, line II-14.

[a]The 1945 figures in this table have been superseded by those in Table IV-b-15; they are included here for comparability with earlier years.

[b]Government corporation obligations fully guaranteed by the U.S. government are included in this table and excluded from U.S. Government Securities, Table IV-b-13d. In the postwar tables they are included with U.S. government securities. The amounts are as follows: 1933—$180 million; 1939—$5,704 million; 1945—$567 million (see Goldsmith, *A Study of Saving*, Vol. III, note to Table W-40, p. 95).

TABLE IV-b-16

Preferred Stock, Assets
(billion dollars)

	1945	1946	1947	1948
1. Nonfarm households	8.15	8.15	8.46	8.74
2. Nonfarm unincorporated business				
3. Agriculture				
4. Nonfinancial corporations	3.47	3.48	3.49	3.50
5. Finance	1.83	2.01	2.12	2.19
b. Govt. insurance and pension funds	.02	.02	.02	.03
f. Investment companies	.25	.24	.25	.27
h. Life insurance	.82	.97	1.03	1.06
i. Fire and casualty insurance	.59	.60	.60	.59
j. Noninsured pension plans	.09	.12	.16	.18
k. Other private insurance	.04	.05	.05	.05
m. Other finance	.02	.01	.01	.01
6. State and local governments				
7. Federal government				
8. Total	13.45	13.64	14.07	14.43
9. Rest of world, assets	.28	.28	.27	.25
10. Total outstanding	13.73	13.92	14.34	14.68

Line

1 Line 8 minus lines 4 and 5.

4-5m Line II-16 of Tables III-4 through III-5m.

8 Line 10 minus line 9.

9 See note to line 9, Table IV-b-17.

10 1949: Goldsmith, *Financial Intermediaries*, Appendix F (supplement), Table F-5.

1945-48 and 1950-58: Cumulated from 1949 figure by the sum of new issues of preferred stock (*Federal Reserve Bulletin*, e.g., December 1956, p. 1346) and sales to individuals of preferred stock of new corporations (see notes to Table IV-b-17a, line 9) minus issues called for payment (see notes to Table IV-b-17a, line 4) and minus conversions of preferred into common (Table IV-b-17a, line 5).

1949	1950	1951	1952	1953	1954	1955	1956	1957	1958	
8.75	8.69	9.14	9.42	9.45	9.44	9.30	9.90	10.33	10.37	1.
										2.
										3.
3.50	3.51	3.51	3.52	3.52	3.53	3.54	3.54	3.55	3.55	4.
2.50	2.81	2.94	3.12	3.47	3.88	4.08	3.95	3.92	4.36	5.
.03	.04	.05	.06	.08	.10	.13	.15	.19	.25	b.
.27	.30	.34	.29	.46	.54	.65	.73	.62	.93	f.
1.26	1.45	1.40	1.49	1.53	1.73	1.74	1.55	1.52	1.56	h.
.65	.68	.72	.80	.85	.90	.90	.82	.84	.83	i.
.21	.27	.36	.41	.48	.53	.58	.64	.68	.73	j.
.06	.06	.05	.05	.05	.05	.05	.04	.04	.04	k.
.02	.01	.02	.02	.02	.03	.03	.02	.03	.02	m.
										6.
										7.
14.75	15.01	15.59	16.06	16.44	16.85	16.92	17.39	17.80	18.28	8.
.25	.25	.27	.27	.28	.30	.31	.32	.32	.33	9.
15.00	15.26	15.86	16.33	16.72	17.15	17.23	17.71	18.12	18.61	10.

TABLE IV-b-17

Common Stock, Assets

(billion dollars)

	1945	1946	1947	1948
1. Nonfarm households	103.47	92.27	90.20	90.41
2. Nonfarm unincorporated business				
3. Agriculture				
4. Nonfinancial corporations	24.20	21.67	21.26	21.39
5. Finance	5.53	5.41	5.55	5.74
b. Govt. insurance and pension funds	.02	.02	.02	.03
c. Commercial banks	.22	.19	.16	.16
d. Mutual savings banks	.14	.15	.15	.16
f. Investment companies	2.65	2.56	2.52	2.56
h. Life insurance	.18	.28	.36	.37
i. Fire and casualty insurance	1.81	1.73	1.76	1.82
j. Noninsured pension plans	.20	.24	.32	.40
k. Other private insurance	.01	.02	.02	.02
m. Other finance	.30	.22	.24	.22
6. State and local governments				
7. Federal government				
8. Total	133.20	119.35	117.01	117.54
9. Rest of world, assets	2.73	2.41	2.21	2.05
10. Rest of world, liabilities	1.26	1.45	1.39	1.34
11. Total domestic outstanding	134.67	120.31	117.83	118.25

Line	
1	Line 8 minus lines 4 and 5.
4-5m	Line II-17 of Tables III-4 through III-5m.
8	Sum of lines 10 and 11, minus line 9.
9	The ratio of total stock held by "rest of the world" (Goldsmith, *National Wealth*, Table B-186, line 5) to total domestic stock outstanding (sum of Table IV-b-17a, line 18, and Table IV-b-16, line 10), multiplied by total domestic common stock outstanding (line 18, Table IV-b-17a).
10	Foreign stock outstanding at end-of-period prices (Table IV-b-17a, line 19).
11	Total domestic common stock outstanding at end-of-period prices (Table IV-b-17a, line 20).

1949	1950	1951	1952	1953	1954	1955	1956	1957	1958	
101.09	125.38	142.96	154.00	151.93	211.34	260.63	273.23	245.79	332.62	1.
										2.
										3.
24.20	29.67	33.65	36.11	35.46	49.13	60.09	62.54	56.12	75.45	4.
7.24	8.80	10.97	13.30	14.11	21.25	26.69	28.39	27.78	39.10	5.
.03	.04	.05	.06	.08	.10	.13	.15	.19	.25	b.
.15	.15	.14	.15	.15	.15	.16	.16	.18	.19	c.
.16	.18	.23	.34	.43	.57	.66	.70	.77	.86	d.
3.24	4.04	5.17	6.29	6.47	9.74	12.10	12.63	11.89	17.15	f.
.46	.65	.82	.96	1.04	1.54	1.89	1.95	1.87	2.55	h.
2.30	2.76	3.15	3.52	3.61	5.04	6.02	6.40	5.83	7.51	i.
.51	.67	1.03	1.55	1.96	3.46	5.07	5.95	6.36	10.07	j.
.02	.03	.04	.04	.04	.06	.06	.06	.06	.08	k.
.37	.28	.34	.39	.33	.59	.60	.39	.63	.44	m.
										6.
										7.
132.53	163.85	187.58	203.41	201.50	281.72	347.41	364.16	329.69	447.17	8.
2.24	2.68	3.18	3.43	3.37	4.96	6.27	6.64	5.77	7.97	9.
1.07	.99	1.01	.91	.72	1.64	2.21	2.17	1.85	3.10	10.
133.70	165.54	189.75	205.93	204.15	285.04	351.47	368.63	333.61	452.04	11.

TABLE IV-b-17-a

Estimate of New Issues of Common Stock and Total Stock Outstanding, Assets

(dollar values in millions)

	1945	1946	1947	1948
1. All domestic stocks	1,533	2,459	1,867	1,632
2. Preferred stocks	758	1,126	761	492
3. Common stock, gross	775	1,333	1,106	1,140
4. Estimated retirements	193	233	164	245
5. Conversions of preferred into common	50	50	50	50
6. New bank and insurance stock included in line 1				
7. NBER estimate of new bank stock		53	44	21
8. NBER estimate of new insurance stock		39	32	−2
9. Sales of stock by privately held corporations	213	496	515	476
10. Net new stock issues, domestic		1,738	1,583	1,440
11. Net new stock issues, foreign		0	−15	15
12. Net new stock issues, total		1,738	1,568	1,455
13. Ratio: end-of-year to initial prices (%)		88.19	96.65	99.17
14. Average monthly stock price index	60.48	69.64	61.22	61.92
15. Ratio: end-of-year to average prices (%)	117.03	89.63	98.55	96.62
16. New issues at end-of-year prices		1,558	1,560	1,391
17. Initial stock at end-of-year prices		118,745	116,273	116,855
18. Total stock at end-of-year prices	134,667	120,303	117,833	118,246
19. Foreign stock outstanding	1,258	1,454	1,387	1,345
20. Total domestic and foreign stock outstanding	135,925	121,757	119,220	119,591

Line

1 SEC data on net change in outstanding corporate securities—new stock issues (*Federal Reserve Bulletin*, e.g., December 1956, p. 1348).

2 SEC data on new security issues—preferred stock (*Federal Reserve Bulletin*, e.g., December 1956, p. 1346).

3 Line 1 minus line 2.

4 SEC worksheets on domestic corporate securities issued and retired—total stock retirements except issues called for payment.

5 Assumed to be $50 million a year.

6 SEC worksheets.

7 The change in capital accounts of all commercial banks (*Federal Reserve Bulletin*, e.g., May 1961, p. 557) minus change in preferred stock of banks held by RFC (*Treasury Bulletin*, Table on "Balance Sheets of U.S. Govt. Corporations and Certain other Business Type Activities" and FRB worksheets) and minus net additions to capital of all banks from profits. The last is the ratio of capital accounts of all banks (see above) to capital accounts of all insured commercial banks (*Annual Report, FDIC*, Table on assets and liabilities of operating banks in U.S.) multiplied by net additions to capital of insured commercial banks from profits (*Ibid.*, Table on earnings, expenses and dividends of insured commercial banks).

8 Change in capital stock of life insurance and fire and casualty insurance companies. For life insurance companies, sources are:
1945-48: Goldsmith, *A Study of Saving*, Vol. I, p. 450, Table I-2, col. 2.
1949-51: *Spectator Life Insurance Yearbook*, e.g., 1954, p. 224a.
1952-58: *Life Insurance Fact Book*, e.g., 1955, p. 56.
The source for fire and casualty insurance companies is *Best's Fire and Casualty Aggregates and Averages*, e.g., 1955, p. 16.

1949	1950	1951	1952	1953	1954	1955	1956	1957	1958	
1,864	2,418	3,366	3,335	2,898	3,862	4,903	5,267	4,712	5,088	1.
425	631	838	564	489	816	635	636	411	571	2.
1,439	1,787	2,528	2,771	2,409	3,046	4,268	4,631	4,301	4,517	3.
197	327	431	250	417	1,201	1,627	1,649	983	1,282	4.
50	50	50	50	50	50	50	50	50	50	5.
	111	147	153	144	224	32	286	236	43	6.
13	74	143	140	113	231	139	396	359	126	7.
83	123	10	43	93	77	142	115	81	56	8.
402	454	455	491	535	613	733	763	762	852	9.
1,790	2,050	2,608	3,092	2,639	2,592	3,673	4,028	4,334	4,276	10.
-18	24	-17	59	-51	256	173	111	35	332	11.
1,772	2,074	2,591	3,151	2,588	2,848	3,846	4,139	4,369	4,608	12.
111.40	122.10	112.98	106.81	97.83	138.13	121.91	103.75	89.42	133.99	13.
60.43	72.87	87.85	93.43	94.08	112.79	149.33	169.98	163.58	170.44	14.
110.29	111.68	104.66	105.11	102.12	117.65	108.33	98.74	91.75	117.99	15.
1,974	2,289	2,729	3,250	2,695	3,049	3,979	3,977	3,976	5,045	16.
131,726	163,248	187,024	202,675	201,456	281,993	347,495	364,654	329,630	446,999	17.
133,700	165,537	189,753	205,925	204,151	285,042	351,474	368,631	333,606	452,044	18.
1,071	991	1,010	914	719	1,637	2,207	2,173	1,853	3,095	19.
134,771	166,528	190,763	206,839	204,870	286,679	353,681	370,804	335,459	455,139	20.

Line

Line	
9	Total cash sales to individuals of stock of new corporations. This is estimated by using the product of the wholesale price index (*Federal Reserve Bulletin*, e.g., December 1956, p. 1356) and an index of incorporations on a 1946-48 base (Dun & Bradstreet, *Statistical Review*, section on new business incorporations in the U.S.) to extrapolate from a figure of \$600 million (the average annual purchase of stock in new corporations by individuals in 1945 to 1948 as estimated on the basis of data in Lawrence Bridge, "The Financing of Investment by New Firms," *Conference on Research in Business Finance*, National Bureau of Economic Research, New York, 1952). Ninety per cent of this amount was estimated to be common stock, on the basis of the relation between preferred and common stock of small corporations for 1931-46, as reported in *Statistics of Income*.
10	Sum of lines 3, 5, 7, 8, and 9, minus the sum of lines 4 and 6.
11	FRB worksheets.
12	Sum of lines 10 and 11.
13 through 15	Table 39, Vol. I of this study.
16	Line 10 multiplied by line 15.
17	1945-49: Line 18 minus line 16. 1950-58: Line 13 times preceding entry on line 18.
18	1945-48: entry for following year, line 17, divided by entry for following year, line 13. 1949: Goldsmith, *Financial Intermediaries*, Appendix F supplement, Table F-5. 1950-58: Line 16 plus line 17.
19	Goldsmith, *National Wealth*, Table B-185, lines 7 and 8, minus foreign bonds outstanding in U.S. (FRB worksheets).
20	Line 18 plus line 19.

TABLE IV-b-17b

Corporate Stock, Assets, 1900-45, Selected Years

(million dollars)

	1900	1912
1. Nonfarm households	10,704	30,112
2. Nonfarm unincorporated business		
3. Agriculture		
4. Nonfinancial corporations	2,818	7,134
5. Finance	380	740
c. Commercial banks	103	284
d. Mutual savings banks	43	41
f. Investment companies		
h. Life insurance	62	84
i. Fire and casualty insurance	121	230
j. Noninsured pension plans		
k. Other private insurance		
l. Finance companies		
m. Other finance	51	101
6. State and local governments		
7. Federal government		2
8. Total	13,902	37,988

Line	
1	Line 8 minus the sum of lines 4, 5, and 7.
4	Table III-4b, lines 16-17.
5	Table III-5o, lines 16-17.
5c	Goldsmith, *Financial Intermediaries*, Table A-3, line 29, plus Table A-4, line 23.
5d	*Ibid.*, Table A-5, line 24.
5f	*Ibid.*, Table A-21, line 14.
5h	*Ibid.*, Table A-8, line 23.
5i	*Ibid.*, Table A-12, line 16, plus Table A-13, line 16.
5j	*Ibid.*, Table A-10, line 6.

TABLE IV-b-18

Equity in Mutual Financial Organizations, Assets

(billion dollars)

	1945	1946	1947	1948
1. Nonfarm households	2.28	2.66	2.87	3.33
2. Nonfarm unincorporated business				
3. Agriculture				
4. Nonfinancial corporations				
5. Finance				
6. State and local governments				
7. Federal government				
8. Total	2.28	2.66	2.87	3.33

Table III-1, line II-18.

1922	1929	1933	1939	1945[a]	
55,520	138,296	57,113	73,231	115,790	1.
					2.
					3.
19,234	42,309	40,473	21,969	28,193	4.
1,339	6,080	3,869	4,359	6,516	5.
508	1,180	992	609	324	c.
48	77	136	136	166	d.
69	2,191	1,006	1,216	2,017	f.
75	352	535	568	999	h.
370	1,511	952	1,458	2,420	i.
18	100	140	210	347	j.
		1	12	43	k.
	19	7			l.
251	650	100	150	200	m.
					6.
		249	572	304	7.
76,093	186,685	101,704	100,131	150,803	8.

Line

5k *Ibid.*, Table A-9, line 19, plus Table A-14, line 9.
5l *Ibid.*, Table A-26, line 6 (1929 and 1933).
5m Line 5 minus the sum of lines 5c through 5m.
7 Table III-7f, line II-16.
8 Goldsmith, *A Study of Saving*, Vol. III, Table W-18, sum of lines II-15 and II-16.

[a] The 1945 figures in this table have been superseded by those in Tables IV-b-16 and IV-b-17; they are included here for comparability with earlier years.

1949	1950	1951	1952	1953	1954	1955	1956	1957	1958
3.71	4.03	4.28	4.59	4.99	5.49	6.10	6.74	7.36	8.04
3.71	4.03	4.28	4.59	4.99	5.49	6.10	6.74	7.36	8.04

TABLE IV-b-19

Equity in Other Business, Assets

(billion dollars)

	1945	1946	1947	1948
1. Nonfarm households	42.13	51.45	59.20	65.22
2. Nonfarm unincorporated business				
3. Agriculture				
4. Nonfinancial corporations				
5. Finance				
6. State and local governments				
7. Federal government	2.34	2.34	.55	.54
8. Total	44.47	53.79	59.75	65.76

Line

1 Table III-1, line II-19.
7 Table III-7, line II-19.
8 Sum of lines 1 and 7.

TABLE IV-b-20

Other Intangible Assets

(million dollars)

	1945	1946	1947	1948
1. Nonfarm households	1.33	1.32	1.33	1.32
2. Nonfarm unincorporated business				
3. Agriculture	1.38	1.54	1.71	1.88
4. Nonfinancial corporations	14.36	13.90	15.77	16.70
5. Finance	9.66	10.90	12.58	12.52
a. Federal Reserve Banks and Treasury monetary funds	2.27	2.65	3.11	3.02
c. Commercial banks	5.54	6.32	7.44	7.18
d. Mutual savings banks	.07	.07	.07	.08
e. Savings and loan associations	.43	.43	.43	.51
f. Investment companies	.03	.04	.03	.05
h. Life insurance	.96	1.03	1.09	1.24
i. Fire and casualty insurance	.14	.12	.14	.15
j. Noninsured pension plans	.04	.07	.10	.13
k. Other private insurance	.02	.03	.03	.03
m. Other finance	.16	.14	.14	.13
6. State and local governments				
7. Federal government	11.12	12.02	14.21	14.98
8. Total	37.85	39.68	45.60	47.40
9. U.S. direct investment abroad	6.72	7.23	8.37	9.62
10. Subscriptions to IMF and IRD		.32	3.38	3.38
11. Assets, adjusted	31.13	32.13	33.85	34.40
12. Discrepancy	8.69	9.53	10.73	12.94
13. Liabilities	39.82	41.66	44.58	47.34

Line

1-7 Line II-20 of Tables III-1 through III-7.
8 Sum of lines 1, 3, 4, 5, and 7.
9 Goldsmith, *National Wealth*, Table B-185, line 3.
10 *Federal Reserve Bulletin*, e.g., March 1959, p. 288.

1949	1950	1951	1952	1953	1954	1955	1956	1957	1958
65.17	71.76	78.94	80.29	82.52	82.72	86.15	91.65	97.17	98.24
.52	.49	.48	.48	.46	.45	.43	.43	.42	.42
65.69	72.25	79.42	80.77	82.98	83.17	86.58	92.08	97.59	98.66

1949	1950	1951	1952	1953	1954	1955	1956	1957	1958	
1.31	1.08	.85	.62	.61	.61	.61	.62	.62	.62	1.
										2.
2.06	2.28	2.48	2.72	2.87	3.11	3.25	3.42	3.59	3.81	3.
17.56	18.12	19.14	22.12	24.75	29.68	34.51	40.50	47.14	48.14	4.
13.25	17.44	18.11	19.11	19.67	20.29	25.26	27.25	28.38	29.78	5.
										a.
3.06	4.40	4.05	4.41	4.38	4.10	5.67	5.88	5.92	5.78	
7.58	10.02	10.60	10.72	10.73	10.99	13.96	14.90	15.11	16.07	c.
.10	.12	.17	.17	.20	.21	.23	.25	.28	.30	d.
.65	.67	.82	1.03	1.26	1.53	1.57	1.77	2.11	2.38	e.
.03	.04	.04	.04	.04	.04	.07	.05	.06	.07	f.
1.33	1.59	1.77	1.95	2.07	2.27	2.48	2.79	3.05	3.25	h.
.17	.19	.24	.28	.34	.39	.43	.47	.55	.55	i.
.16	.19	.22	.30	.41	.52	.58	.82	.93	.98	j.
.03	.04	.04	.04	.05	.05	.06	.07	.08	.08	k.
.14	.18	.16	.17	.19	.19	.21	.25	.29	.32	m.
										6.
12.89	20.36	24.98	21.82	22.35	19.22	23.24	22.03	20.54	18.28	7.
47.07	59.28	65.56	66.39	70.25	72.91	86.87	93.82	100.27	100.63	8.
10.70	11.79	13.09	14.82	16.33	17.63	19.31	22.18	25.24	27.08	9.
3.38	3.38	3.38	3.38	3.38	3.38	3.38	3.42	3.42	3.42	10.
32.99	44.11	49.09	48.19	50.54	51.90	64.18	68.22	71.61	70.13	11.
15.15	13.30	16.58	18.46	20.12	20.80	17.15	18.66	20.04	23.71	12.
48.14	57.41	65.67	66.65	70.66	72.70	81.33	86.88	91.65	93.84	13.

Line

11 Line 8 minus lines 9 and 10.

12 Line 13 minus line 11.

13 Table IV-c-13, line 8.

TABLE IV-c-1

Currency and Demand Deposits, Liabilities

(billion dollars)

	1945	1946	1947	1948
1. Nonfarm households				
2. Nonfarm unincorporated business				
3. Agriculture				
4. Nonfinancial corporations				
5. Finance	185.24	170.36	179.97	182.05
a. Federal Reserve Banks and Treasury monetary funds	65.36	65.50	71.47	75.40
c. Commercial banks	119.88	104.86	108.50	106.65
6. State and local governments				
7. Federal government	2.31	2.44	2.41	2.40
8. Total	187.55	172.80	182.38	184.45

Line	
5	Sum of lines 5a and 5c.
5a	Table III-5a, line III-1.
5c	Table III-5c, line III-1.
7	Table III-7, line III-1.
8	Sum of lines 5 and 7.

TABLE IV-c-2

Other Bank Deposits and Shares, Liabilities

(billion dollars)

	1945	1946	1947	1948
1. Nonfarm households				
2. Nonfarm unincorporated business				
3. Agriculture				
4. Nonfinancial corporations				
5. Finance	53.48	60.03	63.62	66.19
c. Commercial banks	30.34	34.17	35.60	36.23
d. Mutual savings banks	15.38	16.87	17.75	18.39
e. Savings and loan associations	7.39	8.56	9.76	10.97
g. Credit unions	.37	.43	.51	.60
6. State and local governments				
7. Federal government	3.02	3.38	3.52	3.45
8. Total	56.50	63.41	67.14	69.64

Line	
5	Sum of lines 5c, 5d, 5e, and 5g.
5c-7	Line III-2 of Tables III-5c through III-7.
8	Sum of lines 5 and 7.

1949	1950	1951	1952	1953	1954	1955	1956	1957	1958	
										1.
										2.
										3.
										4.
179.36	188.71	199.64	206.62	206.27	208.97	215.69	219.67	218.93	223.18	5.
										a.
70.84	70.41	73.49	75.44	74.73	73.18	73.74	74.52	75.43	73.03	
108.52	118.30	126.15	131.18	131.54	135.79	141.95	145.15	143.50	150.15	c.
										6.
2.38	2.36	2.40	2.44	2.47	2.50	2.51	2.53	2.56	2.60	7.
181.74	191.07	202.04	209.06	208.74	211.47	218.20	222.20	221.49	225.78	8.

1949	1950	1951	1952	1953	1954	1955	1956	1957	1958	
										1.
										2.
										3.
										4.
69.17	71.81	76.73	84.86	94.01	104.50	112.95	122.36	134.69	151.62	5.
36.73	36.96	38.69	41.76	45.16	48.97	50.30	52.37	57.82	65.86	c.
19.27	20.01	20.89	22.59	24.36	26.30	28.13	30.00	31.66	34.01	d.
12.47	13.99	16.11	19.20	22.85	27.25	32.14	37.15	41.91	47.98	e.
.70	.85	1.04	1.31	1.64	1.98	2.38	2.84	3.30	3.77	g.
										6.
3.31	3.04	2.82	2.66	2.47	2.24	1.99	1.74	1.42	1.22	7.
72.48	74.85	79.55	87.52	96.48	106.74	114.94	124.10	136.11	152.84	8.

TABLE IV-c-3

Private Life Insurance Reserves, Liabilities

(billion dollars)

	1945	1946	1947	1948
1. Nonfarm households				
2. Nonfarm unincorporated business				
3. Agriculture				
4. Nonfinancial corporations				
5. Finance	45.34	49.11	52.68	56.51
h. Life insurance	43.57	47.24	50.70	54.44
k. Other private insurance	1.77	1.87	1.98	2.07
6. State and local governments				
7. Federal government				
8. Total	45.34	49.11	52.68	56.51

Line

5	Sum of lines 5h and 5k.
5h	Table III-5h, line III-3.
5k	Table III-5k, line III-3.
8	Same as line 5.

TABLE IV-c-4

Private Pension and Retirement Funds, Liabilities

(billion dollars)

	1945	1946	1947	1948
1. Nonfarm households				
2. Nonfarm unincorporated business				
3. Agriculture				
4. Nonfinancial corporations				
5. Finance	2.68	3.25	3.90	4.55
j. Noninsured pension plans	2.68	3.25	3.90	4.55
6. State and local governments				
7. Federal government				
8. Total	2.68	3.25	3.90	4.55

Table III-5j, line III-4.

1949	1950	1951	1952	1953	1954	1955	1956	1957	1958	
										1.
										2.
										3.
										4.
60.65	64.99	69.31	74.47	79.64	85.68	91.65	97.10	102.20	108.51	5.
58.45	62.67	66.85	71.85	76.84	82.68	88.42	93.71	98.79	104.87	h.
2.20	2.32	2.46	2.62	2.80	3.00	3.23	3.39	3.41	3.64	k.
										6.
										7.
60.65	64.99	69.31	74.47	79.64	85.68	91.65	97.10	102.20	108.51	8.

1949	1950	1951	1952	1953	1954	1955	1956	1957	1958	
										1.
										2.
										3.
										4.
5.26	6.23	7.80	9.52	11.42	14.34	17.35	20.02	22.28	27.80	5.
5.26	6.23	7.80	9.52	11.42	14.34	17.35	20.02	22.28	27.80	j.
										6.
										7.
5.26	6.23	7.80	9.52	11.42	14.34	17.35	20.02	22.28	27.80	8.

TABLE IV-c-5

Government Pension and Insurance Funds, Liabilities

(billion dollars)

	1945	1946	1947	1948
1. Nonfarm households				
2. Nonfarm unincorporated business				
3. Agriculture				
4. Nonfinancial corporations				
5. Finance	25.83	29.50	33.38	36.86
b. Govt. insurance and pension funds	25.83	29.50	33.38	36.86
6. State and local governments				
7. Federal government				
8. Total	25.83	29.50	33.38	36.86

Table III-5b, line III-5.

TABLE IV-c-6

Consumer Debt, Liabilities

(billion dollars)

	1945	1946	1947	1948
1. Nonfarm households	5.36	8.01	11.20	14.00
2. Nonfarm unincorporated business				
3. Agriculture	.35	.46	.56	.65
4. Nonfinancial corporations				
5. Finance				
6. State and local governments				
7. Federal government				
8. Total	5.71	8.47	11.76	14.65

Line

1 Line 8 minus line 3.

3 Non-real estate debt to nonreporting creditors (*Balance Sheet of Agriculture*, e.g., 1958, Table 1) minus farm business trade debt (Table III-3, line III-7) and minus farmers' life insurance company policy loans (see note to Table III-3, line III-10).

8 Table IV-b-6, line 8.

1949	1950	1951	1952	1953	1954	1955	1956	1957	1958	
										1.
										2.
										3.
										4.
39.40	40.71	44.78	49.13	52.51	55.20	58.44	62.02	64.87	66.10	5.
39.40	40.71	44.78	49.13	52.51	55.20	58.44	62.02	64.87	66.10	b.
										6.
										7.
39.40	40.71	44.78	49.13	52.51	55.20	58.44	62.02	64.87	66.10	8.

1949	1950	1951	1952	1953	1954	1955	1956	1957	1958	
16.95	20.94	22.29	26.99	30.92	31.93	38.19	41.89	44.75	44.77	1.
										2.
.64	.83	.82	.91	.90	.99	1.18	1.17	1.15	1.33	3.
										4.
										5.
										6.
										7.
17.59	21.77	23.11	27.90	31.82	32.92	39.37	43.06	45.90	46.10	8.

TABLE IV-c-7

Trade Debt, Liabilities

(billion dollars)

	1945	1946	1947	1948
1. Nonfarm households	.52	.59	.68	.76
2. Nonfarm unincorporated business	3.42	3.33	2.80	3.56
3. Agriculture	.70	.90	1.10	1.40
4. Nonfinancial corporations	19.72	23.45	28.09	28.53
5. Finance	.03	.02	.03	.04
g. Credit unions	.03	.02	.03	.04
6. State and local governments	.55	.70	.85	1.00
7. Federal government	2.70	.70	0	0
8. Total	27.64	29.69	33.55	35.29

Line

1 Trade debt of nonprofit organizations (FRB worksheets).

2 Noncorporate business trade debt was derived from FRB worksheet series on short-term payables to nonbanks. We subtracted from this series loans made by finance companies to noncorporate business (one-half of line II-10, Table III-51) since such loans would not fit our definition of trade debt.

3 Table III-3, line III-7.

4 Meiselman and Shapiro, "Corporate Sources," Table C-1b, line 1 minus lines 2 and 3, and finance company loans to corporate business (one-half of line II-10, Table III-51)—see note to line 2 above.

TABLE IV-c-8

Loans on Securities, Liabilities

(billion dollars)

	1945	1946	1947	1948
1. Nonfarm households	3.34	1.86	1.80	1.68
2. Nonfarm unincorporated business				
3. Agriculture				
4. Nonfinancial corporations	1.40	.49	.16	0
5. Finance	3.74	1.70	.99	1.50
h. Life insurance	.37	0	0	0
m. Other finance	3.37	1.70	.99	1.50
6. State and local governments				
7. Federal government				
8. Total	8.48	4.05	2.95	3.18

Line

1 Sum of the following four items:

a. 125 per cent of Table III-5m-1a, column 1.

b. Commercial bank loans on securities to individuals

1945-46: loans on securities to other than brokers and dealers (*Annual Report, Comptroller of the Currency*, e.g., 1946, Table 29, p. 119) less loans to nonindividuals of $1,771 million in 1945 and $487 million in 1946 (FRB worksheets).

1947-58: *Federal Reserve Bulletin*, e.g., December 1956, p. 1332, less loans to nonindividuals of $165 million in 1947 (FRB worksheets).

c. Line 5d of Table IV-b-8.

d. Foreign customers' debit balances with brokers and dealers (*Treasury Bulletin*, e.g., March 1959, p. 78).

1949	1950	1951	1952	1953	1954	1955	1956	1957	1958	
.80	.90	.90	1.14	1.20	1.30	1.42	1.59	1.73	1.83	1.
3.78	4.52	3.83	4.14	5.24	6.56	7.16	8.10	8.78	9.00	2.
1.60	1.80	2.20	2.30	2.10	2.10	2.10	2.10	2.20	2.30	3.
27.19	35.20	37.48	41.07	41.23	44.63	54.87	60.48	62.50	68.78	4.
.06	.07	.06	.10	.12	.13	.15	.18	.19	.21	5.
.06	.07	.06	.10	.12	.13	.15	.18	.19	.21	g.
1.10	1.20	1.20	1.30	1.40	1.55	1.70	1.80	1.85	2.00	6.
0	1.10	2.70	2.80	2.60	2.37	2.28	2.61	2.77	2.83	7.
34.53	44.79	48.37	52.85	53.89	58.64	69.68	76.86	80.02	86.95	8.

Line

5	Same as line 5g.
5g	Table III-5g, line III-7.
6	Table III-6, line III-7.
7	Table III-7, line III-7.
8	Sum of lines 1 through 7.

1949	1950	1951	1952	1953	1954	1955	1956	1957	1958	
2.00	2.78	2.63	2.84	3.36	4.64	5.39	5.34	4.88	6.20	1.
										2.
										3.
0	0	0	0	0	0	0	0	0	0	4.
1.95	2.02	1.83	2.31	2.61	3.28	3.60	2.98	3.08	3.42	5.
0	0	0	0	0	0	0	0	0	0	h.
1.95	2.02	1.83	2.31	2.61	3.28	3.60	2.98	3.08	3.42	m.
										6.
										7.
3.95	4.80	4.46	5.15	5.97	7.92	8.99	8.32	7.96	9.62	8.

Line

4	Table III-4, line III-8.
5	Sum of lines 5h and 5m.
5h	Table III-5h, line III-8.
5m	Table III-5m, line III-8.
8	Sum of lines 1, 4, and 5.

TABLE IV-c-9

Bank Loans, N.E.C., Liabilities

(billion dollars)

	1945	1946	1947	1948
1. Nonfarm households	.88	.59	.34	.44
2. Nonfarm unincorporated business	3.15	4.60	6.82	6.12
3. Agriculture	1.04	1.29	1.59	1.95
4. Nonfinancial corporations	6.42	9.40	11.06	12.12
5. Finance	1.17	1.76	2.38	2.84
c. Commercial banks	.22	.05	.07	.06
d. Mutual savings banks	a	a	a	a
e. Savings and loan associations	.14	.11	.11	.07
l. Finance companies	.81	1.60	2.20	2.71
6. State and local governments				
7. Federal government	.31	.10	.07	.92
8. Total	12.97	17.74	22.26	24.39

Line

1	Bank loans, n.e.c., of nonprofit organizations (FRB worksheets).
2	Line 8 minus lines 1, 3, 4, 5, and 7.
3-7	Line III-9 of Tables III-3 through III-7.
8	Table IV-b-9, line 10.

TABLE IV-c-9a

Short-Term Bank Loans, N.E.C., Liabilities

(billion dollars)

	1945	1946	1947	1948
1. Nonfarm households	.88	.59	.34	.44
2. Nonfarm unincorporated business	2.68	3.83	5.85	5.10
3. Agriculture	1.04	1.29	1.59	1.95
4. Nonfinancial corporations	4.03	5.52	6.13	6.69
5. Finance	1.17	1.76	2.38	2.84
c. Commercial banks	.22	.05	.07	.06
d. Mutual savings banks	0	0	0	0
e. Savings and loan associations	.14	.11	.11	.07
l. Finance companies	.81	1.60	2.20	2.71
6. State and local governments				
7. Federal government	.31	.10	.07	.92
8. Total	10.11	13.09	16.36	17.94

Table IV-c-9 minus Table IV-c-9b.

1949	1950	1951	1952	1953	1954	1955	1956	1957	1958	
.44	.71	.70	.64	.56	.68	1.36	1.49	1.70	2.12	1.
5.83	7.96	7.16	7.64	7.45	8.56	10.05	10.72	10.63	12.45	2.
2.05	2.52	3.12	3.19	2.76	2.93	3.31	3.28	3.60	4.16	3.
10.19	12.34	17.30	18.49	18.33	17.11	19.38	24.76	26.82	25.94	4.
3.23	4.29	4.25	5.16	5.02	5.02	7.77	7.14	6.77	5.69	5.
.02	.09	.03	.19	.06	.03	.16	.08	.08	.07	c.
a	a	a	a	a	a	a	a	a	.01	d.
.07	.08	.09	.08	.08	.08	.13	.12	.11	.15	e.
3.14	4.12	4.13	4.89	4.88	4.91	7.48	6.94	6.58	5.46	l.
										6.
1.00	.38	.29	.72	2.20	2.27	1.17	.88	.46	.81	7.
22.74	28.20	32.82	35.84	36.32	36.57	43.04	48.27	49.98	51.17	8.

[a]Under $5 million.

1949	1950	1951	1952	1953	1954	1955	1956	1957	1958	
.44	.71	.70	.64	.56	.68	1.36	1.49	1.70	2.12	1.
4.80	6.73	5.63	6.01	5.74	6.80	8.10	8.45	8.22	10.02	2.
2.05	2.52	3.12	3.19	2.76	2.93	3.31	3.28	3.60	4.16	3.
5.63	7.13	11.25	11.30	11.38	10.18	11.22	13.95	14.61	13.23	4.
3.23	4.29	4.25	5.16	5.02	5.02	7.77	7.14	6.77	5.69	5.
.02	.09	.03	.19	.06	.03	.16	.08	.08	.07	c.
0	0	0	0	0	0	0	0	0	.01	d.
.07	.08	.09	.08	.08	.08	.13	.12	.11	.15	e.
3.14	4.12	4.13	4.89	4.88	4.91	7.48	6.94	6.58	5.46	l.
										6.
1.00	.38	.29	.72	2.20	2.27	1.17	.88	.46	.81	7.
17.15	21.76	25.24	27.02	27.66	27.88	32.93	35.19	35.36	36.03	8.

TABLE IV-c-9b

Long-Term Bank Loans, N.E.C., Liabilities

(billion dollars)

	1945	1946	1947	1948
1. Nonfarm households				
2. Nonfarm unincorporated business	.47	.77	.97	1.02
3. Agriculture				
4. Nonfinancial corporations	2.39	3.88	4.93	5.43
5. Finance				
6. State and local governments				
7. Federal government				
8. Total	2.86	4.65	5.90	6.45

SEC worksheets. Estimates are based on Federal Reserve Board commercial loan surveys for 1946, 1955, and 1957.

Line 4 apparently includes loans to finance companies. Term loans to sales finance companies at dates of FRB surveys were as follows:

Nov. 20, 1946	$ 74 million	(*Federal Reserve Bulletin*, May 1947, p. 516)
Oct. 5, 1955	$131 million	(*Ibid.*, April 1959, p. 354)
Oct. 16, 1957	$266 million	(*Ibid.*, April 1959, p. 354)

TABLE IV-c-10

Other Loans, Liabilities

(billion dollars)

	1945	1946	1947	1948
1. Nonfarm households	1.97	1.90	1.95	2.08
2. Nonfarm unincorporated business	.88	1.22	1.68	2.33
3. Agriculture	.80	.82	.85	.93
4. Nonfinancial corporations	.81	.82	.96	1.13
5. Finance	1.71	1.93	2.12	2.12
c. Commercial banks	.28	.21	.16	.13
e. Savings and loan associations	.31	.50	.70	.74
m. Other finance	1.12	1.22	1.26	1.25
6. State and local governments				
7. Federal government				
8. Total	6.17	6.69	7.56	8.59

Line	
1	Sum of: line 5k, Table IV-b-10; line 5b, Table IV-b-10; and 98 per cent of line 5h, Table IV-b-10; minus policy loans to farmers (see note to line III-10, Table III-3).
2	Line 8 minus lines 1, 3, 4, and 5.
3-5m	Line III-10 of Tables III-3 through III-5m.
8	Table IV-b-10, line 10.

1949	1950	1951	1952	1953	1954	1955	1956	1957	1958
1.03	1.23	1.53	1.63	1.71	1.76	1.95	2.27	2.41	2.43
4.56	5.21	6.05	7.19	6.95	6.93	8.16	10.81	12.21	12.71
5.59	6.44	7.58	8.82	8.66	8.69	10.11	13.08	14.62	15.14

Long-term notes payable to banks by finance companies were estimated in the Federal Reserve Board finance company surveys (*Ibid.*, October 1961) as follows:

	June 30, 1960	June 30, 1955
	(millions of dollars)	
Sales finance	353	230
Consumer finance	47	98
Other personal finance	15	n.a.
Business finance	72	n.a.

1949	1950	1951	1952	1953	1954	1955	1956	1957	1958	
2.27	2.45	2.65	2.77	2.98	3.22	3.40	3.67	4.02	4.37	1.
2.42	2.78	3.28	3.59	3.69	3.87	4.88	4.97	5.30	5.42	2.
.96	1.02	1.13	1.21	1.19	1.29	1.34	1.42	1.64	1.87	3.
1.21	1.34	1.49	1.58	1.92	1.65	2.11	1.96	2.33	2.18	4.
2.20	3.19	3.24	3.21	3.25	3.93	4.41	4.22	4.53	5.55	5.
.11	.09	.08	.05	.04	.02	.01	a	.01	a	c.
.70	1.22	1.22	1.37	1.51	1.66	2.34	2.13	2.13	2.44	e.
1.39	1.88	1.94	1.79	1.70	2.25	2.06	2.09	2.39	3.11	m.
										6.
										7.
9.06	10.78	11.79	12.36	13.03	13.96	16.14	16.24	17.82	19.39	8.

[a]Under $5 million.

TABLE IV-c-11

Mortgages, Liabilities
(million dollars)

	1945	1946	1947	1948
1. Nonfarm households	18,453	22,708	27,639	32,781
2. Nonfarm unincorporated business	4,451	4,967	5,555	6,157
3. Agriculture	4,760	4,897	5,064	5,288
4. Nonfinancial corporations	7,872	9,187	10,659	11,972
5. Finance				
6. State and local governments				
7. Federal government				
8. Total	35,536	41,759	48,917	56,198
9. Farm mortgages	4,760	4,897	5,064	5,288
10. Nonfarm mortgages	30,776	36,862	43,853	50,910
11. Life insurance holdings of foreign farm mortgages	n.a.	n.a.	n.a.	n.a.
12. Life insurance holdings of foreign nonfarm mortgages	n.a.	n.a.	n.a.	n.a.

Line

1-8 Sum of corresponding lines in Tables IV-c-11a through IV-c-11d.
9 Table IV-b-12, line 8.
10 Line 8 minus line 9.
11-12 Various issues of *Life Insurance Fact Book* and unpublished figures from Institute of Life Insurance.

TABLE IV-c-11a

One- to Four-Family Nonfarm Residential Mortgages, Liabilities
(million dollars)

	1945	1946	1947	1948	1949
1. Nonfarm households	18,258	22,448	27,336	32,433	36,669
2. Nonfarm unincorporated business					
3. Agriculture					
4. Nonfinancial corporations	333	586	863	846	950
5. Finance					
6. State and local governments					
7. Federal government					
8. Total	18,591	23,034	28,199	33,279	37,619

Line

1 Line 8 minus line 4.
4 FRB worksheets (construction loans).
8 Table IV-b-11a-2, line 8.

1949	1950	1951	1952	1953	1954	1955	1956	1957	1958	
37,039	44,306	51,084	57,808	65,456	74,829	87,364	98,367	107,065	117,052	1.
6,687	7,257	7,910	8,430	8,983	9,727	10,632	11,649	12,577	13,936	2.
5,579	6,118	6,676	7,263	7,772	8,289	9,066	9,908	10,507	11,254	3.
13,371	15,178	16,628	17,916	19,114	20,871	22,875	24,752	26,480	29,671	4.
										5.
										6.
										7.
62,676	72,859	82,298	91,417	101,325	113,716	129,937	144,676	156,629	171,913	8.
5,579	6,118	6,676	7,263	7,772	8,289	9,066	9,908	10,507	11,254	9.
57,097	66,741	75,622	84,154	93,553	105,427	120,871	134,768	146,122	160,659	10.
5	6	7	8	8	9	10	11	11	11	11.
123	168	210	249	288	343	435	558	634	709	12.

1950	1951	1952	1953	1954	1955	1956	1957	1958	1959	
43,904	50,646	57,332	64,940	74,242	86,702	97,622	106,255	116,149		1.
										2.
										3.
1,266	1,065	1,168	1,154	1,435	1,548	1,415	1,362	1,537		4.
										5.
										6.
										7.
45,170	51,711	58,500	66,094	75,677	88,250	99,037	107,617	117,686	130,909	8.

TABLE IV-c-11b

Multifamily Nonfarm Residential Mortgages, Liabilities

(million dollars)

	1945	1946	1947	1948	1949
1. Nonfarm households					
2. Nonfarm unincorporated business	1,645	1,721	1,819	1,986	2,172
3. Agriculture					
4. Nonfinancial corporations	3,038	3,343	3,737	4,348	5,093
5. Finance					
6. State and local governments					
7. Federal government					
8. Total	4,683	5,064	5,556	6,334	7,265

Line

2 FRB worksheets.
4 FRB worksheets.
8 Table IV-b-11a-1, line 8.

TABLE IV-c-11c

Nonfarm Nonresidential Mortgages, Liabilities

(million dollars)

	1945	1946	1947	1948	1949
1. Nonfarm households	195	260	303	348	370
2. Nonfarm unincorporated business	2,806	3,246	3,736	4,171	4,515
3. Agriculture					
4. Nonfinancial corporations	4,501	5,258	6,059	6,778	7,328
5. Finance					
6. State and local governments					
7. Federal government					
8. Total	7,502	8,764	10,098	11,297	12,213

Line

1 Nonprofit organizations' mortgage liability, assumed to be 11.8 per cent of nonfarm nonresidential mortgages held by commercial banks and mutual savings banks (Morris Mendelson, *Flow-of-Funds*, p. I-225).
2 Line 8 minus lines 1 and 4.
4 60 per cent of line 8.
8 Table IV-b-11b, line 8.

1950	1951	1952	1953	1954	1955	1956	1957	1958	1959
2,407	2,653	2,792	2,921	3,022	3,193	3,335	3,453	3,787	4,183
6,034	7,021	7,578	8,094	8,497	9,176	9,748	10,217	11,555	13,019
8,441	9,674	10,370	11,015	11,519	12,369	13,083	13,670	15,342	17,202

1950	1951	1952	1953	1954	1955	1956	1957	1958	1959
402	438	476	516	587	662	745	810	904	1,024
4,850	5,257	5,638	6,062	6,705	7,439	8,314	9,124	10,148	11,211
7,878	8,542	9,170	9,866	10,939	12,151	13,589	14,901	16,579	18,352
13,130	14,237	15,284	16,444	18,231	20,252	22,648	24,835	27,631	30,587

TABLE IV-c-11d

Farm Mortgages, Liabilities

(million dollars)

	1945	1946	1947	1948	1949
1. Nonfarm households					
2. Nonfarm unincorporated business					
3. Agriculture	4,760	4,897	5,064	5,288	5,579
4. Nonfinancial corporations					
5. Finance					
6. State and local governments					
7. Federal government					
8. Total	4,760	4,897	5,064	5,288	5,579

Table IV-b-12, line 8.

TABLE IV-c-11e

Mortgages, Liabilities, 1900-45, Selected Years

(million dollars)

	1900	1912
1. Nonfarm households	2,606	4,059
2. Nonfarm unincorporated business	1,081	1,928
3. Agriculture	2,312	4,348
4. Nonfinancial corporations	778	1,674
5. Finance		
6. State and local governments		
7. Federal government		
8. Total	6,777	12,009

Line

1	Table IV-c-11e-1, line 11.
2	Table IV-c-11e-1, sum of lines 3, 7, and 15.
3	Table III-3b, line III-11.
4	Table IV-c-11e-1, sum of lines 4, 8, 12, and 16.
8	Sum of lines 1 through 4 of this table.

1950	1951	1952	1953	1954	1955	1956	1957	1958	1959
6,118	6,676	7,263	7,772	8,289	9,066	9,908	10,507	11,254	12,291
6,118	6,676	7,263	7,772	8,289	9,066	9,908	10,507	11,254	12,291

1922	1929	1933	1939	1945[a]
8,310	17,985	14,584	15,525	17,661
3,948	7,697	6,169	4,544	4,313
10,786	9,631	7,685	6,586	4,760
4,396	11,169	9,713	8,834	8,818
27,440	46,482	38,151	35,489	35,552

[a]The 1945 figures in this table have been superseded by those in Table IV-c-11; they are included here for comparability with earlier years.

TABLE IV-c-11e-1

Allocation of Mortgage Liabilities by Sector, 1900-45, Selected Years

(million dollars)

	1900	1912	1922	1929	1933	1939	1945
Nonfarm nonresidential mortgages							
1. Total outstanding	1,511	2,669	5,562	11,939	9,414	8,061	7,501
2. Commercial mortgages	1,133	2,002	4,172	8,954	7,060	6,046	5,626
3. Noncorporate	736	1,181	2,211	4,119	3,071	2,418	2,250
4. Corporate	397	821	1,961	4,835	3,989	3,628	3,376
5. Percentage noncorporate	65.0	59.0	53.0	46.0	43.5	40.0	40.0
6. Industrial mortgages	378	667	1,390	2,985	2,354	2,015	1,875
7. Noncorporate	94	92	117	188	134	101	94
8. Corporate	284	575	1,273	2,797	2,220	1,914	1,781
9. Percentage noncorporate	25.0	13.8	8.4	6.3	5.7	5.0	5.0
Nonfarm residential mortgages							
10. 1- to 4-family outstanding	2,659	4,193	8,674	18,912	15,352	16,342	18,591
11. Noncorporate	2,606	4,059	8,310	17,985	14,584	15,525	17,661
12. Corporate	53	134	364	927	768	817	930
13. Percentage corporate	2.0	3.2	4.2	4.9	5.0	5.0	5.0
14. Multifamily outstanding	295	799	2,418	6,000	5,700	4,500	4,700
15. Noncorporate	251	655	1,620	3,390	2,964	2,025	1,969
16. Corporate	44	144	798	2,610	2,736	2,475	2,731
17. Percentage corporate	15.0	18.0	33.0	43.5	48.0	55.0	58.1

Notes to Table IV-c-11e-1

Line	
1	Table IV-b-11c-4, line 8.
2	Line 1 minus line 6.
3	Line 2 multiplied by line 5.
4	Line 2 minus line 3.
5	Goldsmith, *A Study of Saving*, Vol. I, Table R-29, column 3, interpolated on straight line.
6	One-quarter of line 1. See Goldsmith, *A Study of Saving*, Vol. III, note to line III-11 of Table W-29.
7	Line 6 multiplied by line 9.
8	Line 6 minus line 7.
9	Goldsmith, *A Study of Saving*, Vol. I, Table R-29, column 4, interpolated on straight line.
10	Table IV-b-11c-2, line 8.
11	Line 10 minus line 12.
12	Line 10 multiplied by line 13.
13	Goldsmith, *A Study of Saving*, Vol. I, Table R-29, column 1, interpolated on straight line.
14	Table IV-b-11c-3, line 8.
15	Line 14 minus line 16.
16	Line 14 multiplied by line 17.
17	Goldsmith, *A Study of Saving*, Vol. I, Table R-29, column 2, interpolated on straight line.

TABLE IV-c-12

Bonds and Notes, Liabilities

(billion dollars)

	1945	1946	1947	1948
1. Nonfarm households				
2. Nonfarm unincorporated business				
3. Agriculture				
4. Nonfinancial corporations	23.60	24.48	27.32	31.55
5. Finance	.19	.45	.73	1.31
l. Finance companies	.19	.45	.73	1.31
6. State and local governments	21.27	21.14	22.55	24.76
7. Federal government	278.98	259.99	257.69	253.88
a. Direct and guaranteed	277.87	258.74	256.30	252.23
b. Nonguaranteed	1.11	1.25	1.39	1.65
8. Total	324.04	306.06	308.29	311.50

Line

4 Nonfinancial corporation bonds outstanding (Meiselman and Shapiro, "Corporate Sources," Table C-23, line 1), plus commercial paper held outside banks (Table III-51-a, columns 4, 8, and 11), less finance company bonds and notes outstanding (Table III-51, line III-12).

5-5l Table III-51, line III-12.

6 Table III-6, line III-12.

TABLE IV-c-13

Other Liabilities

(billion dollars)

	1945	1946	1947	1948
1. Nonfarm households				
2. Nonfarm unincorporated business				
3. Agriculture				
4. Nonfinancial corporations	28.42	28.84	31.58	33.35
5. Finance	11.21	12.59	12.72	13.66
a. Federal Reserve Banks and Treasury monetary funds	3.89	4.30	3.26	3.11
c. Commercial banks	.63	.84	.99	1.15
d. Mutual savings banks	.05	.07	.09	.09
e. Savings and loan associations	.26	.29	.26	.28
h. Life insurance	.64	.70	.78	.82
i. Fire and casualty insurance	3.85	4.60	5.59	6.43
k. Other private insurance	.07	.08	.10	.10
m. Other finance	1.82	1.71	1.65	1.68
6. State and local governments				
7. Federal government	.19	.23	.27	.33
8. Total	39.82	41.66	44.57	47.34

Line

4 Table III-4, line III-13.

5 Sum of lines 5a through 5m.

5a-5k Line III-13 of Tables III-5a through III-5k.

1949	1950	1951	1952	1953	1954	1955	1956	1957	1958	
										1.
										2.
										3.
34.45	36.06	39.36	44.08	47.43	50.97	53.74	57.41	63.76	69.68	4.
1.83	2.25	2.82	3.36	4.94	5.13	6.76	7.95	9.08	9.09	5.
1.83	2.25	2.82	3.36	4.94	5.13	6.76	7.95	9.08	9.09	l.
27.11	30.22	32.63	35.81	39.39	43.57	47.05	50.37	55.24	61.16	6.
258.07	258.12	261.11	269.12	276.91	280.46	284.04	280.53	280.92	288.49	7.
256.58	256.20	258.95	266.96	274.78	278.35	280.41	276.34	274.62	282.66	a.
1.49	1.92	2.16	2.16	2.13	2.11	3.63	4.19	6.30	5.83	b.
321.46	326.65	335.92	352.37	368.67	380.13	391.59	396.26	409.00	428.42	8.

Line

7 Table III-7, line III-12.

7a Line 7 minus line 7b.

7b Federal Land Banks from Table III-7e, line III-12. Banks for Cooperatives, Federal Home Loan Banks, Federal Intermediate Credit Banks, and Federal National Mortgage Association, from *Federal Reserve Bulletin*, e.g., March 1959, p. 288.

8 Sum of lines 4-7.

1949	1950	1951	1952	1953	1954	1955	1956	1957	1958	
										1.
										2.
										3.
32.69	40.06	47.00	45.60	47.83	48.15	54.70	58.09	60.65	60.84	4.
14.96	16.86	18.03	20.15	21.72	23.16	25.27	27.33	29.47	31.20	5.
										a.
3.41	3.66	3.34	3.88	3.94	3.80	4.67	4.72	4.79	5.06	
1.32	1.90	2.30	2.54	2.65	2.99	3.01	3.56	3.93	3.88	c.
.11	.14	.15	.16	.21	.28	.33	.36	.44	.53	d.
.28	.33	.35	.36	.39	.45	.48	.51	.63	.73	e.
.90	1.01	1.08	1.16	1.26	1.34	1.48	1.67	1.84	1.97	h.
7.20	7.92	8.77	9.85	10.95	11.64	12.42	13.08	14.13	14.97	i.
.12	.13	.14	.16	.17	.19	.21	.22	.24	.26	k.
1.62	1.77	1.90	2.04	2.15	2.47	2.67	3.21	3.47	3.80	m.
										6.
.49	.49	.64	.90	1.11	1.39	1.36	1.46	1.53	1.80	7.
48.14	57.41	65.67	66.65	70.66	72.70	81.33	86.88	91.65	93.84	8.

Line

5m Table III-5m, sum of lines III-1, III-2, and III-13. Deposit liabilities of banks in possessions (Table III-5m-2) are included under "other liabilities" in this table.

7 Table III-7, line III-13.

8 Sum of lines 4, 5, and 7.

SECTION V

Flow of Funds Through Sectors, 1946–58

TABLE V

Annual Flow of Funds Through Sectors—1946

(billion dollars)

	Nonfarm Households (1)	Nonfarm Unincorporated Business (2)	Agriculture (3)	Nonfinancial Corporations (4)	Finance (5)	State and Local Govts. (6)	Federal Govt. (7)	Total (8)
I. Gross capital expenditures								
1. Residential structures	4.89	.13	.42	.29	n.a.	.37	–.12	5.98
2. Nonresidential structures	.32	.74	.46	4.33	.27	1.42	.34	7.88
3. Land								
4. Producer durables	.06	1.59	.97	7.60	.07	.21	.15	10.65
5. Consumer durables	13.71		1.84					15.55
6. Inventories at book value (see note below)		2.09	3.42	11.22	.02	.02	–1.20	15.57
7. Total	18.98	4.55	7.11	23.44	.36	2.02	–.83	55.63
II. Net financial flows								
1. Currency and demand deposits	4.15	.01	.50	1.14	.50	.87	–22.73	–15.56
a. Monetary metals	.05	.01	.01	.01	.41			.49
b. Other	4.10	0	.49	1.13	.09	.87	–22.73	–16.05
2. Other bank deposits and shares	6.38		.20	0	.14	.18	.01	6.91
3. Life insurance reserves	3.53		.19					3.72
4. Pension and retirement funds, private	.57							.57
5. Pension and insurance funds, govt.	3.47		.20					3.67
6. Consumer credit		.33		.57	1.86			2.76
7. Trade credit		.96		3.19	.34		–.80	3.69
8. Loans on securities					–4.40			–4.40
9. Bank loans, n.e.c.					4.97			4.97
10. Other loans	.16				.36		3.17	3.69
11. Mortgages, nonfarm	1.36				4.95	0	–.24	6.07
a. Residential	.89				4.16	0	–.23	4.82
b. Nonresidential	.47				.80		–.01	1.26
12. Mortgages, farm	.12				.20		–.19	.13
13. Securities, U. S. government	–.49		.06	–5.70	–12.09	–.62	.54	–18.30
a. Short-term	.16			–5.10	–13.52	–.10		–18.56
b. Savings bonds	1.20		.06	0	.38			1.64
c. Other long-term	–1.85			–.60	1.05	–.52	.54	–1.38
14. Securities, state and local	–.16			0	.18	–.13	–.02	–.13

15. Securities, other bonds and notes	−1.37			.04	2.55	.01		1.23
16. Securities, preferred stock	0			.01	.18			.19
17. Securities, common stock	1.42			.09	.29			1.80
18. Equity in mutual financial organizations								
19. Equity in other business								
20. Other intangible assets	−.01		.16	−.46	1.23		.90	1.82
21. Total	19.13	1.30	1.31	−1.12	1.24	.31	−19.36	2.81
III. Net changes in liabilities								
1. Currency and demand deposits					−14.94		.13	−14.81
2. Other bank deposits and shares					6.59		.36	6.95
3. Life insurance reserves					3.78			3.78
4. Pension and retirement funds, private					.57			.57
5. Pension and insurance funds, govt.					3.67			3.67
6. Consumer debt	2.65		.11					2.76
7. Trade debt	.07	−.09	.20	3.73	−.01	.15	−2.00	2.05
8. Loans on securities	−1.48			−.91	−2.04			−4.43
9. Bank loans, n.e.c.	−.29	1.45	.25	2.98	.59		−.21	4.77
10. Other loans	−.07	.34	.02	.01	.22			.52
11. Mortgages	4.26	.52	.14	1.32				6.24
12. Bonds and notes				.88	.26	−.13	−18.99	−17.98
13. Other liabilities				.42	1.41		.04	1.87
14. Total	5.14	2.22	.72	8.43	.10	.02	−20.67	−4.04
IV. Net changes in equities								
1. Net issues of common stock				1.49	.25			1.74
2. Net issues of preferred stock				.19	0			.19
3. Saving	32.97	3.63	7.70	12.21	1.26	2.31	.48	60.56
V. Total uses and sources of funds	38.11	5.85	8.42	22.32	1.60	2.33	−20.19	58.44

Note: Inventories at Adjusted Values and Lines Affected

Inventories (adjusted values)		.38	−.06	5.95	.02	.02	−1.20	5.11
Gross capital expenditures	18.98	2.84	3.63	18.17	.36	2.02	−.83	45.17
Saving	32.97	1.92	4.22	6.94	1.26	2.31	.48	50.10
Total uses and sources of funds	38.11	4.14	4.94	17.05	1.60	2.33	−20.19	47.98

Source: For columns 1–7, see Tables VII–1 through VII–7 respectively.

TABLE V

Annual Flow of Funds Through Sectors—1947

(billion dollars)

	Nonfarm House-holds (1)	Nonfarm Unincor-porated Business (2)	Agri-culture (3)	Nonfinan-cial Corpora-tions (4)	Finance (5)	State and Local Govts. (6)	Federal Govt. (7)	Total (8)
I. Gross capital expenditures								
1. Residential structures	7.39	.25	.70	.41	.03	.14	–.08	8.84
2. Nonresidential structures	.44	.64	.73	5.29	.28	2.59	.56	10.53
3. Land								
4. Producer durables	.08	2.47	1.79	11.32	.07	.33	.16	16.22
5. Consumer durables	18.38		2.31					20.69
6. Inventories at book value (see note below)		1.53	3.40	7.15	–.01	.01	–.28	11.80
7. Total	26.29	4.89	8.93	24.17	.37	3.07	.36	68.08
II. Net financial flows								
1. Currency and demand deposits	–.31	.36	–.10	2.20	7.89	.72	–.54	10.22
a. Monetary metals	.03	.01	.01	0	2.22			2.27
b. Other	–.34	.35	–.11	2.20	5.67	.72	–.54	7.95
2. Other bank deposits and shares	3.63		–.08	0	.04	.16	–.01	3.74
3. Life insurance reserves	3.30		.21					3.51
4. Pension and retirement funds, private	.65							.65
5. Pension and insurance funds, govt.	3.79		.09					3.88
6. Consumer credit		.33		.64	2.31			3.28
7. Trade credit		.37		5.86	.13		–.10	6.26
8. Loans on securities					–1.06			–1.06
9. Bank loans, n.e.c.					4.59			4.59
10. Other loans	.04				.33		4.13	4.50
11. Mortgages, nonfarm	1.21				5.83	0	–.04	7.00
a. Residential	.67				5.04	0	–.04	5.67
b. Nonresidential	.54				.78		0	1.32
12. Mortgages, farm	.07				.22		–.12	.17
13. Securities, U. S. government	1.82		.17	–1.20	–4.37	.66	.04	–2.88
a. Short-term	–.42			–.90	–2.83	.30		–3.85
b. Savings bonds	1.81		.17	0	.34			2.32
c. Other long-term	.43			–.30	–1.88	.36	.04	–1.35
14. Securities, state and local	.41			.04	.99	–.05	.02	1.41

15. Securities, other bonds and notes	–.69			.12	3.86	.04		3.33
16. Securities, preferred stock	.31			.01	.10			.42
17. Securities, common stock	1.16			.08	.45			1.69
18. Equity in mutual financial organizations								
19. Equity in other business								
20. Other intangible assets	.01		.17	1.87	1.68		2.19	5.92
21. Total	15.40	1.06	.46	9.62	23.00	1.53	5.57	56.64
III. Net changes in liabilities								
1. Currency and demand deposits					9.60		–.03	9.57
2. Other bank deposits and shares					3.56		.14	3.70
3. Life insurance reserves					3.58			3.58
4. Pension and retirement funds, private					.64			.64
5. Pension and insurance funds, govt.					3.88			3.88
6. Consumer debt	3.19		.10					3.29
7. Trade debt	.09	–.53	.20	4.64	.01	.15	–.70	3.86
8. Loans on securities	–.06			–.33	–.71			–1.10
9. Bank loans, n.e.c.	–.25	2.22	.30	1.66	.62		–.03	4.52
10. Other loans	.05	.46	.03	.14	.19			.87
11. Mortgages	4.93	.59	.17	1.47				7.16
12. Bonds and notes				2.84	.28	1.41	–2.30	2.23
13. Other liabilities				2.74	.16		.04	2.94
14. Total	7.95	2.74	.80	13.16	21.80	1.56	–2.88	45.13
IV. Net changes in equities								
1. Net issues of common stock				1.32	.26			1.58
2. Net issues of preferred stock				.42	0			.42
3. Saving	33.74	3.21	8.59	18.89	1.30	3.04	8.81	77.58
V. Total uses and sources of funds	41.69	5.95	9.39	33.79	23.36	4.60	5.93	124.71

Note: Inventories at Adjusted Values and Lines Affected

Inventories (adjusted values)		.06	–1.73	1.25	–.01	.01	–.28	–.70
Gross capital expenditures	26.29	3.42	3.80	18.27	.37	3.07	.36	55.58
Saving	33.74	1.74	3.46	12.99	1.30	3.04	8.81	65.08
Total uses and sources of funds	41.69	4.48	4.26	27.89	23.36	4.60	5.93	112.21

Source: For columns 1–7, see Tables VII–1 through VII–7 respectively

TABLE V

Annual Flow of Funds Through Sectors—1948

(billion dollars)

	Nonfarm House-holds (1)	Nonfarm Unincor-porated Business (2)	Agri-culture (3)	Nonfinan-cial Corpora-tions (4)	Finance (5)	State and Local Govts. (6)	Federal Govt. (7)	Total (8)
I. Gross capital expenditures								
1. Residential structures	10.59	.46	.75	.70	.04	.02	–.08	12.48
2. Nonresidential structures	.70	.89	.82	6.34	.26	3.67	.83	13.51
3. Land								
4. Producer durables	.13	2.77	2.43	12.49	.07	.42	.23	18.54
5. Consumer durables	20.09		2.76					22.85
6. Inventories at book value (see note below)		1.33	–.30	4.21	–.01	a	.82	6.05
7. Total	31.51	5.45	6.46	23.74	.36	4.11	1.80	73.43
II. Net financial flows								
1. Currency and demand deposits	–2.06	–.15	–.30	.20	4.75	.49	1.08	4.01
a. Monetary metals	.03	0	0	.02	1.50			1.55
b. Other	–2.09	–.15	–.30	.18	3.25	.49	1.08	2.46
2. Other bank deposits and shares	2.18		0	0	.02	.27	0	2.47
3. Life insurance reserves	3.52		.23					3.75
4. Pension and retirement funds, private	.65							.65
5. Pension and insurance funds, govt.	3.49		–.01					3.48
6. Consumer credit		.37		.54	1.98			2.89
7. Trade credit		.40		2.34	.17		0	2.91
8. Loans on securities					.25			.25
9. Bank loans, n.e.c.					2.17			2.17
10. Other loans	–.13				.62		1.67	2.16
11. Mortgages, nonfarm	1.00				5.96	.01	.09	7.06
a. Residential	.59				5.17	.01	.09	5.86
b. Nonresidential	.41				.78		0	1.19
12. Mortgages, farm	.13				.16		–.06	.23
13. Securities, U. S. government	–.23		.22	.80	–5.76	.32	.10	–4.55
a. Short-term	2.11			.90	–6.48	.50		–2.97
b. Savings bonds	1.62		.22	.20	.98			3.02
c. Other long-term	–3.96			–.30	–.26	–.18	.10	–4.60
14. Securities, state and local	.99			.05	1.10	0	.07	2.21

	(1)	(2)	(3)	(4)	(5)	(6)	(7)	(8)
15. Securities, other bonds and notes	−.28			.14	5.17	.17		5.20
16. Securities, preferred stock	.28			.01	.07			.36
17. Securities, common stock	1.23			.08	.27			1.58
18. Equity in mutual financial organizations								
19. Equity in other business								
20. Other intangible assets	−.01		.17	.93	−.06		.77	1.80
21. Total	10.76	.62	.31	5.09	16.86	1.26	3.72	38.62
III. Net changes in liabilities								
1. Currency and demand deposits					2.03		−.01	2.02
2. Other bank deposits and shares					2.55		−.07	2.48
3. Life insurance reserves					3.83			3.83
4. Pension and retirement funds, private					.65			.65
5. Pension and insurance funds, govt.					3.48			3.48
6. Consumer debt	2.80		.09					2.89
7. Trade debt	.08	.76	.30	.44	.01	.15	0	1.74
8. Loans on securities	−.12			−.16	.51			.23
9. Bank loans, n.e.c.	.10	−.70	.36	1.06	.46		.85	2.13
10. Other loans	.13	.65	.08	.17	0			1.03
11. Mortgages	5.14	.60	.22	1.31				7.27
12. Bonds and notes				4.23	.58	2.21	−3.81	3.21
13. Other liabilities				1.77	1.02		.06	2.85
14. Total	8.13	1.31	1.05	8.82	15.12	2.36	−2.98	33.81
IV. Net changes in equities								
1. Net issues of common stock				1.29	.15			1.44
2. Net issues of preferred stock				.29	.05			.34
3. Saving	34.14	4.76	5.72	18.43	1.91	3.01	8.50	76.47
V. Total uses and sources of funds	42.27	6.07	6.77	28.83	17.22	5.37	5.52	112.05

Note: Inventories at Adjusted Values and Lines Affected

Inventories (adjusted values)		.92	1.47	2.06	−.01	[a]	.82	5.26
Gross capital expenditures	31.51	5.04	8.23	21.59	.36	4.11	1.80	72.64
Saving	34.14	4.35	7.49	16.28	1.91	3.01	8.50	75.68
Total uses and sources of funds	42.27	5.66	8.54	26.68	17.22	5.37	5.52	111.26

Source: For columns 1-7, see Tables VII-1 through VII-7 respectively.

[a]$5 million or under.

TABLE V

Annual Flow of Funds Through Sectors—1949

(billion dollars)

	Nonfarm Households (1)	Nonfarm Unincorporated Business (2)	Agriculture (3)	Nonfinancial Corporations (4)	Finance (5)	State and Local Govts. (6)	Federal Govt. (7)	Total (8)
I. Gross capital expenditures								
1. Residential structures	9.45	.51	.70	.78	.07	.25	–.01	11.75
2. Nonresidential structures	.92	.80	.80	6.19	.12	5.06	1.19	15.08
3. Land								
4. Producer durables	.17	2.64	2.64	10.49	.03	.45	.12	16.54
5. Consumer durables	21.94		2.76					24.70
6. Inventories at book value (see note below)		–.95	–3.26	–3.57	a	a	1.36	–6.42
7. Total	32.48	3.00	3.64	13.89	.22	5.76	2.66	61.65
II. Net financial flows								
1. Currency and demand deposits	–2.31	.37	–.40	1.07	–2.79	.23	.38	–3.45
a. Monetary metals	0	.01	.01	0	.22			.24
b. Other	–2.31	.36	–.41	1.07	–3.01	.23	.38	–3.69
2. Other bank deposits and shares	2.48		0	0	.01	.15	.06	2.70
3. Life insurance reserves	3.76		.24					4.00
4. Pension and retirement funds, private	.71							.71
5. Pension and insurance funds, govt.	2.49		.05					2.54
6. Consumer credit		.25		.44	2.26			2.95
7. Trade credit		.06		–.94	.11		0	–.77
8. Loans on securities					.75			.75
9. Bank loans, n.e.c.					–1.62			–1.62
10. Other loans	.16				.12		.67	.95
11. Mortgages, nonfarm	.59				5.01	.09	.48	6.17
a. Residential	.23				4.47	.09	.49	5.28
b. Nonresidential	.36				.54		0	.90
12. Mortgages, farm	.08				.20		.02	.30
13. Securities, U. S. government	.97		.12	1.92	1.13	.02	.08	4.24
a. Short-term	.97			2.30	6.85	.10		10.22
b. Savings bonds	1.30		.12	0	.29			1.71
c. Other long-term	–1.30			–.38	–6.01	–.08	.08	–7.69
14. Securities, state and local	.61			.05	1.49	.28	–.08	2.35

	(1)	(2)	(3)	(4)	(5)	(6)	(7)	(8)
15. Securities, other bonds and notes	−.63			.14	3.71	−.01		3.21
16. Securities, preferred stock	.01			0	.30			.31
17. Securities, common stock	1.13			.09	.57			1.79
18. Equity in mutual financial organizations								
19. Equity in other business								
20. Other intangible assets	−.01		.18	.86	.73		−2.09	−.33
21. Total	10.04	.68	.19	3.63	12.01	.76	−.48	26.83
III. Net changes in liabilities								
1. Currency and demand deposits					−2.68		−.02	−2.70
2. Other bank deposits and shares					2.95		−.14	2.81
3. Life insurance reserves					4.07			4.07
4. Pension and retirement funds, private					.70			.70
5. Pension and insurance funds, govt.					2.54			2.54
6. Consumer debt	2.95		−.01					2.94
7. Trade debt	.04	.22	.20	−1.34	.02	.10	0	−.76
8. Loans on securities	.32			0	.45			.77
9. Bank loans, n.e.c.	0	−.29	.10	−1.93	.39		.08	−1.65
10. Other loans	.19	.09	.03	.08	.08			.47
11. Mortgages	4.26	.53	.29	1.40				6.48
12. Bonds and notes				2.90	.52	2.35	4.19	9.96
13. Other liabilities				−.66	1.32		.16	.82
14. Total	7.76	.55	.61	.45	10.37	2.45	4.27	26.46
IV. Net changes in equities								
1. Net issues of common stock				1.42	.37			1.79
2. Net issues of preferred stock				.29	.03			.32
3. Saving	34.76	3.13	3.22	15.36	1.43	4.07	−2.09	59.88
V. Total uses and sources of funds	42.52	3.68	3.83	17.52	12.21	6.52	2.18	88.46

Note: Inventories at Adjusted Values and Lines Affected

	(1)	(2)	(3)	(4)	(5)	(6)	(7)	(8)
Inventories (adjusted values)		−.49	−1.35	−1.72	a	a	1.36	−2.20
Gross capital expenditures	32.48	3.46	5.55	15.74	.22	5.76	2.66	65.87
Saving	34.76	3.59	5.13	17.21	1.43	4.07	−2.09	64.10
Total uses and sources of funds	42.52	4.14	5.74	19.37	12.21	6.52	2.18	92.68

Source: For columns 1-7, see Tables VII-1 through VII-7 respectively.

[a]$5 million or under.

TABLE V

Annual Flow of Funds Through Sectors—1950

(billion dollars)

	Nonfarm House-holds (1)	Nonfarm Unincor-porated Business (2)	Agri-culture (3)	Nonfinan-cial Corpora-tions (4)	Finance (5)	State and Local Govts. (6)	Federal Govt. (7)	Total (8)
I. Gross capital expenditures								
1. Residential structures	13.18	.46	.78	.82	.05	.28	–.02	15.55
2. Nonresidential structures	1.13	.94	.89	6.52	.30	5.68	1.26	16.72
3. Land								
4. Producer durables	.21	3.06	2.64	11.64	.07	.47	.04	18.13
5. Consumer durables	27.68		3.05					30.73
6. Inventories at book value (see note below)		2.27	5.43	9.77	.01	.02	–.61	16.89
7. Total	42.20	6.73	12.79	28.75	.43	6.45	.67	98.02
II. Net financial flows								
1. Currency and demand deposits	1.90	.22	0	1.31	.07	.46	–.68	3.28
a. Monetary metals	.06	.01	–.01	.01	–1.73			–1.66
b. Other	1.84	.21	.01	1.30	1.80	.46	–.68	4.94
2. Other bank deposits and shares	2.09		0	0	–.05	.10	.01	2.15
3. Life insurance reserves	3.96		.24					4.20
4. Pension and retirement funds, private	.97							.97
5. Pension and insurance funds, govt.	1.56		–.25					1.31
6. Consumer credit		.49		.78	2.90			4.17
7. Trade credit		1.22		11.44	.29		.38	13.33
8. Loans on securities					.80			.80
9. Bank loans, n.e.c.					5.52			5.52
10. Other loans	.55				.61		.70	1.86
11. Mortgages, nonfarm	.37				8.95	.05	.29	9.66
a. Residential	.09				8.29	.05	.29	8.72
b. Nonresidential	.28				.64		0	.92
12. Mortgages, farm	.22				.27		.05	.54
13. Securities, U. S. government	–.33		–.03	2.87	–4.51	.36	–.24	–1.88
a. Short-term	–1.18			3.00	–.32	.30		1.80
b. Savings bonds	.45		–.03	0	.92			1.34
c. Other long-term	.40			–.13	–5.11	.06	–.24	–5.02
14. Securities, state and local	.38			.07	2.29	.30	.07	3.11

	(1)	(2)	(3)	(4)	(5)	(6)	(7)	(8)
15. Securities, other bonds and notes	.03			.03	2.95	.06		3.07
16. Securities, preferred stock	−.06			.01	.30			.25
17. Securities, common stock	1.59			.10	.38			2.07
18. Equity in mutual financial organizations								
19. Equity in other business								
20. Other intangible assets	−.23		.22	.56	4.18		7.47	12.20
21. Total	13.00	1.93	.18	17.17	24.95	1.33	8.05	66.61
III. Net changes in liabilities								
1. Currency and demand deposits					9.39		−.02	9.37
2. Other bank deposits and shares					2.65		−.27	2.38
3. Life insurance reserves					4.29			4.29
4. Pension and retirement funds, private					.98			.98
5. Pension and insurance funds, govt.					1.31			1.31
6. Consumer debt	3.99		.19					4.18
7. Trade debt	.10	.74	.20	8.01	.01	.10	1.10	10.26
8. Loans on securities	.78			0	.07			.85
9. Bank loans, n.e.c.	.27	2.13	.47	2.15	1.06		−.62	5.46
10. Other loans	.18	.36	.06	.13	.99			1.72
11. Mortgages	7.27	.57	.54	1.81				10.19
12. Bonds and notes				1.61	.42	3.11	.05	5.19
13. Other liabilities				7.37	1.85		0	9.22
14. Total	12.59	3.80	1.46	21.08	23.02	3.21	.24	65.40
IV. Net changes in equities								
1. Net issues of common stock				1.60	.45			2.05
2. Net issues of preferred stock				.24	.02			.26
3. Saving	42.61	4.86	11.51	23.00	1.89	4.57	8.48	96.92
V. Total uses and sources of funds	55.20	8.66	12.97	45.92	25.37	7.78	8.72	164.62

Note: Inventories at Adjusted Values and Lines Affected

	(1)	(2)	(3)	(4)	(5)	(6)	(7)	(8)
Inventories (adjusted values)		1.18	1.22	4.81	.01	.02	−.61	6.63
Gross capital expenditures	42.20	5.64	8.58	23.79	.43	6.45	.67	87.76
Saving	42.61	3.77	7.30	18.04	1.89	4.57	8.48	86.66
Total uses and sources of funds	55.20	7.57	8.76	40.96	25.37	7.78	8.72	154.36

Source: For columns 1-7, see Tables VII-1 through VII-7 respectively.

TABLE V

Annual Flow of Funds Through Sectors—1951

(billion dollars)

	Nonfarm House-holds (1)	Nonfarm Unincor-porated Business (2)	Agri-culture (3)	Nonfinan-cial Corpora-tions (4)	Finance (5)	State and Local Govts. (6)	Federal Govt. (7)	Total (8)
I. Gross capital expenditures								
1. Residential structures	13.69	.34	.88	.75	.01	.58	–.01	16.24
2. Nonresidential structures	1.27	1.11	1.00	8.13	.38	6.03	1.20	19.12
3. Land								
4. Producer durables	.24	3.31	2.74	13.80	.10	.53	.10	20.82
5. Consumer durables	26.24		3.09					29.33
6. Inventories at book value (see note below)		.83	3.77	9.75	a	a	–.43	13.92
7. Total	41.44	5.59	11.48	32.43	.49	7.14	.86	99.43
II. Net financial flows								
1. Currency and demand deposits	3.07	1.04	.20	1.82	4.67	.43	.06	11.29
a. Monetary metals	.05	.02	.02	.01	–.05			.05
b. Other	3.02	1.02	.18	1.81	4.72	.43	.06	11.24
2. Other bank deposits and shares	4.20		.07	0	.08	.15	.09	4.59
3. Life insurance reserves	3.92		.24					4.16
4. Pension and retirement funds, private	1.45							1.45
5. Pension and insurance funds, govt.	4.11		–.04					4.07
6. Consumer credit		.30		.51	.53			1.34
7. Trade credit		.22		3.41	.20		.92	4.75
8. Loans on securities					–.34			–.34
9. Bank loans, n.e.c.					4.68			4.68
10. Other loans	–.04				.65		.63	1.24
11. Mortgages, nonfarm	.49				7.69	.07	.62	8.87
a. Residential	.22				6.86	.07	.62	7.77
b. Nonresidential	.27				.83		0	1.10
12. Mortgages, farm	.25				.25		.06	.56
13. Securities, U. S. government	–1.45		.02	.93	2.73	.37	–.09	2.51
a. Short-term	–1.61			.30	–9.21	–.20		–10.72
b. Savings bonds	–.55		.02	0	.02			–.51
c. Other long-term	.71			.63	11.92	.57	–.09	13.74
14. Securities, state and local	.31			.05	1.66	.12	.26	2.40

	(1)	(2)	(3)	(4)	(5)	(6)	(7)	Total
15. Securities, other bonds and notes	.07			.30	4.03	.10		4.50
16. Securities, preferred stock	.45			0	.13			.58
17. Securities, common stock	1.67			.12	.70			2.49
18. Equity in mutual financial organizations								
19. Equity in other business								
20. Other intangible assets	–.23		.20	1.02	.67		4.62	6.28
21. Total	18.27	1.56	.69	8.16	28.33	1.24	7.17	65.42
III. Net changes in liabilities								
1. Currency and demand deposits					10.96		.04	11.00
2. Other bank deposits and shares					4.92		–.22	4.70
3. Life insurance reserves					4.25			4.25
4. Pension and retirement funds, private					1.44			1.44
5. Pension and insurance funds, govt.					4.07			4.07
6. Consumer debt	1.35		–.01					1.34
7. Trade debt	0	–.69	.40	2.28	–.01	0	1.60	3.58
8. Loans on securities	–.15			0	–.19			–.34
9. Bank loans, n.e.c.	–.01	–.80	.60	4.96	–.04		–.09	4.62
10. Other loans	.20	.50	.11	.15	.05			1.01
11. Mortgages	6.78	.65	.56	1.45				9.44
12. Bonds and notes				3.30	.57	2.41	2.99	9.27
13. Other liabilities				6.94	1.14		.15	8.23
14. Total	8.17	–.34	1.66	19.08	27.16	2.41	4.47	62.61
IV. Net changes in equities								
1. Net issues of common stock				2.05	.56			2.61
2. Net issues of preferred stock				.64	–.04			.60
3. Saving	51.54	7.49	10.51	18.82	1.15	5.97	3.56	99.04
V. Total uses and sources of funds	59.71	7.15	12.17	40.59	28.82	8.38	8.03	164.85

Note: Inventories at Adjusted Values and Lines Affected

	(1)	(2)	(3)	(4)	(5)	(6)	(7)	Total
Inventories (adjusted values)		.50	1.54	8.55	[a]	[a]	–.43	10.16
Gross capital expenditures	41.44	5.26	9.25	31.23	.49	7.14	.86	95.67
Saving	51.54	7.16	8.28	17.62	1.15	5.97	3.56	95.28
Total uses and sources of funds	59.71	6.82	9.94	39.39	28.82	8.38	8.03	161.09

Source: For columns 1-7, see Tables VII-1 through VII-7 respectively.

[a] $5 million or under.

TABLE V

Annual Flow of Funds Through Sectors—1952

(billion dollars)

	Nonfarm House-holds (1)	Nonfarm Unincor-porated Business (2)	Agri-culture (3)	Nonfinan-cial Corpora-tions (4)	Finance (5)	State and Local Govts. (6)	Federal Govt. (7)	Total (8)
I. Gross capital expenditures								
1. Residential structures	13.95	.31	.90	.63	.11	.63	−.01	16.52
2. Nonresidential structures	1.18	1.02	1.03	8.82	.21	6.96	1.14	20.36
3. Land								
4. Producer durables	.23	3.28	2.59	14.07	.05	.58	.18	20.98
5. Consumer durables	26.28		2.54					28.82
6. Inventories at book value (see note below)		−.29	−4.99	1.25	a	a	.46	−3.57
7. Total	41.64	4.32	2.07	24.77	.37	8.17	1.77	83.11
II. Net financial flows								
1. Currency and demand deposits	1.89	−.35	−.10	.80	1.15	.47	1.95	5.81
a. Monetary metals	.08	−.01	0	.01	.47			.55
b. Other	1.81	−.34	−.10	.79	.68	.47	1.95	5.26
2. Other bank deposits and shares	7.35		.13	0	.13	.09	.07	7.77
3. Life insurance reserves	4.71		.28					4.99
4. Pension and retirement funds, private	1.61							1.61
5. Pension and insurance funds, govt.	4.36		−.01					4.35
6. Consumer credit		.40		.76	3.63			4.79
7. Trade credit		1.11		3.53	.15		.95	5.74
8. Loans on securities					.70			.70
9. Bank loans, n.e.c.					3.02			3.02
10. Other loans	−.11				.35		.75	.99
11. Mortgages, nonfarm	.56				7.43	.08	.46	8.53
a. Residential	.28				6.66	.08	.46	7.48
b. Nonresidential	.28				.77		0	1.05
12. Mortgages, farm	.25				.25		.09	.59
13. Securities, U. S. government	.23		−.08	−.80	6.38	1.08	.10	6.91
a. Short-term	.75			−1.10	5.41	.70		5.76
b. Savings bonds	.15		−.08	0	.24			.31
c. Other long-term	−.67			.30	.73	.38	.10	.84
14. Securities, state and local	1.16			.06	1.54	.11	.32	3.19

	(1)	(2)	(3)	(4)	(5)	(6)	(7)	(8)
15. Securities, other bonds and notes	−.15			.41	5.05	−.07		5.24
16. Securities, preferred stock	.28			.01	.19			.48
17. Securities, common stock	1.82			.16	1.16			3.14
18. Equity in mutual financial organizations								
19. Equity in other business								
20. Other intangible assets	−.23		.24	2.98	1.01		−3.16	.84
21. Total	23.73	1.16	.46	7.91	32.12	1.76	1.53	68.67
III. Net changes in liabilities								
1. Currency and demand deposits					6.99		.04	7.03
2. Other bank deposits and shares					8.14		−.16	7.98
3. Life insurance reserves					5.09			5.09
4. Pension and retirement funds, private					1.60			1.60
5. Pension and insurance funds, govt.					4.35			4.35
6. Consumer debt	4.70		.09					4.79
7. Trade debt	.24	.31	.10	3.59	.04	.10	.10	4.48
8. Loans on securities	.21			0	.48			.69
9. Bank loans, n.e.c.	−.06	.48	.07	1.19	.91		.43	3.02
10. Other loans	.12	.31	.08	.09	−.03			.57
11. Mortgages	6.72	.52	.59	1.29				9.12
12. Bonds and notes				4.72	.54	3.18	8.01	16.45
13. Other liabilities				−1.40	2.10		.26	.96
14. Total	11.93	1.62	.93	9.48	30.21	3.28	8.68	66.13
IV. Net changes in equities								
1. Net issues of common stock				2.33	.76			3.09
2. Net issues of preferred stock				.45	.02			.47
3. Saving	53.44	3.86	1.60	20.42	1.49	6.65	−5.38	82.08
V. Total uses and sources of funds	65.37	5.48	2.53	32.68	32.48	9.93	3.30	151.77

Note: Inventories at Adjusted Values and Lines Affected

	(1)	(2)	(3)	(4)	(5)	(6)	(7)	(8)
Inventories (adjusted values)		−.08	.75	2.23	[a]	[a]	.46	3.36
Gross capital expenditures	41.64	4.53	7.81	25.75	.37	8.17	1.77	90.04
Saving	53.44	4.07	7.34	21.40	1.49	6.65	−5.38	89.01
Total uses and sources of funds	65.37	5.69	8.27	33.66	32.48	9.93	3.30	158.70

Source: For columns 1-7, see Tables VII-1 through VII-7 respectively.

[a]$5 million or under.

TABLE V

Annual Flow of Funds Through Sectors—1953

(billion dollars)

	Nonfarm Households (1)	Nonfarm Unincorporated Business (2)	Agriculture (3)	Nonfinancial Corporations (4)	Finance (5)	State and Local Govts. (6)	Federal Govt. (7)	Total (8)
I. Gross capital expenditures								
1. Residential structures	15.13	.40	.82	.88	−.01	.52	.02	17.76
2. Nonresidential structures	1.27	1.33	.93	9.61	.33	7.45	1.09	22.01
3. Land								
4. Producer durables	.24	3.68	2.46	14.96	.08	.62	.17	22.21
5. Consumer durables	29.17		2.93					32.10
6. Inventories at book value (see note below)		.42	−4.24	1.80	a	.01	2.88	.87
7. Total	45.81	5.83	2.90	27.25	.40	8.60	4.16	94.95
II. Net financial flows								
1. Currency and demand deposits	.91	−.05	−.10	−.08	−1.18	.60	−1.47	−1.37
a. Monetary metals	.06	.01	−.01	0	−1.16			−1.10
b. Other	.85	−.06	−.09	−.08	−.02	.60	−1.47	−.27
2. Other bank deposits and shares	7.88		.13	0	.08	.33	−.01	8.41
3. Life insurance reserves	4.77		.27					5.04
4. Pension and retirement funds, private	1.94							1.94
5. Pension and insurance funds, govt.	3.42		−.04					3.38
6. Consumer credit		.18		.24	3.51			3.93
7. Trade credit		.58		−.81	.15		−.04	−.12
8. Loans on securities					.80			.80
9. Bank loans, n.e.c.					.38			.38
10. Other loans	.05				.22		.61	.88
11. Mortgages, nonfarm	.75				8.17	.14	.35	9.41
a. Residential	.40				7.34	.14	.35	8.23
b. Nonresidential	.34				.81		0	1.15
12. Mortgages, farm	.20				.21		.10	.51
13. Securities, U. S. government	.19		.10	1.58	3.86	1.31	.02	7.06
a. Short-term	1.02			1.80	11.77	1.20		15.79
b. Savings bonds	−.04		.10	0	−.17			−.11
c. Other long-term	−.79			−.22	−7.75	.11	.02	−8.63
14. Securities, state and local	1.61			.09	2.12	.09	−.33	3.58

	(1)	(2)	(3)	(4)	(5)	(6)	(7)	(8)
15. Securities, other bonds and notes	.12			.18	4.45	.05		4.80
16. Securities, preferred stock	.03			0	.34			.37
17. Securities, common stock	1.52			.13	.89			2.54
18. Equity in mutual financial organizations								
19. Equity in other business								
20. Other intangible assets	–.01		.15	2.63	.56		.53	3.86
21. Total	23.38	.71	.51	3.96	24.56	2.52	–.24	55.40
III. Net changes in liabilities								
1. Currency and demand deposits					–.35		.03	–.32
2. Other bank deposits and shares					9.16		–.19	8.97
3. Life insurance reserves					5.14			5.14
4. Pension and retirement funds, private					1.94			1.94
5. Pension and insurance funds, govt.					3.38			3.38
6. Consumer debt	3.93		–.01					3.92
7. Trade debt	.06	1.10	–.20	.16	.02	.10	–.20	1.04
8. Loans on securities	.52			0	.30			.82
9. Bank loans, n.e.c.	–.08	–.19	–.43	–.16	–.14		1.48	.48
10. Other loans	.21	.10	–.02	.34	.04			.67
11. Mortgages	7.65	.55	.51	1.20				9.91
12. Bonds and notes				3.35	1.58	3.58	7.79	16.30
13. Other liabilities				2.23	1.56		.21	4.00
14. Total	12.29	1.56	–.15	7.12	22.63	3.68	9.12	56.25
IV. Net changes in equities								
1. Net issues of common stock				1.94	.70			2.64
2. Net issues of preferred stock				.39	0			.39
3. Saving	56.90	4.98	3.56	21.76	1.65	7.44	–5.20	91.09
V. Total uses and sources of funds	69.19	6.54	3.41	31.21	24.98	11.12	3.92	150.37

Note: Inventories at Adjusted Values and Lines Affected

Inventories (adjusted values)		.26	–.98	.81	[a]	.01	2.88	2.98
Gross capital expenditures	45.81	5.67	6.16	26.26	.40	8.60	4.16	97.06
Saving	56.90	4.82	6.82	20.77	1.65	7.44	–5.20	93.20
Total uses and sources of funds	69.19	6.38	6.67	30.22	24.98	11.12	3.92	152.48

Source: For columns 1–7, see Tables VII–1 through VII–7 respectively.

[a] $5 million or under.

TABLE V

Annual Flow of Funds Through Sectors—1954

(billion dollars)

	Nonfarm House-holds (1)	Nonfarm Unincor-porated Business (2)	Agri-culture (3)	Nonfinan-cial Corpora-tions (4)	Finance (5)	State and Local Govts. (6)	Federal Govt. (7)	Total (8)
I. Gross capital expenditures								
1. Residential structures	15.74	.36	.78	.83	.02	.32	–.01	18.04
2. Nonresidential structures	1.54	1.55	.89	9.80	.27	8.61	.94	23.60
3. Land								
4. Producer durables	.29	3.48	2.21	14.10	.07	.70	.11	20.96
5. Consumer durables	29.23		2.61					31.84
6. Inventories at book value (see note below)		–.15	–.16	–1.60	–.01	.01	1.24	–.67
7. Total	46.80	5.24	6.33	23.13	.35	9.64	2.28	93.77
II. Net financial flows								
1. Currency and demand deposits	2.20	.53	–.10	2.36	–.93	.33	.03	4.42
a. Monetary metals	.01	.01	0	0	–.27			–.25
b. Other	2.19	.52	–.10	2.36	–.66	.33	.03	4.67
2. Other bank deposits and shares	8.83		.10	.20	.10	.46	.02	9.71
3. Life insurance reserves	5.18		.32					5.50
4. Pension and retirement funds, private	2.05							2.05
5. Pension and insurance funds, govt.	2.71		–.02					2.69
6. Consumer credit		.09		.27	.74			1.10
7. Trade credit		.20		4.31	.16		.23	4.90
8. Loans on securities					1.86			1.86
9. Bank loans, n.e.c.					.60			.60
10. Other loans	.74				.11		–.07	.78
11. Mortgages, nonfarm	.99				10.77	.10	.02	11.88
a. Residential	.43				9.54	.10	.02	10.09
b. Nonresidential	.57				1.22		0	1.79
12. Mortgages, farm	.18				.24		.10	.52
13. Securities, U. S. government	–1.53		.24	–2.29	5.25	1.44	.13	3.24
a. Short-term	–.65			–2.60	–8.67	0		–11.92
b. Savings bonds	.09		.24	0	.09			.42
c. Other long-term	–.97			.31	13.83	1.44	.13	14.74
14. Securities, state and local	.66			.33	3.49	.03	–.33	4.18

15. Securities, other bonds and notes	−.97			−.07	4.31	.20		3.47
16. Securities, preferred stock	−.01			.01	.42			.42
17. Securities, common stock	1.24			.14	1.34			2.72
18. Equity in mutual financial organizations								
19. Equity in other business								
20. Other intangible assets	0		.24	4.93	.62		−3.13	2.66
21. Total	22.27	.82	.78	10.19	29.06	2.56	−3.00	62.68
III. Net changes in liabilities								
1. Currency and demand deposits					2.72		.03	2.75
2. Other bank deposits and shares					10.51		−.23	10.28
3. Life insurance reserves					5.61			5.61
4. Pension and retirement funds, private					2.05			2.05
5. Pension and insurance funds, govt.					2.69			2.69
6. Consumer debt	1.01		.09					1.10
7. Trade debt	.10	1.32	0	3.40	.01	.15	−.23	4.75
8. Loans on securities	1.28			0	.67			1.95
9. Bank loans, n.e.c.	.12	1.11	.17	−1.22	−.01		.07	.24
10. Other loans	.24	.18	.10	−.27	.68			.93
11. Mortgages	9.37	.74	.52	1.76				12.39
12. Bonds and notes				3.54	.19	4.18	3.55	11.46
13. Other liabilities				.32	1.40		.28	2.00
14. Total	12.12	3.35	.88	7.53	26.53	4.33	3.47	58.21
IV. Net changes in equities								
1. Net issues of common stock				1.81	.78			2.59
2. Net issues of preferred stock				.50	−.07			.43
3. Saving	56.95	2.71	6.23	23.48	2.17	7.87	−4.19	95.22
V. Total uses and sources of funds	69.07	6.06	7.11	33.32	29.40	12.20	−.72	156.44

Note: Inventories at Adjusted Values and Lines Affected

Inventories (adjusted values)		−.20	.66	−1.92	−.01	.01	1.24	−.22
Gross capital expenditures	46.80	5.19	7.15	22.81	.35	9.64	2.28	94.22
Saving	56.95	2.66	7.05	23.16	2.17	7.87	−4.19	95.67
Total uses and sources of funds	69.07	6.01	7.93	33.00	29.40	12.20	−.72	156.89

Source: For columns 1-7, see Tables VII-1 through VII-7 respectively.

TABLE V

Annual Flow of Funds Through Sectors—1955

(billion dollars)

	Nonfarm House-holds (1)	Nonfarm Unincor-porated Business (2)	Agri-culture (3)	Nonfinan-cial Corpora-tions (4)	Finance (5)	State and Local Govts. (6)	Federal Govt. (7)	Total (8)
I. Gross capital expenditures								
1. Residential structures	19.84	.40	.76	.99	.01	.26	a	22.26
2. Nonresidential structures	1.66	1.94	.86	11.16	.41	9.92	.85	26.80
3. Land								
4. Producer durables	.32	4.09	2.27	15.35	.10	.75	.05	22.93
5. Consumer durables	36.58		2.54					39.12
6. Inventories at book value (see note below)		.76	−1.37	6.66	a	.01	.14	6.20
7. Total	58.40	7.19	5.06	34.16	.52	10.94	1.04	117.31
II. Net financial flows								
1. Currency and demand deposits	−.75	.29	0	.98	.61	.39	−.41	1.11
a. Monetary metals	.06	.01	.01	.01	−.05			.04
b. Other	−.81	.28	−.01	.97	.66	.39	−.41	1.07
2. Other bank deposits and shares	8.42		.05	−.10	.02	−.06	0	8.33
3. Life insurance reserves	5.26		.30					5.56
4. Pension and retirement funds, private	2.06							2.06
5. Pension and insurance funds, govt.	3.24		0					3.24
6. Consumer credit		.16		.66	5.63			6.45
7. Trade credit		.53		10.86	.38		−.17	11.60
8. Loans on securities					1.08			1.08
9. Bank loans, n.e.c.					6.84			6.84
10. Other loans	−.12				1.29		1.03	2.20
11. Mortgages, nonfarm	1.00				14.00	.12	.32	15.44
a. Residential	.38				12.60	.12	.32	13.42
b. Nonresidential	.62				1.40		0	2.02
12. Mortgages, farm	.22				.36		.19	.77
13. Securities, U. S. government	1.76		.20	3.99	−5.71	.41	.02	.67
a. Short-term	−1.01			3.00	−8.15	−1.60		−7.76
b. Savings bonds	.03		.20	0	−.04			.19
c. Other long-term	2.74			.99	2.48	2.01	.02	8.24
14. Securities, state and local	1.68			.18	1.57	.05	0	3.48

	(1)	(2)	(3)	(4)	(5)	(6)	(7)	Total
15. Securities, other bonds and notes	1.91			.41	3.38	.04		5.74
16. Securities, preferred stock	−.14			.01	.20			.07
17. Securities, common stock	2.13			.19	1.40			3.72
18. Equity in mutual financial organizations								
19. Equity in other business								
20. Other intangible assets	0		.14	4.83	4.96		4.02	13.95
21. Total	26.67	.98	.69	22.01	35.98	.95	5.00	92.28
III. Net changes in liabilities								
1. Currency and demand deposits					6.75		.01	6.76
2. Other bank deposits and shares					8.46		−.25	8.21
3. Life insurance reserves					5.67			5.67
4. Pension and retirement funds, private					2.06			2.06
5. Pension and insurance funds, govt.					3.24			3.24
6. Consumer debt	6.26		.19					6.45
7. Trade debt	.12	.60	0	10.24	.02	.15	−.09	11.04
8. Loans on securities	.75			0	.32			1.07
9. Bank loans, n.e.c.	.68	1.49	.38	2.27	2.76		−1.10	6.48
10. Other loans	.18	1.01	.05	.46	.48			2.18
11. Mortgages	12.54	.90	.78	2.00				16.22
12. Bonds and notes				2.77	1.63	3.48	3.58	11.46
13. Other liabilities				6.55	2.07		−.03	8.59
14. Total	20.53	4.00	1.40	24.29	33.45	3.63	2.12	89.42
IV. Net changes in equities								
1. Net issues of common stock				2.55	1.12			3.67
2. Net issues of preferred stock				0	.08			.08
3. Saving	64.54	4.17	4.35	29.33	1.84	8.26	3.92	116.41
V. Total uses and sources of funds	85.07	8.17	5.75	56.17	36.50	11.89	6.04	209.59

Note: Inventories at Adjusted Values and Lines Affected

	(1)	(2)	(3)	(4)	(5)	(6)	(7)	Total
Inventories (adjusted values)		.56	.26	4.93	a	.01	.14	5.90
Gross capital expenditures	58.40	6.99	6.69	32.43	.52	10.94	1.04	117.01
Saving	64.54	3.97	5.98	27.60	1.84	8.26	3.92	116.11
Total uses and sources of funds	85.07	7.97	7.38	54.44	36.50	11.89	6.04	209.29

Source: For columns 1–7, see Tables VII–1 through VII–7 respectively.

[a] $5 million or under.

TABLE V

Annual Flow of Funds Through Sectors—1956

(billion dollars)

	Nonfarm House-holds (1)	Nonfarm Unincor-porated Business (2)	Agri-culture (3)	Nonfinan-cial Corpora-tions (4)	Finance (5)	State and Local Govts. (6)	Federal Govt. (7)	Total (8)
I. Gross capital expenditures								
1. Residential structures	19.14	.48	.74	1.12	–.01	.28	.02	21.77
2. Nonresidential structures	1.72	2.19	.84	12.64	.51	10.34	1.05	29.29
3. Land								
4. Producer durables	.33	4.59	2.03	19.39	.13	.88	.04	27.39
5. Consumer durables	35.37		2.53					37.90
6. Inventories at book value (see note below)		.69	.85	7.58	a	.02	–.11	9.03
7. Total	56.56	7.95	6.99	40.73	.63	11.52	1.00	125.38
II. Net financial flows								
1. Currency and demand deposits	.96	.35	–.20	.14	2.22	.15	–.30	3.32
a. Monetary metals	.06	.01	.01	.01	.31			.40
b. Other	.90	.34	–.21	.13	1.91	.15	–.30	2.92
2. Other bank deposits and shares	9.14		.05	0	.05	.04	–.03	9.25
3. Life insurance reserves	5.22		.26					5.48
4. Pension and retirement funds, private	2.61							2.61
5. Pension and insurance funds, govt.	3.58		0					3.58
6. Consumer credit		.26		.41	3.02			3.69
7. Trade credit		.89		7.06	.42		.08	8.45
8. Loans on securities					–.68			–.68
9. Bank loans, n.e.c.					5.58			5.58
10. Other loans	–.04				.25		–.03	.18
11. Mortgages, nonfarm	1.49				11.84	.11	.46	13.90
a. Residential	.75				10.18	.11	.46	11.50
b. Nonresidential	.73				1.66		0	2.39
12. Mortgages, farm	.34				.26		.25	.85
13. Securities, U. S. government	1.11		–.11	–4.59	–2.02	.70	.25	–4.66
a. Short-term	1.50			–3.70	6.37	2.20		6.37
b. Savings bonds	–.29		–.11	–.20	–.93			–1.53
c. Other long-term	–.10			–.69	–7.45	–1.50	.25	–9.49
14. Securities, state and local	1.68			.11	1.38	.07	.08	3.32

	(1)	(2)	(3)	(4)	(5)	(6)	(7)	Total
15. Securities, other bonds and notes	1.66			.23	3.88	.01		5.78
16. Securities, preferred stock	.60			0	−.12			.48
17. Securities, common stock	2.17			.19	1.53			3.89
18. Equity in mutual financial organizations								
19. Equity in other business								
20. Other intangible assets	.01		.17	5.99	1.99		−1.21	6.95
21. Total	30.53	1.50	.17	9.54	29.58	1.08	−.45	71.95
III. Net changes in liabilities								
1. Currency and demand deposits					4.04		.02	4.06
2. Other bank deposits and shares					9.43		−.25	9.18
3. Life insurance reserves					5.59			5.59
4. Pension and retirement funds, private					2.60			2.60
5. Pension and insurance funds, govt.					3.58			3.58
6. Consumer debt	3.70		−.01					3.69
7. Trade debt	.17	.94	0	5.61	.03	.10	.33	7.18
8. Loans on securities	−.05			0	−.62			−.67
9. Bank loans, n.e.c.	.13	.67	−.03	5.38	−.63		−.29	5.23
10. Other loans	.27	.09	.08	−.15	−.18			.11
11. Mortgages	11.00	1.02	.84	1.88				14.74
12. Bonds and notes				3.67	1.19	3.32	−3.51	4.67
13. Other liabilities				3.39	1.98		.10	5.47
14. Total	15.22	2.72	.88	19.78	27.00	3.42	−3.60	65.42
IV. Net changes in equities								
1. Net issues of common stock				2.60	1.43			4.03
2. Net issues of preferred stock				.46	.02			.48
3. Saving	71.87	6.73	6.28	27.43	1.75	9.18	4.15	127.39
V. Total uses and sources of funds	87.09	9.45	7.16	50.27	30.20	12.60	.55	197.32

Note: Inventories at Adjusted Values and Lines Affected

	(1)	(2)	(3)	(4)	(5)	(6)	(7)	Total
Inventories (adjusted values)		.19	−.68	4.89	[a]	.02	−.11	4.31
Gross capital expenditures	56.56	7.45	5.46	38.04	.63	11.52	1.00	120.66
Saving	71.87	6.23	4.75	24.74	1.75	9.18	4.15	122.67
Total uses and sources of funds	87.09	8.95	5.63	47.58	30.20	12.60	.55	192.60

Source: For columns 1-7, see Tables VII-1 through VII-7 respectively.

[a] $5 million or under.

TABLE V

Annual Flow of Funds Through Sectors—1957

(billion dollars)

	Nonfarm Households (1)	Nonfarm Unincorporated Business (2)	Agriculture (3)	Nonfinancial Corporations (4)	Finance (5)	State and Local Govts. (6)	Federal Govt. (7)	Total (8)
I. Gross capital expenditures								
1. Residential structures	18.15	.48	.75	1.08	.01	.35	.15	20.97
2. Nonresidential structures	2.02	2.20	.86	13.60	.46	11.96	1.06	32.16
3. Land								
4. Producer durables	.38	4.87	2.06	20.35	.12	1.04	.04	28.86
5. Consumer durables	36.76		2.64					39.40
6. Inventories at book value (see note below)		.31	2.34	2.74	–.01	.01	–.94	4.45
7. Total	57.31	7.86	8.65	37.77	.58	13.36	.31	125.84
II. Net financial flows								
1. Currency and demand deposits	–1.02	.81	–.10	0	2.07	.21	.01	1.98
a. Monetary metals	.17	.03	.03	.02	.73			.98
b. Other	–1.19	.78	–.13	–.02	1.34	.21	.01	1.00
2. Other bank deposits and shares	11.38		.27	0	.04	.38	–.03	12.04
3. Life insurance reserves	4.90		.24					5.14
4. Pension and retirement funds, private	2.89							2.89
5. Pension and insurance funds, govt.	2.86		–.01					2.85
6. Consumer credit		.10		.21	2.53			2.84
7. Trade credit		.28		2.72	.34		–.05	3.29
8. Loans on securities					–.36			–.36
9. Bank loans, n.e.c.					2.06			2.06
10. Other loans	.06				1.31		.63	2.00
11. Mortgages, nonfarm	1.42				8.30	.36	1.27	11.35
a. Residential	.81				6.73	.36	1.27	9.17
b. Nonresidential	.61				1.58		0	2.19
12. Mortgages, farm	.24				.13		.22	.59
13. Securities, U. S. government	–1.14		.06	–.80	–.94	.74	.44	–1.64
a. Short-term	2.38			–.40	2.23	1.30		5.51
b. Savings bonds	–2.27		.06	–.20	–1.40			–3.81
c. Other long-term	–1.25			–.20	–1.78	–.56	.44	–3.35
14. Securities, state and local	2.12			.15	2.33	.07	.20	4.87

	(1)	(2)	(3)	(4)	(5)	(6)	(7)	(8)
15. Securities, other bonds and notes	1.85			.83	7.32	−.10		9.90
16. Securities, preferred stock	.43			.01	−.03			.41
17. Securities, common stock	1.76			.21	2.26			4.23
18. Equity in mutual financial organizations								
19. Equity in other business								
20. Other intangible assets	0		.17	6.64	1.12		−1.49	6.44
21. Total	27.75	1.19	.63	9.97	28.50	1.66	1.20	70.90
III. Net changes in liabilities								
1. Currency and demand deposits					−.67		.03	−.64
2. Other bank deposits and shares					12.40		−.32	12.08
3. Life insurance reserves					5.25			5.25
4. Pension and retirement funds, private					2.89			2.89
5. Pension and insurance funds, govt.					2.85			2.85
6. Consumer debt	2.86		−.02					2.84
7. Trade debt	.14	.68	.10	2.02	.01	.05	.16	3.16
8. Loans on securities	−.46			0	.10			−.36
9. Bank loans, n.e.c.	.21	−.09	.32	2.06	−.37		−.42	1.71
10. Other loans	.35	.33	.22	.37	.30			1.57
11. Mortgages	8.70	.93	.60	1.73				11.96
12. Bonds and notes				6.35	1.12	4.87	.39	12.73
13. Other liabilities				2.56	2.00		.07	4.63
14. Total	11.80	1.85	1.22	15.09	25.87	4.92	−.09	60.66
IV. Net changes in equities								
1. Net issues of common stock				2.94	1.39			4.33
2. Net issues of preferred stock				.37	.04			.41
3. Saving	73.26	7.20	8.06	29.34	1.77	10.10	1.60	131.33
V. Total uses and sources of funds	85.06	9.05	9.28	47.74	29.08	15.02	1.51	196.74

Note: Inventories at Adjusted Values and Lines Affected

Inventories (adjusted values)		.01	.55	1.21	−.01	.01	−.94	.83
Gross capital expenditures	57.31	7.56	6.86	36.24	.58	13.36	.31	122.22
Saving	73.26	6.90	6.27	27.81	1.77	10.10	1.60	127.71
Total uses and sources of funds	85.06	8.75	7.49	46.21	29.08	15.02	1.51	193.12

Source: For columns 1-7, see Tables VII-1 through VII-7 respectively.

TABLE V

Annual Flow of Funds Through Sectors—1958

(billion dollars)

	Nonfarm House-holds (1)	Nonfarm Unincor-porated Business (2)	Agri-culture (3)	Nonfinan-cial Corpora-tions (4)	Finance (5)	State and Local Govts. (6)	Federal Govt. (7)	Total (8)
I. Gross capital expenditures								
1. Residential structures	18.26	.53	.76	1.17	a	.48	.35	21.55
2. Nonresidential structures	2.18	2.21	.86	12.73	.31	13.62	1.20	33.11
3. Land								
4. Producer durables	.41	3.81	2.59	15.64	.08	1.02	.06	23.61
5. Consumer durables	34.04		2.87					36.91
6. Inventories at book value (see note below)		–.02	5.58	–4.44	a	.01	1.97	3.10
7. Total	54.89	6.53	12.66	25.10	.39	15.13	3.58	118.28
II. Net financial flows								
1. Currency and demand deposits	2.84	1.10	.30	1.72	–3.73	.22	0	2.45
a. Monetary metals	.12	.02	.01	.02	–2.22			–2.05
b. Other	2.72	1.08	.29	1.70	–1.51	.22	0	4.50
2. Other bank deposits and shares	13.75		.17	.60	.31	.80	.03	15.66
3. Life insurance reserves	5.24		.29					5.53
4. Pension and retirement funds, private	3.06							3.06
5. Pension and insurance funds, govt.	1.24		–.01					1.23
6. Consumer credit		–.09		.52	–.23			.20
7. Trade credit		.79		7.67	.36		–.60	8.22
8. Loans on securities					1.58			1.58
9. Bank loans, n.e.c.					1.72			1.72
10. Other loans	.78				.35		1.10	2.23
11. Mortgages, nonfarm	1.84				12.18	.42	.11	14.55
a. Residential	.81				10.42	.42	.11	11.76
b. Nonresidential	1.03				1.75		0	2.78
12. Mortgages, farm	.34				.18		.22	.74
13. Securities, U. S. government	–2.03		.09	.19	10.42	–.70	–.09	7.88
a. Short-term	–1.37			.70	.58	–1.10		–1.19
b. Savings bonds	–.90		.09	–.18	–.34			–1.33
c. Other long-term	.24			–.33	10.19	.40	–.09	10.41
14. Securities, state and local	1.42			.13	4.10	.05	.21	5.91

	(1)	(2)	(3)	(4)	(5)	(6)	(7)	(8)
15. Securities, other bonds and notes	.28			−.26	5.95	−.12		5.85
16. Securities, preferred stock	.04			0	.44			.48
17. Securities, common stock	2.16			.23	2.29			4.68
18. Equity in mutual financial organizations								
19. Equity in other business								
20. Other intangible assets	0		.22	1.00	1.40		−2.26	.36
21. Total	30.96	1.80	1.06	11.80	37.35	.67	−1.28	82.36
III. Net changes in liabilities								
1. Currency and demand deposits					4.29		.04	4.33
2. Other bank deposits and shares					17.01		−.20	16.81
3. Life insurance reserves					5.64			5.64
4. Pension and retirement funds, private					3.07			3.07
5. Pension and insurance funds, govt.					1.23			1.23
6. Consumer debt	.02		.18					.20
7. Trade debt	.10	.22	.10	6.28	.02	.15	.06	6.93
8. Loans on securities	1.32			0	.34			1.66
9. Bank loans, n.e.c.	.42	1.82	.56	−.88	−1.08		.35	1.19
10. Other loans	.35	.12	.23	−.15	1.03			1.58
11. Mortgages	9.99	1.36	.75	3.19				15.29
12. Bonds and notes				5.92	.02	5.92	7.57	19.43
13. Other liabilities				.19	1.62		.27	2.08
14. Total	12.20	3.52	1.82	14.55	33.18	6.07	8.09	79.43
IV. Net changes in equities								
1. Net issues of common stock				2.59	1.69			4.28
2. Net issues of preferred stock				.49	0			.49
3. Saving	73.65	4.81	11.90	19.27	2.87	9.73	−5.79	116.44
V. Total uses and sources of funds	85.85	8.33	13.72	36.90	37.73	15.80	2.30	200.63

Note: Inventories at Adjusted Values and Lines Affected

	(1)	(2)	(3)	(4)	(5)	(6)	(7)	(8)
Inventories (adjusted values)		−.06	2.31	−4.84	a	.01	1.97	−.61
Gross capital expenditures	54.89	6.49	9.39	24.70	.39	15.13	3.58	114.57
Saving	73.65	4.77	8.63	18.87	2.87	9.73	−5.79	112.73
Total uses and sources of funds	85.85	8.29	10.45	36.50	37.73	15.80	2.30	196.92

Source: For columns 1-7, see Tables VII-1 through VII-7 respectively.

[a] $5 million or under.

SECTION VI

Flow of Funds Through Finance Subsectors, 1946–58

TABLE VI

Annual Flow of Funds Through Finance Subsectors—1946 (billion dollars)

	Federal Reserve Banks & Treasury Monetary Funds (1)	Govt. Pension and Insurance Funds (2)	Commercial Banks (3)	Mutual Savings Banks (4)
I. Gross capital expenditures	a		.10	.01
II. Net financial flows				
1. Currency and demand deposits	1.26	.01	−1.30	.06
a. Monetary metals	.41			
b. Other	.85	.01	−1.30	.06
2. Other bank deposits and shares			−.01	.15
3. Life insurance reserves				
4. Pension and retirement funds, private				
5. Pension and insurance funds, govt.				
6. Consumer credit			1.19	0
7. Trade credit				
8. Loans on securities			−3.66	0
9. Bank loans, n.e.c.	−.09		5.06	
10. Other loans		−.01		.02
11. Mortgages, nonfarm		0	2.27	.23
a. Residential		0	1.74	.20
b. Nonresidential			.53	.03
12. Mortgages, farm			.18	0
13. Securities, U.S. government	−.92	3.76	−15.83	1.10
a. Short-term	−.90		−13.50	.28
b. Savings bonds		.10	.02	.04
c. Other long-term	−.02	3.66	−2.35	.78
14. Securities, state and local		−.10	.43	−.03
15. Securities, other bonds and notes		0	.35	.17
16. Securities, preferred stock		0		
17. Securities, common stock		0	−.03	.01
18. Equity in mutual financial organizations				
19. Equity in other business				
20. Other intangible assets	.38		.78	0
21. Total	.63	3.66	−10.57	1.71
III. Net changes in liabilities				
1. Currency and demand deposits	.14		−15.02	
2. Other bank deposits and shares			3.83	1.49
3. Life insurance reserves				
4. Pension and retirement funds, private				
5. Pension and insurance funds, govt.		3.67		
6. Consumer debt				
7. Trade debt				
8. Loans on securities				
9. Bank loans, n.e.c.			−.17	0
10. Other loans			−.07	
11. Mortgages				
12. Bonds and notes				
13. Other liabilities	.41		.21	.02
14. Total	.55	3.67	−11.22	1.51
IV. Net changes in equities				
1. Net issues of common stock			.05	
2. Net issues of preferred stock				
3. Saving	.08		.70	.21
V. Total uses and sources of funds	.63	3.66	−10.47	1.72

Savings and Loan Associ- ations (5)	Invest- ment Com- panies (6)	Credit Unions (7)	Life Insur- ance Com- panies (8)	Fire and Casualty Insur- ance Com- panies (9)	Non- insured Pension Plans (10)	Other Private Insur- ance (11)	Finance Com- panies (12)	Other Finance (13)	Total (14)	
.05			.17	.02		a			.36	I.
										II.
.07	0	0	−.01	.19	.02	0	−.01	.21	.50	1.
									.41	
.07	0	0	−.01	.19	.02	0	−.01	.21	.09	
		0		0					.14	2.
										3.
										4.
										5.
.04		.05					.58		1.86	6.
				.17			.18	−.01	.34	7.
								−.74	−4.40	8.
									4.97	9.
		0	−.07			0	.33	.09	.36	10.
1.76	.04	.01	.50	0	.01	.01	.11	.01	4.95	11.
1.73	.04	.01	.31	0	.01	0	.11	.01	4.16	
.04	0		.19	0		.01		0	.80	
			.02			0		0	.20	12.
−.41	−.05	0	1.05	.19	.18	.01		−1.17	−12.09	13.
0			.45	.05				.10	−13.52	
0			.02	.03	.17	0			.38	
−.41	−.05	0	.58	.11	.01	.01		−1.27	1.05	
			−.11	0		.01		−.02	.18	14.
	−.02		1.81	0	.26	.06		−.08	2.55	15.
	−.01		.15	.01	.03	.01		−.01	.18	16.
	.15		.12	.04	.05	.01		−.06	.29	17.
										18.
										19.
0	.01		.07	−.02	.03	0		−.02	1.23	20.
1.46	.12	.06	3.53	.58	.57	.10	1.19	−1.80	1.24	21.
										III.
								−.06	−14.94	1.
1.17		.06						.04	6.59	2.
			3.69			.09			3.78	3.
					.57				.57	4.
									3.67	5.
										6.
		−.01							−.01	7.
			−.37					−1.67	−2.04	8.
−.03							.79		.59	9.
.19								.10	.22	10.
										11.
							.26		.26	12.
.03			.06	.75		.02		−.09	1.41	13.
1.36		.05	3.38	.75	.57	.11	1.05	−1.68	.10	14.
										IV.
	.16		.02	.02			na		.25	1.
							na		0	2.
.15	−.04	.01	.30	−.17			.14	−.12	1.26	3.
1.51	.12	.06	3.70	.60	.57	.11	1.19	−1.80	1.60	V.

TABLE VI

Annual Flow of Funds Through Finance Subsectors—1947 (billion dollars)

	Federal Reserve Banks & Treasury Monetary Funds (1)	Govt. Pension and Insurance Funds (2)	Commercial Banks (3)	Mutual Savings Banks (4)
I. Gross capital expenditures			.11	.01
II. Net financial flows				
1. Currency and demand deposits	5.35	.02	2.21	.02
a. Monetary metals	2.22			
b. Other	3.13	.02	2.21	.02
2. Other bank deposits and shares			0	.05
3. Life insurance reserves				
4. Pension and retirement funds, private				
5. Pension and insurance funds, govt.				
6. Consumer credit			1.31	.02
7. Trade credit				
8. Loans on securities			−1.11	0
9. Bank loans, n.e.c.	−.07		4.66	
10. Other loans		0		−.02
11. Mortgages, nonfarm		0	2.08	.41
a. Residential		0	1.78	.35
b. Nonresidential			.30	.06
12. Mortgages, farm			.12	0
13. Securities, U.S. government	−.79	3.75	−5.56	.20
a. Short-term	−2.40		.40	.05
b. Savings bonds		.10	−.03	.05
c. Other long-term	1.61	3.65	−5.93	.10
14. Securities, state and local		.10	.88	0
15. Securities, other bonds and notes		.01	.06	.32
16. Securities, preferred stock		0		
17. Securities, common stock		0	−.03	0
18. Equity in mutual financial organizations				
19. Equity in other business				
20. Other intangible assets	.46		1.12	0
21. Total	4.95	3.88	5.74	1.00
III. Net changes in liabilities				
1. Currency and demand deposits	5.97		3.64	
2. Other bank deposits and shares			1.43	.88
3. Life insurance reserves				
4. Pension and retirement funds, private				
5. Pension and insurance funds, govt.		3.88		
6. Consumer debt				
7. Trade debt				
8. Loans on securities				
9. Bank loans, n.e.c.			.02	0
10. Other loans			−.05	
11. Mortgages				
12. Bonds and notes				
13. Other liabilities	−1.04		.15	.02
14. Total	4.93	3.88	5.19	.90
IV. Net changes in equities				
1. Net issues of common stock			.04	
2. Net issues of preferred stock				
3. Saving	.02		.62	.11
V. Total uses and sources of funds	4.95	3.88	5.85	1.01

Savings and Loan Associations (5)	Investment Companies (6)	Credit Unions (7)	Life Insurance Companies (8)	Fire and Casualty Insurance Companies (9)	Non-insured Pension Plans (10)	Other Private Insurance (11)	Finance Companies (12)	Other Finance (13)	Total (14)	
.05			.17	.02		a			.37	I.
										II.
0	−.01	.01	.25	.18	.03	0	−.06	−.11	7.89	1.
									2.22	
0	−.01	.01	.25	.18	.03	0	−.06	−.11	5.67	
		−.01		0					.04	2.
										3.
										4.
										5.
.03		.09					.86		2.31	6.
				.10			.01	.02	.13	7.
								.05	−1.06	8.
									4.59	9.
		0	.05			0	.21	.09	.33	10.
1.72	.08	.01	1.42	.01	0	.02	.07	.01	5.83	11.
1.68	.07	.01	1.06	0	0	.01	.07	.01	5.04	
.03	.01		.36	.01		.01		0	.78	
			.10			0		0	.22	12.
−.27	.01	0	−1.61	.59	.16	.01		−.86	−4.37	13.
0			−.53	.15				−.50	−2.83	
0			.02	.04	.16	0			.34	
−.27	.01	0	−1.10	.40	0	.01		−.36	−1.88	
			0	.08		.01		−.08	.99	14.
	−.02		3.02	.06	.31	.07		.03	3.86	15.
	.01		.06	0	.03	0		0	.10	16.
	.15		.09	.13	.08	0		.03	.45	17.
										18.
										19.
0	−.01		.06	.02	.03	0		0	1.68	20.
1.48	.21	.10	3.44	1.17	.64	.12	1.09	−.82	23.00	21.
										III.
								−.01	9.60	1.
1.20		.08						−.03	3.56	2.
			3.47			.11			3.58	3.
					.64				.64	4.
									3.88	5.
										6.
		.01							.01	7.
			0					−.71	−.71	8.
0							.60		.62	9.
.20								.04	.19	10.
										11.
							.28		.28	12.
−.03			.08	.99		.01		−.02	.16	13.
1.37		.09	3.55	.99	.64	.12	.87	−.73	21.80	14.
										IV.
	.17		.01	.02			.02		.26	1.
							0		0	2.
.16	.04	.01	.05	.18		0	.20	−.09	1.30	3.
1.53	.21	.10	3.61	1.19	.64	.12	1.09	−.82	23.36	V.

TABLE VI

Annual Flow of Funds Through Finance Subsectors—1948 (billion dollars)

	Federal Reserve Banks & Treasury Monetary Funds (1)	Govt. Pension and Insurance Funds (2)	Commercial Banks (3)	Mutual Savings Banks (4)
I. Gross capital expenditures	a		.10	.01
II. Net financial flows				
1. Currency and demand deposits	3.03	.08	1.52	−.03
a. Monetary metals	1.50			
b. Other	1.53	.08	1.52	−.03
2. Other bank deposits and shares			−.01	.02
3. Life insurance reserves				
4. Pension and retirement funds, private				
5. Pension and insurance funds, govt.				
6. Consumer credit			1.01	0
7. Trade credit				
8. Loans on securities			.26	0
9. Bank loans, n.e.c.	.13		2.04	
10. Other loans		.02		.02
11. Mortgages, nonfarm		0	1.36	.94
a. Residential		0	1.11	.82
b. Nonresidential			.25	.12
12. Mortgages, farm			.05	.01
13. Securities, U.S. government	.77	3.14	−6.60	−.50
a. Short-term	−7.50		.20	.05
b. Savings bonds		.10	.30	.18
c. Other long-term	8.27	3.04	−7.10	−.73
14. Securities, state and local		.15	.38	.01
15. Securities, other bonds and notes		.06	−.20	.50
16. Securities, preferred stock		.01		
17. Securities, common stock		.01	0	.01
18. Equity in mutual financial organizations				
19. Equity in other business				
20. Other intangible assets	−.09		−.26	.01
21. Total	3.84	3.47	−.45	.99
III. Net changes in liabilities				
1. Currency and demand deposits	3.93		−1.85	
2. Other bank deposits and shares			.63	.64
3. Life insurance reserves				
4. Pension and retirement funds, private				
5. Pension and insurance funds, govt.		3.48		
6. Consumer debt				
7. Trade debt				
8. Loans on securities				
9. Bank loans, n.e.c.			−.01	0
10. Other loans			−.03	
11. Mortgages				
12. Bonds and notes				
13. Other liabilities	−.15		.16	0
14. Total	3.78	3.48	−1.10	.64
IV. Net changes in equities				
1. Net issues of common stock			.02	
2. Net issues of preferred stock				
3. Saving	.06		.73	.36
V. Total uses and sources of funds	3.84	3.47	−.35	1.00

Savings and Loan Associations (5)	Investment Companies (6)	Credit Unions (7)	Life Insurance Companies (8)	Fire and Casualty Insurance Companies (9)	Noninsured Pension Plans (10)	Other Private Insurance (11)	Finance Companies (12)	Other Finance (13)	Total (14)	
.05			.17	.02		a			.36	I.
										II.
.06	0	.01	−.11	.04	.03	0	.18	−.06	4.75	1.
									1.50	
.06	0	.01	−.11	.04	.03	0	.18	−.06	3.25	
		.01		0					.02	2.
										3.
										4.
										5.
.03		.09					.85		1.98	6.
				.08			.02	.07	.17	7.
								−.01	.25	8.
									2.17	9.
		0	.12			0	.36	.10	.62	10.
1.45	.06	.02	2.06	.01	0	.03	−.01	.04	5.96	11.
1.42	.04	.02	1.72	.01	0	.01	−.01	.03	5.17	
.03	.01		.34	.01		.01		.01	.78	
			.10			0		0	.16	12.
−.28	−.05	−.02	−3.27	.49	.13	0		.43	−5.76	13.
−.10			.02	.35				.50	−6.48	
.10			.10	.15	.05	0			.98	
−.28	−.05	−.02	−3.39	−.01	.08	0		−.07	−.26	
			.26	.21		0		.09	1.10	14.
	.01		4.23	.17	.36	.05		−.01	5.17	15.
	.02		.03	−.01	.02	0		0	.07	16.
	.10		.01	.11	.08	0		−.05	.27	17.
										18.
										19.
.08	.02		.15	.01	.03	0		−.01	−.06	20.
1.34	.16	.11	3.58	1.11	.65	.09	1.38	.59	16.86	21.
										III.
								−.05	2.03	1.
1.21		.09						−.02	2.55	2.
			3.74			.09			3.83	3.
					.65				.65	4.
									3.48	5.
										6.
		.01							.01	7.
			0					.51	.51	8.
−.04							.51		.46	9.
.04								−.01	0	10.
										11.
							.58		.58	12.
.02			.04	.84		.01		.10	1.02	13.
1.23		.10	3.78	.84	.65	.10	1.09	.53	15.12	14.
										IV.
	.14		−.01	0			0		.15	1.
							.05		.05	2.
.16	.02	.01	−.02	.29			.24	.06	1.91	3.
1.39	.16	.11	3.75	1.13	.65	.10	1.38	.59	17.22	V.

TABLE VI

Annual Flow of Funds Through Finance Subsectors—1949 (billion dollars)

	Federal Reserve Banks & Treasury Monetary Funds (1)	Govt. Pension and Insurance Funds (2)	Commercial Banks (3)	Mutual Savings Banks (4)
I. Gross capital expenditures	a		.06	a
II. Net financial flows				
1. Currency and demand deposits	.35	−.02	−3.36	0
a. Monetary metals	.22			
b. Other	.13	−.02	−3.36	0
2. Other bank deposits and shares			−.01	−.01
3. Life insurance reserves				
4. Pension and retirement funds, private				
5. Pension and insurance funds, govt.				
6. Consumer credit			1.03	0
7. Trade credit				
8. Loans on securities			.33	0
9. Bank loans, n.e.c.	−.14		−1.48	
10. Other loans		.01		0
11. Mortgages, nonfarm		0	.70	.90
a. Residential		0	.60	.81
b. Nonresidential			.10	.08
12. Mortgages, farm			.04	0
13. Securities, U.S. government	−4.45	2.19	4.38	−.05
a. Short-term	−.40		7.10	−.10
b. Savings bonds		.10	−.05	.02
c. Other long-term	−4.05	2.09	−2.67	.03
14. Securities, state and local		.21	.89	.02
15. Securities, other bonds and notes		.15	.15	.14
16. Securities, preferred stock		0		
17. Securities, common stock		0	−.01	0
18. Equity in mutual financial organizations				
19. Equity in other business				
20. Other intangible assets	.04		.40	.02
21. Total	−4.20	2.54	3.06	1.02
III. Net changes in liabilities				
1. Currency and demand deposits	−4.56		1.87	
2. Other bank deposits and shares			.50	.88
3. Life insurance reserves				
4. Pension and retirement funds, private				
5. Pension and insurance funds, govt.		2.54		
6. Consumer debt				
7. Trade debt				
8. Loans on securities				
9. Bank loans, n.e.c.			−.04	0
10. Other loans			−.02	
11. Mortgages				
12. Bonds and notes				
13. Other liabilities	.30		.17	.02
14. Total	−4.26	2.54	2.48	.90
IV. Net changes in equities				
1. Net issues of common stock			.01	
2. Net issues of preferred stock				
3. Saving	.06		.63	.12
V. Total uses and sources of funds	−4.20	2.54	3.12	1.02

Savings and Loan Associations (5)	Investment Companies (6)	Credit Unions (7)	Life Insurance Companies (8)	Fire and Casualty Insurance Companies (9)	Noninsured Pension Plans (10)	Other Private Insurance (11)	Finance Companies (12)	Other Finance (13)	Total (14)	
.03			.10	.01		a			.22	I.
										II.
.08	0	0	0	.06	.04	.02	.11	−.07	−2.79	1.
									.22	
.08	0	0	0	.06	.04	.02	.11	−.07	−3.01	
		.03		0					.01	2.
										3.
										4.
										5.
.02		.11					1.10		2.26	6.
				.07			.05	−.01	.11	7.
								.42	.75	8.
									−1.62	9.
		0	.18			.01	−.09	.01	.12	10.
1.31	.02	.01	1.92	.01	.01	.03	.09	.01	5.01	11.
1.28	.02	.01	1.60	.01	.01	.02	.09	.02	4.47	
.03	0		.32	0		.01		0	.54	
			.15			.01		0	.20	12.
0	.04	−.02	−1.46	.51	.14	0		−.15	1.13	13.
0			.05	.30				−.10	6.85	
.10			.02	.05	.05	0			.29	
−.10	.04	−.02	−1.53	.16	.09	0		−.05	−6.01	
			.18	.22		−.01		−.02	1.49	14.
	.02		2.57	.09	.34	.06		.19	3.71	15.
	0		.20	.06	.03	0		.01	.30	16.
	.20		.03	.06	.11	0		.18	.57	17.
										18.
										19.
.14	−.02		.09	.02	.03	0		.01	.73	20.
1.55	.26	.13	3.86	1.10	.71	.14	1.26	.58	12.01	21.
										III.
								.01	−2.68	1.
1.50		.10						−.03	2.95	2.
			3.95			.12			4.07	3.
					.70				.70	4.
									2.54	5.
										6.
		.02							.02	7.
			0					.45	.45	8.
0							.43		.39	9.
−.04								.14	.08	10.
										11.
							.52		.52	12.
0			.08	.77		.02		−.04	1.32	13.
1.46		.12	4.03	.77	.70	.14	.96	.53	10.37	14.
										IV.
	.26		.03	.05			.02		.37	1.
							.03		.03	2.
.12	0	.01	−.10	.29			.25	.05	1.43	3.
1.58	.26	.13	3.96	1.11	.71	.14	1.26	.58	12.21	V.

TABLE VI

Annual Flow of Funds Through Finance Subsectors—1950 (billion dollars)

	Federal Reserve Banks & Treasury Monetary Funds (1)	Govt. Pension and Insurance Funds (2)	Commercial Banks (3)	Mutual Savings Banks (4)
I. Gross capital expenditures	a		.12	.01
II. Net financial flows				
1. Currency and demand deposits	−3.38	.46	2.28	−.02
a. Monetary metals	−1.73			
b. Other	−1.65	.46	2.28	−.02
2. Other bank deposits and shares			0	−.05
3. Life insurance reserves				
4. Pension and retirement funds, private				
5. Pension and insurance funds, govt.				
6. Consumer credit			1.66	.02
7. Trade credit				
8. Loans on securities			.22	0
9. Bank loans, n.e.c.	−.01		5.53	
10. Other loans		.02		0
11. Mortgages, nonfarm		.06	1.94	1.55
a. Residential		.06	1.73	1.48
b. Nonresidential			.21	.06
12. Mortgages, farm			.06	.01
13. Securities, U.S. government	1.90	.41	−4.97	−.56
a. Short-term	4.00		−4.30	−.33
b. Savings bonds		.10	.29	.08
c. Other long-term	−2.10	.31	−.96	−.31
14. Securities, state and local		.19	1.57	0
15. Securities, other bonds and notes		.15	.58	−.08
16. Securities, preferred stock		.01		
17. Securities, common stock		.01	0	.02
18. Equity in mutual financial organizations				
19. Equity in other business				
20. Other intangible assets	1.34		2.44	.02
21. Total	−.15	1.31	11.31	.91
III. Net changes in liabilities				
1. Currency and demand deposits	−.43		9.78	
2. Other bank deposits and shares			.23	.74
3. Life insurance reserves				
4. Pension and retirement funds, private				
5. Pension and insurance funds, govt.		1.31		
6. Consumer debt				
7. Trade debt				
8. Loans on securities				
9. Bank loans, n.e.c.			.07	0
10. Other loans			−.02	
11. Mortgages				
12. Bonds and notes				
13. Other liabilities	.25		.58	.03
14. Total	−.18	1.31	10.64	.77
IV. Net changes in equities				
1. Net issues of common stock			.07	
2. Net issues of preferred stock				
3. Saving	.03		.72	.15
V. Total uses and sources of funds	−.15	1.31	11.43	.92

Savings and Loan Associations (5)	Investment Companies (6)	Credit Unions (7)	Life Insurance Companies (8)	Fire and Casualty Insurance Companies (9)	Non-insured Pension Plans (10)	Other Private Insurance (11)	Finance Companies (12)	Other Finance (13)	Total (14)	
.06			.20	.03		a			.43	I.
										II.
.09	.04	.02	.09	.06	.06	.01	.17	.19	.07	1.
									−1.73	
.09	.04	.02	.09	.06	.06	.01	.17	.19	1.80	
		0		0					−.05	2.
										3.
										4.
										5.
.06		.15					1.01		2.90	6.
				.02			.28	−.01	.29	7.
								.58	.80	8.
									5.52	9.
		.01	.17			.01	.30	.10	.61	10.
2.04	.04	.01	3.01	.01	.01	.05	.21	.02	8.95	11.
2.00	.03	.01	2.70	.01	.01	.03	.21	.02	8.29	
.04	0		.30	.01		.02		0	.64	
			.19			.01		0	.27	12.
.03	.02	−.02	−1.83	.35	.22	.01		−.07	−4.51	13.
0			.26	.05				0	−.32	
.10			.05	.11	.19	0			.92	
−.07	.02	−.02	−2.14	.19	.03	.01		−.07	−5.11	
			.10	.31		−.01		.13	2.29	14.
	.04		1.83	.05	.44	.05		−.11	2.95	15.
	.03		.19	.03	.05	0		−.01	.30	16.
	.10		.13	.09	.16	.01		−.14	.38	17.
										18.
										19.
.02	.01		.26	.02	.03	0		.04	4.18	20.
2.24	.28	.17	4.14	.94	.98	.13	1.97	.72	24.95	21.
										III.
								.04	9.39	1.
1.52		.15						.01	2.65	2.
			4.16			.13			4.29	3.
					.98				.98	4.
									1.31	5.
										6.
		.01							.01	7.
			0					.07	.07	8.
.01							.98		1.06	9.
.52								.49	.99	10.
										11.
							.42		.42	12.
.05			.11	.72		.01		.10	1.85	13.
2.10		.16	4.27	.72	.98	.13	1.41	.71	23.02	14.
										IV.
	.25		.06	.06			.01		.45	1.
							.02		.02	2.
.20	.03	.01	.01	.19			.54	.01	1.89	3.
2.30	.28	.17	4.34	.97	.98	.13	1.97	.72	25.37	V.

TABLE VI

Annual Flow of Funds Through Finance Subsectors—1951 (billion dollars)

	Federal Reserve Banks & Treasury Monetary Funds (1)	Govt. Pension and Insurance Funds (2)	Commercial Banks (3)	Mutual Savings Banks (4)
I. Gross capital expenditures	a		.14	.01
II. Net financial flows				
1. Currency and demand deposits	.16	.06	3.92	.07
a. Monetary metals	−.05			
b. Other	.21	.06	3.92	.07
2. Other bank deposits and shares			0	.02
3. Life insurance reserves				
4. Pension and retirement funds, private				
5. Pension and insurance funds, govt.				
6. Consumer credit			.17	0
7. Trade credit				
8. Loans on securities			−.30	0
9. Bank loans, n.e.c.	−.05		4.73	
10. Other loans		.02		0
11. Mortgages, nonfarm		.06	1.00	1.65
a. Residential		.06	.81	1.54
b. Nonresidential			.19	.11
12. Mortgages, farm			.04	0
13. Securities, U.S. government	3.02	3.60	−.51	−1.05
a. Short-term	−2.60		−6.40	.07
b. Savings bonds		0	.02	0
c. Other long-term	5.62	3.60	5.87	−1.12
14. Securities, state and local		.07	1.08	.06
15. Securities, other bonds and notes		.24	−.13	.13
16. Securities, preferred stock		.01		
17. Securities, common stock		.01	−.01	.05
18. Equity in mutual financial organizations				
19. Equity in other business				
20. Other intangible assets	−.35		.58	.05
21. Total	2.78	4.07	10.57	.98
III. Net changes in liabilities				
1. Currency and demand deposits	3.08		7.85	
2. Other bank deposits and shares			1.73	.88
3. Life insurance reserves				
4. Pension and retirement funds, private				
5. Pension and insurance funds, govt.		4.07		
6. Consumer debt				
7. Trade debt				
8. Loans on securities				
9. Bank loans, n.e.c.			−.06	0
10. Other loans			−.01	
11. Mortgages				
12. Bonds and notes				
13. Other liabilities	−.32		.40	.01
14. Total	2.76	4.07	9.91	.89
IV. Net changes in equities				
1. Net issues of common stock			.14	
2. Net issues of preferred stock				
3. Saving	.02		.66	.10
V. Total uses and sources of funds	2.78	4.07	10.71	.99

Savings and Loan Associations (5)	Investment Companies (6)	Credit Unions (7)	Life Insurance Companies (8)	Fire and Casualty Insurance Companies (9)	Noninsured Pension Plans (10)	Other Private Insurance (11)	Finance Companies (12)	Other Finance (13)	Total (14)	
.07			.23	.03		a			.49	I.
										II.
.10	.03	.05	.10	.04	.04	.01	.12	−.03	4.67	1.
									−.05	
.10	.03	.05	.10	.04	.04	.01	.12	−.03	4.72	
		.05		.01					.08	2.
										3.
										4.
										5.
.03		.05					.28		.53	6.
				.12			.05	.03	.20	7.
								−.04	−.34	8.
									4.68	9.
		.01	.18			.01	.27	.16	.65	10.
1.91	−.01	.02	3.01	.01	.04	.05	−.08	.03	7.69	11.
1.87	−.01	.02	2.55	.01	.04	.03	−.08	.02	6.86	
.04	0		.46	.01		.02		0	.83	
			.20			.01		0	.25	12.
.11	0	.02	−2.45	.13	.12	.02		−.28	2.73	13.
.10			.09	−.37				−.10	−9.21	
0			0	.02	−.03	.01			.02	
.01	0	.02	−2.54	.48	.15	.01		−.18	11.92	
			.02	.39		−.01		.05	1.66	14.
	.05		2.71	.05	.88	.06		.04	4.03	15.
	.04		−.05	.04	.09	−.01		.01	.13	16.
	.14		.10	.11	.24	0		.06	.70	17.
										18.
										19.
.15	0		.18	.05	.03	0		−.02	.67	20.
2.30	.25	.20	4.00	.95	1.44	.14	.64	.01	28.33	21.
										III.
								.03	10.96	1.
2.12		.19						0	4.92	2.
			4.11			.14			4.25	3.
					1.44				1.44	4.
									4.07	5.
										6.
		−.01							−.01	7.
			0					−.19	−.19	8.
.01							.01		−.04	9.
0								.06	.05	10.
										11.
							.57		.57	12.
.02			.07	.85		.01		.10	1.14	13.
2.15		.18	4.18	.85	1.44	.15	.58	0	27.16	14.
										IV.
	.40		.01	0			.01		.56	1.
							−.04		−.04	2.
.22	−.15	.02	.04	.13			.10	.01	1.15	3.
2.37	.25	.20	4.23	.98	1.44	.15	.64	.01	28.82	V.

TABLE VI

Annual Flow of Funds Through Finance Subsectors—1952 (billion dollars)

	Federal Reserve Banks & Treasury Monetary Funds (1)	Govt. Pension and Insurance Funds (2)	Commercial Banks (3)	Mutual Savings Banks (4)
I. Gross capital expenditures	a		.11	.01
II. Net financial flows				
1. Currency and demand deposits	1.15	−.11	−.06	0
a. Monetary metals	.47			
b. Other	.68	−.11	−.06	0
2. Other bank deposits and shares			0	.03
3. Life insurance reserves				
4. Pension and retirement funds, private				
5. Pension and insurance funds, govt.				
6. Consumer credit			1.89	.01
7. Trade credit				
8. Loans on securities			.60	0
9. Bank loans, n.e.c.	.14		2.88	
10. Other loans		.01		0
11. Mortgages, nonfarm		.04	1.08	1.46
a. Residential		.04	.92	1.29
b. Nonresidential			.16	.17
12. Mortgages, farm			.05	.01
13. Securities, U.S. government	.90	3.92	1.80	−.40
a. Short-term	1.40		3.40	.08
b. Savings bonds		.10	.02	.01
c. Other long-term	−.50	3.82	−1.62	−.49
14. Securities, state and local		.13	.99	.17
15. Securities, other bonds and notes		.34	−.22	.37
16. Securities, preferred stock		.01		
17. Securities, common stock		.01	.01	.11
18. Equity in mutual financial organizations				
19. Equity in other business				
20. Other intangible assets	.36		.12	0
21. Total	2.55	4.35	9.14	1.76
III. Net changes in liabilities				
1. Currency and demand deposits	1.95		5.03	
2. Other bank deposits and shares			3.07	1.70
3. Life insurance reserves				
4. Pension and retirement funds, private				
5. Pension and insurance funds, govt.		4.35		
6. Consumer debt				
7. Trade debt				
8. Loans on securities				
9. Bank loans, n.e.c.			.16	0
10. Other loans			−.03	
11. Mortgages				
12. Bonds and notes				
13. Other liabilities	.54		.24	.01
14. Total	2.49	4.35	8.47	1.71
IV. Net changes in equities				
1. Net issues of common stock			.14	
2. Net issues of preferred stock				
3. Saving	.06		.64	.06
V. Total uses and sources of funds	2.55	4.35	9.25	1.77

Savings and Loan Associations (5)	Investment Companies (6)	Credit Unions (7)	Life Insurance Companies (8)	Fire and Casualty Insurance Companies (9)	Noninsured Pension Plans (10)	Other Private Insurance (11)	Finance Companies (12)	Other Finance (13)	Total (14)	
.05			.17	.02		a			.37	I.
										II.
.07	−.01	0	.05	.08	−.03	.02	.03	−.04	1.15	1.
									.47	
.07	−.01	0	.05	.08	−.03	.02	.03	−.04	.68	
		.09		.01					.13	2.
										3.
										4.
										5.
.07		.20					1.46		3.63	6.
				.07			.07	.01	.15	7.
								.10	.70	8.
									3.02	9.
		.01	.12			.01	.14	.06	.35	10.
2.83	.01	.03	1.76	.01	.03	.04	.14	0	7.43	11.
2.78	.01	.03	1.40	0	.03	.02	.14	0	6.66	
.06	0		.36	0		.02		0	.77	
			.18			.01		0	.25	12.
.19	−.01	0	−.76	.34	0	.03		.37	6.38	13.
0			−.11	.14				.50	5.41	
0			.01	.01	.01	.08			.24	
.19	−.01	0	−.66	.19	−.01	−.05		−.13	.73	
			−.02	.42		0		−.15	1.54	14.
	.10		3.10	.16	1.06	.07		.07	5.05	15.
	−.05		.09	.08	.06	0		0	.19	16.
	.48		.07	.10	.40	.01		−.03	1.16	17.
										18.
										19.
.21	0		.18	.04	.08	.01		.01	1.01	20.
3.37	.52	.33	4.77	1.31	1.60	.18	1.84	.40	32.12	21.
										III.
								.01	6.99	1.
3.09		.27						.01	8.14	2.
			4.93			.16			5.09	3.
					1.60				1.60	4.
									4.35	5.
										6.
		.04							.04	7.
			0					.48	.48	8.
−.01							.76		.91	9.
.15								−.15	−.03	10.
										11.
							.54		.54	12.
.01			.08	1.08		.02		.12	2.10	13.
3.24		.31	5.01	1.08	1.60	.18	1.30	.47	30.21	14.
										IV.
	.55		.02	.02			.03		.76	1.
							.02		.02	2.
.18	−.03	.02	−.09	.23			.49	−.07	1.49	3.
3.42	.52	.33	4.94	1.33	1.60	.18	1.84	.40	32.48	V.

TABLE VI

Annual Flow of Funds Through Finance Subsectors—1953 (billion dollars)

	Federal Reserve Banks & Treasury Monetary Funds (1)	Govt. Pension and Insurance Funds (2)	Commercial Banks (3)	Mutual Savings Banks (4)
I. Gross capital expenditures	a		.12	.01
II. Net financial flows				
1. Currency and demand deposits	−1.68	−.04	.24	.04
a. Monetary metals	−1.16			
b. Other	−.52	−.04	.24	.04
2. Other bank deposits and shares			0	.02
3. Life insurance reserves				
4. Pension and retirement funds, private				
5. Pension and insurance funds, govt.				
6. Consumer credit			1.60	.01
7. Trade credit				
8. Loans on securities			.40	0
9. Bank loans, n.e.c.	−.13		.51	
10. Other loans		.02		.01
11. Mortgages, nonfarm		.03	.96	1.56
a. Residential		.03	.74	1.45
b. Nonresidential			.22	.11
12. Mortgages, farm			.03	0
13. Securities, U.S. government	1.22	2.69	.11	−.24
a. Short-term	2.20		9.00	.22
b. Savings bonds		0	−.02	−.03
c. Other long-term	−.98	2.69	−8.87	−.43
14. Securities, state and local		.24	.63	.09
15. Securities, other bonds and notes		.40	−.12	.29
16. Securities, preferred stock		.02		
17. Securities, common stock		.02	0	.09
18. Equity in mutual financial organizations				
19. Equity in other business				
20. Other intangible assets	−.03		.01	.03
21. Total	−.62	3.38	4.37	1.90
III. Net changes in liabilities				
1. Currency and demand deposits	−.71		.36	
2. Other bank deposits and shares			3.40	1.77
3. Life insurance reserves				
4. Pension and retirement funds, private				
5. Pension and insurance funds, govt.		3.38		
6. Consumer debt				
7. Trade debt				
8. Loans on securities				
9. Bank loans, n.e.c.			−.13	0
10. Other loans			−.01	
11. Mortgages				
12. Bonds and notes				
13. Other liabilities	.06		.11	.05
14. Total	−.65	3.38	3.73	1.82
IV. Net changes in equities				
1. Net issues of common stock			.11	
2. Net issues of preferred stock				
3. Saving	.03		.65	.09
V. Total uses and sources of funds	−.62	3.38	4.49	1.91

Savings and Loan Associations (5)	Investment Companies (6)	Credit Unions (7)	Life Insurance Companies (8)	Fire and Casualty Insurance Companies (9)	Non-insured Pension Plans (10)	Other Private Insurance (11)	Finance Companies (12)	Other Finance (13)	Total (14)	
.06			.19	.03		a			.40	I.
										II.
.05	.04	.02	.07	.05	.05	.03	.02	−.07	−1.18	1.
									−1.16	
.05	.04	.02	.07	.05	.05	.03	.02	−.07	−.02	
		.06		0					.08	2.
										3.
										4.
										5.
.05		.28					1.57		3.51	6.
				.05			.05	.05	.15	7.
								.40	.80	8.
									.38	9.
		0	.20			.01	.07	−.09	.22	10.
3.57	.01	.03	1.89	.01	.04	.04	.03	0	8.17	11.
3.50	−.01	.03	1.51	0	.04	.02	.03	0	7.34	
.07	0		.38	.01		.02		0	.81	
			.18			0		0	.21	12.
.13	0	−.01	−.42	.21	.16	.02		−.01	3.86	13.
0			−.07	.42				0	11.77	
0			−.02	−.02	−.03	−.05			−.17	
.13	0	−.01	−.33	−.19	.19	.06		−.01	−7.75	
			.15	.75		.01		.25	2.12	14.
	.01		2.71	.12	1.06	.07		−.09	4.45	15.
	.17		.04	.05	.06	0		0	.34	16.
	.19		.05	.14	.45	0		−.05	.89	17.
										18.
										19.
.23	0		.12	.06	.11	.01		.02	.56	20.
4.03	.42	.38	4.99	1.44	1.94	.18	1.74	.41	24.56	21.
										III.
								0	−.35	1.
3.65		.33						.01	9.16	2.
			4.96			.18			5.14	3.
					1.94				1.94	4.
									3.38	5.
										6.
		.02							.02	7.
			0					.30	.30	8.
0							−.01		−.14	9.
.14								−.09	.04	10.
										11.
							1.58		1.58	12.
.03			.10	1.10		.01		.10	1.56	13.
3.82		.35	5.06	1.10	1.94	.19	1.57	.32	22.63	14.
										IV.
	.43		.06	.04			.06		.70	1.
							0		0	2.
.27	−.01	.03	.06	.33			.11	.09	1.65	3.
4.09	.42	.38	5.18	1.47	1.94	.19	1.74	.41	24.98	V.

TABLE VI

Annual Flow of Funds Through Finance Subsectors—1954 (billion dollars)

	Federal Reserve Banks & Treasury Monetary Funds (1)	Govt. Pension and Insurance Funds (2)	Commercial Banks (3)	Mutual Savings Banks (4)
I. Gross capital expenditures	a		.10	.01
II. Net financial flows				
1. Currency and demand deposits	−.52	.32	−1.23	.02
a. Monetary metals	−.27			
b. Other	−.25	.32	−1.23	.02
2. Other bank deposits and shares			0	.03
3. Life insurance reserves				
4. Pension and retirement funds, private				
5. Pension and insurance funds, govt.				
6. Consumer credit			.03	0
7. Trade credit				
8. Loans on securities			.89	.01
9. Bank loans, n.e.c.	.11		.49	
10. Other loans		.02		.01
11. Mortgages, nonfarm		.07	1.65	2.06
a. Residential		.07	1.23	1.88
b. Nonresidential			.42	.18
12. Mortgages, farm			.08	0
13. Securities, U.S. government	−.99	1.44	5.55	−.43
a. Short-term	2.40		−10.60	−.32
b. Savings bonds		0	.01	−.01
c. Other long-term	−3.39	1.44	16.14	−.10
14. Securities, state and local		.31	1.77	.19
15. Securities, other bonds and notes		.49	−.14	.09
16. Securities, preferred stock		.02		
17. Securities, common stock		.02	0	.14
18. Equity in mutual financial organizations				
19. Equity in other business				
20. Other intangible assets	−.28		.26	.01
21. Total	−1.68	2.69	9.35	2.13
III. Net changes in liabilities				
1. Currency and demand deposits	−1.55		4.25	
2. Other bank deposits and shares			3.81	1.94
3. Life insurance reserves				
4. Pension and retirement funds, private				
5. Pension and insurance funds, govt.		2.69		
6. Consumer debt				
7. Trade debt				
8. Loans on securities				
9. Bank loans, n.e.c.			−.03	0
10. Other loans			−.02	
11. Mortgages				
12. Bonds and notes				
13. Other liabilities	−.14		.34	.07
14. Total	−1.69	2.69	8.35	2.01
IV. Net changes in equities				
1. Net issues of common stock			.23	
2. Net issues of preferred stock				
3. Saving	.01		.87	.13
V. Total uses and sources of funds	−1.68	2.69	9.45	2.14

Savings and Loan Associations (5)	Investment Companies (6)	Credit Unions (7)	Life Insurance Companies (8)	Fire and Casualty Insurance Companies (9)	Noninsured Pension Plans (10)	Other Private Insurance (11)	Finance Companies (12)	Other Finance (13)	Total (14)	
.05			.16	.02		a			.35	I.
										II.
.26	0	.05	.02	−.05	0	.02	.05	.13	−.93	1.
									−.27	
.26	0	.05	.02	−.05	0	.02	.05	.13	−.66	
		.07		0					.10	2.
										3.
										4.
										5.
.05		.22					.44		.74	6.
				.06			.11	−.01	.16	7.
								.96	1.86	8.
									.60	9.
		0	.22			.01	−.24	.09	.11	10.
4.15	0	.03	2.49	.01	.03	.06	.22	0	10.77	11.
4.06	0	.03	2.00	0	.03	.02	.22	0	9.54	
.08	0		.49	.01		.04		0	1.22	
			.16			0		0	.24	12.
.10	0	0	−.76	.11	.01	.04		.18	5.25	13.
0			.08	−.53				.30	−8.67	
0			−.01	−.01	.08	.03			.09	
.10	0	0	−.83	.65	−.07	.01		−.12	13.83	
			.55	.78		.02		−.13	3.49	14.
	.14		2.10	.03	1.22	.06		.32	4.31	15.
	.08		.20	.05	.06	0		.01	.42	16.
	.22		.07	.10	.62	.01		.16	1.34	17.
										18.
										19.
.27	0		.20	.05	.11	0		0	.62	20.
4.83	.44	.37	5.25	1.14	2.04	.22	.57	1.71	29.06	21.
										III.
								.02	2.72	1.
4.40		.34						.02	10.51	2.
			5.41			.20			5.61	3.
					2.05				2.05	4.
									2.69	5.
										6.
		.01							.01	7.
			0					.67	.67	8.
0							.02		−.01	9.
.15								.55	.68	10.
										11.
									.19	12.
.06			.08	.69		.02		.28	1.40	13.
4.61		.35	5.49	.69	2.05	.22	.22	1.54	26.53	14.
										IV.
	.46		.04	.03			.02		.78	1.
							−.07		−.07	2.
.27	−.02	.02	−.12	.44			.40	.17	2.17	3.
4.88	.44	.37	5.41	1.16	2.04	.22	.57	1.71	29.40	V.

TABLE VI

Annual Flow of Funds Through Finance Subsectors—1955 (billion dollars)

	Federal Reserve Banks & Treasury Monetary Funds (1)	Govt. Pension and Insurance Funds (2)	Commercial Banks (3)	Mutual Savings Banks (4)
I. Gross capital expenditures	.01		.15	.01
II. Net financial flows				
1. Currency and demand deposits	.05	−.22	.23	−.02
a. Monetary metals	−.05			
b. Other	.10	−.22	.23	−.02
2. Other bank deposits and shares			0	−.05
3. Life insurance reserves				
4. Pension and retirement funds, private				
5. Pension and insurance funds, govt.				
6. Consumer credit			2.36	.02
7. Trade credit				
8. Loans on securities			.59	.01
9. Bank loans, n.e.c.	0		6.84	
10. Other loans		.03		0
11. Mortgages, nonfarm		.04	2.25	2.45
a. Residential		.04	1.71	2.36
b. Nonresidential			.54	.09
12. Mortgages, farm			.14	0
13. Securities, U.S. government	−.15	2.40	−7.39	−.29
a. Short-term	1.30		−8.60	.10
b. Savings bonds		0	−.02	−.03
c. Other long-term	−1.45	2.40	1.23	−.36
14. Securities, state and local		.34	.11	.04
15. Securities, other bonds and notes		.59	.24	−.26
16. Securities, preferred stock		.03		
17. Securities, common stock		.03	.01	.09
18. Equity in mutual financial organizations				
19. Equity in other business				
20. Other intangible assets	1.57		2.97	.02
21. Total	1.47	3.24	8.35	2.01
III. Net changes in liabilities				
1. Currency and demand deposits	.56		6.16	
2. Other bank deposits and shares			1.33	1.83
3. Life insurance reserves				
4. Pension and retirement funds, private				
5. Pension and insurance funds, govt.		3.24		
6. Consumer debt				
7. Trade debt				
8. Loans on securities				
9. Bank loans, n.e.c.			.13	0
10. Other loans			−.01	
11. Mortgages				
12. Bonds and notes				
13. Other liabilities	.87		.02	.05
14. Total	1.43	3.24	7.63	1.88
IV. Net changes in equities				
1. Net issues of common stock			.14	
2. Net issues of preferred stock				
3. Saving	.05		.73	.14
V. Total uses and sources of funds	1.48	3.24	8.50	2.02

Savings and Loan Associations (5)	Investment Companies (6)	Credit Unions (7)	Life Insurance Companies (8)	Fire and Casualty Insurance Companies (9)	Noninsured Pension Plans (10)	Other Private Insurance (11)	Finance Companies (12)	Other Finance (13)	Total (14)	
.07			.24	.03		a			.52	I.
										II.
.19	0	.01	.02	.03	.06	0	.25	.01	.61	1.
									−.05	
.19	0	.01	.02	.03	.06	0	.25	.01	.66	
		.07		0					.02	2.
										3.
										4.
										5.
.08		.34					2.83		5.63	6.
				.09			.24	.05	.38	7.
								.48	1.08	8.
									6.84	9.
		.02	.16			.02	.97	.09	1.29	10.
5.30	−.01	.03	3.24	.01	.04	.08	.53	.04	14.00	11.
5.19	−.01	.03	2.66	0	.04	.03	.53	.02	12.60	
.11	0		.59	.01		.05		.01	1.40	
			.22			0		0	.36	12.
.32	.14	0	−.49	−.14	.30	.07		−.48	−5.71	13.
.10			−.14	−.41				−.50	−8.15	
.03			−.02	−.01	.02	−.01			−.04	
.19	.14	0	−.33	.28	.28	.08		.02	2.48	
			.19	.79		.05		.05	1.57	14.
	.18		1.75	−.01	.91	.02		−.04	3.38	15.
	.11		.01	0	.05	0		0	.20	16.
	.40		.06	.17	.66	0		−.02	1.40	17.
										18.
										19.
.04	.03		.21	.04	.05	.01		.02	4.96	20.
5.93	.85	.47	5.37	.98	2.06	.23	4.82	.20	35.98	21.
										III.
								.03	6.75	1.
4.89		.40						.01	8.46	2.
			5.45			.22			5.67	3.
					2.06				2.06	4.
									3.24	5.
										6.
		.02							.02	7.
			0					.32	.32	8.
.05							2.58		2.76	9.
.68								−.19	.48	10.
										11.
							1.63		1.63	12.
.03			.14	.78		.02		.16	2.07	13.
5.65		.42	5.59	.78	2.06	.24	4.20	.33	33.45	14.
										IV.
	.76		.06	.08			.08		1.12	1.
							.08		.08	2.
.35	.09	.05	−.04	.15			.45	−.13	1.84	3.
6.00	.85	.47	5.61	1.01	2.06	.24	4.82	.20	36.50	V.

TABLE VI

Annual Flow of Funds Through Finance Subsectors—1956 (billion dollars)

	Federal Reserve Banks & Treasury Monetary Funds (1)	Govt. Pension and Insurance Funds (2)	Commercial Banks (3)	Mutual Savings Banks (4)
I. Gross capital expenditures	.01		.18	.01
II. Net financial flows				
1. Currency and demand deposits	.48	.14	1.36	.02
a. Monetary metals	.31			
b. Other	.17	.14	1.36	.02
2. Other bank deposits and shares			0	−.06
3. Life insurance reserves				
4. Pension and retirement funds, private				
5. Pension and insurance funds, govt.				
6. Consumer credit			1.45	.03
7. Trade credit				
8. Loans on securities			−.76	0
9. Bank loans, n.e.c.	−.02		5.60	
10. Other loans		.03		.01
11. Mortgages, nonfarm		.09	1.66	2.29
a. Residential		.09	1.11	2.14
b. Nonresidential			.56	.15
12. Mortgages, farm			.04	0
13. Securities, U.S. government	.22	2.25	−3.04	−.49
a. Short-term	1.40		4.80	−.02
b. Savings bonds		−.10	−.39	−.07
c. Other long-term	−1.18	2.35	−7.45	−.40
14. Securities, state and local		.40	.20	.03
15. Securities, other bonds and notes		.63	−.64	.13
16. Securities, preferred stock		.02		
17. Securities, common stock		.02	0	.04
18. Equity in mutual financial organizations				
19. Equity in other business				
20. Other intangible assets	.21		.94	.02
21. Total	.89	3.58	6.81	2.02
III. Net changes in liabilities				
1. Currency and demand deposits	.78		3.20	
2. Other bank deposits and shares			2.07	1.87
3. Life insurance reserves				
4. Pension and retirement funds, private				
5. Pension and insurance funds, govt.		3.58		
6. Consumer debt				
7. Trade debt				
8. Loans on securities				
9. Bank loans, n.e.c.			−.08	0
10. Other loans			0	
11. Mortgages				
12. Bonds and notes				
13. Other liabilities	.05		.55	.03
14. Total	.83	3.58	5.74	1.90
IV. Net changes in equities				
1. Net issues of common stock			.40	
2. Net issues of preferred stock				
3. Saving	.07		.85	.13
V. Total uses and sources of funds	.90	3.58	6.99	2.03

Savings and Loan Associations (5)	Investment Companies (6)	Credit Unions (7)	Life Insurance Companies (8)	Fire and Casualty Insurance Companies (9)	Noninsured Pension Plans (10)	Other Private Insurance (11)	Finance Companies (12)	Other Finance (13)	Total (14)	
.09			.29	.04		a			.63	I.
										II.
.07	.03	.03	.02	−.07	0	−.01	.03	.12	2.22	1.
									.31	
.07	.03	.03	.02	−.07	0	−.01	.03	.12	1.91	
		.11		0					.05	2.
										3.
										4.
										5.
.08		.33					1.13		3.02	6.
				.14			.18	.10	.42	7.
								.08	−.68	8.
									5.58	9.
		−.01	.23			.01	−.09	.07	.25	10.
4.32	−.01	.06	3.34	.01	.11	.06	−.10	.01	11.84	11.
4.23	−.01	.06	2.53	0	.11	.01	−.10	.01	10.18	
.09	0		.80	.01		.05		0	1.66	
			.21			.01		0	.26	12.
.44	.02	.01	−1.02	−.33	−.20	.03		.09	−2.02	13.
−.10			−.13	.26				.16	6.37	
−.13			−.04	−.07	−.15	.02			−.93	
.67	.02	.01	−.85	−.52	−.05	.01		−.06	−7.45	
			.23	.63		0		−.11	1.38	14.
	.11		2.15	.03	1.59	.06		−.18	3.88	15.
	.08		−.19	−.08	.06	0		−.01	−.12	16.
	.50		.19	.21	.82	0		−.25	1.53	17.
										18.
										19.
.20	−.02		.31	.04	.24	.01		.04	1.99	20.
5.11	.71	.53	5.47	.58	2.60	.17	1.15	−.04	29.58	21.
										III.
								.06	4.04	1.
5.01		.46						.02	9.43	2.
			5.42			.17			5.59	3.
					2.60				2.60	4.
									3.58	5.
										6.
		.03							.03	7.
			0					−.62	−.62	8.
−.01							−.54		−.63	9.
−.21								.03	−.18	10.
										11.
							1.19		1.19	12.
.03			.19	.66		.01		.46	1.98	13.
4.82		.49	5.61	.66	2.60	.17	.65	−.05	27.00	14.
										IV.
	.91		.09	.02			.01		1.43	1.
							.02		.02	2.
.38	−.20	.04	.06	−.06			.47	.01	1.75	3.
5.20	.71	.53	5.76	.62	2.60	.17	1.15	−.04	30.20	V.

TABLE VI

Annual Flow of Funds Through Finance Subsectors—1957 (billion dollars)

	Federal Reserve Banks & Treasury Monetary Funds (1)	Govt. Pension and Insurance Funds (2)	Commercial Banks (3)	Mutual Savings Banks (4)
I. Gross capital expenditures	.01		.17	.01
II. Net financial flows				
1. Currency and demand deposits	1.73	.24	−.15	0
a. Monetary metals	.73			
b. Other	1.00	.24	−.15	0
2. Other bank deposits and shares			0	−.04
3. Life insurance reserves				
4. Pension and retirement funds, private				
5. Pension and insurance funds, govt.				
6. Consumer credit			1.21	0
7. Trade credit				
8. Loans on securities			−.06	−.01
9. Bank loans, n.e.c.	0		2.06	
10. Other loans		.03		.03
11. Mortgages, nonfarm		.02	.57	1.42
a. Residential		.02	.14	1.31
b. Nonresidential			.43	.12
12. Mortgages, farm			.03	0
13. Securities, U.S. government	−.76	1.07	−.31	−.42
a. Short-term	−.70		1.90	.21
b. Savings bonds		−.10	−.47	−.15
c. Other long-term	−.06	1.17	−1.74	−.48
14. Securities, state and local		.45	1.02	.01
15. Securities, other bonds and notes		.96	.60	.74
16. Securities, preferred stock		.04		
17. Securities, common stock		.04	.02	.07
18. Equity in mutual financial organizations				
19. Equity in other business				
20. Other intangible assets	.04		.21	.03
21. Total	1.01	2.85	5.20	1.83
III. Net changes in liabilities				
1. Currency and demand deposits	.91		−1.65	
2. Other bank deposits and shares			5.45	1.66
3. Life insurance reserves				
4. Pension and retirement funds, private				
5. Pension and insurance funds, govt.		2.85		
6. Consumer debt				
7. Trade debt				
8. Loans on securities				
9. Bank loans, n.e.c.			0	0
10. Other loans			0	
11. Mortgages				
12. Bonds and notes				
13. Other liabilities	.07		.37	.08
14. Total	.98	2.85	4.17	1.74
IV. Net changes in equities				
1. Net issues of common stock			.36	
2. Net issues of preferred stock				
3. Saving	.04		.84	.10
V. Total uses and sources of funds	1.02	2.85	5.37	1.84

Savings and Loan Associations (5)	Investment Companies (6)	Credit Unions (7)	Life Insurance Companies (8)	Fire and Casualty Insurance Companies (9)	Noninsured Pension Plans (10)	Other Private Insurance (11)	Finance Companies (12)	Other Finance (13)	Total (14)	
.08			.27	.04		a			.58	I.
										II.
.05	.03	.03	.01	−.01	.06	−.01	.07	.02	2.07	1.
									.73	
.05	.03	.03	.01	−.01	.06	−.01	.07	.02	1.34	
		.08		0					.04	2.
										3.
										4.
										5.
.08		.42					.82		2.53	6.
				.15			.15	.04	.34	7.
								−.29	−.36	8.
									2.06	9.
		.02	.35				.61	.27	1.31	10.
4.28	−.02	0	2.14	0	.17	.02	−.32	.02	8.30	11.
4.19	−.02	0	1.25	−.01	.17	0	−.32	0	6.73	
.08	0		.90	0		.03		.02	1.58	
			.10			0		0	.13	12.
.39	0	−.01	−.53	−.21	−.27	−.01		.12	−.94	13.
.30			−.03	.43				.12	2.23	
−.08			−.10	−.17	−.34	.01			−1.40	
.17	0	−.01	−.40	−.47	.06	−.02		0	−1.78	
			.11	.62		−.02		.14	2.33	14.
	.14		2.67	.18	1.73	.03		.27	7.32	15.
	−.11		−.03	.02	.04	0		.01	−.03	16.
	.90		.07	.10	1.04	0		.02	2.26	17.
										18.
										19.
.34	.01		.26	.08	.11	0		.04	1.12	20.
5.14	.95	.54	5.15	.93	2.89	.03	1.32	.66	28.50	21.
										III.
								.07	−.67	1.
4.76		.46						.07	12.40	2.
			5.23			.02			5.25	3.
				2.89					2.89	4.
									2.85	5.
										6.
		.01							.01	7.
			0					.10	.10	8.
−.01							−.36		−.37	9.
0								.30	.30	10.
										11.
							1.12		1.12	12.
.12			.17	1.05		.02		.12	2.00	13.
4.87		.47	5.40	1.05	2.89	.03	.76	.66	25.87	14.
										IV.
	.98		.06	.02			−.03		1.39	1.
							.04		.04	2.
.35	−.03	.07	−.04	−.10			.54	0	1.77	3.
5.22	.95	.54	5.42	.97	2.89	.03	1.32	.66	29.08	V.

TABLE VI

Annual Flow of Funds Through Finance Subsectors—1958 (billion dollars)

	Federal Reserve Banks & Treasury Monetary Funds (1)	Govt. Pension and Insurance Funds (2)	Commercial Banks (3)	Mutual Savings Banks (4)
I. Gross capital expenditures	a		.11	.01
II. Net financial flows				
1. Currency and demand deposits	−4.13	.13	−.36	0
a. Monetary metals	−2.22			
b. Other	−1.91	.13	−.36	0
2. Other bank deposits and shares			.04	.04
3. Life insurance reserves				
4. Pension and retirement funds, private				
5. Pension and insurance funds, govt.				
6. Consumer credit			.18	.01
7. Trade credit				
8. Loans on securities			.44	0
9. Bank loans, n.e.c.	−.01		1.73	
10. Other loans		.04		.04
11. Mortgages, nonfarm		−.05	2.04	2.10
a. Residential		−.05	1.42	1.93
b. Nonresidential			.62	.17
12. Mortgages, farm			.10	0
13. Securities, U.S. government	2.18	−.62	7.94	−.29
a. Short-term	−.40		.90	−.15
b. Savings bonds		−.10	−.03	−.08
c. Other long-term	2.58	−.52	7.07	−.06
14. Securities, state and local		.46	2.58	.05
15. Securities, other bonds and notes		1.15	.03	.55
16. Securities, preferred stock		.06		
17. Securities, common stock		.06	.01	.09
18. Equity in mutual financial organizations				
19. Equity in other business				
20. Other intangible assets	−.14		.96	.02
21. Total	−2.10	1.23	15.69	2.61
III. Net changes in liabilities				
1. Currency and demand deposits	−2.40		6.65	
2. Other bank deposits and shares			8.04	2.35
3. Life insurance reserves				
4. Pension and retirement funds, private				
5. Pension and insurance funds, govt.		1.23		
6. Consumer debt				
7. Trade debt				
8. Loans on securities				
9. Bank loans, n.e.c.			−.01	.01
10. Other loans			0	
11. Mortgages				
12. Bonds and notes				
13. Other liabilities	.27		−.05	.09
14. Total	−2.13	1.23	14.63	2.45
IV. Net changes in equities				
1. Net issues of common stock			.13	
2. Net issues of preferred stock				
3. Saving	.03		1.04	.17
V. Total uses and sources of funds	−2.10	1.23	15.80	2.62

Savings and Loan Associations (5)	Investment Companies (6)	Credit Unions (7)	Life Insurance Companies (8)	Fire and Casualty Insurance Companies (9)	Noninsured Pension Plans (10)	Other Private Insurance (11)	Finance Companies (12)	Other Finance (13)	Total (14)	
.05			.18	.03					.39	I.
										II.
.27	0	.04	.08	.06	.03	.02	.10	.03	−3.73	1.
									−2.22	
.27	0	.04	.08	.06	.03	.02	.10	.03	−1.51	
		.23		0					.31	2.
										3.
										4.
										5.
.06		.23					−.71		−.23	6.
				.14			.23	−.01	.36	7.
								1.14	1.58	8.
									1.72	9.
		0	.32			.01	−.33	.27	.35	10.
5.62	−.03	.08	1.74	0	.14	.04	.46	.04	12.18	11.
5.51	−.03	.08	.93	0	.14	0	.46	.03	10.42	
.11	0		.81	0		.03		.01	1.75	
			.08			0		0	.18	12.
.65	.14	0	.15	−.06	.03	.06		.24	10.42	13.
−.20			.27	−.08				.24	.58	
0			−.03	−.07	−.01	−.02			−.34	
.85	.14	0	−.09	.09	.05	.08		0	10.19	
			.30	.71		0		0	4.10	14.
	.24		2.42	.09	1.51	.08		−.12	5.95	15.
	.31		.04	−.01	.05	0		−.01	.44	16.
	.66		.02	.14	1.25	.01		.05	2.29	17.
										18.
										19.
.27	.01		.20	0	.05			.03	1.40	20.
6.87	1.33	.58	5.35	1.07	3.06	.24	−.24	1.66	37.35	21.
										III.
								.04	4.29	1.
6.07		.47						.08	17.01	2.
			5.42			.22			5.64	3.
					3.07				3.07	4.
									1.23	5.
										6.
		.02							.02	7.
			0					.34	.34	8.
.04							−1.12		−1.08	9.
.31								.72	1.03	10.
										11.
							.02		.02	12.
.10			.13	.84		.03		.21	1.62	13.
6.52		.49	5.55	.84	3.07	.24	−1.10	1.39	33.18	14.
										IV.
	1.50		.06	−.01			.01		1.69	1.
							0		0	2.
.40	−.17	.09	−.08	.27			.85	.27	2.87	3.
6.92	1.33	.58	5.53	1.10	3.06	.24	−.24	1.66	37.73	V.

Notes to Table VI

Source: Columns 1 through 13—Tables VII-5a through VII-5m respectively. Column 14—Sum of cols. 1 through 13 except for line I; for line I see line I-7 in Table VII-5.

[a]$5 million or under.

Note: Figures may not add to totals because of rounding.

SECTION VII

Sector Flow of Funds, 1946–58

TABLE VII-1

Flow of Funds Through Nonfarm Households

(billion dollars)

	1946	1947	1948	1949
I. Gross capital expenditures				
1. Residential structures	4.89	7.39	10.59	9.45
2. Nonresidential structures	.32	.44	.70	.92
4. Producer durables	.06	.08	.13	.17
5. Consumer durables	13.71	18.38	20.09	21.94
7. Total	18.98	26.29	31.51	32.48
II. Net financial flows				
1. Currency and demand deposits	4.15	–.31	–2.06	–2.31
a. Monetary metals	.05	.03	.03	0
b. Other	4.10	–.34	–2.09	–2.31
2. Other bank deposits and shares	6.38	3.63	2.18	2.48
3. Life insurance reserves	3.53	3.30	3.52	3.76
4. Pension and retirement funds, private	.57	.65	.65	.71
5. Pension and insurance funds, govt.	3.47	3.79	3.49	2.49
10. Other loans	.16	.04	–.13	.16
11. Mortgages, nonfarm	1.36	1.21	1.00	.59
a. Residential	.89	.67	.59	.23
b. Nonresidential	.47	.54	.41	.36
12. Mortgages, farm	.12	.07	.13	.08
13. Securities, U. S. government	–.49	1.82	–.23	.97
a. Short-term	.16	–.42	2.11	.97
b. Savings bonds	1.20	1.81	1.62	1.30
c. Other long-term	–1.85	.43	–3.96	–1.30
14. Securities, state and local	–.16	.41	.99	.61
15. Securities, other bonds and notes	–1.37	–.69	–.28	–.63
16. Securities, preferred stock	0	.31	.28	.01
17. Securities, common stock	1.42	1.16	1.23	1.13
18. Equity in mutual financial organizations[a]				
19. Equity in other business[b]				
20. Other intangible assets	–.01	.01	–.01	1.13
21. Total	19.13	15.40	10.76	10.04
III. Net changes in liabilities				
6. Consumer debt	2.65	3.19	2.80	2.95
7. Trade debt	.07	.09	.08	.04
8. Loans on securities	–1.48	–.06	–.12	.32
9. Bank loans, n.e.c.	–.29	–.25	.10	0
10. Other loans	–.07	.05	.13	.19
11. Mortgages	4.26	4.93	5.14	4.26
14. Total	5.14	7.95	8.13	7.76
IV. Net changes in equities				
3. Saving	32.97	33.74	34.14	34.76
V. Total uses and sources of funds	38.11	41.69	42.27	42.52

Line	
I-1 through I-5	From line 1 of corresponding Tables VIII-a-1 through VIII-a-5.
7	Sum of lines I-1 through I-5.
II-1	Table VIII-b-1, line 1.
1a	Table III-1, line II-1a (first difference).
1b	Table III-1, line II-1b (first difference).
2 through 20	From line 1 of corresponding Tables VIII-b-2 through VIII-b-20.
21	Sum of lines II-1 through II-20.
III-6 through III-11	From line 1 of corresponding Tables VIII-c-6 through VIII-c-11.
14	Sum of lines III-6 through III-11.

1950	1951	1952	1953	1954	1955	1956	1957	1958	
									I.
13.18	13.69	13.95	15.13	15.74	19.84	19.14	18.15	18.26	1.
1.13	1.27	1.18	1.27	1.54	1.66	1.72	2.02	2.18	2.
.21	.24	.23	.24	.29	.32	.33	.38	.41	4.
27.68	26.24	26.28	29.17	29.23	36.58	35.37	36.76	34.04	5.
42.20	41.44	41.64	45.81	46.80	58.40	56.56	57.31	54.89	7.
									II.
1.90	3.07	1.89	.91	2.20	−.75	.96	−1.02	2.84	1.
.06	.05	.08	.06	.01	.06	.06	.17	.12	
1.84	3.02	1.81	.85	2.19	−.81	.90	−1.19	2.72	
2.09	4.20	7.35	7.88	8.83	8.42	9.14	11.38	13.75	2.
3.96	3.92	4.71	4.77	5.18	5.26	5.22	4.90	5.24	3.
.97	1.45	1.61	1.94	2.05	2.06	2.61	2.89	3.06	4.
1.56	4.11	4.36	3.42	2.71	3.24	3.58	2.86	1.24	5.
.55	−.04	−.11	.05	.74	−.12	−.04	.06	.78	10.
.37	.49	.56	.75	.99	1.00	1.49	1.42	1.84	11.
.09	.22	.28	.40	.43	.38	.75	.81	.81	
.28	.27	.28	.34	.57	.62	.73	.61	1.03	
.22	.25	.25	.20	.18	.22	.34	.24	.34	12.
−.33	−1.45	.23	.19	−1.53	1.76	1.11	−1.14	−2.03	13.
−1.18	−1.61	.75	1.02	−.65	−1.01	1.50	2.38	−1.37	
.45	−.55	.15	−.04	.09	.03	−.29	−2.27	−.90	
.40	.71	−.67	−.79	−.97	2.74	−.10	−1.25	.24	
.38	.31	1.16	1.61	.66	1.68	1.68	2.12	1.42	14.
.03	.07	−.15	.12	−.97	1.91	1.66	1.85	.28	15.
−.06	.45	.28	.03	−.01	−.14	.60	.43	.04	16.
1.59	1,67	1.82	1.52	1.24	2.13	2.17	1.76	2.16	17.
									18.
									19.
−.23	−.23	−.23	−.01	0	0	.01	0	0	20.
13.00	18.27	23.73	23.38	22.27	26.67	30.53	27.75	30.96	21.
									III.
3.99	1.35	4.70	3.93	1.01	6.26	3.70	2.86	.02	6.
.10	0	.24	.06	.10	.12	.17	.14	.10	7.
.78	−.15	.21	.52	1.28	.75	−.05	−.46	1.32	8.
.27	−.01	−.06	−.08	.12	.68	.13	.21	.42	9.
.18	.20	.12	.21	.24	.18	.27	.35	.35	10.
7.27	6.78	6.72	7.65	9.37	12.54	11.00	8.70	9.99	11.
12.59	8.17	11.93	12.29	12.12	20.53	15.22	11.80	12.20	14.
									IV.
42.61	51.54	53.44	56.90	56.95	64.54	71.87	73.26	73.65	3.
55.20	59.71	65.37	69.19	69.07	85.07	87.09	85.06	85.85	V.

Line	
IV-3	Sum of lines I-7 and II-21 minus line III-14.
V	Sum of lines I-7 and II-21.

[a] The saving originating in mutual financial organizations (even if actually transferred to households) was treated in an analogous way to corporate saving, so as to avoid double counting of the saving flow (once as saving of households and once as saving of mutual financial organizations).

[b] The saving originating in unincorporated business and in operations of brokers and dealers was treated in an analogous way to corporate saving, so as to avoid double counting of the saving flow.

TABLE VII-2

Flow of Funds Through Unincorporated Nonfarm Business

(billion dollars)

	1946	1947	1948	1949
I. Gross capital expenditures				
1. Residential structures	.13	.25	.46	.51
2. Nonresidential structures	.74	.64	.89	.80
4. Producer durables	1.59	2.47	2.77	2.64
6. Inventories at book value (see note below)	2.09	1.53	1.33	–.95
7. Total	4.55	4.89	5.45	3.00
II. Net financial flows				
1. Currency and demand deposits	.01	.36	–.15	.37
a. Monetary metals	.01	.01	0	.01
b. Other	0	.35	–.15	.36
6. Consumer credit	.33	.33	.37	.25
7. Trade credit	.96	.37	.40	.06
21. Total	1.30	1.06	.62	.68
III. Net changes in liabilities				
7. Trade debt	–.09	–.53	.76	.22
9. Bank loans, n.e.c.	1.45	2.22	–.70	–.29
10. Other loans	.34	.46	.65	.09
11. Mortgages	.52	.59	.60	.53
14. Total	2.22	2.74	1.31	.55
IV. Net changes in equities				
3. Saving	3.63	3.21	4.76	3.13
V. Total uses and sources of funds	5.85	5.95	6.07	3.68

Note: Inventories at Adjusted Value and Lines Affected

	1946	1947	1948	1949
Inventories (adjusted value)	.38	.06	.92	–.49
Gross capital expenditures	2.84	3.42	5.04	3.46
Saving	1.92	1.74	4.35	3.59
Total uses and sources of funds	4.14	4.48	5.66	4.14

Line	
I-1	Table VIII-a-1, line 2.
2	Table VIII-a-2, line 2.
4	Table VIII-a-4, line 2.
6	Table VIII-a-6b, line 2.
7	Sum of lines I-1 through I-6.
II-1	Table VIII-b-1, line 2.
1a	Table III-2, line II-1a (first difference).
1b	Table III-2, line II-1b (first difference).
6	Table VIII-b-6, line 2.
7	Table VIII-b-7, line 2.
21	Sum of lines II-1 through II-7.

1950	1951	1952	1953	1954	1955	1956	1957	1958	
									I.
.46	.34	.31	.40	.36	.40	.48	.48	.53	1.
.94	1.11	1.02	1.33	1.55	1.94	2.19	2.20	2.21	2.
3.06	3.31	3.28	3.68	3.48	4.09	4.59	4.87	3.81	4.
2.27	.83	−.29	.42	−.15	.76	.69	.31	−.02	6.
6.73	5.59	4.32	5.83	5.24	7.19	7.95	7.86	6.53	7.
									II.
.22	1.04	−.35	−.05	.53	.29	.35	.81	1.10	1.
.01	.02	−.01	.01	.01	.01	.01	.03	.02	
.21	1.02	−.34	−.06	.52	.28	.34	.78	1.08	
.49	.30	.40	.18	.09	.16	.26	.10	−.09	6.
1.22	.22	1.11	.58	.20	.53	.89	.28	.79	7.
1.93	1.56	1.16	.71	.82	.98	1.50	1.19	1.80	21.
									III.
.74	−.69	.31	1.10	1.32	.60	.94	.68	.22	7.
2.13	−.80	.48	−.19	1.11	1.49	.67	−.09	1.82	9.
.36	.50	.31	.10	.18	1.01	.09	.33	.12	10.
.57	.65	.52	.55	.74	.90	1.02	.93	1.36	11.
3.80	−.34	1.62	1.56	3.35	4.00	2.72	1.85	3.52	14.
									IV.
4.86	7.49	3.86	4.98	2.71	4.17	6.73	7.20	4.81	3.
8.66	7.15	5.48	6.54	6.06	8.17	9.45	9.05	8.33	V.

1950	1951	1952	1953	1954	1955	1956	1957	1958
1.18	.50	−.08	.26	−.20	.56	.19	.01	−.06
5.64	5.26	4.53	5.67	5.19	6.99	7.45	7.56	6.49
3.77	7.16	4.07	4.82	2.66	3.97	6.23	6.90	4.77
7.57	6.82	5.69	6.38	6.01	7.97	8.95	8.75	8.29

Line	
III-7 through III-11	From line 2 of corresponding Tables VIII-c-7 through VIII-c-11.
14	Sum of lines III-7 through III-11.
IV-3	Sum of lines I-7 and II-21 minus line III-14.
V	Sum of lines I-7 and II-21.

Figures on adjusted inventories are from Table VIII-a-6d.

TABLE VII-3

Flow of Funds Through Agriculture

(billion dollars)

	1946	1947	1948	1949
I. Gross capital expenditures				
1. Residential structures	.42	.70	.75	.70
2. Nonresidential structures	.46	.73	.82	.80
4. Producer durables	.97	1.79	2.43	2.64
5. Consumer durables	1.84	2.31	2.76	2.76
6. Inventories at book value (see note below)	3.42	3.40	−.30	−3.26
7. Total	7.11	8.93	6.46	3.64
II. Net financial flows				
1. Currency and demand deposits	.50	−.10	−.30	−.40
a. Monetary metals	.01	.01	0	.01
b. Other	.49	−.11	−.30	−.41
2. Other bank deposits and shares	.20	−.08	0	0
3. Life insurance reserves	.19	.21	.23	.24
5. Pension and insurance funds, govt.	.20	.09	−.01	.05
13. Securities, U. S. government	.06	.17	.22	.12
b. Savings bonds	.06	.17	.22	.12
20. Other intangible assets	.16	.17	.17	.18
21. Total	1.31	.46	.31	.19
III. Net changes in liabilities				
6. Consumer debt	.11	.10	.09	−.01
7. Trade debt	.20	.20	.30	.20
9. Bank loans, n.e.c.	.25	.30	.36	.10
10. Other loans	.02	.03	.08	.03
11. Mortgages	.14	.17	.22	.29
14. Total	.72	.80	1.05	.61
IV. Net changes in equities				
3. Saving	7.70	8.59	5.72	3.22
V. Total uses and sources of funds	8.42	9.39	6.77	3.83

Note: Inventories at Adjusted Value and Lines Affected

	1946	1947	1948	1949
Inventories (adjusted values)	−.06	−1.73	1.47	−1.35
Gross capital expenditures	3.63	3.80	8.23	5.55
Saving	4.22	3.46	7.49	5.13
Total uses and sources of funds	4.94	4.26	8.54	5.74

Line	
I-1 through I-5	From line 3 of corresponding Tables VIII-a-1 through VIII-a-5.
6	Table VIII-a-6b, line 3.
7	Sum of lines I-1 through I-6.
II-1	Table VII-b-1, line 3.
1a	Table III-3, line II-1a (first difference).
1b	Table III-3, line II-1b (first difference).
2 through 20	From line 3 of corresponding Tables VIII-b-2 through VIII-b-20.
21	Sum of lines II-1 through II-20.

1950	1951	1952	1953	1954	1955	1956	1957	1958	
									I.
.78	.88	.90	.82	.78	.76	.74	.75	.76	1.
.89	1.00	1.03	.93	.89	.86	.84	.86	.86	2.
2.64	2.74	2.59	2.46	2.21	2.27	2.03	2.06	2.59	4.
3.05	3.09	2.54	2.93	2.61	2.54	2.53	2.64	2.87	5.
5.43	3.77	−4.99	−4.24	−.16	−1.37	.85	2.34	5.58	6.
12.79	11.48	2.07	2.90	6.33	5.06	6.99	8.65	12.66	7.
									II.
0	.20	−.10	−.10	−.10	0	−.20	−.10	.30	1.
−.01	.02	0	−.01	0	.01	.01	.03	.01	
.01	.18	−.10	−.09	−.10	−.01	−.21	−.13	.29	
0	.07	.13	.13	.10	.05	.05	.27	.17	2.
.24	.24	.28	.27	.32	.30	.26	.24	.29	3.
−.25	−.04	−.01	−.04	−.02	0	0	−.01	−.01	5.
−.03	.02	−.08	.10	.24	.20	−.11	.06	.09	13.
−.03	.02	−.08	.10	.24	.20	−.11	.06	.09	
.22	.20	.24	.15	.24	.14	.17	.17	.22	20.
.18	.69	.46	.51	.78	.69	.17	.63	1.06	21.
									III.
.19	−.01	.09	−.01	.09	.19	−.01	−.02	.18	6.
.20	.40	.10	−.20	0	0	0	.10	.10	7.
.47	.60	.07	−.43	.17	.38	−.03	.32	.56	9.
.06	.11	.08	−.02	.10	.05	.08	.22	.23	10.
.54	.56	.59	.51	.52	.78	.84	.60	.75	11.
1.46	1.66	.93	−.15	.88	1.40	.88	1.22	1.82	14.
									IV.
11.51	10.51	1.60	3.56	6.23	4.35	6.28	8.06	11.90	3.
12.97	12.17	2.53	3.41	7.11	5.75	7.16	9.28	13.72	V.

1950	1951	1952	1953	1954	1955	1956	1957	1958
1.22	1.54	.75	−.98	.66	.26	−.68	.55	2.31
8.58	9.25	7.81	6.16	7.15	6.69	5.46	6.86	9.39
7.30	8.28	7.34	6.82	7.05	5.98	4.75	6.27	8.63
8.76	9.94	8.27	6.67	7.93	7.38	5.63	7.49	10.45

Line	
III-6 through III-11	From line 3 of corresponding Tables VIII-c-6 through VIII-c-11.
14	Sum of lines III-6 through III-11.
IV-3	Sum of lines I-7 and II-21 minus line III-14.
V	Sum of lines I-7 and II-21.

Figures on adjusted inventories are from Table VIII-a-6d.

TABLE VII-4

Flow of Funds Through Nonfinancial Corporations

(billion dollars)

	1946	1947	1948	1949
I. Gross capital expenditures				
1. Residential structures	.29	.41	.70	.78
2. Nonresidential structures	4.33	5.29	6.34	6.19
4. Producer durables	7.60	11.32	12.49	10.49
6. Inventories at book value (see note below)	11.22	7.15	4.21	−3.57
7. Total	23.44	24.17	23.74	13.89
II. Net financial flows				
1. Currency and demand deposits	1.14	2.20	.20	1.07
a. Monetary metals	.01	0	.02	0
b. Other	1.13	2.20	.18	1.07
2. Other bank deposits and shares	0	0	0	0
6. Consumer credit	.57	.64	.54	.44
7. Trade credit	3.19	5.86	2.34	−.94
13. Securities, U.S. government	−5.70	−1.20	.80	1.92
a. Short-term	−5.10	−.90	.90	2.30
b. Savings bonds	0	0	.20	0
c. Other long-term	−.60	−.30	−.30	−.38
14. Securities, state and local	0	.04	.05	.05
15. Securities, other bonds and notes	.04	.12	.14	.14
16. Securities, preferred stock	.01	.01	.01	0
17. Securities, common stock	.09	.08	.08	.09
20. Other intangible assets	−.46	1.87	.93	.86
21. Total	−1.12	9.62	5.09	3.63
III. Net changes in liabilities				
7. Trade debt	3.73	4.64	.44	−1.34
8. Loans on securities	−.91	−.33	−.16	0
9. Bank loans, n.e.c.	2.98	1.66	1.06	−1.93
10. Other loans	.01	.14	.17	.08
11. Mortgages	1.32	1.47	1.31	1.40
12. Bonds and notes	.88	2.84	4.23	2.90
13. Other liabilities	.42	2.74	1.77	−.66
14. Total	8.43	13.16	8.82	.45
IV. Net changes in equities				
1. Net issues of common stock	1.49	1.32	1.29	1.42
2. Net issues of preferred stock	.19	.42	.29	.29
3. Saving	12.21	18.89	18.43	15.36
V. Total uses and sources of funds	22.32	33.79	28.83	17.52
Note: Inventories at Adjusted Value and Lines Affected				
Inventories (adjusted values)	5.95	1.25	2.06	−1.72
Gross capital expenditures	18.17	18.27	21.59	15.74
Saving	6.94	12.99	16.28	17.21
Total uses and sources of funds	17.05	27.89	26.68	19.37

Line	
I-1 through I-4	From line 4 of corresponding Tables VIII-a-1 through VIII-a-4.
6	Table VIII-a-6b, line 4.
7	Sum of lines I-1 through I-7.
II-1	Table VIII-b-1, line 4.
1a	Table III-4, line II-1a (first difference).
1b	Table III-4, line II-1b (first difference).
2-20	From line 4 of corresponding Tables VIII-b-2 through VIII-b-20.
21	Sum of line II-1 through II-20.

Table 4

1950	1951	1952	1953	1954	1955	1956	1957	1958	
									I.
.82	.75	.63	.88	.83	.99	1.12	1.08	1.17	1.
6.52	8.13	8.82	9.61	9.80	11.16	12.64	13.60	12.73	2.
11.64	13.80	14.07	14.96	14.10	15.35	19.39	20.35	15.64	4.
9.77	9.75	1.25	1.80	−1.60	6.66	7.58	2.74	−4.44	6.
28.75	32.43	24.77	27.25	23.13	34.16	40.73	37.77	25.10	7.
									II.
1.31	1.82	.80	−.08	2.36	.98	.14	0	1.72	1.
.01	.01	.01	0	0	.01	.01	.02	.02	
1.30	1.81	.79	−.08	2.36	.97	.13	−.02	1.70	
0	0	0	0	.20	−.10	0	0	.60	2.
.78	.51	.76	.24	.27	.66	.41	.21	.52	6.
11.44	3.41	3.53	−.81	4.31	10.86	7.06	2.72	7.67	7.
2.87	.93	−.80	1.58	−2.29	3.99	−4.59	−.80	.19	13.
3.00	.30	−1.10	1.80	−2.60	3.00	−3.70	−.40	.70	
0	0	0	0	0	0	−.20	−.20	−.18	
−.13	.63	.30	−.22	.31	.99	−.69	−.20	−.33	
.07	.05	.06	.09	.33	.18	.11	.15	.13	14.
.03	.30	.41	.18	−.07	.41	.23	.83	−.26	15.
.01	0	.01	0	.01	.01	0	.01	0	16.
.10	.12	.16	.13	.14	.19	.19	.21	.23	17.
.56	1.02	2.98	2.63	4.93	4.83	5.99	6.64	1.00	20.
17.17	8.16	7.91	3.96	10.19	22.01	9.54	9.97	11.80	21.
									III.
8.01	2.28	3.59	.16	3.40	10.24	5.61	2.02	6.28	7.
0	0	0	0	0	0	0	0	0	8.
2.15	4.96	1.19	−.16	−1.22	2.27	5.38	2.06	−.88	9.
.13	.15	.09	.34	−.27	.46	−.15	.37	−.15	10.
1.81	1.45	1.29	1.20	1.76	2.00	1.88	1.73	3.19	11.
1.61	3.30	4.72	3.35	3.54	2.77	3.67	6.35	5.92	12.
7.37	6.94	−1.40	2.23	.32	6.55	3.39	2.56	.19	13.
21.08	19.08	9.48	7.12	7.53	24.29	19.78	15.09	14.55	14.
									IV.
1.60	2.05	2.33	1.94	1.81	2.55	2.60	2.94	2.59	1.
.24	.64	.45	.39	.50	0	.46	.37	.49	2.
23.00	18.82	20.42	21.76	23.48	29.33	27.43	29.34	19.27	3.
45.92	40.59	32.68	31.21	33.32	56.17	50.27	47.74	36.90	V.
4.81	8.55	2.23	.81	−1.92	4.93	4.89	1.21	−4.84	
23.79	31.23	25.75	26.26	22.81	32.43	38.04	36.24	24.70	
18.04	17.62	21.40	20.77	23.16	27.60	24.74	27.81	18.87	
40.96	39.39	33.66	30.22	33.00	54.44	47.58	46.21	36.50	

Line	
III-7 through III-13	From line 4 of corresponding Tables VIII-c-7 through VIII-c-13.
14	Sum of lines III-7 through III-13.
IV-1	Table VIII-d-1, line 4.
2	Table VIII-d-2, line 4.
3	Sum of lines I-7 and II-21 minus the sum of lines III-14, IV-1 and IV-2.
V	Sum of lines I-7 and II-21.

Figures on adjusted inventories are from Table VIII-a-6d.

TABLE VII-5

Flow of Funds Through Total Finance

(billion dollars)

	1946	1947	1948	1949
I. Gross capital expenditures				
1. Residential structures	n.a.	.03	.04	.07
2. Nonresidential structures	.27	.28	.26	.12
4. Producer durables	.07	.07	.07	.03
6. Inventories	.02	–.01	–.01	a
7. Total	.36	.37	.36	.22
II. Net financial flows				
1. Currency and demand deposits	.50	7.89	4.75	–2.79
a. Monetary metals	.41	2.22	1.50	.22
b. Other	.09	5.67	3.25	–3.01
2. Other bank deposits and shares	.14	.04	.02	.01
6. Consumer credit	1.86	2.31	1.98	2.26
7. Trade credit	.34	.13	.17	.11
8. Loans on securities	–4.40	–1.06	.25	.75
9. Bank loans, n.e.c.	4.97	4.59	2.17	–1.62
10. Other loans	.36	.33	.62	.12
11. Mortgages, nonfarm	4.95	5.83	5.96	5.01
a. Residential	4.16	5.04	5.17	4.47
b. Nonresidential	.80	.78	.78	.54
12. Mortgages, farm	.20	.22	.16	.20
13. Securities, U.S. government	–12.09	–4.37	–5.76	1.13
a. Short-term	–13.52	–2.83	–6.48	6.85
b. Savings bonds	.38	.34	.98	.29
c. Other long-term	1.05	–1.88	–.26	–6.01
14. Securities, state and local	.18	.99	1.10	1.49
15. Securities, other bonds and notes	2.55	3.86	5.17	3.71
16. Securities, preferred stock	.18	.10	.07	.30
17. Securities, common stock	.29	.45	.27	.57
20. Other intangible assets	1.23	1.68	–.06	.73
21. Total	1.24	23.00	16.86	12.01
III. Net changes in liabilities				
1. Currency and demand deposits	–14.94	9.60	2.03	–2.68
2. Other bank deposits and shares	6.59	3.56	2.55	2.95
3. Life insurance reserves	3.78	3.58	3.83	4.07
4. Pension and retirement funds, private	.57	.64	.65	.70
5. Pension and insurance funds, govt.	3.67	3.88	3.48	2.54
7. Trade debt	–.01	.01	.01	.02
8. Loans on securities	–2.04	–.71	.51	.45
9. Bank loans, n.e.c.	.59	.62	.46	.39
10. Other loans	.22	.19	0	.08
12. Bonds and notes	.26	.28	.58	.52
13. Other liabilities	1.41	.16	1.02	1.32
14. Total	.10	21.80	15.12	10.37
IV. Net changes in equities				
1. Net issues of common stock	.25	.26	.15	.37
2. Net issues of preferred stock	0	0	.05	.03
3. Saving	1.26	1.30	1.91	1.43
V. Total uses and sources of funds	1.60	23.36	17.22	12.21

Line	
I-1 through I-4	From line 5 of corresponding Tables VIII-a-1 through VIII-a-4.
6	Table VIII-a-6b, line 5.
7	Sum of lines I-1 through I-6.

1950	1951	1952	1953	1954	1955	1956	1957	1958	
									I.
.05	.01	.11	−.01	.02	.01	−.01	.01	a	1.
.30	.38	.21	.33	.27	.41	.51	.46	.31	2.
.07	.10	.05	.08	.07	.10	.13	.12	.08	4.
.01	a	a	a	−.01	a	a	−.01	a	6.
.43	.49	.37	.40	.35	.52	.63	.58	.39	7.
									II.
.07	4.67	1.15	−1.18	−.93	.61	2.22	2.07	−3.73	1.
−1.73	−.05	.47	−1.16	−.27	−.05	.31	.73	−2.22	
1.80	4.72	.68	−.02	−.66	.66	1.91	1.34	−1.51	
−.05	.08	.13	.08	.10	.02	.05	.04	.31	2.
2.90	.53	3.63	3.51	.74	5.63	3.02	2.53	−.23	6.
.29	.20	.15	.15	.16	.38	.42	.34	.36	7.
.80	−.34	.70	.80	1.86	1.08	−.68	−.36	1.58	8.
5.52	4.68	3.02	.38	.60	6.84	5.58	2.06	1.72	9.
.61	.65	.35	.22	.11	1.29	.25	1.31	.35	10.
8.95	7.69	7.43	8.17	10.77	14.00	11.84	8.30	12.18	11.
8.29	6.86	6.66	7.34	9.54	12.60	10.18	6.73	10.42	
.64	.83	.77	.81	1.22	1.40	1.66	1.58	1.75	
.27	.25	.25	.21	.24	.36	.26	.13	.18	12.
−4.51	2.73	6.38	3.86	5.25	−5.71	−2.02	−.94	10.42	13.
−.32	−9.21	5.41	11.77	−8.67	−8.15	6.37	2.23	.58	
.92	.02	.24	−.17	.09	−.04	−.93	−1.40	−.34	
−5.11	11.92	.73	−7.75	13.83	2.48	−7.45	−1.78	10.19	
2.29	1.66	1.54	2.12	3.49	1.57	1.38	2.33	4.10	14.
2.95	4.03	5.05	4.45	4.31	3.38	3.88	7.32	5.95	15.
.30	.13	.19	.34	.42	.20	−.12	−.03	.44	16.
.38	.70	1.16	.89	1.34	1.40	1.53	2.26	2.29	17.
4.18	.67	1.01	.56	.62	4.96	1.99	1.12	1.40	20.
24.95	28.33	32.12	24.56	29.06	35.98	29.58	28.50	37.35	21.
									III.
9.39	10.96	6.99	−.35	2.72	6.75	4.04	−.67	4.29	1.
2.65	4.92	8.14	9.16	10.51	8.46	9.43	12.40	17.01	2.
4.29	4.25	5.09	5.14	5.61	5.67	5.59	5.25	5.64	3.
.98	1.44	1.60	1.94	2.05	2.06	2.60	2.89	3.07	4.
1.31	4.07	4.35	3.38	2.69	3.24	3.58	2.85	1.23	5.
.01	−.01	.04	.02	.01	.02	.03	.01	.02	7.
.07	−.19	.48	.30	.67	.32	−.62	.10	.34	8.
1.06	−.04	.91	−.14	−.01	2.76	−.63	−.37	−1.08	9.
.99	.05	−.03	.04	.68	.48	−.18	.30	1.03	10.
.42	.57	.54	1.58	.19	1.63	1.19	1.12	.02	12.
1.85	1.14	2.10	1.56	1.40	2.07	1.98	2.00	1.62	13.
23.02	27.16	30.21	22.63	26.53	33.45	27.00	25.87	33.18	14.
									IV.
.45	.56	.76	.70	.78	1.12	1.43	1.39	1.69	1.
.02	−.04	.02	0	−.07	.08	.02	.04	0	2.
1.89	1.15	1.49	1.65	2.17	1.84	1.75	1.77	2.87	3.
25.37	28.82	32.48	24.98	29.40	36.50	30.20	29.08	37.73	V.

All lines II, III, IV, and V in this table are the sum of the corresponding lines in Tables VII-5a through VII-5m. The same figures appear in the corresponding lines of the last column of the tables in Section VI.

[a]$5 million or under.

Figures may not add to totals because of rounding.

TABLE VII-5a

Flow of Funds Through Federal Reserve Banks and Treasury Monetary Funds

(billion dollars)

	1946	1947	1948	1949
I. Gross capital expenditures				
7. Total	a	a	a	a
II. Net financial flows				
1. Currency and demand deposits	1.26	5.35	3.03	.35
a. Monetary metals	.41	2.22	1.50	.22
b. Other	.85	3.13	1.53	.13
9. Bank loans, n.e.c.	−.09	−.07	.13	−.14
13. Securities, U.S. government	−.92	−.79	.77	−4.45
a. Short-term	−.90	−2.40	−7.50	−.40
b. Savings bonds				
c. Other long-term	−.02	1.61	8.27	−4.05
20. Other intangible assets	.38	.46	−.09	.04
21. Total	.63	4.95	3.84	−4.20
III. Net changes in liabilities				
1. Currency and demand deposits	.14	5.97	3.93	−4.56
13. Other liabilities	.41	−1.04	−.15	.30
14. Total	.55	4.93	3.78	−4.26
IV. Net changes in equities				
3. Saving	.08	.02	.06	.06
V. Total uses and sources of funds	.63	4.95	3.84	−4.20

Line

I-7	Table VIII-a-7, line 5a.
II-1	Table VIII-b-1, line 5a.
1a	Table III-5a, line II-1a (first difference).
1b	Table III-5a, line II-1b (first difference).
9-20	From line 5a of corresponding Tables VIII-b-9 through VIII-b-20.
21	Sum of lines II-1 through II-20.

1950	1951	1952	1953	1954	1955	1956	1957	1958	
									I.
a	a	a	a	a	.01	.01	.01	a	7.
									II.
−3.38	.16	1.15	−1.68	−.52	.05	.48	1.73	−4.13	1.
−1.73	−.05	.47	−1.16	−.27	−.05	.31	.73	−2.22	
−1.65	.21	.68	−.52	−.25	.10	.17	1.00	−1.91	
−.01	−.05	.14	−.13	.11	0	−.02	0	−.01	9.
1.90	3.02	.90	1.22	−.99	−.15	.22	−.76	2.18	13.
4.00	−2.60	1.40	2.20	2.40	1.30	1.40	−.70	−.40	
−2.10	5.62	−.50	−.98	−3.39	−1.45	−1.18	−.06	2.58	
1.34	−.35	.36	−.03	−.28	1.57	.21	.04	−.14	20.
−.15	2.78	2.55	−.62	−1.68	1.47	.89	1.01	−2.10	21.
									III.
−.43	3.08	1.95	−.71	−1.55	.56	.78	.91	−2.40	1.
.25	−.32	.54	.06	−.14	.87	.05	.07	.27	13.
−.18	2.76	2.49	−.65	−1.69	1.43	.83	.98	−2.13	14.
									IV.
.03	.02	.06	.03	.01	.05	.07	.04	.03	3.
−.15	2.78	2.55	−.62	−1.68	1.48	.90	1.02	−2.10	V.

Line	
III-1	Table VIII-c-1, line 5a.
13	Table VIII-c-13, line 5a.
14	Sum of lines III-1 and III-13.
IV-3	Sum of lines I-7 and II-21 minus line III-14.
V	Sum of lines I-7 and II-21.

[a] $5 million or under.
Figures may not add to totals because of rounding.

TABLE VII-5b

Flow of Funds Through Government Pension and Insurance Funds

(billion dollars)

	1946	1947	1948	1949
I. Gross capital expenditures				
II. Net financial flows				
1. Currency and demand deposits	.01	.02	.08	−.02
a. Monetary metals				
b. Other	.01	.02	.08	−.02
10. Other loans	−.01	0	.02	.01
11. Mortgages, nonfarm	0	0	0	0
a. Residential	0	0	0	0
b. Nonresidential				
13. Securities, U.S. government	3.76	3.75	3.14	2.19
a. Short-term				
b. Savings bonds	.10	.10	.10	.10
c. Other long-term	3.66	3.65	3.04	2.09
14. Securities, state and local	−.10	.10	.15	.21
15. Securities, other bonds and notes	0	.01	.06	.15
16. Securities, preferred stock	0	0	.01	0
17. Securities, common stock	0	0	.01	0
21. Total	3.66	3.88	3.47	2.54
III. Net changes in liabilities				
5. Pension and insurance funds, govt.	3.67	3.88	3.48	2.54
14. Total	3.67	3.88	3.48	2.54
IV. Net changes in equities				
V. Total uses and sources of funds	3.66	3.88	3.47	2.54

Line	
II-1	Table VIII-b-1, line 5b.
1b	Table III-5b, line II-1b (first difference).
10-17	From line 5b of corresponding Tables VIII-b-10 through VIII-b-17.
21	Sum of lines II-1 through II-17.

1950	1951	1952	1953	1954	1955	1956	1957	1958	
									I.
									II.
.46	.06	−.11	−.04	.32	−.22	.14	.24	.13	1.
.46	.06	−.11	−.04	.32	−.22	.14	.24	.13	
.02	.02	.01	.02	.02	.03	.03	.03	.04	10.
.06	.06	.04	.03	.07	.04	.09	.02	−.05	11.
.06	.06	.04	.03	.07	.04	.09	.02	−.05	
.41	3.60	3.92	2.69	1.44	2.40	2.25	1.07	−.62	13.
.10	0	.10	0	0	0	−.10	−.10	−.10	
.31	3.60	3.82	2.69	1.44	2.40	2.35	1.17	−.52	
.19	.07	.13	.24	.31	.34	.40	.45	.46	14.
.15	.24	.34	.40	.49	.59	.63	.96	1.15	15.
.01	.01	.01	.02	.02	.03	.02	.04	.06	16.
.01	.01	.01	.02	.02	.03	.02	.04	.06	17.
1.31	4.07	4.35	3.38	2.69	3.24	3.58	2.85	1.23	21.
									III.
1.31	4.07	4.35	3.38	2.69	3.24	3.58	2.85	1.23	5.
1.31	4.07	4.35	3.38	2.69	3.24	3.58	2.85	1.23	14.
									IV.
1.31	4.07	4.35	3.38	2.69	3.24	3.58	2.85	1.23	V.

Line	
III-5 through III-14	Table VIII-c-5, line 5b.
V	Same as line II-21.

Figures may not add to totals because of rounding.

TABLE VII-5c

Flow of Funds Through Commercial Banks

(billion dollars)

	1946	1947	1948	1949
I. Gross capital expenditures				
7. Total	.10	.11	.10	.06
II. Net financial flows				
1. Currency and demand deposits	−1.30	2.21	1.52	−3.36
a. Monetary metals				
b. Other	−1.30	2.21	1.52	−3.36
2. Other bank deposits and shares	−.01	0	−.01	−.01
6. Consumer credit	1.19	1.31	1.01	1.03
8. Loans on securities	−3.66	−1.11	.26	.33
9. Bank loans, n.e.c.	5.06	4.66	2.04	−1.48
11. Mortgages, nonfarm	2.27	2.08	1.36	.70
a. Residential	1.74	1.78	1.11	.60
b. Nonresidential	.53	.30	.25	.10
12. Mortgages, farm	.18	.12	.05	.04
13. Securities, U.S. government	−15.83	−5.56	−6.60	4.38
a. Short-term	−13.50	.40	.20	7.10
b. Savings bonds	.02	−.03	.30	−.05
c. Other long-term	−2.35	−5.93	−7.10	−2.67
14. Securities, state and local	.43	.88	.38	.89
15. Securities, other bonds and notes	.35	.06	−.20	.15
17. Securities, common stock	−.03	−.03	0	−.01
20. Other intangible assets	.78	1.12	−.26	.40
21. Total	−10.57	5.74	−.45	3.06
III. Net changes in liabilities				
1. Currency and demand deposits	−15.02	3.64	−1.85	1.87
2. Other bank deposits and shares	3.83	1.43	.63	.50
9. Bank loans, n.e.c.	−.17	.02	−.01	−.04
10. Other loans	−.07	−.05	−.03	−.02
13. Other liabilities	.21	.15	.16	.17
14. Total	−11.22	5.19	−1.10	2.48
IV. Net changes in equities				
1. Net issues of common stock	.05	.04	.02	.01
3. Saving	.70	.62	.73	.63
V. Total uses and sources of funds	−10.47	5.85	−.35	3.12

Line	
I-7	Table VIII-a-7, line 5c.
II-1	Table VIII-b-1, line 5c.
1b	Table III-5c, line II-1b (first difference).
2-20	From line 5c of corresponding Tables VIII-b-2 through VIII-b-20.
21	Sum of lines II-1 through II-20.

1950	1951	1952	1953	1954	1955	1956	1957	1958	
									I.
.12	.14	.11	.12	.10	.15	.18	.17	.11	7.
									II.
2.28	3.92	−.06	.24	−1.23	.23	1.36	−.15	−.36	1.
2.28	3.92	−.06	.24	−1.23	.23	1.36	−.15	−.36	
0	0	0	0	0	0	0	0	.04	2.
1.66	.17	1.89	1.60	.03	2.36	1.45	1.21	.18	6.
.22	−.30	.60	.40	.89	.59	−.76	−.06	.44	8.
5.53	4.73	2.88	.51	.49	6.84	5.60	2.06	1.73	9.
1.94	1.00	1.08	.96	1.65	2.25	1.66	.57	2.04	11.
1.73	.81	.92	.74	1.23	1.71	1.11	.14	1.42	
.21	.19	.16	.22	.42	.54	.56	.43	.62	
.06	.04	.05	.03	.08	.14	.04	.03	.10	12.
−4.97	−.51	1.80	.11	5.55	−7.39	−3.04	−.31	7.94	13.
−4.30	−6.40	3.40	9.00	−10.60	−8.60	4.80	1.90	.90	
.29	.02	.02	−.02	.01	−.02	−.39	−.47	−.03	
−.96	5.87	−1.62	−8.87	16.14	1.23	−7.45	−1.74	7.07	
1.57	1.08	.99	.63	1.77	.11	.20	1.02	2.58	14.
.58	−.13	−.22	−.12	−.14	.24	−.64	.60	.03	15.
0	−.01	.01	0	0	.01	0	.02	.01	17.
2.44	.58	.12	.01	.26	2.97	.94	.21	.96	20.
11.31	10.57	9.14	4.37	9.35	8.35	6.81	5.20	15.69	21.
									III.
9.78	7.85	5.03	.36	4.25	6.16	3.20	−1.65	6.65	1.
.23	1.73	3.07	3.40	3.81	1.33	2.07	5.45	8.04	2.
.07	−.06	.16	−.13	−.03	.13	−.08	0	−.01	9.
−.02	−.01	−.03	−.01	−.02	−.01	0	0	0	10.
.58	.40	.24	.11	.34	.02	.55	.37	−.05	13.
10.64	9.91	8.47	3.73	8.35	7.63	5.74	4.17	14.63	14.
									IV.
.07	.14	.14	.11	.23	.14	.40	.36	.13	1.
.72	.66	.64	.65	.87	.73	.85	.84	1.04	3.
11.43	10.71	9.25	4.49	9.45	8.50	6.99	5.37	15.80	V.

Line	
III-1 through III-13	From line 5c of corresponding Tables VIII-c-1 through VIII-c-13.
14	Sum of lines III-1 through III-13.
IV-1	Table VIII-d-1, line 5c.
3	Sum of lines I-7 and II-21, minus the sum of lines III-14 and IV-1.
V	Sum of lines I-7 and II-21.

Figures may not add to totals because of rounding.

TABLE VII-5d

Flow of Funds Through Mutual Savings Banks

(billion dollars)

	1946	1947	1948	1949
I. Gross capital expenditures				
7. Total	.01	.01	.01	a
II. Net financial flows				
1. Currency and demand deposits	.06	.02	−.03	0
a. Monetary metals				
b. Other	.06	.02	−.03	0
2. Other bank deposits and shares	.15	.05	.02	−.01
6. Consumer credit	0	.02	0	0
8. Loans on securities	0	0	0	0
10. Other loans	.02	−.02	.02	0
11. Mortgages, nonfarm	.23	.41	.94	.90
a. Residential	.20	.35	.82	.81
b. Nonresidential	.03	.06	.12	.08
12. Mortgages, farm	0	0	.01	0
13. Securities, U.S. government	1.10	.20	−.50	−.05
a. Short-term	.28	.05	.05	−.10
b. Savings bonds	.04	.05	.18	.02
c. Other long-term	.78	.10	−.73	.03
14. Securities, state and local	−.03	0	.01	.02
15. Securities, other bonds and notes	.17	.32	.50	.14
17. Securities, common stock	.01	0	.01	0
20. Other intangible assets	0	0	.01	.02
21. Total	1.71	1.00	.99	1.02
III. Net changes in liabilities				
2. Other bank deposits and shares	1.49	.88	.64	.88
9. Bank loans, n.e.c.	0	0	0	0
13. Other liabilities	.02	.02	0	.02
14. Total	1.51	.90	.64	.90
IV. Net changes in equities				
3. Saving	.21	.11	.36	.12
V. Total uses and sources of funds	1.72	1.01	1.00	1.02

Line	
I-7	Table VIII-a-7, line 5d.
II-1	Table VIII-b-1, line 5d.
1b	Table III-5d, line II-1b (first difference).
2-20	From line 5d of corresponding Tables VIII-b-2 through VIII-b-20.
21	Sum of lines II-1 through II-20.

1950	1951	1952	1953	1954	1955	1956	1957	1958	
									I.
.01	.01	.01	.01	.01	.01	.01	.01	.01	7.
									II.
−.02	.07	0	.04	.02	−.02	.02	0	0	1.
−.02	.07	0	.04	.02	−.02	.02	0	0	
−.05	.02	.03	.02	.03	−.05	−.06	−.04	.04	2.
.02	0	.01	.01	0	.02	.03	0	.01	6.
0	0	0	0	.01	.01	0	−.01	0	8.
0	0	0	.01	.01	0	.01	.03	.04	10.
1.55	1.65	1.46	1.56	2.06	2.45	2.29	1.42	2.10	11.
1.48	1.54	1.29	1.45	1.88	2.36	2.14	1.31	1.93	
.06	.11	.17	.11	.18	.09	.15	.12	.17	
.01	0	.01	0	0	0	0	0	0	12.
−.56	−1.05	−.40	−.24	−.43	−.29	−.49	−.42	−.29	13.
−.33	.07	.08	.22	−.32	.10	−.02	.21	−.15	
.08	0	.01	−.03	−.01	−.03	−.07	−.15	−.08	
−.31	−1.12	−.49	−.43	−.10	−.36	−.40	−.48	−.06	
0	.06	.17	.09	.19	.04	.03	.01	.05	14.
−.08	.13	.37	.29	.09	−.26	.13	.74	.55	15.
.02	.05	.11	.09	.14	.09	.04	.07	.09	17.
.02	.05	0	.03	.01	.02	.02	.03	.02	20.
.91	.98	1.76	1.90	2.13	2.01	2.02	1.83	2.61	21.
									III.
.74	.88	1.70	1.77	1.94	1.83	1.87	1.66	2.35	2.
0	0	0	0	0	0	0	0	.01	9.
.03	.01	.01	.05	.07	.05	.03	.08	.09	13.
.77	.89	1.71	1.82	2.01	1.88	1.90	1.74	2.45	14.
									IV.
.15	.10	.06	.09	.13	.14	.13	.10	.17	3.
.92	.99	1.77	1.91	2.14	2.02	2.03	1.84	2.62	V.

Line	
III-2 through III-13	From line 5d of corresponding Tables VIII-c-2 through VIII-c-13.
14	Sum of lines III-2 through III-13.
IV-3	Sum of lines I-7 and II-21 minus line III-14.
V	Sum of lines I-7 and II-21.

[a]$5 million or under.
Figures may not add to totals because of rounding.

TABLE VII-5e

Flow of Funds Through Savings and Loan Associations

(billion dollars)

	1946	1947	1948	1949
I. Gross capital expenditures				
7. Total	.05	.05	.05	.03
II. Net financial flows				
1. Currency and demand deposits	.07	0	.06	.08
a. Monetary metals				
b. Other	.07	0	.06	.08
6. Consumer credit	.04	.03	.03	.02
11. Mortgages, nonfarm	1.76	1.72	1.45	1.31
a. Residential	1.73	1.68	1.42	1.28
b. Nonresidential	.04	.03	.03	.03
13. Securities, U.S. government	−.41	−.27	−.28	0
a. Short-term	0	0	−.10	0
b. Savings bonds	0	0	.10	.10
c. Other long-term	−.41	−.27	−.28	−.10
20. Other intangible assets	0	0	.08	.14
21. Total	1.46	1.48	1.34	1.55
III. Net changes in liabilities				
2. Other bank deposits and shares	1.17	1.20	1.21	1.50
9. Bank loans, n.e.c.	−.03	0	−.04	0
10. Other loans	.19	.20	.04	−.04
13. Other liabilities	.03	−.03	.02	0
14. Total	1.36	1.37	1.23	1.46
IV. Net changes in equities				
3. Saving	.15	.16	.16	.12
V. Total uses and sources of funds	1.51	1.53	1.39	1.58

Line	
I-7	Table VIII-a-7, line 5e.
II-1	Table VIII-b-1, line 5e.
1b	Table III-5e, line II-1b (first difference).
6-20	From line 5e of corresponding Tables VIII-b-6 through VIII-b-20.
21	Sum of lines II-1 through II-20.

1950	1951	1952	1953	1954	1955	1956	1957	1958	
									I.
.06	.07	.05	.06	.05	.07	.09	.08	.05	7.
									II.
.09	.10	.07	.05	.26	.19	.07	.05	.27	1.
.09	.10	.07	.05	.26	.19	.07	.05	.27	
.06	.03	.07	.05	.05	.08	.08	.08	.06	6.
2.04	1.91	2.83	3.57	4.15	5.30	4.32	4.28	5.62	11.
2.00	1.87	2.78	3.50	4.06	5.19	4.23	4.19	5.51	
.04	.04	.06	.07	.08	.11	.09	.08	.11	
.03	.11	.19	.13	.10	.32	.44	.39	.65	13.
0	.10	0	0	0	.10	−.10	.30	−.20	
.10	0	0	0	0	.03	−.13	−.08	0	
−.07	.01	.19	.13	.10	.19	.67	.17	.85	
.02	.15	.21	.23	.27	.04	.20	.34	.27	20.
2.24	2.30	3.37	4.03	4.83	5.93	5.11	5.14	6.87	21.
									III.
1.52	2.12	3.09	3.65	4.40	4.89	5.01	4.76	6.07	2.
.01	.01	−.01	0	0	.05	−.01	−.01	.04	9.
.52	0	.15	.14	.15	.68	−.21	0	.31	10.
.05	.02	.01	.03	.06	.03	.03	.12	.10	13.
2.10	2.15	3.24	3.82	4.61	5.65	4.82	4.87	6.52	14.
									IV.
.20	.22	.18	.27	.27	.35	.38	.35	.40	3.
2.30	2.37	3.42	4.09	4.88	6.00	5.20	5.22	6.92	V.

Line	
III-2 through III-13	From line 5e of corresponding Tables VIII-c-2 through VIII-c-13.
14	Sum of lines III-1 through III-14.
IV-3	Sum of lines I-7 and II-21 minus line III-14.
V	Sum of lines I-7 and II-21.

Figures may not add to totals because of rounding.

TABLE VII-5f

Flow of Funds Through Investment Companies

(billion dollars)

	1946	1947	1948	1949
I. Gross capital expenditures				
II. Net financial flows				
1. Currency and demand deposits	0	−.01	0	0
a. Monetary metals				
b. Other	0	−.01	0	0
11. Mortgages, nonfarm	.04	.08	.06	.02
a. Residential	.04	.07	.04	.02
b. Nonresidential	0	.01	.01	0
13. Securities, U.S. government	−.05	.01	−.05	.04
a. Short-term				
b. Savings bonds				
c. Other long-term	−.05	.01	−.05	.04
15. Securities, other bonds and notes	−.02	−.02	.01	.02
16. Securities, preferred stock	−.01	.01	.02	0
17. Securities, common stock	.15	.15	.10	.20
20. Other intangible assets	.01	−.01	.02	−.02
21. Total	.12	.21	.16	.26
III. Net changes in liabilities				
IV. Net changes in equities				
1. Net issues of common stock	.16	.17	.14	.26
3. Saving	−.04	.04	.02	0
V. Total uses and sources of funds	.12	.21	.16	.26

Line	
II-1	Table VIII-b-1, line 5f.
1b	Table III-5f, line II-1b (first difference).
11-20	From line 5f of corresponding Tables VIII-b-11 through VIII-b-20.
21	Sum of lines II-1 through II-20.

1950	1951	1952	1953	1954	1955	1956	1957	1958	
									I.
									II.
.04	.03	−.01	.04	0	0	.03	.03	0	1.
.04	.03	−.01	.04	0	0	.03	.03	0	
.04	−.01	.01	.01	0	−.01	−.01	−.02	−.03	11.
.03	−.01	.01	−.01	0	−.01	−.01	−.02	−.03	
0	0	0	0	0	0	0	0	0	
.02	0	−.01	0	0	.14	.02	0	.14	13.
.02	0	−.01	0	0	.14	.02	0	.14	
.04	.05	.10	.01	.14	.18	.11	.14	.24	15.
.03	.04	−.05	.17	.08	.11	.08	−.11	.31	16.
.10	.14	.48	.19	.22	.40	.50	.90	.66	17.
.01	0	0	0	0	.03	−.02	.01	.01	20.
.28	.25	.52	.42	.44	.85	.71	.95	1.33	21.
									III.
									IV.
.25	.40	.55	.43	.46	.76	.91	.98	1.50	1.
.03	−.15	−.03	−.01	−.02	.09	−.20	−.03	−.17	3.
.28	.25	.52	.42	.44	.85	.71	.95	1.33	V.

Line	
IV-1	Table VIII-d-1, line 5f.
3	Line II-21 minus line IV-1.
V	Same as line II-21.

Figures may not add to totals because of rounding.

TABLE VII-5g

Flow of Funds Through Credit Unions

(billion dollars)

	1946	1947	1948	1949
I. Gross capital expenditures				
II. Net financial flows				
1. Currency and demand deposits	0	.01	.01	0
a. Monetary metals				
b. Other	0	.01	.01	0
2. Other bank deposits and shares	0	−.01	.01	.03
6. Consumer credit	.05	.09	.09	.11
10. Other loans	0	0	0	0
11. Mortgages, nonfarm	.01	.01	.02	.01
a. Residential	.01	.01	.02	.01
13. Securities, U.S. government	0	0	−.02	−.02
c. Other long-term	0	0	−.02	−.02
21. Total	.06	.10	.11	.13
III. Net changes in liabilities				
2. Other bank deposits and shares	.06	.08	.09	.10
7. Trade debt	−.01	.01	.01	.02
14. Total	.05	.09	.10	.12
IV. Net changes in equities				
3. Saving	.01	.01	.01	.01
V. Total uses and sources of funds	.06	.10	.11	.13

Line	
II-1	Table VIII-b-1, line 5g.
1b	Table III-5g, line II-1b (first difference).
2-13c	From line 5g of corresponding Tables VIII-b-11 through VIII-b-20.
21	Sum of lines II-1 through II-20.
III-2	Table VIII-c-2, line 5g.
7	Table VIII-c-7, line 5g.
14	Sum of lines III-2 and III-7.

1950	1951	1952	1953	1954	1955	1956	1957	1958	
									I.
									II.
.02	.05	0	.02	.05	.01	.03	.03	.04	1.
.02	.05	0	.02	.05	.01	.03	.03	.04	
0	.05	.09	.06	.07	.07	.11	.08	.23	2.
.15	.05	.20	.28	.22	.34	.33	.42	.23	6.
.01	.01	.01	0	0	.02	−.01	.02	0	10.
.01	.02	.03	.03	.03	.03	.06	0	.08	11.
.01	.02	.03	.03	.03	.03	.06	0	.08	
−.02	.02	0	−.01	0	0	.01	−.01	0	13.
−.02	.02	0	−.01	0	0	.01	−.01	0	
.17	.20	.33	.38	.37	.47	.53	.54	.58	21.
									III.
.15	.19	.27	.33	.34	.40	.46	.46	.47	2.
.01	−.01	.04	.02	.01	.02	.03	.01	.02	7.
.16	.18	.31	.35	.35	.42	.49	.47	.49	14.
									IV.
.01	.02	.02	.03	.02	.05	.04	.07	.09	3.
.17	.20	.33	.38	.37	.47	.53	.54	.58	V.

Line	
IV-3	Line II-21 minus line III-14.
V	Same as line II-21.

Figures may not add to totals because of rounding.

TABLE VII-5h

Flow of Funds Through Life Insurance Companies

(billion dollars)

	1946	1947	1948	1949
I. Gross capital expenditures				
7. Total	.17	.17	.17	.10
II. Net financial flows				
1. Currency and demand deposits	−.01	.25	−.11	0
a. Monetary metals				
b. Other	−.01	.25	−.11	0
10. Other loans	−.07	.05	.12	.18
11. Mortgages, nonfarm	.50	1.42	2.06	1.92
a. Residential	.31	1.06	1.72	1.60
b. Nonresidential	.19	.36	.34	.32
12. Mortgages, farm	.02	.10	.10	.15
13. Securities, U.S. government	1.05	−1.61	−3.27	−1.46
a. Short-term	45	−.53	.02	.05
b. Savings bonds	.02	.02	.10	.02
c. Other long-term	.58	−1.10	−3.39	−1.53
14. Securities, state and local	−.11	0	.26	.18
15. Securities, other bonds and notes	1.81	3.02	4.23	2.57
16. Securities, preferred stock	.15	.06	.03	.20
17. Securities, common stock	.12	.09	.01	.03
20. Other intangible assets	.07	.06	.15	.09
21. Total	3.53	3.44	3.58	3.86
III. Net changes in liabilities				
3. Life insurance reserves	3.69	3.47	3.74	3.95
8. Loans on securities	−.37	0	0	0
13. Other liabilities	.06	.08	.04	.08
14. Total	3.38	3.55	3.78	4.03
IV. Net changes in equities				
1. Net issues of common stock	.02	.01	−.01	.03
3. Saving	.30	.05	−.02	−.10
V. Total uses and sources of funds	3.70	3.61	3.75	3.96

Line	
I-7	Table VIII-a-7, line 5h.
II-1	Table VIII-b-1, line 5h.
1b	Table III-5h, line II-1b (first difference).
10-20	From line 5h of corresponding Tables VIII-b-10 through VIII-b-20.
21	Sum of lines II-1 through II-20.

1950	1951	1952	1953	1954	1955	1956	1957	1958	
									I.
.20	.23	.07	.19	.16	.24	.29	.27	.18	7.
									II.
.09	.10	.05	.07	.02	.02	.02	.01	.08	1.
.09	.10	.05	.07	.02	.02	.02	.01	.08	
.17	.18	.12	.20	.22	.16	.23	.35	.32	10.
3.01	3.01	1.76	1.89	2.49	3.24	3.34	2.14	1.74	11.
2.70	2.55	1.40	1.51	2.00	2.66	2.53	1.25	.93	
.30	.46	.36	.38	.49	.59	.80	.90	.81	
.19	.20	.18	.18	.16	.22	.21	.10	.08	12.
−1.83	−2.45	−.76	−.42	−.76	−.49	−1.02	−.53	.15	13.
.26	.09	−.11	−.07	.08	−.14	−.13	−.03	.27	
.05	0	.01	−.02	−.01	−.02	−.04	−.10	−.03	
−2.14	−2.54	−.66	−.33	−.83	−.33	−.85	−.40	−.09	
.10	.02	−.02	.15	.55	.19	.23	.11	.30	14.
1.83	2.71	3.10	2.71	2.10	1.75	2.15	2.67	2.42	15.
.19	−.05	.09	.04	.20	.01	−.19	−.03	.04	16.
.13	.10	.07	.05	.07	.06	.19	.07	.02	17.
.26	.18	.18	.12	.20	.21	.31	.26	.20	20.
4.14	4.00	4.77	4.99	5.25	5.37	5.47	5.15	5.35	21.
									III.
4.16	4.11	4.93	4.96	5.41	5.45	5.42	5.23	5.42	3.
0	0	0	0	0	0	0	0	0	8.
.11	.07	.08	.10	.08	.14	.19	.17	.13	13.
4.27	4.18	5.01	5.06	5.49	5.59	5.61	5.40	5.55	14.
									IV.
.06	.01	.02	.06	.04	.06	.09	.06	.06	1.
.01	.04	−.09	.06	−.12	−.04	.06	−.04	−.08	3.
4.34	4.23	4.94	5.18	5.41	5.61	5.76	5.42	5.53	V.

Line	
III-3-13	From line 5h of corresponding Tables VIII-c-3 through VIII-c-13.
14	Sum of lines III-3 through III-13.
IV-1	Table VIII-d-1, line 5h.
3	Sum of lines I-7 and II-21 less lines III-14 and IV-1.
V	Sum of lines I-7 and II-21.

Figures may not add to totals because of rounding.

TABLE VII-5i

Flow of Funds Through Fire and Casualty Insurance Companies

(billion dollars)

	1946	1947	1948	1949
I. Gross capital expenditures				
7. Total	.02	.02	.02	.01
II. Net financial flows				
1. Currency and demand deposits	.19	.18	.04	.06
a. Monetary metals				
b. Other	.19	.18	.04	.06
2. Other bank deposits and shares	0	0	0	0
7. Trade credit	.17	.10	.08	.07
11. Mortgages, nonfarm	0	.01	.01	.01
a. Residential	0	0	.01	.01
b. Nonresidential	0	.01	.01	0
13. Securities, U.S. government	.19	.59	.49	.51
a. Short-term	.05	.15	.35	.30
b. Savings bonds	.03	.04	.15	.05
c. Other long-term	.11	.40	−.01	.16
14. Securities, state and local	0	.08	.21	.22
15. Securities, other bonds and notes	0	.06	.17	.09
16. Securities, preferred stock	.01	0	−.01	.06
17. Securities, common stock	.04	.13	.11	.06
20. Other intangible assets	−.02	.02	.01	.02
21. Total	.58	1.17	1.11	1.10
III. Net changes in liabilities				
13. Other liabilities	.75	.99	.84	.77
14. Total	.75	.99	.84	.77
IV. Net changes in equities				
1. Net issues of common stock	.02	.02	0	.05
3. Saving	−.17	.18	.29	.29
V. Total uses and sources of funds	.60	1.19	1.13	1.11

Line	
I-7	Table VIII-a-7, line 5i.
II-1	Table VIII-b-1, line 5i.
1b	Table III-5i, line II-1b (first difference).
2-20	From line 5i of corresponding Tables VIII-b-2 through VIII-b-20.
21	Sum of lines II-1 through II-20.

1950	1951	1952	1953	1954	1955	1956	1957	1958	
									I.
.03	.03	.02	.03	.02	.03	.04	.04	.03	7.
									II.
.06	.04	.08	.05	−.05	.03	−.07	−.01	.06	1.
.06	.04	.08	.05	−.05	.03	−.07	−.01	.06	
0	.01	.01	0	0	0	0	0	0	2.
.02	.12	.07	.05	.06	.09	.14	.15	.14	7.
.01	.01	.01	.01	.01	.01	.01	0	0	11.
.01	.01	0	0	0	0	0	−.01	0	
.01	.01	0	.01	.01	.01	.01	0	0	
.35	.13	.34	.21	.11	−.14	−.33	−.21	−.06	13.
.05	−.37	.14	.42	−.53	−.41	.26	.43	−.08	
.11	.02	.01	−.02	−.01	−.01	−.07	−.17	−.07	
.19	.48	.19	−.19	.65	.28	−.52	−.47	.09	
.31	.39	.42	.75	.78	.79	.63	.62	.71	14.
.05	.05	.16	.12	.03	−.01	.03	.18	.09	15.
.03	.04	.08	.05	.05	0	−.08	.02	−.01	16.
.09	.11	.10	.14	.10	.17	.21	.10	.14	17.
.02	.05	.04	.06	.05	.04	.04	.08	0	20.
.94	.95	1.31	1.44	1.14	.98	.58	.93	1.07	21.
									III.
.72	.85	1.08	1.10	.69	.78	.66	1.05	.84	13.
.72	.85	1.08	1.10	.69	.78	.66	1.05	.84	14.
									IV.
.06	0	.02	.04	.03	.08	.02	.02	−.01	1.
.19	.13	.23	.33	.44	.15	−.06	−.10	.27	3.
.97	.98	1.33	1.47	1.16	1.01	.62	.97	1.10	V.

Line	
III-13	Table VIII-c-13, line 5i.
14	Same as line III-13.
IV-1	Table VIII-d-1, line 5i.
3	Sum of lines I-7 and II-21 minus lines III-14 and IV-1.
V	Sum of lines I-7 and II-21.

Figures may not add to total because of rounding.

TABLE VII-5j

Flow of Funds Through Noninsured Pension Plans

(million dollars)

	1946	1947	1948	1949
I. Gross capital expenditures				
II. Net financial flows				
1. Currency and demand deposits	21	32	31	43
a. Monetary metals				
b. Other	21	32	31	43
11. Mortgages, nonfarm	6	4	4	6
a. Residential	6	4	4	6
13. Securities, U.S. government	176	163	133	143
b. Savings bonds	170	160	50	52
c. Other long-term	6	3	83	91
15. Securities, other bonds and notes	258	308	355	340
16. Securities, preferred stock	29	32	24	33
17. Securities, common stock	49	78	76	110
20. Other intangible assets	29	27	31	33
21. Total	568	644	654	708
III. Net changes in liabilities				
4. Pension and retirement funds, private	568	645	654	705
14. Total	568	645	654	705
IV. Net changes in equities				
V. Total uses and sources of funds	568	644	654	708

Line

II-1 through II-16	From corresponding lines (first difference) of Table III-5j.
17	See notes to Table VIII-b-17, line 5j.
20	Table III-5j, line II-20 (first difference).
21	Sum of lines II-1 through II-20.

1950	1951	1952	1953	1954	1955	1956	1957	1958	
									I.
									II.
62	41	−26	49	−02	57	−05	63	30	1.
62	41	−26	49	−02	57	−05	63	30	
7	45	33	37	33	36	109	171	137	11.
7	45	33	37	33	36	109	171	137	
216	123	−3	162	8	302	−203	−274	33	13.
188	−27	9	−27	79	19	−153	−336	−13	
28	150	−12	189	−71	283	−50	62	46	
442	875	1063	1064	1219	906	1588	1734	1508	15.
54	89	59	62	57	49	60	40	50	16.
163	236	398	454	622	660	815	1043	1253	17.
31	33	77	113	108	54	241	113	54	20.
975	1442	1601	1941	2045	2064	2605	2890	3065	21.
									III.
976	1444	1602	1939	2046	2063	2605	2892	3067	4.
976	1444	1602	1939	2046	2063	2605	2892	3067	14.
									IV.
975	1442	1601	1941	2045	2064	2605	2890	3065	V.

Line	
III-4	Table VIII-c-4, line 5j.
14	Same as line III-4.
V	Same as line II-21 (total uses of funds do not equal net changes in liabilities because of rounding).

TABLE VII-5k

Flow of Funds Through Other Private Insurance

(million dollars)

	1946	1947	1948	1949
I. Gross capital expenditures				
7. Total	3	3	3	2
II. Net financial flows				
1. Currency and demand deposits	3	1	3	20
a. Monetary metals				
b. Other	3	1	3	20
10. Other loans	–3	2	3	7
11. Mortgages, nonfarm	6	19	26	34
a. Residential	0	6	14	21
b. Nonresidential	6	13	12	13
12. Mortgages, farm	1	1	2	7
13. Securities, U.S. government	8	9	0	5
b. Savings bonds	0	0	0	0
c. Other long-term	8	9	0	5
14. Securities, state and local	9	13	0	–6
15. Securities, other bonds and notes	58	67	54	62
16. Securities, preferred stock	12	2	0	5
17. Securities, common stock	6	5	1	4
20. Other intangible assets	5	2	4	1
21. Total	105	121	93	139
III. Net changes in liabilities				
3. Life insurance reserves	92	110	89	125
13. Other liabilities	16	14	7	16
14. Total	108	124	96	141
IV. Net changes in equities				
V. Total uses and sources of funds	108	124	96	141

Line	
I-7	For method of derivation of figures see notes to Table VIII-a-7, line 5k.
II-1 through II-16	From corresponding lines (first difference) of Table III-5k.
17	See notes to Table VIII-b-17, line 5k.
20	Table III-5k, line II-20 (first difference).
21	Sum of lines II-1 through II-20.

1950	1951	1952	1953	1954	1955	1956	1957	1958	
									I.
3	3	3	3	2	4	4	4	3	7.
									II.
6	10	16	31	16	−4	−10	−8	24	1.
6	10	16	31	16	−4	−10	−8	24	
6	9	7	7	7	17	12	3	13	10.
46	51	41	39	55	79	63	25	36	11.
28	29	21	16	20	28	13	−4	3	
18	22	20	23	35	51	50	29	33	
8	11	11	2	1	−4	6	2	3	12.
8	18	28	15	39	71	26	−11	61	13.
0	10	80	−50	30	−10	20	10	−20	
8	8	−52	65	9	81	6	−21	81	
−9	−8	−5	8	25	47	−3	−15	4	14.
51	55	68	74	59	18	64	28	83	15.
5	−8	0	−2	0	−5	−3	−3	3	16.
6	4	6	2	14	4	4	3	6	17.
2	2	6	7	3	10	10	5	5	20.
129	144	178	183	219	233	169	29	238	21.
									III.
126	136	160	176	196	217	166	18	215	3.
6	11	21	10	25	20	7	15	26	13.
132	147	181	186	221	237	173	33	241	14.
									IV.
132	147	181	186	221	237	173	33	241	V.

Line	
III-3	Table VIII-c-3, line 5k.
13	Table III-5k, line III-13 (first difference).
14	Sum of lines III-3 and III-13.
V	Sum of lines I-7 and II-21.

TABLE VII-5k-1

Flow of Funds Through Fraternal Orders

(million dollars)

	1946	1947	1948	1949
I. Gross capital expenditures				
7. Total	3	3	3	2
II. Net financial flows				
1. Currency and demand deposits	−2	−4	−4	11
10. Other loans	−4	0	0	3
11. Mortgages, nonfarm	6	16	23	30
12. Mortgages, farm	1	1	2	7
13. Securities, U.S. government	−10	−10	−23	−14
14. Securities, state and local	9	13	0	−6
15. Securities, other bonds and notes	55	63	50	51
16. Securities, preferred stock	12	2	0	5
17. Securities, common stock	6	4	1	3
20. Other intangible assets	5	0	3	0
21. Total	78	85	52	90
III. Net changes in liabilities				
3. Life insurance reserves	65	74	48	76
13. Other liabilities	16	14	7	16
14. Total	81	88	55	92
IV. Net changes in equities				
V. Total uses and sources of funds	81	88	55	92

Line	
I-7	Table VII-5k, line I-7.
II-1 through II-16	From corresponding line (first difference) of Table III-5k-1.
17	Table VIII-b-17, line 5k.
20	Table III-5k-1, line II-20 (first difference).
21	Sum of lines II-1 through II-20.

1950	1951	1952	1953	1954	1955	1956	1957	1958	
									I.
3	3	3	3	2	4	4	4	3	7.
									II.
−5	−4	−1	4	4	−8	−6	0	4	1.
2	4	1	2	5	6	3	0	8	10.
31	42	31	30	42	79	50	18	28	11.
8	11	11	2	1	−4	6	2	3	12.
−17	−17	−15	−12	−24	−1	−16	−23	−15	13.
−10	−9	−6	7	24	45	−3	−16	2	14.
48	49	61	39	41	−3	51	24	62	15.
4	−8	0	−3	−1	−5	−4	−3	2	16.
6	3	5	−1	11	2	3	3	3	17.
1	3	1	0	1	5	7	4	−2	20.
68	74	88	68	104	116	91	9	95	21.
									III.
66	66	70	61	81	100	88	−2	72	3.
6	11	21	10	25	20	7	15	26	13.
72	77	91	71	106	120	95	13	98	14.
									IV.
71	77	91	71	106	120	95	13	98	V.

Line

III-3 Table VIII-c-3, line 5k.
13 Table III-5k-1, line III-13 (first difference).
14 Sum of lines III-3 and III-13.

V Sum of lines I-7 and II-21.

Figures may not add to totals because of rounding.

TABLE VII-51

Flow of Funds Through Finance Companies

(million dollars)

	1946	1947	1948	1949
I. Gross capital expenditures				
II. Net financial flows				
1. Currency and demand deposits	–9	–62	175	111
a. Monetary metals				
b. Other	–9	–62	175	111
6. Consumer credit	584	865	847	1099
7. Trade credit	175	6	18	46
10. Other loans	334	211	355	–88
11. Mortgages, nonfarm	110	68	–12	89
a. Residential	110	68	–12	89
21. Total	1194	1088	1383	1257
III. Net changes in liabilities				
9. Bank loans, n.e.c.	793	598	507	433
12. Bonds and notes	259	275	581	522
14. Total	1052	873	1088	955
IV. Net changes in equities				
1. Net issues of common stock	n.a	20	0	20
2. Net issues of preferred stock	n.a	0	50	30
3. Saving	142	195	245	252
V. Total uses and sources of funds	1194	1088	1383	1257

Line	
II-1 through II-11a	From corresponding line (first difference) of Table III-51.
21	Sum of lines II-1 through II-11.
III-9	Table III-51, line III-9 (first difference).
12	Table III-51, line III-12 (first difference).
14	Sum of lines III-9 and III-12.

1950	1951	1952	1953	1954	1955	1956	1957	1958	
									I.
									II.
168	118	33	21	50	254	27	67	105	1.
168	118	33	21	50	254	27	67	105	
1010	285	1457	1567	439	2826	1131	815	−706	6.
284	47	70	53	108	243	185	151	234	7.
302	272	136	74	−245	966	−90	610	−329	10.
210	−82	144	26	221	527	−104	−325	457	11.
210	−82	144	26	221	527	−104	−325	457	
1974	640	1840	1741	573	4816	1149	1318	−239	21.
									III.
984	8	760	−9	24	2576	−542	−360	−1117	9.
423	567	536	1581	194	1629	1194	1124	15	12.
1407	575	1296	1572	218	4205	652	764	−1102	14.
									IV.
10	10	30	60	20	80	10	−30	10	1.
20	−40	20	0	−70	80	20	40	0	2.
537	95	494	109	405	451	467	544	853	3.
1974	640	1840	1741	573	4816	1149	1318	−239	V.

Line	
IV-1	Table VIII-d-1, line 51.
2	Table VIII-d-2, line 51.
3	Line II-21 minus the sum of lines III-14, IV-1 and IV-2.
V	Same as line II-21.

Figures may not add to totals because of rounding.

TABLE VII-5m

Flow of Funds Through Other Finance

(billion dollars)

	1946	1947	1948	1949
I. Gross capital expenditures				
II. Net financial flows				
1. Currency and demand deposits	.21	–.11	–.06	–.07
a. Monetary metals				
b. Other	.21	–.11	–.06	–.07
7. Trade credit	–.01	.02	.07	–.01
8. Loans on securities	–.74	.05	–.01	.42
10. Other loans	.09	.09	.10	.01
11. Mortgages, nonfarm	.01	.01	.04	.01
a. Residential	.01	.01	.03	.02
b. Nonresidential	0	0	.01	0
12. Mortgages, farm	0	0	0	0
13. Securities, U.S. government	–1.17	–.86	.43	–.15
a. Short-term	.10	–.50	.50	–.10
b. Savings bonds				
c. Other long-term	–1.27	–.36	–.07	–.05
14. Securities, state and local	–.02	–.08	.09	–.02
15. Securities, other bonds and notes	–.08	.03	–.01	.19
16. Securities, preferred stock	–.01	0	0	.01
17. Securities, common stock	–.06	.03	–.05	.18
20. Other intangible assets	–.02	0	–.01	.01
21. Total	–1.80	–.82	.59	.58
III. Net changes in liabilities				
1. Currency and demand deposits	–.06	–.01	–.05	.01
2. Other bank deposits and shares	.04	–.03	–.02	–.03
8. Loans on securities	–1.67	–.71	.51	.45
10. Other loans	.10	.04	–.01	.14
13. Other liabilities	–.09	–.02	.10	–.04
14. Total	–1.68	–.73	.53	.53
IV. Net changes in equities				
3. Saving	–.12	–.09	.06	.05
V. Total uses and sources of funds	–1.80	–.82	.59	.58

Line	
II-1	Table VIII-b-1, line 5m.
1b	Table III-5m, line II-1b (first difference).
7-20	From line 5m of corresponding Tables VIII-b-7 through VIII-b-20.
21	Sum of lines II-1 through II-20.
III-1	Table III-5m, line III-1 (first difference).
2	Table III-5m, line III-2 (first difference).
8	Table VIII-c-8, line 5m.
10	Table VIII-c-10, line 5m.
13	Table III-5m, line III-13 (first difference).
14	Sum of lines III-1 through III-13.

1950	1951	1952	1953	1954	1955	1956	1957	1958	
									I.
									II.
.19	−.03	−.04	−.07	.13	.01	.12	.02	.03	1.
.19	−.03	−.04	−.07	.13	.01	.12	.02	.03	
−.01	.03	.01	.05	−.01	.05	.10	.04	−.01	7.
.58	−.04	.10	.40	.96	.48	.08	−.29	1.14	8.
.10	.16	.06	−.09	.09	.09	.07	.27	.27	10.
.02	.03	0	0	0	.04	.01	.02	.04	11.
.02	.02	0	0	0	.02	.01	0	.03	
0	0	0	0	0	.01	0	.02	.01	
0	0	0	0	0	0	0	0	0	12.
−.07	−.28	.37	−.01	.18	−.48	.09	.12	.24	13.
0	−.10	.50	0	.30	−.50	.16	.12	.24	
−.07	−.18	−.13	−.01	−.12	.02	−.06	0	0	
.13	.05	−.15	.25	−.13	.05	−.11	.14	0	14.
−.11	.04	.07	−.09	.32	−.04	−.18	.27	−.12	15.
−.01	.01	0	0	.01	0	−.01	.01	−.01	16.
−.14	.06	−.03	−.05	.16	−.02	−.25	.02	.05	17.
.04	−.02	.01	.02	0	.02	.04	.04	.03	20.
.72	.01	.40	.41	1.71	.20	−.04	.66	1.66	21.
									III.
.04	.03	.01	0	.02	.03	.06	.07	.04	1.
.01	0	.01	.01	.02	.01	.02	.07	.08	2.
.07	−.19	.48	.30	.67	.32	−.62	.10	.34	8.
.49	.06	−.15	−.09	.55	−.19	.03	.30	.72	10.
.10	.10	.12	.10	.28	.16	.46	.12	.21	13.
.71	0	.47	.32	1.54	.33	−.05	.66	1.39	14.
									IV.
.01	.01	−.07	.09	.17	−.13	.01	0	.27	3.
.72	.01	.40	.41	1.71	.20	−.04	.66	1.66	V.

Line

IV-3 Line II-21 minus line III-14.

V Same as line II-21.

TABLE VII-5m-1

Flow of Funds Through Brokers and Dealers

(billion dollars)

	1946	1947	1948	1949
I. Gross capital expenditures				
II. Net financial flows				
1. Currency and demand deposits	.24	−.10	−.07	−.07
8. Loans on securities	−.72	.05	−.03	.40
13. Securities, U.S. government	−1.10	−.72	.61	−.06
14. Securities, state and local	0	−.10	.02	−.02
15. Securities, other bonds and notes	−.09	.03	−.03	.16
16. Securities, preferred stock				.01
17. Securities, common stock	−.06	.03	−.05	.18
21. Total	−1.73	−.81	.45	.60
III. Net changes in liabilities				
8. Loans on securities	−1.67	−.71	.51	.44
10. Other loans	.06	−.02	−.09	.12
14. Total	−1.61	−.73	.42	.56
IV. Net changes in equities				
3. Saving	−.12	−.08	.03	.04
V. Total uses and sources of funds	−1.73	−.81	.45	.60

Line	
II-1 through II-16	From corresponding line (first difference) of Table III-5m-1.
17	Table VIII-b-17, line 5m.
21	Sum of lines II-1 through II-17.
III-8	Table III-5m-1, line III-8 (first difference).
10	Table III-5m-1, line III-10 (first difference).
14	Sum of lines III-8 and III-10.

1950	1951	1952	1953	1954	1955	1956	1957	1958	
									I.
									II.
.15	−.03	−.06	−.08	.08	−.03	.01	−.01	0	1.
.57	−.08	.08	.40	.88	.48	.04	−.37	1.06	8.
−.12	−.28	.30	−.01	.06	−.48	−.02	.23	.17	13.
.12	.01	−.16	.20	−.13	0	−.20	.10	.02	14.
−.10	.05	.06	−.07	.27	0	−.23	.23	−.21	15.
				.01	0	−.01	.01	−.01	16.
−.14	.05	−.03	−.05	.15	−.02	−.26	0	.04	17.
.48	−.28	.19	.39	1.32	−.05	−.67	.19	1.07	21.
									III.
.07	−.19	.48	.30	.67	.32	−.62	.10	.34	8.
.42	−.06	−.19	−.01	.50	−.24	−.02	.10	.49	10.
.49	−.25	.29	.29	1.17	.08	−.64	.20	.83	14.
									IV.
−.01	−.03	−.10	.10	.15	−.13	−.03	−.01	.24	3.
.48	−.28	.19	.39	1.32	−.05	−.67	.19	1.07	V.

Line

IV-3 Line II-21 minus line III-14.

V Same as line II-21.

Figures may not add to totals because of rounding.

TABLE VII-6

Flow of Funds Through State and Local Governments

(billion dollars)

	1946	1947	1948	1949
I. Gross capital expenditures				
1. Residential structures	.37	.14	.02	.25
2. Nonresidential structures	1.42	2.59	3.67	5.06
4. Producer durables	.21	.33	.42	.45
6. Inventories	.02	.01	a	a
7. Total	2.02	3.07	4.11	5.76
II. Net financial flows				
1. Currency and demand deposits	.87	.72	.49	.23
a. Monetary metals				
b. Other	.87	.72	.49	.23
2. Other bank deposits and shares	.18	.16	.27	.15
11. Mortgages, nonfarm	0	0	.01	.09
a. Residential	0	0	.01	.09
13. Securities, U.S. government	−.62	.66	.32	.02
a. Short-term	−.10	.30	.50	.10
b. Savings bonds				
c. Other long-term	−.52	.36	−.18	−.08
14. Securities, state and local	−.13	−.05	0	.28
15. Securities, other bonds and notes	.01	.04	.17	−.01
21. Total	.31	1.53	1.26	.76
III. Net changes in liabilities				
7. Trade debt	.15	.15	.15	.10
12. Bonds and notes	−.13	1.41	2.21	2.35
14. Total	.02	1.56	2.36	2.45
IV. Net changes in equities				
3. Saving	2.31	3.04	3.01	4.07
V. Total uses and sources of funds	2.33	4.60	5.37	6.52

Line

I-1 through I-4	From line 6 of corresponding Tables VIII-a-1 through VIII-a-4.
6	Table VIII-a-6b, line 6.
7	Sum of lines I-1 through I-6.
II-1	Table VIII-b-1, line 6.
1b	Table III-6, line II-1b (first difference).
2-15	From line 6 of corresponding Tables VIII-b-2 through VIII-b-15.
21	Sum of lines II-1 through II-15.

1950	1951	1952	1953	1954	1955	1956	1957	1958	
									I.
.28	.58	.63	.52	.32	.26	.28	.35	.48	1.
5.68	6.03	6.96	7.45	8.61	9.92	10.34	11.96	13.62	2.
.47	.53	.58	.62	.70	.75	.88	1.04	1.02	4.
.02	a	a	.01	.01	.01	.02	.01	.01	6.
6.45	7.14	8.17	8.60	9.64	10.94	11.52	13.36	15.13	7.
									II.
.46	.43	.47	.60	.33	.39	.15	.21	.22	1.
.46	.43	.47	.60	.33	.39	.15	.21	.22	
.10	.15	.09	.33	.46	−.06	.04	.38	.80	2.
.05	.07	.08	.14	.10	.12	.11	.36	.42	11.
.05	.07	.08	.14	.10	.12	.11	.36	.42	
.36	.37	1.08	1.31	1.44	.41	.70	.74	−.70	13.
.30	−.20	.70	1.20	0	−1.60	2.20	1.30	−1.10	
.06	.57	.38	.11	1.44	2.01	−1.50	−.56	.40	
.30	.12	.11	.09	.03	.05	.07	.07	.05	14.
.06	.10	−.07	.05	.20	.04	.01	−.10	−.12	15.
1.33	1.24	1.76	2.52	2.56	.95	1.08	1.66	.67	21.
									III.
.10	0	.10	.10	.15	.15	.10	.05	.15	7.
3.11	2.41	3.18	3.58	4.18	3.48	3.32	4.87	5.92	12.
3.21	2.41	3.28	3.68	4.33	3.63	3.42	4.92	6.07	14.
									IV.
4.57	5.97	6.65	7.44	7.87	8.26	9.18	10.10	9.73	3.
7.78	8.38	9.93	11.12	12.20	11.89	12.60	15.02	15.80	V.

Line	
III-7	Table VIII-c-7, line 6.
12	Table VIII-c-12, line 6.
14	Sum of lines III-7 through III-12.
IV-3	Sum of lines I-7 and II-21 minus line III-14.
V	Sum of lines I-7 and II-21.

[a] $5 million or under.

Figures may not add to totals because of rounding.

TABLE VII-7

Flow of Funds Through Federal Government (Civil Only)

(billion dollars)

	1946	1947	1948	1949
I. Gross capital expenditures				
1. Residential structures	−.12	−.08	−.08	−.01
2. Nonresidential structures	.34	.56	.83	1.19
4. Producer durables	.15	.16	.23	.12
6. Inventories	−1.20	−.28	.82	1.36
7. Total	−.83	.36	1.80	2.66
II. Net financial flows				
1. Currency and demand deposits	−22.73	−.54	1.08	.38
a. Monetary metals				
b. Other	−22.73	−.54	1.08	.38
2. Other bank deposits and shares	.01	−.01	0	.06
7. Trade credit	−.80	−.10	0	0
10. Other loans	3.17	4.13	1.67	.67
11. Mortgages, nonfarm	−.24	−.04	.09	.48
a. Residential	−.23	−.04	.09	.49
b. Nonresidential	−.01	0	0	0
12. Mortgages, farm	−.19	−.12	−.06	.02
13. Securities, U.S. government	.54	.04	.10	.08
c. Other long-term	.54	.04	.10	.08
14. Securities, state and local	−.02	.02	.07	−.08
19. Equity in other business[b]				
20. Other intangible assets	.90	2.19	.77	−2.09
21. Total	−19.36	5.57	3.72	−.48
III. Net changes in liabilities				
1. Currency and demand deposits	.13	−.03	−.01	−.02
2. Other bank deposits and shares	.36	.14	−.07	−.14
7. Trade debt	−2.00	−.70	0	0
9. Bank loans, n.e.c.	−.21	−.03	.85	.08
12. Bonds and notes	−18.99	−2.30	−3.81	4.19
13. Other liabilities	.04	.04	.06	.16
14. Total	−20.67	−2.88	−2.98	4.27
IV. Net changes in equities				
3. Saving	.48	8.81	8.50	−2.09
V. Total uses and sources of funds	−20.19	5.93	5.52	2.18

Line

I-1 through I-4	From line 7 of corresponding Tables VIII-a-1 through VIII-a-4.
6	Table VIII-a-6b, line 7.
7	Sum of lines I-1 through I-6.
II-1	Table VIII-b-1, line 7.
1b	Table III-7, line II-1b (first difference).
2-20	From line 7 of corresponding Tables VIII-b-2 through VIII-b-20.
21	Sum of lines II-1 through II-20.
III-1 through III-13	From line 7 of corresponding Tables VIII-c-1 through VIII-c-13.
14	Sum of lines III-1 through III-13.

1950	1951	1952	1953	1954	1955	1956	1957	1958	
									I.
−.02	−.01	−.01	.02	−.01	[a]	.02	.15	.35	1.
1.26	1.20	1.14	1.09	.94	.85	1.05	1.06	1.20	2.
.04	.10	.18	.17	.11	.05	.04	.04	.06	4.
−.61	−.43	.46	2.88	1.24	.14	−.11	−.94	1.97	6.
.67	.86	1.77	4.16	2.28	1.04	1.00	.31	3.58	7.
									II.
−.68	.06	1.95	−1.47	.03	−.41	−.30	.01	0	1.
−.68	.06	1.95	−1.47	.03	−.41	−.30	.01	0	
.01	.09	.07	−.01	.02	0	−.03	−.03	.03	2.
.38	.92	.95	−.04	.23	−.17	.08	−.05	−.60	7.
.70	.63	.75	.61	−.07	1.03	−.03	.63	1.10	10.
.29	.62	.46	.35	.02	.32	.46	1.27	.11	11.
.29	.62	.46	.35	.02	.32	.46	1.27	.11	
0	0	0	0	0	0	0	0	0	
.05	.06	.09	.10	.10	.19	.25	.22	.22	12.
−.24	−.09	.10	.02	.13	.02	.25	.44	−.09	13.
−.24	−.09	.10	.02	.13	.02	.25	.44	−.09	
.07	.26	.32	−.33	−.33	0	.08	.20	.21	14.
									19.
7.47	4.62	−3.16	.53	−3.13	4.02	−1.21	−1.49	−2.26	20.
8.05	7.17	1.53	−.24	−3.00	5.00	−.45	1.20	−1.28	21.
									III.
−.02	.04	.04	.03	.03	.01	.02	.03	.04	1.
−.27	−.22	−.16	−.19	−.23	−.25	−.25	−.32	−.20	2.
1.10	1.60	.10	−.20	−.23	−.09	.33	.16	.06	7.
−.62	−.09	.43	1.48	.07	−1.10	−.29	−.42	.35	9.
.05	2.99	8.01	7.79	3.55	3.58	−3.51	.39	7.57	12.
0	.15	.26	.21	.28	−.03	.10	.07	.27	13.
.24	4.47	8.68	9.12	3.47	2.12	−3.60	−.09	8.09	14.
									IV.
8.48	3.56	−5.38	−5.20	−4.19	3.92	4.15	1.60	−5.79	3.
8.72	8.03	3.30	3.92	−.72	6.04	.55	1.51	2.30	V.

Line	
IV-3	Sum of lines I-7 and II-21 minus line III-14.
V	Sum of lines I-7 and II-21.

[a]$5 million or under.

[b]The retained surplus originating in government monetary agencies was recorded as surplus retained in these agencies—the exchange equalization fund, and production credit associations—although they were transferred to the government budget. This was done to avoid double counting of retained surplus (net saving): once as saving of the federal government and once as saving of the above-mentioned organizations.

Figures may not add to totals because of rounding.

TABLE VII-7-1

Flow of Funds Through the Government Sector (Civil and Military)

(billion dollars)

	1946	1947	1948	1949
I. Gross capital expenditures				
1. Residential structures	−.12	−.07	−.05	.02
2. Nonresidential structures	1.10	1.13	1.21	1.51
4. Producer durables	2.53	1.79	1.85	2.26
6. Inventories	−1.07	−.12	1.16	2.08
7. Total	2.44	2.73	4.17	5.87
II. Net financial flows				
1. Currency and demand deposits	−22.73	−.54	1.08	.38
a. Monetary metals				
b. Other	−22.73	−.54	1.08	.38
2. Other bank deposits and shares	.01	−.01	0	.06
7. Trade credit	−.80	−.10	0	0
10. Other loans	3.17	4.13	1.67	.67
11. Mortgages, nonfarm	−.24	−.04	.09	.48
a. Residential	−.23	−.04	.09	.49
b. Nonresidential	−.01	0	0	0
12. Mortgages, farm	−.19	−.12	−.06	.02
13. Securities, U.S. government	.54	.04	.10	.08
c. Other long-term	.54	.04	.10	.08
14. Securities, state and local[b]	−.02	.02	.07	−.08
19. Equity in other business				
20. Other intangible assets	.90	2.19	.77	−2.09
21. Total	−19.36	5.57	3.72	−.48
III. Net changes in liabilities				
1. Currency and demand deposits	.13	−.03	−.01	−.02
2. Other bank deposits and shares	.36	.14	−.07	−.14
7. Trade debt	−2.00	−.70	0	0
9. Bank loans, n.e.c.	−.21	−.03	.85	.08
12. Bonds and notes	−18.99	−2.30	−3.81	4.19
13. Other liabilities	.04	.04	.06	.16
14. Total	−20.67	−2.88	−2.98	4.27
IV. Net changes in equities				
3. Saving	3.75	11.18	10.87	1.12
V. Total uses and sources of funds	−16.92	8.30	7.89	5.39

Line	
I-1 through I-4	From lines 7 and 9 of corresponding Tables VIII-a-1 through VIII-a-4.
6	Table VII-a-6b, lines 7 and 9.
7	Sum of lines I-1 through I-6.
II and III	Same as Table VII-7.

1950	1951	1952	1953	1954	1955	1956	1957	1958	
									I.
0	0	.01	.02	−.01	a	.02	.15	.35	1.
1.71	2.62	3.52	3.44	2.78	2.73	2.93	2.89	3.13	2.
3.02	7.19	15.98	18.32	15.05	13.04	14.04	14.78	15.02	4.
.13	.71	1.96	4.21	2.82	1.61	1.43	.83	3.80	6.
4.86	10.52	21.47	25.99	20.64	17.38	18.42	18.65	22.30	7.
									II.
−.68	.06	1.95	−1.47	.03	−.41	−.30	.01	0	1.
−.68	.06	1.95	−1.47	.03	−.41	−.30	.01	0	
.01	.09	.07	−.01	.02	0	−.03	−.03	.03	2.
.38	.92	.95	−.04	.23	−.17	.08	−.05	−.60	7.
.70	.63	.75	.61	−.07	1.03	−.03	.63	1.10	10.
.29	.62	.46	.35	.02	.32	.46	1.27	.11	11.
.29	.62	.46	.35	.02	.32	.46	1.27	.11	
0	0	0	0	0	0	0	0	0	
.05	.06	.09	.10	.10	.19	.25	.22	.22	12.
−.24	−.09	.10	.02	.13	.02	.25	.44	−.09	13.
−.24	−.09	.10	.02	.13	.02	.25	.44	−.09	
.07	.26	.32	−.33	−.33	0	.08	.20	.21	14.
									19.
7.47	4.62	−3.16	.53	−3.13	4.02	−1.21	−1.49	−2.26	20.
8.05	7.17	1.53	−.24	−3.00	5.00	−.45	1.20	−1.28	21.
									III.
−.02	.04	.04	.03	.03	.01	.02	.03	.04	1.
−.27	−.22	−.16	−.19	−.23	−.25	−.25	−.32	−.20	2.
1.10	1.60	.10	−.20	−.23	−.09	.33	.16	.06	7.
−.62	−.09	.43	1.48	.07	−1.10	−.29	−.42	.35	9.
.05	2.99	8.01	7.79	3.55	3.58	−3.51	.39	7.57	12.
0	.15	.26	.21	.28	−.03	.10	.07	.27	13.
.24	4.47	8.68	9.12	3.47	2.12	−3.60	−.09	8.09	14.
									IV.
12.67	13.22	14.32	16.63	14.17	20.26	21.57	19.94	12.93	3.
12.91	17.69	23.00	25.75	17.64	22.38	17.97	19.85	21.02	V.

Line	
IV-3	Sum of lines I-7 and II-21 minus line III-14.
V	Sum of lines I-7 and II-21.

[a] $5 million or under.
[b] See Table VII-7, note b.
Figures may not add to totals because of rounding.

SECTION VIII

Transaction Flow of Funds, 1946–58

TABLE VIII-a-1

Uses of Funds: Gross Investment in Residential Structures, Original Cost

(billion dollars)

	1946	1947	1948	1949
1. Nonfarm households	4.89	7.39	10.59	9.45
2. Nonfarm unincorporated business	.13	.25	.46	.51
3. Agriculture	.42	.70	.75	.70
4. Nonfinancial corporations	.29	.41	.70	.78
5. Finance	n.a.	.03	.04	.07
6. State and local governments	.37	.14	.02	.25
7. Federal government (civil)	−.12	−.08	−.08	−.01
8. Total	5.98	8.84	12.48	11.75
9. Military expenditures	a	.01	.03	.03
10. Total, including military	5.98	8.85	12.51	11.78

All data not otherwise specified below are from Raymond W. Goldsmith, *The National Wealth of the United States in the Postwar Period,* Princeton University Press for NBER, 1962, Appendix B.

<u>Line</u>

1	Sum of Tables B-15, col. 1, and B-164, col. 1.
2	Sum of Tables B-52, col. 1; B-53, col. 1; and B-146, col. 1.
3	Table B-60, col. 1 plus proportionate share of Table B-63, col. 1.
4 & 5	Sum of Tables B-5, col. 1; B-7, col. 1; and B-8, col. 1; minus Tables B-15, col. 1; B-52, col. 1; B-53, col. 1.
4	The above total minus line 5 of this table.

TABLE VIII-a-1a

Uses of Funds: Gross Investment in Residential Structures, Constant 1947-49 Prices

(billion dollars)

	1946	1947	1948	1949
1. Nonfarm households	6.40	7.99	10.17	9.26
2. Nonfarm unincorporated business	.17	.28	.47	.50
3. Agriculture	.56	.72	.72	.71
4. Nonfinancial corporations	.37	.45	.68	.75
5. Finance	n.a.	.03	.04	.06
6. State and local governments	.46	.15	−.01	.24
7. Federal government (civil)	−.21	−.14	−.15	−.02
8. Total	7.75	9.48	11.92	11.50
9. Military expenditures	.01	.01	.03	.03
10. Total, including military	7.76	9.49	11.95	11.53

Source: Unless specified below, figures for all lines are obtained from same sources as in Table VIII-a-1, except that col. 2 of the respective source tables, rather than col. 1, is used.

<u>Line</u>

5	The same method as used for Table VIII-a-1, line 5. The method for original cost was modified by converting first differences of the value of holdings to constant prices by the application of the average yearly index for multifamily dwellings from Table B-9, col. 2.

[a]$5 million or under.

1950	1951	1952	1953	1954	1955	1956	1957	1958	
13.18	13.69	13.95	15.13	15.74	19.84	19.14	18.15	18.26	1.
.46	.34	.31	.40	.36	.40	.48	.48	.53	2.
.78	.88	.90	.82	.78	.76	.74	.75	.76	3.
.82	.75	.63	.88	.83	.99	1.12	1.08	1.17	4.
.05	.01	.11	−.01	.02	.01	−.01	.01	a	5.
.28	.58	.63	.52	.32	.26	.28	.35	.48	6.
−.02	−.01	−.01	.02	−.01	a	.02	.15	.35	7.
15.55	16.24	16.52	17.76	18.04	22.26	21.77	20.97	21.55	8.
.02	.01	.02	a	a	a	a	a	a	9.
15.57	16.25	16.54	17.76	18.04	22.26	21.77	20.97	21.55	10.

Line

5 Based on holdings of life insurance sector as determined from various issues of *Life Insurance Fact Book*, e.g., 1957, p. 78.

Gross expenditures are estimated by adding depreciation calculated on the basis of 50-year life to first difference of holdings. (The estimate for 1947 was possible after an estimate was made for the 1946 end-of-year figure for life insurance holdings of residential buildings. This was computed as a quarter of total real estate held by life insurance at the end of 1946, i.e., $735 million.)

6 Sum of Tables B-144, col. 1, and B-147, col. 1.

7 Sum of Tables B-162, col. 1, and B-165, col. 1.

8 Sum of lines 1 through 7.

9 Table B-177, col. 1.

10 Sum of lines 8 and 9.

[a] $5 million or under.

1950	1951	1952	1953	1954	1955	1956	1957	1958	
12.26	11.81	11.73	12.49	13.10	16.01	14.79	13.77	13.73	1.
.44	.29	.26	.32	.29	.30	.35	.34	.37	2.
.76	.78	.79	.72	.68	.65	.62	.61	.61	3.
.76	.64	.52	.71	.67	.77	.83	.78	.83	4.
.05	.01	.09	a	.02	.01	−.01	.01	a	5.
.24	.49	.53	.42	.27	.21	.21	.27	.36	6.
−.04	−.02	−.03	.01	−.02	a	.01	.12	.26	7.
14.47	14.00	13.89	14.67	15.01	17.95	16.80	15.90	16.16	8.
.01	.01	.02	a	a	a	a	a	a	9.
14.48	14.01	13.91	14.67	15.01	17.95	16.80	15.90	16.16	10.

TABLE VIII-a-1b

Uses of Funds: Net Investment in Residential Structures, Depreciation at Replacement Cost

(billion dollars)

	1946	1947	1948	1949
1. Nonfarm households	1.48	3.19	5.73	4.58
2. Nonfarm unincorporated business	−.20	−.14	.01	.05
3. Agriculture	.10	.28	.29	.25
4. Nonfinancial corporations	.04	.12	.37	.43
5. Finance	n.a.	.02	.03	.06
6. State and local governments	.34	.10	−.03	.20
7. Federal government (civil)	−.19	−.15	−.16	−.07
8. Total	1.57	3.42	6.24	5.50
9. Military expenditures	a	.01	.03	.03
10. Total, including military	1.57	3.43	6.27	5.53

Source: Unless specified below, figures for all lines are obtained from same sources as in Table VIII-a-1, except that col. 8 of the respective source tables, rather than col. 1, is used.

Line

5 Based on holdings of life insurance sector as determined from various issues of *Life Insurance Fact Book*, e.g., 1957, p. 78.

[a] $5 million or under.

TABLE VIII-a-1c

Uses of Funds: Net Investment in Residential Structures, Constant 1947-49 Prices

(billion dollars)

	1946	1947	1948	1949
1. Nonfarm households	1.98	3.47	5.54	4.50
2. Nonfarm unincorporated business	−.26	−.14	.04	.06
3. Agriculture	.13	.29	.28	.25
4. Nonfinancial corporations	.06	.13	.35	.42
5. Finance	n.a.	.02	.03	.06
6. State and local governments	.43	.10	−.06	.19
7. Federal government (civil)	−.30	−.22	−.22	−.08
8. Total	2.04	3.65	5.96	5.40
9. Military expenditures	a	.01	.03	.03
10. Total, including military	2.04	3.66	5.99	5.43

Source: Unless specified below, figures for all lines are obtained from same sources as in Table VIII-a-1, except that col. 7 of the respective source tables, rather than col. 1, is used.

Line

5 The same method as used for Table VIII-a-1b, line 5. The adjustment for price changes is by the application of the average yearly index for multifamily dwellings from Table B-9, col. 2.

[a] $5 million or under.

1950	1951	1952	1953	1954	1955	1956	1957	1958	
7.90	7.82	7.75	8.65	9.11	12.79	11.53	10.10	9.90	1.
−.02	−.19	−.23	−.17	−.21	−.19	−.14	−.17	−.13	2.
.31	.36	.36	.27	.23	.19	.15	.14	.14	3.
.44	.33	.18	.41	.34	.47	.56	.48	.53	4.
.05	.01	.10	−.02	.01	a	−.02	a	−.01	5.
.22	.52	.55	.42	.22	.14	.15	.22	.34	6.
−.09	−.08	−.08	−.06	−.08	−.07	−.06	.14	.32	7.
8.81	8.77	8.63	9.50	9.62	13.33	12.17	10.91	11.09	8.
.01	a	.02	a	a	a	a	−.01	−.01	9.
8.82	8.77	8.65	9.50	9.62	13.33	12.17	10.90	11.08	10.

1950	1951	1952	1953	1954	1955	1956	1957	1958	
7.36	6.76	6.53	7.15	7.60	10.33	8.92	7.67	7.45	1.
a	−.16	−.19	−.12	−.16	−.14	−.10	−.12	−.09	2.
.30	.31	.32	.24	.20	.16	.12	.11	.11	3.
.41	.29	.15	.32	.28	.37	.42	.35	.38	4.
.04	.01	.09	−.01	.01	a	−.01	a	−.01	5.
.18	.44	.46	.34	.18	.12	.12	.17	.27	6.
−.11	−.08	−.09	−.05	−.08	−.06	−.04	.10	.24	7.
8.18	7.57	7.27	7.87	8.03	10.78	9.43	8.28	8.35	8.
.01	a	.02	a	a	a	a	a	a	9.
8.19	7.57	7.29	7.87	8.03	10.78	9.43	8.28	8.35	10.

TABLE VIII-a-2

Uses of Funds: Gross Investment in Nonresidential Structures, Original Cost

(billion dollars)

	1946	1947	1948	1949
1. Nonfarm households	.32	.44	.70	.92
2. Nonfarm unincorporated business	.74	.64	.89	.80
3. Agriculture	.46	.73	.82	.80
4. Nonfinancial corporations	4.33	5.29	6.34	6.19
5. Finance	.27	.28	.26	.12
6. State and local governments	1.42	2.59	3.67	5.06
7. Federal government (civil)	.34	.56	.83	1.19
8. Total	7.88	10.53	13.51	15.08
9. Military expenditures	.76	.57	.38	.32
10. Total, including military	8.64	11.10	13.89	15.40

Source: All data not otherwise specified below are from Goldsmith, *National Wealth*, Appendix B.

Line

1 Sum of Tables B-38, col. 1 and B-39, col. 1.

2 Sum of Table B-44, cols. 5, 8, 11, 15, 18 and Table B-46, col. 4.

3 Table B-61, col. 1 plus proportionate share of Table B-63, col. 1.

4 & 5 Sum of Tables B-101, col. 1; B-102, col. 1; B-103, col. 1; B-104, col. 1; B-46, col. 3; B-109, col. 1; and one-half of Table B-107, col. 1, plus B-108, col. 1; minus Table B-44, cols. 5, 8, 11, 15, and 18.

TABLE VIII-a-2a

Uses of Funds: Gross Investment in Nonresidential Structures, Constant 1947-49 Prices

(billion dollars)

	1946	1947	1948	1949
1. Nonfarm households	.48	.48	.68	.88
2. Nonfarm unincorporated business	1.02	.69	.86	.77
3. Agriculture	.60	.77	.79	.79
4. Nonfinancial corporations	5.60	5.65	6.13	5.95
5. Finance	.35	.30	.26	.12
6. State and local governments	1.85	2.79	3.53	4.93
7. Federal government (civil)	.44	.61	.80	1.13
8. Total	10.34	11.29	13.05	14.57
9. Military expenditures	.99	.62	.37	.31
10. Total, including military	11.33	11.91	13.42	14.88

Source: Unless specified below, figures for all lines are obtained from same source as in Table VIII-a-2, except that col. 2 of the respective source tables, rather than col. 1, is used.

Line

2 Sum of Table B-45, cols. 1 through 5 and Table B-39, col. 2.

4 & 5 Sum of Tables B-101 through B-104, col. 2; B-39, col. 2; B-109, col. 2; and one-half of Tables B-107, col. 2, and B-108, col. 2; minus Table B-45, cols. 1 through 5.

1950	1951	1952	1953	1954	1955	1956	1957	1958	
1.13	1.27	1.18	1.27	1.54	1.66	1.72	2.02	2.18	1.
.94	1.11	1.02	1.33	1.55	1.94	2.19	2.20	2.21	2.
.89	1.00	1.03	.93	.89	.86	.84	.86	.86	3.
6.52	8.13	8.82	9.61	9.80	11.16	12.64	13.60	12.73	4.
.30	.38	.21	.33	.27	.41	.51	.46	.31	5.
5.68	6.03	6.96	7.45	8.61	9.92	10.34	11.96	13.62	6.
1.26	1.20	1.14	1.09	.94	.85	1.05	1.06	1.20	7.
16.72	19.12	20.36	22.01	23.60	26.80	29.29	32.16	33.11	8.
.45	1.42	2.38	2.35	1.84	1.88	1.88	1.83	1.93	9.
17.17	20.54	22.74	24.36	25.44	28.68	31.17	33.99	35.04	10.

Line

4 The above total minus line 5 of this table.

5 Calculated on the basis of assumed 80%-20% relationship between nonresidential structures and producer durables, as applied to the allocation of total expenditures for financial corporations (as cited in note to Table VIII-a-7, line 5) less residential structures and inventories.

6 Sum of Tables B-137, col. 1; B-138, col. 1; and B-141, col. 1.

7 Sum of Tables B-158, col. 1 and B-160, col. 1.

8 Sum of lines 1-7.

9 Sum of Tables B-166, col. 6, and B-178, col. 1.

10 Sum of lines 8 and 9.

1950	1951	1952	1953	1954	1955	1956	1957	1958	
1.06	1.12	1.01	1.04	1.22	1.28	1.28	1.43	1.50	1.
.89	.96	.87	1.09	1.26	1.56	1.66	1.58	1.54	2.
.86	.89	.87	.79	.75	.72	.67	.66	.66	3.
6.03	6.85	7.20	7.61	7.72	8.56	9.01	9.15	8.38	4.
.28	.32	.17	.26	.22	.31	.36	.31	.20	5.
5.54	5.48	6.03	6.37	7.43	8.40	8.33	9.31	10.56	6.
1.15	1.03	.94	.87	.73	.64	.74	.72	.78	7.
15.81	16.65	17.09	18.03	19.33	21.47	22.05	23.16	23.62	8.
.42	1.22	1.96	1.93	1.52	1.51	1.44	1.34	1.39	9.
16.23	17.87	19.05	19.96	20.85	22.98	23.49	24.50	25.01	10.

Line

4 The above total minus line 5 of this table.

5 The above total was allocated between financial and nonfinancial corporations according to the proportion of financial corporations in Table VIII-a-2 (line 5) to all corporations in that table (lines 4 & 5).

9 Sum of Tables B-167, col. 6, and B-178, col. 2.

TABLE VIII-a-2b

Uses of Funds: Net Investment in Nonresidential Structures, Depreciation at Replacement Cost
(billion dollars)

	1946	1947	1948	1949
1. Nonfarm households	-.02	-.02	.17	.37
2. Nonfarm unincorporated business	.20	-.05	.12	.03
3. Agriculture	.10	.27	.32	.30
4. Nonfinancial corporations	1.49	1.79	2.35	1.97
5. Finance	.03	.03	.04	.05
6. State and local governments	-.70	-.01	.69	2.06
7. Federal government (civil)	-.12	-.04	.14	.48
8. Total	.98	1.97	3.83	5.26
9. Military expenditures	.06	-.27	-.53	-.50
10. Total, including military	1.04	1.70	3.30	4.76

Source: Unless specified below, figures for all lines are obtained from same source as in Table VIII-a-2, except that col. 8 of the respective source tables, rather than col. 1, is used.

Line

2 Sum of Tables B-47, cols. 3, 6, 9; B-48, col. 9, and one-half of cols. 3 and 6; and B-39, col. 8.

4 & 5 Sum of Tables B-101 through B-104, col. 8; B-39, col. 8; B-109, col. 8; and one-half of Tables B-107 and B-108, col. 8; minus Tables B-47, cols. 3, 6, 9; B-48, col. 9, and one-half of cols. 3 and 6.

TABLE VIII-a-2c

Uses of Funds: Net Investment in Nonresidential Structures, Constant 1947-49 Prices
(billion dollars)

	1946	1947	1948	1949
1. Nonfarm households	-.04	-.03	.16	.36
2. Nonfarm unincorporated business	.28	-.05	.12	.03
3. Agriculture	.12	.30	.30	.30
4. Nonfinancial corporations	1.76	1.70	2.11	1.73
5. Finance	.04	.03	.04	.05
6. State and local governments	-.93	-.01	.67	2.00
7. Federal government (civil)	-.21	-.05	.14	.46
8. Total	1.02	1.89	3.54	4.93
9. Military expenditures	.08	-.28	-.50	-.51
10. Total, including military	1.10	1.61	3.04	4.42

Source: Unless specified below, figures for all lines are obtained from same source as in Table VIII-a-2, except that col. 7 of the respective source tables, rather than col. 1, is used.

Line

2 Sum of Tables B-47, cols. 2, 5, 8; B-48, col. 8, and one-half of cols. 2 and 5; and B-39, col. 7.

1950	1951	1952	1953	1954	1955	1956	1957	1958	
.57	.66	.54	.58	.82	.90	.92	1.16	1.26	1.
.15	.24	.14	.39	.58	.94	1.09	1.00	.94	2.
.37	.41	.41	.31	.26	.22	.17	.16	.15	3.
2.24	3.38	3.63	4.24	4.18	5.28	6.23	6.42	4.98	4.
.05	.07	.08	.10	.10	.14	.17	.17	.13	5.
2.61	2.67	3.27	3.59	4.65	5.71	5.72	6.94	8.29	6.
.52	.38	.28	.18	−.01	−.14	.01	.04	.25	7.
6.51	7.81	8.35	9.39	10.58	13.05	14.31	15.89	16.00	8.
−.40	.51	1.39	1.35	.77	.76	.66	.48	.52	9.
6.11	8.32	9.74	10.74	11.35	13.81	14.97	16.37	16.52	10.

Line

4 The above total minus line 5 of this table.

5 The above total was allocated between financial and nonfinancial corporations according to the proportion of nonresidential structures assets held by financial corporations (Table I, line I-2, col. 5) to nonresidential structure assets held by all corporations (Table I, line I-2, cols. 4 and 5).

9 Sum of Tables B-171, cols. 2 and 3, and B-178, col. 8.

1950	1951	1952	1953	1954	1955	1956	1957	1958	
.53	.58	.46	.48	.65	.70	.68	.82	.87	1.
.14	.21	.11	.32	.48	.75	.82	.72	.66	2.
.35	.38	.35	.26	.22	.18	.13	.12	.11	3.
1.92	2.74	2.87	3.28	3.21	4.00	4.46	4.33	3.29	4.
.05	.06	.06	.07	.08	.11	.12	.11	.09	5.
2.52	2.36	2.82	3.05	3.99	4.81	4.59	5.40	6.45	6.
.46	.32	.22	.13	−.02	−.12	−.02	.01	.15	7.
5.97	6.65	6.89	7.59	8.61	10.43	10.78	11.51	11.62	8.
−.38	.42	1.13	1.11	.64	.60	.48	.35	.37	9.
5.59	7.07	8.02	8.70	9.25	11.03	11.26	11.86	11.99	10.

Line

4 & 5 Sum of Tables B-101 through B-104, col. 7; Table B-39, col. 7; B-109, col. 7; and one-half of Tables B-107 and B-108, col. 7; minus Table B-47, cols. 2, 5, 8; Table B-48, col. 8, and one-half of cols. 2 and 5.

4 The above total minus line 5 of this table.

5 The same method as used for Table VIII-a-2b, line 5.

9 Sum of Tables B-170, cols. 2 and 3, and B-178, col. 7.

TABLE VIII-a-4

Uses of Funds: Gross Investment in Producer Durables, Original Cost

(billion dollars)

	1946	1947	1948	1949
1. Nonfarm households	.06	.08	.13	.17
2. Nonfarm unincorporated business	1.59	2.47	2.77	2.64
3. Agriculture	.97	1.79	2.43	2.64
4. Nonfinancial corporations	7.60	11.32	12.49	10.49
5. Finance	.07	.07	.07	.03
6. State and local governments	.21	.33	.42	.45
7. Federal government (civil)	.15	.16	.23	.12
8. Total	10.65	16.22	18.54	16.54
9. Military expenditures	2.38	1.63	1.62	2.14
10. Total, including military	13.03	17.85	20.16	18.68

Source: All data not otherwise specified below are from Goldsmith, *National Wealth*, Appendix B.

Line

1 Table B-40, col. 1.
2 Col. 1 of Tables B-49, B-50, and B-51.
3 Col. 1 of Tables B-64, B-65, and B-67.
4 & 5 Table B-99, col. 1; minus col. 1 of Tables B-49, B-50, and B-40.

TABLE VIII-a-4a

Uses of Funds: Gross Investment in Producer Durables, Constant 1947-49 Prices

(billion dollars)

	1946	1947	1948	1949
1. Nonfarm households	.07	.09	.12	.16
2. Nonfarm unincorporated business	1.96	2.65	2.74	2.49
3. Agriculture	1.24	2.01	2.41	2.39
4. Nonfinancial corporations	9.23	11.91	12.35	10.04
5. Finance	.08	.08	.07	.03
6. State and local governments	.26	.35	.42	.42
7. Federal government (civil)	.19	.17	.22	.11
8. Total	13.03	17.26	18.33	15.64
9. Military expenditures	2.96	1.77	1.61	2.01
10. Total, including military	15.99	19.03	19.94	17.65

Source: Unless specified below, figures for all lines are obtained from same source as in Table VIII-a-4, except that col. 2 of the respective source tables, rather than col. 1, is used.

Line

4 & 5 Table B-111, col. 1, minus col. 2 of Tables B-49, B-50, and B-40.
4 The above total minus line 5 of this table.

1950	1951	1952	1953	1954	1955	1956	1957	1958	
.21	.24	.23	.24	.29	.32	.33	.38	.41	1.
3.06	3.31	3.28	3.68	3.48	4.09	4.59	4.87	3.81	2.
2.64	2.74	2.59	2.46	2.21	2.27	2.03	2.06	2.59	3.
11.64	13.80	14.07	14.96	14.10	15.35	19.39	20.35	15.64	4.
.07	.10	.05	.08	.07	.10	.13	.12	.08	5.
.47	.53	.58	.62	.70	.75	.88	1.04	1.02	6.
.04	.10	.18	.17	.11	.05	.04	.04	.06	7.
18.13	20.82	20.98	22.21	20.96	22.93	27.39	28.86	23.61	8.
2.98	7.09	15.80	18.15	14.94	12.99	14.00	14.74	14.96	9.
21.11	27.91	36.78	40.36	35.90	35.92	41.39	43.60	38.57	10.

Line

4 The above total minus line 5 of this table.
5 See notes to Table VIII-a-2, line 5.
6 Sum of Tables B-139, col. 1 and B-142, col. 1.
7 Sum of Tables B-159, col. 1 and B-161, col. 1.
8 Sum of lines 1-7.
9 Sum of Tables B-166, col. 4 and B-178A, col. 1.
10 Sum of lines 8 and 9.

1950	1951	1952	1953	1954	1955	1956	1957	1958	
.19	.21	.19	.20	.24	.25	.25	.27	.28	1.
2.85	2.87	2.78	3.11	2.94	3.36	3.56	3.57	2.72	2.
2.37	2.28	2.09	2.00	1.79	1.82	1.57	1.51	1.81	3.
10.87	11.70	11.86	12.38	11.49	12.16	14.45	14.24	10.74	4.
.07	.08	.04	.07	.06	.08	.09	.08	.05	5.
.43	.45	.49	.52	.58	.60	.66	.74	.71	6.
.04	.09	.16	.14	.09	.04	.03	.03	.04	7.
16.82	17.68	17.61	18.42	17.19	18.31	20.61	20.44	16.35	8.
2.75	5.97	13.01	14.76	11.99	10.12	10.16	10.08	9.98	9.
19.57	23.65	30.62	33.18	29.18	28.43	30.77	30.52	26.33	10.

Line

5 The above total was allocated between financial and nonfinancial corporations according to the proportion of financial corporations in Table VIII-a-4 (line 5) to all corporations in that table (lines 4 and 5).
9 Sum of Tables B-167, col. 4, and B-178A, col. 2.

TABLE VIII-a-4b

Uses of Funds: Net Investment in Producer Durables, Depreciation at Replacement Cost

(billion dollars)

	1946	1947	1948	1949
1. Nonfarm households	.03	.05	.08	.11
2. Nonfarm unincorporated business	.81	1.48	1.52	1.11
3. Agriculture	.23	.86	1.24	1.18
4. Nonfinancial corporations	3.69	6.46	6.75	3.86
5. Finance	.02	.03	.03	.02
6. State and local governments	.09	.17	.23	.23
7. Federal government (civil)	−.56	−.64	−.52	−.37
8. Total	4.31	8.41	9.33	6.14
9. Military expenditures	−13.08	−13.19	−10.93	−8.26
10. Total, including military	−8.77	−4.78	−1.60	−2.12

Source: Unless specified below, figures for all lines are obtained from same source as in Table VIII-a-4, except that col. 8 of the respective source tables, rather than col. 1, is used.

Line	
4 & 5	Table B-117, col. 1, minus col. 8 of Tables B-49, B-50, and B-40.
4	The above total minus line 5 of this table.

TABLE VIII-a-4c

Uses of Funds: Net Investment in Producer Durables, Constant 1947-49 Prices

(billion dollars)

	1946	1947	1948	1949
1. Nonfarm households	.04	.05	.08	.10
2. Nonfarm unincorporated business	1.00	1.59	1.50	1.05
3. Agriculture	.29	.97	1.23	1.07
4. Nonfinancial corporations	4.50	6.79	6.68	3.71
5. Finance	.02	.03	.03	.02
6. State and local governments	.10	.18	.23	.21
7. Federal government (civil)	−.68	−.69	−.51	−.35
8. Total	5.27	8.92	9.24	5.81
9. Military expenditures	−16.29	−14.26	−10.82	−7.75
10. Total, including military	−11.02	−5.34	−1.58	−1.94

Source: Unless specified below, figures for all lines are obtained from same source as in Table VIII-a-4, except that col. 7 of the respective source tables, rather than col. 1, is used.

Line	
4 & 5	Table B-116, col. 1; minus col. 7 of Tables B-49, B-50, and B-40.
4	The above total minus line 5 of this table

1950	1951	1952	1953	1954	1955	1956	1957	1958	
.14	.15	.12	.12	.15	.14	.12	.14	.12	1.
1.27	1.12	.83	1.03	.64	.99	1.18	1.09	−.25	2.
1.02	.87	.55	.33	.0	−.14	−.09	−.62	−.15	3.
4.26	5.67	5.28	5.60	4.32	3.95	7.28	7.53	2.70	4.
.02	.03	.03	.03	.02	.02	.04	.04	.02	5.
.22	.24	.27	.28	.31	.29	.33	.39	.28	6.
−.23	−.11	−.01	−.02	−.08	−.12	−.13	−.12	−.09	7.
6.70	7.97	7.07	7.37	5.36	5.13	8.73	8.45	2.63	8.
−6.22	−2.18	5.18	5.06	.33	−2.11	−1.84	−1.74	1.57	9.
.48	5.79	12.25	12.43	5.69	3.02	6.89	6.71	4.20	10.

Line

5 The above total was allocated between financial and nonfinancial corporations according to the proportion of producer durable assets held by financial corporations (Table I, line I-4, col. 5) to producer durable assets held by all corporations (Table I, line I-4, cols. 4 and 5).

9 Sum of Tables B-171, cols. 1 and 7, and B-178A, col. 8.

1950	1951	1952	1953	1954	1955	1956	1957	1958	
.13	.13	.10	.10	.12	.12	.09	.10	.08	1.
1.18	.97	.70	.86	.53	.82	.90	.78	−.19	2.
.91	.72	.43	.27	a	−.03	−.34	−.37	−.10	3.
3.98	4.76	4.40	4.57	3.42	3.00	5.26	5.09	1.70	4.
.02	.02	.02	.02	.02	.02	.03	.03	.01	5.
.20	.20	.23	.23	.26	.23	.25	.28	.20	6.
−.21	−.09	a	−.02	−.07	−.10	−.10	−.08	−.06	7.
6.21	6.71	5.88	6.03	4.28	4.06	6.09	5.83	1.64	8.
−5.71	−1.82	4.27	4.11	.27	−1.65	−1.34	−1.20	−1.05	9.
.50	4.89	10.15	10.14	4.55	2.41	4.75	4.63	.59	10.

Line

5 The same method as used for Table VIII-a-4b, line 5.

9 Sum of Tables B-170, cols. 1 and 7, and B-178A, col. 7.

[a] $5 million or under.

TABLE VIII-a-5
Uses of Funds: Gross Investment in Consumer Durables, Original Cost
(billion dollars)

	1946	1947	1948	1949
1. Nonfarm households	13.71	18.38	20.09	21.94
2. Nonfarm unincorporated business				
3. Agriculture	1.84	2.31	2.76	2.76
4. Nonfinancial corporations				
5. Finance				
6. State and local governments				
7. Federal government				
8. Total	15.55	20.69	22.85	24.70

Source: All data not otherwise specified are from Goldsmith, *National Wealth*, Appendix B.

TABLE VIII-a-5a
Uses of Funds: Gross Investment in Consumer Durables, Constant 1947-49 Prices
(billion dollars)

	1946	1947	1948	1949
1. Nonfarm households	16.47	19.30	19.74	21.22
2. Nonfarm unincorporated business				
3. Agriculture	2.19	2.43	2.71	2.59
4. Nonfinancial corporations				
5. Finance				
6. State and local governments				
7. Federal government				
8. Total	18.66	21.73	22.45	23.81

Source: All data not otherwise specified are from Goldsmith, *National Wealth*, Appendix B.

TABLE VIII-a-5b
Uses of Funds: Net Investment in Consumer Durables, Depreciation at Replacement Cost
(billion dollars)

	1946	1947	1948	1949
1. Nonfarm households	5.28	7.65	7.33	7.73
2. Nonfarm unincorporated business				
3. Agriculture	.76	.96	1.14	.96
4. Nonfinancial corporations				
5. Finance				
6. State and local governments				
7. Federal government				
8. Total	6.04	8.61	8.47	8.69

Source: All data not otherwise specified are from Goldsmith, *National Wealth*, Appendix B.

1950	1951	1952	1953	1954	1955	1956	1957	1958	
27.68	26.24	26.28	29.17	29.23	36.58	35.37	36.76	34.04	1.
									2.
3.05	3.09	2.54	2.93	2.61	2.54	2.53	2.64	2.87	3.
									4.
									5.
									6.
									7.
30.73	29.33	28.82	32.10	31.84	39.12	37.90	39.40	36.91	8.

Line

1 Col. 1 of Tables B-18 and B-32.
3 Col. 1 of Tables B-71 and B-66.
8 Sum of lines 1 and 3.

1950	1951	1952	1953	1954	1955	1956	1957	1958	
26.91	23.76	23.74	26.47	27.31	34.05	32.78	33.13	30.67	1.
									2.
3.01	2.76	2.27	2.71	2.30	2.43	2.27	2.25	2.39	3.
									4.
									5.
									6.
									7.
29.92	26.52	26.01	29.18	29.61	36.48	35.05	35.38	33.06	8.

Line

1 Sum of Tables B-19, col. 1, and B-32, col. 2.
3 Sum of Tables B-72, col. 1, and B-66, col. 2.
8 Sum of lines 1 and 3.

1950	1951	1952	1953	1954	1955	1956	1957	1958	
11.75	7.26	5.91	7.56	6.75	12.15	8.60	7.20	2.98	1.
									2.
1.10	.67	−.06	.40	−.26	−.26	−.27	−.49	−.43	3.
									4.
									5.
									6.
									7.
12.85	7.93	5.85	7.96	6.49	11.89	8.33	6.71	2.55	8.

Line

1 Sum of Tables B-25, col. 1, and B-32, col. 8.
3 Sum of Tables B-78, col. 1, and B-66, col. 8.
8 Sum of lines 1 and 3.

TABLE VIII-a-5c

Uses of Funds: Net Investment in Consumer Durables, Constant 1947-49 Prices

(billion dollars)

	1946	1947	1948	1949
1. Nonfarm households	6.31	8.06	7.24	7.39
2. Nonfarm unincorporated business				
3. Agriculture	.89	1.01	1.12	.85
4. Nonfinancial corporations				
5. Finance				
6. State and local governments				
7. Federal government				
8. Total	7.20	9.07	8.36	8.24

Source: All data not otherwise specified are from Goldsmith, *National Wealth*, Appendix B.

TABLE VIII-a-6b

Uses of Funds: Inventories at Book Value, Original Cost

(billion dollars)

	1946	1947	1948	1949
1. Nonfarm households				
2. Nonfarm unincorporated business	2.09	1.53	1.33	−.95
3. Agriculture	3.42	3.40	−.30	−3.26
4. Nonfinancial corporations	11.22	7.15	4.21	−3.57
5. Finance	.02	−.01	−.01	a
6. State and local governments	.02	.01	a	a
7. Federal government (civil)	−1.20	−.28	.82	1.36
8. Total	15.57	11.80	6.05	−6.42
9. Military expenditures	.13	.16	.34	.72
10. Total, including military	15.70	11.96	6.39	−5.70

Source: All data not otherwise specified below are from Goldsmith, *National Wealth*, Appendix B.

Line

2 Table B-130, col. 6.
3 First differences in Table B-97, col. 1.
4 & 5 Table B-130, col. 5.
4 The above total minus line 5 of this table.
5 First differences of inventories of financial corporations from *Statistics of Income*, Part II.

1950	1951	1952	1953	1954	1955	1956	1957	1958	
11.38	6.68	5.57	7.10	6.57	11.49	8.36	7.03	3.46	1.
									2.
1.07	.63	.06	.42	–.06	a	–.20	–.22	–.09	3.
									4.
									5.
									6.
									7.
12.45	7.31	5.63	7.52	6.51	11.49	8.16	6.81	3.37	8.

Line

1 Sum of Tables B-24, col. 1, and B-32, col. 7.
3 Sum of Tables B-77, col. 1, and B-66, col. 7.
8 Sum of lines 1 and 3.

[a]$5 million or under.

1950	1951	1952	1953	1954	1955	1956	1957	1958	
									1.
2.27	.83	–.29	.42	–.15	.76	.69	.31	–.02	2.
5.43	3.77	–4.99	–4.24	–.16	–1.37	.85	2.34	5.58	3.
9.77	9.75	1.25	1.80	–1.60	6.66	7.58	2.74	–4.44	4.
.01	a	a	a	–.01	a	a	–.01	a	5.
.02	a	a	.01	.01	.01	.02	.01	.01	6.
–.61	–.43	.46	2.88	1.24	.14	–.11	–.94	1.97	7.
16.89	13.92	–3.57	.87	–.67	6.20	9.03	4.45	3.10	8.
.74	1.14	1.50	1.33	1.58	1.47	1.54	1.77	1.83	9.
17.63	15.06	–2.07	2.20	.91	7.67	10.57	6.22	4.93	10.

Line

6 First differences in Table B-156, col. 4.
7 First differences in Table B-156, col. 2.
8 Sum of lines 1-7.
9 First differences in Table B-179, col. 8, and Table B-180, col. 1.
10 Sum of lines 8 and 9.

[a]$5 million or under.

TABLE VIII-a-6c

Uses of Funds: Inventories, Constant 1947-49 Prices

(billion dollars)

	1946	1947	1948	1949
1. Nonfarm households				
2. Nonfarm unincorporated business	.56	.01	.57	−.31
3. Agriculture	−.18	−1.86	1.59	−1.22
4. Nonfinancial corporations	6.89	1.50	1.30	−1.11
5. Finance	.01	−.01	−.01	a
6. State and local governments	a	a	a	a
7. Federal government (civil)	−2.05	−.51	.97	1.73
8. Total	5.23	−.87	4.42	−.91
9. Military expenditures	.14	.16	.33	.72
10. Total, including military	5.37	−.71	4.75	−.19

Source: All data not otherwise specified below are from Goldsmith, *National Wealth*, Appendix B.

Line

2 Table B-131, col. 6.
3 First differences of Table B-97, col. 4.
4 & 5 Table B-131, col. 5.
4 The above total minus line 5 of this table.
5 First differences of inventories of financial corporations from *Statistics of Income*, deflated by fourth quarter averages of B.L.S. monthly index of wholesale prices for commodities other than farm products and foods, *Federal Reserve Bulletin*, various issues, e.g., March 1957, p. 468.

TABLE VIII-a-6d

Uses of Funds: Inventories at Adjusted Values

(billion dollars)

	1946	1947	1948	1949
1. Nonfarm households				
2. Nonfarm unincorporated business	.38	.06	.92	−.49
3. Agriculture	−.06	−1.73	1.47	−1.35
4. Nonfinancial corporations	5.95	1.25	2.06	−1.72
5. Finance	.02	−.01	−.01	a
6. State and local governments	.02	.01	a	a
7. Federal government (civil)	−1.20	−.28	.82	1.36
8. Total	5.11	−.70	5.26	−2.20
9. Military expenditures	.13	.16	.34	.72
10. Total, including military	5.24	−.54	5.60	−1.48

Source: All data not otherwise specified below are from Goldsmith, *National Wealth*, Appendix B.

Line

2 Table B-130, col. 12.
3 Unpublished figures of the agricultural market service for livestock and crops. For crops the figures were adjusted to exclude the annual change in quantity, valued at average annual prices of corn and wheat stored on farms under the commodity credit corporation loan (see Table B-96).
4 & 5 Table B-130, col. 11.

1950	1951	1952	1953	1954	1955	1956	1957	1958	
									1.
.77	.43	−.06	.18	−.14	.12	.05	.07	−.11	2.
.82	.68	.44	−.59	.59	.34	−.54	.47	2.25	3.
3.96	7.35	1.96	.71	−1.45	3.31	3.74	1.30	−3.97	4.
.01	a	a	a	−.01	a	a	−.01	a	5.
a	a	.01	.01	.01	.01	.01	.01	.01	6.
−1.25	−.40	.69	3.10	1.67	.87	−.65	−1.35	2.40	7.
4.31	8.06	3.04	3.41	.67	4.65	2.61	.49	.58	8.
.73	1.00	1.42	1.29	1.46	1.39	1.50	1.89	2.09	9.
5.04	9.06	4.46	4.70	2.13	6.04	4.11	2.38	2.67	10.

Line

6 Table B-156, col. 3 (first differences).
7 Table B-156, col. 1 (first differences).
8 Sum of lines 1-7.
9 Sum of Tables B-170, col. 6 and B-170, col. 5.
10 Sum of lines 8 and 9.

[a]$5 million or under.

1950	1951	1952	1953	1954	1955	1956	1957	1958	
									1.
1.18	.50	−.08	.26	−.20	.56	.19	.01	−.06	2.
1.22	1.54	.75	− 98	.66	.26	−.68	.55	2.31	3.
4.81	8.55	2.23	.81	−1.92	4.93	4.89	1.21	−4.84	4.
.01	a	a	a	−.01	a	a	−.01	a	5.
.02	a	a	.01	.01	.01	.02	.01	.01	6.
−.61	−.43	.46	2.88	1.24	.14	−.11	−.94	1.97	7.
6.63	10.16	3.36	2.98	−.22	5.90	4.31	.83	−.61	8.
.74	1.14	1.50	1.33	1.58	1.47	1.54	1.77	1.83	9.
7.37	11.30	4.86	4.31	1.36	7.37	5.85	2.60	1.22	10.

Line

4 The above total minus line 5 of this table.
5 See note to Table VIII-a-6b, line 5.
6 First differences in Table B-156, col. 4.
7 First differences in Table B-156, col. 2.
8 Sum of lines 1-7.
9 First differences in Table B-179, col. 8, plus Table B-180, col. 1.
10 Sum of lines 8 and 9.

[a]$5 million or under.

TABLE VIII-a-7

Uses of Funds: Gross Investment, Inventories at Book Value, Original Cost

(billion dollars)

	1946	1947	1948	1949
1. Nonfarm households	18.98	26.29	31.51	32.48
2. Nonfarm unincorporated business	4.55	4.89	5.45	3.00
3. Agriculture	7.11	8.93	6.46	3.64
4. Nonfinancial corporations	23.44	24.17	23.74	13.89
5. Finance	.36	.37	.36	.22
a. Federal Reserve Banks and Treasury monetary funds	a	a	a	a
c. Commercial banks	.10	.11	.10	.06
d. Mutual savings banks	.01	.01	.01	a
e. Savings and loan associations	.05	.05	.05	.03
h. Life insurance	.17	.17	.17	.10
i. Fire and casualty insurance	.02	.02	.02	.01
k. Other private insurance [a]				
6. State and local governments	2.02	3.07	4.11	5.76
7. Federal government (civil)	−.83	.36	1.80	2.66
8. Total	55.63	68.08	73.43	61.65
9. Military expenditures	3.27	2.37	2.37	3.21
10. Total, including military	58.90	70.45	75.80	64.86

Source: Unless otherwise specified below, all figures are the sum of corresponding lines in Table VIII-a-1 through VIII-a-5 and VIII-a-6b.

Line

5 Derived by allocating gross capital expenditures (at original cost) of all corporations between financial and nonfinancial corporations in the proportion of 1.5 to 98.5. This ratio is based on *Statistics of Income* data; the average relative share of gross depreciable assets of financial corporations in gross depreciable assets of all corporations is 1.5 per cent during the years 1945-57.

1950	1951	1952	1953	1954	1955	1956	1957	1958	
42.20	41.44	41.64	45.81	46.80	58.40	56.56	57.31	54.89	1.
6.73	5.59	4.32	5.83	5.24	7.19	7.95	7.86	6.53	2.
12.79	11.48	2.07	2.90	6.33	5.06	6.99	8.65	12.66	3.
28.75	32.43	24.77	27.25	23.13	34.16	40.73	37.77	25.10	4.
.43	.49	.37	.40	.35	.52	.63	.58	.39	5.
a	a	a	a	a	.01	.01	.01	a	a.
.12	.14	.11	.12	.10	.15	.18	.17	.11	c.
.01	.01	.01	.01	.01	.01	.01	.01	.01	d.
.06	.07	.05	.06	.05	.07	.09	.08	.05	e.
.20	.23	.17	.19	.16	.24	.29	.27	.18	h.
.03	.03	.02	.03	.02	.03	.04	.04	.03	i.
									k.
6.45	7.14	8.17	8.60	9.64	10.94	11.52	13.36	15.13	6.
.67	.86	1.77	4.16	2.28	1.04	1.00	.31	3.58	7.
98.02	99.43	83.11	94.95	93.77	117.31	125.38	125.84	118.28	8.
4.19	9.66	19.70	21.83	18.36	16.34	17.42	18.34	18.72	9.
102.21	109.09	102.81	116.78	112.13	133.65	142.80	144.18	137.00	10.

Line 5 was allocated among its subsectors in the following proportions:

Line	Distribution (per cent)	Net Change in Tangible Assets, 1945-58 (billion dollars)
5a	1.1	.06
5c	28.8	1.55
5d	2.0	.11
5e	13.9	.75
5h	46.5	2.50
5i	6.5	.35
5k	.7	.04
Residual	.4	.02
Total	100.0	5.38

These weights represent each institution's share of the change in the value of tangible assets of all financial institutions between 1945 and 1958. Tangible assets were measured at book value (see Table III-5n).

[a] $5 million or under.

TABLE VIII-a-7a

Uses of Funds: Gross Investment, Constant 1947-49 Prices

(billion dollars)

	1946	1947	1948	1949
1. Nonfarm households	23.42	27.86	30.71	31.52
2. Nonfarm unincorporated business	3.71	3.63	4.64	3.45
3. Agriculture	4.41	4.07	8.22	5.26
4. Nonfinancial corporations	22.09	19.51	20.46	15.63
5. Finance	.44	.40	.36	.21
6. State and local governments	2.57	3.29	3.94	5.59
7. Federal government (civil)	−1.63	.13	1.84	2.95
8. Total	55.01	58.89	70.17	64.61
9. Military expenditures	4.10	2.56	2.34	3.07
10. Total, including military	59.11	61.45	72.51	67.68

Sum of corresponding lines in Tables VIII-a-1a, VIII-a-2a, VIII-a-4a, VIII-a-5a, and VIII-a-6c.

TABLE VIII-a-7b

Uses of Funds: Net Investment, Depreciation at Replacement Cost, Inventories at Book Value

(billion dollars)

	1946	1947	1948	1949
1. Nonfarm households	6.77	10.87	13.31	12.79
2. Nonfarm unincorporated business	2.90	2.82	2.98	.24
3. Agriculture	4.61	5.77	2.69	−.57
4. Nonfinancial corporations	16.44	15.52	13.68	2.69
5. Finance	.07	.07	.09	.13
6. State and local governments	−.25	.27	.89	2.49
7. Federal government (civil)	−2.07	−1.11	.28	1.40
8. Total	28.47	34.21	33.92	19.17
9. Military expenditures	−12.89	−13.29	−11.09	−8.01
10. Total, including military	15.58	20.92	22.83	11.16

Sum of corresponding lines in Tables VIII-a-1b, VIII-a-2b, VIII-a-4b, VIII-a-5b, and VIII-a-6b.

1950	1951	1952	1953	1954	1955	1956	1957	1958	
40.42	36.90	36.67	40.20	41.87	51.59	49.10	48.60	46.18	1.
4.95	4.55	3.85	4.70	4.35	5.34	5.62	5.56	4.52	2.
7.82	7.39	6.46	5.63	6.11	5.96	4.59	5.50	7.72	3.
21.62	26.54	21.54	21.41	18.43	24.80	28.03	25.47	15.98	4.
.41	.41	.30	.33	.29	.40	.44	.39	.25	5.
6.21	6.42	7.06	7.32	8.29	9.22	9.21	10.33	11.64	6.
−.10	.70	1.76	4.12	2.47	1.55	.13	−.48	3.48	7.
81.33	82.91	77.64	83.71	81.81	98.86	97.12	95.37	89.77	8.
3.91	8.20	16.41	17.98	14.97	13.02	13.10	13.31	13.46	9.
85.24	91.11	94.05	101.69	96.78	111.88	110.22	108.68	103.23	10.

1950	1951	1952	1953	1954	1955	1956	1957	1958	
20.36	15.89	14.32	16.91	16.83	25.98	21.17	18.60	14.26	1.
3.67	2.00	.45	1.67	.86	2.50	2.82	2.23	.54	2.
8.23	6.08	−3.73	−2.93	.07	−1.36	.81	1.53	5.29	3.
16.71	19.13	10.34	12.05	7.24	16.36	21.65	17.17	3.77	4.
.13	.11	.21	.11	.12	.16	.19	.20	.14	5.
3.07	3.43	4.09	4.30	5.19	6.15	6.22	7.56	8.92	6.
−.41	−.24	.65	2.98	1.07	−.19	−.29	−.88	2.45	7.
51.76	46.40	26.33	35.09	31.38	49.60	52.57	46.41	35.37	8.
−5.87	−.53	8.09	7.74	2.68	.12	.36	.50	3.91	9.
45.89	45.87	34.42	42.83	34.06	49.72	52.93	46.91	39.28	10.

TABLE VIII-a-7c

Uses of Funds: Net Investment, Constant 1947-49 Prices

(billion dollars)

	1946	1947	1948	1949
1. Nonfarm households	8.29	11.55	13.02	12.35
2. Nonfarm unincorporated business	1.58	1.41	2.23	.83
3. Agriculture	1.25	.71	4.52	1.25
4. Nonfinancial corporations	13.21	10.12	10.44	4.75
5. Finance	.07	.07	.09	.13
6. State and local governments	−.40	.27	.84	2.40
7. Federal government (civil)	−3.24	−1.47	.38	1.76
8. Total	20.76	22.66	31.52	23.47
9. Military expenditures	−16.07	−14.37	−10.96	−7.51
10. Total, including military	4.69	8.29	20.56	15.96

Sum of corresponding lines in Tables VIII-a-1c, VIII-a-2c, VIII-a-4c, VIII-a-5c, and VIII-a-6c.

TABLE VIII-a-7d

Uses of Funds: Gross Investment, Inventories at Adjusted Value

(billion dollars)

	1946	1947	1948	1949
1. Nonfarm households	18.98	26.29	31.51	32.48
2. Nonfarm unincorporated business	2.84	3.42	5.04	3.46
3. Agriculture	3.63	3.80	8.23	5.55
4. Nonfinancial corporations	18.17	18.27	21.59	15.74
5. Finance	.36	.37	.36	.22
a. Federal Reserve Banks and Treasury monetary funds	a	a	a	a
c. Commercial banks	.10	.11	.10	.06
d. Mutual savings banks	.01	.01	.01	a
e. Savings and loan association	.05	.05	.05	.03
h. Life insurance	.17	.17	.17	.10
i. Fire and casualty insurance	.02	.02	.02	.01
k. Other private insurance [a]				
6. State and local governments	2.02	3.07	4.11	5.76
7. Federal government (civil)	−.83	.36	1.80	2.66
8. Total	45.17	55.58	72.64	65.87
9. Military expenditures	3.27	2.37	2.37	3.21
10. Total, including military	48.44	57.95	75.01	69.08

Line

1-5, 6-10 Sum of corresponding lines in Tables VIII-a-1, VIII-a-2, VIII-a-4, VIII-a-5, and VIII-a-6d.
5a-5m See note to Table VIII-a-7, lines 5a-5m.

[a] $5 million or under.

1950	1951	1952	1953	1954	1955	1956	1957	1958	
19.40	14.15	12.66	14.83	14.94	22.64	18.05	15.62	11.86	1.
2.09	1.45	.56	1.24	.71	1.55	1.67	1.45	.27	2.
3.45	2.72	1.60	.60	.95	.65	−.83	.11	2.28	3.
10.27	15.14	9.38	8.88	5.46	10.68	13.88	11.07	1.40	4.
.12	.09	.17	.08	.10	.13	.14	.13	.09	5.
2.90	3.00	3.52	3.63	4.44	5.17	4.97	5.86	6.93	6.
−1.11	−.25	.82	3.16	1.50	.59	−.81	−1.32	2.73	7.
37.12	36.30	28.71	32.42	28.10	41.41	37.07	32.92	25.56	8.
−5.35	−.40	6.84	6.51	2.37	.34	.64	1.04	1.41	9.
31.77	35.90	35.55	38.93	30.47	41.75	37.71	33.96	26.97	10.

1950	1951	1952	1953	1954	1955	1956	1957	1958	
42.20	41.44	41.64	45.81	46.80	58.40	56.56	57.31	54.89	1.
5.64	5.26	4.53	5.67	5.19	6.99	7.45	7.56	6.49	2.
8.58	9.25	7.81	6.16	7.15	6.69	5.46	6.86	9.39	3.
23.79	31.23	25.75	26.26	22.81	32.43	38.04	36.24	24.70	4.
.43	.49	.37	.40	.35	.52	.63	.58	.39	5.
a	a	a	a	a	.01	.01	.01	a	a.
.12	.14	.11	.12	.10	.15	.18	.17	.11	c.
.01	.01	.01	.01	.01	.01	.01	.01	.01	d.
.06	.07	.05	.06	.05	.07	.09	.08	.05	e.
.20	.23	.17	.19	.16	.24	.29	.27	.18	h.
.03	.03	.02	.03	.02	.03	.04	.04	.03	i.
									k.
6.45	7.14	8.17	8.60	9.64	10.94	11.52	13.36	15.13	6.
.67	.86	1.77	4.16	2.28	1.04	1.00	.31	3.58	7.
87.76	95.67	90.04	97.06	94.22	117.01	120.66	122.22	114.57	8.
4.19	9.66	19.70	21.83	18.36	16.34	17.42	18.34	18.72	9.
91.95	105.33	109.74	118.89	112.58	133.35	138.08	140.56	133.29	10.

TABLE VIII-a-7e
Uses of Funds: Net Investment, Depreciation at Replacement Cost, Inventories at Adjusted Value

(billion dollars)

	1946	1947	1948	1949
1. Nonfarm households	6.73	10.89	13.36	12.93
2. Nonfarm unincorporated business	1.19	1.35	2.57	.70
3. Agriculture	1.13	.64	4.46	1.34
4. Nonfinancial corporations	11.17	9.62	11.53	4.54
5. Finance	.07	.07	.09	.13
6. State and local governments	−.25	.27	.89	2.49
7. Federal government (civil)	−2.07	−1.11	.28	1.40
8. Total	17.97	21.73	33.18	23.53
9. Military expenditures	−12.89	−13.29	−11.09	−8.01
10. Total, including military	5.08	8.44	22.09	15.52

Sum of corresponding lines in Tables VIII-a-1b, VIII-a-2b, VIII-a-4b, VIII-a-5b, and VIII-a-6d.

TABLE VIII-b-1
Uses of Funds: Net Change in Currency and Demand Deposits

(billion dollars)

	1946	1947	1948	1949
1. Nonfarm households	4.15	−.31	−2.06	−2.31
2. Nonfarm unincorporated business	.01	.36	−.15	.37
3. Agriculture	.50	−.10	−.30	−.40
4. Nonfinancial corporations	1.14	2.20	.20	1.07
5. Finance	.50	7.89	4.74	−2.79
a. Federal Reserve Banks and Treasury monetary funds	1.26	5.35	3.03	.35
b. Govt. insurance and pension funds	.01	.02	.08	−.02
c. Commercial banks	−1.30	2.21	1.52	−3.36
d. Mutual savings banks	.06	.02	−.03	0
e. Savings and loan associations	.07	0	.06	.08
f. Investment companies	0	−.01	0	0
g. Credit unions	0	.01	.01	0
h. Life insurance	−.01	.25	−.11	0
i. Fire and casualty insurance	.19	.18	.04	.06
j. Noninsured pension plans	.02	.03	.03	.04
k. Other private insurance	0	0	0	.02
l. Finance companies	−.01	−.06	.17	.11
m. Other finance	.21	−.11	−.06	−.07
6. State and local governments	.87	.72	.49	.23
7. Federal government	−22.73	−.54	1.08	.38
8. Total	−15.56	10.22	4.00	−3.45
9. Rest of world, assets	.07	.05	.34	−.01
10. Monetary metals	.36	1.32	1.48	.23
11. Mail float	.90	−.95	−.31	.46
12. Commercial bank cash items: in process of collection	.58	1.11	−.45	.52
13. Currency and demand deposit assets, adjusted	−14.37	9.11	2.10	−2.71
14. Discrepancy	−.38	.47	−.03	0
15. Currency and demand deposits, liabilities	−14.75	9.58	2.07	−2.71

Table IV-b-1, first difference.

1950	1951	1952	1953	1954	1955	1956	1957	1958	
20.50	16.06	14.50	17.10	17.02	26.19	21.39	18.95	14.61	1.
2.58	1.67	.66	1.51	.81	2.30	2.32	1.93	.50	2.
4.02	3.85	2.01	.33	.89	.27	−.72	−.26	2.02	3.
11.75	17.93	11.32	11.06	6.92	14.63	18.96	15.64	3.37	4.
.13	.11	.21	.11	.12	.16	.19	.20	.14	5.
3.07	3.43	4.09	4.30	5.19	6.15	6.22	7.56	8.92	6.
−.41	−.24	.65	2.98	1.07	−.19	−.29	−.88	2.45	7.
41.64	42.81	33.44	37.39	32.02	49.51	48.07	43.14	32.01	8.
−5.87	−.53	8.09	7.74	2.68	.12	.36	.50	3.91	9.
35.77	42.28	41.53	45.13	34.70	49.63	48.43	43.64	35.92	10.

1950	1951	1952	1953	1954	1955	1956	1957	1958	
1.90	3.07	1.89	.91	2.20	−.75	.96	−1.02	2.84	1.
.22	1.04	−.35	−.05	.53	.29	.35	.81	1.10	2.
0	.20	−.10	−.10	−.10	0	−.20	−.10	.30	3.
1.31	1.82	.80	−.08	2.36	.98	.14	0	1.72	4.
.08	4.67	1.14	−1.17	−.94	.62	2.20	2.07	−3.72	5.
−3.38	.16	1.15	−1.68	−.52	.05	.48	1.73	−4.13	a.
.46	.06	−.11	−.04	.32	−.22	.14	.24	.13	b.
2.28	3.92	−.06	.24	−1.23	.23	1.36	−.15	−.36	c.
−.02	.07	0	.04	.02	−.02	.02	0	0	d.
.09	.10	.07	.05	.26	.19	.07	.05	.27	e.
.04	.03	−.01	.04	0	0	.03	.03	0	f.
.02	.05	0	.02	.05	.01	.03	.03	.04	g.
.09	.10	.05	.07	.02	.02	.02	.01	.08	h.
.06	.04	.08	.05	−.05	.03	−.07	−.01	.06	i.
.07	.04	−.03	.05	0	.06	−.01	.06	.03	j.
.01	.01	.01	.04	.01	0	−.01	−.01	.02	k.
.17	.12	.03	.02	.05	.26	.02	.07	.11	l.
.19	−.03	−.04	−.07	.13	.01	.12	.02	.03	m.
.46	.43	.47	.60	.33	.39	.15	.21	.22	6.
−.68	.06	1.95	−1.47	.03	−.41	−.30	.01	0	7.
3.29	11.29	5.80	−1.36	4.41	1.12	3.30	1.98	2.46	8.
−.10	−.43	.20	−.25	.09	−.05	.22	.17	.08	9.
−1.68	0	.52	−.63	−.31	.01	.37	.91	−1.99	10.
.88	.04	1.53	.20	−1.75	1.50	.07	−1.29	−1.25	11.
2.32	.39	.13	0	−.12	3.25	.60	−.18	.88	12.
8.07	11.29	7.14	−.78	2.94	5.81	3.82	−.23	4.16	13.
1.26	−.32	−.12	.46	−.21	.92	.18	−.48	.13	14.
9.33	10.97	7.02	−.32	2.73	6.73	4.00	−.71	4.29	15.

TABLE VIII-b-2

Uses of Funds: Net Change in Other Bank Deposits and Shares

(billion dollars)

	1946	1947	1948	1949
1. Nonfarm households	6.38	3.63	2.18	2.48
2. Nonfarm unincorporated business				
3. Agriculture	.20	−.08	0	0
4. Nonfinancial corporations	0	0	0	0
5. Finance	.14	.04	.02	.01
c. Commercial banks	−.01	0	−.01	−.01
d. Mutual savings banks	.15	.05	.02	−.01
g. Credit unions	0	−.01	.01	.03
i. Fire and casualty insurance	0	0	0	0
6. State and local governments	.18	.16	.27	.15
7. Federal government	.01	−.01	0	.06
8. Total	6.91	3.74	2.47	2.70
9. Rest of world, assets	0	−.01	.03	.14
10. Total liabilities	6.91	3.73	2.50	2.84

Table IV-b-2, first difference.

TABLE VIII-b-3

Uses of Funds: Net Change in Life Insurance Policy Reserves

(billion dollars)

	1946	1947	1948	1949
1. Nonfarm households	3.53	3.30	3.52	3.76
2. Nonfarm unincorporated business				
3. Agriculture	.19	.21	.23	.24
4. Nonfinancial corporations				
5. Finance				
6. State and local governments				
7. Federal government				
8. Total domestic purchases	3.72	3.51	3.75	4.00
9. Rest of world, assets	.07	.07	.08	.08
10. Total domestic policy reserve, net changes in liability	3.79	3.58	3.83	4.08

Line

1 Line 8 minus line 3.
3 First differences of Table IV-b-3, line 3.
8 Line 10 less line 9.

1950	1951	1952	1953	1954	1955	1956	1957	1958	
2.09	4.20	7.35	7.88	8.83	8.42	9.14	11.38[a]	13.75	1.
									2.
0	.07	.13	.13	.10	.05	.05	.27	.17	3.
0	0	0	0	.20	−.10	0	0	.60	4.
−.05	.08	.13	.08	.10	.02	.05	.04[a]	.31	5.
0	0	0	0	0	0	0	0	.04	c.
−.05	.02	.03	.02	.03	−.05	−.06	−.04	.04	d.
0	.05	.09	.06	.07	.07	.11	.08[a]	.23	g.
0	.01	.01	0	0	0	0	0	0	i.
.10	.15	.09	.33	.46	−.06	.04	.38	.80	6.
.01	.09	.07	−.01	.02	0	−.03	−.03	.03	7.
2.15	4.59	7.77	8.41	9.71	8.33	9.25	12.04	15.66	8.
.22	.11	.20	.55	.55	−.13	−.09	−.03	1.06	9.
2.37	4.70	7.97	8.96	10.26	8.20	9.16	12.01	16.72	10.

[a]Based on a corrected figure for credit unions.

1950	1951	1952	1953	1954	1955	1956	1957	1958	
3.96	3.92	4.71	4.77	5.18	5.26	5.22	4.90	5.24	1.
									2.
.24	.24	.28	.27	.32	.30	.26	.24	.29	3.
									4.
									5.
									6.
									7.
4.20	4.16	4.99	5.04	5.50	5.56	5.48	5.14	5.53	8.
.08	.09	.10	.10	.11	.12	.10	.11	.12	9.
4.28	4.25	5.09	5.14	5.61	5.68	5.58	5.25	5.65	10.

Line

9 First differences of Table IV-b-3, line 9.
10 Table VIII-c-3, line 5.

TABLE VIII-b-4

Uses of Funds: Net Change in Private Pension and Retirement Funds

(billion dollars)

	1946	1947	1948	1949
1. Nonfarm households	.57	.65	.65	.71
2. Nonfarm unincorporated business				
3. Agriculture				
4. Nonfinancial corporations				
5. Finance				
6. State and local governments				
7. Federal government				
8. Total	.57	.65	.65	.71

See note to line 5j, Table VIII-c-4.

TABLE VIII-b-5

Uses of Funds: Net Change in Government Pension and Insurance Funds

(billion dollars)

	1946	1947	1948	1949
1. Nonfarm households	3.47	3.79	3.49	2.49
2. Nonfarm unincorporated business				
3. Agriculture	.20	.09	−.01	.05
4. Nonfinancial corporations				
5. Finance				
6. State and local governments				
7. Federal government				
8. Total	3.67	3.88	3.48	2.54

Table IV-b-5, first difference.

TABLE VIII-b-6

Uses of Funds: Net Change in Consumer Credit

(billion dollars)

	1946	1947	1948	1949
1. Nonfarm households				
2. Nonfarm unincorporated business	.33	.33	.37	.25
3. Agriculture				
4. Nonfinancial corporations	.57	.64	.54	.44
5. Finance	1.86	2.32	1.98	2.25
c. Commercial banks	1.19	1.31	1.01	1.03
d. Mutual savings banks	0	.02	0	0
e. Savings and loan associations	.04	.03	.03	.02
g. Credit unions	.05	.09	.09	.11
l. Finance companies	.58	.87	.85	1.09
6. State and local governments				
7. Federal government				
8. Total	2.76	3.29	2.89	2.94

Table IV-b-6, first difference.

1950	1951	1952	1953	1954	1955	1956	1957	1958	
.97	1.45	1.61	1.94	2.05	2.06	2.61	2.89	3.06	1.
									2.
									3.
									4.
									5.
									6.
									7.
.97	1.45	1.61	1.94	2.05	2.06	2.61	2.89	3.06	8.

1950	1951	1952	1953	1954	1955	1956	1957	1958	
1.56	4.11	4.36	3.42	2.71	3.24	3.58	2.86	1.24	1.
									2.
−.25	−.04	−.01	−.04	−.02	0	0	−.01	−.01	3.
									4.
									5.
									6.
									7.
1.31	4.07	4.35	3.38	2.69	3.24	3.58	2.85	1.23	8.

1950	1951	1952	1953	1954	1955	1956	1957	1958	
									1.
.49	.30	.40	.18	.09	.16	.26	.10	−.09	2.
									3.
.78	.51	.76	.24	.27	.66	.41	.21	.52	4.
2.91	.53	3.63	3.50	.74	5.63	3.02	2.53	−.23	5.
1.66	.17	1.89	1.60	.03	2.36	1.45	1.21	.18	c.
.02	0	.01	.01	0	.02	.03	0	.01	d.
.06	.03	.07	.05	.05	.08	.08	.08	.06	e.
.15	.05	.20	.28	.22	.34	.33	.42	.23	g.
1.02	.28	1.46	1.56	.44	2.83	1.13	.82	−.71	l.
									6.
									7.
4.18	1.34	4.79	3.92	1.10	6.45	3.69	2.84	.20	8.

TABLE VIII-b-7

Uses of Funds: Net Change in Trade Credit

(billion dollars)

	1946	1947	1948	1949
1. Nonfarm households				
2. Nonfarm unincorporated business	.96	.37	.40	.06
3. Agriculture				
4. Nonfinancial corporations	3.19	5.86	2.34	−.94
5. Finance	.33	.13	.17	.10
i. Fire and casualty insurance	.17	.10	.08	.07
l. Finance companies	.17	.01	.02	.04
m. Other finance	−.01	.02	.07	−.01
6. State and local governments				
7. Federal government	−.80	−.10	0	0
8. Total	3.68	6.26	2.91	−.78
9. Net trade credit	1.63	2.40	1.17	−.02
10. Trade debt	2.05	3.86	1.74	−.76

Table IV-b-7, first difference.

TABLE VIII-b-8

Uses of Funds: Net Change in Loans on Securities

(billion dollars)

	1946	1947	1948	1949
1. Nonfarm households				
2. Nonfarm unincorporated business				
3. Agriculture				
4. Nonfinancial corporations				
5. Finance	−4.40	−1.06	.25	.75
c. Commercial banks	−3.66	−1.11	.26	.33
d. Mutual savings banks	0	0	0	0
m. Other finance	−.74	.05	−.01	.42
6. State and local governments				
7. Federal government				
8. Total	−4.40	−1.06	.25	.75
9. Rest of world, assets	.01	−.01	−.03	0
10. Discrepancy	−.04	−.03	.01	.02
11. Total liabilities	−4.43	−1.10	.23	.77

Table IV-b-8, first difference.

1950	1951	1952	1953	1954	1955	1956	1957	1958	
									1.
1.22	.22	1.11	.58	.20	.53	.89	.28	.79	2.
									3.
11.44	3.41	3.53	−.81	4.31	10.86	7.06	2.72	7.67	4.
.30	.19	.15	.16	.15	.39	.42	.34	.37	5.
.02	.12	.07	.05	.06	.09	.14	.15	.14	i.
.29	.04	.07	.06	.10	.25	.18	.15	.24	l.
−.01	.03	.01	.05	−.01	.05	.10	.04	−.01	m.
									6.
.38	.92	.95	−.04	.23	−.17	.08	−.05	−.60	7.
13.34	4.74	5.74	−.11	4.89	11.61	8.45	3.29	8.23	8.
3.08	1.16	1.26	−1.15	−1.93	2.64	1.27	.13	1.30	9.
10.26	3.58	4.48	1.04	6.82	8.97	7.18	3.16	6.93	10.

1950	1951	1952	1953	1954	1955	1956	1957	1958	
									1.
									2.
									3.
									4.
.80	−.34	.70	.80	1.86	1.08	−.68	−.36	1.58	5.
.22	−.30	.60	.40	.89	.59	−.76	−.06	.44	c.
0	0	0	0	.01	.01	0	−.01	0	d.
.58	−.04	.10	.40	.96	.48	.08	−.29	1.14	m.
									6.
									7.
.80	−.34	.70	.80	1.86	1.08	−.68	−.36	1.58	8.
.02	−.01	0	−.01	0	−.02	.01	.01	.01	9.
.03	.01	−.01	.03	.09	.01	0	−.01	.07	10.
.85	−.34	.69	.82	1.95	1.07	−.67	−.36	1.66	11.

TABLE VIII-b-9

Uses of Funds: Net Change in Bank Loans

(billion dollars)

	1946	1947	1948	1949
1. Nonfarm households				
2. Nonfarm unincorporated business				
3. Agriculture				
4. Nonfinancial corporations				
5. Finance	4.97	4.59	2.17	−1.62
a. Federal Reserve Banks and Treasury monetary funds	−.09	−.07	.13	−.14
c. Commercial banks	5.06	4.66	2.04	−1.48
6. State and local governments				
7. Federal government				
8. Total	4.97	4.59	2.17	−1.62
9. Rest of world, liabilities	.20	.07	.04	.03
10. Total liabilities	4.77	4.52	2.13	−1.65

Table IV-b-9, first difference.

TABLE VIII-b-10

Uses of Funds: Net Change in Other Loans

(billion dollars)

	1946	1947	1948	1949
1. Nonfarm households	.16	.04	−.13	.16
2. Nonfarm unincorporated business				
3. Agriculture				
4. Nonfinancial corporations				
5. Finance	.37	.33	.61	.12
b. Govt. insurance and pension funds	−.01	0	.02	.01
d. Mutual savings banks	.02	−.02	.02	0
g. Credit unions	0	0	0	0
h. Life insurance	−.07	.05	.12	.18
k. Other private insurance	0	0	0	.01
l. Finance companies	.34	.21	.35	−.09
m. Other finance	.09	.09	.10	.01
6. State and local governments				
7. Federal government	3.17	4.13	1.67	.67
8. Total	3.70	4.50	2.15	.95
9. Rest of world, liabilities	3.18	3.63	1.12	.48
10. Total liabilities	.52	.87	1.03	.47

Table IV-b-10, first difference.

1950	1951	1952	1953	1954	1955	1956	1957	1958	
									1.
									2.
									3.
									4.
5.52	4.68	3.02	.38	.60	6.84	5.58	2.06	1.72	5.
									a.
−.01	−.05	.14	−.13	.11	0	−.02	0	−.01	
5.53	4.73	2.88	.51	.49	6.84	5.60	2.06	1.73	c.
									6.
									7.
5.52	4.68	3.02	.38	.60	6.84	5.58	2.06	1.72	8.
.06	.06	0	−.10	.35	.37	.35	.35	.53	9.
5.46	4.62	3.02	.48	.25	6.47	5.23	1.71	1.19	10.

1950	1951	1952	1953	1954	1955	1956	1957	1958	
.55	−.04	−.11	.05	.74	−.12	−.04	.06	.78	1.
									2.
									3.
									4.
.62	.65	.33	.23	.10	1.28	.26	1.31	.35	5.
.02	.02	.01	.02	.02	.03	.03	.03	.04	b.
0	0	0	.01	.01	0	.01	.03	.04	d.
.01	.01	.01	0	0	.02	−.01	.02	0	g.
.17	.18	.12	.20	.22	.16	.23	.35	.32	h.
.01	.01	0	.01	.01	.01	.02	0	.01	k.
.31	.27	.13	.08	−.25	.97	−.09	.61	−.33	l.
.10	.16	.06	−.09	.09	.09	.07	.27	.27	m.
									6.
.70	.63	.75	.61	−.07	1.03	−.03	.63	1.10	7.
1.87	1.24	.97	.89	.77	2.19	.19	2.00	2.23	8.
.14	.24	.40	.22	−.16	.01	.09	.42	.66	9.
1.72	1.01	.57	.67	.93	2.18	.10	1.58	1.57	10.

TABLE VIII-b-11

Uses of Funds: Net Change in Nonfarm Mortgages

(billion dollars)

	1946	1947	1948	1949
1. Nonfarm households	1.36	1.21	1.00	.59
2. Nonfarm unincorporated business				
3. Agriculture				
4. Nonfinancial corporations				
5. Finance	4.96	5.83	5.96	5.02
b. Govt. insurance and pension funds	0	0	0	0
c. Commercial banks	2.27	2.08	1.36	.70
d. Mutual savings banks	.23	.41	.94	.90
e. Savings and loan associations	1.76	1.72	1.45	1.31
f. Investment companies	.04	.08	.06	.02
g. Credit unions	.01	.01	.02	.01
h. Life insurance	.50	1.42	2.06	1.92
i. Fire and casualty insurance	0	.01	.01	.01
j. Noninsured pension plans	.01	0	0	.01
k. Other private insurance	.01	.02	.03	.03
l. Finance companies	.11	.07	–.01	.09
m. Other finance	.01	.01	.04	.01
6. State and local governments	0	0	.01	.09
7. Federal government	–.24	–.04	.09	.48
8. Total	6.09	6.99	7.06	6.19

Table IV-b-11, first difference.
Figures may not add to totals because of rounding.

TABLE VIII-b-11a

Uses of Funds: Net Change in Nonfarm Residential Mortgages

(billion dollars)

	1946	1947	1948	1949
1. Nonfarm households	.89	.67	.59	.23
2. Nonfarm unincorporated business				
3. Agriculture				
4. Nonfinancial corporations				
5. Finance	4.16	5.03	5.17	4.46
b. Govt. insurance and pension funds	0	0	0	0
c. Commercial banks	1.74	1.78	1.11	.60
d. Mutual savings banks	.20	.35	.82	.81
e. Savings and loan associations	1.73	1.68	1.42	1.28
f. Investment companies	.04	.07	.04	.02
g. Credit unions	.01	.01	.02	.01
h. Life insurance	.31	1.06	1.72	1.60
i. Fire and casualty insurance	0	0	.01	.01
j. Noninsured pension plans	.01	0	0	.01
k. Other private insurance	0	.01	.01	.02
l. Finance companies	.11	.07	–.01	.09
m. Other finance	.01	.01	.03	.02
6. State and local governments	0	0	.01	.09
7. Federal government	–.23	–.04	.09	.49
8. Total	4.82	5.66	5.86	5.27

Table IV-b-11a, first difference.
Figures may not add to totals because of rounding.

1950	1951	1952	1953	1954	1955	1956	1957	1958	
.37	.49	.56	.75	.99	1.00	1.49	1.42	1.84	1.
									2.
									3.
									4.
8.94	7.70	7.43	8.16	10.77	14.00	11.84	8.30	12.17	5.
.06	.06	.04	.03	.07	.04	.09	.02	−.05	b.
1.94	1.00	1.08	.96	1.65	2.25	1.66	.57	2.04	c.
1.55	1.65	1.46	1.56	2.06	2.45	2.29	1.42	2.10	d.
2.04	1.91	2.83	3.57	4.15	5.30	4.32	4.28	5.62	e.
.04	−.01	.01	.01	0	−.01	−.01	−.02	−.03	f.
.01	.02	.03	.03	.03	.03	.06	0	.08	g.
3.01	3.01	1.76	1.89	2.49	3.24	3.34	2.14	1.74	h.
.01	.01	.01	.01	.01	.01	.01	0	0	i.
.01	.04	.03	.04	.03	.04	.11	.17	.14	j.
.05	.05	.04	.04	.06	.08	.06	.02	.04	k.
.21	−.08	.14	.03	.22	.53	−.10	−.32	.46	l.
.02	.03	0	0	0	.04	.01	.02	.04	m.
.05	.07	.08	.14	.10	.12	.11	.36	.42	6.
.29	.62	.46	.35	.02	.32	.46	1.27	.11	7.
9.64	8.88	8.53	9.40	11.88	15.44	13.90	11.35	14.54	8.

1950	1951	1952	1953	1954	1955	1956	1957	1958	
.09	.22	.28	.40	.43	.38	.75	.81	.81	1.
									2.
									3.
									4.
8.30	6.86	6.66	7.35	9.54	12.60	10.18	6.73	10.40	5.
.06	.06	.04	.03	.07	.04	.09	.02	−.05	b.
1.73	.81	.92	.74	1.23	1.71	1.11	.14	1.42	c.
1.48	1.54	1.29	1.45	1.88	2.36	2.14	1.31	1.93	d.
2.00	1.87	2.78	3.50	4.06	5.19	4.23	4.19	5.51	e.
.03	−.01	.01	−.01	0	−.01	−.01	−.02	−.03	f.
.01	.02	.03	.03	.03	.03	.06	0	.08	g.
2.70	2.55	1.40	1.51	2.00	2.66	2.53	1.25	.93	h.
.01	.01	0	0	0	0	0	−.01	0	i.
.01	.04	.03	.04	.03	.04	.11	.17	.14	j.
.03	.03	.02	.02	.02	.03	.01	0	0	k.
.21	−.08	.14	.03	.22	.53	−.10	−.32	.46	l.
.02	.02	0	0	0	.02	.01	0	.03	m.
.05	.07	.08	.14	.10	.12	.11	.36	.42	6.
.29	.62	.46	.35	.02	.32	.46	1.27	.11	7.
8.73	7.77	7.48	8.24	10.09	13.42	11.50	9.17	11.74	8.

TABLE VIII-b-11a-1

Uses of Funds: Net Change in Nonfarm Residential Mortgages, Multifamily

(billion dollars)

	1946	1947	1948	1949
1. Nonfarm households	13	17	.12	.03
2. Nonfarm unincorporated business				
3. Agriculture				
4. Nonfinancial corporations				
5. Finance	.25	.32	.66	.83
b. Govt. insurance and pension funds	0	0	0	0
c. Commercial banks	.05	.06	04	.05
d. Mutual savings banks	.06	.10	.27	.28
e. Savings and loan associations	.05	.05	.05	.01
h. Life insurance	.07	.10	.27	.45
i. Fire and casualty insurance	0	0	.01	.01
k. Other private insurance	0	0	.01	.02
l. Finance companies	.01	.01	0	.01
6. State and local governments	0	0	0	.05
7. Federal government	0	0	0	.02
8. Total	.38	.49	.78	.93

Table IV-b-11a-1, first difference.
Figures may not add to totals because of rounding.

TABLE VIII-b-11a-2

Uses of Funds: Net Change in Nonfarm Residential Mortgages, One- to Four-Family

(billion dollars)

	1946	1947	1948	1949
1. Nonfarm households	.75	.50	.49	.18
2. Nonfarm unincorporated business				
3. Agriculture				
4. Nonfinancial corporations				
5. Finance	3.92	4.70	4.51	3.64
b. Govt. insurance and pension funds	0	0	0	0
c. Commercial banks	1.69	1.72	1.07	.55
d. Mutual savings banks	.14	.25	.55	.53
e. Savings and loan associations	1.68	1.64	1.37	1.28
f. Investment companies	.04	.06	.04	.02
g. Credit unions	.01	.01	.02	.01
h. Life insurance	.24	.95	1.45	1.15
j. Noninsured pension plans	.01	0	0	.01
k. Other private insurance	0	0	0	0
l. Finance companies	.10	.06	−.01	.08
m. Other finance	.01	.01	.02	.01
6. State and local governments	0	0	0	.05
7. Federal government	−.23	−.04	.08	.47
8. Total	4.44	5.16	5.08	4.34

Table IV-b-11a-2, first difference.
Figures may not add to totals because of rounding.

1950	1951	1952	1953	1954	1955	1956	1957	1958	
–.03	–.03	0	0	.03	.07	.09	.09	.15	1.
									2.
									3.
									4.
1.19	1.20	.65	.47	.38	.61	.52	.28	1.17	5.
.03	.03	.02	.01	.04	.02	.04	.01	–.03	b.
.23	.04	–.06	–.04	–.05	–.04	–.05	0	.20	c.
.54	.52	.42	.27	.25	.26	.24	.19	.40	d.
0	.14	–.03	.14	.06	.20	.23	.20	.61	e.
.32	.42	.26	.08	.04	.15	.06	–.06	0	h.
.01	.01	0	0	0	0	0	–.01	0	i.
.02	.02	.02	.01	.01	.02	0	–.01	0	k.
.04	.02	.02	0	.03	0	0	–.04	0	l.
.02	.04	.04	.07	.05	.06	.06	.18	.21	6.
0	.02	.01	.10	.04	.11	.04	.04	.14	7.
1.18	1.23	.70	.64	.50	.85	.71	.59	1.67	8.

1950	1951	1952	1953	1954	1955	1956	1957	1958	
.11	24	.28	.40	.39	.31	.67	.72	.66	1.
									2.
									3.
									4.
7.12	5.66	6.01	6.87	9.16	11.98	9.65	6.45	9.23	5.
.03	.03	.02	.02	.04	.02	.05	01	–.02	b.
1.51	.77	.98	.77	1.27	1.75	1.16	.14	1.22	c.
.95	1.02	.86	1.18	1.63	2.10	1.89	1.12	1.53	d.
2.00	1.73	2.80	3.35	4.00	5.00	4.00	3.99	4.89	e.
.03	–.01	.01	.01	0	–.01	–.01	–.02	–.03	f.
.01	02	.03	.03	.03	.03	.06	0	.08	g.
2.38	2.13	1.15	1.44	1.96	2.51	2.47	1.31	.93	h.
.01	.04	.03	.04	03	.04	.11	.17	.14	j.
01	.01	0	.01	.01	0	.01	.01	0	k.
.17	–.10	.13	.02	.19	.52	–.10	–.29	.46	l.
.02	.02	0	0	0	.02	.01	0	.03	m.
.03	.04	.04	.07	.05	.06	.05	.18	.21	6.
.29	.60	.46	.25	–.02	.22	.42	1.23	–.03	7.
7.55	6.54	6.79	7.59	9.58	12.57	10.79	8.58	10.07	8.

TABLE VIII-b-11a-3

Uses of Funds: Net Change in Nonfarm Residential Mortgages, Multifamily, Conventional

(billion dollars)

	1946	1947	1948	1949
1. Nonfarm households and others	.17	–.03	.01	–.18
2. Nonfarm unincorporated business				
3. Agriculture				
4. Nonfinancial corporations				
5. Finance	.23	.19	.17	.12
c. Commercial banks	.05	–.03	–.10	–.12
d. Mutual savings banks	.06	07	.17	.12
e. Savings and loan associations	.04	.04	.05	0
h. Life insurance	.08	.11	.05	.12
6. State and local governments				
7. Federal government	0	0	0	0
8. Total	.40	.16	.18	–.06

Table IV-b-11a-3, first difference (note changes in coverage).
Figures may not add to totals because of rounding.

TABLE VIII-b-11a-4

Uses of Funds: Net Change in Nonfarm Residential Mortgages, Multifamily, FHA-Insured

(billion dollars)

	1946	1947	1948	1949
1. Nonfarm households and others	–.02	.22	.13	.30
2. Nonfarm unincorporated business				
3. Agriculture				
4. Nonfinancial corporations				
5. Finance	–.01	.12	.46	.67
c. Commercial banks	0	.09	.14	.17
d. Mutual savings banks	.01	.03	.10	.16
e. Savings and loan associations	0	.01	0	.01
h. Life insurance	–.01		.22	.33
6. State and local governments				
7. Federal government	n.a.	n.a.	n.a.	.02
8. Total	–.03	.34	.59	.99

Table IV-b-11a-4, first difference (note changes in coverage).
Figures may not add to totals because of rounding.

1950	1951	1952	1953	1954	1955	1956	1957	1958	
−.32	.28	.27	.08	.09	.30	.16	−.02	.14	1.
									2.
									3.
									4.
.40	.45	.20	.42	.30	.63	.58	.16	.85	5.
.06	.03	.07	.06	.02	0	−.07	−.16	−.05	c.
.24	.10	.07	.18	.15	.25	.31	.17	.25	d.
0	.15	−.02	.13	.06	.20	.23	.18	.60	e.
.10	17	.08	.05	.07	.17	.11	−.03	.04	h.
									6.
0	.01	.01	.03	.03	.04	.03	.02	.01	7.
.09	.74	.48	.53	.42	.97	.77	.16	1.00	8.

1950	1951	1952	1953	1954	1955	1956	1957	1958	
.41	−.19	−.18	.01	.07	−.12	.03	.24	.19	1.
									2.
									3.
									4.
.67	.67	.39	.02	0	−.06	−.10	.17	.36	5.
.16	.01	−.13	−.10	−.07	−.04	.01	.16	.25	c.
.29	.42	.35	.09	.10	.01	−.06	.02	.14	d.
.0	−.01	−.01	.01	−.01	−.01	0	.03	.01	e.
.22	.25	.18	.02	−.03	−.02	−.05	−.04	−.04	h.
									6.
−.01	.01	0	.07	.01	.07	.01	.02	.12	7.
1.07	.49	.21	.10	.08	−.11	−.06	.43	.67	8.

TABLE VIII-b-11a-5

Uses of Funds: Net Change in Nonfarm Residential Mortgages, One- to Four-Family, Conventional

(billion dollars)

	1946	1947	1948	1949
1. Nonfarm households and others	.92	.66	.23	.50
2. Nonfarm unincorporated business				
3. Agriculture				
4. Nonfinancial corporations				
5. Finance	1.92	1.46	1.78	1.44
c. Commercial banks	.96	.71	.41	.14
d. Mutual savings banks	−.02	−.02	.08	.07
e. Savings and loan associations	.84	.58	.87	.95
h. Life insurance	.14	.19	.42	.29
6. State and local governments				
7. Federal government	−.21	−.15	−.12	−.14
8. Total	2.63	1.97	1.89	1.80

Table IV-b-11a-5, first difference (note changes in coverage).
Figures may not add to totals because of rounding.

TABLE VIII-b-11a-6

Uses of Funds: Net Change in Nonfarm Residential Mortgages, One- to Four-Family, FHA- and VA-Insured

(billion dollars)

	1946	1947	1948	1949
1. Nonfarm households and others	–	−.01	.34	−.12
2. Nonfarm unincorporated business				
3. Agriculture				
4. Nonfinancial corporations				
5. Finance	1.83	3.09	2.65	2.06
c. Commercial banks	.74	1.00	.66	.41
d. Mutual savings banks	.16	.27	.47	.46
e. Savings and loan associations	.85	1.05	.50	.33
h. Life insurance	.10	.76	1.02	.86
6. State and local governments				
7. Federal government	−.02	.11	.20	.60
8. Total	1.81	3.19	3.19	2.54

Table IV-b-11a-6, first difference (note changes in coverage).
Figures may not add to totals because of rounding.

1950	1951	1952	1953	1954	1955	1956	1957	1958	
.85	−.12	.44	.69	.68	.10	.76	−.08	.87	1.
									2.
									3.
									4.
3.05	2.54	3.79	4.08	4.82	5.51	5.06	5.04	6.10	5.
.73	.19	.50	.39	.72	.91	.74	.59	1.08	c.
.16	.22	.10	.14	.21	.24	.20	.23	.27	d.
1.48	1.54	2.50	2.63	3.14	3.58	3.16	3.49	4.27	e.
.68	.59	.69	.92	.75	.78	.96	.73	.48	h.
									6.
−.21	.12	.07	.11	.08	.11	0	.32	.17	7.
3.69	2.54	4.30	4.88	5.58	5.72	5.82	5.28	7.14	8.

1950	1951	1952	1953	1954	1955	1956	1957	1958	
−.42	.42	.10	−.09	.05	.92	.09	.87	.66	1.
									2.
									3.
									4.
3.77	3.11	2.00	2.67	4.05	5.83	4.46	1.52	2.47	5.
.78	.58	.47	.38	.55	.84	.42	−.45	.14	c.
.78	.80	.76	1.04	1.42	1.85	1.69	.89	1.26	d.
.51	.19	.31	.72	.86	1.41	.84	.50	.62	e.
1.70	1.54	.46	.52	1.21	1.73	1.51	.58	.45	h.
									6.
.50	.48	.39	.14	−.10	.11	.42	.91	−.20	7.
3.85	4.01	2.49	2.72	4.00	6.86	4.97	3.30	2.93	8.

TABLE VIII-b-11b

Uses of Funds: Net Change in Nonfarm Nonresidential Mortgages

(million dollars)

	1946	1947	1948	1949
1. Nonfarm households	469	543	407	359
2. Nonfarm unincorporated business				
3. Agriculture				
4. Nonfinancial corporations				
5. Finance	799	793	792	559
c. Commercial banks	528	300	254	104
d. Mutual savings banks	30	64	124	84
e. Savings and loan associations	35	34	29	26
f. Investment companies	4	8	10	4
h. Life insurance	191	365	344	325
i. Fire and casualty insurance	2	6	6	4
k. Other private insurance	6	13	12	13
m. Other finance	3	3	13	−1
6. State and local governments				
7. Federal government	−6	−2	0	−2
8. Total	1,262	1,334	1,199	916

Table IV-b-11b, first difference.
Figures may not add to totals because of rounding.

TABLE VIII-b-12

Uses of Funds: Net Change in Farm Mortgages

(billion dollars)

	1946	1947	1948	1949
1. Nonfarm households	.12	.07	.13	.08
2. Nonfarm unincorporated business				
3. Agriculture				
4. Nonfinancial corporations				
5. Finance	.20	.22	.15	.19
c. Commercial banks	.18	.12	.05	.04
d. Mutual savings banks	0	0	.01	0
h. Life insurance	.02	.10	.10	.15
k. Other private insurance	0	0	0	.01
m. Other finance	0	0	0	0
6. State and local governments				
7. Federal government	−.19	−.12	−.06	.02
8. Total	.13	.17	.22	.29

Table IV-b-12, first difference.
Figures may not add to totals because of rounding.

1950	1951	1952	1953	1954	1955	1956	1957	1958	
276	274	277	344	570	622	734	613	1,028	1.
									2.
									3.
									4.
642	833	771	816	1,220	1,399	1,662	1,573	1,768	5.
207	191	158	219	421	542	556	428	625	c.
65	110	170	112	184	91	153	118	172	d.
41	38	57	71	83	106	87	85	112	e.
5	−1	2	1	−1	−1	−1	−3	−4	f.
303	464	355	377	493	588	804	897	814	h.
6	6	4	10	6	8	9	3	3	i.
18	22	20	23	35	51	50	29	33	k.
−3	3	5	3	−1	14	4	16	13	m.
									6.
−1	0	−1	0	0	0	0	0	0	7.
917	1,107	1,047	1,160	1,790	2,021	2,396	2,186	2,796	8.

1950	1951	1952	1953	1954	1955	1956	1957	1958	
.22	.25	.25	.20	.18	.22	.34	.24	.34	1.
									2.
									3.
									4.
.27	.25	.25	.21	.24	.36	.25	.13	.19	5.
.06	.04	.05	.03	.08	.14	.04	.03	.10	c.
.01	0	.01	0	0	0	0	0	0	d.
.19	.20	.18	.18	.16	.22	.21	.10	.08	h.
.01	.01	.01	0	0	0	.01	0	0	k.
0	0	0	0	0	0	0	0	0	m.
									6.
.05	.06	.09	.10	.10	.19	.25	.22	.22	7.
.54	.56	.59	.51	.52	.77	.84	.59	.75	8.

TABLE VIII-b-13

Uses of Funds: Net Acquisition of U. S. Government Securities

(billion dollars)

	1946	1947	1948	1949
1. Nonfarm households	−.49	1.82	−.23	.97
2. Nonfarm unincorporated business				
3. Agriculture	.06	.17	.22	.12
4. Nonfinancial corporations	−5.70	−1.20	.80	1.92
5. Finance	−12.09	−4.37	−5.76	1.14
a. Federal Reserve Banks and Treasury monetary funds	−.92	−.79	.77	−4.45
b. Govt. insurance and pension funds	3.76	3.75	3.14	2.19
c. Commercial banks	−15.83	−5.56	−6.60	4.38
d. Mutual savings banks	1.10	.20	−.50	−.05
e. Savings and loan associations	−.41	−.27	−.28	0
f. Investment companies	−.05	.01	−.05	.04
g. Credit unions	0	0	−.02	−.02
h. Life insurance	1.05	−1.61	−3.27	−1.46
i. Fire and casualty insurance	.19	.59	.49	.51
j. Noninsured pension plans	.18	.16	.13	.15
k. Other private insurance	.01	.01	0	0
m. Other finance	−1.17	−.86	.43	−.15
6. State and local governments	−.62	.66	.32	.02
7. Federal government	.54	.04	.10	.08
8. Total	−18.30	−2.88	−4.55	4.25
9. Rest of world, assets	−.47	.60	.08	.10
10. Difference between obligor and holder records, all banks	−.36	−.16	.40	0
11. Total liabilities	−19.13	−2.44	−4.07	4.35

Table IV-b-13, first difference.

TABLE VIII-b-13a

Uses of Funds: Net Acquisition of Short-Term U. S. Government Securities

(billion dollars)

	1946	1947	1948	1949
1. Nonfarm households	.16	−.42	2.11	.97
2. Nonfarm unincorporated business				
3. Agriculture				
4. Nonfinancial corporations	−5.10	−.90	.90	2.30
5. Finance	−13.52	−2.83	−6.48	6.85
a. Federal Reserve Banks and Treasury monetary funds	−.90	−2.40	−7.50	−.40
c. Commercial banks	−13.50	.40	.20	7.10
d. Mutual savings banks	.28	.05	.05	−.10
e. Savings and loan associations	0	0	−.10	0
h. Life insurance	.45	−.53	.02	.05
i. Fire and casualty insurance	.05	.15	.35	.30
m. Other finance	.10	−.50	.50	−.10
6. State and local governments	−.10	.30	.50	.10
7. Federal government				
8. Total	−18.56	−3.85	−2.97	10.22
9. Rest of world, assets	−.54	−.75	.47	.28
10. Total liabilities	−19.10	−4.60	−2.50	10.50

Table IV-b-13a, first difference.
Figures may not add to totals because of rounding.

1950	1951	1952	1953	1954	1955	1956	1957	1958	
−.33	−1.45	.23	.19	−1.53	1.76	1.11	−1.14	−2.03	1.
									2.
−.03	.02	−.08	.10	.24	.20	−.11	.06	.09	3.
2.87	.93	−.80	1.58	−2.29	3.99	−4.59	−.80	.19	4.
−4.52	2.73	6.38	3.85	5.25	−5.71	−2.02	−.94	10.42	5.
1.90	3.02	.90	1.22	−.99	−.15	.22	−.76	2.18	a.
.41	3.60	3.92	2.69	1.44	2.40	2.25	1.07	−.62	b.
−4.97	−.51	1.80	.11	5.55	−7.39	−3.04	−.31	7.94	c.
−.56	−1.05	−.40	−.24	−.43	−.29	−.49	−.42	−.29	d.
.03	.11	.19	.13	10	.32	.44	.39	.65	e.
.02	0	−.01	0	0	.14	.02	0	.14	f.
−.02	.02	0	−.01	0	0	.01	−.01	0	g.
−1.83	−2.45	−.76	−.42	−.76	−.49	−1.02	−.53	.15	h.
.35	.13	.34	.21	.11	−.14	−.33	−.21	−.06	i.
.21	.12	0	.16	.01	.30	−.20	−.27	.03	j.
.01	.02	.03	.01	.04	.07	.03	−.01	.06	k.
−.07	−.28	.37	−.01	.18	−.48	.09	.12	.24	m.
.36	.37	1.08	1.31	1.44	.41	.70	.74	−.70	6.
−.24	−.09	.10	.02	.13	.02	.25	.44	−.09	7.
−1.89	2.51	6.91	7.05	3.24	.67	−4.66	−1.64	7.88	8.
1.45	−.05	1.03	.57	.43	1.17	.25	−.17	.05	9.
.06	.29	.07	.20	−.10	.22	.34	.09	.11	10.
−.38	2.75	8.01	7.82	3.57	2.06	−4.07	−1.72	8.04	11.

1950	1951	1952	1953	1954	1955	1956	1957	1958	
−1.18	−1.61	.75	1.02	−.65	−1.01	1.50	2.38	−1.37	1.
									2.
									3.
3.00	.30	−1.10	1.80	−2.60	3.00	−3.70	−.40	.70	4.
−.32	−9.21	5.41	11.77	−8.67	−8.15	6.36	2.23	.58	5.
4.00	−2.60	1.40	2.20	2.40	1.30	1.40	−.70	−.40	a.
−4.30	−6.40	3.40	9.00	−10.60	−8.60	4.80	1.90	.90	c.
−.33	.07	.08	.22	−.32	.10	−.02	.21	−.15	d.
0	.10	0	0	0	.10	−.10	.30	−.20	e.
.26	.09	−.11	−.07	.08	−.14	−.13	−.03	.27	h.
.05	−.37	.14	.42	−.53	−.41	.26	.43	−.08	i.
0	−.10	.50	0	.30	−.50	.16	.12	.24	m.
.30	−.20	.70	1.20	0	−1.60	2.20	1.30	−1.10	6.
									7.
1.80	−10.72	5.76	15.79	−11.92	−7.76	6.36	5.51	−1.19	8.
.90	−.28	1.24	.71	.12	.66	1.04	−.01	−.01	9.
2.70	−11.00	7.00	16.50	−11.80	−7.10	7.40	5.50	−1.20	10.

TABLE VIII-b-13b
Uses of Funds: Net Acquisition of U.S. Savings Bonds
(billion dollars)

	1946	1947	1948	1949
1. Nonfarm households	1.20	1.81	1.62	1.30
2. Nonfarm unincorporated business				
3. Agriculture	.06	.17	.22	.12
4. Nonfinancial corporations	0	0	.20	0
5. Finance	.38	.34	.98	.29
b. Govt. insurance and pension funds	.10	.10	.10	.10
c. Commercial banks	.02	–.03	.30	–.05
d. Mutual savings banks	.04	.05	.18	.02
e. Savings and loan associations	0	0	.10	.10
h. Life insurance	.02	.02	.10	.02
i. Fire and casualty insurance	.03	.04	.15	.05
j. Noninsured pension plans	.17	.16	.05	.05
k. Other private insurance	0	0	0	0
6. State and local governments				
7. Federal government				
8. Total	1.64	2.32	3.02	1.71
9. Total liabilities	1.64	2.32	3.02	1.71

Table IV-b-13b, first difference.

TABLE VIII-b-13c
Uses of Funds: Net Acquisition of Long-Term U.S. Government Securities Other Than Savings Bonds
(billion dollars)

	1946	1947	1948	1949
1. Nonfarm households	–1.85	.43	–3.96	–1.30
2. Nonfarm unincorporated business				
3. Agriculture				
4. Nonfinancial corporations	–.60	–.30	–.30	–.38
5. Finance	1.05	–1.88	–.26	–6.00
a. Federal Reserve Banks and Treasury monetary funds	–.02	1.61	8.27	–4.05
b. Govt. insurance and pension funds	3.66	3.65	3.04	2.09
c. Commercial banks	–2.35	–5.93	–7.10	–2.67
d. Mutual savings banks	.78	.10	–.73	.03
e. Savings and loan associations	–.41	–.27	–.28	–.10
f. Investment companies	–.05	.01	–.05	.04
g. Credit unions	0	0	–.02	–.02
h. Life insurance	.58	–1.10	–3.39	–1.53
i. Fire and casualty insurance	.11	.40	–.01	.16
j. Noninsured pension plans	.01	0	.08	.10
k. Other private insurance	.01	.01	0	0
m. Other finance	–1.27	–.36	–.07	–.05
6. State and local governments	–.52	.36	–.18	–.08
7. Federal government	.54	.04	.10	.08
8. Total	–1.38	–1.35	–4.60	–7.66
9. Rest of world, assets	.07	1.35	–.39	–.18
10. Difference between obligor and holder records, all banks	–.36	–.16	.40	0
11. Total liabilities	–1.67	–.16	–4.59	–7.86

Table IV-b-13c, first difference.

1950	1951	1952	1953	1954	1955	1956	1957	1958	
.45	−.55	.15	−.04	.09	.03	−.29	−2.27	−.90	1.
									2.
−.03	.02	−.08	.10	.24	.20	−.11	.06	.09	3.
0	0	0	0	0	0	−.20	−.20	−.18	4.
.92	.02	.24	−.17	.09	−.04	−.93	−1.40	−.34	5.
.10	0	.10	0	0	0	−.10	−.10	−.10	b.
.29	.02	.02	−.02	.01	−.02	−.39	−.47	−.03	c.
.08	0	.01	−.03	−.01	−.03	−.07	−.15	−.08	d.
.10	0	0	0	0	.03	−.13	−.08	0	e.
.05	0	.01	−.02	−.01	−.02	−.04	−.10	−.03	h.
.11	.02	.01	−.02	−.01	−.01	−.07	−.17	−.07	i.
.19	−.03	.01	−.03	.08	.02	−.15	−.34	−.01	j.
0	.01	.08	−.05	.03	−.01	.02	.01	−.02	k.
									6.
									7.
1.34	−.51	.31	−.11	.42	.19	−1.53	−3.81	−1.33	8.
1.34	−.51	.31	−.11	.42	.19	−1.53	−3.81	−1.33	9.

1950	1951	1952	1953	1954	1955	1956	1957	1958	
.40	.71	−.67	−.79	−.97	2.74	−.10	−1.25	.24	1.
									2.
									3.
−.13	.63	.30	−.22	.31	.99	−.69	−.20	−.33	4.
−5.12	11.92	.73	−7.75	13.83	2.48	−7.45	−1.77	10.18	5.
−2.10	5.62	−.50	−.98	−3.39	−1.45	−1.18	−.06	2.58	a.
.31	3.60	3.82	2.69	1.44	2.40	2.35	1.17	−.52	b.
−.96	5.87	−1.62	−8.87	16.14	1.23	−7.45	−1.74	7.07	c.
−.31	−1.12	−.49	−.43	−.10	−.36	−.40	−.48	−.06	d.
−.07	.01	.19	.13	.10	.19	.67	.17	.85	e.
.02	0	−.01	0	0	.14	.02	0	.14	f.
−.02	.02	0	−.01	0	0	.01	−.01	0	g.
−2.14	−2.54	−.66	−.33	−.83	−.33	−.85	−.40	−.09	h.
.19	.48	.19	−.19	.65	.28	−.52	−.47	.09	i.
.02	.15	−.01	.19	−.07	.28	−.05	.07	.04	j.
.01	.01	−.05	.06	.01	.08	.01	−.02	.08	k.
−.07	−.18	−.13	−.01	−.12	.02	−.06	0	0	m.
.06	.57	.38	.11	1.44	2.01	−1.50	−.56	.40	6.
−.24	−.09	.10	.02	.13	.02	.25	.44	−.09	7.
−5.03	13.74	.84	−8.63	14.74	8.24	−9.49	−3.34	10.40	8.
.55	.23	−.21	−.14	.31	.51	−.79	−.16	.06	9.
.06	.29	.07	.20	−.10	.22	.34	.09	.11	10.
−4.42	14.26	.70	−8.57	14.95	8.97	−9.94	−3.41	10.57	11.

TABLE VIII-b-14

Uses of Funds: Net Acquisition of State and Local Government Securities

(billion dollars)

	1946	1947	1948	1949
1. Nonfarm households	–.16	.41	.99	.61
2. Nonfarm unincorporated business				
3. Agriculture				
4. Nonfinancial corporations	0	.04	.05	.05
5. Finance	.18	0.99	1.10	1.49
b. Govt. insurance and pension funds	–.10	.10	.15	.21
c. Commercial banks	.43	.88	.38	.89
d. Mutual savings banks	–.03	0	.01	.02
h. Life insurance	–.11	0	.26	.18
i. Fire and casualty insurance	0	.08	.21	.22
k. Other private insurance	.01	.01	0	–.01
m. Other finance	–.02	–.08	.09	–.02
6. State and local governments	–.13	–.05	0	.28
7. Federal government	–.02	.02	.07	–.08
8. Total	–.13	1.41	2.21	2.35

Table IV-b-14, first difference.

TABLE VIII-b-15

Uses of Funds: Net Acquisition of Other Bonds and Notes

(billion dollars)

	1946	1947	1948	1949
1. Nonfarm households	–1.37	–.69	–.28	–.63
2. Nonfarm unincorporated business				
3. Agriculture				
4. Nonfinancial corporations	.04	.12	.14	.14
5. Finance	2.55	3.85	5.17	3.71
b. Govt. insurance and pension funds	0	.01	.06	.15
c. Commercial banks	.35	.06	–.20	.15
d. Mutual savings banks	.17	.32	.50	.14
f. Investment companies	–.02	–.02	.01	.02
h. Life insurance	1.81	3.02	4.23	2.57
i. Fire and casualty insurance	0	.06	.17	.09
j. Noninsured pension plans	.26	.31	.35	.34
k. Other private insurance	.06	.06	.06	.06
m. Other finance	–.08	.03	–.01	.19
6. State and local governments	.01	.04	.17	–.01
7. Federal government				
8. Total	1.23	3.32	5.20	3.21
9. Rest of world, assets	–.04	–.04	–.05	.04
10. Rest of world, liabilities	–.09	.02	.08	–.01
11. Total liabilities	1.28	3.26	5.07	3.26

Table IV-b-15, first difference.

1950	1951	1952	1953	1954	1955	1956	1957	1958	
.38	.31	1.16	1.61	.66	1.68	1.68	2.12	1.42	1.
									2.
									3.
.07	.05	.06	.09	.33	.18	.11	.15	.13	4.
2.29	1.66	1.54	2.12	3.49	1.57	1.38	2.33	4.11	5.
.19	.07	.13	.24	.31	.34	.40	.45	.46	b.
1.57	1.08	.99	.63	1.77	.11	.20	1.02	2.58	c.
0	.06	.17	.09	.19	.04	.03	.01	.05	d.
.10	.02	−.02	.15	.55	.19	.23	.11	.30	h.
.31	.39	.42	.75	.78	.79	.63	.62	.71	i.
−.01	−.01	0	.01	.02	.05	0	−.02	.01	k.
.13	.05	−.15	.25	−.13	.05	−.11	.14	0	m.
.30	.12	.11	.09	.03	.05	.07	.07	.05	6.
.07	.26	.32	−.33	−.33	0	.08	.20	.21	7.
3.11	2.40	3.19	3.58	4.18	3.48	3.32	4.87	5.92	8.

1950	1951	1952	1953	1954	1955	1956	1957	1958	
.03	.07	−.15	.12	−.97	1.91	1.66	1.85	.28	1.
									2.
									3.
.03	.30	.41	.18	−.07	.41	.23	.83	−.26	4.
2.95	4.03	5.05	4.46	4.30	3.38	3.88	7.32	5.95	5.
.15	.24	.34	.40	.49	.59	.63	.96	1.15	b.
.58	−.13	−.22	−.12	−.14	.24	−.64	.60	.03	c.
−.08	.13	.37	.29	.09	−.26	.13	.74	.55	d.
.04	.05	.10	.01	.14	.18	.11	.14	.24	f.
1.83	2.71	3.10	2.71	2.10	1.75	2.15	2.67	2.42	h.
.05	.05	.16	.12	.03	−.01	.03	.18	.09	i.
.44	.88	1.06	1.07	1.21	.91	1.59	1.73	1.51	j.
.05	.06	.07	.07	.06	.02	.06	.03	.08	k.
−.11	.04	.07	−.09	.32	−.04	−.18	.27	−.12	m.
.06	.10	−.07	.05	.20	.04	.01	−.10	−.12	6.
									7.
3.07	4.50	5.24	4.81	3.46	5.74	5.78	9.90	5.85	8.
0	.01	.04	.04	.03	−.04	.05	.11	.04	9.
.61	.40	.02	−.05	−.22	−.22	.41	.42	.43	10.
2.46	4.11	5.26	4.90	3.71	5.92	5.42	9.59	5.46	11.

TABLE VIII-b-16

Uses of Funds: Net Acquisition of Preferred Stock

(billion dollars)

	1946	1947	1948	1949
1. Nonfarm households	0	.31	.28	.01
2. Nonfarm unincorporated business				
3. Agriculture				
4. Nonfinancial corporations	.01	.01	.01	0
5. Finance	.18	.11	.07	.31
b. Govt. insurance and pension funds	0	0	.01	0
f. Investment companies	−.01	.01	.02	0
h. Life insurance	.15	.06	.03	.20
i. Fire and casualty insurance.	.01	0	−.01	.06
j. Noninsured pension plans	.03	.04	.02	.03
k. Other private insurance	.01	0	0	.01
m. Other finance	−.01	0	0	.01
6. State and local governments				
7. Federal government				
8. Total domestic acquisitions	.19	.43	.36	.32
9. Rest-of-world purchases of domestic issues	0	−.01	−.02	0
10. Total domestic net issues	.19	.42	.34	.32

All lines except 5k from Table IV-b-16, first difference.
Line 5k, see note to Table VII-5k, line II-16.

1950	1951	1952	1953	1954	1955	1956	1957	1958	
−.06	.45	.28	.03	−.01	−.14	.60	.43	.04	1.
									2.
									3.
.01	0	.01	.0	.01	.01	0	.01	0	4.
.31	.13	.18	.35	.41	.20	−.13	−.03	.44	5.
.01	.01	.01	.02	.02	.03	.02	.04	.06	b.
.03	.04	−.05	.17	.08	.11	.08	−.11	.31	f.
.19	−.05	.09	.04	.20	.01	−.19	−.03	.04	h.
.03	.04	.08	.05	.05	0	−.08	.02	−.01	i.
.06	.09	.05	.07	.05	.05	.06	.04	.05	j.
0	−.01	0	0	0	0	−.01	0	0	k.
−.01	.01	0	0	.01	0	−.01	.01	−.01	m.
									6.
									7.
.26	.58	.47	.38	.41	.07	.47	.41	.48	8.
0	.02	0	.01	.02	.01	.01	0	.01	9.
.26	.60	.47	.39	.43	.08	.48	.41	.49	10.

TABLE VIII-b-17

Uses of Funds: Net Acquisition of Common Stock

(billion dollars)

	1946	1947	1948	1949
1. Nonfarm households	1.42	1.16	1.23	1.13
2. Nonfarm unincorporated business				
3. Agriculture				
4. Nonfinancial corporations	.09	.08	.08	.09
5. Finance	.29	.46	.27	.57
b. Govt. insurance and pension funds	0	0	.01	0
c. Commercial banks	–.03	–.03	0	–.01
d. Mutual savings banks	.01	0	.01	0
f. Investment companies	.15	.15	.10	.20
h. Life insurance	.12	.09	.01	.03
i. Fire and casualty insurance	.04	.13	.11	.06
j. Noninsured pension plans	.05	.08	.08	.11
k. Other private insurance	.01	.01	0	0
m. Other finance	–.06	.03	–.05	.18
6. State and local governments				
7. Federal government				
8. Total domestic acquisitions	1.80	1.70	1.58	1.79
9. Acquisitions from rest of world	0	–.02	.02	–.02
10. Acquisitions from domestic sector	1.80	1.72	1.56	1.81
11. Rest-of-world purchases of domestic issues	–.06	–.14	–.12	–.02
12. Total domestic net issues	1.74	1.58	1.44	1.79

Line

1 Line 8 minus lines 4 and 5.
4 Estimated as 5 per cent of line 8.
5 Sum of lines 5b through 5m.
5b First difference of Table IV-b-17, line 5b.
5c First difference of Table IV-b-17, line 5c.
5d First difference of Table IV-b-17, line 5d (data assumed to be book values).
5f Total corporate stocks (data from FRB worksheets underlying *Flow of Funds/Saving Accounts 1946-1960, Supplement 5,* Dec. 1961) minus preferred stocks (Table VIII-b-16, line 5f).
5h Total corporate stocks (see source, line 5f) minus preferred stocks (Table VIII-b-16, line 5h).
5i Total corporate stocks (see source, line 5f) minus preferred stocks (Table VIII-b-16, line 5i).
5j *1946-50*: First difference of Table IV-b-17 line 5j, stock outstanding at book value.
1951-58: Total corporate stocks (data from FRB as in line 5f, Supplement 5, p. 50) less preferred stocks (Table VIII-b-16, line 5j).

1950	1951	1952	1953	1954	1955	1956	1957	1958	
1.59	1.67	1.82	1.52	1.24	2.13	2.17	1.76	2.16	1.
									2.
									3.
.10	.12	.16	.13	.14	.19	.19	.21	.23	4.
.38	.70	1.17	.89	1.35	1.40	1.53	2.26	2.29	5.
.01	.01	.01	.02	.02	.03	.02	.04	.06	b.
0	−.01	.01	0	0	.01	0	.02	.01	c.
.02	.05	.11	.09	.14	.09	.04	.07	.09	d.
.10	.14	.48	.19	.22	.40	.50	.90	.66	f.
.13	.10	.07	.05	.07	.06	.19	.07	.02	h.
.09	.11	.10	.14	.10	.17	.21	.10	.14	i.
.16	.24	.41	.45	.63	.66	.82	1.04	1.25	j.
.01	0	.01	0	.01	0	0	0	.01	k.
−.14	.06	−.03	−.05	.16	−.02	−.25	.02	.05	m.
									6.
									7.
2.07	2.49	3.15	2.54	2.73	3.72	3.89	4.23	4.68	8.
.02	−.02	.06	−.05	.26	.17	.11	.04	.33	9.
2.05	2.51	3.09	2.59	2.47	3.55	3.78	4.19	4.35	10.
									11.
0	.10	0	.05	.12	.12	.25	.14	−.07	
2.05	2.61	3.09	2.64	2.59	3.67	4.03	4.33	4.28	12.

Line

5k For fraternal orders: total corporate stocks (see source, line 5f) less preferred stocks (first difference of line II-16 in Table III-5k-1). For other subgroups: first difference of line II-17 in Tables III-5k-2 and III-5k-3.

5m For brokers and dealers: total corporate stocks (see source, line 5f) less preferred stocks (first difference of line II-16 in Table III-5m-1). For other subgroups: first difference of line II-17 in Tables III-5m-2 and III-5m-3.

8 Sum of lines 9 and 10.

9 Table IV-b-17a, line 11.

10 Line 12 minus line 11.

11 Total corporate stocks (from *Treasury Bulletin*, June 1959, p. 65, Table 3) minus preferred stock (Table VIII-b-16, line 9).

12 Table IV-b-17a, line 10.

TABLE VIII-b-17-1

Uses of Funds: Net Acquisition of Corporate Stock

(billion dollars)

	1946	1947	1948	1949
1. Nonfarm households	1.42	1.47	1.51	1.14
2. Nonfarm unincorporated business				
3. Agriculture				
4. Nonfinancial corporations	.10	.09	.09	.09
5. Finance	.47	.57	.34	.88
b. Govt. insurance and pension funds	0	0	.02	0
c. Commercial banks	−.03	−.03	0	−.01
d. Mutual savings banks	.01	0	.01	0
f. Investment companies	.14	.16	.12	.20
h. Life insurance	.27	.15	.04	.23
i. Fire and casualty insurance	.05	.13	.10	.12
j. Noninsured pension plans	.08	.12	.10	.14
k. Other private insurance	.02	.01	0	.01
m. Other finance	−.07	.03	−.05	.19
6. State and local governments				
7. Federal government				
8. Sum of lines 9 and 10	1.99	2.13	1.94	2.11
9. Acquisitions from rest of world	0	−.02	.02	−.02
10. Acquisitions from domestic sector	1.99	2.15	1.92	2.13
11. Rest-of-world purchases of domestic issues	−.06	−.15	−.14	−.02
12. Total domestic net issues	1.93	2.00	1.78	2.11

Sum of Tables VIII-b-16 and VIII-b-17.

1950	1951	1952	1953	1954	1955	1956	1957	1958	
1.53	2.12	2.10	1.55	1.23	1.99	2.77	2.19	2.20	1.
									2.
									3.
.11	.12	.17	.13	.15	.20	.19	.22	.23	4.
.69	.83	1.35	1.24	1.76	1.60	1.40	2.23	2.73	5.
.02	.02	.02	.04	.04	.06	.04	.08	.12	b.
0	−.01	.01	0	0	.01	0	.02	.01	c.
.02	.05	.11	.09	.14	.09	.04	.07	.09	d.
.13	.18	.43	.36	.30	.51	.58	.79	.97	f.
.32	.05	.16	.09	.27	.07	0	.04	.06	h.
.12	.15	.18	.19	.15	.17	.13	.12	.13	i.
.22	.33	.46	.52	.68	.71	.88	1.08	1.30	j.
.01	−.01	.01	0	.01	0	−.01	0	.01	k.
−.15	.07	−.03	−.05	.17	−.02	−.26	.03	.04	m.
									6.
									7.
2.33	3.07	3.62	2.92	3.14	3.79	4.36	4.64	5.16	8.
.02	−.02	.06	−.05	.26	.17	.11	.04	.33	9.
2.31	3.09	3.56	2.97	2.88	3.62	4.25	4.60	4.83	10.
									11.
0	.12	0	.06	.14	.13	.26	.14	−.06	
2.31	3.21	3.56	3.03	3.02	3.75	4.51	4.74	4.77	12.

TABLE VIII-b-20

Uses of Funds: Net Change in Other Intangible Assets

(billion dollars)

	1946	1947	1948	1949
1. Nonfarm households	−.01	.01	−.01	−.01
2. Nonfarm unincorporated business				
3. Agriculture	.16	.17	.17	.18
4. Nonfinancial corporations	−.46	1.87	.93	.86
5. Finance	1.24	1.68	−.06	.73
a. Federal Reserve Banks and Treasury monetary funds	.38	.46	−.09	.04
c. Commercial banks	.78	1.12	−.26	.40
d. Mutual savings banks	0	0	.01	.02
e. Savings and loan associations	0	0	.08	.14
f. Investment companies	.01	−.01	.02	−.02
h. Life insurance	.07	.06	.15	.09
i. Fire and casualty insurance	−.02	.02	.01	.02
j. Noninsured pension plans	.03	.03	.03	.03
k. Other private insurance	0	0	0	0
m. Other finance	−.02	0	−.01	.01
6. State and local governments				
7. Federal government	.90	2.19	.77	−2.09
8. Total	1.83	5.92	1.80	−.33
9. U.S. direct investment abroad	.51	1.14	1.25	1.08
10. Subscriptions to IMF and IBRD	0	3.06	0	0
11. Line 8 minus lines 9 and 10	1.32	1.72	.55	−1.41
12. Discrepancy	.53	1.18	2.23	2.21
13. Liabilities	1.85	2.90	2.78	.80

All lines except line 5k, from Table IV-b-20.
Line 5k, see note to Table VII-5k, line II-20.

1950	1951	1952	1953	1954	1955	1956	1957	1958	
−.23	−.23	−.23	−.01	0	0	.01	0	0	1.
									2.
.22	.20	.24	.15	.24	.14	.17	.17	.22	3.
.56	1.02	2.98	2.63	4.93	4.83	5.99	6.64	1.00	4.
4.19	.67	1.00	.56	.62	4.97	1.99	1.13	1.40	5.
									a.
1.34	−.35	.36	−.03	−.28	1.57	.21	.04	−.14	
2.44	.58	.12	.01	.26	2.97	.94	.21	.96	c.
.02	.05	0	.03	.01	.02	.02	.03	.02	d.
.02	.15	.21	.23	.27	.04	.20	.34	.27	e.
.01	0	0	0	0	.03	−.02	.01	.01	f.
.26	.18	.18	.12	.20	.21	.31	.26	.20	h.
.02	.05	.04	.06	.05	.04	.04	.08	0	i.
.03	.03	.08	.11	.11	.06	.24	.11	.05	j.
0	0	.01	.01	0	.01	.01	.01	.01	k.
.04	−.02	.01	.02	0	.02	.04	.04	.03	m.
									6.
7.47	4.62	−3.16	.53	−3.13	4.02	−1.21	−1.49	−2.26	7.
12.21	6.28	.83	3.86	2.66	13.96	6.95	6.45	.36	8.
1.09	1.30	1.73	1.51	1.30	1.68	2.87	3.06	1.84	9.
0	0	0	0	0	0	.04	0	0	10.
11.12	4.98	−.90	2.35	1.36	12.28	4.04	3.39	−1.48	11.
−1.85	3.28	1.88	.56	.68	−3.65	1.51	1.38	3.68	12.
9.27	8.26	.98	4.01	2.04	8.63	5.55	4.77	2.20	13.

TABLE VIII-c-1

Sources of Funds: Net Change in Currency and Demand Deposits

(billion dollars)

	1946	1947	1948	1949
1. Nonfarm households				
2. Nonfarm unincorporated business				
3. Agriculture				
4. Nonfinancial corporations				
5. Finance	−14.88	9.61	2.08	−2.69
a. Federal Reserve Banks and Treasury monetary funds	.14	5.97	3.93	−4.56
c. Commercial banks	−15.02	3.64	−1.85	1.87
6. State and local governments				
7. Federal government	.13	−.03	−.01	−.02
8. Total	−14.75	9.58	2.07	−2.71

Table IV-c-1, first difference.

TABLE VIII-c-2

Sources of Funds: Net Change in Other Bank Deposits and Shares

(billion dollars)

	1946	1947	1948	1949
1. Nonfarm households				
2. Nonfarm unincorporated business				
3. Agriculture				
4. Nonfinancial corporations				
5. Finance	6.55	3.59	2.57	2.98
c. Commercial banks	3.83	1.43	.63	.50
d. Mutual savings banks	1.49	.88	.64	.88
e. Savings and loan associations	1.17	1.20	1.21	1.50
g. Credit unions	.06	.08	.09	.10
6. State and local governments				
7. Federal government	.36	.14	−.07	−.14
8. Total	6.91	3.73	2.50	2.84

Table IV-c-2, first difference.

1950	1951	1952	1953	1954	1955	1956	1957	1958	
									1.
									2.
									3.
									4.
9.35	10.93	6.98	−.35	2.70	6.72	3.98	−.74	4.25	5.
									a.
−.43	3.08	1.95	−.71	−1.55	.56	.78	.91	−2.40	
9.78	7.85	5.03	.36	4.25	6.16	3.20	−1.65	6.65	c.
									6.
−.02	.04	.04	.03	.03	.01	.02	.03	.04	7.
9.33	10.97	7.02	−.32	2.73	6.73	4.00	−.71	4.29	8.

1950	1951	1952	1953	1954	1955	1956	1957	1958	
									1.
									2.
									3.
									4.
2.64	4.92	8.13	9.15	10.49	8.45	9.41	12.33	16.93	5.
.23	1.73	3.07	3.40	3.81	1.33	2.07	5.45	8.04	c.
.74	.88	1.70	1.77	1.94	1.83	1.87	1.66	2.35	d.
1.52	2.12	3.09	3.65	4.40	4.89	5.01	4.76	6.07	e.
.15	.19	.27	.33	.34	.40	.46	.46	.47	g.
									6.
−.27	−.22	−.16	−.19	−.23	−.25	−.25	−.32	−.20	7.
2.37	4.70	7.97	8.96	10.26	8.20	9.16	12.01	16.73	8.

TABLE VIII-c-3

Sources of Funds: Life Insurance Policy Reserves
(billion dollars)

	1946	1947	1948	1949
1. Nonfarm households				
2. Nonfarm unincorporated business				
3. Agriculture				
4. Nonfinancial corporations				
5. Finance	3.78	3.58	3.83	4.08
h. Life insurance	3.69	3.47	3.74	3.95
k. Other private insurance	.09	.11	.09	.13
6. State and local governments				
7. Federal government				
8. Total	3.78	3.58	3.83	4.08

Line

5 Sum of lines 5h and 5k.

5h First differences of line 5h in Table IV-c-3 adjusted for capital gain or loss accruing to policy holders of mutual companies which purchased common stock. About three-fifths of all policy holders reserves were issued by mutual companies. These policy holders own and control the mutual insurance organizations. (See *Life Insurance Fact Book*: 1960, p. 15.) The method of adjustment is shown in Table VIII-c-3a.

TABLE VIII-c-3a

Sources of Funds: Adjustment for Capital Gain or Loss, Life Insurance Companies

	Common Stock			
Year	Net Changes in Holding (billion dollars) (1)	Net Changes at Cost (billion dollars) (2)	Amount Due to Price Changes (billion dollars) (3)	Changes in Holding of Common Stock Due to Price Changes (per cent) (4)
1946	.10	.12	−.02	−11.1
1947	.08	.09	−.01	−3.6
1948	.01	.01	0	0
1949	.09	.03	.06	16.2
1950	.19	.13	.06	13.0
1951	.17	.10	.07	10.8
1952	.14	.07	.07	8.5
1953	.08	.05	.03	3.1
1954	.50	.07	.43	41.3
1955	.35	.06	.29	18.8
1956	.06	.19	−.13	−6.9
1957	−.08	.07	−.15	−7.7
1958	.68	.02	.66	35.3

Col. 1: Table III-5h, line II-17, first difference.
Col. 2: Table VIII-b-17, line 5h.
Col. 3: Col. 1 minus col. 2. This is the difference between the market value and the value at original cost.
Col. 4: Col. 3 as per cent of line II-17 in Table III-5h, lagged by one year.

1950	1951	1952	1953	1954	1955	1956	1957	1958	
									1.
									2.
									3.
									4.
4.29	4.25	5.09	5.14	5.61	5.67	5.59	5.25	5.64	5.
4.16	4.11	4.93	4.96	5.41	5.45	5.42	5.23	5.42	h.
.13	.14	.16	.18	.20	.22	.17	.02	.22	k.
									6.
									7.
4.29	4.25	5.09	5.14	5.61	5.67	5.59	5.25	5.64	8.

Line

5k First difference of line 5k in Table IV-c-3 adjusted for capital gain or loss accruing to policy holders of fraternal orders which purchased common stock and tangible assets. The reason for adjustment of policy holdings is given in Table III-5k-1, line III-3.

8 Same as line 5.

Common Stocks Price Index: Percentage Changes from Year to Year (5)	Net Changes in Policy Reserves Holdings (6)	Adjusted Net Changes in Policy Holdings (7)
−11.9	3.67	3.69
−3.2	3.46	3.47
−1.0	3.74	3.74
11.4	4.01	3.95
22.2	4.22	4.16
12.9	4.18	4.11
6.9	5.00	4.93
−2.2	4.99	4.96
38.1	5.84	5.41
21.9	5.74	5.45
3.7	5.29	5.42
−10.5	5.08	5.23
34.0	6.08	5.42

Col. 5: Standard & Poor Common Stock Price Index. See Goldsmith and Lipsey, *Studies in the National Balance Sheet*, Vol. I, Part Two, Table 39.

Col. 6: Table III-5h, line III-3, first difference.

Col. 7: Col. 6 minus col. 3.

TABLE VIII-c-4

Sources of Funds: Private Pension and Retirement Funds

(billion dollars)

	1946	1947	1948	1949
1. Nonfarm households				
2. Nonfarm unincorporated business				
3. Agriculture				
4. Nonfinancial corporations				
5. Finance	.57	.65	.65	.71
j. Noninsured pension plans	.57	.65	.65	.71
6. State and local governments				
7. Federal government				
8. Total	.57	.65	.65	.71

1946-50: First differences of line 5j in Table IV-c-4 which estimates common stock at book value.

TABLE VIII-c-4a

Sources of Funds: Adjustment for Capital Gain or Loss, Noninsured Pension Funds

	Common Stock		
Year	Net Changes in Holdings (billion dollars) (1)	Net Purchases at Cost (billion dollars) (2)	Amount Due to Price Changes (billion dollars) (3)
1951	.36	.24	.12
1952	.52	.41	.11
1953	.41	.45	-.04
1954	1.50	.63	.87
1955	1.61	.66	.95
1956	.88	.82	.06
1957	.41	1.04	-.63
1958	3.71	1.25	2.46

Col. 1: Table III-5j, line II-17, first differences.
Col. 2: Table VIII-b-17, line 5j.
Col. 3: Col. 1 minus col. 2. This is the difference between market value and the value at cost.
Col. 4: Col. 3 as per cent of line II-17 in Table III-5j, lagged by one year.

1950	1951	1952	1953	1954	1955	1956	1957	1958	
									1.
									2.
									3.
									4.
.97	1.45	1.61	1.94	2.05	2.06	2.61	2.89	3.06	5.
.97	1.45	1.61	1.94	2.05	2.06	2.61	2.89	3.06	j.
									6.
									7.
.97	1.45	1.61	1.94	2.05	2.06	2.61	2.89	3.06	8.

1951-58: First differences of line 5j in Table IV-c-4 adjusted for capital gain or loss due to the purchase and holding of common stock by pension funds (see Table VIII-c-4a).

Changes in Holding of Common Stock Due to Price Changes (per cent) (4)	Common Stocks Price Index: Percentage Changes from Year to Year (5)	Net Changes in Pension Reserves Holdings (6)	Adjusted Net Changes in Pension Holdings (7)
17.9	12.9	1.57	1.45
10.6	6.9	1.72	1.61
−2.6	−2.1	1.90	1.94
44.3	38.1	2.92	2.05
27.5	21.9	3.01	2.06
11.8	3.7	2.67	2.61
−10.6	−10.5	2.26	2.89
38.7	34.0	5.52	3.06

Col. 5: Standard & Poor Common Stock Price Index. See Goldsmith and Lipsey, *National Balance Sheet*, Vol. I, Part Two, Table 39.
Col. 6: Table IV-c-4, line 5j, first differences.
Col. 7: Col. 6 minus col. 3.

TABLE VIII-c-5

Sources of Funds: Net Change in Government Pension and Insurance Funds

(billion dollars)

	1946	1947	1948	1949
1. Nonfarm households				
2. Nonfarm unincorporated business				
3. Agriculture				
4. Nonfinancial corporations				
5. Finance	3.67	3.88	3.48	2.54
b. Govt. insurance and pension funds	3.67	3.88	3.48	2.54
6. State and local governments				
7. Federal government				
8. Total	3.67	3.88	3.48	2.54

Table IV-c-5, first difference.

TABLE VIII-c-6

Sources of Funds: Net Change in Consumer Debt

(billion dollars)

	1946	1947	1948	1949
1. Nonfarm households	2.65	3.19	2.80	2.95
2. Nonfarm unincorporated business				
3. Agriculture	.11	.10	.09	-.01
4. Nonfinancial corporations				
5. Finance				
6. State and local governments				
7. Federal government				
8. Total	2.76	3.29	2.89	2.94

Table IV-c-6, first difference.

TABLE VIII-c-7

Sources of Funds: Net Change in Trade Debt

(billion dollars)

	1946	1947	1948	1949
1. Nonfarm households	.07	.09	.08	.04
2. Nonfarm unincorporated business	-.09	-.53	.76	.22
3. Agriculture	.20	.20	.30	.20
4. Nonfinancial corporations	3.73	4.64	.44	-1.34
5. Finance	-.01	.01	.01	.02
g. Credit unions	-.01	.01	.01	.02
6. State and local governments	.15	.15	.15	.10
7. Federal government	-2.00	-.70	0	0
8. Total	2.05	3.86	1.74	-.76

Table IV-c-7, first difference.

1950	1951	1952	1953	1954	1955	1956	1957	1958	
									1.
									2.
									3.
									4.
1.31	4.07	4.35	3.38	2.69	3.24	3.58	2.85	1.23	5.
1.31	4.07	4.35	3.38	2.69	3.24	3.58	2.85	1.23	b.
									6.
									7.
1.31	4.07	4.35	3.38	2.69	3.24	3.58	2.85	1.23	8.

1950	1951	1952	1953	1954	1955	1956	1957	1958	
3.99	1.35	4.70	3.93	1.01	6.26	3.70	2.86	.02	1.
									2.
.19	−.01	.09	−.01	.09	.19	−.01	−.02	.18	3.
									4.
									5.
									6.
									7.
4.18	1.34	4.79	3.92	1.10	6.45	3.69	2.84	.20	8.

1950	1951	1952	1953	1954	1955	1956	1957	1958	
.10	0	.24	.06	.10	.12	.17	.14	.10	1.
.74	−.69	.31	1.10	1.32	.60	.94	.68	.22	2.
.20	.40	.10	−.20	0	0	0	.10	.10	3.
8.01	2.28	3.59	.16	3.40	10.24	5.61	2.02	6.28	4.
.01	−.01	.04	.02	.01	.02	.03	.01	.02	5.
.01	−.01	.04	.02	.01	.02	.03	.01	.02	g.
.10	0	.10	.10	.15	.15	.10	.05	.15	6.
1.10	1.60	.10	−.20	−.23	−.09	.33	.16	.06	7.
10.26	3.58	4.48	1.04	4.75	11.04	7.18	3.16	6.93	8.

TABLE VIII-c-8

Sources of Funds: Net Change in Loans on Securities

(billion dollars)

	1946	1947	1948	1949
1. Nonfarm households	−1.48	−.06	−.12	.32
2. Nonfarm unincorporated business				
3. Agriculture				
4. Nonfinancial corporations	−.91	−.33	−.16	0
5. Finance	−2.04	−.71	.51	.45
h. Life insurance	−.37	0	0	0
m. Other finance	−1.67	−.71	.51	.45
6. State and local governments				
7. Federal government				
8. Total	−4.43	−1.10	.23	.77

Table IV-c-8, first difference.

TABLE VIII-c-9

Sources of Funds: Net Change in Bank Loans, N.E.C.

(billion dollars)

	1946	1947	1948	1949
1. Nonfarm households	−.29	−.25	.10	0
2. Nonfarm unincorporated business	1.45	2.22	−.70	−.29
3. Agriculture	.25	.30	.36	.10
4. Nonfinancial corporations	2.98	1.66	1.06	−1.93
5. Finance	.59	.62	.46	.39
c. Commercial banks	−.17	.02	−.01	−.04
d. Mutual savings banks	0	0	0	0
e. Savings and loan associations	−.03	0	−.04	0
l. Finance companies	.79	.60	.51	.43
6. State and local governments				
7. Federal government	−.21	−.03	.85	.08
8. Total	4.77	4.52	2.13	−1.65

Table IV-c-9, first difference.

1950	1951	1952	1953	1954	1955	1956	1957	1958	
.78	−.15	.21	.52	1.28	.75	−.05	−.46	1.32	1.
									2.
									3.
0	0	0	0	0	0	0	0	0	4.
.07	−.19	.48	.30	.67	.32	−.62	.10	.34	5.
0	0	0	0	0	0	0	0	0	h.
.07	−.19	.48	.30	.67	.32	−.62	.10	.34	m.
									6.
									7.
.85	−.34	.69	.82	1.95	1.07	−.67	−.36	1.66	8.

1950	1951	1952	1953	1954	1955	1956	1957	1958	
.27	−.01	−.06	−.08	.12	.68	.13	.21	.42	1.
2.13	−.80	.48	−.19	1.11	1.49	.67	−.09	1.82	2.
.47	.60	.07	−.43	.17	.38	−.03	.32	.56	3.
2.15	4.96	1.19	−.16	−1.22	2.27	5.38	2.06	−.88	4.
1.06	−.04	.91	−.14	0	2.75	−.63	−.37	−1.08	5.
.07	−.06	.16	−.13	−.03	.13	−.08	0	−.01	c.
0	0	0	0	0	0	0	0	.01	d.
.01	.01	−.01	0	0	.05	−.01	−.01	.04	e.
.98	.01	.76	−.01	.03	2.57	−.54	−.36	−1.12	l.
									6.
−.62	−.09	.43	1.48	.07	−1.10	−.29	−.42	.35	7.
5.46	4.62	3.02	.48	.25	6.47	5.23	1.71	1.19	8.

TABLE VIII-c-9a

Sources of Funds: Net Change in Short-Term Bank Loans
(billion dollars)

	1946	1947	1948	1949
1. Nonfarm households	−.29	−.25	.10	0
2. Nonfarm unincorporated business	1.15	2.02	−.75	−.30
3. Agriculture	.25	.30	.36	.10
4. Nonfinancial corporations	1.49	.61	.56	−1.06
5. Finance	.59	.62	.46	.39
c. Commercial banks	−.17	.02	−.01	−.04
d. Mutual savings banks	0	0	0	0
e. Savings and loan associations	−.03	0	−.04	0
l. Finance companies	.79	.60	.51	.43
6. State and local governments				
7. Federal government	−.21	−.03	.85	.08
8. Total	2.98	3.27	1.58	−.79

Table IV-c-9a, first difference.

TABLE VIII-c-9b

Sources of Funds: Net Change in Long-Term Bank Loans
(billion dollars)

	1946	1947	1948	1949
1. Nonfarm households				
2. Nonfarm unincorporated business	.30	.20	.05	.01
3. Agriculture				
4. Nonfinancial corporations	1.49	1.05	.50	−.87
5. Finance				
6. State and local governments				
7. Federal government				
8. Total	1.79	1.25	.55	−.86

Table IV-c-9b, first difference.

TABLE VIII-c-10

Sources of Funds: Net Change in Other Loans
(billion dollars)

	1946	1947	1948	1949
1. Nonfarm households	−.07	.05	.13	.19
2. Nonfarm unincorporated business	.34	.46	.65	.09
3. Agriculture	.02	.03	.08	.03
4. Nonfinancial corporations	.01	.14	.17	.08
5. Finance	.22	.19	0	.08
c. Commercial banks	−.07	−.05	−.03	−.02
e. Savings and loan associations	.19	.20	.04	−.04
m. Other finance	.10	.04	−.01	.14
6. State and local governments				
7. Federal government				
8. Total	.52	.87	1.03	.47

Table IV-c-10, first difference.
Figures may not add to totals because of rounding.

1950	1951	1952	1953	1954	1955	1956	1957	1958	
.27	−.01	−.06	−.08	.12	.68	.13	.21	.42	1.
1.93	−1.10	.38	−.27	1.06	1.30	.35	−.23	1.80	2.
.47	.60	.07	−.43	.17	.38	−.03	.32	.56	3.
1.50	4.12	.05	.08	−1.20	1.04	2.73	.66	−1.38	4.
1.06	−.04	.91	−.14	0	2.75	−.63	−.37	−1.08	5.
.07	−.06	.16	−.13	−.03	.13	−.08	0	−.01	c.
0	0	0	0	0	0	0	0	.01	d.
.01	.01	−.01	0	0	.05	−.01	−.01	.04	e.
.98	.01	.76	−.01	.03	2.57	−.54	−.36	−1.12	l.
									6.
−.62	−.09	.43	1.48	.07	−1.10	−.29	−.42	.35	7.
4.61	3.48	1.78	.64	.22	5.05	2.26	.17	.67	8.

1950	1951	1952	1953	1954	1955	1956	1957	1958	
									1.
.20	.30	.10	.08	.05	.19	.32	.14	.02	2.
									3.
.65	.84	1.14	−.24	−.02	1.23	2.65	1.40	.50	4.
									5.
									6.
									7.
.85	1.14	1.24	−.16	.03	1.42	2.97	1.54	.52	8.

1950	1951	1952	1953	1954	1955	1956	1957	1958	
.18	.20	.12	.21	.24	.18	.27	.35	.35	1.
.36	.50	.31	.10	.18	1.01	.09	.33	.12	2.
.06	.11	.08	−.02	.10	.05	.08	.22	.23	3.
.13	.15	.09	.34	−.27	.46	−.15	.37	−.15	4.
.99	.05	−.03	.04	.68	.48	−.19	.31	1.02	5.
−.02	−.01	−.03	−.01	−.02	−.01	0	0	0	c.
.52	0	.15	.14	.15	.68	−.21	0	.31	e.
.49	.06	−.15	−.09	.55	−.19	.03	.30	.72	m.
									6.
									7.
1.72	1.01	.57	.67	.93	2.18	.10	1.58	1.57	8.

TABLE VIII-c-11
Sources of Funds: Net Change in Mortgage Liabilities
(million dollars)

	1946	1947	1948	1949
1. Nonfarm households	4,255	4,931	5,142	4,258
2. Nonfarm unincorporated business	516	588	602	530
3. Agriculture	137	167	224	291
4. Nonfinancial corporations	1,315	1,472	1,313	1,399
5. Finance				
6. State and local governments				
7. Federal government				
8. Total	6,223	7,158	7,281	6,478
9. Farm mortgages	137	167	224	291
10. Nonfarm mortgages	6,086	6,991	7,057	6,187
11. Life insurance holdings of foreign farm mortgages				
12. Life insurance holdings of foreign nonfarm mortgages				

Table IV-c-11, first difference.

TABLE VIII-c-11a
Sources of Funds: Net Change in Nonfarm Residential Mortgages, One-to Four-Family
(million dollars)

	1946	1947	1948	1949
1. Nonfarm households	4,190	4,888	5,097	4,236
2. Nonfarm unincorporated business				
3. Agriculture				
4. Nonfinancial corporations	253	277	−17	104
5. Finance				
6. State and local governments				
7. Federal government				
8. Total	4,443	5,165	5,080	4,340

Table IV-c-11a, first difference.

TABLE VIII-c-11b
Sources of Funds: Net Change in Nonfarm Residential Mortgages, Multifamily
(million dollars)

	1946	1947	1948	1949
1. Nonfarm households				
2. Nonfarm unincorporated business	76	98	167	186
3. Agriculture				
4. Nonfinancial corporations	305	394	611	745
5. Finance				
6. State and local governments				
7. Federal government				
8. Total	381	492	778	931

Table IV-c-11b, first difference.

1950	1951	1952	1953	1954	1955	1956	1957	1958	
7,267	6,778	6,724	7,648	9,373	12,535	11,003	8,698	9,988	1.
570	653	520	553	744	905	1,017	928	1,358	2.
539	558	587	509	517	777	842	599	747	3.
1,807	1,450	1,288	1,198	1,757	2,004	1,877	1,728	3,191	4.
									5.
									6.
									7.
10,183	9,439	9,119	9,908	12,391	16,221	14,739	11,953	15,284	8.
539	558	587	509	517	777	842	599	747	9.
9,644	8,881	8,532	9,399	11,874	15,444	13,897	11,354	14,537	10.
1	1	1	0	1	1	0	0		11.
45	42	39	39	55	92	123	76	75	12.

1950	1951	1952	1953	1954	1955	1956	1957	1958	
7,235	6,742	6,686	7,608	9,302	12,460	10,920	8,633	9,894	1.
									2.
									3.
316	−201	103	−14	281	113	−133	−53	175	4.
									5.
									6.
									7.
7,551	6,541	6,789	7,594	9,583	12,573	10,787	8,580	10,069	8.

1950	1951	1952	1953	1954	1955	1956	1957	1958	
									1.
235	246	139	129	101	171	142	118	334	2.
									3.
941	987	557	516	403	679	572	469	1,338	4.
									5.
									6.
									7.
1,176	1,233	696	645	504	850	714	587	1,672	8.

TABLE VIII-c-11c

Sources of Funds: Net Change in Nonfarm Nonresidential Mortgages

(million dollars)

	1946	1947	1948	1949
1. Nonfarm households	65	43	45	22
2. Nonfarm unincorporated business	440	490	435	344
3. Agriculture				
4. Nonfinancial corporations	757	801	719	550
5. Finance				
6. State and local governments				
7. Federal government				
8. Total	1,262	1,334	1,199	916

Table IV-c-11c, first difference.

TABLE VIII-c-11d

Sources of Funds: Net Change in Farm Mortgages

(million dollars)

	1946	1947	1948	1949
1. Nonfarm households				
2. Nonfarm unincorporated business				
3. Agriculture	137	167	224	291
4. Nonfinancial corporations				
5. Finance				
6. State and local governments				
7. Federal government				
8. Total	137	167	224	291

Table IV-c-11d, first difference.

1950	1951	1952	1953	1954	1955	1956	1957	1958	
32	36	38	40	71	75	83	65	94	1.
335	407	381	424	643	734	875	810	1,024	2.
									3.
550	664	628	696	1,073	1,212	1,438	1,312	1,678	4.
									5.
									6.
									7.
917	1,107	1,047	1,160	1,787	2,021	2,396	2,187	2,796	8.

1950	1951	1952	1953	1954	1955	1956	1957	1958	
									1.
									2.
539	558	587	509	517	777	842	599	747	3.
									4.
									5.
									6.
									7.
539	558	587	509	517	777	842	599	747	8.

TABLE VIII-c-12

Sources of Funds: Net Change in Other Bonds and Notes

(billion dollars)

	1946	1947	1948	1949
1. Nonfarm households				
2. Nonfarm unincorporated business				
3. Agriculture				
4. Nonfinancial corporations	.88	2.84	4.23	2.90
5. Finance	.26	.28	.58	.52
l. Finance companies	.26	.28	.58	.52
6. State and local governments	−.13	1.41	2.21	2.35
7. Federal government	−18.99	−2.30	−3.81	4.19
a. Direct and guaranteed	−19.13	−2.44	−4.07	4.35
b. Nonguaranteed	.14	.14	.26	−.16
8. Total	−17.98	2.23	3.21	9.96

Table IV-c-12, first difference.

TABLE VIII-c-13

Sources of Funds: Net Change in Other Liabilities

(billion dollars)

	1946	1947	1948	1949
1. Nonfarm households				
2. Nonfarm unincorporated business				
3. Agriculture				
4. Nonfinancial corporations	.42	2.74	1.77	−.66
5. Finance	1.39	.12	.95	1.30
a. Federal Reserve Banks and Treasury monetary funds	.41	−1.04	−.15	.30
c. Commercial banks	.21	.15	.16	.17
d. Mutual savings banks	.02	.02	0	.02
e. Savings and loan associations	.03	−.03	.02	0
h. Life insurance	.06	.08	.04	.08
i. Fire and casualty insurance	.75	.99	.84	.77
k. Other private insurance	.02	.01	.01	.02
m. Other finance	−.11	−.06	.03	−.06
6. State and local governments				
7. Federal government	.04	.04	.06	.16
8. Total	1.85	2.90	2.78	.80

All lines except line 5k—from Table IV-c-13, first difference.
Line 5k—see note to line III-13, Table VII-5k.
Figures may not add to totals because of rounding.

1950	1951	1952	1953	1954	1955	1956	1957	1958	
									1.
									2.
									3.
1.61	3.30	4.72	3.35	3.54	2.77	3.67	6.35	5.92	4.
.42	.57	.54	1.58	.19	1.63	1.19	1.13	.01	5.
.42	.57	.54	1.58	.19	1.63	1.19	1.13	.01	l.
3.11	2.41	3.18	3.58	4.18	3.48	3.32	4.87	5.92	6.
.05	2.99	8.01	7.79	3.55	3.58	−3.51	.39	7.57	7.
−.38	2.75	8.01	7.82	3.57	2.06	−4.07	−1.72	8.04	a.
.43	.24	0	−.03	−.02	1.52	.56	2.11	−.47	b.
5.19	9.27	16.45	16.30	11.46	11.46	4.67	12.74	19.42	8.

1950	1951	1952	1953	1954	1955	1956	1957	1958	
									1.
									2.
									3.
7.37	6.94	−1.40	2.23	.32	6.55	3.39	2.56	.19	4.
1.90	1.17	2.12	1.57	1.44	2.11	2.06	2.14	1.74	5.
									a.
.25	−.32	.54	.06	−.14	.87	.05	.07	.27	
.58	.40	.24	.11	.34	.02	.55	.37	−.05	c.
.03	.01	.01	.05	.07	.05	.03	.08	.09	d.
.05	.02	.01	.03	.06	.03	.03	.12	.10	e.
.11	.07	.08	.10	.08	.14	.19	.17	.13	h.
.72	.85	1.08	1.10	.69	.78	.66	1.05	.84	i.
.01	.01	.02	.01	.02	.02	.01	.02	.03	k.
.15	.13	.14	.11	.32	.20	.54	.26	.33	m.
									6.
0	.15	.26	.21	.28	−.03	.10	.07	.27	7.
9.27	8.26	.98	4.01	2.04	8.63	5.55	4.77	2.20	8.

TABLE VIII-d-1

Sources of Funds: Net Issue of Common Stock

(billion dollars)

	1946	1947	1948	1949
1. Nonfarm households				
2. Nonfarm unincorporated business				
3. Agriculture				
4. Nonfinancial corporations	1.49	1.32	1.29	1.42
5. Finance	.25	.26	.15	.37
c. Commercial banks	.05	.04	.02	.01
f. Investment companies	.16	.17	.14	.26
h. Life insurance	.02	.01	−.01	.03
i. Fire and casualty insurance	.02	.02	0	.05
l. Finance companies	n.a.	.02	0	.02
6. State and local governments				
7. Federal government				
8. Total domestic issues	1.74	1.58	1.44	1.79

Line	
4	Line 8 less line 5.
5	Sum of lines 5c through 5l.
5c	Table IV-b-17a, line 7.
5f	1946-47: Irwin Friend, *Individual Saving*, New York, 1954, pp. 235 and 242.
	1948-58: SEC worksheets of March 12, 1959, *Domestic Corporate Securities Issued and Retired.*
5h	See note to Table IV-b-17a, line 8.
5i	Same as line 5h.

TABLE VIII-d-2

Sources of Funds: Net Issue of Preferred Stock

(billion dollars)

	1946	1947	1948	1949
1. Nonfarm households				
2. Nonfarm unincorporated business				
3. Agriculture				
4. Nonfinancial corporations	.19	.42	.29	.29
5. Finance	n.a.	0	.05	03
l. Finance companies	n.a.	0	.05	03
6. State and local governments				
7. Federal government				
8. Total	.19	.42	.34	.32

Line	
4	Line 8 less line 5l.
5l	Obtained by the same method as Table VIII-d-1, line 5l.
8	Table VIII-b-16, line 10.

1950	1951	1952	1953	1954	1955	1956	1957	1958	
									1.
									2.
									3.
1.60	2.05	2.33	1.94	1.81	2.55	2.60	2.94	2.59	4.
.45	.56	.76	.70	.78	1.12	1.43	1.39	1.69	5.
.07	.14	.14	.11	.23	.14	.40	.36	.13	c.
.25	.40	.55	.43	.46	.76	.91	.98	1.50	f.
.06	.01	.02	.06	.04	.06	.09	.06	.06	h.
.06	0	.02	.04	.03	.08	.02	.02	−.01	i.
.01	.01	.03	.06	.02	.08	.01	−.03	.01	l.
									6.
									7.
2.05	2.61	3.09	2.64	2.59	3.67	4.03	4.33	4.28	8.

Line

51 NBER sample of 70 finance companies in Richard T. Selden, "Trends and Cycles in the Commercial Paper Market" (forthcoming occasional paper). Figures as they were available in January 1962. The sample covers 90-95 per cent of all finance companies as measured in term of total assets. The total assets of the ten largest companies were $6,961 million, or 85 per cent of total assets ($8,068 million) of the sampled companies in 1953; they were therefore about 75 per cent of total assets of all companies. This same ratio was applied to common stock outstanding of the ten largest companies. The common stocks outstanding were recorded at book value; the net issues of common stock were computed as first difference of common stock outstanding.

8 Table IV-b-17a, line 10.

1950	1951	1952	1953	1954	1955	1956	1957	1958	
									1.
									2.
									3.
.24	.64	.45	.39	.50	0	.46	.37	.49	4.
.02	−.04	.02	0	−.07	.08	.02	.04	0	5.
.02	−.04	.02	0	−.07	.08	.02	.04	0	l.
									6.
									7.
.26	.60	.47	.39	.43	.08	.48	.41	.49	8.

TABLE VIII-d-3

Sources of Funds: Gross Saving, Inventories at Book Value

(billion dollars)

	1946	1947	1948	1949
1. Nonfarm households	32.97	33.74	34.14	34.76
2. Nonfarm unincorporated business	3.63	3.21	4.76	3.13
3. Agriculture	7.70	8.59	5.72	3.22
4. Nonfinancial corporations	12.21	18.89	18.43	15.36
5. Finance	1.26	1.30	1.91	1.43
a. Federal Reserve Banks and Treasury monetary funds	.08	.02	.06	.06
c. Commercial banks	.70	.62	.73	.63
d. Mutual savings banks	.21	.11	.36	.12
e. Savings and loan associations	.15	.16	.16	.12
f. Investment companies	–.04	.04	.02	0
g. Credit unions	.01	.01	.01	.01
h. Life insurance	.30	.05	–.02	–.10
i. Fire and casualty insurance	–.17	.18	.29	.29
l. Finance companies	.14	.20	.24	.25
m. Other finance	–.12	–.09	.06	.05
6. State and local governments	2.31	3.04	3.01	4.07
7. Federal government (civil)	.48	8.81	8.50	–2.09
8. Total	60.56	77.58	76.47	59.88
9. Federal government (military)	3.27	2.37	2.37	3.21
10. Total, including military	63.83	79.95	78.84	63.09

Line

1 through 7 From line IV-3 of corresponding Tables VII-1 through VII-7.
8 Sum of lines 1 through 7.

TABLE VIII-d-3b

Sources of Funds: Net Saving, Inventories at Book Value

(billion dollars)

	1946	1947	1948	1949
1. Nonfarm households	20.76	18.32	15.94	15.07
2. Nonfarm unincorporated business	1.98	1.14	2.29	.37
3. Agriculture	5.20	5.43	1.95	–.99
4. Nonfinancial corporations	5.21	10.24	8.37	4.16
5. Finance	.97	1.00	1.64	1.34
6. State and local governments	.04	.24	–.21	.80
7. Federal government (civil)	–.76	7.34	6.98	–3.35
8. Total	33.40	43.71	36.96	17.40
9. Federal government (military)	–12.89	–13.29	–11.09	–8.01
10. Total, including military	20.51	30.42	25.87	9.39

Gross saving (Table VIII-d-3) minus depreciation (Table VIII-a-7 minus Table VIII-a-7b).

1950	1951	1952	1953	1954	1955	1956	1957	1958	
42.61	51.54	53.44	56.90	56.95	64.54	71.87	73.26	73.65	1.
4.86	7.49	3.86	4.98	2.71	4.17	6.73	7.20	4.81	2.
11.51	10.51	1.60	3.56	6.23	4.35	6.28	8.06	11.90	3.
23.00	18.82	20.42	21.76	23.48	29.33	27.43	29.34	19.27	4.
1.89	1.15	1.49	1.65	2.17	1.84	1.75	1.77	2.87	5.
.03	.02	.06	.03	.01	.05	.07	.04	.03	a.
.72	.66	.64	.65	.87	.73	.85	.84	1.04	c.
.15	.10	.06	.09	.13	.14	.13	.10	.17	d.
.20	.22	.18	.27	.27	.35	.38	.35	.40	e.
.03	−.15	−.03	−.01	−.02	.09	−.20	−.03	−.17	f.
.01	.02	.02	.03	.02	.05	.04	.07	.09	g.
.01	.04	−.09	.06	−.12	−.04	.06	−.04	−.08	h.
.19	.13	.23	.33	.44	.15	−.06	−.10	.27	i.
.54	.10	.49	.11	.40	.45	.47	.54	.85	l.
.01	.01	−.07	.09	.17	−.13	.01	0	.27	m.
4.57	5.97	6.65	7.44	7.87	8.26	9.18	10.10	9.73	6.
8.48	3.56	−5.38	−5.20	−4.19	3.92	4.15	1.60	−5.79	7.
96.92	99.04	82.08	91.09	95.22	116.41	127.39	131.33	116.44	8.
4.19	9.66	19.70	21.83	18.36	16.34	17.42	18.34	18.72	9.
101.11	108.70	101.78	112.92	113.58	132.75	144.81	149.67	135.16	10.

Line

9 Table VII-7-1, line IV-3, minus Table VII-7, line IV-3.
10 Sum of lines 8 and 9.

1950	1951	1952	1953	1954	1955	1956	1957	1958	
20.77	25.99	26.12	28.00	26.98	32.12	36.48	34.55	33.02	1.
1.80	3.90	−.01	.82	−1.67	−.52	1.60	1.57	−1.18	2.
6.95	5.11	−4.20	−2.27	−.03	−2.07	.10	.94	4.53	3.
10.96	5.52	5.99	6.56	7.59	11.53	8.35	8.74	−2.06	4.
1.59	.77	1.33	1.36	1.94	1.48	1.31	1.39	2.62	5.
1.19	2.26	2.57	3.14	3.42	3.47	3.88	4.30	3.52	6.
7.40	2.46	−6.50	−6.38	−5.40	2.69	2.86	.41	−6.92	7.
50.66	46.01	25.30	31.23	32.83	48.70	54.58	51.90	33.53	8.
−5.87	−.53	8.09	7.74	2.68	.12	.36	.50	3.91	9.
44.79	45.48	33.39	38.97	35.51	48.82	54.94	52.40	37.44	10.

TABLE VIII-d-3d

Sources of Funds: Gross Saving, Inventories at Adjusted Value

(billion dollars)

	1946	1947	1948	1949
1. Nonfarm households	32.97	33.74	34.14	34.76
2. Nonfarm unincorporated business	1.92	1.74	4.35	3.59
3. Agriculture	4.22	3.46	7.49	5.13
4. Nonfinancial corporations	6.94	12.99	16.28	17.21
5. Finance	1.26	1.30	1.91	1.43
a. Federal Reserve Banks and Treasury monetary funds	.08	.02	.06	.06
c. Commercial banks	.70	.62	.73	.63
d. Mutual savings banks	.21	.11	.36	.12
e. Savings and loan associations	.15	.16	.16	.12
f. Investment companies	−.04	.04	.02	0
g. Credit unions	.01	.01	.01	.01
h. Life insurance	.30	.05	−.02	−.10
i. Fire and casualty insurance	−.17	.18	.29	.29
l. Finance companies	.14	.20	.24	.25
m. Other finance	−.12	−.09	.06	.05
6. State and local governments	2.31	3.04	3.01	4.07
7. Federal government (civil)	.48	8.81	8.50	−2.09
8. Total	50.10	65.08	75.68	64.10
9. Federal government (military)	3.27	2.37	2.37	3.21
10. Total, including military	53.37	67.45	78.05	67.31

Line

1 and 5 through 7	From line IV-3 of corresponding Tables VII-1 through VII-7.
2 through 4	From note to corresponding lines in Table VII-2 through VII-4.
8	Sum of lines 1 through 7.

TABLE VIII-d-3e

Sources of Funds: Net Saving, Inventories at Adjusted Value

(billion dollars)

	1946	1947	1948	1949
1. Nonfarm households	20.76	18.32	15.94	15.07
2. Nonfarm unincorporated business	.27	−.33	1.88	.83
3. Agriculture	1.72	.30	3.72	.92
4. Nonfinancial corporations	−.06	4.34	6.22	6.01
5. Finance	.97	1.00	1.64	1.34
6. State and local governments	.04	.24	−.21	.80
7. Federal government (civil)	−.76	7.34	6.98	−3.35
8. Total	22.94	31.21	36.17	21.62
9. Federal government (military)	−12.89	−13.29	−11.09	−8.01
10. Total, including military	10.05	17.92	25.08	13.61

Gross Saving (Table VIII-d-3d) minus depreciation (Table VIII-a-7d minus Table VIII-a-7e).

1950	1951	1952	1953	1954	1955	1956	1957	1958	
42.61	51.54	53.44	56.90	56.95	64.54	71.87	73.26	73.65	1.
3.77	7.16	4.07	4.82	2.66	3.97	6.23	6.90	4.77	2.
7.30	8.28	7.34	6.82	7.05	5.98	4.75	6.27	8.63	3.
18.04	17.62	21.40	20.77	23.16	27.60	24.74	27.81	18.87	4.
1.89	1.15	1.49	1.65	2.17	1.84	1.75	1.77	2.87	5.
.03	.02	.06	.03	.01	.05	.07	.04	.03	a.
.72	.66	.64	.65	.87	.73	.85	.84	1.04	c.
.15	.10	.06	.09	.13	.14	.13	.10	.17	d.
.20	.22	.18	.27	.27	.35	.38	.35	.40	e.
.03	−.15	−.03	−.01	−.02	.09	−.20	−.03	−.17	f.
.01	.02	.02	.03	.02	.05	.04	.07	.09	g.
.01	.04	−.09	.06	−.12	−.04	.06	−.04	−.08	h.
.19	.13	.23	.33	.44	.15	−.06	−.10	.27	i.
.54	.10	.49	.11	.40	.45	.47	.54	.85	l.
.01	.01	−.07	.09	.17	−.13	.01	0	.27	m.
4.57	5.97	6.65	7.44	7.87	8.26	9.18	10.10	9.73	6.
8.48	3.56	−5.38	−5.20	−4.19	3.92	4.15	1.60	−5.79	7.
86.66	95.28	89.01	93.20	95.67	116.11	122.67	127.71	112.73	8.
4.19	9.66	19.70	21.83	18.36	16.34	17.42	18.34	18.72	9.
90.85	104.94	108.71	115.03	114.03	132.45	140.09	146.05	131.45	10.

Line

9 Table VII-7-1, line IV-3 minus Table VII-7, line IV-3.
10 Sum of lines 8 and 9.

1950	1951	1952	1953	1954	1955	1956	1957	1958	
20.77	25.99	26.12	28.00	26.98	32.12	36.48	34.55	33.02	1.
.71	3.57	.20	.66	−1.72	−.72	1.10	1.27	−1.22	2.
2.74	2.88	1.54	.99	.79	−.44	−1.43	−.85	1.26	3.
6.00	4.32	6.97	5.57	7.27	9.80	5.66	7.21	−2.46	4.
1.59	.77	1.33	1.36	1.94	1.48	1.31	1.39	2.62	5.
1.19	2.26	2.57	3.14	3.42	3.47	3.88	4.30	3.52	6.
7.40	2.46	−6.50	−6.38	−5.40	2.69	2.86	.11	−6.92	7.
40.40	42.25	32.23	33.34	33.28	48.40	49.86	48.28	29.82	8.
−5.87	−.53	8.09	7.74	2.68	.12	.36	.50	3.91	9.
34.53	41.72	40.32	41.08	35.96	48.52	50.22	48.78	33.73	10.